KARLA ZIMMERMAN

CHICAGO
CITY GUIDE

INTRODUCING CHICAGO

The city of Chicago rises high above the waters of Lake Michigan

PETER PTSCHELINZEW

The sun dips. Skyscraper lights flicker on, ricocheting around the steely towers. Then Beethoven's Ninth Symphony fills the twilight air. People on blankets spread as far as the eye can see.

They chat, clink beer bottles and hoist burly slices of pizza – a Chicago-style picnic, blending high culture and earthy pleasures. That's how it's done here, whether at a free concert by the Grant Park Orchestra or at the Art Institute, where the revered lion sculptures don hockey helmets for the Blackhawks' Stanley Cup win.

Chicago often gets 'discovered' for its cultural cool, perhaps never more so than when a local guy named Barack Obama got elected President of the United States. The spotlight swung to the nation's third-largest city. 'Wow,' visitors said. 'Look at that high-flying architecture. That blue, sailboat-dotted water stretching over the horizon. That whimsical public art studding the street corners.'

The accolades continued: 'Hey, there's a globe-spanning foodie culture. And loads of Beard-award-winning chefs. And the continent's top restaurant, Alinea, cooks in the Windy City.'

Then the deal sealer: 'Megabashes like Lollapalooza, Blues Fest and Pitchfork rock downtown almost every weekend in summer, while smaller concerts happen *every night* at Millennium Park for *free!*'

Chicagoans shook their heads and smiled, too polite to point out that, yes, that's Chicago, and it has been here – right at the nation's core – all along.

2

CHICAGO LIFE

If you want your finger on America's pulse, you don't head to New York or LA. The heart beats in Chicago. That's why businesses have come here for decades to test new products, be they Broadway shows or Costco caskets. Whether they make it to your local shelf depends on what the pragmatic but open-minded people of the Windy City have to say.

A spirit of inventiveness lingers from the days when Chicago built the first skyscraper. Big, bold ideas are still encouraged. You'll see it in groundbreaking theater productions, chefs' bubbling kitchens and the green architecture rising from city streets (Chicago has more LEED-certified buildings than anywhere else in the country).

For most of the past decade, the pace of change here has been fast and grand. Development swept through downtown and spilled over its edges. Mod Millennium Park led the way, The Donald popped the top on his new Trump Tower, and the Art Institute built a wing huge enough to make it the second-largest art museum in the nation.

Chicago actually added to its 2.8 million population, but there was a flip side. Taxes went up (becoming the country's steepest), which angered citizens and drove away some businesses. Traffic gridlocked, to the point where Chicago now ranks second only to LA. And segregation deepened, a remnant of historical immigration patterns and policies that put blacks, whites and Latinos in specific pockets of the city. The debate continues on how to deal with these issues.

In the meantime, locals continue to dash for the beaches, ballparks and beer gardens when the weather warms. Soak it up while you can, they say, because once winter hits, it's time to hibernate. Thank goodness for the slew of neighborhood taverns to socialize in, where chances are equal that you'll find an avant-garde jazz band, a poetry reading or a Bears or Hawks game on TV – and quite possibly all three.

Hit Chicago's eating streets for an encounter with a local legend: the humble deep-dish pizza

HIGHLIGHTS

❶ Chicago Blues Festival
Rock to fret-bending licks at the world's largest blues fest (p14).

❷ St Patrick's Day
No, you're not seeing things – they really do dye the river green (p13).

❸ Taste of Chicago
Loosen the belt before gorging on a park full of food (p14).

❹ Lollapalooza
Bodysurf through three days of rock bands (p15).

CHUCK ECKERT/ALAMY

GARY HEBDING JR/ALAMY

CITY OF FESTIVALS

The Windy City whoops it up like there's no tomorrow. Between March and September alone it throws 200 free festivals. Whether they honor Mexican independence or giant floating turkeys is irrelevant – Chicago just wants an excuse to crank tunes, blast fireworks and party in the streets.

PETER PTSCHELINZEW

TIM MOSENFELDER/GETTY IMAGES

ARTS APPRECIATION

Chicago treats its world-class operas and circus-punk marching bands with equal reverence. Same goes for its glitzy Broadway-style theaters and roll-the-dice-for-admission-price storefront stages. While you can find anything in a museum or on a stage here, specialties include blues, jazz, improv comedy and theater.

CHARLES COOK

CHARLES COOK

❶ Theater District
Catch a show at the Chicago Theatre (p60), a historic venue downtown.

❷ Art Institute of Chicago
View a quarter-million Monets, Renoirs and other colorful masters (p52).

❸ Pilsen Murals
See eye-popping scenes splashed across Little Mexico's buildings (p107).

❹ Green Mill
Relive Chicago's dark past at Al Capone's old speakeasy (p191).

RICHARD CUMMINS

CHARLES COOK

FOODIE FAVORITES

For years epicures wrote off Chicago as a meaty backwater. Then chef by chef, restaurant by restaurant, the city built a scene of plenty. Suddenly, foodies are bypassing the coasts, heading to the heartland. Critics agree: the eateries here might just be the USA's best.

❶ Ethnic Eats
Explore Chicago's global restaurants, such as Mexican favorite Nuevo Leon (p173).

❷ Chicago Hot Dog
Bite into a famed Vienna dog laden with peppers, pickles and more (p154).

❸ Farmers' Markets
Reduce your food miles by eating locally produced items (p157).

❹ Neighborhood Joints
Seek out local neighborhood eateries, such as the Chicago Diner (p160).

RAY LASKOWITZ

RICHARD CUMMINS

RICK GERHARTER

CHARLES COOK

6

1 Millennium Park
Look at the city reflect off *Cloud Gate* by Arish Kapoor, 2005 (p53).

2 Rookery
See Frank Lloyd Wright's atrium overhaul (p56).

3 Tribune Tower
Identify shards from global monuments in the Gothic building's base (p64).

4 Willis Tower
Skyrocket to the top of the USA's tallest building (p56).

JOHN SONES

RICHARD CUMMINS

STEELY SKYLINE

Hard to believe all this height came compliments of a cow. When Mrs O'Leary's bovine kicked over the lantern that burned down the city in 1871, it created the blank canvas that allowed Chicago's mighty architecture to flourish.

RICHARD CUMMINS

RICHARD I'ANSON

RICHARD CUMMINS

SPORTS FANATICS

In warm weather Chicagoans dash like sun-starved maniacs for the parks and beaches to cycle, swim and skate. When the weather sucks, they hibernate (often in bars) and watch sports on TV. Year-round, they cheer on their baseball, hockey, football and basketball teams.

CHARLES COOK

PETER PTSCHELINZEW

① Lake Michigan Beaches
Build sandcastles, spike volleyballs or swim in the waves (p219).

② Watch a Game in a Bar
Join locals anytime, anywhere in the city's favorite pastime (p177).

③ Chicago Cubs
Watch baseball's favorite losing team play at historic Wrigley Field (p220).

④ Chicago Marathon
Join one million spectators feeling the pain of 45,000 runners (p16).

TANNEN MAURY/EPA/CORBIS

CONTENTS

THE AUTHOR

Karla Zimmerman

Karla lives in Chicago, where she has been eating deep-dish pizza (Giordano's preferred) and cheering on the hopeless Cubs for more than 20 years. Like most Chicagoans, she's a little bit silly in love with her town and will talk your ear off about its sky-high architecture, rockin' arts, global neighborhoods and character-filled dive bars. Come wintertime, the words she uses get a bit more colorful, especially if she's just shoveled her car out of a snowbank.

Karla writes travel features for newspapers, books, magazines and websites. She has authored or coauthored several Lonely Planet guidebooks covering the USA, Canada, the Caribbean and Europe. For more on the Windy City, see her blog, My Kind of Town & Around (www.mykindoftownandaround .blogspot.com).

KARLA'S TOP CHICAGO DAY

I take the El toward downtown, and the skyline zooms into focus. Soon the train is rumbling through the Loop (p52), so close to the buildings I can practically touch them. I disembark near Millennium Park (p53) and admire 'the Bean' as it reflects the skyline and Crown Fountain's gargoyle people as they spit water. Then I cross the Nichols Bridgeway to the Art Institute for a peek at the Modern Wing's Picassos and Matisses, and the Main Wing's Renoirs and Gauguins.

Arted out, I hop on the Red Line and head due north to Wrigley Field (p84) to catch a Cubs game. If the sun is shining and the breeze is blowing, there's nowhere in the city that beats an afternoon spent here; if the sun is obscured and the breeze blizzardlike, that sucks, but at least tickets are easier to come by. I order a hot dog and an Old Style beer and sigh as the Cubs get clobbered.

Nothing soothes the soul like a slice of banana cream, so it's off to Hoosier Mama Pie Company (p168) in east Ukrainian Village. Yes, it's out of the way, but this is crazy-good pie. Now I'm just a few El stops from groovy browsing on Milwaukee Ave, so I drop in to see what's stacking the shelves at Quimby's zine shop (p139), Myopic Books (p139) and Reckless Records (p140). And it dawns on me: I should probably have some dinner to soak up my dessert. The bike-messenger hangout Handlebar (p165) dishes up veg-friendly stews and sandwiches a few blocks away.

It's getting late, but I make one more stop. The Hideout (p193) is a tucked-away bar hosting indie-oriented rock, folk and country musicians. I stop in for a set, then cab it home, convinced once again that Chicago is my kind of town.

So you've decided to visit the Windy City. Excellent choice. You'll be well entertained, given all the festivals and attractions. The top sights are conveniently plunked near downtown – and what's not in the center is easily accessible by public transportation (ie the El trains) – so you don't have to worry about having a car. And Chicago's prices won't break the bank, especially with a bit of advance planning. What are you waiting for? Let's go…

WHEN TO GO

Wicked weather slaps the city between November and March. It gets nastiest in January, with temperatures hovering around 24°F (-4°C) and blasting snow and wind added for emphasis. This is when everyone stays inside and drinks.

When the sun begins to shine again and warmth creeps through the skyscrapers, from April through October, everyone flings open their doors and makes a greedy dash for the outdoor festivals, ballparks, beaches and beer gardens. This is the best time to visit Chicago. It's no surprise that this is also the city's peak season, specifically June through August, when summer temperatures average 85°F (29°C).

FESTIVALS

Chicago stages an insane number of festivals, concerts and events. The moment the thermometer registers a single degree above freezing, you can count on some group lugging a stage and speakers to Grant Park to celebrate the good news. Between March and September alone, the city throws around 200 free day- or weekend-long shindigs.

Grant Park hosts most of the outdoor biggies, such as Blues Fest, Jazz Fest and Taste of Chicago. Many of the major parades take place nearby along S Columbus Dr. We've highlighted some of our favorite events here, but this is by no means a comprehensive list. For the whole enchilada, check with the Mayor's Office of Special Events (☎ live 312-744-3315, recorded 312-744-3370; www.cityofchicago.org/specialevents). Another good resource is Metromix (www.chicago.metromix.com/festivals). The Arts (p201) and Nightlife (p189) chapters contain further information on music, theater, dance, film and literary festivals.

January
POLAR ADVENTURE DAYS
☎ 312-742-7529; www.chicagoparkdistrict.com
On select weekends throughout the winter, the Chicago Parks District hosts free family events on Northerly Island, with sled dogs, ice sculptures and snowshoeing. Mush!

CHINESE NEW YEAR PARADE
www.chicagochinatown.org
Loads of spectators line Wentworth Ave in Chinatown to watch dragons dance, firecrackers burst and marching bands bang their gongs. The exact date varies according to the ancient Chinese calendar, but it's typically in late January or early to mid-February.

February
CHICAGO AUTO SHOW
www.chicagoautoshow.com
Detroit, Tokyo and Bavaria introduce their latest and finest vehicles to hordes of excited gearheads in a huge mid-February show at McCormick Place.

BLACK HISTORY MONTH
☎ 877-244-2246
The city hosts events and exhibits from north to south and everywhere in between to celebrate African American history throughout the month.

WINTER DANCE
☎ 312-744-3315; www.explorechicago.org
The party moves to Millennium Park for this cold-weather version of SummerDance (see p14), with live DJ sets and free ice-skating and ice dance lessons on weekends throughout February.

March
POLAR PLUNGE   1st Sun in Mar
☎ 312-527-3743; www.chicagopolarplunge.org
Watch 1500 people experience extreme shrinkage as they jump into Lake Michigan from North Ave Beach. The event is a fundraiser for the local Special Olympics.

CHICAGO INTERNATIONAL MOVIES AND MUSIC FESTIVAL
www.cimmfest.org
CIMM Fest, as it's called, reels through the Windy City for a long weekend in early March. It presents movies. And music. And movies about music, which is the main gist. Screenings and concerts take place at various Wicker Park venues and at the Chicago Cultural Center.

CHIDITAROD
www.chiditarod.org
More than 100 teams compete in this crazy-costume, Burning Man–esque version of the Iditarod (the famed Alaskan sled-dog race), which swaps humans for huskies and shopping carts for sleds. The goal is to pick up 40lb of canned food for local pantries along the Near West Side route. Held on a Saturday in early March.

ST PATRICK'S DAY PARADE
www.chicagostpatsparade.com
It's a city institution: after the parade along S Columbus Dr, the local plumbers union dyes the Chicago River shamrock green (pouring in the secret, biodegradable coloring near the N Columbus Dr bridge). Then everyone drinks beer. Held the Saturday before March 17.

GREEK INDEPENDENCE DAY PARADE
☎ 773-775-4949; www.enosis.org
Hellenic pride overtakes Greektown in this celebration and parade, typically held the Sunday closest to March 25. The action centers on Halsted St, from Randolph to Van Buren Sts.

April
CHICAGO EDIBLE BOOKS FESTIVAL
Apr 1
www.colum.edu/book_and_paper
Part of an internationally celebrated event on April 1, Chicago's version is sponsored by Columbia College's Center for Books & Paper Arts. You get one hour to view the entries before – that's right – you eat them.

CHICAGO IMPROV FESTIVAL
☎ 773-935-9810; www.chicagoimprovfestival.org
The town that invented improv comedy happily hosts its preeminent festival for a week in mid- to late April, spitballing yucks at venues around the city.

ARTROPOLIS
www.artropolischicago.com
It's three international art shows rolled into one at the Merchandise Mart. Art Chicago features established artists, NEXT shows off newbies, and the International Antique Fair displays, well, antiques. Several museums and galleries hold simultaneous events. Held late-month over a long weekend.

May
POLISH CONSTITUTION DAY PARADE
1st Sat in May
☎ 773-745-7799; www.may3parade.org
Accordion-fueled polka'ing and lots of kielbasa bring out Chicago's mighty Polish community (the world's second-largest after Warsaw). The event celebrates Europe's first democratic constitution, signed in 1791. The parade starts in Grant Park and goes up S Columbus Dr.

CINCO DE MAYO FESTIVAL & PARADE
☎ 773-843-9738; www.el5demayo.org
Commemorating the Mexican army's routing of the French in 1862, this three-day, family-friendly bash draws more than 350,000 people to Douglas Park near Pilsen with food, music and carnival rides the first weekend in May. Sunday's colorful parade along Cermak Ave (beginning at Damen Ave) marks the finale.

CELTIC FEST CHICAGO
☎ 312-744-3315; www.celticfestchicago.us
Bagpipers, storytellers and Celtic culture let loose in Millennium Park during a weekend in early May. The traditional 'Men in Kilts Leg Contest' is always a hairy good time.

ANARCHIST FILM FESTIVAL
http://home.comcast.net/~more_about_it
Fight the power by checking out this festival's radical works by and about anarchists. Topics might cover everything from revolution in Oaxaca, Mexico to national identity card use in the UK. Screenings usually occur over two weekends early in the month at various cafes and cultural centers.

BIKE THE DRIVE

last Sun in May

☎ 312-427-3325, ext 251; www.bikethedrive.org
There's one day a year when you don't
need to worry about cars knocking you
off your bicycle. Starting at 5:30am,
automobiles are banned from Lake Shore
Dr, and 20,000 two-wheelers take to the
road. Riding 15 miles along the car-free
lakefront as the sun busts out is a thrill.
Pancakes and live music follow in Grant
Park. It costs $40 to $55 to participate;
proceeds go to the nonprofit Active
Transportation Alliance.

June

CHICAGO GOSPEL FESTIVAL

☎ 312-744-3315; www.chicagogospelmusic
festival.us
Praise the Lord and say hallelujah for the
choirs singing their souls out in Millennium
Park. The free fest usually takes place
during a weekend in early June.

CHICAGO BLUES FESTIVAL

☎ 312-744-3315; www.chicagobluesfestival.us
It's the globe's biggest free blues fest, with
three days of the music that made Chicago
famous. More than 640,000 people unfurl
blankets by the multiple stages that take
over Grant Park in early June.

PRINTERS ROW LIT FEST

☎ 312-222-3986; www.printersrowlitfest.org
This popular free event, sponsored by the
Chicago Tribune, features thousands of rare
and not-so-rare books for sale, plus author
readings. The browsable booths line the
500 to 700 blocks of S Dearborn St in early
June.

JUST FOR LAUGHS CHICAGO

www.justforlaughschicago.com
Montreal's famous comedy festival
exported to Chicago in 2009, and for five
days mid-month more than 100 funny
people – including some Very Big Names –
make 'em laugh at theaters around town.

ANDERSONVILLE MIDSOMMARFEST

☎ 773-664-4682; www.andersonville.org
The Swedes in Andersonville gather round
the maypole mid-month to sing, dance and
eat lingonberries during the weekend-long
festivities.

PUERTO RICAN PARADE & FIESTAS PUERTORRIQUEÑAS

☎ 773-292-1414; www.prparadechicago.org
Chicago's large Puerto Rican community
waves its flag in mid-June. The party starts
downtown with a Saturday parade along
S Columbus Dr, followed by carnival rides
and pork-filled eats at the Humboldt Park
festival.

GRANT PARK MUSIC FESTIVAL

☎ 312-742-7638; www.grantparkmusic
festival.com
The Grant Park Orchestra, composed of top
musicians from symphonies around the
globe, plays free concerts in Millennium
Park's Pritzker Pavilion on Wednesday,
Friday and Saturday evenings from mid-
June through mid-August. It's a summer
ritual to bring wine and a picnic and soak
up the ambience as the sun dips, the
skyscraper lights flicker on, and glorious
music fills the night air.

SUMMERDANCE

☎ 312-742-4007; www.chicagosummerdance.org
Boogie at the Spirit of Music Garden in
Grant Park with a multiethnic mash-up
of locals. Bands play rumba, samba and
other world beats preceded by fun dance
lessons – all free. It starts at 6pm Thursday
to Saturday, and 4pm Sunday, from mid-
June until late August.

TASTE OF CHICAGO

☎ 312-744-3315; www.tasteofchicago.us
This late-month, 10-day food festival in
Grant Park draws hordes for a smorgasbord
of ethnic, meaty, sweet and other local
edibles – much of it served on a stick.
Bring your wallet, extra napkins and
your patience for long lines and crowd
jostling. Several stages host free live
music, including big-name bands (rock
on, Stevie Wonder). The Taste closes
around July 4th.

CHICAGO UNDERGROUND FILM FEST (CUFF)

www.cuff.org
Independent, experimental and
documentary films from around the
world screen at CUFF, the edgier, younger
sibling of the Chicago International Film
Festival (p16). Venues include various small

theaters and galleries. Held over a week in late June.

PRIDE PARADE
last Sun in June

☎ 773-348-8243; www.chicagopridecalendar.org
Colorful floats and risqué revelers pack Halsted St in Boystown. It's the gay and lesbian communities' main event, and more than 450,000 Chicagoans come to the party.

July

INDEPENDENCE DAY FIREWORKS
July 4

Pyrotechnics light up the night sky at Navy Pier, with synchronized shows blasting north (near Montrose Beach) and south (near 63rd St Beach). Note this is not your dad's firework display – Chicago ended its three-decades-long whopper of a show in 2010 due to budget constraints and replaced it with this smaller arsenal.

CHICAGO FOLK & ROOTS FESTIVAL

☎ 773-728-6000; www.chicagofolkandroots.org
Mid-month, one of Chicago's coolest organizations – the Old Town School of Folk Music – throws this two-day party in northside Welles Park, featuring everything from alt-country to Zimbabwean vocalists.

OLD ST PAT'S WORLD'S LARGEST BLOCK PARTY

www.worldslargestblockparty.com
It may be a church – Chicago's oldest, in fact – but St Pat's knows how to throw a party. Booze, bands and beautiful people are all here, and the West Loop event supposedly has brought together several couples over the years. The mingling takes place on a Friday and Saturday in mid-July.

WEST FEST

www.westfestchicago.com
This neighborhood festival rocks harder than most by staging a well-curated lineup of bands, including some pretty damn great national names. The dog-friendly, kid-friendly, weekend shindig takes place on Chicago Ave in Ukrainian Village in mid-July.

PITCHFORK MUSIC FESTIVAL

www.pitchforkmusicfestival.com
It's sort of Lollapalooza Jr, only for bespectacled indie-rock fans. Sonic Youth, the Flaming Lips and other indie heroes shake up Union Park on a typically sweltering weekend, Friday through Sunday, in mid-July. A day pass costs $40; tickets go on sale in February and become scarce by show time.

August

LOLLAPALOOZA

☎ 888-512-7469; www.lollapalooza.com
Once upon a time, this mondo rock fest traveled city to city. Now its permanent home is here in Chicago. It's a raucous event, with 130 bands – including many A-listers – spilling off eight stages in Grant Park the first Friday to Sunday in August.

Ticket prices vary, depending on how early you buy. A limited batch usually goes on sale in early March. These are the cheapest to obtain, since the band lineups haven't been finalized and you're buying on spec. The next ticket round goes up for grabs in early April; you get a bit more information on who's playing at this point, so tickets cost a bit more. By showtime, a three-day pass costs about $215; day passes are about $90. While tickets don't always sell out, advance purchases can help you save significant bucks. Keep a close eye on the website for updates.

NORTHALSTED MARKET DAYS

☎ 773-883-0500; www.northalsted.com
Prepare to see some wild costumes and booths at Market Days, the Midwest's biggest two-day street fair, which spans six blocks of Halsted St in Boystown. Locals gay and straight alike check out crafty vendors and the ample live music. It's held in early to mid-August.

BUD BILLIKEN PARADE
2nd Sat in Aug

☎ 877-244-2246; www.budbillikenparade.com
Held on the second Saturday of the month, this huge parade (the USA's largest African American one) features drill teams, dancers and floats. It runs along Martin Luther King Jr Dr, from 39th St to 51st St, and wraps up with a picnic in Washington Park afterwards.

ELVIS IS ALIVE 5K
☎ 773-305-3338; www.fleetfeetchicago.com/htm/events_races_elvis.asp
Shimmy into your white jumpsuit, glue on the sideburns and energize with a peanut-butter-and-banana sandwich for this annual race through Grant Park, held sometime around August 16th, the day Elvis died. A postrun party in the park follows.

VIVA! CHICAGO LATIN MUSIC FESTIVAL
☎ 312-744-3315; www.vivachicago.us
Held during a mid-month weekend in Millennium Park, the free fest features salsa, merengue, mariachi and Spanish pop music delivered by well-known acts.

CHICAGO AIR & WATER SHOW
☎ 312-744-3370; www.chicagoairandwatershow.us
On Saturday and Sunday afternoon, the third weekend in August, the latest military hardware buzzes the lakefront from Diversey Pkwy south to Oak St Beach, rattling all the buildings' windows in between. North Ave Beach is the best place for viewing.

AFRICAN FESTIVAL OF THE ARTS
☎ 773-955-2787; www.africanfestivalchicago.com
Soulful music and ethnic eats bring crowds to Washington Park for this annual event, usually held over the Labor Day weekend.

CHICAGO JAZZ FEST
☎ 312-744-3315; www.chicagojazzfestival.us
Chicago's longest-running free music fest attracts top names on the local and national jazz scene. Miles Davis, Dave Brubeck and Charlie Haden are among those who have headlined. It's held over Labor Day weekend in Grant Park, with some shows spilling into Millennium Park and the Chicago Cultural Center.

September
WINDY CITY WINE FESTIVAL
☎ 847-382-1480; www.windycitywinefestival.com
Vendors pour more than 250 global vinos by Buckingham Fountain, and a cool $25 gets you 10 tastings plus cooking demos and free music acts. It's held the second weekend in September.

GERMAN-AMERICAN FESTIVAL
☎ 630-653-3018; www.germanday.com
Don the lederhosen and raise a frothy stein at this annual event in the old German 'hood of Lincoln Square. The Von Steuben Parade marches through on Saturday (*Ferris Bueller's Day Off* fans will remember it as the parade Ferris joins when he sings aboard a float).

WORLD MUSIC FESTIVAL
☎ 312-742-1938; www.worldmusicfestival.org
Musicians and bands from around the world tote their bouzoukis, ouds and other exotic instruments to Chicago for a week's worth of performances late month. Shows take place at venues throughout town, with the Chicago Cultural Center anchoring it all.

October
CHICAGO COUNTRY MUSIC FESTIVAL
☎ 312-744-3315; www.chicagocountrymusicfestival.us
Millennium Park fills up once again, this time with cowboy-boot-wearin' folks for a weekend early in the month. The music spans the gamut from slick new artists to old-school favorites like Loretta Lynn and Kenny Rogers.

CHICAGO INTERNATIONAL FILM FESTIVAL
☎ 312-683-0121; www.chicagofilmfestival.com
This is the city's main film event. It typically shows a few big-name flicks among the myriad not-so-big-name flicks, and brings a few big-name Hollywood stars to town to add a glamorous sheen to the proceedings. It's unspools over two weeks, starting early in the month, at varying venues.

CHICAGO MARATHON
☎ 312-904-9800; www.chicagomarathon.com
More than 45,000 runners from all over the globe compete on the 26-mile course through the city's heart, cheered on by a million spectators. Held on a Sunday in October (when the weather can be pleasant or absolutely freezing), it's considered one of the world's top five marathons.

CHICAGO BOOK FESTIVAL
☎ 312-747-4999; www.chicagopubliclibrary foundation.org
The Chicago Public Library organizes special readings, lectures and book events throughout the month at its citywide branches. Many festivities revolve around the 'One Book, One Chicago' program, where everyone – including Mayor Daley – reads the same book (past selections have included Elie Wiesel's *Night* and Jane Austen's *Pride & Prejudice*).

CHICAGOWEEN
☎ 312-744-3315; www.explorechicago.org
From mid-October through Halloween, the city transforms Daley Plaza into Pumpkin Plaza and sets up a Haunted Village for kids.

DAY OF THE DEAD CELEBRATIONS
☎ 312-738-1503; www.nationalmuseumof mexicanart.org
The National Museum of Mexican Art in Pilsen puts on thought-provoking Day of the Dead events running from October to mid-December.

November
CHICAGO HUMANITIES FESTIVAL
☎ 312-661-1028; www.chicagohumanities.org
Put on your thinking cap: for two weeks in early November, a citywide series of chin-stroking talks, panels, readings, performances, exhibits and screenings take place, all focusing on a single, academic topic (it was 'the body' in 2010).

MAGNIFICENT MILE LIGHTS FESTIVAL
www.magnificentmilelightsfestival.com
During this free pre-Thanksgiving fest, Mickey Mouse and a posse of family-friendly musicians kick off the holiday season by turning on the Mag Mile's one million lights, which twinkle on into January.

THANKSGIVING DAY PARADE
4th Thu In Nov
www.chicagofestivals.org
Around 400,000 shivering souls show up to see giant helium balloons, floats, marching bands, and local and national celebrities at the annual turkey day parade. It glides along State St from Congress to Randolph Sts.

TREE LIGHTING CEREMONY
4th Thu in Nov
☎ 312-744-3315
The mayor flips the switch to light up Chicago's Christmas tree in Daley Plaza on Thanksgiving Day.

December
CHRISTKINDLMARKET
www.christkindlmarket.com
This traditional German holiday market takes over Daley Plaza in December, wafting sausages, roasted nuts and spiced wine along with Old World handicrafts. It starts around Thanksgiving and goes on until Christmas Eve.

ZOOLIGHTS
☎ 312-742-2000; www.lpzoo.org
As if the predatory cats weren't interesting enough, Lincoln Park Zoo gets gussied up for the holidays with sparkling trees, Santa spotting and seasonal displays throughout December.

WINTER WONDERFEST AT NAVY PIER
☎ 312-595-7437; www.winterwonderfest.com
With ice-skating, rides and an eye-popping indoor display throughout December, Chicago's most popular tourist attraction goes all out for the holidays, and then out with a bang during its New Year's Eve fireworks show.

HOW MUCH?
Gallon of gas $3.30
Liter of water $1.50
Bottle of Old Style beer $3
Souvenir T-shirt from the Hideout $15
Italian beef sandwich $5
El fare $2.25
Green Mill martini $8.50
Near North hotel room approximately $159
Blues club cover charge $15
Small bag of Garrett's caramel popcorn $4.50

lonelyplanet.com

GETTING STARTED COSTS & MONEY

COSTS & MONEY

Chicago is cheaper than its big-city coastal counterparts. In general, eating and drinking prices are reasonable, and there are loads of free concerts and cultural festivals for entertainment. Accommodation prices are another story.

Your hotel room can cost an awful lot. The rack rates on rooms here are shocking. This is partially because of the 15.4% hotel tax levied by the city, which Chicago depends on to maintain its parks and public buildings. But the city is only partially to blame for the price tags on hotel and motel rooms. Business travelers are the other culprits. Because of the huge number of conventioneers in Chicago at any given moment, hotel rooms are almost always at a premium. And unlike leisure travelers, the business travelers (1) have to come here whether they want to or not, and (2) get reimbursed for their lodging costs.

A standard midrange room costs between $150 and $225 per night with tax. Sadly, $35 hostel beds and other budget properties are thin on the ground. The best way to save money is to shop around as much as possible on the internet. Sometimes the room price listed on a discount travel website can be $100 lower than the price quoted by the hotel reservation agent. For tips on bidding for rooms, see the boxed text, p232. For other lodging-related tips and tricks, see Saving Strategies (p227).

Food is typically good value in the Windy City. Lunch at a sit-down restaurant costs about $15 per person, including a nonalcoholic drink and a tip. Double it for dinner at a mid-range restaurant or pub. If you want to spend more, Chicago has plenty of upscale places where you can do just that and easily rack up a $200 tab for top-end molecular gastronomy. Chicago's ample ethnic eats – Mexican, Indian, Middle Eastern and Vietnamese food – are the budgeteer's friend. So are the myriad burger and hot dog joints, where you can feast for less than $10. A pint of beer averages $6.

The premier museums charge around $20 for admission. Many have scattered free days (see p111), and discount cards are available (see p268). Other top attractions, including Millennium Park, Navy Pier and Lincoln Park Zoo, don't cost a dime. Discount ticket brokers such as Goldstar (www.goldstar.com) and Hot Tix (www.hottix.org) slash prices in half for theater and sports events.

The El offers an economical way to get around at $2.25 per ride ($5.75 for a day pass). Taxi fares mount quickly – even a short ride of just a few miles will cost $10.

All in all, once you conquer the accommo-dation issue, you're looking at a reasonably priced holiday in Chicago compared to other big cities.

INTERNET RESOURCES

DailyCandy (www.dailycandy.com/chicago) Get the girly fashion and shopping lowdown.

Richard M Daley's YouTube channel (www.youtube.com /mayordaley) Da Mayor spouts on YouTube.

ADVANCE PLANNING

First and foremost, book your lodging ahead of time. Not only will this help avoid unpleasant surprises like the International Screwdriver Association taking up every room in town, but you'll cut costs off the outrageous rack rates. See p227 for detailed advice on saving strategies.

Foodies who crave dinner at top-end restaurants like Alinea (p156), Topolobampo (p150) and Schwa (p165) should make reservations six to eight weeks in advance.

Three weeks or so before your trip, sign up online with national ticket broker Goldstar (www.goldstar.com) to be privy to half-price seats for a huge array of theater performances, sports events (including White Sox, Bulls and Cubs rooftop seats) and even local boat tours.

While you can get half-price theater tickets on the day of performances from Hot Tix (www.hottix.org), popular shows often sell out. If you have your heart set on a particular performance, keep an eye on the Hot Tix website a few weeks before your arrival and see if your show has a pattern of available tickets. If not, book ahead.

Pitchfork and especially Lollapalooza fans can save money by buying tickets in advance. Keep an eye on the events' websites starting in February; see p15 for details. If you're coming to town for these fests or any other big summer music bash, definitely secure lodging in advance.

You'll save more time than money by ordering your CTA train passes (p265) in advance, but didn't someone once say 'time is money'?

Finally, folks who enjoy DIY walking tours should download the several audio excursions the city has to offer. The MP3s cover everything from Loop architecture to blues sights; see p272 for a list of what's on offer.

18

Explore Chicago (www.explorechicago.org) The city's official portal, with excellent neighborhood information and a Twitter feed of day-by-day free events.

Gapers Block (www.gapersblock.com) Hip, playful reports on the latest news, cultural happenings and political shenanigans afoot in the Windy City.

Hot Rooms (www.hotrooms.com) Peruse this Chicago-centric hotel room consolidator to save a few bucks. If nothing else, you can take the prices you find here and try to beat 'em on Hotwire or Priceline.

HuffPost Chicago (www.huffingtonpost.com/chicago) Amalgamates news from major local sources.

Lonely Planet (www.lonelyplanet.com) Succinct summaries on travelling to most places on earth; postcards from other travelers; and the Thorn Tree bulletin board, where you can ask questions before you go or dispense advice when you get back.

LTHForum (www.lthforum.com) Foodies, this one's for you: wide-ranging talk about the local restaurant scene from a dedicated community of food lovers.

VegIllinois.com Chicago (www.vegchicago.com) Guide to local vegetarian and vegan restaurants and markets.

SUSTAINABLE CHICAGO

You can tread gently on the earth and still have a first-class visit to the Windy City. You're spoiled for choice if you wish to avoid flying here. Chicago is an Amtrak (p266), Megabus (p264) and Greyhound (p264) hub, so take your pick of these lower-impact modes of travel. Once in town, ditch the car. Public transportation goes to most visitor-oriented places; taking the train or bus not only cuts down on emissions, but allows you to avoid

top picks

ECOFRIENDLY BUSINESSES

- Working Bikes Cooperative (p216)
- Hotel Felix (p234)
- Xoco (p153)
- Greenheart Shop (p138)
- City Provisions (p160)
- Green City Market (p157)
- Bleeding Heart Bakery (p161)

the megahassle of trying to find parking (and paying the absurd price for it).

Heck, if you really want to do it right, buy a recycled two-wheeler from Working Bikes Cooperative (p216) for $50 or so. The cost won't be much more than a daily bike rental, plus when you're finished you can donate it back to the group.

It's getting easier and easier to eat sustainably, thanks to farmers' markets and a growing list of restaurants that source ingredients locally. See Farmers' markets (p157) and the Local Beet (www.thelocalbeet.com), a locavore website, for suggestions.

As for lodging, most of the city's properties do the usual by asking visitors to reuse towels and sheets. Approximately 15 downtown hotels have received Green Seal certification; see p229 for more on the subject.

Chicago continues its role as an architectural innovator and leads the nation in green building design; see p39 for details.

HISTORY

ONIONS, FORTS AND MASSACRES

The Potawatomi Indians were the first folks in town, and they gave the name 'Checagou' – or wild onions – to the area around the Chicago River's mouth. Needless to say, they weren't particularly pleased when the first settlers arrived in 1803. The newcomers built Fort Dearborn on the river's south bank, on marshy ground under what is today's Michigan Ave Bridge (look for plaques in the sidewalk marking the spot at the corner of Michigan Ave and Wacker Dr).

The Potawatomi's resentment toward their new neighbors mounted, and bad things ensued. In 1812, the natives – in cahoots with the British (their allies in the War of 1812) – slaughtered 52 settlers fleeing the fort. The massacre took place near what is today Hillary Rodham Clinton Women's Park (p117). During the war this had been a strategy employed throughout the frontier: the British sought the allegiance of various Indian tribes through trade and other deals, and the Indians paid them back by killing American settlers. The people killed in Chicago had simply waited too long to flee the rising tension and found themselves caught.

After the war ended, everyone let bygones be bygones and hugged it out for the sake of the fur trade.

REAL ESTATE BOOM

Chicago was incorporated as a town in 1833, with a population of 340. Within three years land speculation rocked the local real estate market; lots that sold for $33 in 1829 now went for $100,000. Construction on the Illinois & Michigan Canal – a state project linking the Great Lakes to the Illinois River and thus to the Mississippi River and the Atlantic coast – fueled the boom. Swarms of laborers swelled the population to more than 4100 by 1837, and Chicago became a city.

Within 10 years, more than 20,000 people lived in what had become the region's dominant city. The rich Illinois soil supported thousands of farmers, and industrialist Cyrus Hall McCormick moved his reaper factory to the city to serve them. He would soon control one of the Midwest's major fortunes and have a big mansion on Astor St (see p73).

In 1848 the canal opened. Shipping flowed through the area and had a marked economic effect on the city. A great financial institution, the Chicago Board of Trade, opened to handle the sale of grain by Illinois farmers, who now had greatly improved access to Eastern markets.

Railroad construction began soon thereafter, and tracks radiated out from Chicago. The city quickly became the hub of America's freight and passenger trains, a position it would hold for the next 100 years.

RING ON THE BACON

By the end of the 1850s, immigrants had poured into the city, drawn by jobs on the railroads that served the ever-growing agricultural trade. Twenty million bushels of produce were

TIMELINE

Late 1600s	1779	1803
The Potawatomi Indians have the land to themselves. They paddle their birchbark canoes, fish and ponder a name for the place. How about Checagou (Wild Onions), after the local plants growing here?	Jean Baptiste Pointe du Sable, an enterprising gent of African and Caribbean descent, sails down from Québec and sets up a fur-trading post on the Chicago River. He is the city's first settler.	More settlers arrive and build Fort Dearborn at the river's mouth. The Potawatomi locals do not send a fruit basket to their new neighbors. Rather, they massacre the settlers nine years later.

shipped through Chicago annually by then. The population topped 100,000.

The city's location smack-dab in the middle of the country made it a favorite meeting spot, a legacy that continues to this day (which is why you're paying out the nose for your hotel room). In 1860 the Republican Party held its national political convention in Chicago and selected Abraham Lincoln, a lawyer from Springfield, Illinois, as its presidential candidate.

Like other northern cities, Chicago profited from the Civil War, which boosted business in the burgeoning steel and toolmaking industries, and provided plenty of freight for the railroads and canal. In 1865, the year the war ended, another event took place that profoundly affected the city for the next century: the Union Stockyards opened on the South Side.

Chicago's rail network and the invention of the iced refrigerator car meant that meat could be shipped for long distances, satiating hungry carnivores all the way east to New York and beyond. The stockyards soon became the major meat supplier to the nation. But besides bringing great wealth to a few and jobs to many, the yards were also a source of water pollution (see the boxed text, p124).

STOP THE BACON!

The stockyard effluvia polluted not only the Chicago River but also Lake Michigan. Flowing into the lake, the fouled waters spoiled the city's source of fresh water and caused cholera and other epidemics that killed thousands. In 1869 the Water Tower and Pumping Station built a 2-mile tunnel into Lake Michigan and began bringing water into the city from there; it was hoped that this set-up would skirt the contaminated areas. Alas, the idea proved resoundingly inadequate, and outbreaks of illness continued.

top picks

BOOKS ON CHICAGO'S HISTORY

Beyond the history classics (*Chicago: City on the Make* by Nelson Algren, 1951; *Boss: Richard J Daley of Chicago* by Mike Royko, 1971; and *Working: What People Do All Day and How They Feel About What They Do* by Studs Terkel, 1974), here are some more recent additions to the Chicago bookshelf:

- Sin in the Second City (Karen Abbott, 2007) In the early 1900s, sisters Minna and Ada Everleigh opened a brothel called the Everleigh Club in Chicago's notorious Levee district. Their courtesans entertained Prince Henry of Prussia and author Theodore Dreiser, plus moguls and senators. The ladies dined on gourmet food, read Balzac and started a culture war that rocked the nation.
- Murder City: The Bloody History of Chicago in the Twenties (Michael Lesy, 2007) Chicago in the 1920s was America's murder capital – professionals and amateurs alike snuffed each other out with reckless abandon. The book shows that these crimes of loot and love may be the progenitors of our modern age.
- Richard Nickels' Chicago, Photographs of a Lost City (Richard Cahan & Michael Williams, 2006) Nickels was a photographer and preservationist. He snapped buildings in Chicago in the 1950s and '60s, at a point when big construction was really starting to take hold and change the city.
- Encyclopedia of Chicago (2004) The Newberry Library and the Chicago History Museum put together this all-encompassing guide to Windy City history.
- Historic Photos of Chicago Crime (John Russick, 2007) A compilation of 200 photos of Al Capone and fellow thugs, from bloody cadavers to one of Capone at a White Sox game.

1837	1865	1871
Chicago incorporates as a city (population: 4170). It's a happenin' place, having sky-rocketed from just 340 people four years earlier. And it continues to boom – within 10 years 16,000 folks call the city home.	The Union Stockyards open, and millions of cows get the ax. Thanks to new train tracks and refrigerated railcars, Chicago can send its bacon afar and becomes 'hog butcher for the world' (per poet Carl Sandburg).	The Great Fire torches the entire inner city. Mrs O'Leary's cow takes the blame, though it's eventually determined that Daniel 'Peg Leg' Sullivan kicked over the lantern that started the blaze.

Two years later, engineers deepened the Illinois & Michigan Canal so they could alter the Chicago River's course and make it flow south, away from the city. Sending waste and sewage down the reversed river provided relief for Chicago residents and helped ease lake pollution, but it was not a welcome change for those living near what had become the city's drainpipe. A resident of Morris, about 60 miles downstream, wrote: 'What right has Chicago to pour its filth down into what was before a sweet and clean river, pollute its waters, and materially reduce the value of property on both sides of the river and canal, and bring sickness and death to the citizens?' The guy had a point.

The river occasionally still flowed into the lake after heavy rains; it wasn't permanently reversed until 1900, when the huge Chicago Sanitary & Ship Canal opened.

BURN BABY BURN – CHICAGO INFERNO

On October 8, 1871, the Chicago fire started just southwest of downtown. For more than 125 years, legend has had it that a cow owned by a certain Mrs O'Leary kicked over a lantern, which ignited some hay, which ignited some lumber, which ignited the whole town. The image of the hapless heifer has endured despite evidence that the fire was actually the fault of Daniel 'Peg Leg' Sullivan, who dropped by the barn on an errand, accidentally started the fire himself and then tried to blame it on the bovine. (The Chicago City Council officially passed a resolution in 1997 absolving the O'Leary family of blame.)

However it started, the results of the Chicago fire were devastating. It burned for three days, killing 300 people, destroying 18,000 buildings and leaving 90,000 people homeless. 'By morning 100,000 people will be without food and shelter. Can you help us?' was the message sent East by Mayor Roswell B Mason as Chicago and City Hall literally burned down around him.

The dry conditions and mostly wood buildings set the stage for a runaway conflagration, as a hot wind carried flaming embers to unburned areas, which quickly caught fire. The primitive, horse-drawn fire-fighting equipment could do little to keep up with the spreading blaze. Almost every structure was destroyed or gutted in the area bounded by the river on the west, what's now Roosevelt Rd to the south and Fullerton Ave to the north.

Mayor Mason did earn kudos for his skilful handling of Chicago's recovery. His best move was to prevent the aldermen on the city council from getting their hands on the millions of dollars in relief funds that Easterners had donated after the mayor's fireside plea, thus ensuring that the money actually reached the rabble living in the rubble.

MAKE BIG PLANS

Despite the human tragedy, the fire taught the city some valuable lessons – namely, don't build everything from wood. Chicago reconstructed with modern materials, and created space for new industrial and commercial buildings.

The world's best architects poured into the city during the 1880s and '90s to take advantage of the situation. They had a blank canvas to work with, a city giving them lots of dough, and pretty much the green light to use their imaginations to the fullest. The world's first skyscraper soon popped up in 1885. Several other important buildings (see p56) also rose during the era, spawning the Chicago Style of architecture. Daniel Burnham was one of the premier designers running the show, and he summed up the city's credo best: 'Make no little plans,' he counseled Chicago's leaders in 1909, 'for they have no magic to stir men's blood… Make big plans.'

1880s	1885	1886
People start calling Chicago the 'Windy City' – not because of its blustery weather, but because of its big-mouthed local citizenry who constantly brag about the town's greatness.	The world's first steel-frame 'skyscraper,' the Home Insurance Building, rises up on the skyline. It's 10 stories (138ft) tall and paves the way for big things to come.	Workers fight for their right to an eight-hour workday and decent pay by holding a rally at Haymarket Sq. The cops come, bombs explode, anarchists take the blame and the modern labor movement is born.

22

FIVE FIGURES WHO CHANGED CHICAGO HISTORY

Daniel Burnham Designer of the 'Chicago Plan,' Burnham played a principal role in developing the Chicago School of architecture and oversaw the beaux-arts buildings of the 1893 World's Expo.

Al Capone Many historians say the city's corruption legacy stems from this notorious gangster and racketeer.

Chess Brothers Leonard and Phil are the dudes who brought the electric blues – and ultimately rock 'n' roll – to the world from their Near South Side studio.

Richard J Daley Chicago politics have never been the same since Mayor Daley number one ruled the roost with iron fists from 1955 to 1976.

Mrs O'Leary's cow When it kicked over the lantern that burned down the city, it created the blank canvas that allowed Chicago's sky-scraping architecture to flourish.

GIMME A BREAK

Labor unrest had been brewing in the city for a few years. In 1876, organized strikes began in the railroad yards as workers demanded an eight-hour workday and rest breaks. The turbulence spread to the McCormick Reaper Works, which was then Chicago's largest factory. The police and federal troops broke up the strikes, killing 18 civilians and injuring hundreds more.

By then, May 1 had become the official day of protest for labor groups in Chicago. On that day in 1886, 60,000 workers went on strike, once again demanding an eight-hour workday. As usual, police attacked the strikers at locations throughout the city. Three days later, self-described anarchists staged a protest in Haymarket Sq; out of nowhere a bomb exploded, killing seven police officers. The government reacted strongly to what became known as the Haymarket Riot. Eight anarchists were convicted of 'general conspiracy to murder' and four were hanged, although only two had been present at the incident and the bomber was never identified. A sculpture marks the square today (see p106 for details).

THE WHITE CITY DEBUTS

The 1893 World's Expo marked Chicago's showy debut on the international stage. The event centered on a grand complex of specially built structures lying just south of Hyde Park. They were painted white and were brilliantly lit by electric searchlights, which is how the 'White City' tag came to be. Designed by architectural luminaries such as Daniel Burnham, Louis Sullivan and Frederick Law Olmsted, the fairgrounds were meant to show how parks, streets and buildings could be designed in a harmonious manner that would enrich the chaotic urban environment.

Open for only five months, the exposition attracted 27 million visitors, many of whom rode the newly built El train to and from the Loop. The fair offered wonders heretofore unknown to the world: long-distance phone calls, the first moving pictures (courtesy of Thomas Alva Edison's Kinetoscope), the first Ferris wheel and the first zipper. Businessmen were in awe of the first vertical file (invented by Melvil Dewey, of Dewey Decimal System fame) and children were taken with a new gum called Juicy Fruit. It was at this fair that Pabst beer won the blue ribbon that has been part of its name ever since.

1893	1900	1908
The World's Expo opens near Hyde Park, and Chicago grabs the global spotlight for the wonders it unveils, including the Ferris wheel, movies, Cracker Jack, Pabst beer and the vertical filing cabinet.	In an engineering feat, Chicago reverses the flow of the Chicago River, forever ingratiating itself with its downstate neighbors as waste now streams in their direction.	Chicago Cubs win the World Series. 'Let's do this again soon,' the team says. But curses involving goats, fans named Bartman and general all-round crappy teams keep them winless for the next 100 years. And counting…

top picks

HISTORIC SITES

- St Valentine's Day Massacre Site (p81)
- Water Tower (p71)
- Haymarket Square (p106)
- Graceland Cemetery (p89)
- Nuclear Energy sculpture (p124)

The entire assemblage made a huge impact worldwide, and the fair's architects were deluged with commissions to redesign cities. The buildings themselves, despite their grandeur, were short lived, having been built out of a rough equivalent of plaster of Paris that barely lasted through the fair. The only survivor was the Fine Arts Building, which was revamped to become the Museum of Science & Industry (p119).

Around this time, society legend Bertha Palmer was following the lead of other Chicago elite by touring Paris. A prescient art collector, she nabbed Monets, Renoirs and other impressionist works before they had achieved acclaim. Her collection later formed the core of the Art Institute (p52).

THE GREAT MIGRATION

In 1910 eight out of 10 blacks still lived in the southern states of the old Confederacy. Over the next decade a variety of factors combined to change that, as more than two million African Americans moved north in what came to be known as the Great Migration.

Chicago played a pivotal role in this massive population shift, both as an impetus and as a destination. Articles in the black-owned and nationally circulated *Chicago Defender* proclaimed the city a worker's paradise and a place free from the horrors of Southern racism. Ads from Chicago employers also promised jobs to anyone willing to work.

These lures, coupled with glitzy images of thriving neighborhoods like Bronzeville (p122), inspired thousands to relocate. Chicago's black population zoomed from 44,103 in 1910 to 109,458 in 1920 and continued growing. The migrants, often poorly educated sharecroppers with big dreams, found a reality not as rosy as promised. In 1919 white gangs from Bridgeport led days of rioting that killed 23 local black residents and 15 white ones. Employers were ready with the promised jobs, but many hoped to rid their factories of white unionized workers by replacing them with blacks, which further exacerbated racial tensions. Blacks were also restricted to living in South Side ghettos by openly prejudicial real estate practices that kept them from buying or renting homes elsewhere in the city. The South Side remains predominantly black to this day.

BOOZE FUELS THE MACHINE

Efforts to make the United States 'dry' had never found great favor in Chicago, especially among the city's vast numbers of German and Irish immigrants. During the 20th century's first two decades, the political party that could portray itself as the 'wettest' would win the local elections. Thus the nationwide enactment of Prohibition in 1920 (the federal constitutional amendment making alcohol consumption illegal) was destined to meet resistance in Chicago, where voters had gone six to one against the law in an advisory referendum. However, few could have predicted how efforts to flout Prohibition would forever mark Chicago's image on a global scale, thanks to a gent named Al Capone (see the boxed text, p81).

1915	1929	1931
The *Eastland* steamboat, filled with picnickers, capsizes in the Chicago River while still tied to the dock by LaSalle St Bridge; 844 people die, though the water there is only 20ft deep.	Prohibition conflict comes to a head when seven people are killed in a gang shoot-out between gangster Al Capone and Bugs Moran. The day becomes known as the St Valentine's Day Massacre.	After years of running the murderous Chicago Outfit and supplying the nation with illegal booze during Prohibition, Capone goes to jail for tax evasion. There he's called 'the wop with the mop.'

An important year for the city, 1933 saw Prohibition repealed and a thirsty populace return openly to the bars. Another world's fair, this time called the Century of Progress, opened on the lakefront south of Grant Park and promised a bright future filled with modern conveniences. Then, in the same year, Ed Kelly became mayor. With the help of party boss, Pat Nash, he strengthened Chicago's Democratic Party, creating the legendary 'machine' that would control local politics for the next 50 years. Politicians doled out thousands of city jobs to people who worked hard to make sure their patrons were reelected. The same was true for city vendors and contractors, whose continued prosperity was tied to their donations.

WINDY CITY INGENUITY

Chicago has wowed the world with inventions and discoveries:

- roller skates (1884)
- the cafeteria (1895)
- Hostess Twinkies (1930)
- pinball (1930)
- Oscar Mayer 'Wienermobile' (1936)
- controlled atomic reaction (1942)
- daytime TV soap operas (1949)
- spray paint (1949)
- Weber Grill (1951)
- Lava Lite 'Lava Lamps' (1965)
- house music (1977)

DA MAYOR #1: RICHIE J DALEY

The zenith of the machine's power began with the election of Richard J Daley in 1955. Initially thought to be a mere party functionary, Daley was reelected mayor five times before dying while still in office in 1976. With an uncanny understanding of machine politics and how to use it to halt dissent, he dominated the city in a way no mayor had before. His word was law, and the city council routinely approved all his actions, lest a dissenter find his or her ward deprived of vital city services.

Under 'the Boss's' rule, corruption was rampant. A 1957 *Life* magazine report called Chicago's cops the most corrupt in the nation. Although Daley and the machine howled with indignation over the article, further exposés by the press revealed that some cops and politicians were in cahoots with various crime rings.

Chicago's voting practices were also highly suspect, never more so than in 1960 when John F Kennedy ran for president of the United States against Richard Nixon, then vice president. The night of the election, the results were so close nationwide that the outcome hinged on the vote in Illinois.

Mayor Daley called up Kennedy and assured him that 'with a little bit of luck and the help of a few close friends, you're going to carry Illinois.' Kennedy did win Illinois, by 10,000 votes, and that granted him the presidency. For many, that was the perfect embodiment of electoral politics in Chicago, a city where the slogan has long been 'Vote early and vote often,' and voters have been known to rise from the grave to cast ballots.

HIPPIES & RIOTS COME TO TOWN

The year 1968 proved an explosive one for Chicago. When Martin Luther King Jr was assassinated in Memphis, Tennessee, Chicago's West Side exploded in riots and went up in smoke. Whole stretches of the city were laid to waste, and Daley and the many black politicians in the machine were helpless to stop the violence. Worse yet, the city's hosting of the Democratic

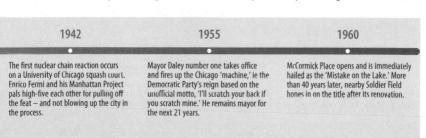

1942	1955	1960
The first nuclear chain reaction occurs on a University of Chicago squash court. Enrico Fermi and his Manhattan Project pals high-five each other for pulling off the feat – and not blowing up the city in the process.	Mayor Daley number one takes office and fires up the Chicago 'machine,' ie the Democratic Party's reign based on the unofficial motto, 'I'll scratch your back if you scratch mine.' He remains mayor for the next 21 years.	McCormick Place opens and is immediately hailed as the 'Mistake on the Lake.' More than 40 years later, nearby Soldier Field hones in on the title after its renovation.

National Convention in August degenerated into a fiasco of such proportions that its legacy dogged Chicago for decades.

With the war in Vietnam escalating and general unrest quickly spreading through the USA, the convention became a focal point for protest groups of all stripes. Yet despite the tempest brewing, Mayor Daley insisted the city would continue its plans to host the big event. Word leaked out that protesters would converge on Chicago, sparking authorities' strategy to crack the head of anybody who got in the way. Local officials shot down all of the protesters' requests for parade permits, despite calls from the press and other politicians to uphold the civil right of free assembly.

Enter Abbie Hoffman, Jerry Rubin, Rennie Davis, Tom Hayden, Bobby Seale and David Dellinger – members of the soon-to-become 'Chicago Seven.' They called for a mobilization of 500,000 protesters to converge on Chicago. As the odds of confrontation became high, many moderate protesters decided not to attend. When the convention opened, there were just a few thousand young protesters in the city. But Daley and his allies spread rumors to the media to bolster the case for their aggressive preparations, including a claim that LSD would be dumped into the city's water supply.

The force amassed amounted to 11,900 Chicago police officers, 7500 Army troops, 7500 Illinois National Guardsmen and 1000 Secret Service agents for the August 25–30 convention. The first few nights police staged raids on protesters attempting to camp in Lincoln Park. The cops moved in with tear gas and billy clubs, singling out some individuals – including several news reporters – for savage attacks.

The action then shifted to Grant Park, across from the Conrad Hilton (now the Chicago Hilton & Towers), where the main presidential candidates were staying. Protesters attempted to march to the site, and the police again met them with tear gas and nightsticks and threw many through the hotel's plate-glass windows. The media widely covered the incident, which investigators later termed a 'police riot.'

It was all scrutinized in a federal government–funded study to determine the cause of the violence. Who was to blame? Mostly the Chicago police, the study said. Mayor Daley disagreed and issued the police a pay raise.

The long-term effects of the riots were far greater that anyone could have guessed. The Democratic candidate for president, Hubert Humphrey, was left without liberal backing after his tacit support of Daley's tactics, and as a result, Republican Richard Nixon was elected president. Chicago was left with a huge black eye for decades.

POLISHING THE RUST

Meanwhile, the city's economy was hitting the skids. In 1971 financial pressures caused the last of the Chicago stockyards to close, marking the end of one of the city's most infamous enterprises. Factories and steel mills were also shutting down as companies moved to the suburbs or the southern USA, where taxes and wages were lower. Chicago and much of the Midwest earned the moniker 'Rust Belt,' describing the area's shrunken economies and rusting factories.

But two events happened in the 1970s that were harbingers of the city's more promising future. The world's tallest building (at the time), the Sears Tower (later renamed Willis Tower), opened in the Loop in 1974, beginning a development trend that would spur the creation of

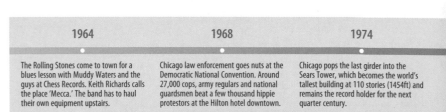

1964	1968	1974
The Rolling Stones come to town for a blues lesson with Muddy Waters and the guys at Chess Records. Keith Richards calls the place 'Mecca.' The band has to haul their own equipment upstairs.	Chicago law enforcement goes nuts at the Democratic National Convention. Around 27,000 cops, army regulars and national guardsmen beat a few thousand hippie protestors at the Hilton hotel downtown.	Chicago pops the last girder into the Sears Tower, which becomes the world's tallest building at 110 stories (1454ft) and remains the record holder for the next quarter century.

thousands of high-paying white-collar jobs. And in 1975, the Water Tower Place shopping mall brought new life to N Michigan Ave.

The city's first and only female mayor – the colorful Jane Byrne – took the helm in 1979. She opened Chicago up to filmmakers, allowing the producers of *The Blues Brothers* to demolish part of the Daley Center. Moviemaking remains an important city revenue generator today.

Byrne's reign was followed by that of Harold Washington, Chicago's first black mayor, in 1983. His legacy was the success of the African American politicians who followed him. Democrat Carol Moseley-Braun's election to the US senate in 1992 can be credited in part to Washington's political trailblazing. Barack Obama is another name that comes to mind.

DA MAYOR #2: RICHIE M DALEY

In 1989 Chicago elected Richard M Daley, the son of Richard J Daley, to finish the remaining two years of Harold Washington's mayoral term (Washington died in office).

Like his father, Daley had an uncanny instinct for city politics. First, he made nice with state officials, who handed over hundreds of millions of public dollars. Among the projects that bore fruit were an O'Hare airport expansion, a huge addition to the McCormick Place Convention Center and the reconstruction of Navy Pier. He also restructured old, semi-independent bureaucracies such as the Park District and the Department of Education. And he entertained the city as well. Daley proved himself prone to amusing verbal comments, such as this classic, his explanation for why city health inspectors had closed down so many local restaurants: 'If a rat is on your sandwich, you hope to know it before. If a mouse is on your salad, it's common sense.'

Despite falling to the third-largest US city, population-wise, in the 1990 census (behind New York and LA), Chicago enjoyed a good decade in the '90s. In 1991 the Chicago Bulls won the first of six national basketball championships. The 1994 World Cup soccer opening ceremony focused international attention on the city. And in 1996 a 28-year-old demon was exorcised when the Democratic National Convention returned to Chicago. Officials spent millions of dollars spiffing up the city, and thousands of cops underwent sensitivity training on how to deal with protestors. The convention went off like a dream and left Chicagoans believing they were on a roll.

And when you're on a roll, who else do you thank but the guy who seems to have made it all possible? Daley won his reelection bids in 1991, 1995, 1999, 2003 and 2007, pretty much by a landslide every time.

That's not to say the guy didn't have issues. In 2003 he bulldozed the lakefront commuter airport of Meigs Field in a show of power (see Northerly Island, p114). In 2005, the 'Hired Truck scandal' cast an awkward shadow over his administration, when it was discovered that city staff had been accepting bribes in exchange for giving lucrative trucking contracts to companies that never actually did any work. In 2008 he leased the city's parking meters to a private firm, which promptly raised rates and irked locals. And in 2009, he failed to bring the Olympics to Chicago after much fanfare and money spent on the bid.

In 2010, Daley announced he would not seek office for a seventh term, that it was 'time to move on.' He was Chicago's longest-running mayor, with 22 years under his belt. The previous record holder? His dad, whose record was...21 years.

At press time, there was no clear front-runner as to who'd fill Daley's shoes.

1989	2008	2010
Mayor Daley number two takes office, continuing the machine legacy of his dad. His reign is highlighted by midnight bulldozings and shiny park unveilings. He ends up ruling the city even longer than his pa.	Local boy Barack Obama stands in the frosty, electric air of Grant Park and gives his acceptance speech as President of the United States. Chicagoans swell with pride. Yes we can, indeed.	The Blackhawks win the Stanley Cup, and two million fans jam downtown for a ticker-tape parade. It's much needed consolation after 2009, when Oprah announced she's leaving and the city loses its Olympic bid.

THE CITY THAT WORKS

Chicago is often called 'the city that works', which has several interpretations. It can refer to the populace with its hard-working, no-nonsense, traditional Midwestern ethics. It can refer to the ambitious civic projects the city undertakes, like its skyscrapers, parks and river-altering sanitation system. Or it can refer to the much publicized culture of corruption, in which patronage greases the wheels that make things happen in local government. For the record: 28 city council members have been convicted of wrongdoing (mostly kickbacks) since 1972.

A lot of Chicagoans sigh when they hear about the shenanigans at City Hall. Then they point out all the flowers planted along the streets downtown, and how the once-trashed sidewalks are now clean. How Millennium Park gleams, even though it opened four years late and hundreds of millions of dollars over budget (thanks to the original contractor, who was the mayor's friend). What's a little graft when the city looks so *good*?

Chicago felt the impact of the global financial crisis – unemployment up, budgets down, some city services cut. Its unemployment rate hovers just above the national average. Recently there've been spotlight-grabbing high points (local boy Barack Obama becomes President) and low points (Olympic bid loss, Spire construction halted). But the city just picks itself up and gets on with its next sky-bound project.

As a wise man named Burnham once said, 'Make big plans. Aim high in hope and work.' Exactly what Chicago continues to do.

ARTS

There's no greater summation of Chicago's devotedly earnest, if slightly awkward, embrace of the arts than a column by Mike Royko that was written after the unveiling of Picasso's *Untitled*. City politicos hoped that the unpainted, three-dimensional hunk of cubist steel would symbolize the city's cultural rebirth. Royko, the voice of Chicago's working class, saw it differently – first, as merely 'a long stupid face [that] looks like some giant insect that is about to eat a smaller, weaker insect' and then, after some reflection, the spirit of Chicago's sometimes brutal devotion to progress. Both perspectives were correct; such juxtapositions of class, convention and perspective make the city's artistic landscape so deeply, inexhaustibly stimulating.

These contrasts fuel Chicago's creative engine by way of high-concept installations that occupy erstwhile warehouses, challenging symphonic works played for picnicking families in the park and poetry readings that are nearly a contact sport. The dedication to populist artistic ideals – most visible in the numerous free summer festivals and ubiquitous public art – lend Chicago artists a unique relationship to their spectators. By pushing boundaries in front of broad audiences, Chicago has shaped one major international movement after another, from beat poetry to house music to modern dance.

No area of Chicago arts has seen a greater recent explosion than the theater scene. The stages here have drawn international attention, exemplified by the twinkling marquees and gilded palaces of the Loop, residencies by celebrated dramatists such as John Malkovich, and the sheer volume of makeshift productions that defy every convention. Major names in theater, like Goodman and Steppenwolf, routinely stage premieres by world-famous playwrights, while small companies such as the House Theater and Redmoon represent the amusing vanguard of the form. Even though the buildings that house the Goodman and Lookingglass theaters are some of Chicago's newest cultural landmarks, many of the city's smaller theater companies and music ensembles are transient, setting up productions in whatever space they can get their hands on. If you encounter a company that does not have an address in the following chapters, check local papers and websites to see where they've set up shop.

The visual arts flourish here, too. The city's largest concentration of galleries has outgrown the River North district, migrating to the West Loop and south to the gentrifying Latino neighborhood of Pilsen. Art students and upstarts who can't get their creations on walls have a tendency to take matters into their own hands, skirting through the night streets with a variety of guerilla expressions, plastering up political posters and elevating that much maligned Chicago invention, spray paint, to a highly stylized form.

There are few cities in the United States that can boast such engaging, affordable options for art lovers, and none that can do so with such little pretension. Find a copy of that Royko column and read it in the shadow of the Picasso; you'll have all the inspiration you'll need.

PAINTING & VISUAL ARTS

Nowhere is it easier to see the great chasms and curious bridges of the city's artistic efforts than in the visual arts. While galleries and critics might still highlight the divide between Chicago's various niches, the creators themselves muddle the lines. Take the recent work of painter Kerry James Marshall, who plays with comics and superheroes, or an artist like Chris Ware (p33), who draws comics with architectural perfectionism. Photographer Rashid Johnson evokes 19th-century photographic techniques and elements of hip-hop, while muralist Dzine (pronounced 'design') draws inspiration from Chicago's hip-hop graffiti movement to create outdoor works on the large scale of 19th-century muralists.

All of these juxtapositions may well have rankled the fat-cat industrialists who raised marble halls and funded collections of old and new European art 100 years ago, but Chicago's public has always embraced pioneering forms. Consider society matron Bertha Palmer, who fostered the city's artistic edge in the late 1800s when she collected impressionist paintings in Europe that later became the Art Institute's core.

Since then, local artists have contributed to every major international movement – from Archibald Motley Jr portraits of roaring South Side jazz clubs in the 1920s to today's big local names like mosaic artist Juan Chavez and multimedia provocateurs Matthew Hoffman and Sabrina Raaf.

Works by Chicago's younger artists demonstrate that the modern art community has few discernable commonalities. If there is such a thing as a 'Chicago style,' the man with the best idea of its definition might be former gallery owner and writer Paul Klein, who launched a movement in 2005 to open a modern museum devoted exclusively to Chicago art. Though that organization is still a pipe dream, Klein's website Art Letter (www.artletter.com) provides an illuminating look at the city's current scene.

In 2009, the Art Institute of Chicago upped the local ante considerably when it opened its Modern Wing. Providing an extra 264,000 sq ft of gallery space – increasing the already huge museum by 35% – the wing has allowed long-hidden works by Picasso, Brancusi and the like to shine, while providing opportunities to view new, cutting-edge multimedia art.

Gallery Districts & Festivals

Chicago has three main gallery-rich neighborhoods, which are the best places to see younger artists and the stars of tomorrow. The most illustrious is the River North neighborhood (p65). These galleries sell major works by both local and international artists, and host a busy scene of openings and events. It makes a fun afternoon of browsing, but if you have to ask, you probably can't afford it.

More recently developed gallery districts in the West Loop (p103) and Pilsen (p108) are good options as well. The former brings Chicago edgier works of younger artists, including many painters, photographers and mixed-media artists of modest renown. Taking something home still won't be cheap – anywhere from $500 to $5000 – but most of the galleries are a bit more exciting than their vetted neighbors north of the river. Pilsen is the youngest and most casual gallery district; work here is largely by Chicago locals and there is a good deal of folk art. To

top picks

ART SPACES

- Art Institute of Chicago (p52) Art fans better block out a full day for the whopping collection (the nation's second largest).
- Chicago Cultural Center (p58) The exhibits span the gamut and change often, but they're always free to peruse.
- National Museum of Mexican Art (p107) This ambitious, free institution is home to the nation's most exciting Mexican and Mexican American artists.
- Museum of Contemporary Art (p73) The challenging collection at the MCA continues to push boundaries.
- Museum of Contemporary Photography (p115) Tidy and engaging (and free), this is a great stop in the South Loop.

BACKGROUND ARTS

a smaller extent, Wicker Park and Bronzeville also have gallery clusters. The former offers scrappy up-and-comers (mostly in the Flat Iron Building; see p94), while the latter focuses on art from the African diaspora.

The River North and the West Loop (which are located near each other) host a joint gallery hop the first Thursday of every month. Pilsen hosts art walks on the second Friday of each month. A roundup of other local happenings can be found through the Chicago Art Dealers Association (CADA; www.chicagoartdealers.org) or by browsing through Chicago Gallery News (www.chicagogallerynews.com).

The biggest annual event in Chicago visual arts is Artropolis (www.artropolischicago.com), an international contemporary art fair at the end of April that takes place in the Merchandise Mart; see p13 for details.

PUBLIC ART

Chicago has a standard-setting public policy that has made the city an international center for public art: in 1978, the city council approved an ordinance stipulating that a percentage of costs for constructing or renovating municipal buildings be set aside for the commission or purchase of artworks. The result finds downtown riddled with gaping art lovers taking in a collection that's as much a part of the city's character as its groundbreaking architecture.

The most prominent of these public works go well beyond the staring eyes of the Picasso and Millennium Park's 'Bean.' Alexander Calder has three major works in the city, both completed in 1974. The most visible of these is the arching red *Flamingo*, which sits in front of the Federal Center Plaza at Dearborn and Adams Sts. *The Universe* is hardly out of the way for most travelers to the city – its colorful, moving shapes grace the lobby of the Willis Tower, while *Flying Dragon* floats in the Art Institute's North McCormick Courtyard. Joan Miró's *Chicago* – originally titled *The Sun, The Moon and One Star* – is within a short walk, as is an expansive mosaic by Chagall. As for the 'Bean,' it's just one of the monumental works of art that have been crammed into Millennium Park, which itself should count as an elegant masterpiece that mirrors the city's pragmatic approach to the arts. For the must-sees downtown, turn to the Loop Public Art (p59).

You'll also see murals around town, many done by youngsters in the city's Gallery 37 program, which offers arts mentoring and job training to school kids. Pilsen's murals (p107), painted by neighborhood artists, are another highlight.

MUSIC

It's hard to tell what sounds more sincere – Frank Sinatra swinging about 'one town that won't let you down' or Wilco ruing being 'far, far away from those city lights,' hip-hop chart-topper Kanye West rhyming about watching the 'fireworks over Lake Michigan' or Magic Sam wanting to get back to his 'sweet home Chicago.' No foolin': every single facet of American music has the grubby fingerprints of Chicago music makers all over it. The birthplace of electric blues and house music, Chicago also fosters a vibrant independent rock scene, boundary-leaping jazzers and several world-class orchestras. From top to bottom Chicago's music embodies the noblest characteristics of the city itself: musicians are resourceful and hard working, sweating it out in muggy blues clubs, long orchestra seasons, DIY punk shows and everyplace in between.

Chicago Blues

The most iconoclastic of Chicago forms comes in one color: blue. Bluesmen set up in the open-air markets of Maxwell St in the 1930s, and by 1936 Chicago had become a regional hub of the genre when Delta bluesman Robert Johnson first recorded 'Sweet Home Chicago.' But what distinguishes Chicago blues from Johnson's original ode is simple: volume. Chicago blues is defined by the plugged-in electric guitars typified by genre fathers Muddy Waters and Howlin' Wolf. Fifties and '60s bluesmen like Willie Dixon, Jimmy Reed and Elmore James, and later champions like Buddy Guy and Koko Taylor, became national stars. These days, Chicago's blues are still playing much the same song they were 40 years ago, but it's a proud one – synonymous with screaming guitars, rolling bass and R&B-inflected rhythms. You can still shake it to blues at clubs all over town (p190).

25 ESSENTIAL CHICAGO SONGS

This sampling of great songs about Chicago and by Chicago musicians is not for the narrow-minded, but neither are the city's wildly eclectic music makers. Load this on the ole iPod, and you'll hear a bit of the city's far-reaching musical spectrum – from the scrappy punks who ramble through local dive bars, to the iconic vocalists of Chicago blues. At 25 songs, this list is woefully abbreviated; it'd be just as easy to list 25,000.

- 'Champagne & Reefer' by Muddy Waters
- 'Sister Havana' by Urge Overkill
- 'Ten-Day Interval' by Tortoise
- 'That's All I Need' by Magic Sam
- 'Plutonian Nights' by Sun Ra
- 'I'll Take You There' by the Staples Singers
- 'Boogie Chillen' by John Lee Hooker
- 'Oh Messy Life' by Cap'n Jazz
- 'Via Chicago' by Wilco
- 'Dolphins' by the Sea and Cake
- 'Rocket Ride' by Felix Da Housecat
- 'We Should Have Never Lived Like We Were Skyscrapers' by Chin Up Chin Up
- 'Wang Dang Doodle' by Koko Taylor
- 'Fever' by Buddy Guy
- 'In The Ghetto' by Elvis Presley
- 'Let's Groove' by Earth, Wind and Fire
- 'Champion' by Kanye West
- 'Hold On, Hold On' by Neko Case
- 'Suitcase (For Ray Charles, Elvin Jones and Steve Lacy)' by Vandermark 5
- 'Goin' To Chicago' by Kurt Elling
- 'Sweet Home Chicago' by Robert Johnson (covered by The Blues Brothers)
- 'Tonight, Tonight' by Smashing Pumpkins
- 'My Kinda Town' by Frank Sinatra
- 'Can You Feel It' by Mr Fingers
- 'Three Hundred Pounds Of Joy' by Howlin' Wolf

House History

Finding the roots of the city's other taste-making musical export is relatively easy: it began in the early '80s at a now-defunct West Side nightclub called the Warehouse, where DJ Frankie Knuckles got tired of spinning disco and added samples of European electronic music and beats from this new-fangled invention, the stand-alone drum machine. Uninterested in appealing to commercial radio, the tracks used deep, pounding bass beats and instrumental samples made for dancing. DJs such as Derrick Carter and Larry Heard revolutionized the form and huge second wave stars like Felix Da Housecat and DJ Sneak took Chicago's thump worldwide. The club scene was all about big beats, wild parties and drugged-out dancing, until the late '90s, when police cracked down and the trend boiled over. In the years since, the scene has matured – no more pacifiers and glow sticks – while continuing to innovate. For the skinny on today's best clubs, see the Nightlife chapter's Clubs section (p195).

Jazz, Rock, Hip-Hop and Gospel

Chicago's many other musical forms are no less noble, but slightly less idiosyncratic on the national stage. The Green Mill (p191) is ground zero for jazz in the city, with hot acts smoking up the stage nightly. For cutting-edge jazz, the name to know is AACM, a Chicago-based organization that formed in the 1960s and was a big inspiration for recent scenemakers like Peter Brotzmann and Ken Vandermark, the latter a MacArthur 'genius' grant recipient.

Chicago's underground rock community has filled an important niche during the past two decades through established indie labels such as Drag City and Touch & Go, and younger feisty upstarts like Flameshovel Records. The reigning kings of Chicago rock are (arguably) still Wilco.

FIVE CHICAGO RECORD LABELS THAT CHANGED THE WORLD

From Chess Records in the '40s and '50s to Thrill Jockey today, Chicago labels have long been the trailblazing leaders in new music. Five labels deserve special credit for making Chicago such a musical hotbed over the past five decades.

Bloodshot (www.bloodshotrecords.com) For over 15 years this label has put out some of the best records in the left-of-center American roots genre that fuses punk rock with old-school country, alt-country or (the label's preferred moniker) insurgent country.

Chess Records When the blues left the Delta and migrated north, its home in Chicago was Chess Records. Run by two brothers, Leonard and Phil Chess, the label helped launch the careers of Muddy Waters, Howlin' Wolf and legendary harmonica player Little Walter. Chess engineered its records to match the tone of its artists, creating an aggressive, redlining blues sound that remains synonymous with Chicago. The label also served as a catalyst for early rock 'n' roll, recording sessions by Chuck Berry, Bo Diddley and the Rolling Stones.

Delmark Records (www.delmark.com) The oldest independent jazz and blues label in the country, Delmark Records has inspired countless small startups around the world, determined to promote the pioneers and mavericks of the two genres. Delmark was founded in 1953 by a 21-year-old music fan named Bob Koester, who, before his leap into the music recording business, had been selling out-of-print blues and jazz records from his dorm room. Over its 50-year life, the label has released blues works by artists like Junior Wells, Otis Rush, Little Walter and Sunnyland Slim, and jazz records by the Art Ensemble of Chicago, Sun Ra and Dinah Washington. Koester also runs the Jazz Record Mart (p131), a wax junkie's heaven in Near North.

Thrill Jockey (www.thrilljockey.com) When indie rock began to incorporate elements of jazz in the mid-1990s, Thrill Jockey documented the moment. Started by New York transplant Bettina Richards, the independent label has been the celebrated home of local bands such as Tortoise, and the Sea and Cake. The label isn't limited to the 'postrock' bands that made it famous, however, with signings from local countryish acts like Freakwater and Califone to abstract European electronica artists such as Mouse on Mars. Thanks to its consistently solid output and extremely high cachet, Thrill Jockey has opened the minds of indie music fans worldwide to new genres and styles.

Wax Trax! It's hard to say what would have happened to industrial music in the '80s without the tireless work of local label Wax Trax! Along with bringing the raw, electronic mayhem of European artists such as KMFDM and Front 242 to the USA, Wax Trax! issued works by fledgling domestic acts such as Ministry and Meat Beat Manifesto. Though the label is now defunct, you can hear highlights in the extensive 3-CD box set *Black Box: Wax Trax! Records, The First 13 Years*.

For hip-hop, the heavyweight champ is Kanye 'George Bush doesn't care about black people' West, son of the former head of Chicago State University's English department. West put Chicago on the hip-hop map, opening the door for fresh underground names like Lupe Fiasco, Twista and Kid Sister.

Folk and gospel are destination-oriented genres in the city: troubadours hold down open mics and play the north-side Old Town School of Folk Music (p194), while gospel churches raise the roof on the South Side. Two worthy destinations for old-school Sunday morning gospel are Greater Salem Missionary Baptist Church (p122), where famed gospel matron Mahalia Jackson was a member, and Pilgrim Baptist Church (p122). If you plan on raising the roof at Pilgrim Baptist, call ahead; a fire gutted its original location in 2006, and during the lengthy rebuilding process services have been held in a temporary location across the street at the Thomas A Dorsey Center.

THEATER

Since the London *Guardian* named Chicago the theater capital of the USA in 2004, the city has vigorously defended the title with a greater number of productions and more enthusiastic audiences. The Broadway blockbusters in the Loop continue to draw hordes, but the more intimate dramatic performances happen at Steppenwolf (p206), Lincoln Park's landmark stage. Since 1976 Steppenwolf's matchless reputation has been earned by stunning talent and groundbreaking programming. Known heavyweights like Joan Allen, John Malkovich and Gary Sinise are alumna, and they exemplify Chicago's bare-knuckled, physical style of acting. It feels particularly raw when you take in a smaller production by any one of the city's DIY companies, which mostly operate in the further-out regions of the city.

But back in the Loop, you'll hardly be victim to another dreary performance of *Phantom*. The new millennium saw numerous renovations and openings including the gorgeous Cadillac Palace Theater and the Chicago Theater, and the Loop is often a pre-Broadway proving ground.

COMEDY & IMPROV

You're sitting in the back of a darkened theater, when suddenly, the man behind you screams in a shrill, ear-piercing falsetto, 'Blow up doll!' This startles the woman to your left, who promptly, cupping her hands around her mouth, yells 'Alpaca! Alpaca! Alpaca!'

'Did someone say "runny eggs?",' says the man on the stage. 'Let's go with runny eggs.' For a moment things seem pretty odd…and then the man on stage starts to sing Wagnerian opera about getting marital counseling with a plate of runny eggs.

Along with Wonder Bread, spray paint and house music, add improvised comedy to the heap of Chicago's wide-reaching cultural contributions. Were it not for Chicago's Second City comedy troupe – a performance of intentionally unstructured skits by the Compass Players in a Hyde Park bar in 1955 – the proverbial chicken might still be crossing the road of American comedy. Since 1959, the Compass Players' original gag incorporating audience suggestions into quick-witted comedy has become standard fare at the Second City Theater (p199), and made Chicago comedy synonymous with audience participation. The company has produced some of the country's most capable funny-bone ticklers in John Belushi, Stephen Colbert, Steve Carell and Tina Fey.

It's a good idea to double check newspaper listings before you go rolling into Second City with the hope of offering your hill-arious suggestion. Second City stages a surprisingly large variety of shows – some of which are scripted and nearly serious. If you find the offering at Second City and its sundry training stages unappealing or a bit too expensive, consider one of the other places to catch improv all over town, including iO (p198) – which was called ImprovOlympic until a run-in with the International Olympic Committee – or ComedySportz (p198).

For those of you who are not content to simply witness the tomfoolery, there are opportunities that go well beyond just screaming out suggestions from the back row. For information about improv classes, check out the websites for both Second City (www.secondcity.com) and iO (www.ioimprov.com).

LITERATURE

'Yet once you've come to be part of this particular patch, you'll never love another,' wrote Chicago literary star Nelson Algren about his hometown. 'Like loving a woman with a broken nose, you may well find lovelier lovelies. But never a lovely so real.'

CHICAGO, COMICS CAPITAL

The city's long history as a capital for comics goes *waaay* back, to an ambitious tyke named Walt Disney, who studied art at a school on Michigan Ave that would one day become the Art Institute. His Mickey Mouse keeps good company with classic fish-wrap heroes like Brenda Star and Dick Tracy, both of whom were born in Chicago. Today, illustrator Dick Locher writes the Dick Tracy strip – he's also the Pulitzer Prize–winning editorial cartoonist whose work appears in *Tribune*.

The edgier side of the comic world these days can be seen in the work of Jeffrey Brown and Oak Park artist Chris Ware. Ware's amazingly distinct catalogue of work has graced the pages of the *Reader,* the *New Yorker* and the *New York Times,* and has been compiled in many hardback books (such as *Jimmy Corrigan* – see p35). Wares has eclectic influences, but shows great attention to 20th-century American aesthetics in both cartooning and graphic design, and precise, geometrical layouts.

Brown is known for a pair of coming-of-age graphic novels, *Clumsy* and *Unlikely*, which generated great local acclaim. He's part of a collective of talented young graphic novelists called the Holy Consumption (www.theholyconsumption.com), which also includes Anders Nilsen, John Hankiewicz and Paul Hornschemeier. The Holy Consumption catalogues some five years of autobiographical whimsy – not the kind of thing to discover if you want to have a productive day at work.

A selection of work by other local artists and graphic novelists can be found at Quimby's (p139) and Chicago Comics (p135), two great emporiums for comics and graphic novels.

Chicago writers have started to love that woman with a broken nose a whole lot, and though the lit scene may be outshined by lovelier lovelies in the USA, the attention to and activity within the community has dramatically flourished in recent years. It might not be too evident at the often scrappy events that are just as likely to take place in a bar as a bookstore, but the number of blogs (see p211) and monthly events that have sprung up are a good indication of how the scene has blossomed.

The small indie publisher Featherproof (www.featherproof.com) shows the local spirit. It prints idiosyncratic fiction books, most by urban authors (including many locals) and many with a humorous slant. The website offers free minibooks to download and fold yourself. Or check out Chicago writers in the literary publication Another Chicago Magazine (www.anotherchicagomagazine.net), whose self-effacing title perfectly exemplifies the literary scene's underdog spirit.

One meeting place for Chicago's hipster writers who want to give something back to the community is 826 Chicago. Modeled after Dave Eggers' successful 826 Valencia tutoring center in San Francisco, this storefront on Milwaukee Ave has a facetious retail section called The Boring Store (p141) in front – worth a trip in its own right for the wacky spy gear – and a tutoring center in back.

Two annual events are prime for book lovers: the *Tribune*-sponsored Printers Row Lit Fest (www .printersrowlitfest.org) during a weekend in June, which spotlights loads of local authors; and the Chicago Humanities Festival (www.chicagohumanities.org) in early November, which offers a two-week schedule of readings and discussions by a heady roster of fiction writers and poets. The newcoming literature and publisher's festival, Printers' Ball (www.printersball.org), is a bit more underground.

And by golly, the whole city reads together as part of the Chicago Public Library's 'One Book, One Chicago' book club program. Even the mayor turns the pages of James Baldwin, Jane Austen or whatever the selection is each spring and fall.

Poetry & Spoken Word

Chicago is home to the nation's gold standard of poetic journals, *Poetry*. Long a bellwether for the academic establishment, the attractive little journal got a nice financial boost in 2002 when pharmaceutical heiress and longtime amateur poet Ruth Lilly bequeathed $100 million to its publisher, Chicago's Modern Poetry Association. Since then, former Wall St investment banker John Barr has taken over as president of the organization, creating a number of lucrative poetry prizes (which include the prestigious Ruth Lilly prize, naturally) and the 'American Life in Poetry' project (www.americanlifeinpoetry.org), which provides a free weekly column for print and online publications about poetry.

Nothing could be more unlike the quietly scholarly verse of *Poetry* than spending a night at the venerated Uptown Poetry Slam (p211), held at the Green Mill. For a paltry admission fee, the Uptown Poetry Slam features guest performers from around the country, an open mic for newcomers, and its famous slam competition, widely considered to be the birthplace of performance-oriented verse.

For a list of regular readings in the city, see Readings & Spoken Word (p210) or you can visit the excellent site maintained by the Chicago Poetry Center (www.poetrycenter.org).

DANCE

Like many of the city's other expressive hallmarks, jazz dance is an art form based on jarring contradictions. At its core it relies on exceedingly controlled yet fluidly expressive motion. The invention of the style is credited to legendary Chicago dance teacher Gus Giordano, and the exhilarating performances by his namesake company (these days overseen by his daughter) will quickly annihilate any unsavory associations with campy 'jazz hands' or show-stopping 'razzle-dazzle.'

Though Giordano's name tops the list of innovators, it's but one in Chicago's crowded landscape of A-list companies. The Joffrey Ballet (p208) settled in Chicago in 1995 to revive the city's awareness of ballet. It recently built a glassy, state-of-the-art practice space and training academy in the Theater District. Hubbard St Dance Chicago (p208) keeps the attention of an international community with its modern moves. Additionally, the dance program at Columbia College supplies dancers and choreographers to the innovative fledgling companies that set up

CHICAGO BOOKS

- *One More Time: The Best of Mike Royko* (Mike Royko, 1999) – Few give you a better introduction to the city's socio-political landscape than this child of Polish and Ukrainian origins and voice of the city's working class. His view on dirty politics and daily life in Chicago at the now-defunct *Daily News* won him a Pulitzer in 1972. This collection compiles earnest, snappy, often poignant vignettes of Chicago life.
- *Working: What People Do All Day and How They Feel About What They Do* (Studs Terkel, 1974) – This exploration of the meaning of work for people in all walks of life is a seminal text for 'the city that works.'
- *The Man With the Golden Arm* (Nelson Algren, 1949) – A tale of a drug-addicted kid on Division St, this won the National Book Award in 1950. These days a walk down the same stretch of Division is more likely to get you addicted to clothes from Urban Outfitters.
- *The Adventures of Augie March* (Saul Bellow, 1953) – Often listed among the best American novels, Bellow's masterwork portrays a destitute boy growing up in Depression-era Chicago (much like the author himself). Bellow died in 2005, but he's still celebrated as a godfather of the city's fiction world.
- *I Sailed With Magellan* (Stuart Dybek, 2004) – Dybek's intertwined short stories follow down-and-out characters on Chicago's South Side, with a vibe á la Algren.
- *The Devil In White City* (Eric Larson, 2004) – A gripping bit of nonfiction about when the World's Columbian Exposition, held in Chicago in 1893, became the playground for one of America's first serial killers.
- *Jimmy Corrigan, the Smartest Kid on Earth* (Chris Ware, 2000) – Ware's graphic novel, about a lonely guy with a superhero imagination, flashes between modern Chicago and the 1893 World's Fair. The *New Yorker* called it 'the first formal masterpiece of the medium.'
- *Annie Allen* (Gwendolyn Brooks, 1949) – This collection of poems made Brooks the first African American writer ever to receive a Pulitzer Prize.
- *Windy City Blues* (Sara Paretsky, 1996) – Paretsky's short-story collection stars her beloved character VI Warshawski, a karate-chopping, opera-loving local detective.
- *Presumed Innocent* (Scott Turow, 1987) – The ace work of crime fiction by Chicago's smartest genre novelist.
- *Freakonomics* (Steven Levitt, 2005) – The University of Chicago economics professor stayed atop bestseller lists for a long time with this shrewd analysis of the 'hidden side of everything.'
- *The Jungle* (Upton Sinclair, 1906) – This epic is set on the brutal, blood-soaked floors of Chicago's South Side meatpacking plants. It cast a bright light on the inhumane working conditions faced by local immigrant communities, and it was a catalyst for reform.
- *The House on Mango Street* (Sandra Cisneros, 1984) – This set of interconnected vignettes is set in a Mexican American Chicago barrio.
- *Sister Carrie* (Theodore Dreiser, 1900) – Once a larger-than-life figure in Chicago's literary world, Dreiser tells the story of a small-town girl seduced by the big city.
- *The Great Perhaps* (Joe Meno, 2009) – Chicagoan and paleontologist Jonathan Caspar has a seizure whenever he sees clouds. A giant squid and homicidal pigeons also play roles in local author Meno's whimsical novel about a disintegrating family.

shop in performance spaces around the city. Aside from listings in the *Reader* and *Time Out*, the best resource about dance in the city is the site of See Chicago Dance (www.seechicagodance.com).

CINEMA & TELEVISION

Chicago is sad about its turn of fortune in the TV taping biz. First Jerry Springer packed up and moved to Connecticut. Then Oprah announced she's ending her show after 25 years in the Windy City. She's not pulling the plug until September 2011, so you may still have a chance to catch a free taping of the Oprah Winfrey Show (p103). But tickets have always been near impossible to procure. You have to sign up online and become a 'member' to submit a request. Last-minute tickets sometimes surface on the website, but again, you must be registered to be eligible to grab them.

An equally memorable, though less syndicated, taping can be seen at the city's inimitable kids' dance party, Chic-A-Go-Go (www.roctober.com/chicagogo). It's pretty fun to watch little tykes cavort around the room *Soul Train*-style to of-the-minute rock bands. The show is hosted by the deliriously chipper Miss Mia and her little buddy Ratso, a puppet. It airs on cable channel 19.

To attend a free taping, check the website for dates and locations, which vary. There are usually some at Millennium Park.

Now that Oprah, Jerry and Ratso are out of the way (you can sort out the similarities and differences for yourself), it's worth noting that Chicago's much varied presence on the big screen has only gotten more prevalent in the past decade. For a list of Chicago cinematic classics see the boxed text below.

One reason that Chicago has been so convivial to those shiny-faced Hollywood types is that the film industry brings money to the city's coffers. Illinois extends hefty tax breaks to production companies filming in the state, and Chicago is at the heart of the action. Check with the Chicago Film Office (☎ 312-744-6415; www.chicagofilmoffice.us) to see what might be filming when you're in town. Better yet, check the 'Casting Calls' section and see if there's a role for you.

ARCHITECTURE

Ever since the Great Fire of 1871 made the city a blank canvas, Chicago has been home to some of the nation's most exciting architecture. For residents, the skyline is more a part of daily life than a backdrop, and the buildings are both tenderly adored and vehemently hated.

CHICAGO FILM & TELEVISION

- *Oprah* – Though Oprah's quitting her gabby show in September 2011 after 25 years of dominance, Harpo Studios will remain in the West Loop to produce...well, we're not sure what.
- *The Untouchables* (1987, director Brian De Palma) – Chicago playwright David Mamet wrote the screenplay for this edge-of-the-seat drama about Eliot Ness' takedown of Al Capone.
- *The Blues Brothers* (1980, director John Landis) – In perhaps the best-known Chicago movie, Second City alums John Belushi and Dan Aykroyd tear up the city, including City Hall.
- *Ferris Bueller's Day Off* (1986, director John Hughes) – A cinematic ode to Chicago from the director who set almost all of his movies, from *Breakfast Club* to *Home Alone,* in and around the Windy City. This one revolves around a rich North Shore teen discovering the joys of Chicago.
- *The Dark Knight* (2008, director Christopher Nolan) – Chicago stands in for brooding Gotham in this megabudget Batman flick. And the scene where the Joker blows up the hospital? The crew blew up the old Brach's Candy Factory as a stand-in.
- *Public Enemies* (2009, director Michael Mann) – Johnny Depp plays bank robber John Dillinger, the FBI's first 'public enemy number one,' who was shot outside the Biograph Theater. Chicago locations feature prominently.
- *Cadillac Records* (2008, director Darnell Martin) – The film takes liberties with the Chess Records blues-to-rock story (including changing the label's name), but there's a high-wattage cast, including Beyonce as Etta James.
- *Hoop Dreams* (1994, director Steve James) – This stirring documentary follows the high-school basketball careers of two African American teenagers from the South Side. The filmmakers interview the young men and their families, coaches, teachers and friends over several years, showing how the dream of playing college and pro ball – and escaping the ghetto – influences their life choices.
- *Check Please!* – The everyman diners of Chicago pull no punches on this popular dining show, which is constantly the talk of the dining community.
- *High Fidelity* (2000, director Stephen Frears) – This Chicago version of Nick Hornby's classic paean to music nerds stars Chicagoan John Cusack as a man uncommitted about commitment. The record-store set for the film was located at Milwaukee Ave and Honore St in Wicker Park.
- *Chic-A-Go-Go* – Indie rock bands, a little rat puppet and gyrating sugar-high youngsters make this Chicago's best cable access staple.
- *The Breakfast Club* (1985, director John Hughes) – Sure, it's set in a fictional suburb, but this is Molly Ringwald in all her mopey brilliance.
- *Chicago* (2002, director Rob Marshall) – All the razzle-dazzle nods to the city's jazz dance legacy in this sturdy theatrical adaptation.
- *Nothing Like the Holidays* (2008, director Alfredo De Villa) – A Puerto Rican family in Humboldt Park faces what may be their last Christmas together. Comedy, shot on location with an ensemble of well-known Hollywood actors.
- *Candyman* (1992, director Bernard Rose) – Yeah, it's campy, gory and pretty stupid, but soon this slasher flick will be the best memento of the demolished Cabrini-Green slums. Plus, it's scored by Philip Glass!

CHICAGO SCHOOL (1872-99) & PRAIRIE SCHOOL (1895-1915)

Though the 1871 fire didn't seem like an opportunity at the time, it made Chicago what it is today. The chance to reshape the burned downtown drew young, ambitious architects including Dankmar Adler, Daniel Burnham, John Root and Louis Sullivan. These men saw the scorched Loop as a sandbox for innovation, and they rapidly built bigger, better commercial structures over the low roughshod buildings that immediately went up after the fire. These men and their colleagues made up the Chicago School (which some say practiced the Commercial Style), which stressed economy, simplicity and function. Using steel framing and high-speed elevators, these architects created their pinnacle achievement: the modern skyscraper.

The earliest buildings of the Chicago School, such as the Auditorium Building (Map pp54-5; 430 S Michigan Ave) and the original Monadnock Building (p56) used thick bases to support the towering walls above. William Le Baron Jenney, the architect who constructed the world's first iron-and-steel-framed building in the 1880s, soon had a studio in Chicago, where he trained a crop of architects who pushed the city skyward through internal frames. The Monadnock itself is a good starting place to get a practical sense of how quickly these innovations were catching on: the original northern half of the building consists of more traditional load-bearing walls that are 6ft thick at the bottom, while the southern half, constructed only two years later, uses the then-revolutionary metal frame for drastically thinner walls that go just as high.

No matter how pragmatic these builders were in inspiration, the steel-framed boxes they erected never suffered from lack of adornment. Maverick firms like Alder & Sullivan and Burnham & Root used a simple, bold geometric language to rebuild downtown in style. Look for strong vertical lines crossed by horizontal bands, contrasted with the sweeping lines of bay windows, curved corners and grand entrances. For more on the city's Chicago School buildings and their locations, see Famous Loop Architecture, p56.

It was the *protégé* of Louis Sullivan, Frank Lloyd Wright, who would endow Chicago with its most distinctive style, the Prairie School. Wright, a spottily educated ladies' man from Oak Park, was the residential designer for the Alder & Sullivan firm until 1893, when his commissions outside the firm led to his dismissal. Forced into his own practice, he set up a small studio in Oak Park and by 1901 had built 50 structures in the area. For details on visiting, see p248.

In the next 15 years Wright's Prairie Houses contrasted the grand edifices of the Chicago School with their modest charms. The buildings stress low-slung structures with dominant horizon lines, flat roofs, overhanging eaves and an unadorned open space that hoped to mirror the Midwestern landscape. To blend visually, they used natural, neutral materials like brick, limestone and copper. Of all the Prairie Style homes from Wright's hand, the Robie House (p119) is the most dramatic and successful. It's a measuring stick by which all other buildings in the style are often compared and is alone worth the trip to Hyde Park. A bit of Wright's early work is nearer to the city center – the 1894 Robert W Roloson Houses (p122) in Bronzeville, which were designed while Wright still worked for Alder & Sullivan and are his only set of row houses. Wright's notable colleagues in the Prairie Style include Walter Burley Griffin, Marion Mahony Griffin, George W Maher and Robert C Spencer.

BEAUX ARTS (1893-1920) & ART DECO (1920-1939)

While the Chicago and Prairie Schools were forward-looking inventions that grew from the marshy shore of Lake Michigan, beaux arts, named for the École des Beaux-Arts in Paris, took after a French fad that stressed antiquity. Proud local builders like Louis Sullivan hated the style, and he didn't mince words, claiming that it set the course of American architecture back 'for half a century from its date, if not longer.' Sullivan aside, these buildings are pleasing today for their eclectic mixed bag of Classical Roman and Greek elements: stately columns, cornices and facades crowded with statuary. The popularity of the style was spurred by Daniel Burnham's colossal, classical-influenced buildings, such as the 'White City', at the 1893 World's Expo. After Burnham's smash hit there, it became a dominant paradigm for the next two decades and a welcome contrast to the dirty, overcrowded slums that came with Chicago's urban explosion.

The impressive echoes of the White City are seen in some of the city's civic landmarks, including the Art Institute (p52) and the Chicago Cultural Center (p58). The latter began in 1897 as the Chicago Public Library and housed a donated collection of some 8000 books sent by

British citizens after the Great Fire. (Many were even autographed by the donors, such as Thomas Carlyle, Lord Tennyson and Benjamin Disraeli.) While the books have since been moved to the Harold Washington Library, the magnificent gilded ceilings and classical details remain.

After the decline in popularity of beaux arts, Chicago designers found inspiration from another French movement: art deco. The style may have been as ornamental as beaux arts, but instead of columns and statues it took on sharp angles, reflective surfaces and a modern palette of blacks, silvers and greens in more geometric elements. Sadly, there are few remaining buildings in the Loop that characterize this style, and the one that does, the Carbide and Carbon Building, has now become the Hard Rock Hotel Chicago (p228). If you can pull yourself away from the Sammy Hagar memorabilia, check out the building's polished black granite, green terra-cotta and gold crown – all colorful signals of the deco palate – which is rumored to be designed to look like a champagne bottle.

The Carbide and Carbon Building was one of the city's last structures in the style, which withered during WWII.

CHICAGO ARCHITECTURE TODAY

The city has had its ups and downs in the last half century or so. It led the architectural world when Ludwig Mies van der Rohe pioneered the new International Style in the 1950s. The steel frame that once revolutionized the Chicago skyline was again seminal, though now no longer hidden on the inside of walls – the International Style was all about exposed

top picks

NOTABLE CHICAGO BUILDINGS

- Chicago Cultural Center (p58) Exemplifying the beaux-arts style, this is a must for travelers, who will stand agape at the gilded details.
- Chicago Board of Trade (p59) Alvin Meyer's art-deco masterpiece is topped by a 31ft statue of the Roman goddess of agriculture.
- Chicago Federal Center (p58) The Loop's sole work by Ludwig Mies van der Rohe, a contemporary masterstroke that demonstrates the open, universal space he favored.
- Jay Pritzker Pavilion (p53) This acoustically awesome performance space is ideal for an afternoon in the park.
- Marina City (p65) Wilco fans aside, these giant corn cobs are strangely charming, especially when they light up at Christmas.
- Robie House (p119) The low eves and graceful lines of this Frank Lloyd Wright building were emulated around the world.
- Rookery (p56) Frank Lloyd Wright's Prairie School–styled atrium is the perfect place to view the city's structural innovations.
- Tribune Tower (p64) The lower level of this building has a wall with stones from the Taj Mahal, Notre Dame, the Great Pyramid, the Alamo, Lincoln's Tomb, the Great Wall of China and more.
- Willis Tower (p56) It kept its crown as the world's tallest building for nearly a quarter century; it remains the USA's tallest. You might recognize more by its old name – the Sears Tower (changed in 2009).

metal and glass, and represents most peoples' image of the modern skyscraper. From 1950 through 1980, the Chicago architectural partnership of Skidmore, Owings & Merrill dominated the cityscape by further developing Mies' ideas. The prominent firm continues to hold sway on the global stage, most recently as the designer of Dubai's Burj Khalifa.

The late '90s sparked a slew of development downtown, leading to a front-page op-ed by Mayor Daley with a headline screaming, 'No More Ugly Buildings.' The *Sun-Times* piece took local architects and developers to task for betraying Chicago with a crop of unsightly condos and townhouse developments. For this, we can blame the big, bad '80s, when real estate prices in the Loop went stratospheric and development sprawled in the Near North, South Loop and Near South.

The past decade has been marked by great triumphs including Millennium Park, and great controversies, such as the Spire (p65). Love it or hate it, Trump Tower rose to take its position as the city's second-tallest structure in 2009. The same year, Jeanne Gang's Aqua Tower, with its spectacularly undulating balconies, was named the skyscraper of the year. And the city leads the nation in ecofriendly, LEED-certified construction – all of which keeps Chicago's architectural reputation sky-high.

HANDS-ON CHICAGO

Want to lend a hand to the environment while you're in town? Check out these groups for their occasional volunteering events:

- Alliance for the Great Lakes (www.greatlakes.org) Holds 'adopt a beach' cleanups along Lake Michigan.
- Chicago Conservation Corps (www.chicagoconservationcorps.org) The Department of Environment manages this group, which brings together volunteers and students for a variety of projects citywide.
- Friends of the Chicago River (www.chicagoriver.org) Works on projects to stop erosion, reduce flooding and remove pollutants.
- Friends of the Parks (www.fotp.org) Picks up trash and plants flowers in Chicago's parks.

Museum of Mexican Art, and the transportation department has put 170 diesel-electric buses into service, with more to come (900 hybrids were supposed to be in service already, but funding issues have slowed down the switchover).

Oddly, one of the most common green initiatives – recycling – lags in Chicago. Some big residential buildings have private recycling services. And some neighborhoods have 'blue carts' that get emptied by city garbage collectors. But a citywide pick-up system for all citizens? Doesn't exist. The absence of a deposit on bottles or cans further lowers the incentive to recycle. The city does have 33 facilities (mostly in parks) where residents can drop off their recycling, but overall the grim statistic is this: just 8% of waste from the city's 600,000 homes with city garbage services is being recycled, according to a recent Department of Environment study.

Most city initiatives come out of the Department of Environment. A great resource for individuals is the city's Center for Green Technology (☎ 312-746-9642; www.cityofchicago.org/Environment /GreenTech), which has helpful hints and equipment for everything from building a greenhouse to composting to installing a rain barrel.

URBAN PLANNING & DEVELOPMENT

Chicago isn't building all those downtown condos and offices willy-nilly. No sir, Chicago has a plan. And that plan is called the 'Chicago Metropolis 2020 Plan,' which pronounces that any new major construction must have a green roof and must adhere to new energy and zoning codes that include sustainable principles, among other things. Recently city designers broadened the plan to 'Go to 2040,' with facets to make Chicago a high-speed regional transportation hub, to boot.

So the city is trying. Unfortunately, it dug itself a large hole back in its younger days. Chicago's highway system is inadequate and can't handle the exhaustive amount of vehicle traffic between downtown and the city's far-flung neighborhoods and suburbs. Public transportation could help, but only if you happen to live on the predominately white and moneyed North Side. Suburban residents don't have a lot to choose from besides Metra trains (which aren't very frequent), and residents in the lower-income West and South Side neighborhoods are limited to irregular buses. The latter areas don't even have good highway access, a remnant of the days of segregation when blacks were isolated in certain pockets of the city.

GOVERNMENT & POLITICS

Chicago's official motto is 'City in a Garden,' but the late *Tribune* columnist Mike Royko wrote that it would be more appropriate to change it to 'Where's mine?' because it often seems that's how things work around here. Corruption has long been an issue in Chicago.

The local government consists of the mayor and a council of 50 alderman (each elected every four years). Maintaining so many politicians and their related offices and staffs is expensive, but proposals to shrink the city council always run aground for the simple reason that the voters like things as they are. Certainly, this amount of bureaucracy is ripe for abuse and corruption (more on that later), but for the average Chicagoan it works well. You got a pothole in front of your house? Somebody stole your trash can? The neighbor's leaving banana peels all over your stoop? Mundane as they are, these are the kinds of matters that directly affect people's lives, and they can be taken care of with a call to the alderman.

With the districts so small in size, the politicians and their staffs can't afford to anger any voters – angry voters start voting for somebody else. Because of this, the aldermen (the term refers to both men and women) are constantly trying to put themselves in a position to do someone a favor. During your visit to Chicago, you'll likely see traces of this mercenary friendliness on billboards and bus shelter ads – aldermen rent them out to help spread their phone numbers and offers of help to their constituents.

Politics is a popular spectator sport in Chicago, in part because of the ongoing scandals associated with the aldermen and other elected officials. For the record: 28 city council members have been convicted of wrongdoing (mostly kickbacks) since 1972. As an example, look at the Hired Truck scandal, which sparked in 2005. That's when it was discovered that various city staff had been accepting bribes in exchange for giving lucrative trucking contracts to companies that never actually did any work. The investigation got wider and wider, eventually looking into City Hall hiring practices overall, and went higher and higher up the political ladder. As of July 2010, 49 people had been charged in the investigation and 46 had been convicted. The Mayor has remained out of the fire so far, though there are certainly questions about his knowledge of the patronage system at work in his administration. And while he still won his postscandal election handily, some of his long-time alderman pals suffered from the fallout and got booted in the subsequent elections.

Things aren't much tidier at the state government level. Above Mayor Daley and the aldermen is Illinois' governor. You may have heard of Rod Blagojevich, a Democrat who replaced incumbent George Ryan in 2003. (Ryan was later convicted on federal racketeering charges as part of the Hired Truck scandal.) Blagojevich (aka 'Blago') was impeached in 2009 after the feds charged him with corruption on an audacious scale. He was caught on tape supposedly trying to sell Barack Obama's senate seat to the highest bidder. In his famous, expletive-laden quote, Blago said he had something 'golden' and he wasn't giving it up for nothing.

The incident blew up and drew national attention to Chicago's corruption problems. Blago went on a media blitz, appearing on shows with everyone from Barbara Walters to Donald Trump. His first trial ended in a hung jury on 23 of 24 counts (he was found guilty of lying to the FBI). At press time, he was slated to go on trial again in 2011.

Ah, politics.

MEDIA
NEWSPAPERS

Chicago is a newspaper town, one of the few cities in the country to support two competing dailies, the *Chicago Tribune* and the *Sun-Times* – though it should be noted both papers filed for bankruptcy recently (they continue to operate in the interim).

YOU'RE BEING WATCHED

Better think twice before running that red light. Or robbing that store. Chicago has the most extensive and sophisticated video surveillance system in the country.

In the past decade, the city has linked thousands of cameras in a network that blankets the city. They're on street poles and skyscrapers, in buses and in tunnels. Officials won't confirm the number of cameras, but estimates range from 10,000 to 15,000. All the data feeds in to a command center at the Office of Emergency Management, though there's way too much of it for real-time monitoring.

The police department installed many of the cameras in high-crime hot spots, but private businesses and even home owners contribute their data, too. Whenever a citizen makes an emergency call, the system identifies the caller's location and pulls the video feed from the nearest camera. Police say it has been effective in fighting crime (even murderers have been caught on camera). Privacy advocates worry citizens' rights are being compromised, that the system is growing too rapidly and with too little public input.

Big Brother or not, the system is changing what it means to be in public in Chicago. And seriously, if you run a red light at certain intersections (which should have a sign warning it's 'photo enforced'), you'll get an action shot in the mail, along with a ticket for $100.

OBAMA-RAMA

These days, Chicago's most famous resident is a guy named Barack Obama – aka President of the United States.

The former community organizer started his political career by representing his Hyde Park/Kenwood district in the Illinois Senate in 1996. In 2000, he tried to kick it up a notch by running for a US House seat, but he went up against a highly entrenched local politician, and lost. So he regrouped and ran for a vacant US Senate seat in 2004. Bingo: he won in the largest landslide victory in Illinois history.

His career picked up steam from there big-time. First came 'the speech' – a stirring oration Obama gave at the Democratic National Convention in Boston in 2004. Afterward, more than one pundit commented on Obama's presidential bearing; CNN called him a 'rock star.' Public opinion was so high he decided to run for the White House.

The pundits didn't really think he could do it. Remember, though, this is the guy who titled his 2006 book *The Audacity of Hope*.

By 2008, he'd won the highest office in the land – the first black man in history to do so. Chicago went wild. Obama's South Side barber was giving press interviews. The Cultural Center was selling Obama finger puppets. Oprah was crying tears of Obama joy. The city was giddy its local boy had hit the big time. And so had the city, at least for a while. Chicago was suddenly 'discovered' for its coolness and named to all kinds of 'hot' lists.

The cruddy economy eventually took its toll on both Obama and the city he stands for, so neither flies as high as during that moment in November '08. Not to say they won't again. In the meantime, locals still swell with pride when, say, Obama wins the Nobel Prize. Or just comes home for a visit.

The *Chicago Tribune* (www.chicagotribune.com) is the more highbrow of the two, and excels at arts and culture coverage. The newspaper also produces a free digest version for 20-something readers titled *Red Eye*. And it doesn't stop there: the Tribune Company conglomerate counts the local WGN TV and radio stations among its holdings. At press time, the whole shebang was up for sale. There's no buyer yet, and it's likely the pieces will be sold off separately, altering Chicago's mediascape in a big way. (The Cubs baseball team was the first piece to go; a private buyer purchased it in 2009.)

The *Sun-Times* (www.suntimes.com) is a tabloid and, true to its format, usually grabs attention with a provocative front-page story. It offers more in-depth sports coverage. Frankly, it's a lot more fun to read than the Trib. Its most famous scribe is movie reviewer Roger Ebert.

The best weekly publication in the city is the free *Chicago Reader* (www.chicagoreader.com). The entertainment paper offers good, independent politics and media coverage, plus a catalog of everything going on in town, from theater to live music to offbeat films to performance art. Its music coverage is particularly impressive, and there are popular advice columns and lots of kinky classified ads. Reading it all can take up the better part of a very pleasurable morning. Alas, the paper has changed publishers a few times in recent years, and always seems to emerge a bit thinner.

Other arts papers include *New City* (www.newcity.com), a slim weekly that is a little edgier than the *Reader;* the *Onion* satirical news weekly, which features Chicago-specific entertainment listings in its 'AV Club' section; and the monthly *UR*, which offers extensive coverage of DJ and club culture. The *Chicago Free Press* (www.chicagofreepress.com) and *Windy City Times* (www.windycitymediagroup.com) are the main gay weeklies, with local, national and entertainment news.

MAGAZINES

The weekly *Time Out Chicago* (www.timeoutchicago.com) launched in 2005, much to the displeasure of the *Reader*. The magazine eschews the *Reader*'s deeper journalism for short, colorful articles and a week's worth of the best entertainment events, shopping sales, museum and gallery exhibits, restaurants, and gay and lesbian goings-on. If you're planning on staying more than a couple of days in the Windy City, *Time Out Chicago* is a worthwhile investment.

Monthly *Chicago Magazine* (www.chicagomag.com) features articles and culture coverage slanted towards upscale readers. For visitors it offers good restaurant listings (indexed by food type, location, cost and more). Its Sales Check e-newsletter is a must for hard-core shoppers looking for the latest sales and events; see the Shopping chapter (p128) for sign-up information.

Moguls and would-be moguls consult *Crain's Chicago Business* (www.chicagobusiness.com), a business tabloid that regularly scoops the dailies despite being a weekly.

Venus Magazine (www.venuszine.com) is a hip, arts-oriented quarterly zine for women that's produced in Chicago. You can pick up it, as well as other offbeat publications, at Quimby's (p139).

RADIO

WGN (720AM) broadcasts many of its shows from its street-level studio in the Tribune Tower on N Michigan Ave. You can press your nose up against the glass and make faces at the hosts.

WBEZ (91.5FM), the National Public Radio affiliate, is well funded and ever-expanding. It's the home station for the hit NPR shows *This American Life* and *Wait, Wait Don't Tell Me*. The studios are located on Navy Pier; the website (www.chicagopublicradio.org) is a great source for local news. And if you happen to be listening at 7:59pm on Saturdays you're in for a special treat: *The Annoying Music Show* presents 'the most awful music ever recorded.' Because it's so harmful to the ears, the show only runs for one minute.

WBBM (780AM) blares news headlines all day long, with traffic reports every 10 minutes. Conservative WLS (890AM) is where you'll find Rush Limbaugh and friends. And if you're just hungry for the latest sports scores, tune into the ESPN-run WMVP (1000AM) or the local WSCR (670AM).

You'll find the most interesting music on WXRT (93.1FM), a rock station that aggressively avoids falling into any canned format trap. Other notables include the eclectic college stations for the University of Chicago (WHPK, 88.5FM), Loyola (WLUW, 88.7FM) and Northwestern (WNUR, 89.3FM).

TELEVISION

Chicago's local network affiliates are little different from their counterparts in other large cities. They are WLS (channel 7, the ABC affiliate), WMAQ (channel 5, the NBC affiliate), WBBM (channel 2, the CBS affiliate) and WFLD (channel 32, the Fox affiliate).

Other stations in town have their own niches. WGN (channel 9) is owned – at least for now – by the Tribune Company. Its meteorologist, Tom Skilling, is something of a cult figure in Chicago TV for his scientific, incredibly technical weather forecasts. He won't just tell you that it's hailing, but *why* it's hailing. WGN also shows many of the baseball games played by the Cubs, and carries Bulls and Blackhawks games as well. WTTW (channel 11) is a good public broadcasting station, home of the beloved restaurant-review show *Check Please!*, as well as *Chicago Tonight* at 7pm weekdays, which takes an in-depth look at one of the day's news stories. CLTV is a local 24-hour cable news station (part-owned by the *Tribune*).

FASHION

Chicago is a casual town. The apex of fashion for most men is a pair of khakis and a Gap button-down shirt. Women's dress is similarly low-key, valuing comfort over high

top picks

CHICAGO BLOGS

- Chicagoist (www.chicagoist.com) Covers the city in all its quirky glory. Topics range from how to neuter feral alley cats to local microbrews to hot bands and festivals around town. It's written from a snarky 20-something viewpoint.
- Second City Cop (http://secondcitycop.blogspot .com) Day job: gun-totin' Chicago law man. Secondary job: blogger who lets loose on the mayor, gangbangers and police department honchos. It's a conservative, frontline look at what cops face, both on the streets and inside the department walls. Check it for the latest scandals afoot.
- Clout City (http://blogs.chicagoreader.com/politics) The *Reader's* political beat reporter provides the scoop on the antics at City Hall.
- Chicago Now (www.chicagonow.com) The *Tribune* owns this community where locals and *Trib* staffers let loose on sports (anyone for 'Cubs in Haiku'?), politics, real estate – there's even a former Playboy Playmate who dishes on high-society functions (lookin' at you, Candid Candace).
- Vocalo blogs (http://blogs.vocalo.org) It's just a handful of bloggers, but they're cream of the crop for food, music and media.

fashion. In the scorching summer, much of the population looks like they're heading off for a lifeguard shift at the local pool – flip-flops, shorts and T-shirts are acceptable attire most everywhere in the city. (Though arctic-cold air-conditioning in shops and movie theaters can sometimes make tank tops a regrettable choice.) In winter, fashion disappears entirely beneath layers of Thinsulate, Gore-Tex and North Face merchandise.

But if you want a pair of hoity-toity Jimmy Choo shoes, Chicago's got 'em. All the big-name designers are here and prance their wares around Oak and Rush Sts. So you too can be like a Gold Coast matron and accessorize those shoes with a Prada purse and a Hermès scarf. Much more popular for urban fashionistas are the boutiques of Wicker Park and Ukrainian Village, where hip international labels mix it up on the racks with high-concept, high-priced outfits from local designers. These sleek little stores have virtually eliminated the lag between Milan runways and Chicago shop displays, allowing Chicagoans to spend $200 on a belt just like they do in New York.

Chicago even boasts its own underground fashion scene. Hipsters proudly sport the latest creations from local button maker Busy Beaver (www.busybeaver.net), and attend unfussy fashion shows staged by Creative Lounge Chicago (www.chicagocreativelounge.org). Thanks to the presence of the Art Institute of Chicago and its fashion program, a lot of budding designers do their thing in the city.

If you plan on hitting the clubs while you're in town, tight black clothing is the rule for both men and women. Some clubs don't allow blue jeans, tennis shoes or baseball caps; if you only brought Levi's and Adidas and still want to go dancing, do yourself a favor and call ahead to make sure there won't be a problem.

CHICAGOESE 101

Use this list to help decipher the local lingo you may encounter.

Downstate – Used by Windy City residents to refer to the rest of Illinois (ie everywhere outside of Chicago).

The Drive – Lake Shore Dr (also referred to as 'LSD').

The Ike – The Eisenhower Expressway (aka I-290).

A Polish – Short for a Polish sausage sandwich (or sammich, as the case may be).

Wet – How to order extra juice on your Italian beef sandwich.

Stoopin' – Socializing on the front porch of a home or apartment, usually with friends and beers.

LANGUAGE

As elsewhere in the USA, English is the major language spoken in Chicago. In the heart of the ethnic enclaves you'll hear Spanish, Polish, Chinese or Russian, but almost all business is conducted in English. Midwestern accents tend to be a bit flat with just a touch of nasal twang, but compared to other parts of the USA, most of the English you'll hear is pretty standard – the middle of the country has always produced a large share of plainspoken TV announcers.

Chicagoans do have their own, special accent. Remember the old *Saturday Night Live* skit where heavy-set Chicago sports fans sat around eating 'sassages' and 'sammiches' and referring to their football team as 'Dah Bears' and their city leader as 'Dah Mare'? It's for real, and you'll hear it in various enclaves of the city (mostly in southside neighborhoods around US Cellular Field and Midway Airport, and northwestside neighborhoods near O'Hare Airport).

NEIGHBORHOODS

top picks

What's your recommendation? www.lonelyplanet.com/chicago

Chicago prides itself on being a 'city of neighborhoods,' each one marked by its own look, feel and foods. Ethnicity characterizes many areas: enticing fragrances waft from varied home grounds in the city's vibrant Mexican, Polish, Chinese, Puerto Rican, Vietnamese and Indian communities.

Most draws for visitors cluster in Chicago's geographic center. The bull's eye is the Loop, the city's historic and business

'A wealth of galleries, historical sights and architectural wonders pop up in the neighborhoods beyond downtown'.

core circled by train tracks (hence the name). Its hubbub spills over into the Near North. Together, these two sight-heavy, shop-and-hotel-laden areas – Millennium Park, the Art Institute, the Magnificent Mile, Navy Pier and much more – could occupy an entire week. But don't give in to temptation and spend your whole trip here. These outlying areas are where locals live, eat, drink and watch their beloved sports teams – they're the places to go for the 'real' Chicago.

Take the gilded Gold Coast, for instance, where you can gaze longingly at mansions inhabited by folks living the high life, same as they've been doing for 120 years. Further north historic Old Town brings up the curtain for Second City improv, and Lincoln Park lets college students and yuppies commune through beautiful parklands and swanky restaurants.

Keep moving north and you'll find Lake View – a hub for bars and shops, both gay and straight, as well as the Cathedral of Baseball, Wrigley Field. Beyond lies Uptown's 'Little Saigon' and European-vibed Andersonville. Both are prime for delicious browsing. Uptown also holds a clutch of historic music venues, including Al Capone's favorite jazz club.

From there, Bucktown and Wicker Park beckon to the southwest with vintage shops and DJ-spinning sushi lounges, while Ukrainian Village gives hipsters an edgier playground next door. Logan Square and Humboldt Park carry on the trendiness, though in a more relaxed manner. Some of Chicago's most inventive eateries – Hot Doug's, Kuma's and Bonsoiree – have set up shop in these two arty, come-one-come-all districts.

A quick ride west of downtown, the Near West Side has hot restaurants, avant-garde galleries and Oprah's studio. Neighboring Pilsen, a focal point for the city's mighty Mexican community, offers taquerias and cinnamon-scented churro vendors alongside groovy galleries on its mural-splashed streets.

The South Loop and Near South Side glitter with new condo high-rises. In addition to its resident shiny young urbanites, the area swarms with visitors who come to gawk at the Shedd Aquarium, Adler Planetarium, the Field Museum and Soldier Field. Further down, on the South Side, Hyde Park is Obama's old stomping ground – a leafy, bookish retreat centered on the gothic University of Chicago.

The El trains clatter through it all and unify the areas. It's easy to find your way around once you understand the orderly city plan. Chicago's streets are laid out on a grid and numbered; Madison and State Sts in the Loop are the grid's center. As you go north, south, east or west from here, each increase of 800 in street numbers corresponds to one mile. At every increase of 400, there is a major arterial street. For instance, Division St (1200 N) is followed by North Ave (1600 N) and Armitage Ave (2000 N), at which point you're 2.5 miles north of downtown.

Got it? Good. Now let's get moving.

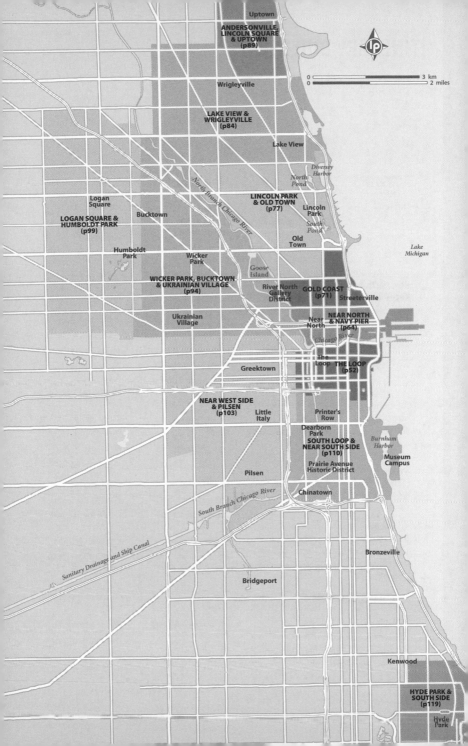

Uptown

**ANDERSONVILLE,
LINCOLN SQUARE
& UPTOWN
(p89)**

Wrigleyville

**LAKE VIEW &
WRIGLEYVILLE
(p84)**

Lake View

*Diversey
Harbor*

*North
Pond*

**LINCOLN PARK
& OLD TOWN
(p77)**

Lincoln
Park

*South
Pond*

Old
Town

Logan
Square

Bucktown

**LOGAN SQUARE &
HUMBOLDT PARK
(p99)**

Humboldt
Park

Wicker
Park

*Goose
Island*

River North
Gallery
District

**GOLD COAST
(p71)**

Streeterville

*Lake
Michigan*

**WICKER PARK, BUCKTOWN
& UKRAINIAN VILLAGE
(p94)**

Ukrainian
Village

Near
North

**NEAR NORTH
& NAVY PIER
(p64)**

Chicago River

The
Loop

**THE LOOP
(p52)**

Greektown

**NEAR WEST SIDE
& PILSEN
(p103)**

Little
Italy

Printer's
Row

Dearborn
Park

**SOUTH LOOP &
NEAR SOUTH SIDE
(p110)**

*Burnham
Harbor*

**Museum
Campus**

Prairie Avenue
Historic District

Pilsen

Chinatown

South Branch Chicago River

Sanitary Drainage and Ship Canal

Bronzeville

Bridgeport

Kenwood

**HYDE PARK &
SOUTH SIDE
(p119)**

*Hyde
Park*

0   3 km
0   2 miles

ITINERARY BUILDER

Mix and match your own Chicago adventure: take your pick of recommended sights, shops, eateries, nightlife and entertainment in Chicago's key neighborhoods listed in our Itinerary Builder.

ACTIVITIES	Sights	Shopping	Eating
The Loop	Millennium Park (p53) Art Institute of Chicago (p52) Famous Loop Architecture (p56)	Poster Plus (p129) Chicago Architecture Foundation Shop (p130) Chicago's Downtown Farmstand (p129)	Cafecito (p149) Lou Mitchell's (p149) Gage (p148)
Near North & Navy Pier	Navy Pier (p68) Tribune Tower (p64) Smith Museum of Stained Glass Windows (p69)	Garrett Popcorn (p131) Levi's Store (p130) Jazz Record Mart (p131)	Xoco (p153) Purple Pig (p153) Giordano's (p152)
Gold Coast	John Hancock Center (p71) Museum of Contemporary Art (p73) Astor Street (p73)	Burton Snowboards (p133) Denim Lounge (p133) Water Tower Place (p133)	Tempo Cafe (p155) Kendall College Dining Room (p155) Gibson's (p154)
Lincoln Park & Old Town	Lincoln Park Zoo (p80) Lincoln Park Conservatory (p80) Biograph Theater (p80)	Spice House (p134) Rotofugi (p135) Dave's Records (p134)	Alinea (p156) Wiener's Circle (p158) Aloha Eats (p158)
Lake View & Wrigleyville	Wrigley Field (p84)	Threadless (p136) Chicago Comics (p135) Strange Cargo (p136)	Terragusto (p159) Victory's Banner (p161) Chilam Balam (p159)
Wicker Park, Bucktown & Ukrainian Village	Polish Museum of America (p95) Nelson Algren House (p94)	Renegade Handmade (p139) Quimby's (p139) Boring Store (p141)	Handlebar (p165) Hoosier Mama Pie Co (p168) West Town Tavern (p167)
South Loop & Near South Side	Field Museum of Natural History (p110) Shedd Aquarium (p111) Willie Dixon's Blues Heaven (p116)	Giftland (p144) Ten Ren Tea & Ginseng Company (p144) Aji Ichiban (p143)	Yolk (p174) Joy Yee's Noodle Shop (p175) Epic Burger (p174)

AREA

HOW TO USE THIS TABLE

The table below allows you to plan a day's worth of activities in any area of the city. Simply select which area you wish to explore, and then mix and match from the corresponding listings to build your day. The first item in each cell represents a well-known highlight of the area, while the other items are more off-the-beaten-track gems.

Drinking and Nightlife	Sports & Activities	Arts
Cal's Bar (p179)	Millennium Park Workouts (p214) Millennium Park Ice Skating (p217) Critical Mass (p216)	Grant Park Music Festival (p204) Chicago Symphony Orchestra (p203) Goodman Theatre (p205)
Billy Goat Tavern (p179) Clark St Ale House (p179) Terrace at Trump Tower (p179)	Bike Chicago (p216)	Chicago Shakespeare Theater (p205)
Coq d'Or (p180) Underground Wonder Bar (p192) Signature Lounge (p180)	Oak Street Beach (p219) Wateriders (p220)	Lookingglass Theatre Company (p205)
Second City (p199) Old Town Ale House (p181) Delilah's (p180)	North Avenue Beach (p219) Diversey Driving Range (p217)	Steppenwolf Theater (p206) Facets Multimedia (p209) Victory Gardens Theater (p207)
Hungry Brain (p182) Metro (p193) Ginger Man (p182)	Chicago Cubs (p220) Moksha Yoga (p215) Diversey-River Bowl (p216)	Music Box Theater (p210)
Hideout (p193) Matchbox (p185) Violet Hour (p186)	Bikram Yoga (p215) Ruby Room (p214)	Danny's Reading Series (p211) Chopin Theatre (p207)
Velvet Lounge (p192) Little Branch Cafe (p187) Jazz Showcase (p191)	12th Street Beach (p219) Sledding at Soldier Field (p217) Chicago White Sox (p221)	Elastic Arts Foundation (p208) Dance Center at Columbia College (p208) SummerDance (p208)

GREATER CHICAGO

INFORMATION			
Chopping Block	(see 15)		
Old Town School of Folk Music	(see 28)		
SIGHTS	(p45)		
Capone's Chicago Home	1 E6		
Devon Ave	2 D2		
Greater Salem Missionary			
Baptist Church	3 D6		
Ida B Wells House	4 E5		
Illinois Institute of Technology	5 D5		
Leather Archives & Museum	6 D2		
McCormick-Tribune Campus			
Center	(see 5)		
Meyers Ace Hardware Store	(see 12)		
Mt Carmel Cemetery	7 A4		
Muddy Waters' House	8 E5		
Pilgrim Baptist Church	9 E5		
Robert W Roloson Houses	10 E5		
Salem Baptist Church	11 E7		
SR Crown Hall	(see 5)		
State Street Village	12 E5		
Supreme Life Building	13 D5		
Union Stockyards Gate	14 E5		
Victory Monument			

SHOPPING	(p127)	
Chopping Block	15 D3	
Merz Apothecary	(see 15)	
Timeless Toys	(see 15)	

EATING	(p145)	
Army & Lou's	16 E6	
Bistro Campagne	(see 28)	
Eli's Cheesecake Factory	17 B3	
Lem's Bar-B-Q House	(see 21)	
Mysore Woodlands	18 D2	
Sabri Nehari	19 D2	
Smoque	20 C3	
Soul Vegetarian East	21 E6	
Udupi Palace	22 D2	

DRINKING	(p177)	
Bernice's Tavern	23 D5	
Chicago Brauhaus	(see 15)	
Schaller's Pump	24 D5	

NIGHTLIFE	(p189)	
Abbey Pub	25 C3	
Lee's Unleaded Blues	26 E6	
New Apartment Lounge	27 E6	
Old Town School of Folk Music	28 D3	

THE ARTS	(p201)	
Book Cellar	(see 15)	
Next Theater Company	29 D1	
Paper Machete	(see 28)	
Side Project Theater	30 D2	

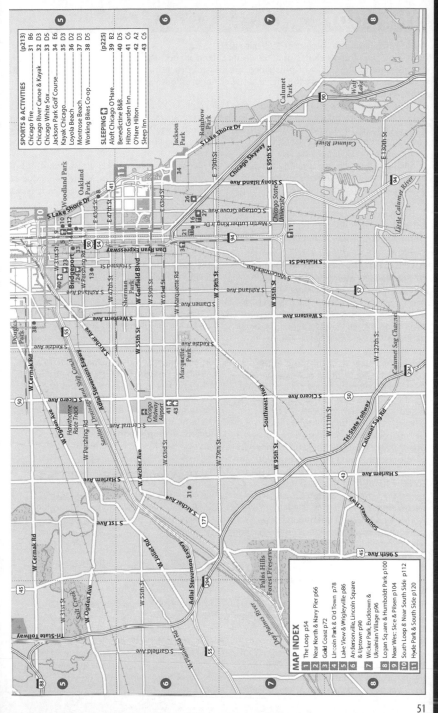

THE LOOP

Drinking p179; Eating p148; Shopping p128; Sleeping p227

The Loop is Chicago's center of action – its financial and historic heart – and it pulses with energy. Tumultuous tides of pinstriped businessfolk rush the sidewalks, while clattering El trains roar overhead. Above the melee, a towering forest of steel and stone soaks in the sun (or snow, as the case may be).

But it's not all work-work-work here. The Loop is also Chicago's favorite playground. Grant Park unfurls a sprawling green buffer between the skyscrapers and Lake Michigan. Millennium Park is Grant's crown jewel, sparkling in the northwest corner. Both host bashes galore, especially in summer when everything from Blues Fest to Lollapalooza to the Grant Park Orchestra makes sweet music for the masses.

Such green spaces are amazing when you consider the area was once a marshy landfill full of 'dumphills' where 'dog fights alternated with wrestling bouts' and 'the winter's residue of deceased animals lent an added something to the vernal breezes,' as the *Chicago Daily News* put it in the early 1900s.

It smells a lot rosier these days, which is good news since visitors will spend significant time here. The Loop is home to big-ticket sights like the Art Institute, the neon-lit Theater District, all the major festivals and parades, and the city's world-famous architecture and public art.

ART INSTITUTE OF CHICAGO Map pp54-5

☎ 312-443-3600; www.artic.edu/aic; 111 S Michigan Ave; adult/under 14yr/student $18/free/12, admission free 5-8pm Thu & daily in Feb; ☷ 10:30am-5pm Mon-Wed, to 8pm Thu & Fri, 10am-5pm Sat & Sun, closed Fri evening in winter; Ⓜ Brown, Orange, Green, Purple, Pink Line to Adams

The second-largest art museum in the country, the Art Institute of Chicago has the kind of celebrity-heavy collection that routinely draws gasps from patrons. Grant Wood's stern *American Gothic*? Check. Edward Hopper's lonely *Nighthawks*? Yep. Georges Seurat's *A Sunday Afternoon on La Grand Jatte*? Here. The museum's collection of impressionist and postimpressionist paintings is second only to those in France, and the number of surrealist works – especially boxes by Joseph Cornell – is tremendous.

The Modern Wing opened in 2009, increasing capacity by about 35%. Dazzling with natural light, it has allowed works by Picasso, Miró, Brancusi and the like to shine, as well as providing opportunities to view new, cutting-edge multimedia work. Added bonus: the wing connects to Millennium Park via the mod, pedestrian-only Nichols Bridgeway. The silver arch leaves from the 3rd-floor sculpture garden, which is free to the public.

Other collections include ancient Egyptian, Greek and Roman art; Chinese, Japanese and Korean art from the past 5000 years; European decorative arts since the 12th century; European art from the 15th to 19th centuries; textiles; furniture; 20th-century paintings and sculpture; and ever so much more.

Friend, you're going to need a plan to make it through here with your feet still intact. When you enter, ask for the Visitor Guide booklet with maps and 'what to see in an hour' instructions. Ask if there's a 60-minute Highlights Tour (free), led by a docent. They depart from Gallery 100 between 12pm and 2pm (and 7pm on Thursday evening, when museum admission is free). Or rent an audio tour ($7). They come in different lengths and styles, with the

TRANSPORTATION – THE LOOP

Bus Number 56 runs along Milwaukee Ave from Wicker Park into the Loop; 151 comes down Michigan Ave from the lakefront in the north.

El All lines converge in the Loop; find your destination and take your pick.

Metra Trains going south to Hyde Park and on into Indiana depart from Millennium Station; most other trains depart from Ogilvie or Union stations.

Parking It'll cost you more to park in the Loop than anywhere else in the city. Meters cost $4.25 per hour (they'll likely be more by the time you're reading this). Parking lots cost about $29 per day. East Monroe Garage (S Columbus Dr btwn Randolph & Monroe Sts; per 12/24hr $16/23) is one of the cheapest.

Director's Tour the standout for cutting to the chase and guiding you to 40 top masterpieces.

Curators often give lectures on various artists and artworks. Many talks are free with admission; inquire at the entrance to see if anything sparks your interest. The Ryan Education Center has drop-in drawing and painting classes and much more for kids.

And just when you thought you were finished: more artwork awaits outside. Edward Kemeys' bronze **lions** have become Chicago icons since they began flanking the entrance to the Art Institute in 1894. The **Stock Exchange Arch**, located on the museum's northeast side, is not so much a statue as a relic amputated from the great Stock Exchange building when it was demolished in 1972. The *AIA Guide to Chicago* calls it the 'Wailing Wall of Chicago's preservation movement.' On the museum's southeast side, Augustus Saint-Gaudens' **Sitting Lincoln** shows lonely 'Honest Abe' in his office chair. Feel his isolation?

Allow at least two hours to browse the Art Institute's highlights; art buffs should allocate much longer. The main entrance is on Michigan Ave (where it meets Adams St). The Modern Wing entrance is on Monroe St. Both have stores that carry an awesome collection of posters of the museum's famous works.

top picks

ART INSTITUTE'S UNEXPECTED GEMS

- **Great Hall of Arms and Armor** – Enough of the paintings already! Let's joust!
- **Thorne Miniature Rooms** – These miniatures span 500 years of interiors, all as delicate as they are beautiful.
- **Paperweight Collection** – We know what you're thinking: 'Paperweights? I'm here for art!' But this collection of 1400 ornate desk accessories will amaze.
- **North McCormick Courtyard** – Rewards include fresh air and Alexander Calder's *Flying Dragon*, a little buddy to his similarly vivid *Flamingo* in the Loop.

MILLENNIUM PARK Map pp54-5

☎ 312-742-1168; www.millenniumpark.org; Welcome Center, 201 E Randolph St; admission free; 6am-11pm; Ⓜ Brown, Orange, Green, Purple, Pink Line to Randolph or Madison

Rising up boldly from Grant Park's northwest corner (between Monroe and Randolph Sts), Millennium Park is a treasure trove of free and arty sights. Frank Gehry's 120ft-high swooping silver band shell anchors what is, in essence, an outdoor modern design gallery. It includes Jaume Plensa's 50ft-high **Crown Fountain**, which projects video images of locals spitting out water gargoyle-style; the Gehry-designed **BP Bridge** that spans Columbus Dr and offers great skyline views; and the **McCormick-Tribune Ice Rink** (p217), which fills with skaters in winter (and al fresco diners in summer). But the thing that has become the park's biggest draw is 'the Bean' – officially titled **Cloud Gate** – Anish Kapoor's ridiculously smooth, 110-ton, silver-drop sculpture (see the boxed text, p56).

Locals and visitors alike find it hard to resist such playful art, as you'll see from all the folks splashing around in Crown Fountain and touching the Bean. The newest installment is the **Nichols Bridgeway**, which arches from the park up to the Art Institute's 3rd-floor contemporary sculpture garden (free to view). If the crowds at these favorite spots are too much, walk through the peaceful **Lurie Garden**, which uses native plants to form a botanical tribute to Illinois' tall-grass prairie.

An hour-long stroll is the best way to take it all in. The Millennium Park Greeter Service offers **free walking tours** (11:30am & 1pm) in summer; departure is from the Welcome Center. Or download a similar tour for your mobile device and do it yourself: www.antennaaudio.com/millenniumpark.shtml.

Oh, but there's more free summer fun. Millennium's acoustically awesome band shell – aka **Pritzker Pavilion** – hosts free concerts at 6:30pm most nights (new music on Monday; world music and jazz on Thursday; classical music on Wednesday, Friday and Saturday), as well as daily concerts at noon. The **Grant Park Orchestra** (p204) plays the classical shows; they're a summertime ritual, requiring a picnic and a bottle of wine. Each Saturday **free exercise classes** (tai chi 8am, yoga 9am, Pilates 10am, dance

THE LOOP

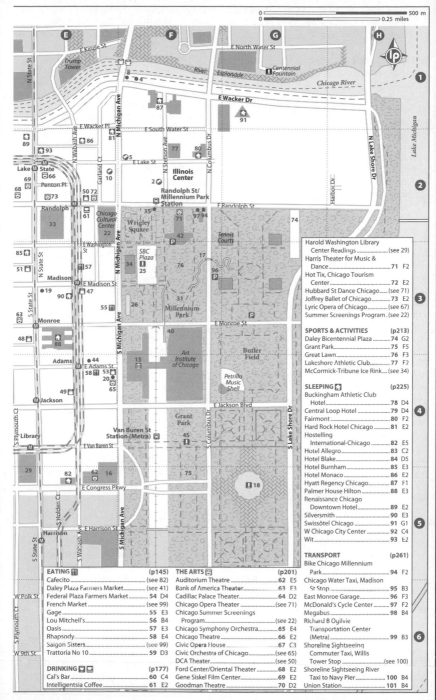

lonelyplanet.com

NEIGHBORHOODS THE LOOP

ENVIRONMENT & PLANNING

THE LAND

Chicago's dominant feature is green-glinting Lake Michigan, which laps the city's entire eastern edge. Its ugly stepsibling is the Chicago River, which flows through downtown and has been rerouted, polluted and abused for most of the city's history.

Thankfully, the city woke up to environmental concerns in the 1980s and started to give the river some love. After monitoring and remediation efforts, the levels of toxic chemicals in the river have declined. Bass fishing has actually become a popular pastime on the upper reaches of the river. The city has also put in a series of public river walkways, and mandated developers working along the riverfront to do the same. You won't see Chicagoans swimming in it any time soon, but a lot of them are kayaking down it, signifying the river is finally making a comeback.

Also thriving is the city's population of wild animals. Coyote and deer both live in the large parks on the city's outskirts, and have been known to wander into the Loop. For instance, in 2007 a coyote sauntered into a downtown Quizno's sandwich shop during the lunchtime rush; he sat in a beverage cooler until animal control workers were able to catch and release him back into the woods several hours later. Raccoons are also plentiful, and if you drive through suburban neighborhoods like Oak Park at night, your car headlights are likely to catch them as they bound across the road.

No animal species does better in Chicago than the rat. Walk through any alley and you'll see the 'Target: Rats' sign that explains when the most recent dose of poison was laid out for the wee beasties. A pet peeve of Mayor Daley's, the rats have met a formidable foe in the city's Department of Streets & Sanitation. One brigade of agents actually patrols the alleys of infested neighborhoods, attacking the rodents with golf clubs. 'We work as a team,' one employee reported to the *Sun-Times*. 'One will whack, while the other one will get the final kill.'

Visitors to Chicago in the summer should be sure to keep an eye out for an infestation of a more beautiful sort. Lightning bugs – flying beetles with phosphorescent abdomens – are prevalent in Chicago in July and August. A park full of their twinkling lights is one of the most beautiful things you'll see in the Windy City.

GREEN CHICAGO

During his tenure, Mayor Richard M Daley pledged to make Chicago 'the greenest city in the US,' and he took several admirable ecosteps toward that end. In 2001 he planted a 'green roof' atop City Hall, complete with native prairie flowers and honeybees. It has been quite an energy-saving success, and many other buildings downtown followed suit. The city now boasts about 500 green roofs, according to the Department of Environment, covering 7 million sq ft. Impressive, until you realize that's a bit less than one-tenth of 1% of Chicago's half-million-plus buildings.

With all the green roofs, perhaps it's no surprise that Chicago has more LEED-certified (Leadership in Energy and Environmental Design) buildings than anywhere in the country. Behemoths like the Merchandise Mart and the Willis Tower have been retrofitted to meet LEED standards. And the city adopted ecosensitive construction standards for new public structures, so that libraries, schools and fire stations will also meet LEED guidelines.

The city has planted thousands of trees throughout Chicago's neighborhoods and parks. It has solar panels on buildings including the Field Museum, the Art Institute and the National

FIVE CHICAGO ARCHITECTS TO KNOW

- Louis Sullivan – Chicago's architectural founding father.
- Frank Lloyd Wright – Sullivan's student, who took the Prairie Style to global renown.
- Daniel Burnham – The man with the Plan (the 1909 urban plan that preserved Chicago's lakefront).
- Ludwig Mies van der Rohe – His 'less is more' motto and simple, boxy designs influenced modern skyscrapers.
- Jeanne Gang – Her 2009 Aqua Tower in the Loop is the world's tallest building designed by a woman.

11am) take place on the Great Lawn. And the Family Fun Tent provides free kids' activities daily between 10am and 3pm.

WILLIS TOWER Map pp54–5

☎ 312-875-9696; www.the-skydeck.com; 233 S Wacker Dr; Skydeck admission adult/3–11yr $16/11; ⏲ 9am-10pm Apr-Sep, 10am-8pm Oct-Mar; Ⓜ Brown, Orange, Purple, Pink Line to Quincy

Yes, you're at the right place. Willis Tower was the Sears Tower until mid-2009, when insurance broker Willis Group Holdings bought the naming rights. No matter what you call it, it's still the USA's tallest building, and its 103rd-floor Skydeck puts visitors way up in the clouds.

The observation platform draws more than one million people per year who are eager to ascend the 1454ft structure (most of which is mundane office space). Enter via Jackson Blvd, then take the elevator down to the waiting area, where you go through security and pay admission.

Next comes a 10-minute, factoid-filled film in which you learn that there are 43,000 miles of phone cable, 2232 steps to the roof, and that the tower height is the equivalent of 313 Oprahs (or 262 Michael Jordans). And then: the ear-popping, 70-second elevator ride to the top. From here, the entire city stretches below, and you can see exactly how Chicago is laid out. On good days you can see for 40 to 50 miles, as far as Indiana, Michigan and Wisconsin. On hazy or stormy days you won't see much at all, so don't bother.

Willis' newest to-do is the 'Ledge.' There are four ledges actually, on the deck's west side. They're like glass-encased boxes hanging out from the building's frame. Step onto the see-through floor for a feeling of mid-air suspension and a knee-buckling view straight below.

On busy days the Skydeck's wait can be an hour or longer; peak times are in summer, between 11am and 4pm Friday through Sunday. Buying your tickets online can save some time.

For those who prefer a drink with their vista, the John Hancock Center (p71) is a better choice.

FAMOUS LOOP ARCHITECTURE
Map pp54–5

Sure, there's the Willis Tower. But it's just one in a long line of high-flying buildings in Chicago. Ever since the city presented the world with the first skyscraper in 1885, it has thought big with its architecture and pushed the envelope of modern design. The Loop is ground zero for gawking.

The following buildings represent the pioneering Chicago School style, stressing economy, simplicity and function. Daniel Burnham and Louis Sullivan were the era's ideas men. For details, see p37.

Architecture buffs on a pilgrimage bow down first to the Monadnock Building (53 W Jackson Blvd), two buildings in one that depict a crucial juncture in skyscraper development. The north half is the older, traditional design from 1891 (with thick, load-bearing walls), while the south is the newer, mod half (with a metal frame that allows for jazzier-looking walls and bigger windows). See the difference?

The 1888 Rookery (209 S LaSalle St) looks hulking and fortresslike outside, but it's

THE MAGIC BEAN

'That's it?' Many Chicagoans fumed when Millennium Park's premier sculpture was unveiled in 2004. 'We pay $23 million, and we get a kidney-shaped hunk of metal?'

Poor Anish Kapoor. First, the artist loftily named his piece *Cloud Gate*, but that degenerated into 'the Bean,' which is what everyone immediately began calling it. Next, he had to unveil the piece before it was finished. Kapoor was still polishing and grinding the 168 stainless steel plates that comprise the Bean when the city showed it to the public. The surface was supposed to be seamless – and it is now. But it wasn't in 2004, and so soon after its debut it went back under wraps.

'We pay $23 million, get a hunk of metal, and now *we can't even see it*?' The locals were more incensed than ever.

But then a funny thing happened. When the Bean came back out again in 2006, people began to marvel at it, despite their better judgment. They admired the way it reflects both the sky and the skyline. They liked that you could get right up under it and touch its silvery smoothness. They liked the way it looked in pictures, which is how it became one of the city's most photographed images. Soon the Bean was a symbol of Chicago, of the city's hip, cutting-edge mentality. And the locals couldn't be more proud. Didn't they say it was fabulous all along?

ART INSTITUTE'S GREATEST HITS

We'd tell you what room each painting is in, except ongoing renovations keep altering the landscape. Ask a docent for the latest locations.

- *American Gothic* by Grant Wood – The artist, a lifelong resident of Iowa, used his sister and his dentist as models for the two stern-faced farmers.
- *The Bedroom* by Vincent van Gogh – It depicts the sleeping quarters of the artist's house in Arles. It's the second of three versions of the painting, executed during Van Gogh's 1889 stay at an asylum.
- *Nighthawks* by Edward Hopper – His lonely, poignant snapshot of four solitary souls at a neon-lit diner was inspired by a Greenwich Ave restaurant in Manhattan.
- *A Sunday Afternoon on La Grande Jatte* by Georges Seurat – Get close enough for the painting to break down into its component dots, and you'll see why it took Seurat two long years to complete his pointillist masterpiece.
- *Stack of Wheat* by Claude Monet – Paintings of the 15ft-tall stacks located in the artist's farmhouse grounds in Giverny were part of a series that effectively launched Monet's career when they sold like hotcakes at a show he organized in 1891.
- *Paris Street; Rainy Day* by Gustave Caillebotte – An engineer by training, Caillebotte straddled the line between the realism that dominated the established art world of his day and the looser, more experimental approach of his impressionist contemporaries.
- *Inventions of the Monsters* by Salvador Dalí – Painted in Austria immediately before the Nazi annexation; the title refers to a Nostradamus prediction that the apparition of monsters presages the outbreak of war. The artist's profile is visible in the lower left corner, along with that of his wife, Gala.
- *The Old Guitarist* by Pablo Picasso – The elongated figure is from the artist's Blue Period, reflecting not only Picasso's color scheme but his mindset as a poor, lonely artist in Paris in the early years.
- *America Windows* by Marc Chagall – Chagall created the huge, blue stained-glass pieces to celebrate the USA's bicentennial.

light and airy inside thanks to Frank Lloyd Wright's atrium overhaul. Step inside and have a look. Pigeons used to roost here, hence the name.

Weep all you want over the old Marshall Field's (111 N State St) becoming Macy's; the building remains a classic no matter who's in it. The iconic bronze corner clocks on the outside have given busy Loop workers the time for over 100 years now. Inside, a 6000-sq-ft dome designed by Louis Comfort Tiffany caps the north-side atrium; 50 artists toiled for 18 months to make it. The best view is from Ladies' Lingerie, on the 5th floor.

Carson Pirie Scott & Co (1 S State St) was originally criticized as being too ornamental to serve as a retail building. You be the judge, as you admire Louis Sullivan's superb metalwork around the main entrance at State and Madison Sts. Though Sullivan insisted that 'form follows function,' it's hard to see his theory at work in this lavishly flowing cast iron. Amid the flowing botanical and geometric forms, look for Sullivan's initials, LHS. The century-old department store vacated the building in 2007, and it has become office space.

The architects behind the Marquette Building (140 S Dearborn St) made natural light

and ventilation vital components. While that's nice, the most impressive features are the sculptured panels and mosaics that recall the exploits of French explorer Jacques Marquette; look for them above the entrance and in the lobby (where there's also a free little exhibit on Chicago School architecture).

With its 16 stories of shimmering glass, framed by brilliant white terra-cotta details, the Reliance Building (1 W Washington St) is a breath of fresh air. The structure's lightweight internal metal frame – much of which was erected in only 15 days – supports a glass facade that gives it a feeling of lightness, a style that didn't become universal until after WWII. Today the Reliance houses the chic Hotel Burnham (p228). Added historical bonus: Al Capone's dentist drilled teeth in what's now room 809.

Another terra-cotta beauty is the 1904 Santa Fe Building (224 S Michigan Ave), where architect Daniel Burnham kept his offices. Enter the lobby and look up at the vast light well Burnham placed in the center – he gave this same feature to the Rookery. Appropriately enough, the Santa Fe Building now houses the Chicago Architecture Foundation.

top picks

ART LOVERS' FAVORITES

- Art Institute of Chicago (p52) The nation's second-largest art museum shows everything from Monet to modern works to paperweights.
- The Picasso (opposite) Bird, dog, woman? You decide what the public artwork is. And feel free to slide down the sloping base.
- Museum of Contemporary Art (p73) Consider it the Art Institute's brash, rebellious sibling.
- The Bean (p56) Join the masses swarming the silver-drop sculpture to see the skyline reflection.
- Pilsen (p107) This neighborhood is an exciting trove of mural-splashed buildings, casual galleries and the folk-art-rich National Museum of Mexican Art.

And last, but certainly not least, no discussion of famed Loop architecture is complete without mentioning the boxy, metal-and-glass International Style of Ludwig Mies van der Rohe. His Kluczynski Building (230 S Dearborn St), part of the Chicago Federal Center, is a prime example; he designed many more buildings at the Illinois Institute of Technology (p123).

CHICAGO ARCHITECTURE FOUNDATION Map pp54-5
☎ 312-922-3432; www.architecture.org; 224 S Michigan Ave; admission free; ☼ 9am-6:30pm; Ⓜ Brown, Orange, Green, Purple, Pink Line to Adams

CAF is the premier keeper of Chicago's architectural flame. Dip in to check out the galleries. The 'You Are Here' display provides an excellent overview of renowned local structures. You can also get the lowdown on CAF's extensive list of boat, bus and walking tours (p272) and make bookings. The foundation's shop (p130) sells stacks of books about local buildings and architects if you prefer to do it yourself.

BUCKINGHAM FOUNTAIN Map pp54-5
☼ 10am-11pm mid-Apr-mid-Oct; Ⓜ Red Line to Harrison

This is one of the world's largest squirters, with a 1.5 million gallon capacity and a 15-story-high spray. Wealthy widow Kate Sturges Buckingham gave the magnificent structure to the city in 1927 in memory of her brother, Clarence. She also wisely left an endowment to maintain and operate it. The central fountain symbolizes Lake Michigan, with the four water-spouting sea creatures representing the surrounding states.

The fountain lets loose on the hour. Like so much in life, the spray begins small. Each successive basin fills, stimulating more jets, then it climaxes as the central fountain spurts up to its full 150ft. The crowd sighs in awe and is thankful that smoking is allowed. At night (8pm and thereafter) multicolored lights and music accompany the show.

CHICAGO CULTURAL CENTER Map pp54-5
☎ 312-744-6630; www.chicagoculturalcenter.org; 78 E Washington St; admission free; ☼ 8am-7pm Mon-Thu, 8am-6pm Fri, 9am-6pm Sat, 10am-6pm Sun; Ⓜ Brown, Orange, Green, Purple, Pink Line to Randolph

Heaps of freebies fill the block-long Cultural Center. In addition to housing one of the city's two visitors centers – with free maps, concierge advice and Chicago Greeter tours – the building hosts free jazz, blues, classical and world music lunchtime concerts (☼ 12:15pm Mon-Fri), as well as ongoing art exhibitions. In summer, free foreign films (☼ 6:30pm Wed & 2pm Sat, early May-early Sep) show in the 2nd-floor Claudia Cassidy Theater. Check the daily schedule posted at the entrances (at both Randolph and Washington Sts) to see what's going on each day.

The exquisite beaux arts building began its life as the Chicago Public Library back in 1897, and the Gilded Age interior mixes white Carrara and green Connemara marble throughout. The building also contains two domes by Louis Comfort Tiffany, including the world's largest stained-glass Tiffany dome, on the 3rd floor (where the circulation desk for the library used to be). The splendor of the building was meant to inspire the rabble toward loftier goals.

Excellent building tours (☎ 312-742-1190; admission free; ☼ 1:15pm Wed, Fri & Sat) leave from the Randolph St lobby. There's also a cafe on the Randolph side (beside the Visitors Center), the Chicago Publishers Gallery (providing local books, magazines and comics to browse at the cafe or various seating nooks) and free wi-fi throughout the building.

NEIGHBORHOODS THE LOOP

WHAT THE EL WAS THAT NOISE?

Novelist Nelson Algren called them Chicago's 'rusty iron heart.' And Chicago's El trains – short for 'elevated trains' – definitely occupy a prized place in the popular consciousness of the city. From El-related blogs (see http://www .chicagonow.com/blogs/cta-tattler/) to locals wearing T-shirts emblazoned with their favorite transit lines, the El trains have been both a mode of transportation and a mover of souls since they made their debut in the Loop in 1897.

Back then (as now) the Union Loop El trains ran on electricity rather than cables or steam. The whole electric train thing was still a new idea at the time, and the Union Loop was viewed with skepticism and more than a little fear by some residents. The medical profession didn't exactly help matters, either. The New York Academy of Medicine published a paper that year claiming that the elevated trains 'prevented the normal development of children, threw convalescing patients into relapses, and caused insomnia, exhaustion, hysteria, paralysis, meningitis, deafness and death.'

Though the case for meningitis might have been a *little* overstated, visitors to Chicago who stand under one of the trains as they pass will attest to the risk of deafness. In fact, a group of students from Columbia College conducted a study in 2005 that found the screeching from the train cars exceeded legal levels on several of the tracks. Most Chicagoans, though, just shrug off any attempts to make changes to the system that has been rattling Loop windows and sending cars screeching overhead for over 100 years. It may be rusty, but it's their heart all the same.

PUBLIC ART Map pp54-5

Chicago has commissioned several puzzling public artworks over the decades. The granddaddy is Pablo Picasso's work, known to everyone as 'the Picasso' (50 W Washington St). The artist was 82 when the work was commissioned. The US Steel Works in Gary, Indiana, made it to Picasso's specifications and erected it in 1967. When Chicago tried to pay Picasso for the work, he refused the money, saying the sculpture was meant as a gift to the city. At the time, many locals thought it was hideous and should be torn down and replaced with a statue of Cubs' great Ernie Banks.

Joan Miró's work The Sun, the Moon and One Star, known now as Miró's Chicago (69 W Washington St), is across the street. Miró hoped to evoke the 'mystical force of a great earth mother' with this 40ft sculpture, made of various metals, cement and tile in 1981.

French sculptor Jean Dubuffet created Monument with Standing Beast (100 W Randolph St), which everyone just calls 'Snoopy in a Blender,' at around the same time. The white fiberglass work looks a little like in-flated puzzle pieces and has a definite Keith Haring feel to it. As you can see by the large number of kids crawling around inside, it's definitely a hands-on piece of art.

Russian-born artist Marc Chagall loved Chicago, and in 1974 he donated a grand mosaic called the Four Seasons (plaza at Dearborn & Monroe Sts) to the city. Using thousands of bits of glass and stone, the artist portrayed six scenes of the city in hues reminiscent of the Mediterranean coast of France, where he kept his studio. Chagall continued to make further adjustments, such as updating the skyline, after the work arrived in Chicago.

A few blocks south on Dearborn, Alexander Calder's soaring red-pink sculpture Flamingo (plaza at Dearborn & Adams Sts) provides some much needed relief from the stark facades of the federal buildings around it. Calder dedicated the sculpture in October 1974 by riding into the Loop on a bandwagon pulled by 40 horses, accompanied by a circus parade.

For the locations of more public artworks stashed around the city, pick up a copy of the highly useful Chicago Public Art Guide at any visitors center, or check the website www.cityofchicago.org/publicart. And don't forget to visit the Bean (p56), the reigning Loop fave.

CHICAGO BOARD OF TRADE Map pp54-5

141 W Jackson Blvd; Ⓜ Brown, Orange, Purple, Pink Line to LaSalle

The Board of Trade is a 1930 art deco gem. Inside, manic traders swap futures and options – a mysterious process that has something to do with corn. Or maybe it's wheat. A small visitors center (☎ 312-435-3590; admission free; ◷ 8am-4pm Mon-Fri) tries to explain it. Or just stay outside and gaze up at the giant statue of Ceres, the goddess of agriculture, that tops the building.

The Board of Trade merged with the Chicago Mercantile Exchange in 2007, and most operations are now in this building so security is tight. The only way to get beyond the visitors center – and see the trading floor in action – is via the Chicago

Architecture Foundation's occasional lunchtime tours (www.architecture.org; $10).

MONEY MUSEUM Map pp54–5
☎ 312-322-2400; www.chicagofed.org; 230 S LaSalle St; admission free; ☯ 9am-4pm Mon-Fri; Ⓜ Brown, Orange, Purple, Pink Line to Quincy
This small museum in the Federal Reserve Bank of Chicago is fun for a quick browse. The best exhibits include a giant glass cube stuffed with one million $1 bills (demonstrating the size of so much money, which weighs 2000lb), and a counterfeit display differentiating real bills from fakes. Learn why we call $1000 a 'grand,' and snap a sweet photo standing next to the $20 million–stuffed briefcase. You'll also get a free bag of shredded currency to take home. The museum is a school group favorite. At 1pm there's a 45-minute guided tour. When you enter the building, look for the 'visitors center' sign (it doesn't say 'Money Museum'), and note you'll have to go through a metal detector.

CHICAGO THEATRE Map pp54–5
☎ 312-462-6363; www.thechicagotheatre.com; 175 N State St; Ⓜ Brown, Green, Orange, Purple, Pink Line to State
Everyone from Duke Ellington to Frank Sinatra to Prince has taken the stage here over the years (and left their signature on the famous backstage walls). The real showstopper, though, is the opulent French baroque architecture, including the lobby modeled on the Palace of Versailles. Opened in 1921, the theater originally screened silent movies with a full orchestra and white-gloved ushers leading patrons to their seats. Tickets cost just 50¢ so rich and poor alike could revel in the splendor. Today it's a concert venue. Tours ($12) are available most days (excluding Friday and Sunday) in summer, less often the rest of the year. At the very least, take a gander at the six-story sign out front; it's an official landmark.

DALEY PLAZA Map pp54–5
50 W Washington St; Ⓜ Blue Line to Washington
The Picasso sculpture marks the heart of Daley Plaza, which is the place to be come lunchtime, particularly when the weather warms. You never know what will be going on – dance performances, bands, ethnic festivals, holiday celebrations, a farmers'

PEDWAY
Come wintertime, when the going gets tough and icy sleet knifes your face, head down to the Pedway. Chicago has a 40-block labyrinth of underground walkways, built in conjunction with the subway trains. The system isn't entirely connected (ie it would be difficult to walk from one end of the Loop to the other entirely underground), and you'll find that you rise to the surface in the oddest places, say an apartment building, a hotel lobby or Macy's. The walkways are also hit-or-miss for amenities: some have coffee shops and fast-food outlets tucked along the way, some have urine smells. The city posts 'Pedway' signs aboveground at points of entry. City Hall is a good place to dive under. Download a DIY map at www.chicagopedwaytour.com. Or take a guided excursion with a local improv actor via Chicago Elevated (☎ 773-593-4873; www.chicagoelevated.com; 45min tour $5).

market (☯ 7am-3pm Thu) – but you do know it'll be free.

The plaza also remains a pilgrimage site to many as the location where the Blues Brothers drove through and crashed into the Richard J Daley Center's plate-glass windows.

City Hall rises to the plaza's west over Clark St. Da Mayor rules from here. To make a point about how the city could conserve energy, he planted the roof with prairie flowers and let loose 200,000 honey bees. The nature experiment was a success – other 'green' roofs have blossomed throughout Chicago, and the bees' sweet wares are sold to make money for kids' art programs. Alas, visitors are not permitted on the roof.

HAROLD WASHINGTON LIBRARY CENTER Map pp54–5
☎ 312-747-4300; www.chipublib.org; 400 S State St; admission free; ☯ 9am-9pm Mon-Thu, to 5pm Fri & Sat, 1-5pm Sun; Ⓜ Brown, Orange, Purple, Pink Line to Library
This grand, art-filled building with free internet and wi-fi is Chicago's whopping main library. Major authors give readings here, and exhibits are constantly shown in the galleries. The light-drenched, 9th-floor Winter Garden is a sweet hideaway for reading, writing or just taking a load off, though you'll have to hike to get there. Take the escalators to the 3rd floor (home of the browsable newspapers and

computer commons), then transfer to the elevator to go up six more floors. And those green copper creatures staring down from the exterior roof? They're wise old owls.

ROUTE 66 SIGN Map pp54–5
Adams St btwn Michigan & Wabash Aves; Ⓜ Brown, Orange, Green, Purple, Pink Line to Adams
Attention Route 66 buffs: the Mother Road's starting point is here. Look for the sign that marks the spot on Adams St's north side as you head west toward Wabash Ave. For further details on the nostalgic, corn-dog-laden highway, see p257.

UNION STATION Map pp54–5
☎ 312-655-2385; 225 S Canal St; Ⓜ Brown, Orange, Purple, Pink Line to Quincy
This wonderfully restored 1925 building, designed by Graham, Burnham and Company (Daniel Burnham's successors), looks like it stepped right out of a gangster movie. In fact, it's been used to great effect in exactly this way. Remember director Brian de Palma's classic *The Untouchables*, when Elliott Ness loses his grip on the baby carriage during the shoot-out with Al Capone's henchmen? And the carriage bounces down the stairs in slow motion? Those steps are right here, baby; they're the north ones from Canal St to the waiting room. Come during the day when Amtrak and Metra riders stride through the space, which is dappled with bright shafts of sunlight from the banks of windows.

RIVERWALK Map pp54–5
Chicago River waterfront along Wacker Dr, btwn N Lake Shore Dr & N Franklin St; Ⓜ Brown, Orange, Green, Purple, Pink, Blue Line to Clark
Clasping the Chicago River's south side along Wacker Dr, this mile-long promenade provides a peaceful spot to take a break from your hectic shopping or sightseeing schedule. Access it from the stairs at any bridge. Outdoor cafes dot the way, with a Vietnam veteran's memorial (near N Wabash Ave), a small river history museum (at N Michigan Ave) and sightseeing boats sprinkled in.

To the east, between Columbus and Lake Shore Drs on the river's north side, Centennial Fountain shoots a massive arc of water across the river. It spurts for 10 minutes straight every hour on the hour, from 10am to 2pm and again from 5pm to midnight. The exercise is meant to commemorate the labor-intensive reversal of the Chicago River in 1900, which tidily began sending all of the city's wastes downriver rather than into the lake. (Chicago's neighbors downstate, as you can imagine, do not go out of their way to celebrate this feat of civil engineering; see p21.)

A POSTCARD PERSPECTIVE
Walking Tour
Why buy postcards when you can make your own? A camera, comfortable shoes, a day spent clicking away at Loop sights and you'll have your own picture-postcard perspective of the city.

1 Picasso
It's a baboon, it's a babe, it's a babe's private parts. The artist never would say what the 1967 iron sculpture represents. Nevertheless, the untitled Picasso (p59) has become a well-known Chi-town symbol. The most intriguing perspective may just be laying faceup, camera angled, looking at the nose of the beast.

2 Miró's Chicago
For more landmark public art, cross the street to Miró's Chicago (p59). Spanish artist Joan Miró unveiled his robot/pagan fertility goddess-like sculpture in 1981. Today, nearby office workers use the statue's base as a smoker's lounge; feel free to crop.

3 Chicago Theatre
What could be more postcard perfect than a six-story-high lighted sign spelling the town's name? Any time is fine to capture the 1920s marquee for the Chicago Theatre (opposite), but if your tour falls on a cloudy day, that would eliminate harsh shadows.

4 Old Marshall Field's Clock
'Meeting under the clock' has been a Chicago tradition since 1897, when Marshall Field installed the elaborate timepiece at Washington and State. (Before that, patrons stuck notes for rendezvous-ing friends on the building.) A photo beneath the clock (now Macy's, p57) is a must.

5 Chicago Cultural Center
The 38ft-diameter Tiffany dome at the Chicago Cultural Center (p58), the world's largest, is well

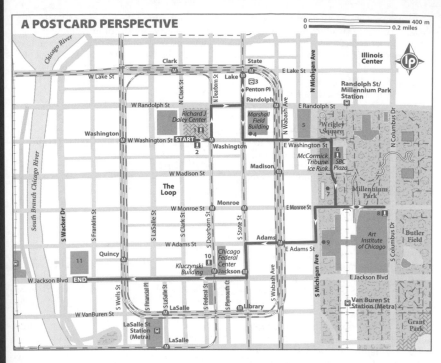

A POSTCARD PERSPECTIVE

worth photographing (as is the 1897 building's hodgepodge of Greek, Roman and European architectural styles). But you're really here to get inspiration from the architectural photos in the Landmark Chicago Gallery.

6 Cloud Gate

Plenty of Kodak moments happen at the 24-acre Millennium Park; your first stop, the sculpture Chicagoans call 'the Bean' (officially known as *Cloud Gate*, p56). Stand on the west side of the giant mirrored blob, hold the camera at waist level and you can take a self-portrait with a skyline background.

7 Crown Fountain

Geysers spout from the ground in front of two 50ft LED screens projecting images of peoples' faces. When an open-mouthed guy or gal appears, the Crown Fountain (p53) spouts water as if spitting. Use a fast shutter speed, and stick to a side view unless you've got a waterproof camera.

8 Chicago Stock Exchange Arch

Many of renowned early-20th-century architect Louis Sullivan's buildings have

been demolished. But you can get up close to his exquisite terra-cotta ornamentation at the Chicago Stock Exchange Arch, which was rescued and placed outside the Art Institute (p52). A telephoto lens can isolate the detail.

9 Art Institute Lions

Around the front of the Art Institute (p52) stand two 1894 bronze lions – city mascots of sorts. They wore helmets when the Blackhawks won the 2010 Stanley Cup, and White Sox caps during the 2005 pennant. Zoom in for a striking profile shot silhouetted against city buildings.

10 Flamingo

Alexander Calder's Flamingo (p59) is another easily recognized piece of monumental public art in Chicago. That bright red paint job should photograph well, especially if you frame it against Mies van der Rohe's ground-breaking 1974 glass-and-steel Kluczynski Building (p58) in the Chicago Federal Center.

11 Willis Tower

Aligning the building's edge on a slight diagonal will add dynamism to a shot of the 1454ft-tall Willis Tower (p56), the tallest US building (pre- and post–World Trade Center). A final photo from the 103rd-floor Skydeck sums it up: high-rises galore, lake beyond – that's the Loop.

NEAR NORTH & NAVY PIER

Drinking p179; Eating p149; Shopping p130; Sleeping p230

The Loop may be where Chicago fortunes are made, but the Near North is where those fortunes are spent. The neighborhood's song is a heady choir of salespeople's greetings, excited shoppers cooing and the crackle of goods being swaddled in paper. All of it backed by the steady beat of cash registers opening and closing.

The epicenter is the upscale shopping haven of N Michigan Ave, also known as the Magnificent Mile (Mag Mile). Stretching north from the Chicago River to Oak St, the road is silly with multistory malls, high-end department stores and outlets of big-name national chains. More than 450 shops ka-ching in the tidy span. Property developer Arthur Rubloff decreed the avenue 'magnificent' right after WWII to drum up business. He wasn't far from the mark, thanks to buildings like the Tribune Tower and the Wrigley Building that already anchored the scene.

In the River North area, west of State St, art is the big business. What was formerly a grimy, noisy assortment of warehouses and factories has become Chicago's most prestigious gallery district – a bastion of high ceilings, hardwood floors, and expensive paintings and sculpture.

Jutting off Near North's eastern end is Navy Pier, which attracts more visitors than any other sight in Chicago. It's a cavalcade of kid- and teen-oriented shops, rides, attractions and a big freakin' Ferris wheel, though adults will appreciate the criminally overlooked Smith Museum of Stained Glass Windows and the many opportunities for romantic, windswept strolling. It's about a 15-minute hoof from Michigan Ave.

NEAR NORTH

MAGNIFICENT MILE Map pp66-7
www.themagnificentmile.com; Michigan Ave; Ⓜ Red Line to Grand

The city likes to claim that the Magnificent Mile, or 'Mag Mile' as it's widely known, is one of the top five shopping streets in the world. It's a bit of a boast, because most of the retailers here are just high-end department stores and national chains that are available throughout the country. Granted, the Mag Mile versions are more slicked up than usual, and their vacuum-packed proximity on Michigan Ave between the Chicago River and Oak St is handy. Probably what's most magnificent is the millions of dollars they ring up annually. The road does go all out in December with a festive spread of tree lights and holiday adornments.

TRIBUNE TOWER Map pp66-7
435 N Michigan Ave; Ⓜ Red Line to Grand

Colonel Robert McCormick, eccentric owner of the *Chicago Tribune,* collected – and asked his reporters to send – rocks from famous buildings and monuments around the world. He stockpiled pieces of the Taj Mahal, Westminster Abbey, the Great Pyramid and 120 or so others, which are now embedded around the tower's base. And the tradition continues: a twisted piece from the World Trade Center wreckage was added recently. The unusual 'bricks' are all marked and viewable from street level. To learn more, dial ☎ 312-222-8687 on your mobile phone to listen to a self-guided audio tour.

WRIGLEY BUILDING Map pp66-7
400 N Michigan Ave; Ⓜ Red Line to Grand

The Wrigley Building glows as white as the Doublemint Twins' teeth, day or night. Chewing-gum guy William Wrigley built it that way on purpose, because he wanted it to be attention grabbing like a billboard. More than 250,000 glazed terra-cotta tiles make up the facade; a computer database tracks each one and when each needs to be cleaned and polished. Banks of megawatt lamps on the river's south side light up the tiles each night.

TRANSPORTATION – NEAR NORTH & NAVY PIER

Bus Number 151 runs along N Michigan Ave; 66 heads east on Chicago Ave to Navy Pier.

El Red Line to Grand for the Magnificent Mile's south end and River North; Red Line to Chicago for the Mag Mile's north end.

Parking The further you get away from the Mag Mile, the more common the metered parking ($2.50 per hour, but slated to go up). Parking at Navy Pier's garage costs $20 to $24 per day.

HOLY NAME CATHEDRAL Map pp66-7

☎ 312-787-8040; www.holynamecathedral.org;
735 N State St; admission free; ☾ 7am-7pm;
Ⓜ Red Line to Chicago

Holy Name Cathedral is the seat of
Chicago's Catholic Church and where its
powerful cardinals do their preaching. Built
in 1875 to a design by the unheralded
Patrick Keely, the cathedral has been
remodeled several times, most recently
after a fire in 2009. Thus the bullet holes
from a Capone-era hit across the street (see
the boxed text, p81) are no longer visible.

The cathedral provides a quiet place for
contemplation, unless the excellent choirs
are practicing, in which case it's an entertaining respite. Open most of the day, the
cathedral holds frequent services. Check
out the sanctuary's ceiling while you're
inside. The hanging red hats are for Holy
Name's deceased cardinals; the hats remain
until they turn to dust.

MERCHANDISE MART Map pp66-7

☎ 800-677-6278; www.mmart.com;
222 Merchandise Mart Plaza; admission free;
☾ 9am-6pm Mon-Fri, 10am-3pm Sat; Ⓜ Brown,
Purple Line to Merchandise Mart

Run by the Kennedy family, the Merchandise
Mart is the world's largest commercial
building and largest LEED-certified building
(Silver status, thanks in part to a hefty
thermal storage facility). Spanning two city
blocks, the 1931 behemoth has its own zip
code and gives most of its copious space to
wholesale showrooms for home furnishing
and design professionals. The first two floors
are mall-like and open to the public. To go
beyond these you must be escorted by an
interior designer, architect or other industry
professional. Tours (☎ 312-527-7762; 60min tour
$12) are available sporadically; call for the
schedule. The Mart also hosts occasional
design shows that are open to the public;
check the 'events' section of the website for
details.

Outdoors on the Mart's river side, a col-
lection of heads on poles rise up like giant
Pez dispensers. This is the Merchant's Hall of
Fame, and the creepy busts depict famous
local retailers such as Marshall Field and
Frank Woolworth.

RIVER NORTH GALLERIES Map pp66-7

www.chicagoartdealers.org; near intersection of
W Superior & N Franklin Sts; Ⓜ Brown, Purple Line
to Chicago

The River North district is the most
established of Chicago's three gallery-rich
zones (West Loop and Pilsen are the other
two), with art from top international names
and price tags to match. It claims to be the
largest concentration of private galleries
in the US outside Manhattan. Most are
very welcoming, and together they open
their doors for a festive art hop on the first
Thursday of every month (which is held in
conjunction with the younger, edgier West
Loop galleries; see p103). Pick up a gallery
map at any of the venues to help find
artwork to your liking.

Some of our favorites:

Catherine Edelman Gallery (☎ 312-266 2350; www
.edelmangallery.com; 300 W Superior St; ☾ 10am-
5:30pm Tue-Sat) If you love photography, drop by this
place where artworks range from traditional landscapes to
mixed-media photo-based collages.

Jean Albano Gallery (☎ 312-440-0770; www.jean
albano-artgallery.com; 215 W Superior St; ☾ 10am-
5pm Tue-Fri, 11am-5pm Sat) The contemporary art here
includes paintings, drawings and interesting textile works.

Zolla-Lieberman Gallery (☎ 312-944-1990; www
.zollaliebermangallery.com; 325 W Huron St; ☾ 10am-
5:30pm Tue-Fri, 11am-5:30pm Sat) The first gallery to
arrive in River North back in the '70s (when the area
looked more like the West Loop does today), it shows cool,
contemporary art by established and emerging artists.

MARINA CITY Map pp66-7

300 N State St; Ⓜ Brown, Orange, Green, Purple,
Pink, Blue Line to Clark

THE DOWNWARD SPIRE

Remember the Chicago Spire (400 N Lake Shore Dr), uberarchitect Santiago Calatrava's new building that was set to
become the nation's tallest? At 2000ft, it would've dwarfed the Willis Tower. Excitement was high (pun!), and nicknames
for the twisting design abounded – The Twizzler, The Drill Bit, The Vibrator among them. Developers broke ground in
2007, but construction came screeching to a halt in late 2008 when the economy went limp and funds dried up. Now
there's a dormant 76ft-deep, 110ft-wide hole in the ground at downtown's pricey edge. The developers vow they'll get
the money and finish the Spire. If not, it might live up to its less savory nickname: 'The Big Screw.'

INFORMATION

American Express	1 D4
Bobby's Bike Hike	(see 108)
British Consulate	(see 26)
Chopping Block	(see 22)
Fort Dearborn Station Post Office	2 C4
German Consulate	(see 97)
Indian Consulate	3 E5
Italian Consulate	(see 53)
Mystic Blue Cruises	4 H5
Northwestern Memorial Hospital	5 D4
Untouchable Gangster Tours	6 C4
Walgreens	7 D3
Weird Chicago Tours	8 C4
Wendella Sightseeing Boats	9 D5
Windy	10 G5

SIGHTS (p64)

Beer Garden	11 H4
Carousel	12 G4
Catherine Edelman Gallery	13 B4
Centennial Fountain	14 E5
Chicago Children's Museum	15 G4
Chicago Spire	16 F5
Ferris Wheel	17 G4
Holy Name Cathedral	18 C3
IMAX Theater	19 G4
Jean Albano Gallery	20 B4
Marina City	21 C5
Merchandise Mart	22 B5
Moody Church	23 C3
Skyline Stage	(see 73)
Smith Museum of Stained Glass Windows	24 H4
Tribune Tower	25 D5
Wrigley Building	26 D5
Zolla-Lieberman Gallery	27 B4

SHOPPING (p127)

Abraham Lincoln Book Shop	28 B3
Apple Store	29 D4
Chicago Tribune Store	(see 25)
Crate & Barrel	30 D4
Garrett Popcorn	31 D4
Jazz Record Mart	32 D5
Levi's Store	33 D4
Merchandise Mart	(see 22)
Niketown	34 D4
Shops at North Bridge	35 D4
Sports Authority	36 C4
Zara	37 D4

EATING (p145)

Bandera	38 D4
Billy Goat Tavern	(see 60)
Cafe Iberico	39 C3
Chicago Chop House	40 C4
Cyrano's Bistrot	41 B4
Eggsperience	42 C4
Elate	(see 90)
Fox & Obel/Atrium Wine Bar	43 E5
Gene and Georgetti	44 B5
Gino's East	45 B4
Giordano's	46 D3
Graham Elliot	47 B4
Green Door Tavern	48 B4
Lou Malnati's	49 D5
Mr Beef	50 B4
Nacional 27	(see 27)
NoMi	(see 98)
Pizzeria Uno	51 D4
Portillo's	52 C4
Purple Pig	53 D5
Second City Pizza Tours	(see 46)
Shaw's Crab House	54 C5
Sunda	55 C5
Topolobampo/Frontera Grill	56 C5
Tru	57 D4
Whole Foods	58 C4
Xoco	59 C5

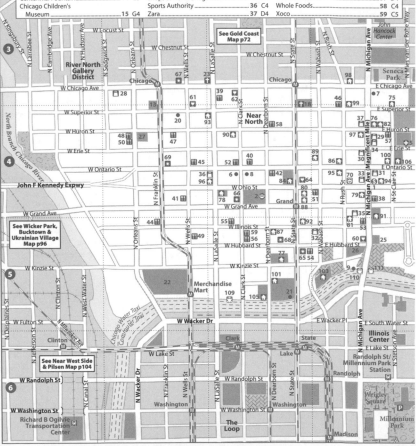

Scale	
0 ——————— 500 m	
0 ——————— 0.25 miles	

E

DRINKING 🍷 (p177)
Billy Goat Tavern 60 D5
Brehon Pub 61 B3
Clark St Ale House 62 C3
Harry Caray's 63 G5
Pop's for Champagne 64 C4
Purple Pig .... (see 53)
Terrace at Trump Tower .... (see 103)

NIGHTLIFE 🎵 (p189)
Andy's 65 C5
Blue Chicago 66 C4
Enclave 67 B3
Howl At the Moon 68 C5
Ontourage .... (see 45)
Sound-Bar 69 B4

THE ARTS (p201)
600 N Michigan Theaters 70 D4
AMC River East 71 E4
Chicago Shakespeare
    Theater 72 G4
Skyline Stage 73 G4

SPORTS & ACTIVITIES 🏊 (p213)
Bike Chicago Navy Pier .... (see 107)
Ohio St Beach 74 F4

F

SLEEPING 🛏 (p225)
Affinia Chicago 75 D3
Allerton Hotel 76 D4
Amalfi Hotel Chicago 77 C5
Best Western River North 78 C4
Chicago Marriott Hotel
    Downtown 79 D4
Comfort Inn & Suites
    Downtown 80 C4
Conrad Chicago 81 D5
Crowne Plaza Avenue Hotel 82 D4
Doubletree Magnificent Mile 83 E4
Embassy Suites
    Chicago-Downtown 84 C4
Embassy Suites
    Chicago-Lakefront 85 E4
Four Points Chicago
    Downtown 86 D4
Hampton Inn &
    Suites-Chicago Downtown 87 C5
Hilton Garden Inn 88 C4
Hotel Cass... 89 D4
Hotel Felix 90 C4
Hotel Inter-Continental
    Chicago 91 D4
Hotel Palomar 92 C5
Howard Johnson Inn 93 C4
Inn of Chicago 94 D4

G

James.. 95 D4
Ohio House Motel 96 C4
Omni Chicago Hotel 97 D4
Park Hyatt 98 D3
Peninsula.. 99 D3
Red Roof Inn 100 D4
Sax Chicago 101 C5
Sheraton Chicago Hotel &
    Towers... 102 E5
Trump Hotel & Tower 103 D5
W Chicago-Lakeshore 104 F4
Westin River North 105 C5
Wyndham Chicago 106 D4

TRANSPORT (p261)
Bike Chicago Navy Pier 107 G5
Bobby's Bike Hike............................ 108 E5
Chicago Water Taxi, La Salle St
    Stop.. 109 C5
Chicago Water Taxi, Michigan
    Ave Stop... 110 D5
Shoreline Sightseeing Commuter
    Taxi, Michigan Ave Stop........... 111 D5
Shoreline Sightseeing Lake Taxi
    to Shedd Aquarium 112 G5
Shoreline Sightseeing River Taxi
    to Willis Tower 113 F5

For some postmodern fun, check out the twin 'corncob' towers of the 1962 mixed-use Marina City. Designed by Bertrand Goldberg, it has become an iconic part of the Chicago skyline, showing up on the cover of the Wilco CD *Yankee Hotel Foxtrot*. The condos that top the spiraling parking garages are especially picturesque at Christmas, when owners decorate the balconies with a profusion of lights.

NAVY PIER

NAVY PIER Map pp66-7

☎ 312-595-7437; www.navypier.com; 600 E Grand Ave; admission free; ⏲ 10am-10pm Sun-Thu, to midnight Fri & Sat, earlier closing times Sep-May; 🚌 124

Navy Pier was once the city's municipal wharf. Today it's Chicago's most visited attraction, with eight million people per year flooding its half-mile length. Locals

top picks

FOR CHILDREN

- Chicago Children's Museum (right) Climb, dig and splash in this educational playland on Navy Pier; follow with an expedition down the carnival-like wharf itself.
- Chicago's beaches (p219) The pint-sized waves are perfect for pint-sized swimmers.
- Crown Fountain at Millennium Park (p53) It's like swimming in art.
- Field Museum of Natural History (p110) Dinosaurs! Need we say more?
- Shedd Aquarium (p111) The top-notch collection of fish and marine mammals makes for a whale of a good time.
- Lincoln Park Zoo (p80) The African exhibit and farm-in-the-zoo are always young-crowd pleasers.
- Art Institute of Chicago (p52) Join in games, story times and drop-in drawing and painting classes at the made-for-kids Ryan Education Center.
- Museum of Science & Industry (p119) This huge museum will leave even the most energetic child happily spent after a few educational hours.
- American Girl Place (p134) Young ladies sip tea and get new hair-dos with their dolls at this multistory girl-power palace.
- Time Out Chicago Kids (p267) Check the daily online listings to find the best kid-friendly events and activities during your visit.

may groan about its commercialization, but even they can't refute the brilliant lakefront views, cool breezes and whopping fireworks displays on Wednesdays (9:30pm) and Saturdays (10:15pm) in summer.

The place will certainly blow the minds of children under 12, thanks to the pier's collection of high-tech rides, hands-on fountains, fast-food restaurants and trinket vendors. For the childless, Navy Pier's charms revolve around the views and the stomach-curdling ride on the gigantic, 150ft Ferris wheel (per ride $6). It's much more exciting than any Ferris wheel has a right to be, mostly because of the dizzying height of the thing. The carousel (per ride $5) is another classic, with bobbing carved horses and organ music. There's also an 18-hole minigolf course and hot-air balloon ride (adult/child $25/15). A flotilla of competing tour boats departs from the pier's southern side; see p272 for details.

Navy Pier isn't all about rides and cotton candy, though. Many of those eight million visitors actually come here on business – the eastern end of the structure consists of exposition space managed in conjunction with McCormick Place.

A variety of acts appear through the summer at the Skyline Stage, a 1500-seat rooftop venue with a glistening white canopy. An IMAX Theater (☎ 312-595-5629; www .imax.com/chicago; tickets $11-15) and the Chicago Shakespeare Theater (p205) also call the pier home.

In summer Shoreline Sightseeing (☎ 312-222-9328; www.shorelinesightseeing.com; adult/child $7/4) runs a handy water taxi between Navy Pier, the river near the Willis Tower and the Shedd Aquarium.

Eating or drinking in a quality, noncheesy place is tough on the pier. The best bet is the Beer Garden (www .chicagosbestbeergarden.com; ⏲ from 11am daily late May-Sept, Fri-Sun only Oct) or Harry Caray's (p182), especially if you're a Chicago sports fan (there's a mini museum inside).

CHICAGO CHILDREN'S MUSEUM

Map pp66-7

☎ 312-527-1000; www.chicagochildrensmuseum .org; Navy Pier; admission $10, free Thu after 5pm; ⏲ 10am-5pm, to 8pm Thu; 🚌 124

The target audience of this attraction will love the place. Designed to challenge the imaginations of toddlers through to 10-year-olds, the colorful and lively museum near the main entrance to Navy Pier gives its wee visitors enough hands-on exhibits to keep them climbing and creating for hours.

Among the favorites, Dinosaur Expedition explores the world of paleontology and lets kids excavate 'bones.' They can expend more energy by climbing a ropey schooner and bowling in a faux alley. And Waterways lets them get wet (and learn about hydroelectric power) just when they've finally dried off from the Navy Pier fountains. Hint: crowds are often lighter on weekday afternoons.

The museum is planning a move to larger, specially built digs at Grant Park's northern edge in a few years.

SMITH MUSEUM OF STAINED GLASS WINDOWS Map pp66-7

☎ 312-595-5024; Navy Pier; admission free; ☻ 10am-10pm Sun-Thu, to midnight Fri & Sat, earlier closing times Sep-May; ☒ 124

Navy Pier doesn't promote this free, impressive attraction very well, but visitors who wander along the lower-level terraces of Festival Hall will discover the country's first museum dedicated entirely to stained glass. Many of the 150 pieces on display were made in Chicago (a stained-glass hub in the late 1800s, thanks to the influx of European immigrants), and most hung at one point in Chicago churches, homes or office buildings. Even if you think stained glass is something for blue-haired grandmas, you should make a point of coming by; the articulately explained

collection ranges from typical Victorian religious themes to far-out political designs (the Martin Luther King Jr one is especially noteworthy). And fans of Louis Comfort Tiffany will rejoice to find 13 of his works hanging here.

ABOVE, ON & IN THE WATER
Walking Tour

Recreational playground, drinking-water source, transportation lane – Lake Michigan is the watery lifeblood of the city. There's no better place to experience its numerous facets than around Navy Pier.

1 Navy Pier

Opened in 1914, Navy Pier (opposite) has seen use as a busy inland port, a naval installation, a university campus, a convention center and today's entertainment complex. Despite the amusement rides, food and shops you still get a real sense of the water as you walk along the pier's 3000ft expanse.

2 USS Chicago Anchor

Follow the quieter northern path to the pier's east end for the best views. The WWII-era USS *Chicago* anchor is a Navy memorial that reminds us of the nearly 200 planes that met a watery end training here in the 1940s. (On a calm day you can see them underwater from the John Hancock observatory.)

3 Grand Ballroom

One of the few remaining 1916 buildings, the rotund Grand Ballroom still has 30,000 lights

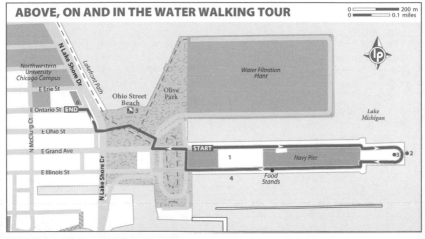

WALK FACTS

tracing the arcs of its dome. With 180 degrees of water views out the windows, wouldn't a party here be grand? The historic buildings adjacent (now meeting spaces) once held a military mess hall, and later the University of Illinois cafeteria.

4 Boat Rides

Enough history already, you want to get on the water. No problem. Power boats, sightseeing or dinner-dance cruises, and a

sail-powered tall ship all dock along the south side of the pier (see p263). The best deal is the water taxi (p263) that takes you to Museum Campus for $7.

5 Ohio Street Beach

If you want to brave the cool water (about 70°F/21°C in August) you can do so at Ohio Street Beach (p219). Just as many people sit on the concrete steps and look at the waves lapping the north shore as sink their toes in the sand.

6 W Chicago-Lakeshore

If you're loaded, you've booked a high-floor junior suite at the W (p231) for an unbeatable private lake lookout. Otherwise, take the elevator up to the 33rd-floor bar, Whisky Sky. Bonus on summer Wednesday and Saturday nights: you can see Navy Pier's fireworks.

GOLD COAST

Drinking p180; Eating p154; Shopping p132; Sleeping p236

In its most pristine reaches, the Gold Coast outshines even its gilded name, the well-heeled historic mansions glinting with an unselfconscious wealth. When you stroll through the neighborhood, especially the Astor St area, you'll take in some of the most beautiful old homes in Chicago, if not the country. With a little imagination, you can almost see the late-19th-century moguls who settled the area brandishing diamond-tipped canes at each other, and cradling their tiny dogs on the carriage rides to their Loop offices.

To get a feel for the Gold Coast's moneyed present, spend an afternoon browsing luxuriant designer wares around Oak and Rush Sts, or an evening among the glittering high heels and good cheekbones of the neighborhood's nightlife. On Friday evening, see-and-be-seen crowds glide through bars and restaurants at Rush and State Sts, where businessmen carve porterhouses while downing martinis and ogling the action – no wonder locals call the area the 'Viagra Triangle.' For window-shopping and people-watching, Chicago offers no finer spectacle.

The further you move away from the lake, the less rarefied the Gold Coast's air. At one time, the Cabrini-Green housing project, one of the city's most bleak, sat at the western edge of the neighborhood. Today it's being demolished, and its residents relocated far away to the Chicago suburbs. True to Gold Coast form, developers have drawn up plans for luxury town houses that will eventually sweep across the valuable 70-acre plot of land.

JOHN HANCOCK CENTER Map pp72-3

☎ 888-875-8439; www.hancock-observatory.com; 875 N Michigan Ave; adult/5-12yr $15/10; 🕐 9am-11pm; Ⓜ Red Line to Chicago

Chicago's third-tallest skyscraper (at 1127ft) is our favorite place to get high. In many ways the view here surpasses the one at Willis Tower, as the Hancock is closer to the lake and a little further north. Plus, you have a couple of options for taking in the view – one of which saves money *and* provides liquid refreshment.

So here's the deal: you can pay the admission price and ascend to the 94th-floor observatory. Recently revamped, it provides visitors with an edifying audio tour that gives a city history overview (good anecdotes from local newspaper journalists). There's the 'skywalk', a sort of screened-in porch that lets you feel the wind and hear the city sounds. And there's a sweet photo op where you get to 'clean' the skyscraper's windows. The observatory is probably your place if you have kids or if you're a newbie and want to beef up your Chicago knowledge.

Otherwise, shoot up to the 96th-floor lounge, where the view is free if you buy a drink ($6 to $14). That's right, here you'll get a glass of wine and a comfy seat while staring out at almost identical views from a few floors *higher*. The lounge's elevators are to the right of the cashier's desk for the observatory.

Random strange factoids: a stuntman in a Spider-Man costume set out to climb to the top of the Hancock Center using suction cups in 1981. The man in question, 'Spider Dan' Goodwin, succeeded despite a questionable intervention attempt by the Chicago Fire Department, who tried to discourage the climb by spraying him with water from their fire hoses. Also, Chicago comedian Chris Farley lived here, and was found dead from a drug overdose in his 60th-floor apartment in 1997.

WATER TOWER Map pp72-3

806 N Michigan Ave; Ⓜ Red Line to Chicago

Believe it or not, the 154ft Water Tower, a city icon and focal point of the Mag Mile, once dwarfed all the surrounding buildings. Built in 1869, the Water Tower and its associated building, the Pumping Station

TRANSPORTATION – GOLD COAST

Bus Number 151 runs along N Michigan Ave; 70 runs along Division St before swooping south to the Newberry Library.

El Red Line to Clark/Division for the northern reaches; Red Line to Chicago for the southern areas.

Parking Resident-only streets stymie street parking. Try LaSalle St, much of which is unmetered.

GOLD COAST

N North Park Ave

W Scott St

N Clybourn Ave

N Cleveland Ave

W Division St

N Howe St

N Larrabee St

N Cambridge Ave

W Elm St

N Cleveland Ave

W Hobble St

Cabrini-Green

N Cleveland Ave

W Oak St

N Orleans St

Goose Island

●43

N Hooker St

N North Branch St

N Kingsbury St

N Larrabee St

N Cambridge Ave

N Mohawk St

N Cleveland Ave

N Hudson Ave

N Sedgwick St

W Locust St

🍴28

N Cleveland Ave

North Branch Chicago River

River North Gallery District

See Wicker Park, Bucktown & Ukrainian Village Map p96

Chicago Ⓜ

W Chicago Ave

Ⓜ

(aka the Water Works) across the street, were constructed with local yellow limestone in a Gothic style popular at the time. This stone construction and lack of flammable interiors saved them in 1871, when the Great Chicago Fire roared through town; they're the only downtown buildings that survived.

The Water Tower was the great hope of Chicago when it first opened, one part of a great technological breakthrough that was going to provide fresh, clean water for the city from intake cribs set far out in Lake Michigan. Before then, the city's drinking water had come from shore-side collection basins that sucked in sewage-laden water and industrial runoff from the Chicago River. Garnished with the occasional school

of small fish, it all ended up in the sinks and bathtubs of unhappy Chicago residents.

Though the fish problem was solved by the new system, the plan was ultimately a failure. Sewage from the river, propelled by spring rains, made its way out to the new intake bins. The whole smelly situation didn't abate until the Chicago River was reversed in the 1890s (when engineers used canals and locks to send sewage *away* from Lake Michigan). By 1906 the Water Tower was obsolete, and only public outcry saved it from demolition three times. Whether Oscar Wilde would have joined the preservationists is debatable: when he visited Chicago in 1881 he called the Water Tower 'a castellated monstrosity with salt and pepper boxes stuck all over it.' Restoration

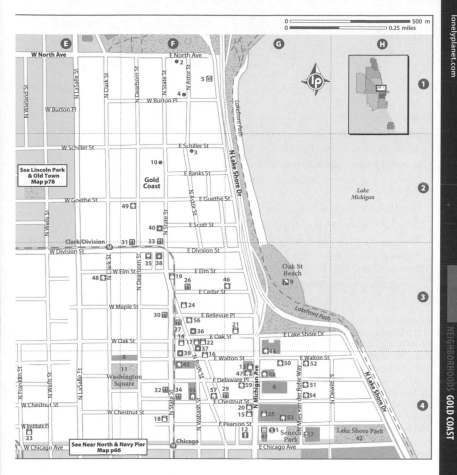

in 1962 ensured the tower's survival, and today it houses the City Gallery (☎ 312-742-0808; admission free; ☉ 10am-6:30pm Mon-Sat, to 5pm Sun), showcasing Chicago-themed works by local photographers. The Pumping Station across the street houses a visitors center (p275) with free wi-fi, comfy public seating and a pie cafe.

MUSEUM OF CONTEMPORARY ART (MCA) Map pp72-3
☎ 312-280-2660; www.mcachicago.org; 220 E Chicago Ave; adult/13-18yr $12/7, admission free Tue; ☉ 10am-8pm Tue, to 5pm Wed-Sun; Ⓜ Red Line to Chicago

Consider it the Art Institute's brash, rebellious sibling, with especially strong minimalist and surrealist collections and permanent works by Franz Kline, René

Magritte, Cindy Sherman and Andy Warhol. Covering art from 1945 forward, the MCA's collection spans the gamut, from Jenny Holzer's LED *Truisms* to Joseph Beuys' austere *Felt Suit,* with displays arranged to blur the boundaries between painting, photography, sculpture, video and other media. The museum also regularly hosts dance, film and speaking events from an international array of contemporary artists, and the traveling exhibits it pulls in are A-list. The museum's shop wins big points for its jewelry pieces and colorful children's toys.

ASTOR STREET Map pp72-3
Ⓜ Red Line to Clark/Division
In 1882 Bertha and Potter Palmer were the power couple of Chicago. His web of

IT'S FREE

Have a thin wallet? Chicago makes it easy by serving up many top sights and activities without charge. And we're not even counting the internationally renowned downtown summer bashes like Blues Fest and Jazz Fest (see Festivals, p12). Many museums also have free days; see p111 for details.

Millennium Park (p53) Listen to classical concerts; perspire in Pilates classes; tour avant-garde artworks; ice-skate in skyscrapers' shadows – the park is ground zero for cool, fun freebies.

Navy Pier (p68) Stroll for sweet views and the tucked-away stained-glass museum.

SummerDance (p14) Boogie down with dance lessons and live world music.

Chicago beaches (p219) Play in the waves at 30-plus sand crescents along the lakefront.

Second City post-show improv (p199) Guffaw during a raucous set after the evening's main performance.

Chicago Cultural Center (p58) Choose from lunchtime concerts, foreign films, art exhibits, browsable comic books, wi-fi and more.

Lincoln Park Zoo (p80) Wander by pygmy hippos, gorillas and roaring lions.

Empty Bottle Monday night concerts (p193) Rock out to edgy indie bands for nix to start the week.

Downloadable tours (p272) Let Buddy Guy lead you to blues sites and poets take you to literary sites.

National Museum of Mexican Art (p107) Ponder a millennium's worth of color-splashed folk art, paintings and artifacts at the USA's largest Latino arts center.

Museum of Contemporary Photography (p115) View this small but mighty collection of pix.

businesses included the city's best hotel and a huge general merchandise store that he later sold to a clerk named Marshall Field. When they later relocated north from Prairie Ave to a crenellated castle of a mansion at what is now 1350 N Lake Shore Dr, the Palmers set off a lemminglike rush of Chicago's wealthy to the neighborhood around them. The mansions sitting along Astor St, especially the 1300 to 1500 blocks, reflect the grandeur of that heady period.

While he was still working for Louis Sullivan, Frank Lloyd Wright (who was 19 at the time) designed the large but only 11-room Charnley-Persky House (☎ 312-915-0105; www.charnleyhouse.org; 1365 N Astor St; tours Wed free, Sat $15; ☉ noon Wed all year, 10am & noon Sat Apr-Nov, 10am only Dec-Mar), and proclaimed with his soon-to-be-trademarked bombast that it was the 'first modern building.' Why? Simply because it did away with Victorian gaudiness in favor of plain, abstract forms that went on to become the modern style. It was completed in 1892 and now houses the Society of Architectural Historians.

The Cyrus McCormick Mansion (1500 N Astor St) is one of the neighborhood's standouts. The 1893 neoclassical home was designed by New York architect Stanford White. McCormick and his family had the whole place to themselves, but it's now divided

up into condos. It's still the high-rent district – a three-bedroom, three-bathroom unit goes for $1.75 million (washer and dryer included).

The 1885 mansion that serves as the Archbishop's Residence (1555 N State St) spans the entire block to Astor. This sweet crib, complete with 19 chimneys, is one of the many perks that comes with leading the Chicago Catholic Archdiocese. Seven archbishops have lived here, and world leaders from Franklin D Roosevelt to Pope John Paul II have crashed at the residence while in town.

Don't forgot to check out another special house in the 'hood: Hugh Hefner's first Playboy Mansion is nearby (see opposite).

OAK STREET BEACH Map pp72-3
☉ dawn-dusk; Ⓜ Red Line to Clark/Division
There aren't many cities outside of Florida that offer such an abundance of sand and (miniaturized) surf this close to their major business districts. Oak St Beach makes for a wonderful respite and offers a lower-key experience than certain beaches further north, where you're likely to get a volleyball spiked on your head if you're not paying attention. The 'beachstro' provides nourishment.

INTERNATIONAL MUSEUM OF SURGICAL SCIENCE Map pp72-3

☎ 312-642-6502; www.imss.org; 1524 N Lake Shore Dr; adult/student $10/6, admission free Tue; ⊙ 10am-4pm Tue-Sun May-Sep, closed Sun Oct-Apr; Ⓜ Red Line to Clark/Division or ☐ 151

Home to an eclectic (and sometimes chilling) collection of surgical gear, the Museum of Surgical Science has fascinating thematic displays, such as the one on bloodletting. A collection of 'stones' (as in 'kidney' and 'gall-') and the somewhat alarming ancient Roman vaginal speculum leave lasting impressions. For those who've always wanted to see an iron lung, here's your chance. And about that hemorrhoid surgery toolkit...

NEWBERRY LIBRARY Map pp72-3

☎ 312-943-9090; www.newberry.org; 60 W Walton St; admission free; ⊙ 9am-5pm Tue-Fri, to 1pm Sat; Ⓜ Red Line to Chicago

Humanities nerds and those trying to document far-flung branches of their family tree will have a field day at this research library. Entry requires a library card, but one-day passes are available for curious browsers; you must be 16 or older to be admitted. Once inside, you can pester the patient librarians with requests for help in tracking down all manner of historical ephemera. (The collection is noncirculating, though, so don't expect to take that 1st edition of the King James Bible home with you.) The Newberry often features interesting special exhibits, and has a bookstore where you can pick up such treatises as *Buffy the Vampire Slayer and Philosophy*, and cool vintage Chicago travel posters. Free tours of the impressive building take place at 3pm Thursday and 10:30am Saturday.

ORIGINAL PLAYBOY MANSION

Map pp72-3

1340 N State St; Ⓜ Red Line to Clark/Division

The sexual revolution pretty much started in the basement 'grotto' of this 1899 mansion. Chicago magazine impresario Hugh Hefner bought it in 1959 and dubbed it the first Playboy Mansion, even hanging a brass plate over the door warning 'If You Don't Swing, Don't Ring.' Alas, Chicago became too square for Hef by the mid '70s, so he packed up and built a new Playboy

Mansion in LA, which is where he remains today, in his pajamas.

After he left, he donated the State St building to the School of the Art Institute for a dorm (imagine the pick-up lines!). It was gutted in 1993 and turned into four very staid but very expensive condos.

Playboy, now run by Hugh's daughter Christine, maintains its corporate headquarters in Chicago, and Walton St (at Michigan Ave) has been named 'Honorary Hugh M Hefner Way' in an official tip of the hat to Hef.

WASHINGTON SQUARE Map pp72-3

btwn N Clark St, N Dearborn St, W Delaware Pl, W Walton St; Ⓜ Red Line to Chicago

This plain-looking park across from the Newberry Library has had both a colorful history and a tragic one. In the 1920s it was known as 'Bughouse Sq' because of the communists, socialists, anarchists and other -ists who gave soapbox orations here. Clarence Darrow and Carl Sandburg are among the respected speakers who climbed up and shouted.

In the 1970s, when it was a gathering place for young male prostitutes, it gained tragic infamy as the preferred pick-up spot of mass murderer John Wayne Gacy. Gacy took his victims back to his suburban home, where he killed them and buried their bodies in the basement. Convicted on 33 counts of murder (although the actual tally may be higher), he was executed in 1994.

Today the square bears little trace of its past lives – except for one weekend a year in late July. That's when the Bughouse Debates occur, and orators return to holler at each other.

LIVING WELL
Walking Tour

Wish you had a lifestyle of the rich and famous? Live it up for a day on the Gold Coast.

1 Four Seasons Hotel

OK, so you may not be able to afford $500 a night at the Four Seasons (p236), but you can at least start your afternoon tour in style. Book a vanilla-sugar exfoliating rub, then relax in the serene spa lounge. Or pop by for tea in the palm-laden lobby-level Conservatory.

LIVING WELL

WALK FACTS

Start Four Seasons Hotel
End International Museum of Surgical Science
Distance 1.25 miles
Time Three or more hours (with drinks and massage)

3 Oak St Boutiques

Next, peruse the window displays of the tony Oak St boutiques, between N Michigan and N Rush Sts (see p132). What can't you live without? That hand-folded Hermès tie, a Prada purse, the perfect pair of Jimmy Choo pumps? They're all here and more.

4 Original Playboy Mansion

Hugh Hefner turned this building into the original Playboy Mansion (p75) in 1959. He not only lived and partied here, but published *Playboy* here. That's how the whole jammie-wearing thing came about. He was working around the clock from home, so he just quit bothering to get dressed.

5 Astor St Mansions

Stroll north on leafy Astor St to ogle the fine 19th-century homes (p73) built by Chicago's elite. The Charnley-Persky House, designed by both Louis Sullivan and Frank Lloyd Wright, and the Cyrus McCormick Mansion, onetime home to a local industrialist, are just two of the many on show.

6 International Museum of Surgical Science

This mansion was put to a different purpose: holding an iron lung, a Roman speculum and other surgical artifacts for the International Museum of Surgical Science (p75). Dr Max Thorek, founder of the International College of Surgeons, started this odd institution back in 1950.

2 John Hancock Center

Meander across the street to the John Hancock Center (p71) and take the elevator to the 96th-floor Signature Lounge. Order a glass of sparkling Rheinland cuvée and the artisanal cheese plate to go with your million-dollar view.

LINCOLN PARK & OLD TOWN

Drinking p180; Eating p156; Shopping p134; Sleeping p239

Home to Chicago's yuppie population, Lincoln Park bustles with well-heeled residents walking dogs, Rollerblading and pushing babies around in $300 strollers. Local curmudgeons grouse that the neighborhood is a soulless victim of gentrification, but the area has some undeniable charms, including many great restaurants (such as Alinea, North America's top-ranked eatery), cute boutiques, Steppenwolf and other provocative theaters, blues clubs and a couple of gangster sights. The yuppieness (and prices) are further tempered by DePaul University and its large student population, near the intersection of Lincoln and Fullerton Ave.

Lincoln Park also has the park itself, a well-loved playland. Almost 50% larger than Central Park in New York, the park offers Chicagoans a chance to celebrate summer with an oasis of ponds and paths, plus roaring lions, fidgety monkeys and an ark's worth of other critters hanging out in the park's free zoo. North Ave Beach washes up to the south side; it's one of the biggest and most active sandlots in the city.

Old Town was the epicenter of Chicago's hippie culture in the 1960s. Artists and longhairs flocked here to tune in, turn on and drop their money on cool black-light posters and bongs from head shops. A few smoke shops, trippy aquarium vendors and other holdovers from the old days remain, but now stylish boutiques and eateries stuff the neighborhood, which abuts Lincoln Park's greenery and the Gold Coast's mansions. Wells St is the main vein, and most visitors make a pilgrimage here at some point – it's the home of improv bastion Second City.

LINCOLN PARK Map pp78-9

🚌 151

The neighborhood gets its name from this park, Chicago's largest. Its 1200 acres stretch for 6 miles, from North Ave north to Diversey Pkwy, where it narrows along the lake and continues until the end of Lake Shore Dr. The park's many lakes, trails and paths make it an excellent place for recreation. Cross-country skiing in the winter and sunbathing in warmer months are just two of the activities Chicagoans enjoy in Lincoln Park. Many buy picnic vittles from the markets on Clark St and Diversey Pkwy.

Most of Lincoln Park's pleasures are natural, though one of its joys is sculptor Augustus Saint-Gaudens' Standing Lincoln, which shows the 16th president deep in contemplation right before he delivers a great speech. Saint-Gaudens based the work on casts made of Lincoln's face and hands while Lincoln was alive. The statue stands in its own garden east of the Chicago History Museum. The artist also sculpted a Sitting Lincoln, which rests its rump by the Art Institute.

Near the southeast corner of LaSalle Dr and Clark St, the Couch Mausoleum is the sole reminder of the land's pre-1864 use: the entire area was a municipal cemetery. Many of the graves contained hundreds of dead prisoners from Camp Douglas, a horrific prisoner-of-war stockade on the city's

TRANSPORTATION – LINCOLN PARK & OLD TOWN

Bus Number 151 runs north from downtown via Michigan Ave and Lake Shore Dr and is good for reaching all the sites in the park itself; 22 connects the Loop to Lincoln Park (the 'hood) and runs along Clark St.

El Brown, Purple or Red Line to Fullerton or the Brown or Purple Line to Armitage for Lincoln Park; Brown or Purple Line to Sedgwick, or the Red Line to Clark/Division for Old Town.

Parking Lincoln Park is a headache. If you're stuck for a spot, consider heading out to the meters along Diversey Harbor. Old Town has plenty of cars competing for its plentiful meters. Try the pay garage at Piper's Alley, at North Ave and Wells St.

South Side during the Civil War. Removing the bodies from the designated park area proved a greater undertaking than the city could stomach and, today, if you were to start digging at the south end of the park, you'd be liable to make some ghoulish discoveries.

From a little dock in front of pretty Café Brauer, a 1908 Prairie School architectural creation, you can rent two-person paddleboats and cruise the South Pond, south of the zoo. The rental season is roughly May through September.

LINCOLN PARK & OLD TOWN

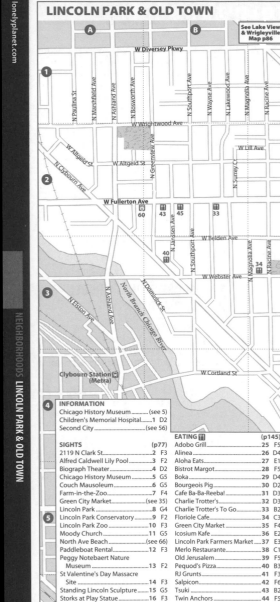

See Lake View & Wrigleyville Map p86

See Wicker Park, Bucktown & Ukrainian Village Map p96

NEIGHBORHOODS LINCOLN PARK & OLD TOWN

INFORMATION
Chicago History Museum .... (see 5)
Children's Memorial Hospital 1 D2
Second City .... (see 56)

SIGHTS (p77)
2119 N Clark St 2 F3
Alfred Caldwell Lily Pool 3 F2
Biograph Theater 4 D2
Chicago History Museum 5 G5
Couch Mausoleum 6 G5
Farm-in-the-Zoo 7 F4
Green City Market .... (see 35)
Lincoln Park 8 G4
Lincoln Park Conservatory 9 F2
Lincoln Park Zoo 10 F3
Moody Church 11 G5
North Ave Beach .... (see 66)
Paddleboat Rental 12 F3
Peggy Notebaert Nature
   Museum 13 F2
St Valentine's Day Massacre
   Site 14 F3
Standing Lincoln Sculpture 15 G5
Storks at Play Statue 16 F3

SHOPPING (p127)
Barker & Meowsky 17 C4
Crossroads Trading Co. 18 E1
Dave's Records 19 E1
Lori's, The Sole of Chicago 20 D3
Lululemon Athletica 21 D3
Rotofugi 22 C1
Spice House 23 F5
Vosges Haut-Chocolat 24 D4

EATING (p145)
Adobo Grill 25 F5
Alinea 26 D4
Aloha Eats 27 E1
Bistrot Margot 28 F5
Boka 29 D4
Bourgeois Pig 30 D2
Cafe Ba-Ba-Reeba! 31 D3
Charlie Trotter's 32 D3
Charlie Trotter's To Go 33 B2
Floriole Cafe 34 C3
Green City Market 35 F4
Icosium Kafe 36 E2
Lincoln Park Farmers Market 37 E3
Merlo Restaurante 38 C1
Old Jerusalem 39 F5
Pequod's Pizza 40 B3
RJ Grunts 41 F3
Salpicon 42 F6
Tsuki 43 B2
Twin Anchors 44 F5
Via Carducci 45 B2
Wiener's Circle 46 E1

DRINKING (p177)
Delilah's 47 C1
Goose Island Brewery 48 C4
Old Town Ale House 49 F5
Red Rooster Cafe & Wine Bar 50 D3
Rose's Lounge 51 C1
Weeds 52 D5

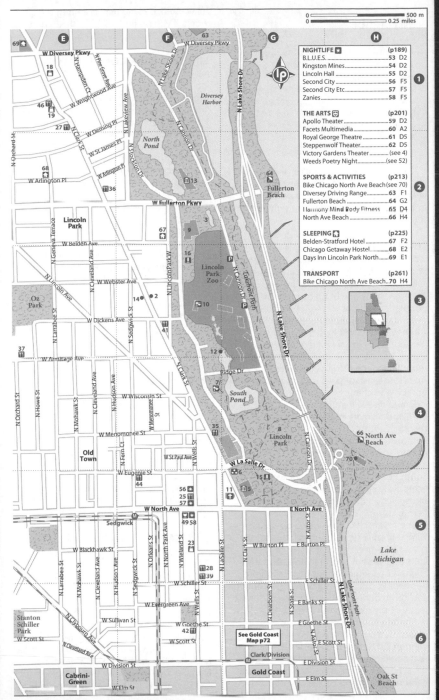

0 ━━━━━━━ 500 m
0 ┈┈┈┈┈┈┈ 0.25 miles

NIGHTLIFE ★	(p189)
B.L.U.E.S.	**53** D2
Kingston Mines	**54** D2
Lincoln Hall	**55** D2
Second City	**56** F5
Second City Etc	**57** F5
Zanies	**58** F5

THE ARTS 🎭	(p201)
Apollo Theater	**59** D2
Facets Multimedia	**60** A2
Royal George Theatre	**61** D5
Steppenwolf Theater	**62** D5
Victory Gardens Theater	(see 4)
Weeds Poetry Night	(see 52)

SPORTS & ACTIVITIES	(p213)
Bike Chicago North Ave Beach	(see 70)
Diversey Driving Range	**63** F1
Fullerton Beach	**64** G2
Harmony Mind Body Fitness	**65** D4
North Ave Beach	**66** H4

SLEEPING 🛏	(p225)
Belden-Stratford Hotel	**67** F2
Chicago Getaway Hostel	**68** E2
Days Inn Lincoln Park North	**69** E1

TRANSPORT	(p261)
Bike Chicago North Ave Beach	**70** H4

NEIGHBORHOODS **LINCOLN PARK & OLD TOWN**

SWEET RIDE

One of Chicago's essential experiences is riding the El, and taking the Brown Line into the Loop is the optimal way to do it. Get on in Lincoln Park at either the Fullerton or Armitage stops, take a seat by the window, and watch as the train clatters downtown, swinging past skyscrapers so close you can almost touch them. Stay aboard as the El loops the Loop, and get off at the Clark stop if you want to remain downtown. Rides cost $2.25.

The outdoor Green City Market (www .chicagogreencitymarket.org) offers heirloom veggies, homemade pies and much more at Lincoln Park's south end from mid-May through October.

LINCOLN PARK ZOO Map pp78-9

☎ 312-742-2000; www.lpzoo.com; 2200 N Cannon Dr; admission free; ☼ 10am-4:30pm Nov-Mar, to 5pm Apr-Oct, to 6:30pm Sat & Sun Jun-Aug; 🚌 151
The free zoo is one of Chicago's most popular attractions. Top of the exhibit heap is the naturalistic Regenstein African Journey. Adults will love the cuddly, perpetually puzzled-looking meerkats, and kids will scream with disgusted glee at the room filled with hissing cockroaches. The Ape House also pleases with its swingin' gorillas and chimps.

Farm-in-the-Zoo features a full range of barnyard animals in a faux farm setting at the zoo's south end, and offers frequent demonstrations of cow milking, horse grooming and other chores. The half-mile-long Nature Boardwalk circles the adjacent South Pond and teaches about wetlands ecology; keep an eye out for endangered birds such as the black-crowned night heron.

The rest of the zoo – which opened in 1868 – is fairly typical. The exhibits for the lions and other big cats and for the sea lions are fine but unremarkable. And the cramped penguin habitat borders on depressing. Still, free is a good price, and if you come during colder months you'll have many of the exhibits to yourself.

The zoo has multiple entrances around its perimeter. The Gateway Pavilion (on Cannon Dr) is the main one, where you can rent strollers, pick up a free map and see the schedule for the day's feedings, training demonstrations and zookeeper talks. Drivers be warned: parking here is among the city's worst. If you do find a spot in the Cannon Dr lot, it costs $19 for four hours.

LINCOLN PARK CONSERVATORY
Map pp78-9

☎ 312-742-7736; 2391 N Stockton Dr; admission free; ☼ 9am-5pm; 🚌 151
'It's like a free trip around the world,' one visitor said after walking through the conservatory's 3 acres of desert palms, jungle ferns and tropical orchids. We couldn't agree more, especially in winter, when the glass-bedecked hothouse remains a soothing 75°F escape from the icy winds raging outside. Just south, the 1887 statue Storks at Play has enchanted generations of Chicagoans. Real birds fill the landscape immediately northeast, at the corner of Fullerton Pkwy and Cannon Dr, around the Alfred Caldwell Lily Pool. The Prairie-style garden, whose stonework resembles the stratified canyons of the Wisconsin Dells, is an important stopover for migrating species. It's a magical, dragonfly-dappled refuge, open from late April through November.

NORTH AVENUE BEACH Map pp78-9

cnr North Ave & Lake Shore Dr; admission free; ☼ dawn-dusk; 🚌 151
Chicago's most popular beach gives off a southern California vibe. Countless volleyball nets draw scores of skimpy-suited beautiful people to the sand. Dodgeball and roller-hockey leagues collide in beachside rinks, while the steamship-inspired beach house contains a party-hearty cafe. A short walk on the curving breakwater any time of year yields postcard city views from a spot that seems almost a world apart. Lifeguards watch the beach throughout summer.

BIOGRAPH THEATER Map pp78-9

2433 N Lincoln Ave; Ⓜ Red, Brown, Purple Line to Fullerton
In 1934, the 'lady in red' betrayed gangster John Dillinger at this theater, which used to show movies. It started out as a date – Dillinger took new girlfriend Polly Hamilton to the show, and Polly's roommate Anna Sage tagged along, wearing a red dress. Alas, Dillinger was a notorious bank robber and the FBI's very first 'Public Enemy Number One.' Sage also had troubles with the law, and was about to be deported.

To avoid it, she agreed to set Dillinger up. FBI agents shot him in the alley beside the theater. The venue now hosts plays by the Victory Gardens Theater (p207).

PEGGY NOTEBAERT NATURE MUSEUM Map pp78-9
☎ 773-755-5100; www.naturemuseum.org; 2430 N Cannon Dr; adult/3-12yr $9/6, admission by

CAPONE'S CHICAGO

Chicagoans traveling the world often experience an unusual phenomenon when others ask where they're from. When they answer 'Chicago,' the local drops into a crouch and yells something along the lines of 'Rat-a-tat-a-tat, Al Capone!' Although civic boosters bemoan Chicago's long association with a scar-faced hoodlum, it's an image that has been burned into the public consciousness by movies such as *The Untouchables* and *Public Enemies,* and other aspects of pop culture.

Capone was the mob boss in Chicago from 1924 to 1931, when he was brought down on tax evasion charges by Elliot Ness, the federal agent whose task force earned the name 'The Untouchables' because its members were supposedly impervious to bribes. (This wasn't a small claim, given that thousands of Chicago police and other officials were on the take, some of them raking in more than $1000 a week.)

Capone came to Chicago from New York in 1919. He quickly moved up the ranks to take control of the city's South Side in 1924, expanding his empire by making 'hits' on his rivals. These acts, which usually involved bullets shot out of submachine guns, were carried out by Capone's lieutenants. Incidentally, Capone earned the nickname 'Scarface' not because he ended up on the wrong side of a bullet but because a dance-hall fight left him with a large scar on his left cheek.

The success of the Chicago mob was fueled by Prohibition. Not surprisingly, the citizens' thirst for booze wasn't eliminated by government mandate, and gangs made fortunes dealing in illegal beer, gin and other intoxicants. Clubs called 'speakeasies' were highly popular and were only marginally hidden from the law, an unnecessary precaution given that crooked cops were usually the ones working the doors. Commenting on the hypocrisy of a society that would ban booze and then pay him a fortune to sell it, Capone said: 'When I sell liquor, they call it bootlegging. When my patrons serve it on silver trays on Lake Shore Dr, they call it hospitality.'

It's a challenge to find traces of the Capone era in Chicago. The city takes a dim view of Chicago's gangland past, with nary a brochure or exhibit on Capone or his cronies (though the Chicago History Museum shop does have a good selection of books on the topic). Many of the actual sites have been torn down – some of the more notable survivors.

Capone's Chicago Home (Map pp50-1; 7244 S Prairie Ave) This South Side home was built by Capone and mostly used by his wife, Mae, son Sonny and other relatives. It's privately owned and in a sketchy area, so use caution when visiting.

City Hall (Map pp54-5; 121 N La Salle St) This building was the workplace of some of Capone's best pals. During William 'Big Bill' Thompson's successful campaign for mayor in 1927, Al donated well over $100,000.

Green Mill (Map p90; 4802 N Broadway St) This tavern was one of Capone's favorite nightspots. During the mid-1920s the cover for the speakeasy in the basement was $10. You can still listen to jazz in its swank setting today (see p191).

Holy Name Cathedral (Map pp66-7; 735 N State St) Two gangland murders took place near this church. In 1924, North Side boss Dion O'Banion was gunned down in his florist shop (738 N State St) after he crossed Capone. In 1926, his successor, Hymie Weiss, died en route to church in a hail of Capone-ordered bullets emanating from a window at 740 N State.

Maxwell St Police Station (Map pp104-5; 943 W Maxwell St) This station, two blocks west of Halsted St, exemplified the corruption rife in the Chicago Police Department in the 1920s. At one time, five captains and about 400 uniformed police here were on the take.

Mt Carmel Cemetery (Map pp50-1; cnr Roosevelt & S Wolf Rds, Hillside) Capone is now buried in this cemetery in Hillside, west of Chicago. He and his relatives were moved here in 1950. Al's simple gray gravestone, which has been stolen and replaced twice, is concealed by a hedge. It reads 'Alphonse Capone, 1899–1947, My Jesus Mercy.' Capone's neighbors include old rivals Dion O'Banion and Hymie Weiss. Both tried to rub out Capone, who returned the favor in a far more effective manner.

St Valentine's Day Massacre Site (Map pp78-9; 2122 N Clark St) In perhaps the most infamous event of the Capone era, seven members of the Bugs Moran gang were lined up against a garage wall and gunned down by mobsters dressed as cops. After that, Moran cut his losses and Capone gained control of Chicago's North Side vice. The garage was torn down in 1967 to make way for a retirement home, and the facility's landscaped parking lot now lies at the site. A house (2119 N Clark St) used as a lookout by the killers stands across the street.

donation Thu; ⊙ 9am-4:30pm Mon-Fri, 10am-5pm Sat & Sun; ⊜ 151

Located near the zoo, this hands-on museum allows you to do everything from walking through a fluttering butterfly haven to engineering your own river system. Other exhibits show how many different wild animals live in urban Chicago, both inside and out. The museum is geared mostly to kids, who are given free rein to explore, scamper and climb while they learn. In winter, the Green City Market sets up inside twice per month on Saturdays.

CHICAGO HISTORY MUSEUM Map pp78-9

☎ 312-642-4600; www.chicagohistory.org; 1601 N Clark St; adult/under 13yr $14/free, admission free Mon; ⊙ 9:30am-4:30pm Mon-Sat, noon-5pm Sun; Ⓜ Brown, Purple Line to Sedgwick or ⊜ 22

The History Museum is the top stop for people curious about Chicago's storied past, including both its troubling and triumphant chapters. Multimedia displays cover the Great Fire and the 1968 Democratic Convention, and detail local inventions such as the skyscraper, the nuclear reactor and the birth control pill. President Lincoln's deathbed is here. So is one of the city's best photo opportunities: the chance to dress up in a Chicago hot dog costume. Ask for the free audio tour to enhance your visit. The on-site bookstore stocks hard-to-find local history tomes, including some scholarly looks at the city's gangsters.

MOODY CHURCH Map pp78-9

☎ 312-943-0466; www.moodychurch.org; 1630 N Clark St; Ⓜ Brown, Purple Line to Sedgwick or ⊜ 22

Directly across from the Chicago History Museum stands the hulking nondenominational Moody Church, started by 19th-century missionary Dwight Moody. He also founded the Moody Bible Institute in the Gold Coast, and was basically the Billy Graham of his age – a charismatic preacher who took his literal interpretations of the Bible to audiences around the world. During the 1893 World's Expo, Moody organized huge Christian revivalist events under enormous tents in Jackson Park, hoping to warn fair-goers away from the moral ruin awaiting them on the Midway and in Chicago's infamous Levee District. This Clark St structure, which can hold almost 4000 worshippers, was built in 1925. Tours are available by request.

THE ZOO & BEYOND
Walking Tour

Looking to entertain the little ones? A day in Lincoln Park will keep you busy without breaking the bank. Generations of Chicagoans having been coming here to what's now one of the last free zoos in the country.

1 Lincoln Park Zoo

Stroll through recreated regions in the African Journey and watch Primate House monkeys play at the two best exhibits at the zoo (p80). Can your kids identify the smallest member of the bear family? The big beast prized for its horns? The panda of a different color?

2 RJ Grunts

Moving fast, you can hit the highlights of the zoo in two hours or so, before heading to RJ Grunts (p157) for lunch. The hostess will store your stroller while you order a chocolate-peanut-butter-banana milkshake and burgers. The menu, and the hubbub, are entirely kid-friendly.

WALK FACTS

Start Lincoln Park Zoo
End North Ave Beach
Distance 2 miles
Time Four to five hours (or as long as your kids hold out)
Fuel Stop Ice-cream stand at Café Brauer

THE ZOO AND BEYOND

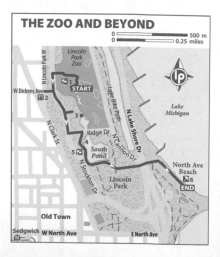

3 Café Brauer Paddleboat Rental

To work off any sugar-fueled energy, head to the paddleboat rental (p77) next to the 1908 Prairie School–style Café Brauer (snacks available). It's a unique experience out on South Pond, with the skyline looming ahead and birds and frogs chirping in the background.

4 Nature Boardwalk

Hop on the Nature Boardwalk (p80), a half-mile path around the pond's wetlands ecosystem. Zoo staff roll by with 'curiosity carts' to entertain and educate kids about local ecology.

5 Farm-in-the-Zoo

Next it's the big ol' barn and the Farm-in-the-Zoo (p80). Little ones seem to love petting sheep, watching chicks hatch and learning how to milk a cow. Parents like that this, too, is free. By now you've spent more than four hours in the park. If you have enough energy to continue…

6 North Avenue Beach

Walk south along the pond and turn east past ballfields before you cross the bridge to North Avenue Beach (p80). Grab a refreshment, rent a beach chair and watch your kids construct castles in the sand. The point's city skyline view is an ideal background for a family photo.

LAKE VIEW & WRIGLEYVILLE

Drinking p181; Eating p159; Shopping p135; Sleeping p239

Lake View is the overarching name of this good-time neighborhood, inhabited mostly by 20- and 30-somethings. Wrigleyville is the pocket that surrounds star attraction Wrigley Field. The neighborhood has become a magnet for singles, who frolic and cruise in the ridiculous number of bars and restaurants lining Clark St and Southport Ave. It's usually well mannered by day, with an impish dose of carousing by night. But when the Cubs play at Wrigley, look out: 40,000 fans descend on the 'hood, and the party kicks into high gear.

Wrigleyville has been the subject of controversy recently. Developers want to build an eight-story retail space with a hotel, condos and big-box retailers across from the ballpark at Clark and Addison Sts. Various neighborhood groups have protested, saying not only would the development displace many current business stalwarts (an improv theater, a diner, several bars and restaurants), but it would ruin the area's charm, now a hodge-podge of single-story, independently owned businesses. Developers counter by saying they'd be making better use of the congested space, ultimately helping the neighborhood grow in a sustainable way. Stay tuned for the ensuing battle, with Wrigleyville's 'tradition' versus 'suburbanization' on the line.

Either the rainbow flags or the abundance of hot, well-dressed men will tip you off to the fact that you've arrived in Boystown. The well-heeled hub of Chicago's gay community, it bustles on Broadway St during the day and gets hedonistic on Halsted St at night. It's also the place to come if you accidentally left those fur-lined handcuffs at home; the shops here are known for their quirky, fun and sex-friendly vibe.

Though the crowds may be straighter in Belmont, just west of Boystown, the shopping scene here is equally wild. This is the youngest-feeling of Lake View's pockets, and the stores here cater to the lifestyle whims of local goths, punks and kitschy hipsters. Whether you need hair dye, a Fender Telecaster or a vintage Morrissey T-shirt, you can count on the endearingly attitude-heavy emporiums here to come through for you.

The Southport Corridor, along Southport Ave between Belmont Ave and Irving Park Rd, is more staid; it's for those who outgrew their Belmont lifestyle and now need a designer wardrobe for their toddler.

For all its copious energy, Lake View has little in the way of historic sights or cultural attractions beyond the ballpark. Just bring your credit cards, your walking shoes and a festive attitude, and you'll be set.

WRIGLEY FIELD Map pp86–7

☎ 773-404-2827; www.cubs.com; 1060 W Addison St; Ⓜ Red Line to Addison

Built in 1914 and named for the chewing-gum guy, Wrigley Field – aka The Friendly Confines – is the second-oldest baseball park in the major leagues. It's filled with legendary traditions and curses (see the boxed text, p221), and has a team that suffers from the longest dry spell in US sports history. The hapless Cubbies haven't won a championship since 1908, a sad record unmatched in pro football, hockey or basketball.

If the team is playing a home game, you can peep through the 'knothole,' a garage-door-sized opening on Sheffield Ave, and watch the action for free. Baseball fanatics can take a 90-minute stadium tour ($25) that goes through the clubhouse, the dugouts and the press box. Tours take place on various days when the Cubs are out of town; check the website for the schedule. Reservations required.

Statues of Cubs heroes ring the stadium. Ernie Banks, aka 'Mr Cub', stands near the main entrance. The shortstop/first baseman was the team's first African American player. Billy 'Sweet-Swinging' Williams

TRANSPORTATION – LAKE VIEW & WRIGLEYVILLE

Bus Number 152 traces Addison St; 22 follows Clark St; 8 runs along Halsted St.

El Red Line Addison stop for Wrigleyville; Brown, Purple and Red Line Belmont stop for Belmont and Boystown.

Parking In a word: nightmare. Especially in Wrigleyville, where side streets are resident-only. Take the train or bring a really good audiobook to listen to as you try to find parking.

wields his mighty bat by the Captain Morgan Club bar. And mythic TV sportscaster Harry Caray dons his barrel-sized eyeglasses in front of the bleacher entrance. Caray was known for broadcasting among the raucous bleacher fans while downing a few Budweisers himself (it's said the sculptors mixed a dash of his favorite beer in with the white bronze used for the statue).

BOYSTOWN Map pp86-7

btwn Halsted & Broadway Sts, Belmont Ave & Addison St; Ⓜ Red Line to Addison

What the Castro is to San Francisco, Boystown is to the Windy City. The mecca of queer Chicago (especially for men), the streets of Boystown are full of rainbow flags and packed with bars, shops and restaurants catering to the residents of the gay neighborhood. For more info on gay Chicago, see the boxed text, p195.

ALTA VISTA TERRACE Map pp86-7

btwn Byron & Grace Sts; Ⓜ Red Line to Sheridan

Chicago's first designated historic district is worthy of the honor. Developer Samuel Eberly Gross recreated a block of London row houses on Alta Vista Tce in 1904. The 20 exquisitely detailed homes on either side of the street mirror each other diagonally, and the owners have worked hard at maintaining the spirit of the block. Individuality isn't dead, however – head to the back of the west row and you'll notice that the back of every house has grown in dramatically different fashions.

CUBBYVILLE
Walking Tour

You don't even have to go into the stadium to enjoy a Cub-filled day around Wrigley Field. Game day fun starts early – get to the area several hours before the first pitch.

1 Sluggers

Warm up for your A-game at Sluggers (p215). The sports bar's four batting cages offer differing speeds. So, even if you're not Sammy Sosa, you've got a shot. A few brewskies beforehand will warm up that stiff body. Drinking heavily (but responsibly) is a way of life in Wrigleyville. Moving on...

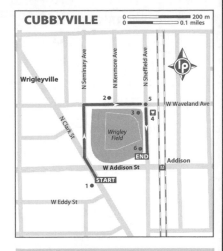

WALK FACTS

Start Sluggers
End Knothole, Wrigley Field
Distance 0.75 miles
Time 1.5 hours (more depending how long you drink)
Fuel Stop Murphy's Bleachers

2 Corner of Kenmore & Waveland Avenues

Once the game's started, head to the corner to hang out with the ball hawks. The professionals set up chairs and wait to snag errant home runs that fly over the wall. No kid stuff, this – ball hawks have filed lawsuits when a ball was knocked out of their hands.

3 Harry Caray Statue

Stop and pay homage to Harry Caray, the legendary sports commentator who was more fan than formal announcer. ('Holy Cow!') You'll likely have to line up to get a picture with his statue guarding the bleacher entrance at Wrigley Field (opposite) – though he's been dead since 1998 he's still quite popular.

4 Murphy's Bleachers

You've heard of the infamous bleacher bums (of whom Caray was one)? Join the loud crowd by heading to Murphy's (p182). Stand around in the yard across from the bleacher entrance swilling beer and debating the Cubs' chances. You may want to practice mouthing off – rowdiness rules in the coveted seats.

LAKE VIEW & WRIGLEYVILLE

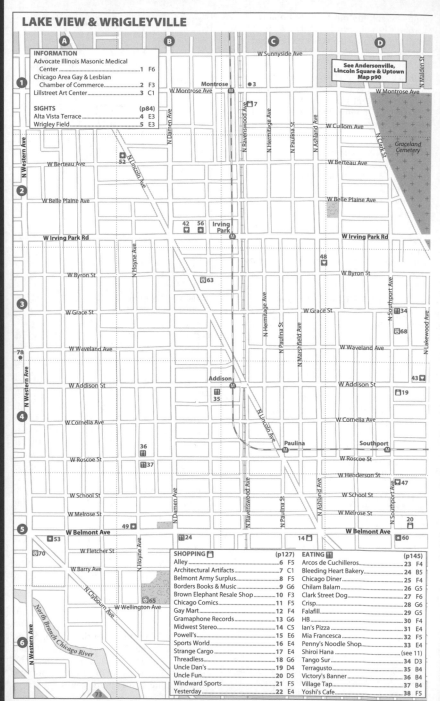

INFORMATION		
Advocate Illinois Masonic Medical		
Center	1	F6
Chicago Area Gay & Lesbian		
Chamber of Commerce	2	F3
Lillstreet Art Center	3	C1
SIGHTS		(p84)
Alta Vista Terrace	4	E3
Wrigley Field	5	E3

SHOPPING	(p127)
Alley	6 F5
Architectural Artifacts	7 C1
Belmont Army Surplus	8 F5
Borders Books & Music	9 G6
Brown Elephant Resale Shop	10 F3
Chicago Comics	11 F5
Gay Mart	12 F4
Gramaphone Records	13 G6
Midwest Stereo	14 C5
Powell's	15 E6
Sports World	16 E4
Strange Cargo	17 E4
Threadless	18 G6
Uncle Dan's	19 D4
Uncle Fun	20 D5
Windward Sports	21 F5
Yesterday	22 E4

EATING	(p145)
Arcos de Cuchilleros	23 F4
Bleeding Heart Bakery	24 B5
Chicago Diner	25 F4
Chilam Balam	26 G5
Clark Street Dog	27 F6
Crisp	28 G6
Falafill	29 G5
HB	30 F4
Ian's Pizza	31 E4
Mia Francesca	32 F5
Penny's Noodle Shop	33 E4
Shiroi Hana	(see 11)
Tango Sur	34 D3
Terragusto	35 B4
Victory's Banner	36 B4
Village Tap	37 B4
Yoshi's Cafe	38 F5

NEIGHBORHOODS LAKE VIEW & WRIGLEYVILLE

DRINKING 🍷	(p177)
Closet	39 G4
Duke of Perth	40 G6
Ginger Man	41 E3
Globe Pub	42 B2
Guthrie's	43 D4
Harry Caray's	44 F4
Hungry Brain	(see 53)
L&L	45 F5
Murphy's Bleachers	46 F3
Southport Lanes	47 D5
Ten Cat Tavern	48 C3

NIGHTLIFE 🎵	(p189)
Beat Kitchen	49 B5
Berlin	50 F5
ComedySportz	51 F5
Corn Productions	52 B2
Hungry Brain	53 A5
Hydrate	54 F4
IO (ImprovOlympic)	55 E4

Katerina's	56 B2
Metro	57 E3
Playground Improv Theatre	58 F5
Rockit	59 E3
Schubas	60 D5
Sidetrack	61 F4
Smart Bar	(see 57)
Spin	62 F5

THE ARTS 🎭	(p201)
American Theater Company	63 B3
Brew & View	64 F5
Chicago Moving Co	65 B6
Landmark's Century Centre	66 G6
Mary-Arrchie Theatre Company	67 F3
Music Box Theatre	68 D3
Theatre Building	69 E5
Viaduct Theatre	70 A5

SPORTS & ACTIVITIES	(p213)
Aveda Institute	71 G6

Captain Morgan Club	72 E4
Chicago Cubs	(see 5)
Diversey-River Bowl	73 A6
Fitness Formula Club	74 F5
Moksha Yoga	75 F5
Rink at Wrigley	(see 5)
Sluggers	76 E4
Southport Lanes	(see 47)
Sydney R Marovitz Golf Course	77 G3
Waveland Bowl	78 A3
Waveland Tennis Courts	79 G3

SLEEPING 🛏	(p225)
Best Western Hawthorne Terrace	80 G4
City Suites Hotel	81 G5
Majestic Hotel	82 G4
Old Chicago Inn	83 F5
Villa Toscana	84 F4
Willows Hotel	85 G6

0 ——————— 500 m
0 ——————— 0.25 miles

W Irving Park Rd

Hebrew Cemetery
Wunders Cemetery

Sheridan
W Dakin St
W Byron St
W Sheridan Rd

W Grace St

W Grace St

W Bradley Pl

Wrigleyville

Wrigley Field

Addison
W Addison St
W Brompton Ave

W Eddy St
W Cornelia Ave
W Cornelia Ave
W Stratford Pl

W Newport Ave
W Hawthorne Pl

W Roscoe St
W Roscoe St

W Buckingham Pl
Boystown
W Aldine Ave

W Aldine Ave
W Melrose St
Belmont
W Belmont Ave
W Belmont Ave

Belmont

W Briar Pl
Lake View
W Briar Pl
W Barry Ave
W Barry Ave
W Barry Ave

W Fletcher St
W Nelson St

W Wellington Ave
Wellington
W Oakdale Ave

W Barry Ave

W Surf St
W Surf St
Diversey
W Diversey Pkwy
W Diversey Pkwy

Lincoln Park
Lake Michigan
Belmont Harbor
Belmont Rocks
Lakefront Path
Diversey Harbor

See Lincoln Park & Old Town Map p78

5 Waveland & Sheffield Avenues

As you're walking around the stadium, look up. The buildings along Waveland and Sheffield have been bought up and turned into corporate hospitality lounges. Rooftop seats (see p220 for ticket info) provide a unique perspective down onto the field. Watch from here and you get food and drink included.

6 Knothole

A 2006 expansion of the Wrigley Field (p84) bleachers beefed up the eastern wall. The franchise left a 20ft-long opening (with iron bars) so you can peek into the game at field level. The right-field vantage point is a bit skewed – but it's free. Now go watch the game.

ANDERSONVILLE, LINCOLN SQUARE & UPTOWN

Drinking p183; Eating p162; Shopping p137; Sleeping p240

These northern neighborhoods are good for a delicious browse. Andersonville is an old Swedish enclave centered on Clark St, where timeworn European-tinged businesses and bakeries mix with new foodie restaurants, funky boutiques, vintage shops and gay and lesbian bars. Places like the butter-lovin' Swedish Bakery carry on the legacy of the original inhabitants, but the residential streets are now home mostly to creative types, young professionals and folks (especially women) who fly the rainbow flag.

Uptown, the scrappy neighborhood to the south of Andersonville, has a fascinating history of its own. Al Capone often drank here at his favorite speakeasy, the Green Mill (still a jazz venue today; see p191). It's also where his gang stored their bootleg booze (in tunnels under the club) after it came off boats in nearby Lake Michigan. Circa 1915, the neighborhood was the epicenter of moviemaking in the United States. Yep, before there was Hollywood, there was Uptown, cranking out the country's silent films and harboring contract players like Charlie Chaplin and WC Fields.

Uptown's most recent cultural contributions are the kind you eat with chopsticks. Hole-in-the-wall Asian eateries along Argyle St have earned this area the name 'Little Saigon' and made it a mecca for fans of Vietnamese food.

West of Uptown lies Lincoln Square, an old German enclave that has blossomed into an eating, drinking and shopping destination with a Euro-vibe reminiscent of Andersonville.

ANDERSONVILLE

SWEDISH AMERICAN MUSEUM CENTER Map p90

☎ 773-728-8111; www.swedishamericanmuseum.org/; 5211 N Clark St; adult/child $4/3; ⊙ 10am-4pm Mon-Fri, 11am-4pm Sat & Sun; Ⓜ Red Line to Berwyn

The permanent collection at this small storefront museum focuses on the lives of the Swedes who originally settled Chicago. In that sense it reflects the dreams and aspirations of many of the groups who have poured into the city since it was founded. You can check out some of the items people felt were important to bring with them on their journey to America. Butter churns, traditional bedroom furniture, religious relics and more are all included. The children's section lets kids climb around on a steamship and milk fake cows.

ROSEHILL CEMETERY Map p90

☎ 773-561-5940; 5800 N Ravenswood Ave; ⊙ 8am-5pm Mon-Sat, 10am-4pm Sun; 🚌 84

The entrance gate to Chicago's largest cemetery is worth the trip alone. Designed by WW Boyington (the architect who created the old Water Tower on Michigan Ave), the entry looks like a cross between high Gothic and low Disney. Through the gates you'll see the graves of plenty of

TRANSPORTATION – ANDERSONVILLE, LINCOLN SQUARE & UPTOWN

Bus Number 151 runs along Sheridan Rd; 22 travels on Clark St.

El Take the Red Line to Berwyn, six blocks east of Clark St, for Andersonville; take the Red Line to Argyle for Argyle St; the Red Line's Lawrence stop is good for trips to lower Uptown; Red Line to Sheridan for Graceland Cemetery and around. For Lincoln Sq, take the Brown Line to Western.

Parking Meter and on-street parking are available in Andersonville and Uptown, though big concerts at Uptown's music venues can make things hairy.

Chicago bigwigs, from Chicago mayors and a US vice president to meat man Oscar Mayer. You'll also find some of the weirdest grave monuments in the city, including a postal train and a huge carved boulder from a Civil War battlefield in Georgia. More than one ghost story started here; keep an eye out for vapors as night falls.

UPTOWN

GRACELAND CEMETERY Map p90

☎ 773-525-1105; 4001 N Clark St; ⊙ 8am-4:30pm; Ⓜ Red Line to Sheridan

ANDERSONVILLE, LINCOLN SQUARE & UPTOWN

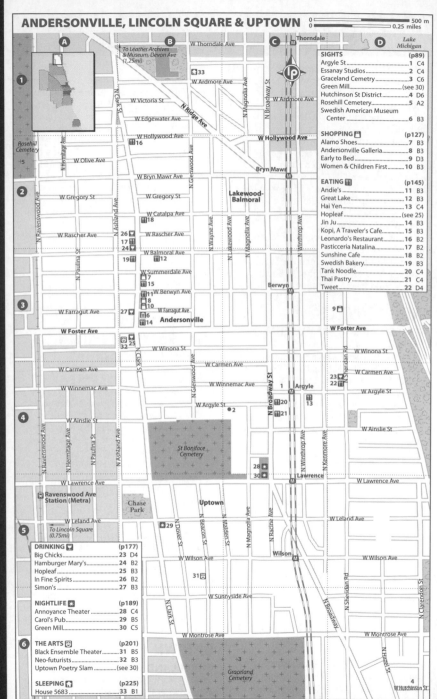

SIGHTS	(p89)
Argyle St	1 C4
Essanay Studios	2 C4
Graceland Cemetery	3 C6
Green Mill	(see 30)
Hutchinson St District	4 D6
Rosehill Cemetery	5 A2
Swedish American Museum Center	6 B3

SHOPPING 🛍	(p127)
Alamo Shoes	7 B3
Andersonville Galleria	8 B3
Early to Bed	9 D3
Women & Children First	10 B3

EATING 🍴	(p145)
Andie's	11 B3
Great Lake	12 B3
Hai Yen	13 C4
Hopleaf	(see 25)
Jin Ju	14 B3
Kopi, A Traveler's Cafe	15 B3
Leonardo's Restaurant	16 B2
Pasticceria Natalina	17 B2
Sunshine Cafe	18 B2
Swedish Bakery	19 B3
Tank Noodle	20 C4
Thai Pastry	21 C4
Tweet	22 D4

DRINKING 🍷	(p177)
Big Chicks	23 D4
Hamburger Mary's	24 B2
Hopleaf	25 B3
In Fine Spirits	26 B2
Simon's	27 B3

NIGHTLIFE ★	(p189)
Annoyance Theater	28 C4
Carol's Pub	29 B5
Green Mill	30 C5

THE ARTS 🎭	(p201)
Black Ensemble Theater	31 B5
Neo-futurists	32 B3
Uptown Poetry Slam	(see 30)

SLEEPING 🛏	(p225)
House 5683	33 B1

Graceland Cemetery is the final resting place for some of the biggest names in Chicago history. Most of the notable tombs lie around the lake, in the northern half of the 121 acres. Pick up a free map at the entrance to navigate the swirl of paths and streets.

Many of the memorials relate to the lives of the dead in symbolic and touching ways: National League founder William Hulbert lies under a baseball; hotelier Dexter Graves lies under a work titled *Eternal Silence*; and George Pullman, the railroad car magnate who sparked so much labor unrest, lies under a hidden fortress designed to prevent angry union members from digging him up.

Daniel Burnham, who did so much to design Chicago, gets his own island. Photographer Richard Nickel, who helped form Chicago's budding preservation movement and was killed during the demolition of his beloved Chicago Stock Exchange Building, has a stone designed by admiring architects. Other notables interred here include architects John Wellborn Root, Louis Sullivan and Ludwig Mies van der Rohe, plus retail magnate Marshall Field and power couple Potter and Bertha Palmer.

ARGYLE STREET Map opposite
btwn Broadway St & Sheridan Rd;
M Red Line to Argyle
Also known as 'Little Saigon.' Many residents came here as refugees from the Vietnam War and subsequently filled the storefronts with pho-serving lunch spots, bubble-tea-pouring bakeries and shops with exotic goods from the homeland. The pagoda-shaped Argyle El station, painted in the auspicious colors of green and red, puts you in the fishy-smelling heart of it. The area is great for a wander (even if it looks a

top picks

PLACES TO ESCAPE THE CROWDS

- Graceland Cemetery (p89)
- Harold Washington Winter Garden (p60)
- 12th Street Beach (p114)
- The Ancient Egyptian and Southeast Asian galleries of the Art Institute (p52)
- Lincoln Park Conservatory (p80)

top picks

FAVORITE TOURS

- Chicago Architecture Foundation (p272) Gawk at Chicago's famed skyscrapers on a boat or walking tour.
- Fork & the Road (p160) Bike from restaurant to restaurant to meet chefs and chow down.
- Bobby's Bike Hike (p272) Pedal along the lakefront or into far-flung neighborhoods like Hyde Park.
- Weird Chicago Tours (p272) Take a bus to ghost, gangster and red-light sites.
- Wateriders (p220) Paddle through downtown's skyscraper canyon.

little scruffy). The businesses spill out onto Broadway St, as well.

ESSANAY STUDIOS Map opposite
1333-1345 W Argyle St; M Red Line to Argyle
Back before the talkies made silent film obsolete, Chicago reigned supreme as the number one producer of movie magic in the USA. Essanay churned out silent films with soon-to-be household names like WC Fields, Charlie Chaplin and Gilbert M Anderson (aka 'Bronco Billy,' the trailblazing star of the brand-new Western genre and cofounder of Essanay). Filming took place at the studio, but also in the surrounding neighborhoods. Getting the product out the door and into theaters was more important than producing artful, well-made films, so editing was viewed somewhat circumspectly. As a result, it was common in the early Essanay films to see local children performing unintentional cameos, or bits of familiar neighborhoods poking into the edge of 'California' mesas. Essanay folded in 1917, about the time that many of its actors were being lured to the bright lights of a still-nascent Hollywood. These days, the building belongs to a local college, but the company's terra-cotta Indian head logo remains above the door at 1345.

HUTCHINSON STREET DISTRICT
Map opposite
M Red Line to Sheridan
In marked contrast to some of Uptown's seedier areas, the Hutchinson St District is a

well-maintained area perfect for a genteel promenade. Homes here were built in the early 1900s and represent some of the best examples of Prairie School residences in Chicago. Several of the homes along Hutchinson St – including the one at 839 Hutchinson St – are the work of George W Maher, a famous student of Frank Lloyd Wright. Also of note are 817 Hutchinson St and 4243 Hazel St.

LEATHER ARCHIVES & MUSEUM
Map p90

☎ 773-761-9200; www.leatherarchives.org; 6418 N Greenview Ave; admission $10; ⊗ 11am-7pm Thu & Fri, to 5pm Sat & Sun; ☒ 22
Who knew? Ben Franklin liked to be flogged, and Egypt's Queen Hatshepsut had a foot fetish. The Leather Archives & Museum reveals this and more in its displays of leather, fetish and S&M subcultures. The on-site shop sells posters, pins and other 'pervertibles.'

DEVON AVENUE Map p90

intersection of Devon & Western Aves; Ⓜ Brown Line to Western, transfer to ☒ 49B
OK, it's technically not in Andersonville or Uptown, but about a mile and a half north. Often called Chicago's 'International Marketplace,' Devon Ave is an ethnic mash-up where Indian women in jewel-toned saris glide past Muslim men in white skullcaps, and Russian women in bright lipstick shop beside Orthodox men in black yarmulkes. It's a fun destination for shopping (see p138) and serial grazing on the samosas, kebabs, kosher doughnuts and other snack-shop items. Or get curried away with a full meal (p164).

SWEET TREATS
Walking Tour
It's a pity that you're only walking a third of a mile, because you'll need more than that to work off all the sugar. This tour is best in late afternoon, when the bars and restaurants are open.

1 Hopleaf
Start your tempting tour at Hopleaf (p184). If you can look past the 200 types of beer on the menu, the cashew-butter-and-fig-jam sandwich provides the base you'll need for the blood sugar onslaught to come. Then again,

you could jump right in with the oatmeal stout chocolate brownie.

2 Swedish American Museum Center
At the shop for the Swedish American Museum Center (p89), pick up a baking cookbook and some lingonberry jam so you can make your own goodies (it also sells cookies). Upstairs in the museum, letters and belongings shed light on the lives of the neighborhood's first immigrants.

3 Andersonville Galleria
Pop in to the multilevel Andersonville Galleria (p137), where 90 indie vendors have banded together to sell their homemade wares – including indulgences like Grown Up Kid Stuff's rich chocolate sauce and Terry's Toffee's signature item (so good it's served at the Academy Awards each year).

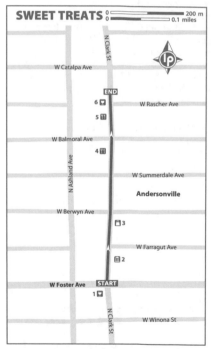

WALK FACTS

Start Hopleaf
End In Fine Spirits
Distance 0.33 miles
Time A couple of hours

4 Swedish Bakery

Allergy sufferers beware, almonds are very popular in Swedish pastries; they're infused in many of the cakes, cookies and confections at the landmark Swedish Bakery (p163). Take a number and wait to order your chocolate-almond-buttercream macaroons or frog-shaped almond cake.

5 Pasticceria Natalina

Shortly after opening in 2007, Pasticceria Natalina (p163) was already drawing comments like 'best bakery in Chicago.' The flaky pastry of the cannoli, stuffed with imported fresh sheep's milk ricotta, is the star at this Sicilian bakery. But there's the chocolate-hazelnut biscotti and the tiramisu to try...

6 In Fine Spirits

Toss back a few cocktails at In Fine Spirits (p183) and you're guaranteed sweet dreams. The Iberian Escape provides a three-flight dessert wine tour of Spain and Portugal. Or go crazy with a Rhubarb Julep, a Sazerac or any of the 30 other cocktails poured with artisanal booze.

WICKER PARK, BUCKTOWN & UKRAINIAN VILLAGE

Drinking p184; Eating p164; Shopping p138; Sleeping p241

If you want to get a taste of artsy young Chicago, wander up Milwaukee Ave near Damen Ave in Wicker Park on a Friday night. You'll pass booming bars, packed restaurants and stages hosting indie rock on one side of the street and shushed underground author readings on the other. By Saturday morning the scene shifts to the dozens of cool vintage stores, in-the-know record shops and buzzing brunch spots. Buttressed by the slightly fancier Bucktown and slightly scruffier Ukrainian Village, this neighborhood has a lot happening, so strap on some comfortable (hip) sneakers and take it block by block.

Although signs of the community's past are fading fast, there are plenty of traces of the Eastern European immigrants who founded it, especially in the western reaches of Ukrainian Village. A stroll here will take you past Ukrainian scrawl on shop windows, Orthodox churches and proud, if humble, corner taverns where immigrants have long quenched their thirst.

Milwaukee, North and Damen Aves are the main veins through the neighborhood. Division St is also chockablock. Once a polka-bar-lined thoroughfare known as the 'Polish Broadway,' it's now stuffed with the requisite sushi lounges and crafty boutiques. That's gentrification for you, and it's transformed Wicker Park, Bucktown and Ukie Village in a big way.

WICKER PARK & BUCKTOWN

WICKER PARK Map pp96-7
btwn N Damen Ave, W Schiller St & N Wicker Park Ave; Ⓜ Blue Line to Damen

Sure, Chicago invented the zipper and a handful of other bric-a-brac. The city's true legacy, though, will be in a strange softball game invented here. Aptly named, 16-Inch Softball uses the same rules as normal softball, but with shorter games, a bigger, squishier ball and a complete lack of gloves or mitts on the fielders. They've been playing it in Chicago for over 75 years, and Wicker Park is a prime place to see the unique local sport played by die-hard fanatics. And for travelers suffering withdrawal from the pooch left at home, Wicker Park's dog park is a great way to get in some quality canine time.

TRANSPORTATION – WICKER PARK, BUCKTOWN & UKRAINIAN VILLAGE

Bus Number 50 runs up Damen Ave; 72 runs along North Ave; 70 travels along Division St.

El Blue Line to Damen Ave for Wicker Park and Bucktown; Blue Line to Division or Chicago for Ukrainian Village.

Parking Meter and free on-street parking are at a premium in Wicker Park and Bucktown; they're widely available in Ukrainian Village.

NELSON ALGREN HOUSE Map pp96-7
1958 W Evergreen Ave; Ⓜ Blue Line to Damen

You can't go inside, but on the third floor of this apartment building writer Nelson Algren created some of his greatest works about life in the once down-and-out neighborhood. He won the 1950 National Book Award for his novel *The Man with the Golden Arm*, set on Division St near Milwaukee Ave (about a half-mile southeast). *A Walk on the Wild Side* contains the classic advice: 'Never play cards with a man called Doc. Never eat at a place called Mom's. Never sleep with a woman whose troubles are worse than your own.' And his short *Chicago: City on the Make* summarizes 120 years of thorny local history and is the definitive read on the city's character.

FLAT IRON BUILDING Map pp96-7
www.flatironartists.com; 1579 N Milwaukee Ave; Ⓜ Blue Line to Damen

A warren of galleries, studios and workshops burrows in the landmark Flat Iron Building. Contemporary painters, realist photographers, digital animators, pop-art printmakers, experimental videographers and metal sculptors fill the spaces. There's an open house on the first Friday of every month (admission $5), as well as larger group shows in mid-September and around the winter holidays. Keep an eye on telephone poles around the area for flyers detailing the latest shows and open-houses in the 'hood.

POLISH MUSEUM OF AMERICA
Map pp96-7

☎ 773-384-3352; www.polishmuseumofamerica.org; 984 N Milwaukee Ave; adult/senior & student $7/5; ⊙ 11am-4pm, closed Thu; Ⓜ Blue Line to Division

If you don't know Pulaski from a pierogi, this is the place to get the scoop on Polish culture. It's one of the oldest ethnic museums in the country, and while you won't find high-tech 3-D virtual roller-coaster rides or IMAX screens, you will get a chance to learn about some of the Poles who helped shape Chicago's history. (Casimir Pulaski, by the way, was a Polish hero in the American Revolution who was known as the 'father of the American cavalry' and the guy who saved George Washington's life at the Battle of Brandywine.) Traditional Polish costumes, WWII artifacts and folk art pieces contribute to the storytelling.

UKRAINIAN VILLAGE
CHURCHES OF UKRAINIAN VILLAGE Map pp96-7
🚌 66

The domes of the neighborhood's majestic churches pop out over the treetops in Ukrainian Village. Take a minute to wander by St Nicholas Ukrainian Catholic Cathedral (☎ 773-276-4537; www.stnicholaschicago.org; 2238 W Rice St), which is the less traditional of the neighborhood's main churches. Its 13 domes represent Christ and the Apostles. The intricate mosaics – added to the 1915 building in 1988 – owe their inspiration to the Cathedral of St Sophia In Kiev. Saints Volodymyr & Olha Church (☎ 312-829-5209; www.stsvo.org; 739 N Oakley Blvd) was founded by traditionalists from St Nicholas, who broke away over liturgical differences and built this showy church in 1975. It makes up for its paucity of domes (only five) with a massive mosaic of the conversion of Grand Duke Vladimir of Kiev to Christianity in AD 988. Holy Trinity Russian Orthodox Cathedral (☎ 773-486-6064; www.holytrinitycathedral.net; 1121 N Leavitt St) looks like it was scooped straight out of the Russian countryside and deposited in the neighborhood. But famed Chicago architect Louis Sullivan actually designed the 1903 beauty and its octagonal dome, front bell tower, and stucco and wood-framed exterior. Czar Nicholas II helped fund the structure, which

top picks
OFFBEAT MUSEUMS

- **International Museum of Surgical Science** (p75) Ogle the iron lung, kidney stones and surgical art.
- **Leather Archives & Museum** (p92) Explore leather, fetish and S&M subcultures.
- **Money Museum** (p60) Snap the obligatory photo with the $20 million briefcase.
- **Polish Museum of America** (left) Learn about Pulaski and all the other 'skis who influenced Chicago.

is now a city landmark. Cathedral staff give tours of the gilded interior every Saturday from 11am to 4pm.

UKRAINIAN INSTITUTE OF MODERN ART Map pp96-7
☎ 773-227-5522; www.uima-chicago.org; 2320 W Chicago Ave; admission free; ⊙ noon-4pm Wed-Sun; 🚌 66

The 'Ukrainian' in the name is somewhat of a misnomer, as this bright white storefront showcases local artists of all ethnicities. The space has earned a reputation for putting together playful and provocative exhibits, done in a host of different media.

DIVISION STREET JAUNT
Walking Tour
There's the old Division St, the one of polka bars and gritty taverns where Nelson Algren used to prowl, and then there's the new Division St, with burger lounges where DJs spin. This tour wanders by both.

1 Algren Fountain
In the park between Milwaukee and Ashland Aves and Division St, a fountain dedicated to Nelson Algren spouts. Algren wrote about Division St in *The Man with the Golden Arm*, the tale of a heroin addict when life in these parts meant fewer premium tequila shots.

2 Podhalanka
No DJs here. Podhalanka (p166) is old-world Wicker Park, a hole-in-the-wall pierogi and borscht restaurant that's like eating at your grandma's house c 1984. A picture of Pope John Paul II hangs on the wall and stares out

WICKER PARK, BUCKTOWN & UKRAINIAN VILLAGE

0 — 500 m
0 — 0.25 miles

SIGHTS (p94)
Flat Iron Building...1 B8
Holy Trinity Russian Orthodox Cathedral...2 B6
Nelson Algren House...3 C5
Polish Museum of America...4 D6
Saints Volodymyr & Olha Church...5 B7
St Nicholas Ukrainian Catholic Cathedral...6 B7
Ukrainian Institute of Modern Art...7 A7
Wicker Park...8 B5

SHOPPING (p127)
Akira...9 C7
Beadniks...10 B5
Boring Store...11 C5
City Sole/Niche...12 A7
Dusty Groove...13 D6
Free People...14 C6
Greenheart Shop...15 C6
Handmade Market...(see 77)
John Fluevog Shoes...16 B8
Levi's Store...17 B8
Ms Catwalk...18 B3
Myopic Books...19 B8
Paper Doll...20 B5
Penelope's...21 C6
Quimby's...22 C7
Reckless Records...23 B8
Red Balloon Co...24 B2
Renegade Handmade...25 C5
Threadless...26 C6
T-shirt Deli...27 B4
Una Mae's Freak Boutique...28 C5
Uprise Skateboards...29 B3
US #1...30 C5
Vive La Femme...31 B2

EATING (p145)
Alliance Bakery...32 C5
Bari Foods...33 E8
Big Star Taqueria...34 B8
Bite Cafe...(see 77)
Crust...35 B5
Dee's Place...36 B5
El Taco Veloz...37 C7
Flo...38 D7
Green Zebra...39 D7
Handlebar...40 A4
Hoosier Mama Pie Company...41 D7
Hot Chocolate...42 A6
Irazu...43 A3
Lazo's Tacos...44 A3
Letizia's Natural Bakery...45 B5
Margie's...46 A3
Milk & Honey...47 C5

Mirai Sushi...48 B5
Mr Brown's Lounge...49 A7
Piece...50 B8
Podhalanka...51 D5
Schwa...52 D4
Sultan's Market...53 A8
Tecalitlan...54 C7
Twisted Spoke...55 E8
Vienna Beef Factory Store & Cafe...56 B1
West Town Tavern...57 D7
Wicker Park & Bucktown Farmers Market...(see 8)

DRINKING (p177)
Bluebird...58 B3
Danny's...59 B2
Ed & Jean's...60 B3
Filter...61 C5
Gold Star Bar...62 C6
Happy Village...63 C6
Innertown Pub...64 C6
Map Room...65 B3
Matchbox...66 E7
Ola's Liquor...67 B6
Quenchers...68 A1
Rainbo Club...69 B6
Richard's Bar...70 F8
Rodan...71 B8
Violet Hour...72 B8

NIGHTLIFE (p189)
Beauty Bar...73 D7
Darkroom...74 B7
Davenport's Piano Bar & Cabaret...75 C5
Debonair Social Club...(see 1)
Double Door...76 B8
Empty Bottle...77 A6
Funky Buddha Lounge...78 F8
Hideout...79 D4
Phyllis' Musical Inn...80 C5
Piece...(see 50)
Subterranean...81 A8

N Damen Ave
N Montana St
W Fullerton Ave
N Western Ave
N Leavitt St
W Webster Ave
W Shakespeare Ave
W Charleston St
W Dickens Ave
W McLean Ave
Bucktown
W Homer St
W Cortland St
W Churchill St
Holstein Park
N Oakley Ave
N Milwaukee Ave
N Winnebago Ave
W St Paul Ave
W Wabansia Ave
W Bloomingdale Ave
W North Ave
W Le Moyne St
N Lister Ave
N Elston Ave
John F Kennedy Expwy
N Dominick St
N Ashland Ave
Clybourn Station (Metra)
N Southport Ave
N Ada St
N Besly Ct
N Hermitage Ave
N Paulina St
N Marshfield Ave
N Wood St
N Honore St
N Wolcott Ave
N Winchester Ave
N Damen Ave
Churchill Field Park
W Willow St
W Moffat St
W Cortland St
W Armitage Ave
Wicker Park
See Enlargement
N Hoyne Ave
N Leavitt St
W Pierce Ave
W Le Moyne St
N Oakley Ave
N Concord Pl
W Caton St

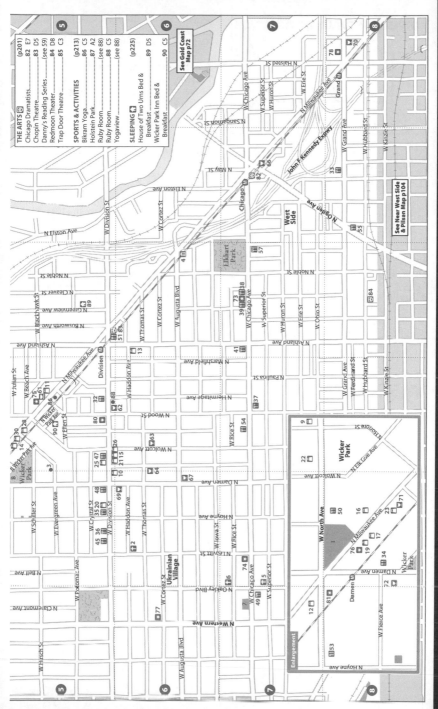

See Gold Coast Map p72

See Near West Side & Pilsen Map p104

DIVISION ST JAUNT

WALK FACTS

Start Algren Fountain
End Nelson Algren House
Distance 0.75 miles
Time 20 minutes to walk; two hours to eat, drink and browse

longingly at the whopping portions set on green vinyl placemats.

3 Phyllis' Musical Inn
Time to pop in to one of the street's few original businesses left standing. Phyllis' Musical Inn (p194) was once a polka hall, and it

remains one of the corridor's best bars – an unpretentious dive with scrappy live bands nightly and an outdoor basketball court.

4 Renegade Handmade
Moving west, Division St starts to drift into hipness with shops like Renegade Handmade (p139). Crafts sold at a local DIY arts fair – pillows, prints, buttons, guitar straps – were so popular that they spawned their own shop.

5 Beadniks
You're in the thick of the cool boutiques now – ecogoods, trendy kids' wear, nifty gifty things. Incense wafts from the open door as you pass Beadniks (p138). Pick up supplies, or make a necklace in-store. They'll help you string together your baubles for a small fee.

6 Nelson Algren's House
Yes, we know: we've veered off Division St. But on the 3rd floor of the house (p94) at 1958 W Evergreen Ave, Nelson Algren took the wisdom he accumulated on Division ('never play cards with a man called Doc') and transformed it into enduring literature.

Drinking p186; Eating p168; Shopping p141

When the Bucktown, Wicker Park and Ukrainian Village hipsters could no longer afford rent in those neighborhoods, they moved west to Logan Square. The mostly Latino neighborhood had a lot to offer, especially around the square (a sort of island formed by strangely intersecting roads). There were old buildings with huge amounts of living space, decent transportation via the Blue Line, tree-shaded boulevards, and cheap eats at the myriad taquerias. It took a while, but stylish restaurants, bars and shops finally caught up with the crowd, and provide the main impetus for visiting today. Because the neighborhood remains primarily residential and spread out over a large area, it feels much more relaxed than the Bucktown, Wicker Park and Ukrainian Village chaos. Gentrification does continue its relentless push here, but thanks to Logan Square's community gardens, neighborhood-run farmers' market and preservation efforts, the area has more or less held on to its dignity.

Humboldt Park, to the south, is where the hipsters priced out of Logan Square ended up. The neighborhood definitely has a rough-around-the-edges feel. It's still heavily Puerto Rican, and is the birthplace of the heart-stopping *jibarito* sandwich (garlic-mayo-slathered steak served between sliced-plantain 'bread'). The eponymous park is the area's focal point.

Both neighborhoods have mansion-strewn streets and unexpectedly grand monuments like the column in Logan Sq and the boathouse in Humboldt Park. Their eating and drinking options – including megahuge crowd pullers such as Hot Doug's (p170) and Kuma's (p169) – make them ideal for an evening out alongside cool-cat locals.

HUMBOLDT PARK Map p100

1400 N Sacramento Ave; www.chicagoparkdistrict .com; 🚌 70 or 72

This 207-acre park, which lends its name to the surrounding neighborhood, comes out of nowhere and gobsmacks you with Mother Nature. A lagoon brushed by native plants takes up much of the green space, and birdsong flickers in the air. The 1907 Prairie School boathouse rises up from the lagoon's edge and serves as the park's showpiece. A gravel path takes off from here and circles the water, where you'll sometimes see people casting fishing lines.

Across the street from the boathouse, on the northwest corner of Humboldt Dr and Division St, lies the Formal Garden, rich with jelly-bean-colored flower beds and a

walk-through fountain. It's a fine place to sit and smell the roses (or whatever flowers are growing currently). Just south, the Institute of Puerto Rican Arts and Culture (🕿 773-486-8345; www.iprac.org; 3015 W Division St) fills the park's old horse stables. If it's open, stroll in and see what free exhibits are showing.

The park has gone through some rough times since it was built in 1869 and named for German naturalist Alexander von Humboldt. It has only come into its own again in the past decade. While it's family-filled by day, it's still pretty rough, and best avoided, at night.

Street vendors and food trucks sell fried plantains, meat dumplings and other Puerto Rican specialties around the edges. Many congregate near Hirsch St and Kedzie Ave, and at Humboldt and Luis Munoz Marin Drs – sniff them out for a picnic. The annual *Fiestas Puertorriqueñas* (Puerto Rican party) takes over the park in mid-June (see p14).

For more in-depth explorations, including the park's wee waterfall, wind turbine and picnic island, download the free audio tour at www.chicagoparkdistrict .com/resources/park_audio_tours /humboldt_park.html.

PASEO BORICUA Map p100

Division St btwn Western Ave & Mozart St; 🚌 70
Paseo Boricua, aka the Puerto Rican Passage, is a mile-long stretch of Division

---

TRANSPORTATION – LOGAN SQUARE & HUMBOLDT PARK

Bus Number 70 travels along Division St to Humboldt Park's heart. Other useful buses are 77 along Belmont Ave and 72 along North Ave.

El Blue Line to Logan Square puts you at the epicenter for that 'hood; Blue Line to California or Western puts you at its fringe.

Parking Street parking isn't bad compared with other neighborhoods, although it can get tight around Logan Sq near Lula Cafe.

LOGAN SQUARE & HUMBOLDT PARK

0 —————— 500 m
0 —————— 0.25 miles

W Roscoe St
John F Kennedy Expwy
W Belmont Ave
Ⓜ Belmont
W Roscoe St
N North Branch Chicago River
W Belmont Ave
W Wellington Ave
W Diversey Ave
W Diversey Ave
W Wrightwood Ave
Logan Square
W Logan Blvd
W Fullerton Ave
W Fullerton Ave
California
W Palmer Sq
Palmer Square Park
W Armitage Ave
W Armitage Ave
W Bloomingdale Ave
W Bloomingdale Ave
W North Ave
W North Ave
Humboldt Park
See Wicker Park, Bucktown & Ukrainian Village Map p96
W Hirsch St
W Division St
W Division St
W Augusta Blvd
W Augusta Blvd
W Grand Ave
W Chicago Ave
W Chicago Ave

INFORMATION	
Specimen/Chicago School of Guitarmaking	1 C6

SIGHTS	(p99)
Boathouse	2 D5
Formal Garden	3 C5
Humboldt Park	4 C5
Illinois Centennial Memorial Column	5 C3
Institute of Puerto Rican Arts and Culture	6 C6
Puerto Rican Flag Sculpture	7 D6

SHOPPING 🛍	(p127)
Wolfbait & B-girls	8 C3

EATING 🍴	(p145)
Bonsoiree	9 D4
Borinquen Restaurant	10 D4
El Cid 2	11 C3
Feed	12 D6
Hot Doug's	13 D1
Kuma's Corner	14 D1
Lula Cafe	15 C3

DRINKING 🍷	(p177)
Fireside Bowl	16 D3
Longman & Eagle	17 C2
Revolution Brewing	18 D3
Small Bar	19 C2
Whirlaway Lounge	20 C3

NIGHTLIFE ★	(p189)
Late Bar	21 B1
Rosa's Lounge	22 B4
Whistler	23 D3

THE ARTS 🎭	(p201)
California Clipper	24 D6
Elastic Arts Foundation	25 B2
Factory Theater	(see 26)
Prop Thtr	26 C1

St stuffed with Puerto Rican shops and restaurants. It's marked at either end by a 45-ton, steel Puerto Rican flag sculpture that arches over the road; the eastern flag stands near Western Ave, while the western one is at Mozart Ave. This area has long been the epicenter of Chicago's 113,000-strong Puerto Rican community.

ILLINOIS CENTENNIAL MEMORIAL COLUMN Map opposite

intersection of Kedzie Blvd, Logan Blvd & Milwaukee Ave; Ⓜ Blue Line to Logan Square
What's that giant phallic thing in the middle of the road, causing traffic to swerve every which way? Excellent question. Most locals have no idea. Turns out it's a monument commemorating the 100th anniversary of Illinois' statehood, by a gent named Henry Bacon – the same architect who created the Lincoln Memorial in Washington DC. The eagle atop the Doric column echoes that on the Illinois state flag. The reliefs of Native Americans, explorers, farmers and laborers represent the great changes the state experienced during its first century.

BOULEVARDS PROMENADE
Walking Tour
The broad green boulevards – Logan, Kedzie, Palmer and Humboldt – that stripe the neighborhood are an official city landmark. Walk along them to glimpse whimsically styled manors c 1900, as well as more recent 'hood highlights.

1 Illinois Centennial Memorial Column
Logan Sq's centerpiece is the 68ft Illinois Centennial Memorial Column (above) erected (OK, bad pun) in 1918 to mark 100 years of statehood. On sunny days folks scramble through the take-your-life-in-your-hands traffic circle to loll on the surrounding grass, people-watch and nibble goodies from the Sunday farmers' market.

2 Wolfbait & B-girls
Cross Logan Blvd to the business-lined square itself. You know a neighborhood's gone trendy when it has a store like Wolfbait & B-girls (p141), where local designers vend funky women's wear and accessories. Weren't you looking for a hand-dyed repurposed minidress made from men's boxer shorts?

BOULEVARDS PROMENADE

WALK FACTS

Start Illinois Centennial Memorial Column
End Humboldt Park
Distance 2 miles
Time 1.5 hours

3 Lula Cafe
Around the corner on Kedzie Blvd, foodies flock to Lula (p169) for the worldly-wise artisan dishes. Grab a sidewalk table and order a tofu-peanut satay while your tablemate tries the duck leg with potato puree. The menu changes frequently, but the from-the-farm credo and laid-back attitude stay the same.

4 Kedzie Boulevard

Continue south on Kedzie Blvd, a prime example of the area's wide, leafy thoroughfares. Several mansions stand sentry for the next half-mile; the best ones are on the street's west side. European immigrants who made their fortunes in Chicago built the manors at the turn of the century. Unwelcome by the Gold Coast's old-money millionaires, the nouveau riche had to move out here.

5 Palmer Square Park

Turn left (east) at Palmer Blvd, the street that rings 7-acre Palmer Sq Park, resting quietly under maple and elm trees and edged by pricey homes. After a quarter-mile you'll come to Humboldt Blvd; turn right (south).

6 Schwinn House

At 2128 N Humboldt Blvd (aka the southwest corner of Palmer and Humboldt) a gent named Ignaz Schwinn used to roll his two-wheeler out of the driveway. Alas, the original mansion is gone now, as is the family-owned bicycle company he launched (though the Schwinn brand still exists under different corporate ownership).

7 Borinquen Restaurant

Continue for three-quarters of a mile on Humboldt Blvd, which is less flashy than its brethren. Turn left (east) at W Wabansia Ave and follow your nose to Borinquen (p169), wellspring of the *jibarito* sandwich. Pack breath mints and a defibrillator for the steak, garlic mayo and fried plantain pileup.

8 Humboldt Park

Fortified, return to Humboldt Blvd, which runs smack into Humboldt Park (p99). Stroll around the lagoon, fish, see Puerto Rican art and munch island snacks from the food carts.

NEAR WEST SIDE & PILSEN

Drinking p187; Eating p170; Shopping p142; Sleeping p241

Ah, meat and art, together at last. At least they are in the West Loop. Akin to New York City's Meatpacking District, in the West Loop chic restaurants, clubs and galleries poke out between meat-processing plants left over from the area's industrial days. Of all people, Oprah was one of the first to see the potential here, and she plunked down her studio in the 'hood years ago. W Randolph St and W Washington Blvd are the main corridors. The area is about 1.25 miles west of the Loop and a bit awkward to reach by El; consider taking a cab.

In addition to the West Loop, the Near West Side includes the ethnic neighborhoods of Greektown (along Halsted St) and Little Italy (along Taylor St). Neither has much in the way of sights, but gustatory tourists will revel in the tavernas and *tzatzikis* (yogurt dip) of the former, and the pastas and lemon ice of the latter. The University of Illinois at Chicago (UIC) lies between the two, and has been on a development rampage that's remaking the neighborhood, mostly for the better.

To the southwest lies Pilsen, the center of Chicago's Mexican community. A trip to this convenient neighborhood – a quick ride on the Pink Line to 18th St – really is like stepping onto the streets of a foreign country. The salsas here scald, the moles soothe, and the sidewalks are filled with umbrella'd food carts that tempt passers-by with a rainbow array of cold, pulpy *agua frescas* (fruit-flavored waters) and spicy-sweet *verduras* (thin slices of melon or cucumber dusted with a chili-powder kick).

Chicago's hipster underground has also been quietly relocating to Pilsen for the last decade or so. The area around 18th and Halsted Sts is a hub for storefront art galleries and painters' spaces. Even the taste-making record label Thrill Jockey has its offices here. And take a gander at the architecture: the original Czechoslovakian settlers not only named the area after their homeland but modeled their three-flats and storefronts on the world they'd left behind. Note, too, how many houses have their front yards several feet below sidewalk level; this is because the city later raised the streets for sewer construction.

NEAR WEST SIDE

HARPO STUDIOS Map pp104-5
www.oprah.com; 1058 W Washington Blvd;
Ⓜ Green, Pink Line to Clinton or 🚍 20
For 25 years *The Oprah Winfrey Show* taped at the studio here, which the media queen owns. But she's packing up and leaving town after September 2011. If you happen to be visiting before that date, you can try to get tickets (see p35). Otherwise, snap a consolation picture with the 'Harpo Studios' sign at the corner of W Randolph and N Carpenter Sts.

WEST LOOP GALLERIES Map pp104-5
near intersection of Peoria St & Washington Blvd;
Ⓜ Green, Pink Line to Clinton or 🚍 20
Tucked between meatpacking plants and warehouses, the galleries of the West Loop are the beachhead for contemporary art in Chicago. Though they're less entrenched than their River North peers, the lower rents here mean larger showrooms. Generally speaking, the galleries also take bigger chances on up-and-coming and controversial artists. Gallery hours typically run from 11am to 5pm, Tuesday to Saturday; admission is free. Check www .westloop.org for listings. Note that owners often take off a week or two in August.

On the first Thursday of every month the galleries stay open later for a festive

TRANSPORTATION – NEAR WEST SIDE & PILSEN

Bus Number 20 runs Loop-bound along Washington St, returns along Madison St; 8 travels along Halsted St; 9 travels north–south on Ashland Ave between Pilsen and Irving Park Rd.

El Pink Line to 18th St for Pilsen; Green, Pink Line to Clinton for the West Loop; Blue Line to UIC-Halsted for Greektown; Pink Line to Polk or Blue Line to Racine for Little Italy; Green Line to Conservatory for Garfield Park Conservatory.

Parking In West Loop free parking is plentiful, especially in the afternoon; Greektown parking can be tough to find but valets abound; Little Italy is fine for free on-street parking. Pilsen has plentiful parking on its side streets.

103

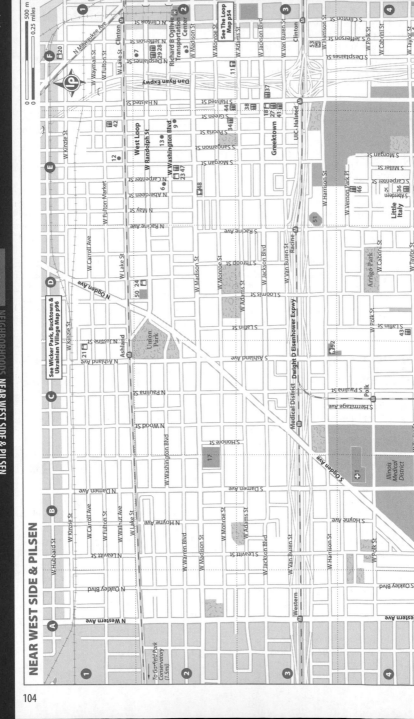

NEAR WEST SIDE & PILSEN

lonelyplanet.com

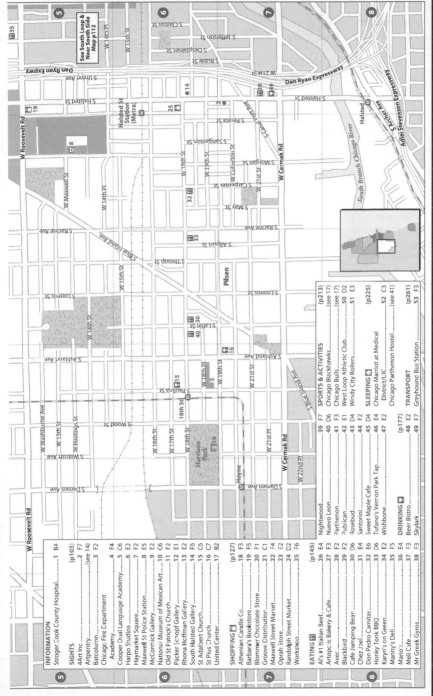

NEIGHBORHOODS NEAR WEST SIDE & PILSEN

INFORMATION	
Stroger Cook County Hospital	1 B4

SIGHTS	(p103)
4Art Inc	2 F7
Artpentry	(see 14)
Batcolumn	3 F2
Chicago Fire Department Academy	4 F4
Cooper Dual Language Academy	5 C6
Harpo Studios	6 E2
Haymarket Square	7 F2
Maxwell St Police Station	8 E5
McCormick Gallery	9 E2
National Museum of Mexican Art	10 C6
Old St Patrick's Church	11 F2
Packer Schopf Gallery	12 E1
Rhona Hoffman Gallery	13 E2
South Halsted Gallery	14 F6
St Adalbert Church	15 C5
St Pius Church	16 C7
United Center	17 B2

SHOPPING	(p127)
Athenian Candle Co	18 F3
Barbara's Bookstore	19 F5
Blommer Chocolate Store	20 F1
Groove Distribution	21 C1
Maxwell Street Market	22 F4
Oprah Store	23 E2
Randolph Street Market	24 D2
Workshop	25 F6

EATING	(p145)
Al's #1 Italian Beef	26 E4
Artopc is Bakery & Cafe	27 F3
Avec	28 F2
Blackbird	29 F2
Cafe Jumping Bean	30 D6
Chez Joel	31 E4
Don Pedro Carnitas	32 E6
Honky Tonk BBQ	33 D6
Karyn's on Green	34 E2
Manny's Deli	35 F5
Mario's	36 E4
Meli Cafe	37 F3
Mr Greek Gyros	38 F3

Nightwood	39 F7
Nuevo Leon	40 D6
Parthenon	41 F3
Publican	42 E1
Rosebud	43 D4
Santorini	44 F2
Sweet Maple Cafe	45 D4
Tufano's Vernon Park Tap	46 E4
Wishbone	47 E2

DRINKING	(p177)
Beer Bistro	48 E2
Skylark	49 F7

SPORTS & ACTIVITIES	(p213)
Chicago Blackhawks	(see 17)
Chicago Bulls	(see 17)
West Loop Athletic Club	50 D2
Windy City Rollers	51 E3

SLEEPING	(p225)
Chicago Marriot at Medical District/UIC	52 C3
Chicago Parthenon Hostel	(see 41)

TRANSPORT	(p261)
Greyhound Bus Station	53 F3

See South Loop & Near South Side Map p112

Pilsen

Harrison Park

105

top picks

CHICAGO PHOTO OPPORTUNITIES

In addition to the sights we've listed in our Postcard Perspective walking tour (p61), get your camera ready for these classic shots:

- Mr Beef sign (p153)
- Wrigley Field front entrance sign (p84)
- Chicago skyline from North Ave Beach (p80)
- 'Chicago' sign at the Brown Line El station
- Harpo Studios sign (p103)

art hop, held in conjunction with the River North galleries (p65).

Some of our favorites among the West Loop's dozen or so galleries:

McCormick Gallery (☎ 312-226-6800; www .thomasmccormick.com; 835 W Washington Blvd)

Packer Schopf Gallery (☎ 312-226-8984; www .packergallery.com; 942 W Lake St)

Rhona Hoffman Gallery (☎ 312-455-1990; www .rhoffmangallery.com; 118 N Peoria)

HAYMARKET SQUARE Map pp104-5
Desplaines St btwn Lake & Randolph Sts; Ⓜ Green, Pink Line to Clinton
The odd-looking bronze statue of some guys on a wagon marks the spot where the world's labor movement began. So the next time you take a lunch break or go home after your eight-hour workday, thank Haymarket Sq, which you're now standing upon.

On May 4, 1886, striking factory workers held a meeting here. A mob of police appeared toward the end of the meeting, which quickly degenerated into chaos – a bomb exploded, killing one policeman and wounding several others. Police began to fire shots into the dispersing crowd, and by the end of the day six more policemen had been shot and killed (most shot down accidentally by other policemen) and 60 others were injured. Eight anarchist leaders, including some of the most prominent speakers and writers of the movement, were eventually arrested and accused of the crime. Despite the fact that the identity of the bomb thrower was never known, that only two of the eight accused actually attended the rally (both were on the speaker's platform – which the current

bronze statue commemorates – in view of police when the bomb went off), and that no evidence linking the accused to the crime was ever produced, all eight were convicted of inciting murder and sentenced to hang. Four of them did soon thereafter. Before dropping from the gallows, leader August Spies uttered the famous words that would later appear on posters and flyers around the world: 'The day will come,' he said from beneath his hood, 'when our silence will be more powerful than the voices you are throttling today.'

BATCOLUMN Map pp104-5
600 W Madison St; Ⓜ Green Line to Clinton
Artist Claes Oldenburg – known for his gigantic shuttlecocks in Kansas City and oversized cherry spoon in Minneapolis – delivered this simple, controversial sculpture to Chicago in 1977. The artist mused that the 96ft bat 'seemed to connect earth and sky the way a tornado does.' Hmm… See it for yourself in front of the Harold Washington Social Security Center.

CHICAGO FIRE DEPARTMENT ACADEMY Map pp104-5
☎ 312-747-7239; 558 W DeKoven St; Ⓜ Blue Line to Clinton
Rarely has a public building been placed in a more appropriate place: the fire department's school stands on the very spot where the 1871 fire began – between Clinton and Jefferson Sts. Although there's no word on whether junk mail still shows up for Mrs O'Leary, the academy trains firefighters so they'll be ready the next time somebody, or some critter, kicks over a lantern (see p22).

OLD ST PATRICK'S CHURCH Map pp104-5
☎ 312-648-1021; www.oldstpats.org; 700 W Adams St; Ⓜ Blue Line to Clinton
A Chicago fire survivor, this 1852 church is not only the city's oldest but also one of its fastest-growing, thanks to the strategies of its politically connected former pastor, Father Jack Wall. Old St Pat's is best known for its year-round calendar of social events for singles, including the enormously popular World's Largest Block Party; this is a weekend-long party with big-name rock bands where Catholic singles can flirt. (No less an authority than Oprah

has proclaimed the block party the best place to meet one's match.) The social programs have certainly boosted Old St Pat's membership, which has gone from four (yes, four) in 1983 to thousands two decades later. The domed steeple signifies the Eastern Church; the spire signifies the Western Church. Call to find out when the church is open so you can see the beautifully restored Celtic-patterned interior.

UNITED CENTER Map pp104-5

☎ 312-455-4650; www.unitedcenter.com; 1901 W Madison St; 🚌 19 or 20

Built for $175 million and opened in 1992, the United Center arena is home to the Bulls (p221) and the Blackhawks (p223), and is the venue for special events such as the circus. The statue of an airborne Michael Jordan in front of the east entrance pays a lively tribute to the man whose talents financed the edifice. The center, surrounded by parking lots, is OK by day but gets pretty edgy at night – unless there's a game, in which case squads of cops are everywhere in order to ensure public safety.

GARFIELD PARK CONSERVATORY
Map pp104-5

☎ 312-746-5100; www.garfieldconservatory.org; 300 N Central Park Ave; admission free; 🕙 9am-5pm Fri-Wed, to 8pm Thu; Ⓜ Green Line to Conservatory

These 4.5 acres under glass are the Park District's pride and joy. Built in 1907, the conservatory completed a multi-million-dollar restoration campaign in 2000, polishing it above and beyond its original splendor. One of the initial designers, Jens Jensen, intended for the palms, ferns and other plants to recreate Chicago's prehistoric landscape. Today the effect continues – all that's missing is a rampaging stegosaurus. Newer halls contain displays of seasonal plants that are especially spectacular in the weeks before Easter. Kids can get dirty with roots and seeds in the Children's Garden. Between May and October the outdoor grounds are open, including the Demonstration Garden, which shows urbanites how to grow veggies, keep bees and compost in city plots; and the Monet Garden, which adapts the Impressionist painter's colorful garden

at Giverny, France. If you drive, lock up: the neighborhood isn't the safest.

PILSEN

NATIONAL MUSEUM OF MEXICAN ART Map pp104-5

☎ 312-738-1503; www.nationalmuseumofmexican art.org; 1852 W 19th St; admission free; 🕙 10am-5pm Tue-Sun; Ⓜ Pink Line to 18th St

Founded in 1982, this vibrant museum – the largest Latino arts institution in the USA – has become one of the city's best. The vivid permanent collection sums up 1000 years of Mexican art and culture through classical paintings, shining gold altars, skeleton-rich folk art, beadwork and much more. The turbulent politics and revolutionary leaders of Mexican history are well represented, including works about Cesar Chavez and Emiliano Zapata. The museum also sponsors readings by top authors and performances by musicians and artists. If you are in town during the fall, be sure to check out the exhibits and celebrations relating to November 1, the Day of the Dead, a traditional Mexican holiday that combines the festive with the religious. The events take place for a month on either side of the day. The on-site store is a winner, with brightly painted Mexican crafts filling the shelves.

PILSEN MURALS Map pp104-5

Ⓜ Pink Line to 18th St

Murals are a traditional Mexican art form, and they're splashed all over Pilsen's buildings. If you arrive by train, your first sighting will be at the Pink Line 18th St station. With the help of his students, local art teacher Francisco Mendoza riotously colored the walls with religious and cultural imagery. The exterior wall of the Cooper Dual Language Academy (1645 W 18th Pl) is the canvas for a 1990s tile mosaic that shows a diverse range of Mexican images, from a portrait of farm-worker advocate Dolores Huerta to the Virgin of Guadalupe. Each summer, art students add more panels. A mural of parishioners eating corn while Jesus looks on graces St Pius Church (1919 S Ashland Ave).

Local artist Jose Guerrero leads the highly recommended Pilsen Mural Tours (☎ 773-342-4191; 1½hr tour $100), where you can learn more about the neighborhood's images; call to arrange an excursion.

PILSEN GALLERIES Map pp104-5

near intersection of Halsted & 18th Sts; 🚌 8

Pilsen is the most casual of Chicago's three main art districts (River North and West Loop are the other two). Works are largely by Chicago locals, and there's a good deal of folk art. A great time to come here is on Second Fridays, when the 20 or so Pilsen galleries – known collectively as the Chicago Arts District (www.chicagoartsdistrict.org) – all stay open late on the second Friday of each month to welcome throngs of wandering art patrons with wine, snacks, and freshly hung paintings, ceramics and photos. It's free, and takes place between 6pm and 10pm. Pick up a map at the office at 1821 S Halsted St.

Regular gallery hours are erratic, though most are closed Sunday and Monday. For the part of Pilsen where the galleries are located, the number 8 Halsted St bus beats the Pink Line train.

The following are some of the best bets in Pilsen:

4Art Inc (☎ 312-850-1816; www.4artinc.com; no 100, 1932 S Halsted St) Specializes in large-scale group shows.

Artpentry (☎ 312-624-8687; 1827 S Halsted St) Urban art, with items like vintage luggage fashioned into speakers. The gallery is usually only open during the art hop.

South Halsted Gallery (☎ 312-804-8962; www .sohachicago.com; 1825 S Halsted St) A husband and wife display their cartoon-y paintings and drawings.

PILSEN CHURCHES Map pp104-5

Ⓜ Pink Line to 18th St

Some wonderful European-influenced churches remain throughout Pilsen. The 1914 St Adalbert Church (1650 W 17th St) features 185ft steeples and is a good example of the soaring religious structures built by Chicago's ethnic populations through thousands of small donations from parishioners, who would cut family budgets to the bone to make their weekly contribution. The rich ornamentation in the interior of this Catholic church glorifies Polish saints and religious figures. The Poles had St Adalbert's; the Irish had St Pius (1919 S Ashland Ave), a Romanesque revival edifice built between 1885 and 1892. Its smooth masonry contrasts with the rough stones of its contemporaries. Catholics of one ethnic group never attended the churches of the others, which explains why this part

of town, with its concentration of Catholic immigrants, is thick with steeples.

WEST LOOP SAMPLER Walking Tour

Cool contemporary art galleries; swank, clubby eateries; and Oprah. A quick walk around the block and you've got it all.

1 Packer Schopf Gallery

Ring the buzzer and find your way up the narrow old stairs to Packer Schopf Gallery (p106). Artists in all media exhibit here, but it's the 'outsider art' that has the sharpest edge. Some exhibits are not for the easily offended.

2 Harpo Studios

The sign at W Randolph and N Carpenter Sts marks the spot of Harpo Studios (p103), where Oprah films. Or 'filmed,' depending on when you're reading this. Even if she's flown the coop, the neighborhood artists and restaurateurs should still be thanking her, because it was Harpo that paved the way for the West Loop's development.

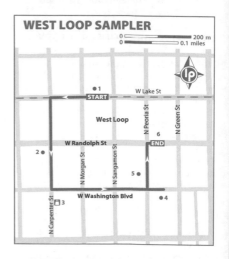

WALK FACTS

Start Packer Schopf Gallery
End Randolph St eateries
Distance 1 mile
Time One hour
Fuel Stop W Randolph St eateries

3 Oprah Store

C'mon, you can't walk by without looking inside the Oprah Store (p142). Pick up a passion journal or a 'receive each day in all its glory' coffee cup. If you lack cash you can ogle the celeb photos and wall-mounted TVs rerunning O's shows.

4 McCormick Gallery

Abstract expressionism and mid-century modern art are the specialties of the McCormick Gallery (p106). Other galleries at the same 835 W Washington address host minishows and the work of 30-something contemporary artists, many of them from the Chicago area.

5 Rhona Hoffman Gallery

At 118 N Peoria St, you'll find one of the several West Loop buildings that contain a veritable warren of galleries. This one includes the Rhona Hoffman Gallery (p106), which has been showing contemporary art from all media since 1976. Both emerging and established artists are represented.

6 W Randolph St eateries

Take your pick of the trendy eateries that keep popping up along W Randolph St, also known as Restaurant Row. The north side of the street, between N Peoria and N Green Sts, is chockablock full of 'em.

SOUTH LOOP & NEAR SOUTH SIDE

Drinking p187; Eating p173; Shopping p143; Sleeping p242

At the turn of the millennium the city went development crazy in the South Loop, putting up high-rise lofts and luxury condos like there was no tomorrow. The prime real estate includes the lower ends of downtown and Grant Park, plus the lakefront Museum Campus and Soldier Field. Young professionals and families couldn't resist, and swarmed in. So did the students of Columbia College, an ever-expanding arts school in the South Loop. Just when the neighborhood seemed to reach its peak, with funky restaurants, retailers and other urban accoutrements up and running, the global recession hit. So now the scene has cooled somewhat, but it shouldn't affect the visitor experience.

What you'll see when you come here – and come here you will, since the South Loop is where the Field Museum, the Shedd Aquarium and Adler Planetarium sit side by side on the lakeshore – is a whole lot of shiny newness. The Museum Campus itself is lovely, jutting out into the blue-green lake and providing breezy skyline views. Tranquil 12th St Beach and Northerly Island, a prairie-grassed nature park, offer escapes if the crowds get to be too much.

Blues fans will want to make the pilgrimage further south to the old Chess Records site, a humble building where Muddy Waters and Howlin' Wolf plugged in their amps and paved the way for rock 'n' roll. History buffs will appreciate mansion-filled Prairie Ave between 16th and 20th Sts, where the millionaires lived before the opium dens and hookers moved in from the Levee District four blocks west.

To top off the wealth of offerings, this part of town is also home to Chicago's small but busy Chinatown, where pork buns, steaming bowls of noodles and imported wares reward an afternoon of exploring.

SOUTH LOOP

FIELD MUSEUM OF NATURAL HISTORY Map pp112-13

☎ 312-922-9410; www.fieldmuseum.org; 1400 S Lake Shore Dr; adult/3-11yr $15/10, some exhibits extra, free 2nd Mon of month; ☻ 9am-5pm, last admission 4pm; ☒ 146

The Field Museum has over 70 PhD-wielding scientists and 20 million artifacts, so you know things are going to be hopping. The big attraction is the *Tyrannosaurus rex* named Sue, a 13ft-tall, 41ft-long beast who menaces the grand space with ferocious aplomb. Sue, the most complete *T rex* ever discovered, takes its name from Sue Hendrickson, the fossil hunter who found the 90%-complete skeleton in South Dakota in 1990.

The head honchos at the Field know how large dinosaurs loom in the grade-school imagination, which is why Sue is just one of many dinosaur-related exhibits here. 'Evolving Planet' has more of the big guys and gals. You can also watch staff paleontologists clean up fossils, learn about the evolution of the massive reptiles, and even find out about *Homo sapiens*' evolutionary ties to the extinct beasts.

A clever blend of the fanciful with a large number of Field artifacts, the 'Inside Ancient Egypt' exhibit recreates an Egyptian burial chamber on three levels. The mastaba (tomb) contains 23 actual mummies and is a reconstruction of the one built for Unis-ankh, the son of the last pharaoh of the Fifth dynasty, who died at age 21 in 2407 BC. The bottom level, with its twisting caverns, is especially worthwhile. Those reeds growing in the stream are real.

Other displays that merit your time include the recently polished Hall of Gems,

---

TRANSPORTATION: SOUTH LOOP & NEAR SOUTH SIDE

Bus Number 146 to the Museum Campus/Soldier Field; 1 to Prairie Ave and sights on S Michigan Ave.

El Red, Green, Orange Lines to Roosevelt for Museum Campus/Soldier Field; Red Line to Harrison for Printer's Row and the photography museum; Red Line to Cermak-Chinatown for Chinatown.

Metra Roosevelt Rd stop for Museum Campus/Soldier Field; 18th St for Prairie Ave Historic District; 23rd St for McCormick Place.

Parking The Museum Campus boasts plenty of lot parking (from $15 per car on nonevent days); meter parking is available but scarce in the South Loop, and readily available in Near South Side.

MUSEUM FREE DAYS

It'll be crowded, and you'll still have to pay extra for special exhibits. But the following museums are free on the days listed (all day, unless indicated otherwise). For top picks of sights and activities that are free 24/7, see p74. Chicago's other big-ticket museums have free days, too – they're just scattered throughout the year. Check the websites of individual attractions for dates.

- Monday: Chicago History Museum (p82), Field Museum of Natural History (p110; second Monday of the month)
- Tuesday: International Museum of Surgical Science (p75), Museum of Contemporary Art (p73)
- Wednesday: Clarke House (p117) and Glessner House (p117)
- Thursday: Art Institute of Chicago (p52; Thu evening), Chicago Children's Museum (p68; Thu evening), Peggy Notebaert Nature Museum (p81)
- Sunday: DuSable Museum of African American History (p122)

the Northwest Coast and Arctic Peoples totem pole collection, and the largest man-eating lion ever caught (he's stuffed and standing sentry on the basement floor).

The basic admission fee covers all of the above. To see bells and whistles such as RoboSue (a dino robot that follows your movements), the 3-D dino movie or any of the special exhibits, it'll cost $7 more. For $29 ($20 for kids) you can get a full-access pass good for all the museum's exhibits.

If there's a dinosaur lover in your life, drop by one of the on-site stores (Sue even has her own store on the upper level).

SHEDD AQUARIUM Map pp112-13

☎ 312-939-2438; www.sheddaquarium.org; 1200 S Lake Shore Dr; adult/3-11yr $27/20, some exhibits extra; ⏰ 9am-6pm Jun-Aug, reduced hr Sep-May; 🚌 146

A huge assortment of finned, gilled, amphibious and other aquatic creatures swims within the kiddie-mobbed, marble-clad confines of the John G Shedd Aquarium. Though it could simply rest on its superlative exhibits – say, beluga whales in a 4-million-gallon aquarium – the Shedd makes a point of trying to tie concepts of ecosystems, food webs and marine

biology into its presentation of supercool animals. Permanent exhibits include the multilevel oceanarium, which mimics ocean conditions off the northwest coast of North America. The beluga whales inside are remarkably cute creatures that come from the pint-sized end of the whale scale. You'll also see Pacific white-sided dolphins, harbor seals and sea otters. Don't linger only on the main floor – you can go underneath the cement seats and watch the mammals from below through viewing windows.

The 'Wild Reef' exhibit will have sharko-philes and sharkophobes equally en-tranced; over two dozen sharks cut through the waters in a simulation of a Philippines reef ecosystem. And the 'Amazon Rising' exhibits offer a captivating look at a year in the Amazon River and rainforest. Some of the newer and special exhibits sell out early in the morning; consider buying tickets on the website beforehand to ensure entry.

The 4-D theater costs $4 extra, and the odd, theatrical 'Fantasea' show costs $2 extra. Check the website for the schedule of free days scattered throughout the year.

The stretch of grass on the lake between the Shedd and the Adler begs for your camera. One look toward the skyline will show you why: the view is good year-round, but on clear winter days, when the lake partially freezes and steam rises off the Loop buildings, it verges on the sensational.

ADLER PLANETARIUM & ASTRONOMY MUSEUM Map pp112-13

☎ 312-922-7827; www.adlerplanetarium.org; 1300 S Lake Shore Dr; adult/3-14yr $10/6, plus $15 for unlimited sky shows; ⏰ 9:30am-6pm Jun-Aug, to 4:30pm Sep-May; 🚌 146

ONLINE TICKETS

Most major sights, including the Art Institute, Shedd Aquarium and Willis Tower, allow you to buy tickets online. The advantage is that you're assured entry and you get to skip the regular ticket lines. The disadvantage is that you have to pay a service fee of $1.50 to $4 per ticket (sometimes it's just per order), and at times the 'will call' line is almost as long as the regular one.

There's really no need to buy tickets in advance during off-peak times. In the summer and for big exhibits, though, it's not a bad idea.

SOUTH LOOP & NEAR SOUTH SIDE

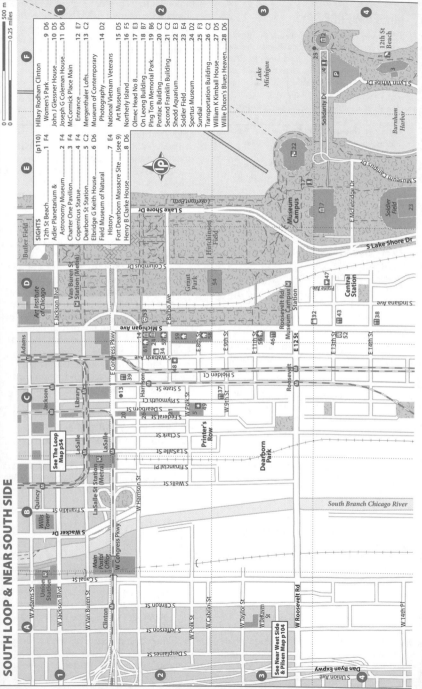

0 _____ 500 m
0 _____ 0.25 miles

Butler Field

Lake Michigan

12th St Beach

S Lynn White Dr

Burnham Harbor

Solidarity Dr

S Lake Shore Dr

Lakefront Path

Museum Campus

Hutchinson Field

Soldier Field

S Museum Campus Dr

E McFetridge Dr

Art Institute of Chicago

E Jackson Blvd

Van Buren St Station (Metra)

S Columbus Dr

Grant Park

S Lake Shore Dr

Roosevelt Rd/Museum Campus Station

Central Station

Plaine Ave

S Indiana Ave

S Michigan Ave

Adams

S Wabash Ave

E Balbo Ave

E 8th St

E 9th St

E 11th St

E 12th St

E 13th St

See The Loop Map p54

Jackson

Library

E Congress Pkwy

Harrison

S State St

S Holden Ct

Roosevelt

W Polk St

W 9th St

W 11th St

W 13th St

LaSalle

LaSalle St Station (Metra)

Quincy

Willis Tower

S Wacker Dr

Franklin St

Main Postal Office

W Harrison St

S Financial Pl

S LaSalle St

S Clark St

S Wells St

Printer's Row

S Plymouth Ct

S Dearborn St

S Federal St

Dearborn Park

W Congress Pkwy

South Branch Chicago River

Union Station

S Canal St

W Jackson Blvd

Clinton

W Adams St

W Van Buren St

W Polk St

S Jefferson St

S Clinton St

S Canal St

W Cabrini St

W Taylor St

W DeKoven St

W Roosevelt Rd

W 14th Pl

S Union Ave

See Near West Side & Pilsen Map p104

Dan Ryan Expwy

S Desplaines St

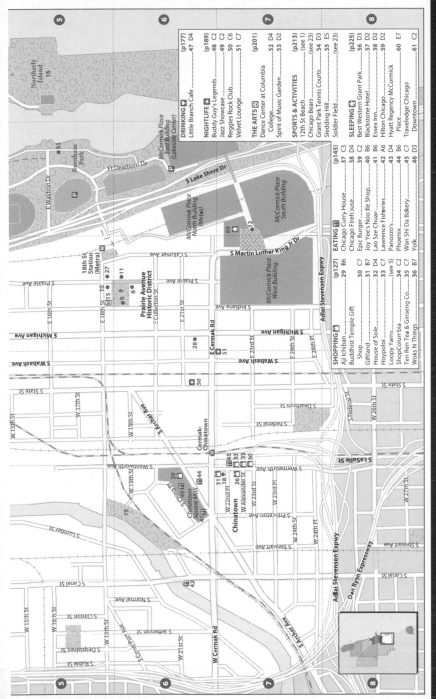

THINGS TO DO WHEN THE WEATHER BLOWS

Don't let the rain, snow and sleet spoil your fun. When the weather sucks, try the following:

- Burrow into the Art Institute (p52) and its vast collection of masterworks.
- Smell the flowers at Lincoln Park Conservatory (p80) or Garfield Park Conservatory (p107).
- Imbibe with locals in a bar – an activity to which we've devoted an entire chapter (p177).
- Brush up on your batting skills at Sluggers (p215).
- Sip tea in Chinatown (p116).
- Visit the whales and dolphins at Shedd Aquarium (p111).
- Unsheathe the credit card and commence shopping at Water Tower Place (p133).
- Hear world music, ogle stained glass and use the free wi-fi at the Chicago Cultural Center (p58).
- Examine mummies, dinosaurs, gemstones and Bushman the stuffed ape at the Field Museum (p110).
- Stop being a wimp – put on your parka and go outside to ice-skate or ride a sled (p217).

Space enthusiasts will get a big bang out of the Adler, the first planetarium built in the western hemisphere. From the entrance, visitors descend below the 1930s building, which has 12 sides, one for each sign of the zodiac. Cosmic films show in the digital theaters and recreate such cataclysmic phenomena as supernovas. Interactive exhibits allow you to simulate cosmic events such as a meteor hitting the earth (this one is especially cool).

Kids gravitate to the Planet Explorers exhibit, where they can climb and crawl over a spacey landscape and 'launch' a rocket. The 3-D lectures are more for adults (that's right: staff give you special eyeglasses to watch presentations like 'where supernovas come from').

The whole place can be easily covered in less than two hours. On the first Friday night of every month – aka Far Out Fridays – the Adler's astronomers bring out their telescopes and let you view the skies along with them (adult/child $20/17).

A 12ft sundial by Henry Moore stands to the side of the main entrance. It's dedicated to the golden years of astronomy, from 1930 to 1980, when so many fundamental discoveries were made using the first generation

of huge telescopes. In the median in front of the entrance, the bronze Copernicus statue shows the 16th-century Polish astronomer Nicolaus Copernicus holding a compass and a model of the solar system. But the best thing about the Adler's entrance? Its front steps, which are the city's most renowned make-out spot (perhaps the romance sparks from the sexy city view).

Check the website for the schedule of free days scattered throughout the year. The Adler is a good option if the Shedd is overrun, as the scene here is usually much quieter.

12TH STREET BEACH Map pp112-13
1200 S Lake Shore Dr; 🚌 146
A path runs south from the planetarium to 12th St Beach, where there are good views of the lake and the fishermen who are likely to be casting there. Despite the beach's proximity to the Museum Campus and its zillions of visitors, the crescent-shaped sand sliver remains bizarrely (but happily) secluded. Beach bonus: if you can't get tickets to see your favorite band at Charter One Pavilion (see Northerly Island), you can sit here and still hear the tunes.

NORTHERLY ISLAND Map pp112-13
www.chicagoparkdistrict.com; 1400 S Lynn White Dr; 🚌 146
A bit further south from the Adler Planetarium and 12th St Beach, Northerly Island was once the busy commuter airport known as Meigs Field. Now it's a prairie-grassed park with walking trails, fishing, bird-watching and the (allegedly temporary) Charter One Pavilion (☎ 312-540-2668; www.charteronepavilion.com) outdoor concert venue. The shift from runway to willowy grasses has its root in a controversial incident that reads a little like a municipal spy thriller, complete with midnight operatives and surprise bulldozings. To sum it up: Mayor Daley wanted the land for a park; businesses wanted to keep it for their private planes. A standoff ensued. Then, one dark night in March 2003, Daley fired up the heavy machinery and razed the airfield while the city slept. His reasoning? Terrorists could attack Chicago with tiny planes launched from Meigs; the airfield was a security liability. Why it couldn't be jackhammered during daylight hours was never answered. But

by 2005 the controversy had died down, and Chicagoans were out in force, happily exploring this beautiful piece of lakefront that had been off-limits for a half-century.

SOLDIER FIELD Map pp112-13

☎ 312-235-7000; www.soldierfield.net; 1410 S Museum Campus Dr; 🚌 146
Built between 1922 and 1926 to pay homage to WWI soldiers, this oft-renovated edifice has been home to everything from civil-rights speeches by Martin Luther King Jr to Brazilian soccer games. It got its latest UFO-landing-upon-a-Greek-ruin look in a controversial 2003 makeover. Prior to that, the stadium's architecture was so noteworthy it was named a National Historic Landmark. Unfortunately, the landmark lacked corporate skyboxes and giant bathrooms, so the city (the venue is owned by the park district) decided it was time for a change. The new look met almost unanimous derision when it was unveiled; critics quickly dubbed it 'the Mistake on the Lake.' The landmark folks agreed and whacked it from their list, saying it jeopardized the national landmark integrity. And that was that. The Bears play football here in the fall and early winter; see p222 for ticket details. Stadium tours are available for groups of 10 or more; call ☎ 312-235-7244 for details. Advance booking is required.

MUSEUM OF CONTEMPORARY PHOTOGRAPHY Map pp112-13

☎ 312-663-5554; www.mocp.org; Columbia College, 600 S Michigan Ave; admission free; 🕐 10am-5pm Mon-Sat, to 8pm Thu, noon-5pm Sun; Ⓜ Red Line to Harrison
This museum focuses on American photography since 1937, and is the only institution of its kind between the coasts. The permanent collection includes the works of Debbie Fleming Caffery, Mark Klett, Catherine Wagner, Patrick Nagatani and 500 more of the best photographers working today. Special exhibitions augment the rotating permanent collection.

SPERTUS MUSEUM Map pp112-13

☎ 312-322-1700; www.spertus.edu; 610 S Michigan Ave; Ⓜ Red Line to Harrison
Located in a glassy mod facility, Spertus explores 5000 years of Jewish faith and culture. Exhibits are on the 9th and 10th

floors. The facility has undergone several changes recently, and appears headed on a course of being open for special exhibits only. Call or check the website for updates, including information on admission prices and opening hours.

OLMEC HEAD NO 8 Map pp112-13

🚌 146
Near the Field Museum, the city has installed Olmec Head No 8. Over 7ft tall, it's a copy of one of the many amazing stone carvings done by the Olmec people more than 3500 years ago in what is now the Veracruz state of Mexico. No one has been able to figure out how the Olmec carved the hard volcanic rock.

PRINTER'S ROW Map pp112-13

Dearborn St btwn W Congress Pkwy & W Polk St; Ⓜ Red Line to Harrison
Chicago was a center for printing at the turn of the 20th century, and the rows of buildings on S Dearborn St from W Congress Pkwy south to W Polk St housed the heart of the city's publishing industry. By the 1970s the printers had left for more economical quarters elsewhere, and the buildings had been largely emptied out, some of them barely getting by on the feeble rents of obscure nonprofit groups.

In the late 1970s savvy developers saw the potential in these derelicts, and one of the most successful gentrification projects in Chicago began. The following describes some of the notable buildings in the area as you travel from north to south.

A snazzy renovation of the Mergenthaler Lofts (531 S Plymouth Ct), the 1886 headquarters for the legendary linotype company, included the artful preservation of a diner storefront. The Pontiac Building (542 S Dearborn St), a classic 1891 design by Holabird & Roche, features the same flowing masonry surfaces as the firm's Monadnock Building to the north.

A massive and once-windowless wreck, the 1911 Transportation Building (600 S Dearborn St) enjoyed a 1980 restoration that assured the neighborhood had arrived. The Second Franklin Building (720 S Dearborn St), a 1912 factory, shows the history of printing on its tiled facade. The roof slopes to allow for a huge skylight over the top floor where books were hand bound; this building existed long before fluorescent lights or high-intensity lamps. The large windows on many of the other buildings in the area served the same purpose.

Once the Chicago terminal of the Santa Fe Railroad, the 1885 Dearborn St Station (47 W Polk St) used to be the premier station for trains to and from California. Today it merely sees the trains of parent-propelled strollers from the Dearborn Park neighborhood, built on the site of the tracks to the south.

NEAR SOUTH SIDE

CHINATOWN Map pp112-13
intersection of Cermak Rd & Wentworth Ave;
Ⓜ Red Line to Cermak-Chinatown
Chinatown's charm is best enjoyed by going from bakery to bakery, nibbling chestnut cakes and almond cookies, then shopping for Hello Kitty trinkets and tea in the small shops. Old Chinatown stretches along Wentworth Ave south of Cermak, and is the neighborhood's traditional retail heart (and a good place to purchase a turtle). Chinatown Square, along Archer Ave north of Cermak, is the newer commerce district; it's filled with restaurants and is at its wonderful noisiest on weekends.

When you're not stuffing your face, you can check out a couple of sights. Ping Tom Memorial Park (300 W 19th St), behind the square, offers dramatic city-railroad-bridge views. The On Leong Building (Pui Tak Center; 2216 S Wentworth Ave) stands out in old Chinatown. It once housed neighborhood service organizations and some illegal gambling operations that led to spectacular police raids. It now houses the Chinese Merchants Association. Built in 1928, the grand structure is a fantasy of Chinese architecture that makes good use of glazed terra-cotta details. Note how the lions guarding the door have twisted their heads so they don't have to risk bad luck by turning their backs to each other.

On Saturdays and Sundays in summer, Chicago Water Taxi (www.chicagowatertaxi.com) runs a groovy boat down the Chicago River from Michigan Ave (the dock is on the bridge's northwest side, by the Wrigley Building) to Ping Tom park. It costs $4 one way, and takes 25 minutes.

WILLIE DIXON'S BLUES HEAVEN
Map pp112-13
☎ 312-808-1286; www.bluesheaven.com; 2120 S Michigan Ave; tours $10; ☀ 11am-4pm Mon-Fri, noon-2pm Sat; 🚇 1

From 1957 to 1967 this humble building was the home of the legendary Chess Records, a temple of blues and a spawning ground of rock 'n' roll. The Chess brothers, two Polish Jews, ran the recording studio that saw – and heard – the likes of Muddy Waters, Bo Diddley, Koko Taylor and others. Chuck Berry recorded four top-10 singles here, and the Rolling Stones named a song '2120 S Michigan Ave' after a recording session at this spot in 1964. (Rock trivia buffs will know that the Stones named themselves after the Muddy Waters song 'Rolling Stone.')

Today the building belongs to Willie Dixon's Blues Heaven, a nonprofit group set up by the late blues great who often recorded at the studios, to promote blues and preserve its legacy. Dixon was the guy who wrote most of Chess' hits and the one who summed up the genre best: 'Blues is the roots, and everything else is the fruits.'

Hard-core blues fans will most appreciate the tours, which go through all the old studios upstairs. Many artifacts – guitars, hats, gold records and whatnot – are on hand as well.

Free blues concerts rock the side garden on summer Thursdays between 6pm and 7pm.

NATIONAL VIETNAM VETERANS ART MUSEUM Map pp112-13
☎ 312-326-0270; www.nvvam.org; 1801 S Indiana Ave; adult/student $10/7; ☀ 10am-5pm Thu-Sat, reduced hr in winter; 🚇 1
Opened in 1996, the National Vietnam Veterans Art Museum displays the art of Americans who served in the military during the war in Vietnam. Spread over three floors in an old commercial building, it features a large and growing collection of haunting, angry, mournful and powerful works by veterans.

Cleveland Wright's *We Regret to Inform You* is a heartbreaking look at a mother in her kitchen at the moment she learns of her son's death. Joseph Fornelli's sculpture *Dressed to Kill* comments on the role of the average grunt in Vietnam. Some 58,000 dog tags hang from the ceiling, a haunting reminder of the Americans who died in the war.

The museum has run into financial troubles recently, and its hours can be erratic. Call before making the trip.

PRAIRIE AVENUE HISTORIC DISTRICT Map pp112-13

🚌 1

By 1900 Chicago's crème de la crème had had enough of the scum de la scum in the nearby neighborhoods. Potter Palmer led a procession of millionaires north to new mansions on the Gold Coast. The once-pristine neighborhood, which lined Prairie Ave for several blocks south of 16th St, fell into quick decline as one mansion after another gave way to warehouses and industry, hookers and gin. Thanks to the efforts of the Chicago Architecture Foundation, a few of the prime homes from the area have been carefully restored. Streets have been closed off, making the neighborhood a good place to stroll. A footbridge over the train tracks links the area to Burnham Park and the Museum Campus.

The John J Glessner House (☎ 312-326-1480; www.glessnerhouse.org; 1800 S Prairie Ave; tours adult/child $10/6, admission free Wed; ⏰ tours 1pm & 3pm Wed-Sun) is the premier survivor of the neighborhood. Famed American architect Henry Hobson Richardson took full advantage of the corner site for this beautiful composition of rusticated granite. Built from 1885 to 1887, the L-shaped house, which surrounds a sunny southern courtyard, got a 100-year jump on the modern craze for interior courtyards. Much of the house's interior is reminiscent of an English manor house, with heavy wooden beams and other English-style details. Additionally, more than 80% of the current furnishings are authentic, thanks to the Glessner family's penchant for family photos.

The nearby Henry B Clarke House (☎ 312-326-1480; 1827 S Indiana Ave; tours adult/child $10/6, admission free Wed; ⏰ tours noon & 2pm Wed-Sun) is the oldest structure in the city. When Caroline and Henry Clarke built this imposing Greek revival home in 1836, log cabins were still the rage in Chicago residential architecture. The sturdy frame paid off – during the past 160 years the house has been moved twice to escape demolition. The present address is about as close as researchers can get to its somewhat undefined original location. The interior has been restored to the period of the Clarkes' occupation, which ended in 1872. A combination ticket (adult/child $15/8) to tour both the Clarke and Glessner houses is available.

Unfortunately, it's not possible for you to visit the following houses, but you can still admire them from the outside. Modeled after 15th-century French châteaux, the William K Kimball House (1801 S Prairie Ave) dates from 1890 to 1892. Both it and the Romanesque Joseph G Coleman House (1811 S Prairie Ave) now serve as the incongruous headquarters for the US Soccer Federation. Limestone puts a glitzy facade on the brick Elbridge G Keith House (1900 S Prairie Ave), an 1870 home.

HILLARY RODHAM CLINTON WOMEN'S PARK Map pp112-13

1827 S Indiana Ave; 🚌 1

Fronting on Prairie Ave, with the Glessner House to the north and the Clarke House to the west, this 4-acre park is named for former first lady, now US Senator, Hillary Rodham Clinton, who grew up in suburban Park Ridge. Since she dedicated the park in 1997, landscapers have added a French garden, a fountain and winding paths. As bright as its future looks, the park has a notorious past. The Fort Dearborn massacre, in which a group of local Native Americans rebelled against the incursion of white settlers, is thought to have occurred on this very spot on August 15, 1812.

MCCORMICK PLACE Map pp112-13

☎ 312-791-7000; www.mccormickplace.com; 2301 S Lake Shore Dr, main entrance on S Martin Luther King Jr Dr; Ⓜ Metra to 23rd St

Called 'the Mistake on the Lake' before the Soldier Field renovation stole the title, the McCormick Place convention center is an economic engine that drives up profits for the city's hotels, restaurants, shops and airlines. 'Vast' isn't big enough to describe it, nor 'huge,' and 'enormous' doesn't work, so settle for whatever word describes the biggest thing you've ever seen. The 2.7 million sq ft of meeting space spreads out over four halls, making this the largest convention center in the country.

UNEXPECTED MUSEUM CAMPUS
Walking Tour

Museum Campus is visited by millions of tourists every year, but the museums and sights still hold some surprises.

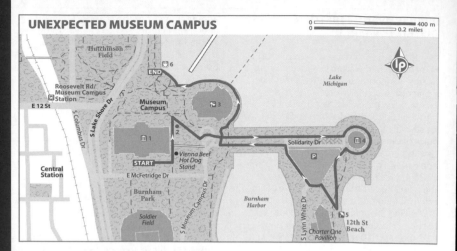

UNEXPECTED MUSEUM CAMPUS

WALK FACTS

Start Field Museum of Natural History
End Water taxi to Navy Pier
Distance 1.5 miles
Time Six hours
Fuel stop Vienna Beef hot dog cart outside Field Museum

1 Field Museum of Natural History

So you've heard of Sue, the *Tyrannosaurus rex* who resides at the Field Museum (p110). But did you know that the museum has hundreds of totem poles from the American northwest? Many of them were shipped to Chicago for the 1893 World's Expo.

2 Olmec Head No 8

Staring out from the Field Museum's lawn, Olmec Head No 8 (p115) is a replica of one of many sculptures the Olmec people carved in Veracruz, Mexico, c 1300 BC. Scholars believe the colossal heads are likenesses of revered Olmec leaders. This guy's noggin weighs in at 1700lb.

3 Shedd Aquarium

Most everyone who comes to Shedd Aquarium (p111) wants to see the beluga whales. But did you know that the players change? Seven North American aquariums cooperate in a breeding program that occasionally relocates members of the 40-strong beluga population. Six calves have been born here since 1998.

4 Adler Planetarium & Astronomy Museum

You knew you could explore black holes and see stars at the Adler Planetarium (p111). But did you realize that from out here, at the end of a peninsula jutting into Lake Michigan, you get some of the most complete city skyline views?

5 12th Street Beach

Beaches are for sand and swimming, and 12th Street Beach (p114) is less populated than most. But it's also a concert venue. If you take your tour when there's a concert at Charter One Pavilion, you can listen for free from the beach.

6 Water Taxi

You planned on taking a bus, or schlepping all the way back to your Near North hotel. But why, when you can take a water taxi (p263) from here all the way to Navy Pier for $7? The sightseeing is thrown in gratis.

Eating p175; Shopping p144; Sleeping p243

Before Hyde Park became known as Barack Obama's neighborhood, its reputation was all about the Gothic buildings and Nobel laureates of the University of Chicago campus, whose student population fills its cafes and defines its options for nightlife. It's a hike from downtown, situated within Chicago's hardscrabble South Side, but if you're willing to make the trip there are some worthy sights, including a stunning example of Frank Lloyd Wright's Prairie School style of architecture and – wait for it – Obama's bulletproof-glass-encased barber chair. Hyde Park is also home to one of the city's most family-friendly museums, the Museum of Science and Industry, where curious exhibits include a live chick hatchery, industrial food production and an entire German U-boat that was captured during WWII.

Two huge parks flank the neighborhood: Washington Park in the west and lagoon-filled Jackson Park to the east. The latter is where the city held the 1893 World's Expo, when Chicago introduced the world to wonders such as the Ferris wheel, moving pictures and the zipper. A long green strip of land called the Midway Plaisance connects Jackson and Washington parks; it's home to an ice rink and college students kicking around soccer balls. Stately Jackson Park Beach and rocky Promontory Point lie along Hyde Park's shoreline and offer cool breezes on hot days.

The intersection of 57th St and S University Ave is a great place to start exploring the gargoyle-cluttered University of Chicago campus. That'll put you close to the cool bookstores, Wright's Robie House and the site where the atomic age began. Obama sites are three-quarters of a mile north in the adjoining Kenwood area.

Beyond Hyde Park, the South Side has its charms, though they take a little digging. Explorers will find neighborhoods that are slowly piecing things together in the shadow of some of the country's bleakest housing projects, the neglected flip side of the immaculately groomed city pictured in Mayor Daley's tourist brochures. Around 74th and 75th Sts you'll find a stretch of soul food, blues and jazz, but you'll need a car to get there.

HYDE PARK

MUSEUM OF SCIENCE & INDUSTRY
Map p120

☎ 773-684-1414; www.msichicago.org; 5700 S Lake Shore Dr; adult/3-11yr $15/10, some exhibits extra; ⏲ 9:30am-5:30pm Jun-Aug, reduced hr Sep-May; 🚌 6 or Ⓜ Metra to 55th-56th-57th

Sure, the nine permanent exhibits of this enormous museum examine just about every aspect of life on Earth, but its pleasures are in the details: chicks struggling to peck their way out of shells in the baby chick hatchery, the whimsical little high jinks of wooden puppets in the Cabaret Mechanical Theatre and the minuscule furnishings in Colleen Moore's fairy castle. If you want to go big, explore the German U-boat captured during WWII ($8 extra to tour it), take a (rather frightening) tour through industrial agriculture, or climb into the life-sized shaft of a coal mine.

The main building of the museum served as the Palace of Fine Arts at the landmark 1893 World's Expo, which was set in the surrounding Jackson Park. When you've had your fill of space capsules, coal mines and Zephyrs at the museum, the park makes an excellent setting to recuperate.

ROBIE HOUSE Map p120

☎ 708-848-1976; www.wrightplus.org; 5757 S Woodlawn Ave; 1hr tours $15; ⏲ 10am-5pm Thu-Mon; 🚌 6 or Ⓜ Metra to 55th-56th-57th

This masterpiece is the ultimate expression of Frank Lloyd Wright's Prairie School style, and it's often listed among the most important structures in American architecture. The low horizontal planes and dramatic cantilevers were meant to mirror the Midwestern landscape, and they're ornamented solely by the exquisite stained-and leaded-glass doors and windows. At the time of publishing the house was undergoing extensive restoration, which had disrupted the tour schedule, so call ahead.

UNIVERSITY OF CHICAGO Map p120

☎ 773-702-1234; www.uchicago.edu; 5801 S Ellis Ave; 🚌 6 or Ⓜ Metra to 55th-56th-57th

Some universities collect football championships. The University of Chicago

HYDE PARK & SOUTH SIDE

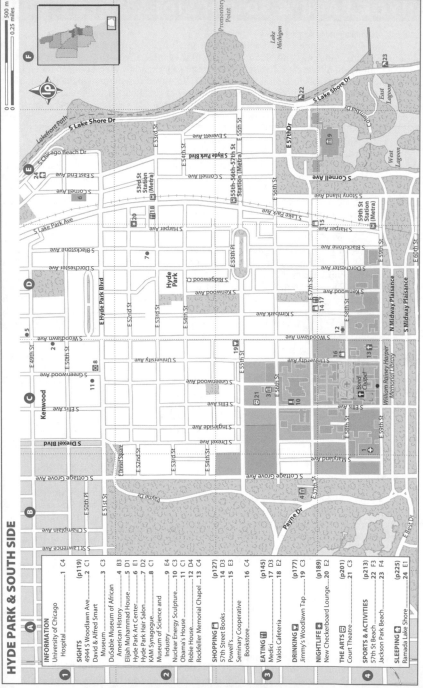

TRANSPORTATION: HYDE PARK & SOUTH SIDE

Bus Number 6 runs from State St in the Loop to 57th St in Hyde Park.

El Green Line to 35th St/Bronzeville/IIT is useful for Bronzeville and the Illinois Institute of Technology sights.

Metra 55th-56th-57th St station for Hyde Park, 53rd St station for Kenwood.

Parking Hyde Park can be tight. Free parking is available on the street and in university parking lots after 4pm weekdays and all day on weekends. If you're really stumped, look south of the Midway Plaisance. Other South Side neighborhoods shouldn't be a problem.

collects Nobel Prizes – 80-plus so far and counting. In particular, the economics department has been a regular winner. Merton Miller, a U of C economics faculty member and a prize winner himself, explained the string of wins to the *Sun-Times*: 'It must be the water; it certainly can't be the coffee.'

The university's classes first met on October 1, 1892. John D Rockefeller was a major contributor to the institution, donating more than $35 million, calling it 'the best investment I ever made in my life.' The original campus was constructed in an English Gothic style. Highlights of a campus tour include the **Rockefeller Memorial Chapel** (5850 S Woodlawn), the exterior of which will send sculpture lovers into paroxysms of joy – the facade bears 24 life-sized religious figures and 53 smaller ones, with even more inside. The **William Rainey Harper Memorial Library** (1116 E 59th St) is another must-see. The long row of arched, two-story windows bathes the 3rd-floor reading room with

light and an almost medieval sense of calm. The **Bond Chapel** (1050 E 59th St) is equally serene. Built in 1926, the exquisite 300-seat chapel is the harmonious creation of the architects, sculptors, woodcarvers and glassmakers who worked together on the project.

On Ellis Ave, between 56th and 57th, sits the 1968 Henry Moore bronze sculpture **Nuclear Energy**, marking the spot where Enrico Fermi and company started the nuclear age (see the boxed text below).

DAVID & ALFRED SMART MUSEUM OF ART Map opposite

☎ 773-702-0200; http://smartmuseum.uchicago.edu; 5550 S Greenwood Ave; admission free; ⏰ 10am-4pm Tue-Fri, 11am-5pm Sat & Sun; 🚍 6 or Ⓜ Metra to 55th-56th-57th

Named after the founders of *Esquire* magazine, who contributed the money to get it started, the official fine arts museum of the university opened in 1974 and expanded in 1999. The 8000 items in the collection include some excellent works from ancient China and Japan, and a colorful and detailed Syrian mosaic from about AD 600. The strength of the collection lies in the paintings and sculpture contemporary to the university's existence, including works by Arthur Davies, Jean Arp, Henry Moore and many others.

OBAMA SITES AND KENWOOD HISTORIC ARCHITECTURE Map opposite

Ⓜ Metra to 53rd

Kenwood, which abuts Hyde Park to the north, has become a tour bus favorite since a certain resident got elected president. Hefty security means you can't get close to **Obama's house** (5046 S Greenwood Ave), but you can stand across the street on Hyde Park Blvd and try to glimpse over the barricades at the redbrick Georgian-style manor. Many

A BOMB IS BORN

At 3:53pm on December 2, 1942, Enrico Fermi looked at a small crowd of men around him and said, 'The reaction is self-sustaining.' The scene was a dank squash court under the abandoned football stadium in the heart of the University of Chicago. With great secrecy, the gathered scientists had just achieved the world's first controlled release of nuclear energy. More than one sigh of relief was heard amid the ensuing rounds of congratulations. The nuclear reactor was supposed to have been built in a remote corner of a forest preserve 20 miles away, but a labor strike had stopped work. The impatient scientists went ahead on campus, despite the objections of many who thought the thing might blow up and take a good part of the city with it. Places such as Los Alamos in New Mexico and Hiroshima and Nagasaki in Japan are more closely linked to the nuclear era, but Chicago is where it began.

historic buildings are nearby. Across the street, the Kehilath Anshe Ma'ariv-Isaiah Israel Temple (KAM Synagogue; ☎ 773-924-1234; 1100 E Hyde Park Blvd) is a domed masterpiece in the Byzantine style with acoustics that are said to be perfect. The house at 4944 S Woodlawn Ave was once home to Muhammad Ali, and Nation of Islam leader Louis Farrakhan currently lives in the 1971 Elijah Muhammad House (4855 S Woodlawn Ave). Returning south, back toward Hyde Park, you can visit Obama's barber Zariff and the bulletproof-glass-encased presidential barber chair at the Hyde Park Hair Salon (5234 S Blackstone Ave).

InstaGreeter (p272) offers free 60-minute walking tours of the neighborhood from the Hyde Park Art Center (5020 S Cornell Ave) between 10am and 3pm on Saturdays in summer.

DUSABLE MUSEUM OF AFRICAN AMERICAN HISTORY Map p120

☎ 773-947-0600; www.dusablemuseum.org; 740 E 56th Pl; adult/child $3/1, admission free Sun; ⏰ 10am-5pm Tue-Sat, noon-5pm Sun; ⛾ 4
This was the first independent museum in the country dedicated to African American art, history and culture. The collection features African American artworks and photography, permanent exhibits that illustrate African Americans' experiences from slavery through the Civil Rights movement, and rotating exhibits that cover topics such as Chicago blues music or the

---

OBAMA'S FOOTPRINTS IN HYDE PARK

The 44th president of the United States has brought an influx of tourists to the South Side. Here are some of the spots where they pay homage.

- Obama Home (p121) You won't get very close (mind the Secret Service guys) but you can still catch a glimpse.
- Hyde Park Hair Salon (above) Home to the presidential barber chair.
- Valois Cafeteria (p176) An of-the-people cafeteria, where the prez enjoyed steak and eggs for breakfast.
- 57th Street Books (p144) Michelle Obama said this bookstore was the family's favorite for browsing.
- Promontory Point Obama used to shoot hoops at the outdoor courts here with his brother-in-law.

Black Panther movement. Housed in a 1910 building, the museum takes its name from Chicago's first permanent settler, Jean Baptiste Pointe du Sable, a French Canadian of Haitian descent.

SOUTH SIDE
BRONZEVILLE HISTORIC BUILDINGS
Map pp50-1

Ⓜ Green Line to 35th-Bronzeville-IIT
Once home to Louis Armstrong and other notables, Bronzeville thrived as the vibrant center of black life in the city from 1920 to 1950, boasting an economic and cultural strength akin to New York's Harlem. Shifting populations, urban decay and the construction of a wall of public housing along State St led to Bronzeville's decline. In the last decade it started its comeback. Many young urban professionals have moved back to the neighborhood, and South Loop development stretches almost all the way here. Still, be careful at night; it's not a good place to be walking around after dark.

Examples of stylish architecture from the past can be found throughout Bronzeville, but some of the buildings are in miserable shape and aren't worthy of more than an inspection of the exterior. You can see some fine homes along two blocks of Calumet Ave between 31st and 33rd Sts, an area known as 'the Gap.' The buildings here include Frank Lloyd Wright's only row houses, the Robert W Roloson Houses (3213-3219 S Calumet Ave).

One of scores of Romanesque houses that date from the 1880s, the Ida B Wells House (3624 S Martin Luther King Jr Dr) is named for its 1920s resident. Wells was a crusading journalist who investigated lynchings and other racially motivated crimes. She coined the line: 'Eternal vigilance is the price of liberty.'

Gospel music got its start at Pilgrim Baptist Church (☎ 312-842-5830; 3301 S Indiana Ave), originally built as a synagogue from 1890 to 1891. Unfortunately, the opulent structure burned to the ground (barring these few exterior walls) in 2006 when a roof repairman lost control of his blowtorch. Gospel fans can make a pilgrimage to two more places further south where the music still soars on Sunday. The Greater Salem Missionary Baptist Church (☎ 773-874-2325; 215 W 71st St) is where gospel great Mahalia Jackson was a lifelong member. Still further south, modern Salem Baptist Church (☎ 773-371-2300; 11800 S Indiana Ave) boasts one of the city's top choral ensembles, and is helmed by the charismatic state senator Reverend James Meeks.

The Supreme Life Building (3501 S Martin Luther King Jr Dr), a 1930s office building, was the spot where John H Johnson Jr, the publishing mogul who founded *Ebony* magazine, got the idea for his empire, which includes *Jet* and other important titles serving African Americans. There's a little neighborhood visitors center that sells old albums and trinkets behind the bank here; enter from 35th St.

In the median at 35th St and Martin Luther King Jr Dr, the Victory Monument was erected in 1928 in honor of the black soldiers who fought in WWI. The figures include a soldier, a mother and Columbia, the mythical figure meant to symbolize the New World.

ILLINOIS INSTITUTE OF TECHNOLOGY Map pp50-1

☎ 312-567-5014; www.mies.iit.edu; 3300 S Federal St; Ⓜ Green Line to 35th-Bronzeville-IIT
A world-class leader in technology, industrial design and architecture, Illinois Institute of Technology (IIT) owes much of its look to legendary architect Ludwig Mies van der Rohe, who fled the Nazis in Germany for Chicago in 1938. From 1940 until his retirement in 1958, Mies designed 22 IIT buildings that reflected his tenets of architecture, combining simple, black-metal frames with glass and brick infills. The look became known as the International Style. The star of the campus and Mies' undisputed masterpiece is SR Crown Hall (3360 S State St), appropriately home to the College of Architecture. The building, close to the center of campus, appears to be a transparent glass box floating between its translucent base and suspended roof. At night it glows from within like an illuminated jewel.

Mies isn't the only architectural hero whose works are on display at IIT. In 2003 the campus opened two other buzz-worthy buildings by world-renowned architects. Dutch architect Rem Koolhaas designed the McCormick Tribune Campus Center (3201 S State St, cnr 33rd) with its simple lines and striking en-tubing of the El tracks that run overhead. This is Koolhaas' only building in the USA. Just south of the Campus Center is the Helmut Jahn–designed State Street Village (cnr 33rd & State Sts). Jahn studied at IIT in his younger days, and his strip of rounded glass-and-steel residence halls is a natural progression from the works of the modernist bigwigs he learned from while here.

You can take a 90-minute docent-led tour ($10; ☉ 10am) that covers all the architectural

BLUES & JAZZ SHRINES FOR DIE-HARDS

You won't find the two spots listed below on the usual tourist itinerary, but hard-core music fans will want to make the effort.

Jazz aficionados often seek out the unassuming Meyers Ace Hardware Store (315 E 35th St, Bronzeville). Why? Because in the 1920s and '30s the building was the Sunset Cafe, where all the greats gigged. Imagine Louis Armstrong blowing his trumpet over by the socket wrenches. Or Earl Hines hammering the piano, down in the plunger aisle. And that was just the house band. Benny Goodman, Jimmy Dorsey and Bix Beiderbecke all launched their careers at the Sunset.

While Chicago landmarked the building, there's no hint of its past life – no plaque marking the spot or jazz tchotchkes for sale. But if David Meyers, the store's owner, is around and not too busy, he'll take you into the back office, which was once the stage. The original red-tinged mural of jazz players splashes across the wall. He'll bring out a box of yellowing news articles about the club and Armstrong's sheet music. He'll even autograph a plunger for you.

A few decades later and a few miles south, a different sound played in the night air – literally different. Guitars screamed and bass lines rolled at new decibel levels, because Muddy Waters and friends had plugged in their amps. So began the electric blues.

At Muddy Waters' house (4339 S Lake Park Ave, Oakland), impromptu jam sessions with pals like Howlin' Wolf and Chuck Berry erupted in the front yard. Waters, of course, was Chicago's main bluesman, so everyone who was anyone came to pay homage. Waters lived here for 20 years, until 1974, but today the building stands vacant in a lonely, tumbledown lot. It's private property, so you can't go inside. A sign commemorates the spot.

You'll need wheels to reach Waters' home, and it's easiest if you have them for Meyers' store (which is about a block from the Supreme Life Building; see above). Daytime is best for visits, as the 'hoods can be edgy at night.

HOG-SQUEAL OF THE UNIVERSE

In *The Jungle*, Upton Sinclair described the Chicago stockyards this way: 'One could not stand and watch very long without becoming philosophical, without beginning to deal in symbols and similes, and to hear the hog-squeal of the universe.'

These were slaughterhouses beyond compare. By the early 1870s they processed more than one million hogs a year and almost as many cattle, plus scores of unlucky sheep, horses and other critters. All of them trundled through the still-standing **Union Stockyards Gate** (Map pp50-1; 850 W Exchange Ave), one of the first commissions of Burnham & Root's young architecture company.

It was a coldly efficient operation. The old saying – that once the animals were in the packinghouses, everything was used but the squeal – was almost true. Some bits of pig debris for which no other use could be found were fed to scavenger pigs, who turned the waste into valuable meat. But a vast amount of waste was simply flushed into the south branch of the Chicago River, flowing into the lake. Beyond the aesthetic and health problems that ensued, the packers had to contend with other consequences of their pollution.

Meat processed in Chicago was shipped in ice-packed railroad cars to the huge markets in the East. The ice was harvested from lakes and rivers each winter and then stored for use all year long. But ice that was taken from the Chicago River returned to its stinky liquid state as it thawed over the meat on the journey east, thus rendering the carcasses unpalatable. The packers finally had to resort to harvesting their ice in huge operations in unpolluted Wisconsin.

highlights; it departs from the information center in the McCormick Tribune Campus Center. The center also rents audio tours.

BRIDGEPORT & UNION STOCKYARDS GATE Map pp50-1

The community of Bridgeport is more noteworthy for its historical role than for tourism, though visitors may find themselves here for a White Sox game. The stockyards were once a major attraction, but they have long since closed and the land is being rapidly covered by new warehouses. Bridgeport is also the traditional home of Chicago's Irish mayors (this is where the Daley dynasty grew up), and remains an enclave of descendants of Irish settlers.

Halsted St, from 31st St south to 43rd St, is Bridgeport's rather uninteresting main drag. Most of the neighborhood lies west of the huge train embankment that itself is west of US Cellular Field. However, Bridgeport extends north of the park all the way to Chinatown and makes for a good walk after a game if you're in a group and don't stray east of the Dan Ryan Expressway.

A tiny vestige of the stockyards lies a block west of the 4100 block of S Halsted St. The Union Stockyards Gate (850 W Exchange Ave) was once the main entrance to the vast stockyards where millions of cows and almost as many hogs met their ends each year. During the 1893 World's Expo the stockyards were a popular tourist draw, with nearly 10,000 people a day making the

trek here to stare, awestruck, as the butchering machine took in animals and spat out blood and meat.

The value of those slaughtered in 1910 was an enormous $225 million. While sanitary conditions eventually improved from the hideous levels documented by Upton Sinclair (see the boxed text above), during the Spanish-American war American soldiers suffered more casualties because of bad cans of meat from the Chicago packing houses than because of enemy fire.

HIGHER LEARNING
Walking Tour

You can learn a lot walking around the University of Chicago's Hyde Park campus and beyond.

1 David & Alfred Smart Museum of Art

Brush up on your art acumen at the Smart Museum (p121). Exhibits here explore the tension between realism and abstraction. Learn about artists from Europe and the Americas from the 19th to the mid-20th century, including Mexican painter Diego Riviera.

2 Nuclear Energy Sculpture

Under the Stagg Field Stadium on the university campus, in secret, scientists initiated the first self-sustaining controlled nuclear reaction on December 2, 1942 – the precursor to the atomic bomb (see the boxed text, p121). Today, the spot is marked by a

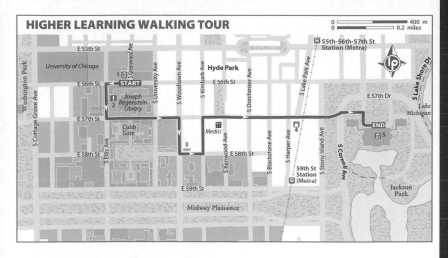

HIGHER LEARNING WALKING TOUR

WALK FACTS

Start Smart Museum of Art
Finish Museum of Science & Industry
Distance 1.25 miles
Time Five hours including browsing time
Fuel Stop Pizza at Medici (p176)

bronze, skull-like sculpture flanking a tennis court. What can we learn from this?

3 Robie House

Frank Lloyd Wright's Robie House (p119) is an excellent opportunity to educate yourself on Prairie School architecture. Notice that by painting out the vertical mortar in the brick facade, and leaving the white horizontal mortar, Wright emphasized the low-lying flatness so essential to his vision.

4 Powell's

Between Kimbark and Harper Aves on E 57th St, there are several new and used bookstores. No matter what subject you want to study – astronomy, architecture, rocket science – you're likely to find a secondhand book about it at Powell's (p144).

5 Museum of Science & Industry

Delve into WWII sea-warfare history at the Museum of Science & Industry (p119). The only German U-505 on US soil is part of a multimedia, multi-million-dollar exhibit. You can also explore a full-scale coal mine or walk through a giant heart here.

top picks

- Chicago Architecture Foundation Shop (p130)
- Boring Store (p141)
- Wolfbait & B-girls (p141)
- Randolph Street Market (p142)
- Spice House (p134)
- Threadless (p136)
- Quimby's (p139)
- Alley (p136)
- Strange Cargo (p136)
- Levi's Store (p130)

SHOPPING

From the glossy department stores of the Magnificent Mile to the gay, goth and comics shops of Lake View to the indie designers of Wicker Park, Chicago is a shopper's destination. The entire family can abuse the credit card here, and an afternoon spent browsing might result in a Crate & Barrel cappuccino maker for mom, a Cubs ball cap for dad, a nipple ring and Darth Vader guitar for the teenage son in a band, a corn-polyester blend jacket for vegetarian sis, and a lucky bingo candle for grandma.

Shopping is in Chicago's blood. The city birthed national retail giants such as Sears, Montgomery Ward, Marshall Field's and Woolworth's. True, three of the four companies no longer exist, victims of big-box retailers and overseas trade. But Chicago is still at its happiest filling shopping bags, and you'll feel the love across town.

Though chains like Old Navy and Target sit on practically every street corner, Chicago has managed to maintain a thriving culture of independent and family-run stores. A friendly Midwestern atmosphere prevails, even among the high-end stores on the Magnificent Mile.

Music, new and retro fashions, art- and architecture-related items and ethnic goods are the city's shopping strengths. For a list of easy-to-obtain local souvenirs, see p130.

Note to serious shoppers: sign up for *Chicago Magazine's* 'Sales Check' e-newsletter (www.chicagomag@salescheck_subscribe) or check the online version at www.chicagomag.com (click the 'Shopping' tab). It's published weekly and lists sales during the upcoming days, as well as new store openings and events. It's a good tool for guidance about where to unsheathe your credit card and how to save a few bucks. Daily Candy (www.dailycandy.com/chicago) is another good resource about fashion goings-on.

SHOPPING AREAS

The shoppers' siren song emanates from Michigan Ave in the Near North, along what's called the Magnificent Mile. It's stuffed with vertical malls and high-end chains and is the busiest shopping area in town. It's particularly festive around the winter holidays. Next door in the Gold Coast, ritzy designers from Paris, Milan and Manhattan mix it up on Oak and Rush Sts.

Moving north and west of downtown, you'll find boutiques filling Wicker Park and Bucktown (mod), Lincoln Park (tony), Lake View (countercultural) and Andersonville (all three).

OPENING HOURS

Typical retail shopping hours are 11am to 7pm Monday to Saturday and noon to 6pm Sunday, though they vary depending on the season, the neighborhood and the amount of foot traffic. Prime shopping areas and malls may stay open until 9pm.

The following listings note stores' hours that stray from these rough standards, as well as any closed days.

CONSUMER TAXES

Chicago's sales tax on goods (excluding food) is 9.75% – the highest in the nation (tied with Los Angeles).

THE LOOP

Shopping in the Loop, filled with iconic department stores in grand old buildings, used to be a legendary experience. Marshall Field's had its flagship store here for over 100 years, where it invented traditions such as the money-back guarantee, the bridal registry and the bargain basement. Around the corner, Carson Pirie Scott was once so prominent it got rock-star architect Louis Sullivan to design its space in the 1890s (see p57 for details). Alas, around 2007, both stores went kaput (Marshall Field's became Macy's; Carson's became office space). While the Loop still has plenty of mondo retailers, they're mostly national chains that have moved in to serve the enormous population of office workers trying to squeeze shopping into their lunch hours.

The stretch of State St between W Randolph and W Washington Sts is known as Block 37, a retail corridor that has been in development for years. Several stores finally opened in late 2009, including some national chains, but also many hip local shops. It's worth a browse, and more retailers supposedly are coming.

GALLERY 37 STORE Map pp54-5   Arts & Crafts
☎ 312-744-7274; 66 E Randolph St; ☺ closed Sun; Ⓜ Brown, Orange, Green, Purple, Pink Line to Randolph

top picks

SHOPPING STRIPS

- Clark Street (p135) Shops on this eclectic strip sell everything from human-sized dog collars to humanities tomes.
- Milwaukee Avenue (p138) Wicker Park's main thoroughfare brims with indie record, book and vintage shops.
- Michigan Avenue, aka the Magnificent Mile (p130) Big-city shopping at its best, with sky-high malls and glossy large-scale retailers.
- Armitage Avenue (p134) Classy yoga togs, haute chocolates and sassy shoes are among the urban accoutrements on offer here.
- Division Street (p138) It explodes with crafters and newbie designers offering locally made, one-of-a-kind wares.

It's a win-win proposition at this nonprofit entity: painters, sculptors and other artists get paid for creating their wares while teaching inner-city teens – who serve as apprentices – to do the same. Their artworks, including paintings, mosaic tables, puppets and carved-wood walking sticks, are sold in the gallery here. Profits return to the organization.

ILLINOIS ARTISANS SHOP
Map pp54-5   Arts & Crafts
☎ 312-814-5321; 2nd level, James R Thompson Center, 100 W Randolph St; ☯ 9am-5pm Mon-Fri; Ⓜ Brown, Orange, Green, Purple, Pink, Blue Line to Clark
The best work of artisans from throughout the state is sold here, including ceramics, wine jugs, glassware, mobiles, toys, and glass and wood coaxed into jewelry. Prices verge on cheap. The enthusiastic staff will tell you all about the people who created the various pieces. The Illinois Art Gallery next door sells paintings and sculptures under the same arrangement.

CENTRAL CAMERA
Map pp54-5   Computers & Electronics
☎ 312-427-5580; 230 S Wabash Ave; Ⓜ Red Line to Jackson
Whatever your photos needs, Central Camera has the answer. If you're traveling with a shutterbug, be sure to avoid this place until the very end of your trip, lest

you risk seeing the sights all by yourself. Once photo-holics step inside the long, narrow store, it will be days before they surface again.

POSTER PLUS
Map pp54-5   Fine Arts
☎ 312-461-9277; 200 S Michigan Ave; Ⓜ Brown, Orange, Green, Purple, Pink Line to Adams
Located across from the Art Institute, this superlative poster store carries reproductions of many of the museum's best-known works, along with a number of fun, Chicago-specific historical prints dating from the late 19th century. Upstairs in the vintage room, European and American poster originals can go for as much as $30,000.

CHICAGO'S DOWNTOWN FARMSTAND
Map pp54-5   Food & Drink
☎ 312-742-8419; www.chicagofarmstand.com; 66 E Randolph St; ☯ 11am-7pm Tue-Fri, to 4pm Sat; Ⓜ Brown, Orange, Green, Purple, Pink Line to Randolph
Chicago's Downtown Farmstand fills its shelves with honey, pastries, produce and other edible products, all made or grown within 250 miles of the city. On Wednesday (11am-1pm) the store hosts free cooking demonstrations of easy recipes using what's newest and freshest that day. On Friday (noon-2pm) local producers come in to share stories and offer tastings of everything from Mayan chocolate cookies to farmstead goat cheese.

5 S WABASH AVE
Map pp54-5   Jewelry
5 S Wabash Ave; ☯ closed Sun; Ⓜ Brown, Orange, Green, Purple, Pink Line to Madison
This old building, located on a block commonly referred to as 'Jewelers Row,' is the center of Chicago's family jeweler trade. Hundreds of shops in here sell every kind of watch, ring, gemstone and bauble imaginable. Most are quick to promise, 'I can get it for you wholesale!'

AKIRA FOOTWEAR
Map pp54-5   Shoes
☎ 312-346-3034; 122 S State St; Ⓜ Red Line to Monroe
This Loop outpost of the trendy local chain offers fun kicks in the most recent styles. Fancy Chuck Taylors, cute silver sandals, colorful rain boots – whatever the look *du jour* is, you'll probably find it on the racks. There's lots of seating to try on your selections, and most items are moderately

priced. A couple of Akira clothing shops are in Wicker Park (see p139).

CHICAGO ARCHITECTURE FOUNDATION SHOP Map pp54-5 Souvenirs
☎ 312-922-3432; 224 S Michigan Ave; Ⓜ Brown, Orange, Green, Pink Line to Adams
Skyscraper playing cards, Frank Lloyd Wright note cards and heaps of books and posters celebrate local architecture at this haven for anyone with an edifice complex. The items make excellent only-in-Chicago-type souvenirs.

SHOP AT THE CULTURAL CENTER Map pp54-5 Souvenirs
☎ 312-742-0079; 78 E Washington St; Ⓜ Brown, Orange, Green, Purple, Pink Line to Randolph
The Chicago Cultural Center's shop is another stellar place for Chicago-oriented souvenirs, especially books by local authors. The Chicago Publishers Gallery is on-site at the center, and so many of the comics, history books, zines and poetry books displayed there are for sale here.

NEAR NORTH & NAVY PIER
The Magnificent Mile, or 'Mag Mile' as it's widely known, encompasses the sleek high-end department stores and national chains

top picks
CLASSIC SOUVENIRS
The ultimate memento from Chicago is a deep-dish pizza. A couple of chains pack pies on dry ice and ship them anywhere in the USA. Try Giordano's (☎ 800-982-1756; www.giordanos.com) or Gino's East (☎ 800-344-5455; www.ginoseast.com). The pie itself costs roughly $25, plus about $25 more for shipping. Suggestions for lighter, less perishable keepsakes:
- A mini Willis Tower replica from the Chicago Architecture Foundation (above).
- Impressionist art posters selected from the Art Institute (p52).
- An iron-on Coach Ditka or an Obama T-shirt from Strange Cargo (p136).
- Jazz or blues CDs found at Jazz Record Mart (opposite).
- Popcorn bought from Garrett Popcorn (opposite).

on Michigan Ave between the river and Oak St. The little stretch sells close to $1 billion worth of goods annually; it's at its frenzied peak during December.

ABRAHAM LINCOLN BOOK SHOP Map pp66-7 Bookstore
☎ 312-944-3085; 357 W Chicago Ave; Ⓨ closed Sun; Ⓜ Brown, Purple Line to Chicago
This hushed, museum-like shop carries new, used and antiquarian books about Honest Abe, the Civil War and the presidency in general. If you want a real, Lincoln-signed White House memo – and have $30,000 to drop on it – you'll walk out of here a satisfied customer. The knowledgeable staff regularly hold open round-table discussions with Civil War scholars.

LEVI'S STORE Map pp66-7 Clothing & Accessories
☎ 312-642-9613; 600 N Michigan Ave; Ⓜ Red Line to Grand
Welcome to denim's mecca. The sheer volume of Levi's for sale here will spin your head: skinny cut? boot-cut? flare 501s? petite? dark washed? They're all in the stacks, in every combination imaginable. Prices span the gamut, from basics at $45 to fashion-forward styles costing upward of $245. There's a second store in Wicker Park (Map pp96-7; 1552 N Milwaukee Ave).

ZARA Map pp66-7 Clothing & Accessories
☎ 312-750-0780; 700 N Michigan Ave; Ⓜ Red Line to Chicago
New products arrive weekly and inventory changes biweekly at Spanish fashion house Zara. It's sort of Gap meets H&M, with youthful, off-the-runway styles at low prices in women's, men's and kids' clothing. The three-story building is Zara's biggest US store.

APPLE STORE Map pp66-7 Computers & Electronics
☎ 312-981-4104; 679 N Michigan Ave; Ⓜ Red Line to Chicago
This bright, airy store offers iPads, iPods and everything else for Mac enthusiasts splayed across butcher-block tables. The user-friendly setup comes with plenty of clued-up staff to answer product questions, a 'genius bar' on the 2nd floor to sort out equipment issues and free internet access on machines throughout the store.

GARRETT POPCORN Map pp66-7 Food & Drink

☎ 312-944-2630; 625 N Michigan Ave; 10am-8pm Mon-Thu, to 10pm Fri & Sat, to 7pm Sun; Ⓜ Red Line to Grand

Like lemmings drawn to a cliff, people form long lines outside this kernel-sized store on the Mag Mile. Granted, the caramel corn is heavenly and the cheese popcorn decadent, but is it worth waiting in the whipping snow for a chance to buy some? Actually, it is. Buy the Chicago Mix, which combines the two flavors. One estimate says Chicagoans wolf down a collective 480,000 pounds per year. The entrance is on Ontario St.

CRATE & BARREL Map pp66-7 Housewares

☎ 312-787-5900; 646 N Michigan Ave; Ⓜ Red Line to Grand

The handsome housewares purveyor started right here in Chicago, and this glassy, sassy uberstore is the flagship. Inside, suburban soccer moms fill their carts with hip but functional lamps, wine goblets, casserole dishes and brass beds, same as the downtown loft nesters shopping beside them.

JAZZ RECORD MART Map pp66-7 Music Store

☎ 312-222-1467; www.jazzmart.com; 27 E Illinois St; Ⓜ Red Line to Grand

You have to hunt for this place, but jazzheads, blues aficionados and vintage vinyl collectors seek it out, as it makes the short list of best records stores in the nation. You can spend hours fingering through the rows of dusty LPs or chatting up owner Bob Koester and his dedicated staff about local blues and jazz. Fans of Chicago blues should stop for a meaningful aural souvenir, especially from the shop's boutique label, Delmark.

MERCHANDISE MART

Map pp66-7 Shopping Mall

☎ 312-527-4141; 222 Merchandise Mart Plaza, W Kinzie & N Well Sts; ⌚ most stores closed Sun; Ⓜ Brown, Purple Line to Merchandise Mart

Beautifully restored in the early 1990s, the Mart contains a modest collection of chain stores on its lower floors. But the real allure lies on the upper floors devoted to distributor showrooms for home furnishings and other interior fittings. As you prowl the halls, you can find next year's hot trends on display today. Technically, only retailers and buyers can shop on most of these floors,

though LuxeHome, with its 100,000 sq ft of kitchen and bathroom fixtures, is open to the public (you must see the concierge to get a free 'guide'). See p65 for further information on the Mart, including tours.

SHOPS AT NORTH BRIDGE

Map pp66-7 Shopping Mall

☎ 312-327-2300; 520 N Michigan Ave; Ⓜ Red Line to Grand

Shops at North Bridge appeals to a less aggressively froufrou demographic than some of the other Mag Mile malls, with stores such as the Ann Taylor Loft, Harley Davidson and the LEGO Store. The multilevel mall connects anchor department store Nordstrom to Michigan Ave via a gracefully curving, shop-lined atrium.

CHICAGO TRIBUNE STORE

Map pp66-7 Souvenirs

☎ 312-222-3080; Tribune Tower, 435 N Michigan Ave; ⌚ closed Sun; Ⓜ Red Line to Grand

CLOTHING SIZES

Women's clothing

Aus/UK	8	10	12	14	16	18
Europe	36	38	40	42	44	46
Japan	5	7	9	11	13	15
USA	6	8	10	12	14	16

Women's shoes

Aus/USA	5	6	7	8	9	10
Europe	35	36	37	38	39	40
France only	35	36	38	39	40	42
Japan	22	23	24	25	26	27
UK	3½	4½	5½	6½	7½	8½

Men's clothing

Aus	92	96	100	104	108	112
Europe	46	48	50	52	54	56
Japan	S		M	M		L
UK/USA	35	36	37	38	39	40

Men's shirts (collar sizes)

Aus/Japan	38	39	40	41	42	43
Europe	38	39	40	41	42	43
UK/USA	15	15½	16	16½	17	17½

Men's shoes

Aus/UK	7	8	9	10	11	12
Europe	41	42	43	44½	46	47
Japan	26	27	27½	28	29	30
USA	7½	8½	9½	10½	11½	12½

Measurements approximate only; try before you buy

top picks

MUSIC STORES

Independent record stores flood Chicago's neighborhoods, supported by the thriving live-music scene in town (see p190). Vinyl geeks will discover heaps of stacks to flip through, while jazz, blues and hip-hop lovers are well positioned for obscure finds.

- **Dusty Groove** (p140)
- **Gramaphone Records** (p136)
- **Jazz Record Mart** (p131)
- **Groove Distribution** (p143)
- **Reckless Records** (p140)

While this small store doesn't have the selection of other souvenir places in Chicago, it does outdo its competitors in *Tribune*-related merchandise. Cubs and Blackhawks hats and jerseys, and books by noted Chicago authors are also available.

NIKETOWN Map pp66-7 · Sportswear
☎ 312-642-6363; 669 N Michigan Ave; Ⓜ Red Line to Chicago

It's no longer the unique, museum-ish store it once was (outlets have cropped up in many other cities), but this Nike temple has all the flash and sparkle you'd expect from the shoe giant. It remains hugely popular, with every swooshed T-shirt, sweatshirt, jersey and high-top imaginable. A free running club takes off from here every Thursday at 6:30pm.

SPORTS AUTHORITY Map pp66-7 · Sportswear
☎ 312-337-6151; 620 N LaSalle St; Ⓜ Red Line to Grand

In a classic rags-to-riches story, Morrie Mages got his start in his family's store in the old Maxwell St Jewish ghetto, where some of the city's leading retailers launched their careers by selling clothes in the period between WWI and WWII. Mages built this into the world's largest sporting-goods store, eventually moving it from Maxwell St into its own renovated eight-story warehouse here. Though Morrie sold the company for a fortune back in 1994, and the store is now owned by national chain Sports Authority, it still continues his discounting philosophy.

GOLD COAST

For years Oak St was where you went for your Hèrmes scarves, Prada handbags and Harry Winston diamonds. And it still is, though many shoppers will tell you Rush St is the new Oak, as luxury retailers now twist around the corner onto that street as well. The corridor is Chicago's swankiest: it's the one place you might experience a bit of haughtiness from shopkeepers.

BORDERS BOOKS & MUSIC
Map pp72-3 · Bookstore
☎ 312-573-0564; 830 N Michigan Ave; ⏰ 9am-11pm Mon-Sat, to 9pm Sun Ⓜ Red Line to Chicago

This humongous Borders, right across from the Water Tower, is always crowded. Thousands of books, including lots of special-interest titles, are spread out over four floors. You'll find a good selection of magazines and newspapers near the main entrance. There's also a branch in Lake View (Map pp86-7; ☎ 773-935-3909; 2817 N Clark St). Both have free wi-fi.

EUROPA BOOKS Map pp72-3 · Bookstore
☎ 312-335-9677; 832 N State St; Ⓜ Red Line to Chicago

As the name promises, this store carries newspapers, magazines and books, primarily in French, German, Spanish, Italian and Portuguese, but also in some non-European languages including Japanese.

OPEN BOOKS Map pp72-3 · Bookstore
☎ 312-475-1355; 213 W Institute Pl; ⏰ 10am-7pm Mon-Sat; Ⓜ Brown, Purple Line to Chicago

Buy a used book here and you're helping to fund this volunteer-based literacy group's programs, which range from in-school reading help to adult creative writing courses. The expansive store has good-quality tomes and plenty of comfy sofas where you can sit and peruse your finds. It's a particularly friendly environment for kids. Books average around $5.

BARNEYS NEW YORK
Map pp72-3 · Clothing & Accessories
☎ 312-587-1700; 15 E Oak St; Ⓜ Red Line to Chicago

Barneys provides the quintessential Gold Coast shopping experience. Its six floors sparkle with mega-high-end designer goods, while the penthouse holds a posh restaurant with a toasty fireplace. The on-site concierge books theater tickets for customers.

DENIM LOUNGE
Map pp72-3   Clothing & Accessories
☎ 312-642-6403; 43 E Oak St; Ⓜ Red Line to Chicago

The entire family can get outfitted in jeans here, from the kiddies on up to mom and dad. It's all cool, easily wearable designer brands, and the four-dimensional fitting station lets you check out the look from every angle in high definition (not always a rewarding feature). The lounge is attached to a hip kids' clothing shop called Madison & Friends.

H&M Map pp72-3   Clothing & Accessories
☎ 312-640-0060; 840 N Michigan Ave; Ⓜ Red Line to Chicago

This Swedish-based purveyor of trendy togs is usually packed with customers clawing the racks for high fashion at low prices. Men and women will find a variety of European-cut styles ranging from business suits to bathing suits. There's another outlet at 22 N State St (Map pp54-5; ☎ 312-263-4436), but this one is bigger.

JIL SANDER Map pp72-3   Clothing & Accessories
☎ 312-335-0006; 48 E Oak St; ⊙ 10am-6pm Mon-Sat; Ⓜ Red Line to Chicago

Jil Sander's minimalist colors and simple designs somehow manage to remain fashionable long after other trendsetters have disappeared from the scene.

BEST BUY Map pp72-3   Computers & Electronics
☎ 312-397-2146; John Hancock Center, 875 N Michigan Ave; Ⓜ Red Line to Chicago

A convenient superstore for those looking to pick up laptop or cell phone supplies, Best Buy offers good prices on things like SIM cards, flash drives, hand-held computing devices and more. Come with a clear idea of what you want, as it can be difficult to flag down staff for help. The store is in the Hancock Center.

ALTERNATIVES Map pp72-3   Shoes
☎ 312-266-1545; 5th fl, 900 N Michigan Ave; Ⓜ Red Line to Chicago

The kinds of shoes that delight the eye and appall the feet are the specialty at this store, located in the 900 N Michigan mall. Featuring one of the most cutting-edge collections in town, its prices will gladden the hearts of budding Imelda Marcoses everywhere. Another outlet is slated to open in Block 37 in the Loop.

JIMMY CHOO Map pp72-3   Shoes
☎ 312-255-1170; 63 E Oak St; Ⓜ Red Line to Chicago

The prices are almost as high as the stiletto heels at Jimmy Choo, revered foot stylist to the rich and famous. Oh, go ahead – be like J Lo and Beyoncé. All it takes is a toss of the head, the willingness to drop $800 on a pair of kicks and the attitude that footwear doesn't make the outfit, it is the outfit.

900 N MICHIGAN Map pp72-3   Shopping Mall
☎ 312-915-3916; 900 N Michigan Ave; Ⓜ Red Line to Chicago

This huge mall is home to an upscale collection of stores including Diesel, Gucci and J Crew, among many others. Water Tower Place is under the same management, and they simply placed all the really expensive stores over here.

WATER TOWER PLACE
Map pp72-3   Shopping Mall
☎ 312-440-3166; 835 N Michigan Ave; Ⓜ Red Line to Chicago

Featuring the coolest fountain in all of Chicago mall-land (you'll see it on your ride up the main escalator), Water Tower Place launched the city's love affair with vertical shopping centers. Many locals swear this first one remains the best one. The mall houses 100 stores on seven levels, including Abercrombie & Fitch, Macy's, Aritzia (the mod Canadian chain), Akira (the hip local clothing vendor) and American Girl Place.

BURTON SNOWBOARDS
Map pp72-3   Sportswear
☎ 312-202-7900; 56 E Walton St; ⊙ 11am-8pm Mon-Sat, to 6pm Sun; Ⓜ Red Line to Chicago

Hey, Midwesterners shred the slopes too, and this is where air dogs come to get their gear. Burton, of course, is the biggest brand in the business. Its multistory Chicago shop carries a sweet selection of boards, jackets, watches and other accessories. There's a chill-out lounge on the top floor where you can check email and watch snowboarding films.

PUMA STORE Map pp72-3 Sportswear

☎ 312-751-8574; 1051 N Rush St; Ⓜ Red Line to Clark/Division

Visiting Puma's minimalist, white-walled store has been described as daytime clubbing. DJs spin tunes (mostly on weekends), and buff young bodies bounce to the beat while checking out men's and women's shoes that are impossible to find anywhere else. The 1st floor is devoted to the brand's sporty urban clothing line.

AMERICAN GIRL PLACE Map pp72-3 Toy Shop

☎ 877-247-5223; www.americangirl.com; Water Tower Place, 835 N Michigan Ave; Ⓜ Red Line to Chicago

This is not your mother's doll shop; it's an *experience*. Here, dolls are treated as real people: the 'hospital' carts them away in wheelchairs for repairs; the cafe seats the dolls as part of the family during tea service; and the dolls' owners – usually outfitted in matching threads, naturally – take classes with their little pals. Creepy? Maybe a little, but the fact that the average shopper's visit lasts three hours is a testament to the immersive environment. There are outlets in many cities now, but this flagship remains the largest and busiest.

FLIGHT 001 Map pp72-3 Travel Accessories

☎ 312-944-1001; 1133 N State St; Ⓜ Red Line to Clark/Division

The brightly colored, hard-shelled luggage and the stock of travel gadgets will get a rise out of any would-be jet-setter. The store is as sleek as can be; you even get cashed out at a retro airline ticket counter.

LINCOLN PARK & OLD TOWN

Lincoln Park contains plenty of tony shops, many of which bunch near the intersection of Halsted St and Armitage Ave. Clark St is also chockablock, though it offers more casual options. The area around North and Clybourn Aves is thick with Pottery Barn, J Crew and other urban-living chains.

CROSSROADS TRADING CO

Map pp78-9 Clothing & Accessories

☎ 773-296-1000; 2711 N Clark St; Ⓜ Brown, Purple Line to Diversey

Crossroads sells funky, name-brand used clothes for men and women that you can count on being in good condition. Lots of jeans usually hang on the racks, including Seven for all Mankind, Citizens of Humanity and Miss Sixty labels. Shoes, coats and handbags are also abundant. You can sell or trade items, too.

SPICE HOUSE Map pp78-9 Food & Drink

☎ 312-274-0378; www.thespicehouse.com; 1512 N Wells St; ⏱ 10am-7pm Mon-Sat, to 5pm Sun; Ⓜ Brown, Purple Line to Sedgwick

A bombardment of peppery fragrance socks you in the nose at this exotic spice house in Old Town, offering delicacies such as black and red volcanic salt from Hawaii and pomegranate molasses among the tidy jars. Best though are the house-made herb blends themed after Chicago neighborhoods, including the piquant 'Argyle St Asian Blend,' allowing you to take home a taste of the city.

VOSGES HAUT-CHOCOLAT

Map pp78-9 Food & Drink

☎ 773-296-9866; 951 W Armitage Ave; Ⓜ Brown, Purple Line to Armitage

Owner-chocolatier Katrina Markoff has earned a national reputation for her brand by blending exotic ingredients like curry powder, chilies and wasabi into her truffles, ice cream and candy bars. They sound weird but taste great, as the abundant samples laid out along the back counter prove. The heaven-sent dark-chocolate blends are the sweets to beat, dressed up with sea salt, 'enchanted mushrooms' and bacon. Yes, bacon.

DAVE'S RECORDS Map pp78-9 Music Store

☎ 773-929-6325; 2604 N Clark St; Ⓜ Brown, Purple Line to Diversey

With a splatter of colored vinyl decorating the back wall, Dave's feels a little like the setting of Nick Hornby's music-nerd classic, *High Fidelity*. CDs? Forget it. MP3s? Never heard of 'em. Dave's doesn't discriminate with genres, but it's for vinyl purists only.

BARKER & MEOWSKY Map pp78-9 Pet Supplies

☎ 773-868-0200; 1003 W Armitage Ave; Ⓜ Brown Line to Armitage

Fido and Fluffy get their due here. Sales staff welcome four-legged visitors with a treat from the all-natural pet food stash, and then the critters are allowed to commence sniffing up and over the fun apparel, beds and carriers. Top wags go to the Chewy Vuitton purse-shaped squeaky toys and Cubs ball caps, the shop's best sellers.

LORI'S, THE SOLE OF CHICAGO
Map pp78-9   Shoes

☎ 773-281-5655; 824 W Armitage Ave; Ⓜ Brown, Purple Line to Armitage

Lori's caters to shoe junkies, who tear through boxes and tissue paper to get at Franco Sarto, Apepazza and other European brands. The general frenzy morphs into a true gorge-fest during season-ending sales in July/August and January/February; lines can form out the door during these sales.

LULULEMON ATHLETICA
Map pp78-9   Sportswear

☎ 773-883-8860; 2104 N Halsted St; Ⓜ Brown Line to Armitage

Canada's famous yoga-wear maker opened shop in Chicago, giving locals access to its colorful togs made of organic cotton, hemp and bamboo. They're flattering, too: the Boogie Pants and Groove Pants 'give every girl a great-looking butt,' swears one devoted customer. Bonus: the shop offers free one-hour yoga classes at 10am Sunday. Call ahead to register; mats are provided.

ROTOFUGI Map pp78-9   Toy Shop
☎ 312-491-9501; www.rotofugi.com; 2780 N Lincoln Ave; Ⓜ Brown, Purple Line to Diversey

---

BRANDS WITH ATTITUDE

The following local brands have racked up impressive indie cachet. Watch for them in shops around town, especially in Wicker Park, Logan Square and Lake View.

Evil Kitty (www.evilkitty.net) Brightly colored, punky, sassy tops, skirts and dresses for women designed by a former Art Institute student.

Busy Beaver Button Company (www.busybeaver .net) Purveyors of ubercool, artist-designed badges. The company also has Button-O Matic vending machines in hot spots like Reckless Records (p140), Hot Doug's (p170) and Uncle Fun (p137).

Shawnimals (www.shawnimals.com) Wacky, huggable, cartoony, Japanese-style plush creatures, each with its own backstory.

Rotofugi has an unusual niche: urban designer toys. The spacey, robot-y, odd vinyl and plush items will certainly distinguish you from the other kids on the block. Graffiti artists and cartoonists use the store as a studio, so it's also a gallery. You can usually find locally designed Shawnimals (see box below) here.

LAKE VIEW & WRIGLEYVILLE

Stuff that's never worn – let alone sold – on Michigan Ave is *de rigueur* on Halsted and Clark Sts in Lake View. Even if you're not buying, the browsing is entertainment in itself. Near Belmont Ave several stores serve the rebellious needs of pierced and spiky-haired youth. On weekend days the sidewalks attract a throng of characters: rich teens from the North Shore, black-clad punks with blond roots and the rest of Lake View's diverse tribes. If you'd prefer a classic designer dress to a nipple ring or a PVC bikini, head to Southport Ave, where a string of upscale clothing boutiques has opened.

ARCHITECTURAL ARTIFACTS
Map pp86-7   Antiques

☎ 773-348-0622; 4325 N Ravenswood Ave; 🕙 10am-5pm; Ⓜ Brown Line to Montrose

This mammoth, 80,000-sq-ft salvage warehouse, located a bit northwest of Lake View proper, is a treasure trove that prompts continual mutterings of 'Where on earth did they find *that*?' Italian marionettes, 1920s French mannequins and Argentinean cast-iron mailboxes rest alongside decorative doors, tiles, stained-glass windows, fireplace mantels and garden furnishings. Be sure to step into the free attached Museum of Historic Chicago Architecture (a work in progress).

CHICAGO COMICS Map pp86-7   Bookstore
☎ 773-528-1983; www.chicagocomics.com; 3244 N Clark St; 🕙 from noon; Ⓜ Red, Brown, Purple Line to Belmont

This comic emporium has won the 'best comic-book store in the USA' honor from all sorts of people who should know. Old Marvel *Superman* back issues share shelf space with hand-drawn works by cutting-edge local artists like Chris Ware, Ivan Brunetti and Dan Clowes (who lived here during his early *Eightball* days). *Simpsons* fanatics will 'd'oh!' with joy at the huge toy selection.

ALLEY Map pp86-7 — Clothing & Accessories

☎ 773-525-3180; www.thealley.com; 3228 N Clark St; Ⓜ Red, Brown, Purple Line to Belmont

A skull and crossbones mark the door at this one-stop counterculture shop. The vast emporium offers everything from pot pipes to band posters to human-sized dog collars. Loud, obnoxious punk-rock tees ('I've got the biggest dick in the band' etc), fetish shoes and leatherwear are some of the house specialties. The scene unfurls through a labyrinth of rooms, including a couple devoted to tattooing and piercing.

BELMONT ARMY SURPLUS

Map pp86-7 — Clothing & Accessories

☎ 773-549-1038; 855 W Belmont Ave; Ⓜ Red, Brown, Purple Line to Belmont

Don't be fooled by the name – the goods at this sprawling store go well beyond combat gear. Fashion-of-the-moment clothes hang from the 1st floor's racks. A rainbow array of Converse, Vans, Adidas, Dr Martens, Red Wing and sky-high goth shoes fills the 2nd floor's shelves. The 3rd floor is where you finally get to the peacoats and other vintage military wares.

STRANGE CARGO

Map pp86-7 — Clothing & Accessories

☎ 773-327-8090; 3448 N Clark St; Ⓜ Red Line to Addison

One of the coolest stores in Chicago for retro T-shirts and thrift-store-esque hipster wear, Strange Cargo also sells wigs, clunky shoes and leather jackets. Buy a vintage-style T-shirt, then use the iron-on machine to enliven it with a message or decal of your choice. There's an excellent selection of kitschy ones featuring Mike Ditka, Harry Caray, the Picasso statue, the Hancock Center and other local icons – all supreme souvenirs.

THREADLESS Map pp86-7 — Clothing & Accessories

☎ 773-525-8640; www.threadless.com; 3011 N Broadway St; Ⓜ Brown, Purple Line to Wellington

Those seeking that perfect ironic, eccentric, limited-edition T-shirt will find it at Threadless. The company runs an ongoing T-shirt design competition on its website in which designers submit ideas and consumers cast votes (750,000 weekly). The

company then releases the seven winning styles in limited quantities of 1500, and they're only available for two weeks. The new designs appear in-store on Friday, before they're posted online on Monday. Prices range from about $15 to $25. Bring back your shopping bag and get $1 off your next purchase. There's a kid-focused outlet at 1905 W Division St (Map pp96-7; ☎ 773-698-7042; Blue Line to Division).

MIDWEST STEREO

Map pp86-7 — Computers & Electronics

☎ 773-975-4250; 1613 W Belmont Ave; ☽ closed Sun; Ⓜ Brown Line to Paulina

This is a hub for DJ gear, both used and new. If you're looking for a basic mixer or a Technics turntable (or a PA system that will quickly make you the talk of your neighborhood), this is your store.

BROWN ELEPHANT RESALE

SHOP Map pp86-7 — Housewares

☎ 773-549-5943; 3651 N Halsted St; Ⓜ Red Line to Addison

Proceeds benefit the Howard Brown Health Center, which specializes in health care for the GLBT communities. The shop has a consistently good selection of books, vintage furniture and kitchen items.

GRAMAPHONE RECORDS

Map pp86-7 — Music Store

☎ 773-472-3683; www.gramaphonerecords.com; 2843 N Clark St; Ⓜ Brown, Purple Line to Diversey

Gramaphone is one of the hippest record stores in Chicago – you'd have to either be a DJ or be dating a DJ to have heard of most of the hip-hop and electronic music sold here. Along with its collection of trendsetting sounds, Gramaphone offers record needles and DJ supplies, and a host of info on upcoming parties.

UNCLE DAN'S Map pp86-7 — Outdoor Gear

☎ 773-348-5800; 3551 N Southport Ave; Ⓜ Brown Line to Southport

This store offers top travel and outdoor gear for those looking to escape the concrete jungle, or at least get some abrasion-reinforced fleece to protect them from the elements. It's a relaxed place to buy hiking boots, camping supplies, backpacks and whatnot without the macho posturing that gear stores sometimes give off.

SPORTS WORLD Map pp86-7   Souvenirs
☎ 312-472-7701; 3555 N Clark St; Ⓜ Red Line to Addison
This store across from Wrigley Field overflows with – that's right, Sherlock – Cubs sportswear. It carries all shapes and sizes of jerseys, T-shirts, sweatshirts and ball caps, plus baby clothes and drink flasks. Surprisingly, the prices aren't bad given the attraction-side location.

WINDWARD SPORTS Map pp86-7 Sportswear
☎ 773-472-6868; www.windwardsports.com; 3317 N Clark St; ☯ closed Tue; Ⓜ Red, Brown, Purple Line to Belmont
One-stop shopping for sporty board gear, whether you're into surfing, windsurfing, kiteboarding, snowboarding or skateboarding. Windward carries the requisite apparel labels, too (Quicksilver, Billabong, Split etc). Staff members are clued in to local boarding hot spots. Ask about various beach rentals of windsurfing equipment during the summer.

GAY MART Map pp86-7   Toy Shop
☎ 773-929-4272; 3457 N Halsted St; Ⓜ Red Line to Addison
The Woolworth's of the strip sells toys, novelties, calendars, souvenirs, you name it. One of the top sellers is Billy, the heroically endowed 'world's first out and proud gay doll.' Ken would just wilt in Billy's presence – that is, if Ken had anything to wilt. Lots of Marvel action figures and 'Homo Depot' buttons, too.

UNCLE FUN Map pp86-7   Toy Shop
☎ 773-477-8223; 1338 W Belmont Ave; ☯ noon-8pm Mon-Fri, 11am-7pm Sat, 11am-5pm Sun; Ⓜ Brown Line to Southport
This oddball toy and novelty shop is one of the best spots in Chicago for goofy gifts, kitschy postcards and vintage games. The shelves are overflowing with strange finds like fake moustache kits, 3-D Jesus postcards and Chinese-made tapestries of the US lunar landing.

YESTERDAY Map pp86-7   Toy Shop
☎ 773-248-8087; 1143 W Addison St; ☯ closed Sun; Ⓜ Red Line to Addison
If you've ever actually lived through the classic 'Mom's thrown out all of my baseball cards' tale, you can come here to find out what a fortune you've lost. Old sports memorabilia is the specialty of this shop, which is even older than some of the goods on sale.

ANDERSONVILLE & UPTOWN
Clark St, north of Foster Ave, is the main commercial drag, and it offers several choices in just a few blocks: antique and resale shops, fashion and furnishing boutiques, old-fashioned toy stores and arty, locally made wares. It's a good place to come for unique, quality goods at relatively decent prices.

ANDERSONVILLE GALLERIA
Map p90   Arts & Crafts
☎ 773-878-8570; 5247 N Clark St; ☯ closed Mon; Red Line to Berwyn
Ninety indie vendors sell their fair-trade and locally made artisan wares in mini-boutiques spread over three floors. Sweets, coffee, clothing, handbags, paintings, photography, jewelry – it's a smorgasbord of cool, crafty goods in a community-oriented marketplace. Support the little guy!

WOMEN & CHILDREN
FIRST Map p90   Bookstore
☎ 773-769-9299; 5233 N Clark St; ☯ 11am-7pm Mon & Tue, 11am-9pm Wed-Fri, 10am-7pm Sat, 11am-6pm Sun; Ⓜ Red Line to Berwyn
A feminist mainstay, this independent bookstore has been around for over 30 years. Book signings and author events happen every week at the welcoming shop, which features fiction and nonfiction by and about women, along with children's books.

EARLY TO BED Map p90   Sex & Fetish
☯ 773-271-1219; 5232 N Sheridan Rd; ☯ noon-7pm Tue, to 8pm Wed-Thu & Sat, to 9pm Fri, to 6pm Sun; Ⓜ Red Line to Berwyn
This low-key, women-owned sex shop is good for novices: it provides explanatory pages and customer reviews throughout the store, so you'll be able to know your anal beads from cock rings from bullet vibes. Also on hand are feather boas, bondage tapes and vegan condoms (made with casein-free latex; casein is a milk-derived product usually used in latex production). Videos and books round out the offerings –

WORTH THE TRIP: LINCOLN SQUARE & DEVON AVE

The old German neighborhood of Lincoln Square has been gentrified, yet its strong European roots continue to flavor its shops, which deserve a visit. It's located between Andersonville and Lake View, to the west; the shopping district is at the intersection of Lincoln, Lawrence and Western Aves. Take the Brown Line to Western.

Chopping Block (Map pp50-1; ☎ 773-472-6700 www.thechoppingblock.net; 4747 N Lincoln Ave; Ⓜ Brown Line to Western) Let's say your recipe calls for Hungarian cinnamon, gray sea salt and Balinese long pepper. Instead of throwing up your hands in despair after searching the local grocery and then calling for a pizza delivery, stop in here for specialty foods, high-end cookware and hard-to-find utensils. Chopping Block also offers cooking classes; see p267 for details.

Merz Apothecary (Map pp50-1; ☎ 773-989-0900; 4716 N Lincoln Ave; ◷ closed Sun) Merz is a true turn-of-the-century European apothecary. Antique pharmacy jars contain herbs, homeopathic remedies, vitamins and supplements, and the shelves are stacked high with skin care, personal care, bath and aromatherapy products from around the world.

Timeless Toys (Map pp50-1; ☎ 773-334-4445; 4749 N Lincoln Ave) This charming independent shop is better described for what it does *not* carry – no Barbies, Harry Potter books or trendy kiddie togs. Instead you'll find high-quality, old-fashioned toys, many of which are made in Germany or other European countries. Have fun playing with the bug magnifiers, microscopes, glitter balls and wooden spinning tops.

Now that you're this far north, why not keep going? Devon Ave is 2 miles up the road and the only place in town to pick up a cell phone, a kosher doughnut and a sari in one fell swoop. Known as Chicago's 'International Marketplace,' Devon Ave is where worlds collide – Indian, Pakistani, Georgian, Russian, Cuban, Hindu, Muslim, Orthodox Jewish – you name the ethnicity and someone from the group has set up a shop or eatery here.

Devon at Western Ave is the main intersection. Indian sari and jewelry shops start near 2600 W Devon; to the west they give way to Jewish and Islamic goods stores, while to the east they trickle out into a gaggle of electronics and dollar stores. It's a good place to stock up on low-cost cell phone necessities, luggage and other travel goods. Or just buy an armful of jangly bangles. If you want to stay for a meal – and you should – see p164 for recommended options. Take the Brown Line to Western and transfer to bus 49B.

the latter include serious resources like sex manuals for rape victims.

ALAMO SHOES Map p90 Shoes
☎ 773-784-8936; 5321 N Clark St; ◷ 9am-8pm Mon-Fri, to 6pm Sat, 10am-6pm Sun; Ⓜ Red Line to Berwyn
This throwback to the 1960s focuses on hip, comfortable shoes for men, women and children. Brands include Dansko, Ecco, Naot, Birkenstock, Keen and Dr Martens, all at good prices. The enthusiastic staffers hop off to the back room and emerge with stacks of boxes until you either find what you want or are entirely walled in by the possibilities.

WICKER PARK, BUCKTOWN & UKRAINIAN VILLAGE

Damen and Milwaukee Aves in Wicker Park are two of the city's best shopping drags. You'll find the more oddball, vintage and thrift shops residing on Milwaukee, while Damen holds a wealth of women's clothing boutiques. To the south, Division St near Damen Ave packs in young designer, children's and crafters' stores.

BEADNIKS Map pp96-7 Arts & Crafts
☎ 773-276-2323; www.beadniks.com/chicago; 1937 W Division St; Ⓜ Blue Line to Division
Incense envelops you at the door, and you know right away you're in for a hippie treat. Mounds of worldly baubles rise up from the tables. African trade beads and Thai silver-dipped beads? Got 'em. Bright-hued stone beads, ceramic beads, glass beads? All present. For $3 the kindly staff will help you string your choices into a necklace. Or take a workshop (two to three hours, $20 to $60) and learn to wield the pliers yourself; they take place most evenings throughout the week. The website has the schedule.

GREENHEART SHOP Map pp96-7 Arts & Crafts
☎ 312-264-1625; 1911 W Division St; Ⓜ Blue Line to Division
This nonprofit, ecofriendly, fair-trade store stocks chocolate from Ghana, banana-fiber

stationery from Uganda, rubber soccer balls from Pakistan and organic cotton baby clothes from, well, Chicago. There's much more, all part of the Center for Cultural Interchange's project that ensures fair wages to artisans.

HANDMADE MARKET Map pp96-7 Arts & Crafts
☎ 773-276-3600; 1035 N Western Ave; ☽ noon-4pm Oct-Apr; 🚌 49
Held the second Saturday of the month at the Empty Bottle (p193), this event showcases Chicago crafters who make funky glass pendants, knitted items, handbags, scarves, journals and greeting cards. The bar serves drinks throughout the event, for those who enjoy sipping while shopping.

RENEGADE HANDMADE
Map pp96-7   Arts & Crafts
☎ 773-227-2707; www.renegadehandmade.com; 1924 W Division St; Ⓜ Blue Line to Division
This store sprung up out of a popular local craft fair. Rather than just selling their goods for two days per year, participants thought it would be a swell idea to have an outlet to sell from year-round. Bravo! The reasonably priced merchandise veers toward mod, such as boho tops, graphic-print guitar straps, journals reconstructed from vintage hardback cookbooks and shadow puppets (why not, eh?).

MYOPIC BOOKS Map pp96-7 Bookstore
☎ 773-862-4882; www.myopicbookstore.com; 1564 N Milwaukee Ave; ☽ 11am-1am Mon-Sat, to 10pm Sun; Ⓜ Blue Line to Damen
Sunlight pours through the windows at Myopic, one of the city's oldest and largest used bookstores. It rambles through three floors, serves coffee and hosts poetry readings (usually on Sunday evenings) and experimental music (on Monday evenings). In other words, it's perfect.

QUIMBY'S Map pp96-7 Bookstore
☎ 773-342-0910; www.quimbys.com; 1854 W North Ave; ☽ noon-9pm Mon-Thu, to 10pm Fri, 11am-10pm Sat, noon-7pm Sun; Ⓜ Blue Line to Damen
The epicenter of Chicago's comic and zine worlds, Quimby's is one of the linchpins of underground culture in the city. Here you can find everything from crayon-powered punk-rock manifestos to slickly produced graphic novels. It's a groovy place for

cheeky literary souvenirs and bizarro readings.

AKIRA Map pp96-7 Clothing & Accessories
☎ 773-489-0818; 1814 W North Ave; Ⓜ Blue Line to Damen
Several fashion design students work here, manning (or woman-ing, to be precise) the denim bar, which is stocked with more than 20 different brands of jeans. There's a focus on up-and-coming and newly popular lines. This particular location is women-oriented, but two other Akira shops – one for men's clothing and one for shoes – hover on the same block.

FREE PEOPLE Map pp96-7 Clothing & Accessories
☎ 773-227-4871; 1464 N Milwaukee Ave; Ⓜ Blue Line to Damen
Owned by the same parent company as Urban Outfitters (young hipster styles) and Anthropologie (older feminine styles), Free People lands in the middle with boho-chic tank tops, cardigan sweaters, herringbone jackets and patterned dresses.

MS CATWALK Map pp96-7 Clothing & Accessories
☎ 773-235-2750; www.mscatwalk.com; 2042 N Damen Ave; ☽ closed Mon; Ⓜ Blue Line to Damen
Ms Catwalk stocks fun, flirty clothing and garnishes for women. T-shirts feature images from Buddha to Supergirl to Junior Mints candies; hoodies, low-rise corduroy pants and big silvery bags accessorize your selection.

PENELOPE'S Map pp96-7 Clothing & Accessories
☎ 773-395-2351; www.shoppenelopes.com; 1913 W Division St; Ⓜ Blue Line to Division
Named after the owners' ridiculously cute pug, Penelope's is a warm boutique for 20- and 30-somethings. It offers both men's and women's fashions (they're new but look thrift-store bought) along with housewares, jewelry and nifty gifty things.

T-SHIRT DELI Map pp96-7 Clothing & Accessories
☎ 773-276-6266; www.tshirtdeli.com; 1739 N Damen Ave; Ⓜ Blue Line to Damen
They take the 'deli' part seriously: after they cook (ie iron a retro design on) your T-shirt, they wrap it in butcher paper and serve it to you with potato chips. Choose from heaps of shirt styles and decals, of which Mao, Sean Connery, Patty Hearst

RETRO CHIC CHICAGO

Much to the chagrin of fashion-forward metropolises New York City and Los Angeles, Chicago is fashion backward, and proud of it. Place the blame – or praise, as the case may be – on its denizens' thrifty Midwestern sensibilities. Folks here don't throw out their old bowling shirts, pillbox hats, faux-fur coats and costume jewelry. Instead, they deposit used duds at vintage or secondhand stores, of which there are hundreds. These places provide a shopping bonanza for bargain seekers patient enough to comb through the racks. The payoff is when you find that perfect 'My Name is Bob' gas station attendant work shirt or chestnut-colored fake mouton coat – both for $5.

For those less patient, several stores have popped up that offer retro-style clothes, but you'll be the first one to wear them.

Lake View, Wicker Park and Bucktown present the most fertile hunting grounds for retro chic styles. We recommend:

- Strange Cargo (p136)
- T-Shirt Deli (p139)
- Una Mae's Freak Boutique (below)
- US #1 (below)

and a red-white-and-blue bong are but the beginning.

UNA MAE'S FREAK BOUTIQUE

Map pp96-7   Clothing & Accessories
☎ 773-276-7002; 1528 N Milwaukee Ave; ⏱ noon-8pm Mon-Fri, 11am-8pm Sat, noon-7pm Sun; Ⓜ Blue Line to Damen
It's unlikely that the solid suburban women who once wore the pillbox hats and fine Republican cloth coats on sale here would ever have thought of themselves as freaks. Along with the vintage wear, Una Mae's has a growing collection of new, cool-cat designer duds and accessories for both men and women.

US #1 Map pp96-7   Clothing & Accessories
☎ 773-489-9428; 1460 N Milwaukee Ave; ⏱ noon-7pm; Ⓜ Blue Line to Damen
From the outside this place looks not so chic. Inside, however, you'll find rack after rack of vintage '70s bowling, Hawaiian and western-wear shirts, as well as towers of old Levi's and designer jeans. The owner knows his stuff, and merch quality is high (though so are some of the prices).

VIVE LA FEMME

Map pp96-7   Clothing & Accessories
☎ 773-772-7429; www.vivelafemme.com; 2048 N Damen Ave; Ⓜ Blue Line to Damen
Plus-size shops for women are often woefully lacking in style. Not so at Vive La Femme, where larger women can find sassy and classy designs in sizes 12 to 24.

PAPER DOLL Map pp96-7   Gifts
☎ 773-227-6950; 2048 W Division St; ⏱ closed Mon; Ⓜ Blue Line to Damen
Stationery rules the house at Paper Doll, and many a Wicker Park thriftster has ordered her wedding cards from the mod assortment on hand. Then, a few years later, she orders her baby announcements from the shop. Kitschy gifts round out the inventory, and eventually that same woman returns to buy *The Three Martini Play Date* book.

DUSTY GROOVE Map pp96-7   Music Store
☎ 773-342-5800; www.dustygroove.com; 1120 N Ashland Ave; ⏱ 10am-8pm; Ⓜ Blue Line to Division
Old-school soul, Brazilian beats, Hungarian disco, bass-stabbing hip-hop – if it's funky, Dusty Groove (which also has its own record label) stocks it. Flip through stacks of vinyl, or get lost amid the tidy shop's CDs. Be sure to check out the dollar bin.

RECKLESS RECORDS Map pp96-7   Music Store
☎ 773-235-3727; 1532 N Milwaukee Ave; ⏱ 10am-10pm Mon-Sat, to 8pm Sun; Ⓜ Blue Line to Damen
Chicago's best indie-rock record and CD emporium allows you to listen to everything before you buy. It's certainly the place to get your finger on the pulse of the local, *au courant* underground scene. There's another outlet in the Loop at 26 E Madison St.

CITY SOLE/NICHE Map pp96-7 Shoes
☎ 773-489-2001; 2001 W North Ave; ⏱ 10am-7pm Mon-Wed, to 8pm Thu & Fri, to 7pm Sat, 11am-6pm Sun; Ⓜ Blue Line to Damen

One of the hippest men's and women's shoe stores in Chicago is divided into two sections. Niche is where high-priced designs dwell, and City Sole is its more down-to-earth cousin. Together they service the neighborhood: punks, young housewives and old Polish women alike.

JOHN FLUEVOG SHOES Map pp96-7 Shoes
☎ 773-772-1983; 1539-1541 N Milwaukee Ave; Ⓜ Blue Line to Damen

Bold and colorful shoes by the eccentric designer are the order of the day at this close-out haven. They come as tough-girl chunky or sex-kitten pointy as you like, and there are equally hip selections for men.

UPRISE SKATEBOARDS Map pp96-7 Sportswear
☎ 773-342-7763; 1820 N Milwaukee Ave; Ⓜ Blue Line to Western

Looking for a Street Sweeper or a pair of Lakais? Uprise is the city's top spot for skateboarders to pick up gear, boards and tips on the local scene. Drop in for a rad T-shirt and to find out where the action is. No attitude here: they're friendly and patient with newbies.

BORING STORE Map pp96-7 Toy Shop
☎ 773-772-8108; 1331 N Milwaukee Ave; ⏱ noon-6pm; Ⓜ Blue Line to Division

The big orange sign out front will have you scratching your head, but do yourself a favor and step inside (don't worry, those 25 surveillance cameras pointed at you are harmless). The place sells crazy-ass spy gear! Mustache disguise kits, underwater voice amplifiers, banana-shaped cases to hide your cell phone in – it's genius. And better yet: profits from sales go toward supporting the after-school writing and tutoring programs that take place on-site at nonprofit group 826CHI.

RED BALLOON CO Map pp96-7 Toy Shop
☎ 773-489-9800; 2060 N Damen Ave; Ⓜ Blue Line to Damen

When hipsters get good jobs and start having kids, this is where they outfit the li'l pups. Adorable clothes, classic children's books and '50s-style wooden block toys prevail in the cozy space.

LOGAN SQUARE & HUMBOLDT PARK

There are not a lot of shops in these neighborhoods, but the stores that are here make up for it in fashionable quality.

WOLFBAIT & B-GIRLS
Map p100 Arts & Crafts
☎ 312-698-8685; www.wolfbaitchicago.com; 3131 W Logan Blvd; ⏱ 10am-7pm Tue-Sat, to 4pm Sun; Ⓜ Blue Line to Logan Square

Old ironing boards serve as display tables; tape measures, scissors and other designers'

CRAFTY CHICAGO

A wave of craftiness has washed over the city, thanks to the success of the Indie Designer Fashion Market (inside the massive Randolph Street Market, p142). Now everyone is opening a store or studio proffering handbags, pendants, scarves and journals that they've stitched, sewed, beaded and glue-gunned themselves. It's great news for shoppers as the items are locally made, often using recycled materials, and they're unique. What's more, many crafters teach how to do it yourself (DIY) via low-key, low-cost workshops on fabric printing, knitting and the like.

Wicker Park is ground zero for the DIY explosion, particularly Division St. Good shops citywide include the following:

- Beadniks (p138)
- Handmade Market (p139)
- Loopy Yarns (p143)
- Renegade Handmade (p139)
- Wolfbait & B-girls (above)
- Andersonville Galleria (p137)

tools hang from vintage hooks. You get that crafting feeling as soon as you walk in, and indeed, Wolfbait & B-girls both sells the wares (tops, dresses, handbags and jewelry) of local indie designers and serves as a working studio for them. Take a fabric book-binding workshop (two hours, $30, materials and drinks included), and who knows? Maybe your stuff will be for sale soon, too.

NEAR WEST SIDE & PILSEN

Ethnic shops and antique markets percolate through the Near West Side neighborhood. Gallery lovers should check out the West Loop's scene (see p103). Pilsen also has galleries (see p108), mostly along Halsted St, while 18th St holds scores of small Mexican shops with a few funky vintage shops tucked in around the edges.

BARBARA'S BOOKSTORE

Map pp104–5   Bookstore
☎ 312-413-2665; www.barbarasbookstore.com; 1218 S Halsted St; 🚍 8
For serious fiction, you can't touch this locally owned chain. Staff members have read what they sell, and touring authors regularly give readings.

WORKSHOP Map pp104–5   Clothing & Accessories
☎ 312-226-9000; 818 W 18th St; 11am–6pm Fri–Sun; 🚍 8
Local designer Annie Novotny of Frei Designs has her workshop in this Pilsen storefront. She's made the front half into a store that sells her skirts, tops and dresses (all made with ecofriendly dyes and fabrics) as well as jewelry and housewares from other ecominded makers. Check out the beeswax candles from the Chicago Honey Co-Op. She also uses the space for occasional sewing classes.

BLOMMER CHOCOLATE STORE

Map pp104–5   Food & Drink
☎ 312-492-1336; 600 W Kinzie St; 🕑 9am–5pm Mon–Fri, to 1pm Sat; Ⓜ Blue Line to Grand
Often in the Loop, a smell wafts through that's so enticing you'd shoot your own mother in the kneecaps to get to it. It comes from Blommer Chocolate Factory, which provides the sweet stuff to big-time

manufacturers such as Fannie May and Nabisco. Luckily, the wee outlet store sells a line of Blommer's own goodies straight to consumers at cut-rate prices. The dark-chocolate-covered almonds reign supreme, and there's a sweet selection of retro candies like Zots, Pop Rocks and Zagnut bars.

OPRAH STORE Map pp104–5   Gifts
☎ 312-633-2100; 37 N Carpenter St; 🕑 10am–5:30pm Mon–Sat, noon–4pm Sun; Ⓜ Green, Pink Line to Clinton or 🚍 20
Located next to Oprah's studio, the shop is filled with her favorite things. Pick up a passion journal, a 'live your own dreams' coffee cup or a pair of Manolo Blahnik pumps – just like Oprah wears! Handicrafts from Africa also brighten the shelves. Celeb photos line the walls, along with mounted TVs re-running O's shows.

MAXWELL STREET MARKET

Map pp104–5   Market
on S Desplaines St btwn Harrison St & Roosevelt Rd; admission free; 🕑 7am–3pm Sun; Ⓜ Blue Line to Clinton
Every Sunday morning hundreds of vendors set up stalls that sell everything from Jesus statues to 10 packs of tube socks to power tools. Don't let the name mislead you: the market is not actually on Maxwell St, though it was for decades until gentrification forced it onward. It has become a hot spot for foodies craving homemade churros, tamales, gorditas and other Mexican noshes, and for folks seeking cheap clothing, electronics and junk galore. The city now runs the market, and it's supposed to be bringing back live blues bands, which were a feature back in the old days.

RANDOLPH STREET MARKET

Map pp104–5   Market
www.randolphstreetmarket.com; 1350 W Randolph St; admission $12; 🕑 10am–5pm Sat, to 4pm Sun, last weekend of the month; 🚍 20
This market, which styles itself on London's Portobello Market, has become quite the to-do in town. It takes place inside the beaux-arts Plumbers Hall, where more than 200 antique dealers hock collectibles, costume jewelry, furniture, books, Turkish rugs and pinball machines. One of the coolest facets is the Indie Designer Fashion Market, where the city's fledgling designers sell their one-of-a-kind skirts,

top picks

MARKET TRAWLING

- Green City Market (p157) The premier farmers' market.
- Maxwell Street Market (opposite) Historic market for socks and hubcaps, now known for its Mexican food stalls.
- Randolph Street Market (opposite) Antiques galore for a $12 admission fee.
- Handmade Market (p139) Monthly DIY crafters' fair held at a bar.
- French Market (p148) Euro-style, with artisanal meats, cheeses, pastries and prepared foods.

shawls, handbags and other pieces. In summer the action spills into the street. A free trolley picks up patrons at Water Tower Place hourly. Note there are no markets in January, April, October and December.

GROOVE DISTRIBUTION

Map pp104-5   Music Store

☎ 312-997-2375; www.groovedis.com; 346 N Justine St; ☻ noon-7pm Tue-Thu, to 9pm Fri, to 3pm Sun; Ⓜ Green, Pink Line to Ashland

Whenever you're at a club, dancing to the beat, Groove is likely the source of the music. The company provides record stores around the world with downtempo, mashups, dubstep, nu jazz, cosmic disco and lotsa that Chicago specialty – house – both on vinyl and CD. You can shop right in their warehouse, which is exactly what discerning DJs do.

ATHENIAN CANDLE CO

Map pp104-5   Religious Items

☎ 312-332-6988; 300 S Halsted St; ☻ closed Wed & Sun; Ⓜ Blue Line to UIC/Halsted

Whether you're hoping to get lucky at bingo, remove a jinx or fall in love, this store promises to help with its array of candles, incense, love potions and miracle oils. Though they've been making candles for the city's Orthodox churches on-site since 1919, the owners aren't devoted to one religion: you'll find Buddha statues, Pope holograms, Turkish evil-eye stones, tarot cards and door *mezuzahs* (parchment inscribed with Hebrew verses from the Torah). Unlike other stores of the ilk, which can be creepy, Athenian is tidy and the staff amiable.

SOUTH LOOP & NEAR SOUTH SIDE

Most of the neighborhood's shopping options are in Chinatown, which sells the same things as every Chinatown the world over: inexpensive groceries and housewares, Hello Kitty trinkets and all the Buddhist altar goods the ancestors require. It makes an entertaining shopping spree post–dim sum or other noodle-y meal. Trendy fashion boutiques are starting to pop up in SoLo (aka South Loop to hipsters).

LOOPY YARNS Map pp112-13   Arts & Crafts

☎ 312-583-9276; www.loopyyarns.com; 47 W Polk St; Ⓜ Red Line to Harrison

This isn't your grandma's knitting shop. Loopy Yarns caters mostly to students from the nearby Art Institute, so the books, patterns, needles, hooks and designer yarns are about as hip as they come. Beginners can learn to knit or crochet in a workshop (two hours, $70 to $90, materials included), while advanced practitioners can learn more complex techniques while making a fair-isle hat or flip-top mittens (two hours, $20 to $60, materials not included). Check the website for the schedule.

SHOPCOLUMBIA Map pp112-13   Arts & Crafts

☎ 312-369-8616; 1st fl, 623 S Wabash Ave; ☻ 11am-5pm Mon-Wed & Fri, to 7pm Thu; Ⓜ Red Line to Harrison

This is Columbia College's student store, where artists and designers in training learn how to market their wares. The shop carries original pieces spanning all media and disciplines: clothes, jewelry, prints, mugs, stationery and more. Proceeds help individual students earn income, and part goes toward student scholarships.

AJI ICHIBAN Map pp112-13   Food & Drink

☎ 312-328-9998; 2117-A S China Pl, Chinatown Sq Mall; Ⓜ Red Line to Cermak-Chinatown

The front sign at this Asian snack and candy store says 'Munchies Paradise,' and so it is. Sweet and salty treats fill the bulk bins, from dried salted plums to chocolate wafer cookies, roasted fish crisps to fruity hard candies. It's all packaged in cool, cartoony wrappers, with plenty of samples out for grabs.

TEN REN TEA & GINSENG CO
Map pp112-13   Food & Drink
☎ 312-842-1171; 2247 S Wentworth Ave; Ⓜ Red Line to Cermak-Chinatown
Ten Ren is *the* place to buy green, red, white and black teas, plus the teacups and teapots to serve them in. They also sell thirst-quenching bubble teas at the counter.

GIFTLAND Map pp112-13   Gifts
☎ 312-225-0088; 2212 S Wentworth Ave; Ⓜ Red Line to Cermak-Chinatown
After you see it, you'll wonder how you've lived without it: a toast-scented Hello Kitty eraser. Giftland stocks a swell supply of pens, stationery, coin purses and backpacks donning the images of Kitty as well as Mashimaro, Pucca, Doraemon and other Asian cartoon characters.

HOYPOLOI Map pp112-13   Housewares
☎ 312-225-6477; 2235 S Wentworth Ave; Ⓜ Red Line to Cermak-Chinatown
Hoypoloi is more upscale than most Chinatown stores – it's actually a gallery filled with Asian artwork, glassware, funky lamps and other interior items. The wind-chime selection wins kudos.

WOKS N THINGS Map pp112-13   Housewares
☎ 312-842-0701; 2234 S Wentworth Ave; Ⓜ Red Line to Cermak-Chinatown
This busy store carries every kind of utensil and cookware you could want – pots, pans, wok brushes, knives. Don't miss the baseball-bat-shaped chopstick holders.

BUDDHIST TEMPLE GIFT
SHOP Map pp112-13   Religious Items
☎ 312-881-0177; 2249 S Wentworth Ave; Ⓜ Red Line to Cermak-Chinatown
Follow your nose into this quiet, incense-wafting storefront to contemplate charms and necklaces (for good luck and happiness), books on how to meditate, Buddha statues and other spiritual items.

HOUSE OF SOLE Map pp112-13   Shoes
☎ 312-834-0909; 1237 S Michigan Ave; ◷ noon-7pm Mon, 11am-8pm Tue-Sat, noon-6pm Sun; Ⓜ Red, Green, Orange Line to Roosevelt

It's not big, but this chic boutique carries an excellent array of mostly European women's brand shoes. The owner knows her straps, heels and trends, and the well-curated selection sends shoe divas swooning.

HYDE PARK & SOUTH SIDE
Bibliophiles should hop on the next Metra train to Hyde Park to check out the great selection of bookstores around the University of Chicago campus.

57TH STREET BOOKS Map p120   Bookstore
☎ 773-684-1300; 1301 E 57th St; ◷ 10am-8pm; Ⓜ Metra to 55th-56th-57th
A serious university demands a serious bookstore, and as you descend the stairs to this basement-level shop you'll know you're in the right place. Its labyrinth of low-slung rooms makes up the kind of old-fashioned bookstore that goes way deeper than the popular titles. It has excellent staff picks and an exhaustive travel section. Seminary Co-op is the sister shop selling academic tomes.

POWELL'S Map p120   Bookstore
☎ 773-955-7780; 1501 E 57th St; ◷ 9am-11pm; Ⓜ Metra to 55th-56th-57th
This leading store for used books can get you just about any title ever published. Shelf after heaving shelf prop up the well-arranged stock. Another outlet is located in Lake View (Map pp86-7; ☎ 773-248-1444; 2850 N Lincoln Ave).

SEMINARY COOPERATIVE
BOOKSTORE Map p120   Bookstore
☎ 773-752-4381; 5757 S University Ave; ◷ 8:30am-8pm Mon-Fri, 10am-6pm Sat, noon-6pm Sun; Ⓜ Metra to 55th-56th-57th
This is the bookstore of choice for several University of Chicago Nobel Prize winners, including Robert Fogel, who says, 'For a scholar, it's one of the great bookstores of the world.' The shop is owned by the same folks as 57th St Books. It's planning a move (down the block to 5751 S Woodlawn Ave) at the end of 2011.

top picks

- Kuma's Corner (p169)
- Xoco (p153)
- Hot Doug's (p170)
- Handlebar (p165)
- Bonsoiree (p168)
- Giordano's (p152)
- Sweet Maple Cafe (p172)
- Chilam Balam (p159)
- Borinquen Restaurant (p169)
- Hoosier Mama Pie Company (p168)

EATING

For years epicures wrote off Chicago as a culinary backwater. Then a funny thing happened: the city won a heap of James Beard awards, and foodie magazines like *Saveur* ranked it as the nation's top restaurant scene.

So get ready: from $225, 24-course meals of 'molecular gastronomy' (more on that later) to $3 pizza slices, from Nepalese dumplings to Cuban sandwiches, from porterhouse steaks to locavore salads, Chicago serves up a plateful.

Perhaps no restaurant sums up the city's whimsical, unpretentious culinary identity as well as Hot Doug's. A humble place located in an out-of-the-way neighborhood, it serves that most quintessential of Chicago dishes: the hot dog. But in this case it's a foie gras and sauternes duck sausage 'dog' with truffle-sauce mustard and foie gras mousse – a tasty, deliriously rich clash of high culture and low, at once traditional and visionary. That's Chicago dining.

Plenty of meat gets carved in the city, a lasting legacy from when Chicago was 'hog butcher for the world.' Steak houses are a dime a dozen downtown, and new restaurants with char-cuterie menus seem to open weekly. That's not to say vegetarians don't get their due. Several restaurants in town are exclusively veggie, including an increasing number of upscale options (see our top veg picks on p161). Locavore fare has come into its own too, and many places source from nearby Midwestern farms and Chicago's Green City Market (p157).

'Molecular gastronomy' is the thing that really weakens foodies' knees, though. A dynamic vanguard of Chicago chefs has helmed the growing trend – a catch-all term for an exciting approach to meal preparation that's more like a science experiment. (What exactly does a 'pillow of lavender air' taste like?) The refined tasting menu at Alinea (p156) is the premier example, and it is often shortlisted as North America's best restaurant.

If getting an authentic taste of the city ranks high on your agenda, break out of the Loop. Restaurant-rich neighborhoods in the Near North, Gold Coast and Wicker Park have a concentration of great eateries at their cores. Logan Square is off the beaten path, but delivers perhaps the most inventive fare of all (Hot Doug's is here, as are several other hot spots). If you're willing to trek further still, immigrant enclaves dish out Vietnamese *banh mi* (baguette sandwiches; Uptown), Mexican *mole* (sauce; Pilsen), Swedish pastries (Andersonville) and much more of the most affordable, genuine fare Chicago has to offer.

Also, if you're interested in bringing along that dusty bottle of Bordeaux – or washing down your pizza with something other than Old Style suds – you're in luck. Many Chicago restaurants have a bring your own beverage (BYOB) policy.

SPECIALTIES

Chicago cooks up three beloved specialties. Deep-dish pizza is foremost. These behemoths are nothing like the flat circular disks known by the same name in the rest of the world. Here they're made in a special pan – kind of like a frying pan without a handle – so the dough, which encases a molten bed of American-style mozzarella cheese and other typical ingredients, is oven fried. The flagship Pizzeria Uno (p152) claims to have invented it in the '40s, but this, like many other fanatical conversations about pizza in the Windy City, will inspire debate. See p152 for suggestions on where to try a slice.

No less iconic is the Chicago-style hot dog, a wiener that's been 'dragged through the garden.' See p154 for the hallmark ingredients of a true dog. And remember rule number one: no ketchup!

The third renowned Chicago specialty is the Italian beef sandwich, and it stacks up like this: thin-sliced, slow-cooked roast beef that's sopped in natural gravy and *giardiniera* (spicy pickled vegetables), then heaped on a hoagie roll. Local immigrants invented it as a low-budget way to feed factory workers in the late 1930s. Try it while you're here – Mr Beef (p153) makes a winner – because you'll be hard-pressed to find one elsewhere on the planet.

Less well known, but equally messy and delicious, is the *jibarito* sandwich, developed at a local Puerto Rican restaurant called Borinquen (p169). It consists of steak covered in garlicky mayo and served between thick, crispy-fried plantain slices, which form the 'bread.' Many restaurants in the Humboldt Park neighborhood have it on the menu.

Finally, we come to brunch, which is much more than a hybrid of breakfast and lunch in Chicago. It's a reverently regarded social event, and most big restaurants take it seriously – as do patrons, which is why lines twist out the door on weekends. For our picks, see p173 or check the Chicago Brunch Blog (www.chicagobrunchblog.com).

THE CITY OF CHAINS

It's strangely fitting that Ray Kroc opened the first McDonald's franchise restaurant in a Chicago 'burb: even top-flight Chicago restaurateurs love to expand their turf into multiple locations. Sometimes – as is the case with Giordano's (p152) and the high-class Taylor Street pasta shop Rosebud (p172) – it's a good thing. In general, though, secondary outlets of local franchises such as the Billy Goat Tavern (p153) are more like the unfortunate sequel to a great movie. When possible, stick with the original location (which we've tried to point out in the listings that follow).

FOOD MEDIA

Chicago is unimpressed by snooty food trends, so it follows that Chicagoans are a self-reliant bunch when it comes to picking where to eat. Case in point? The oft-discussed Check, Please! (www.wttw.com/checkplease), a local channel 11 TV program that sends dining citizens to restaurants across the spectrum to get their straightforward critiques. The show has been flooded with applications from would-be food critics by the tens of thousands – not shocking in a city where a discussion about pizza can end in fisticuffs. See for yourself what locals have to say in the show's entertaining video archives online.

The same instinct has yielded a number of successful websites that feature user reviews. See the boxed text Bytes For Your Bites (p175) for some of the best blogs, review sites and message boards to study before your visit.

PRACTICALITIES
Opening Hours

Most places that serve lunch open around 11am and stay open until 10pm, with fast-food chains and coffee shops opening around 7am and staying open until midnight. The busiest dinner hours are between 6:30pm and

top picks

EAT STREETS
Strike it rich along these well-endowed veins:
- Clark Street, Andersonville (Map p90) Nouveau Korean, home-style Japanese, traditional Belgian and sweet Swedish tempt in a half-mile stretch.
- Randolph Street, West Loop (Map pp104-5) Many of Chicago's best and brightest restaurateurs have set up shop at downtown's edge.
- Division Street, Wicker Park (Map pp96-7) Copious sidewalk seating spills out of hip bistros, sushi lounges and organic bakeries.
- Argyle Street, Uptown (Map p90) Thai and Vietnamese noodle houses steam up their windows along this little corridor.
- 18th Street, Pilsen (Map pp104-5) Taqueria follows taqueria, with barbecue and Mexican bakeries thrown in for good measure.
- Devon Avenue, Far North (Map pp50-1) It's a long haul, but the colorful Indian and Pakistani buffets are worth it.

8:30pm, the lunch rush is usually between 11:30am and 2pm, and breakfast tends to be served from 8am to 10am. On weekends you can get brunch until about 3pm. High-end restaurants in town might not serve lunch and are often closed on Sunday or Monday.

In the listings below, if we say a restaurant is open for 'lunch & dinner' that means it sticks to the typical 11am-to-10pm timeframe daily. If the restaurant's hours vary from this standard, we list them in their entirety. We also note if a restaurant is closed on particular days. Chicago is a late-night diners' paradise, especially on weekends, so see the Midnight Munchies boxed text (p168) for places to get a bite after last call.

How Much?

A sit-down lunch in Chicago will be about $15 per person, including a nonalcoholic drink and a tip. For dinner at a midrange restaurant, expect to pay around $30 per person, including a drink and a tip. Breakfast – say an omelet, hash browns and coffee – will set you back about $10.

If you're watching your budget, eat ethnic. The excellent options for Indian, Thai, Mexican or Chinese will save you money, as will sticking to Chicago's humble favorite: the hot dog.

The following restaurants are grouped by neighborhood and listed in descending price order, with the most expensive options first. Prices listed are for a main course at dinner, unless specified otherwise.

Booking Tables

The rule here is simple: when in doubt, call ahead. This is especially true of fancier places, but most of Chicago's restaurants get busy on the weekends. Certain places won't take a reservation for parties of fewer than four, and some take none at all. If your heart is set on a ballyhooed restaurant like Topolobampo or Alinea, you'll need to reserve six to eight weeks in advance.

Tipping

Adding a tip of 15% to the pretax bill has long been standard for adequate service, though outstanding service might call for as much as 20%. If the service made the meal worse, express your displeasure with a smaller tip; truly awful service warrants no tip and a discussion with the manager, which might be awkward, but may bring a reduced bill. If you're dining with parties of six or more, the gratuity, often as high as 18%, will be added automatically.

For counter service, as in inexpensive cafes or taquerias, there are no hard and fast rules, even with the tip jar prominently displayed. If someone delivers food to the table, it's kind to leave 10% in the tip jar, though takeout orders don't require a tip.

Valet parkers should get anywhere from $2 to $5 when they return your car.

Groceries

A nice summer day in Chicago begs for a picnic. For simple supplies of lunch meat and Wonder Bread (a Chicago original, by the way) find a ubiquitous Jewel (☎ 800-539-3561; www.jewelosco.com), though those with a slightly healthier bent might seek out a Whole Foods (Map pp66-7; ☎ 312-932-9600; 30 W Huron St). The

deli counters at Bari Foods (p168) and Fox & Obel (p152) are first-rate, as are the precooked delicacies at Charlie Trotter's To Go (Map pp78-9; 1337 W Fullerton Ave).

For fresher eats, try the city-sponsored farmers' markets that are common between May and October. Complete schedules can be found on the Chicago farmers' markets website (www.chicagofarmersmarkets.us).

THE LOOP

The Loop's dining scene closely mirrors the different groups you'll elbow past on the sidewalk: early morning coffee shops and lunch counters for office workers, nondescript chain restaurants for the less adventurous conventioneers and tourists, and high-dollar supper clubs that help ease executives through their thick expense accounts. Theatergoers who want to make it through dessert before the curtain rises should call ahead and inform waitstaff about the timeframe as soon as they sit down.

The French Market (Map pp54-5; www.frenchmarketchicago.com; 131 N Clinton St), located in the Ogilvie train station just west of the Loop proper, offers a graze-worthy option. Stalls serving Belgian fries, Montreal-style smoked-meat sandwiches, artisan breads and cheeses, pastries and organic fruits and vegetables stuff the aisles in a Euro-style hall with tables.

RHAPSODY Map pp54-5   American $$
☎ 312-786-9911; 65 E Adams St; mains $19-28; ☻ lunch Mon-Fri, dinner Tue-Sun; Ⓜ Brown, Orange, Green, Purple, Pink Line to Adams
Adjacent to Symphony Center, Rhapsody's dining room opens to a lovely garden – perfect for regaining your strength after a visit to the Art Institute, or dining early before some Mahler. Menu highlights include the herb-crusted halibut and succulent beef tenderloin, with chocolate tart or a flight of five ice cream flavors for dessert. You can always just pop in for a drink and a snack in the lounge.

GAGE Map pp54-5   American $$
☎ 312-372-4243; 24 S Michigan Ave; mains $17-32; ☻ 11am-11pm Mon-Fri, from 10am Sat & Sun; Ⓜ Brown, Orange, Green, Purple, Pink Line to Madison
It's clear from the formidable Scotch egg – a sausage-encased, deep-fried, hard-boiled beast with the girth of a softball – that this

elegant, Irish-tinged gastro pub is serious about its menu. Standards include the Camembert-topped Gage burger ($16, but worth it) and Guinness-battered fish and chips, while more exotic options include roast saddle of elk and barbecue lamb shanks. Ask the knowledgeable servers which beers from the well-curated list best accompany your food. Note the bar stays open later, usually until 2am.

TRATTORIA NO 10 Map pp54-5   Italian $$
☎ 312-984-1718; 10 N Dearborn St; mains $17-29; ❤ lunch Mon-Fri, dinner Mon-Sat; Ⓜ Blue Line to Washington

An ideal stop for ticket holders, this lively bistro is just steps from the Loop theater district. The straightforward menu provides exceptionally flavorful takes on familiar items like ravioli (try the one filled with asparagus tip, *bufala* cheese, and sun-dried tomatoes) and risotto with skirt steak.

LOU MITCHELL'S Map pp54-5   Breakfast $
☎ 312-939-3111; 565 W Jackson Blvd; mains $6-11; ❤ 5:30am-3pm Mon-Sat, 7am-3pm Sun; Ⓜ Blue Line to Clinton

A relic of old Route 66 (it's located a few blocks west of the road's starting point), Lou's coffee shop brings in elbow-to-elbow tourists for breakfast. The omelets hang off the plates, and the fluffy flapjacks and crisp waffles are prepared with practiced perfection. Cups of coffee are bottomless, just like

---

CHICAGO'S CULINARY ROCK STARS

These are the internationally renowned local chefs doing crazy – and crazy-good – stuff with their food.

Rick Bayless He's everywhere: on TV, cooking at the White House, tending the organic garden where he grows the restaurants' herbs, and tending Xoco (p153) and Topolobampo/Frontera Grill (p150).

Grant Achatz He made 'molecular gastronomy' a culinary catchphrase at Alinea (p156).

Graham Elliot He's the tattooed contrarian of the group, turning the usual rules upside down at his restaurant Graham Elliot (p150).

Charlie Trotter He's the rightful father of Chicago's *nouvelle* scene and has been cooking in the style since the 1980s at elegant Charlie Trotter's (p156).

---

the charm of the old-school waiters, who hand out free treats (doughnut holes, ice cream, Milk Duds) to young and old alike.

SAIGON SISTERS Map pp54-5   Vietnamese $
☎ 312-496-0094; 131 N Clinton St; mains $6-8; ❤ 10am-7:30pm Mon-Fri, to 6pm Sat; Ⓜ Green, Pink Line to Clinton

They are indeed two sisters, and they ladle out Vietnamese *pho* (noodle soup) and *banh mi* (baguette sandwiches) in the French Market in the Ogilvie train station. Eclectic creations include the Frenchman (a sandwich of duck confit, candied kumquat and smoked paprika mayonnaise) and the Sun Tanned Cow (with coconut-milk-braised beef ribs, lime leaves and ginger).

OASIS Map pp54-5   Middle Eastern $
☎ 312-443-9534; 21 N Wabash Ave; mains $5-8; ❤ 10am-5pm Mon-Fri, 11am-3pm Sat; Ⓜ Brown, Orange, Green, Purple, Pink Line to Madison

Walk past diamonds, gold and other bling in the jewelers' mall before striking it rich at the cafe in back. Creamy hummus, crisp falafel and other Middle Eastern favorites fill plates at bargain prices. Eat in or carry out to nearby Millennium Park.

CAFECITO Map pp54-5   Latin American $
☎ 312-922-2233; 26 E Congress Pkwy; sandwiches $4-6; ❤ 6am-9pm Mon-Fri, 10am-6pm Sat & Sun; Ⓜ Brown, Orange, Purple, Pink Line to Library

Attached to the hostel and perfect for the hungry, thrifty traveler, Cafecito serves killer Cuban sandwiches layered with citrus-garlic-marinated roasted pork and ham. Strong coffee and hearty egg sandwiches make a fine breakfast. There's free wi-fi; ask at the counter for the password.

NEAR NORTH & NAVY PIER

Flush with tourists, conventioneers and high-rise dwellers, the Near North provides a huge concentration of restaurants to make sure no one goes hungry. Long-standing steak and sea-food houses do the honors alongside French bistros and sceney Asian eateries. You'll catch a whiff of Chicago's acclaimed pizza on nearly every block. Hot-dog and Italian beef shacks waft their scents into the air too.

The options at Navy Pier are less varied, and visitors who plan to dine there will likely leave with a stomach full of McDonald's or other chain-restaurant fare. One alternative is to bring a picnic from nearby Fox & Obel (p152).

TRU Map pp66-7 French $$$

☎ 312-202-0001; 676 N St Clair St; set menus $95-280; ⏲ dinner Mon-Sat; Ⓜ Red Line to Chicago
Rick Tramonto and *Food Network* sweetie Gale Gand opened Tru in 1999, and it's still considered one of the city's best (though Tramonto departed for new ventures in 2010). The French prix fixe menu (from three courses on up) is equally artful and capricious, with highly seasonal offerings, a renowned cheese course and brilliant desserts. As you might expect by the price, the service is ace and a jacket is required for men. Getting a nibble doesn't have to break the bank, though; all prix fixe items are available à la carte in the adjoining lounge.

CHICAGO CHOP HOUSE

Map pp66-7 Steak House $$$
☎ 312-787-7100; 60 W Ontario St; mains $50-100; ⏲ dinner; Ⓜ Red Line to Grand
In the proud tradition of Chicago chops, this comfortable, upscale, independently owned steak house is king. Look forward to perfectly cured meats hand cut on-site, and an atmosphere befitting the city's famous politicos and mob bosses – many of whom look down from framed portraits lining the walls. If you're not up for a slab of meat, you can always pop in to the piano bar and sample the 600-strong wine list.

NOMI Map pp66-7 Fusion $$$

☎ 312-239-4030; 800 N Michigan Ave; mains $35-48; ⏲ breakfast, lunch & dinner; Ⓜ Red Line to Chicago
NoMi is perched on the 7th floor of the Park Hyatt hotel, offering a sleek, art-filled interior and spectacular views over the Magnificent Mile. Dishes combining French fare with Asian flair range from Maine lobster to sushi to black-truffle risotto. Reserve a window table around sunset – it's one of the most romantic experiences that Chicago has to offer. Reservations are required.

TOPOLOBAMPO/FRONTERA GRILL

Map pp66-7 Mexican $$$
☎ 312-661-1434; 445 N Clark St; Topolo mains $35-39, Frontera mains $18-29; ⏲ lunch Tue-Fri, dinner Tue-Sat, brunch Sat; Ⓜ Red Line to Grand
Perhaps you've seen chef-owner Rick Bayless

on TV, stirring up pepper sauces and other jump-off-the-tongue Mexican creations. His isn't your typical taco menu; Bayless uses seasonal, sustainable ingredients for his wood-grilled meats, flavor-packed *mole* sauces, chili-thickened braises and signature margaritas. Though they share the same entrance, Frontera Grill and Topolobampo are actually two separate restaurants: Frontera is the fun, sunny, informal room, while Topolobampo is sleeker with more elegant fare (it's President Obama's favorite eatery; he and the first lady prefer table 65). Both places are always packed. Frontera takes some reservations but mostly seats on a first-come basis. Definitely reserve in advance for Topolobampo (six to eight weeks beforehand recommended). Bayless also operates the lower-priced Xoco next door.

GENE & GEORGETTI

Map pp66-7 Steak House $$$
☎ 312-527-3718; 500 N Franklin St; mains $27-45; ⏲ lunch & dinner Mon-Sat; Ⓜ Brown, Purple Line to Merchandise Mart
For once, a place touting itself as one of Frank Sinatra's favorite restaurants can back it up – a fact evidenced in the framed pic of Ol' Blue Eyes by the door. Old-timers, politicos and crusty regulars are seated downstairs. New-timers, conventioneers and tourists are seated upstairs. The steaks are the same on both levels: thick, well aged and well priced.

GRAHAM ELLIOT

Map pp66-7 New American $$$
☎ 312-624-9975; 217 W Huron St; mains $27-35; ⏲ dinner Mon-Sat; Ⓜ Brown, Purple Line to Chicago
Each meal starts with insanely addictive truffle-oil-and-Parmesan popcorn. Chef Graham Elliot, one of Chicago's young-buck gastro luminaries, then takes whimsy to new levels in such dishes as his foie gras lollypop coated in Pop Rocks and sweetbread hush puppies with anise slaw. Adventurous eaters who appreciate trendy food in an industrial, rock-and-roll atmosphere will like it most. Keep an eye out for his forthcoming sandwich shop.

SHAW'S CRAB HOUSE

Map pp66-7 Seafood $$$
☎ 312-527-2722; 21 E Hubbard St; mains $22-55; ⏲ lunch Mon-Fri, dinner daily, brunch Sun; Ⓜ Red Line to Grand

Shaw's beautiful old dining room and adjoining lounge have an elegant, historic feel, complemented by dark woods and the occasional jazz combo. The efficient servers can tell you what menu selections are freshest, as well as provide a 'sustainable seafood' menu. A crab cake appetizer and key lime pie dessert make faultless bookends to any meal.

SUNDA Map pp66-7   Asian $$
☎ 312-644-0500; 110 W Illinois St; mains $18-32; ◷ lunch Mon-Fri, dinner daily, brunch Sun; Ⓜ Red Line to Grand

When celebrities and star athletes come to town, they beeline to Sunda. Nicole Richie, A-Rod, Jamie Foxx and other scenesters glam it up while swirling specialty cocktails and forking into pan-Asian dishes and sushi, set against a backdrop of black lacquered wood and travertine marble. Make reservations a few weeks in advance for prime-time weekend dinner.

CYRANO'S BISTROT Map pp66-7   French $$
☎ 312-467-0546; 546 N Wells St; mains $18-24; ◷ dinner Mon-Sat; Ⓜ Brown, Purple Line to Merchandise Mart

Chef and owner Didier Durand shares a hometown with literature's Cyrano de Bergerac, for whom he named his casual French restaurant. A very cheerful place, Cyrano's serves a menu of southern French favorites, including numerous roasted meats. A few tables line the street and make a good place to sip one of the many wines on offer while watching the after-work hordes march home.

BANDERA Map pp66-7   American $$
☎ 312-644-3524; 535 N Michigan Ave; mains $16-27; ◷ lunch & dinner; Ⓜ Red Line to Grand

Looking up at the entry to this 2nd-story restaurant on Michigan Ave, you'd have no idea of the gem that waits inside. The red-bedecked Bandera has the comfortable retro feel of an expensive supper club, without the snooty waiters (and at half the price). American classics – meat loaf, grilled fish and rotisserie chicken – predominate here. When you've shopped till you've dropped, this is the place to come pick yourself back up again.

NACIONAL 27 Map pp66-7   Latin American $$
☎ 312-664-2727; 325 W Huron St; mains $15-23; ◷ dinner Mon-Sat; Ⓜ Brown, Purple Line to Chicago

Latin American flavors aren't limited to the menu – salsa dancing breaks out here after 11pm on weekends. Chef Francisco Vilchez mixes things up with a savory pan-American menu. The *ceviche* (raw fish marinated in citrus juice) is revered and comes as part of a four-dish tasting platter. Free salsa lessons push back the tables at 7pm on Thursday.

GINO'S EAST Map pp66-7   Pizza $$
☎ 312-943-1124; 633 N Wells St; small pizzas from $15; ◷ 11am-9:30pm Mon-Sat, from noon Sun; Ⓜ Brown, Purple Line to Chicago

WHEN WILL CHICAGO GET ROLLING?

LA's got them. Portland, Oregon and Austin, Texas have them. Fellow Midwesterners Milwaukee and Minneapolis have them. Crikey, even Hoboken, New Jersey has food trucks. So why doesn't gastronomically progressive Chicago?

The city council has been slow to get on board with the food truck frenzy. Obstacles cited include parking issues (trucks will muck up Chicago's already jammed downtown streets) and regulatory challenges (the trucks will require new health and licensing rules, plus policies to keep them from encroaching on restaurants' territory).

So food truck fans have started to revolt. They've got a website – www.chicagofoodtrucks.com – to gather public support and get the city to change its laws. The movement is led by the chef behind Gaztro-Wagon (www.gaztro-wagon.com), a truck that sells the 'naan-wich' (ingredients such as butternut squash or warm lobster cushioned by Indian naan bread). Yes, Gaztro-Wagon is technically a truck that sells food. But it must adhere to current city regulations, and prepare its items in a licensed kitchen off-site, then simply sell them from the truck.

The same is true of Flirty Cupcakes (www.facebook.com/flirtycupcakes), which zips around the city and suburbs proffering thick-icing treats from a van, and the trucks around Humboldt Park serving Puerto Rican fare – cooks make the food off-site, and they just plate it from the vehicles.

This is the law that food trucksters hope to change. The ball is rolling: a food truck ordinance was introduced in city council and went into committee in summer 2010. Suburban Evanston, next door to Chicago, legalized food trucks a few months later. Foodies are crossing their fingers Chicago is next.

In the great deep-dish pizza wars going on in Chicago, Gino's is easily one of the top-five heavies. And it encourages its customers to do something neither Pizzeria Uno nor Giordano's would allow: cover every available surface (except for the actual food) with graffiti. The pizza is something you'll write home about: the classic stuffed cheese and sausage pie oozes countless pounds of cheese over its crispy cornmeal crust.

ELATE Map pp66-7 — New American $$
☎ 312-202-9900; 111 W Huron St; mains $14-26; ☽ breakfast, lunch & dinner; Ⓜ Red Line to Chicago

Located in the LEED-certified Hotel Felix, Elate sticks to the ecofriendly premise by using mostly local and organic ingredients for its fish and oyster dishes, flatbread pizzas and artisan cured meats. The decor incorporates reclaimed wood and concrete for a mod, rustic look, and natural light pours in the floor-to-ceiling windows. Add the crème brûlée pancakes to the mix, and the significance of the restaurant's name becomes apparent.

PIZZERIA UNO Map pp66-7 — Pizza $$
☎ 312-321-1000; 29 E Ohio St; small pizzas from $12; ☽ 11am-1am Mon-Fri, to 2am Sat, to 11pm Sun; Ⓜ Red Line to Grand

THAT'S AMORE

When pizza first arrived in Chicago it was a scrawny, sickly specimen. It didn't bulk up until 1943. That's when a chef who thought big arrived. He rolled out the mighty dough that cradled the first deep-dish pie – with a full inch of red sauce, chopped plum tomatoes and shredded American-style mozzarella cheese – and the city went gaga.

So who is this genius? It's a matter of dispute. The nod usually goes to Ike Sewell, who owned a restaurant called Uno's. But Ike's cook Malnati claimed he created the gooey-cheesed behemoth. The war over who's first, and best, continues today.

Heft a chunky slice at any of the following establishments:

Gino's East (p151)

Giordano's (p152)

Lou Malnati's (right)

Pequod's Pizza (p157)

Pizano's (p155)

Pizzeria Uno (above)

Ike Sewell supposedly invented Chicago-style pizza here on December 3, 1943, although his claim to fame is hotly disputed. A light, flaky crust holds piles of cheese and an herb-laced tomato sauce. The pizzas take a while, but stick to the pitchers of beer and cheap red wine to kill time, and avoid the salad and other distractions to save room for the main event. If mobs aren't your thing, nearby Giordano's is a swell option.

GIORDANO'S Map pp66-7 — Pizza $$
☎ 312-951-0747; 730 N Rush St; small pizzas from $12; ☽ 11am-11pm Sun-Thu, to midnight Fri & Sat; Ⓜ Red Line to Chicago

The founders of Giordano's, Efren and Joseph Boglio, claim that they got their winning recipe for stuffed pizza from – aww – their mother back in Italy. If you want a slice of heaven, order the 'special,' a stuffed pizza containing sausage, mushroom, green pepper and onions. We think it's the best deep-dish pizza in Chicago.

LOU MALNATI'S Map pp66-7 — Pizza $$
☎ 312-828-9800; 439 N Wells St; small pizzas from $10; ☽ 11am-11pm Mon-Thu, to midnight Fri & Sat, noon-11pm Sun; Ⓜ Brown, Purple Line to Merchandise Mart

It's a matter of dispute, but some say Lou Malnati invented Chicago's deep-dish pizza (he was a cook at Uno's, which also lays claim to the title). Lou certainly concocted the unique 'buttercrust' and the 'sausage crust' (it's literally just meat, no dough) to cradle his tangy toppings.

FOX & OBEL/ATRIUM WINE BAR
Map pp66-7 — American $$
☎ 312-379-0132; 401 E Illinois St; sandwiches $8-13, mains $12-20; ☽ cafe 6am-midnight, wine bar 5-11pm; Ⓜ Red Line to Grand

A short stroll from Navy Pier, this bustling gourmet market has a boon of options for those looking to avoid the area's uninspired chain food. Early in the day, the cafe serves excellent egg dishes; later, it makes sandwiches ranging from upscale (roast beef and blue Brie) to classic (grilled cheese). The attached wine bar kicks it up a notch with seasonal small plates (perhaps spicy grilled tofu) and large ones (maybe pumpkin and duck risotto) served at candlelit tables overlooking the river. Servers pour loads of reasonably priced reds and whites by the glass. The adjoining store is packed with supplies for an idyllic picnic.

PURPLE PIG   Map pp66-7   Mediterranean $$
☎ 312-464-1744; 500 N Michigan Ave; small plates $9; ⏲ 11:30am-midnight Sun-Thu, to 1am Fri & Sat; Ⓜ Red Line to Grand

You'll find 'cheese, swine and wine,' as the tagline says, but also veggie antipasti and Mediterranean seafood. The milk-braised pork shoulder is the hamtastic specialty. Dishes are meant to be shared, and the long list of affordable vinos gets the good times rolling at communal tables both indoors and out.

XOCO   Map pp66-7   Mexican $$
☎ 312-334-3688; 449 N Clark St; mains $8-13; ⏲ 7am-9pm Tue-Thu, to 10pm Fri, 8am-10pm Sat; Ⓜ Red Line to Grand

At Rick Bayless' Mexican street-food restaurant (pronounced 'SHOW-co') everything is sourced from local small farms. Crunch into warm *churros* (spiraled dough fritters) with chili-spiked hot chocolate for breakfast, crusty *tortas* (sandwiches) for lunch and *caldos* (meal-in-a-bowl soups) for dinner. Note the serving schedule: breakfast items until 10:30am, *tortas* after 11am, and nothing but *caldos* after 3pm. Queues can be long; breakfast is the least crowded time.

GREEN DOOR TAVERN
Map pp66-7   Burgers & Hot Dogs $$
☎ 312-664-5496; 678 N Orleans St; mains $8-13; ⏲ lunch & dinner; Ⓜ Brown, Purple Line to Chicago

Ensconced in an 1872 building, the Green Door claims to be Chicago's oldest tavern. This is your place for simple but well-cooked burgers and sandwiches, plus a few pasta dishes, amid old photos and memorabilia. Daily specials (like the $5 cheeseburger and fries on Wednesday) provide substantial savings that can be parlayed into additional microbrews.

CAFE IBERICO   Map pp66-7   Spanish $$
☎ 312-573-1510; 739 N LaSalle St; tapas $6-8; ⏲ lunch & dinner; Ⓜ Brown, Purple Line to Chicago

Iberico's creative tapas burst with flavor. Among the standouts: *salpicon de marisco* (seafood salad with shrimp, octopus and squid), *croquetas de pollo* (chicken and ham

puffs with garlic sauce) and *vieiras a la plancha* (grilled scallops with saffron). The cafe's heady sangria draws wearied Loop workers by the dozen in the summer.

EGGSPERIENCE   Map pp66-7   American $
☎ 312-870-6773; 35 W Ontario St; mains $6-10; ⏲ 24 hr; Ⓜ Red Line to Grand

It's 4am and you're starving? This bright, clean, sprawling 24-hour diner will fix the problem with its big portions of pancakes, omelets, club sandwiches and other staples, plus your very own pot of coffee.

MR BEEF   Map pp66-7   Burgers & Hot Dogs $
☎ 312-337-8500; 666 N Orleans St; mains $4-7; ⏲ 8am-7pm Mon-Thu, to 5am Fri, 10:30am-3:30pm & 10:30pm-5am Sat; Ⓜ Brown, Purple Line to Chicago

At this local classic the Italian beef sandwiches come with long, spongy white buns that begin dribbling (that's a good thing!) after a load of the spicy meat and cooking juices has been ladled on. In a recent episode of the Travel Channel's *Food Wars*, Mr Beef won as Chicago's best beef hands down over its main competitor, Al's. Don't be afraid of the dumpy decor. Eaters from Jerry Springer to Jay Leno have devoured at the picnic-style tables. Cash only.

PORTILLO'S   Map pp66-7   Burgers & Hot Dogs $
☎ 312-587-8910; 100 W Ontario St; mains $4-7; ⏲ 10am-11pm Sun-Thu, to midnight Fri & Sat; Ⓜ Red Line to Grand

Die-hard hot-dog purists might bemoan the lack of true Chicago dogs in the vicinity of tourist hot spots, but this outpost of the local Portillo's chain – gussied up in a *nearly* corny 1930s gangster theme – is the place to get one. Try one of their famous dogs and a slice of the heavenly chocolate cake: far and away the best inexpensive meal in the neighborhood.

BILLY GOAT TAVERN
Map pp66-7   American $
☎ 312-222-1525; lower level, 430 N Michigan Ave; mains $4-6; ⏲ 6am-2am Mon-Fri, 10am-2am Sat & Sun; Ⓜ Red Line to Grand

Literally beneath the pie-eyed mobs on the Magnificent Mile, the subterranean Billy Goat, which enjoyed the fame of John Belushi's *SNL* skit ('Cheezborger! Cheezborger! No fries! Cheeps!'), remains a deserving tourist magnet. Skip the

GONE TO THE DOGS

Like Elvis sightings and fishing stories, the invention of the classic Chicago hot dog is the subject of lore and legend, a long evolution that is much more than the story of wiener meets bun. A real-deal Chicago dog requires a litany of toppings and a sophisticated construction that seems perfectly designed to defy easy consumption.

For the record, a Chicago hot dog begins with an all-beef hot dog, preferably a local Vienna brand. The variation in cooking method is wide – some places steam, others boil and a few grill – but the poppy-seed bun and toppings are musts, as is the strict censure of ketchup. A traditional dog covers most of the essential food groups through the following toppings, although local variations exist:

- diced onions, white or yellow
- diced tomatoes
- sliced cucumbers, possibly slightly pickled
- shredded iceberg lettuce
- diced green bell pepper
- *pepperoncini* (Italian hot and pickled peppers)
- sweet relish, usually a virulent shade of green
- bright yellow mustard
- celery salt

The result? Part salad, part hot dog. It's not hard to find one, either. A great Near North option is Portillo's (p153), which started in a Chicago suburb in the '50s. If you like a little theater with your dog, try Wiener's Circle (p158) in Lincoln Park. For everything from a straight-up Chicago dog to one made with alligator, try Hot Doug's (p170), just north of Logan Sq.

---

franchise locations for the original: a windowless haunt with an entire wall dedicated to former *Tribune* columnist Mike Royko, famously cantankerous Greeks at the grill and scads of old-Chicago charm. Greasy-spoon fare is the only option, and you'll have to order a double cheeseburger if you're interested in tasting meat within the substantial bun. Schlitz on tap helps wash it down.

GOLD COAST

Forty-something gents in power suits who like their steaks rare and their handshakes firm populate the Gold Coast's most time-honored eateries. They're joined by younger singles who are well dressed, well heeled and inclined to enjoy a cocktail or three in the adjoining lounge while they wait for a table. The action centers on Chicago, State and Rush Sts – the so-called Viagra Triangle – and is worth a stroll. If you have to wait a bit for a table during rush hour, all the better: the people-watching is excellent.

MORTON'S Map pp72-3 — Steak House $$$
☎ 312-266-4820; 1050 N State St; mains $30-75; ☽ dinner; Ⓜ Red Line to Clark/Division
Morton's is a chain now, but Chicago is where it all began. The meat here is aged to perfection and displayed tableside

before cooking. See that half a cow? It's the 48oz double porterhouse. Smaller – but still quite dangerous if dropped on your toe – are the fillets, strip steaks and other cuts. The immense baked potatoes could prop up church foundations. Or you could try the hash browns, a superb version of a side dish all too often ignored. Expensive reds anchor the wine list.

GIBSON'S Map pp72-3 — Steak House $$$
☎ 312-266-8999; 1028 N Rush St; mains $30-55; ☽ lunch & dinner; Ⓜ Red Line to Clark/Division
There is a scene nightly at this local original. Politicians, movers, shakers and the shaken-down swirl the famed martinis and compete for prime table space in the buzzing dining room. The bar is a prime stalking place for available millionaires. As for the meat on the plates, the steaks are as good as they come, and ditto for the ginormous lobsters.

SIGNATURE ROOM AT THE 95TH
Map pp72-3 — American $$$
☎ 312-787-9596; John Hancock Center, 875 N Michigan Ave; mains $27-40; ☽ lunch & dinner Mon-Sat, brunch & dinner Sun; Ⓜ Red Line to Chicago
Given that diners spend most of the meal gaping at the soul-stirring views, you'd think the kitchen atop the Hancock

UNDERGROUND SUPPER CLUB

Clandestino (www.clandestinodining.com; multicourse meals $65-85) is an underground 'community dining project,' where chef Efrain Cuevas serves sustainable meals in changing locations like galleries or lofts. Sign up for the online mailing list, and grab a spot when he sends out event invitations.

wouldn't trouble itself with the food, but the chef does a fine job with the fish, steak and pasta dishes, many of which have a seasonal twist. The lunch buffet ($20, served Monday to Saturday) is the best deal for the view, since the price isn't much more than a foodless ticket to the observation deck. Cheapskates should note they can get the same vista for the price of a (costly) beer, one flight up in the Signature Lounge.

MIKE DITKA'S RESTAURANT
Map pp72-3   American $$
☎ 312-587-8989; 100 E Chestnut St; mains $19-38; ⏲ lunch & dinner; Ⓜ Red Line to Chicago
When it's too cold for a tailgate party, come to this spot in the Tremont Hotel owned by the famously cantankerous former coach of the Chicago Bears. The menu is as meaty as you'd expect (the Fridge burger could feed a family for weeks), and fans will love the memorabilia-filled display cases.

PIZANO'S PIZZA Map pp72-3   Pizza $$
☎ 312-751-1766; 864 N State St; large pizzas from $19; ⏲ 11am-11pm Sun-Thu, to 2am Fri & Sat; Ⓜ Red Line to Chicago
Everyone has an opinion on which local pizza is best, including Oprah. And she likes Pizano's. It's a good recommendation for deep-dish newbies, since it's not jaw-breakingly thick. The thin-crust pies that hit the checker-clothed tables win raves too.

KENDALL COLLEGE DINING ROOM
Map pp72-3   New American $$
☎ 312-752-2328; 900 N North Branch St; 3-course menu lunch/dinner $18/29; ⏲ lunch Mon-Fri, dinner Tue-Sat; 🚇 Blue Line to Chicago or 🚌 8
The School of Culinary Arts at Kendall College has turned out a host of local cooking luminaries, and this classy space with river and skyline views is where they honed their chops. Students prepare and

serve inventive contemporary American dishes, with forays into French and international fusion styles, all of which come with white-glove service at fantastic value. Call ahead for reservations (and note the hours can vary depending on the school term schedule).

PJ CLARKE'S Map pp72-3   American $$
☎ 312-664-1650; 1204 N State St; mains $11-19; ⏲ lunch & dinner; Ⓜ Red Line to Clark/Division
Chicago's straight, 30-something singles come to eyeball one another at this upscale restaurant-pub. Classy and cozy, PJ Clarke's specializes in comfort foods with high-end twists, like the béarnaise burger and the teriyaki skirt-steak sandwich.

TEMPO CAFE Map pp72-3   American $
☎ 312-943-3929; 6 E Chestnut St; mains $9-15; ⏲ 24hr; Ⓜ Red Line to Chicago
Bright and cheery, this upscale diner brings most of its meals to the table the way they're meant to be served – in a skillet. Its omelet-centric menu includes all manner of fresh veggies and meat, as well as sandwiches, soups and salads. After the bars close the scene here is chaotic and fun.

ASHKENAZ Map pp72-3   Deli $
☎ 312-944-5006; 12 E Cedar St; mains $8-15; ⏲ 7am-7pm Mon-Sat, to 6pm Sun; Ⓜ Red Line to Clark/Division
There aren't that many kosher delis in Chicago, but the thick stacks of corned beef and pastrami that come from Ashkenaz would stand out anywhere east of New York. Among the pricey options and chain restaurants of the Gold Coast, they offer the best quick lunch in the neighborhood.

FOODLIFE Map pp72-3   Eclectic $
☎ 312-787-7100; 835 N Michigan Ave; mains $7-10; ⏲ 8am-8pm Mon-Thu, to 8:30pm Fri & Sat, to 7pm Sun; Ⓜ Red Line to Chicago
'Call it a restaurant. Call it an eatery. Just don't call it a food court!' demands the mantra of Foodlife – a place with over a dozen different globally themed kitchens featuring gourmet à la carte options in a sleek atmosphere. Situated inside the Water Tower Place shopping center, it's ideal for gangs of shoppers who are so overwhelmed by the Magnificent Mile that they can't come to a consensus.

EATING GOLD COAST

FIRST SLICE CAFE Map pp72-3   Coffee Shop $

☎ 312-202-1227; 163 E Pearson St; mains $5-10;
🕐 8am-7pm Mon-Thu, 8am-6pm Fri, 9am-6pm Sat,
10am-6pm Sun; Ⓜ Red Line to Chicago

Located in the Water Works Visitors Center,
First Slice not only serves made-from-
scratch soups, salads, quiches, sandwiches
and eight different flaky-crusted pies daily,
but proceeds help supply needy local
families with healthy meals. So you're
doing good by eating well.

LINCOLN PARK & OLD TOWN

While some of the world's premier restaurants such as Alinea and Charlie Trotter's
are here, Lincoln Park caters to student tastes
too, thanks to the presence of DePaul University. Halsted St, Lincoln Ave and Fullerton
Ave are good bets to turn up trendy, flirty
eateries – a cupcake bakery here, a sushi
lounge there and a crème-anglaise-pancake-
flipping brunch spot next door – where 20-
and 30-somethings cross paths with yuppie
families.

A bit to the south, Old Town is quieter
and quainter, run through by Wells St and
populated by older diners.

LINCOLN PARK

ALINEA Map pp78-9   New American $$$

☎ 312-867-0110; 1723 N Halsted St; 12-/24-course
menu $150/225; 🕐 dinner Wed-Sun; Ⓜ Red Line
to North/Clybourn

Helmed by superstar chef and James Beard
Award–winner Grant Achatz, the small
room at Alinea is widely regarded as
Chicago's most exciting dinner spot, where
giddy, awestruck culinary cognoscenti
document each course with a digital photo
before eating it. The options are limited
to a 12-course 'tasting' and a 20-plus-
course 'tour', bringing an artistic carnival of
strange pairings served in steel and glass
contraptions. Expect otherworldly single-
bite dishes and futuristic delights like the
duck served with a 'pillow of lavender
air.' The once-in-a-lifetime meal can take
upwards of four hours, and you can add a
note-perfect wine pairing for an additional
fee. *Restaurant Magazine* proclaimed Alinea
North America's top place to indulge.
Reserve well in advance.

CHARLIE TROTTER'S

Map pp78-9   New American $$$

☎ 773-248-6228; 816 W Armitage Ave; multicourse
menus from $135; 🕐 dinner Tue-Sat; Ⓜ Brown,
Purple Line to Armitage

It's no overstatement: Charlie Trotter
is king of Chicago cooking and rightful
father of the *nouvelle* standards exemplified
at Alinea. A notorious perfectionist,
Trotter has never served the same menu
twice. He plates two set multicourse
versions nightly – one vegetarian, one
meaty. Reservations and jackets for men
are required.

BOKA Map pp78-9   New American $$$

☎ 312-337-6070; 1729 N Halsted St; mains $27-36,
6-course menu $85; 🕐 dinner; Ⓜ Red Line to
North/Clybourn

A hip restaurant-lounge hybrid with a
seafood-leaning menu, Boka has become
the pre- and post-theater stomping ground
du jour for younger Steppenwolf patrons.
Order a cocktail at the bar or slip into
one of the booths for small-plate dishes
like mango-laced tabbouleh salad or veal
sweetbreads with Moroccan barbecue
sauce.

MERLO RESTAURANTE

Map pp78-9   Italian $$$

☎ 773-529-0747; 2638 N Lincoln Ave, mains $18-
28; 🚇 Brown Line to Diversey

Bolognese regional fare is the forte of this
cozy family-operated slow-food bistro and
wine bar, where hand-rolled pastas and
steaming dishes of risotto of the day
dominate the menu, offering particular
comfort when the weather turns cold. This
is one place where an otherwise
conservative choice of the *tagliatelle
bolognese* brings a plate of perfectly sweet
and savory meat sauce and ribbons of
homemade pasta that would delight any
Italian grandmother.

CAFE BA-BA-REEBA! Map pp78-9   Spanish $$

☎ 773-935-5000; 2024 N Halsted St; tapas $4-9,
mains $16-22; 🕐 lunch Sat & Sun, dinner daily;
Ⓜ Brown, Purple Line to Armitage

At this long-standing, delightfully ersatz
tapas joint, the garlic-laced sauces may have
you licking the plates. The menu changes
daily but always includes some spicy meats,
marinated fish and heaps of hot or cold
small plates. For a main event, order one

FARMERS' MARKETS

Several local chefs, including Rick Bayless, shop at the Green City Market (Map pp78-9; ☎ 773-880-1266; www.chicagogreencitymarket.org; 1790 N Clark St; ⏲ 7am-1pm Wed & Sat mid-May–late Oct). It's the king of Chicago's farmers' markets, offering heirloom veggies, homemade pies, straight-from-the-farm produce and much more at Lincoln Park's south end.

Many neighborhoods have their own farmers' market. These typically operate from May to October, one day per week between 7am and 1pm. See Chicago's Farmers' markets (www.chicagofarmersmarkets.us) for a complete list. The following are popular:

Daley Plaza Farmers' market At Washington & Dearborn, every Thursday.

Federal Plaza Farmers' market At Adams & Dearborn, every Tuesday.

Lincoln Park Farmers' market At Armitage & Orchard, every Saturday.

Near North Farmers' market At Division & Dearborn, every Saturday.

Wicker Park & Bucktown Farmers' market In Wicker Park, every Sunday.

of the paellas ($11 to $13 per person, minimum two people) as soon as you get seated – they take a while to prepare.

VIA CARDUCCI Map pp78-9   Italian $$
☎ 773-665-1981; 1419 W Fullerton Ave; mains $13-20; ⏲ lunch Mon-Fri, dinner daily; Ⓜ Brown, Purple, Red Line to Fullerton
The simple southern Italian dishes regularly draw moans of delight from diners at this small trattoria. Red-checkered tablecloths complement the baroque murals, and the food leans toward thick tomato-based sauces and amazing sausages.

PEQUOD'S PIZZA Map pp78-9   Pizza $$
☎ 731-327-1512; 2207 N Clybourn Ave; small pizzas from $10; ⏲ 11am-2am Mon-Sat, to midnight Sun; 🚌 9 to Webster
Like the ship in *Moby Dick,* from which this neighborhood restaurant takes its name, Pequod's deep-dish is a thing of legend – head and shoulders above chain competitors because of its caramelized cheese, generous toppings and sweetly flavored sauce. The atmosphere is affably rugged too, with surly waitstaff and graffiti-covered walls.

TSUKI Map pp78-9   Japanese $$
☎ 773-883-8722; 1441 W Fullerton Ave; sushi per piece $3-5, mains $7-14; ⏲ dinner Wed-Sun; Ⓜ Brown, Purple, Red Line to Fullerton
This large urbane sushi destination is beloved for its fresh sashimi and playful approach to traditional rolls. Top picks include the smoked duck *nigiri* (served on top of the rice instead of rolled like maki) and the intriguing pistachio-salmon teriyaki. Soba and udon noodles and tempura round out the menu, which also includes some vegetarian selections. Most items on the simplified lounge menu are $5 or less, making them some of the best nighttime eats around.

ICOSIUM KAFE Map pp78-9   Middle Eastern $$
☎ 773-404-1300; 2433 N Clark St; mains $7-13; ⏲ 10am-10pm Mon-Fri, from 8am Sat & Sun; Ⓜ Brown, Purple, Red Line to Fullerton
It's crepes galore at this exotic Algerian cafe (which sometimes goes by the name Crepe & Coffee Palace). The signature dish comes in varieties both sweet (stuffed with figs, Nutella, Belgian chocolate or berries) and savory (stuffed with chicken, smoked salmon or escargot), alongside robust coffee.

RJ GRUNTS Map pp78-9   Burgers & Hot Dogs $$
☎ 773-929-5363; 2056 N Lincoln Park W; mains $7-12; ⏲ lunch & dinner daily, brunch Sat & Sun; 🚌 22
The very first of the now-ubiquitous Lettuce Entertain You stable of restaurants, RJ Grunts came on to the scene in the 1970s, when Lincoln Park emerged as the young singles' neighborhood of choice. Now, as then, the huge fruit and vegetable bar and burgers are the mainstays. This is a fun postzoo lunch spot; even the pickiest kids (and parents) will find something to love.

BOURGEOIS PIG Map pp78-9   Coffee Shop $
☎ 773-883-5282; 738 W Fullerton Pkwy; mains $7-9; ⏲ 7am-10pm Mon-Sat, from 8am Sun; Ⓜ Brown, Purple, Red Line to Fullerton; Ⓥ
An old-style coffee shop with big, creaking wooden tables and chairs, the Pig serves strong java and whopping sandwiches. It's a convivial place to grab a bite while working through the newspaper or chatting with friends. Tea drinkers and vegetarians will find many options on offer.

ALOHA EATS Map pp78-9 — Hawaiian $
☎ 773-935-6828; 2534 N Clark St; mains $6-9; lunch & dinner; Ⓜ Brown, Purple, Red Line to Fullerton

From *musubis* (rice rolls wrapped in seaweed) to *saimin* (egg noodle soup) to *katsus* (breaded cutlets), it's all about whopping portions of Hawaiian food here. Spam, aka 'the Hawaiian steak,' is the main ingredient in many dishes, including the popular Loco Moco (meat, fried eggs and brown gravy atop rice). Macaroni or fries always arrive on the side. The massive menu includes several tofu and fish options for those watching their girlish figures. The bright-yellow interior and island dishes soothe especially well in winter.

FLORIOLE CAFE Map pp78-9 — Bakery $
☎ 773-883-1313; 1220 W Webster Ave; items $3-8; Ⓨ 7am-3pm Tue-Fri, 8am-4pm Sat & Sun; Ⓜ Brown, Purple, Red Line to Fullerton

The chef got her start selling lemon tarts, twice-baked croissants and rum-tinged *caneles* (a pastry with a custard center and caramelized crust) at the Green Market. She now sells her French-influenced baked goods and ciabatta sandwiches – which use Midwest-sourced meats, cheeses and produce – in an airy, loftlike space punctuated by a big wooden farm table.

WIENER'S CIRCLE
Map pp78-9 — Burgers & Hot Dogs $
☎ 773-477-7444; 2622 N Clark St; mains $3-6; Ⓨ 10:30am-4:30am Sun-Thu, to 5:30am Fri & Sat; Ⓜ Brown, Purple Line to Diversey

Both infamous and revered in Chicago, Wiener's Circle's charred hot dogs and cheddar fries come with a verbal berating that would make a sailor blush. During the day and on weeknights it's a normal hot-dog stand – with damn good food (no less than Rachael Ray and Jerry Springer proclaimed them the best hot dogs in town). The foul-mouthed show is on week-end eves, late night, when the nearby bars close. The f-bombs fly, and sometimes racial epithets erupt between the mostly white clientele and the mostly black staff.

OLD TOWN

SALPICON Map pp78-9 — Mexican $$$
☎ 312-988-7811; 1252 N Wells St, mains $20-30; Ⓨ dinner; Ⓜ Red Line to Clark/Division

Another favorite among Chicago's high-end Mexican restaurants, Priscilla Satkoff's place has elevated *ceviche* and *chiles rellenos* (stuffed poblano peppers that are batter fried) to an art. Many other items come slathered in heavenly *mole* sauce. The festive interior features high ceilings and bold colors. Create bright colors in your head by trying some of the 60 tequilas, including some rare, oak-barrel-aged numbers.

BISTROT MARGOT Map pp78-9 — French $$
☎ 312-587-3660; 1437 N Wells St; mains $19-26; Ⓨ lunch Mon-Fri, brunch Sat & Sun, dinner daily; Ⓜ Brown, Purple Line to Sedgwick

A visit to Bistrot Margot is like a visit to a little Parisian corner bistro in one of the remoter districts. Roast chicken, steak and *frites*, mussels and other coastal shellfish highlight the classic menu. The interior decor mixes dark wood with bright tiles and red booths, and the busy crowd adds to the atmosphere. There are good daily specials, including half-price wine on Monday and a prix fixe menu on Wednesday.

TWIN ANCHORS Map pp78-9 — BBQ $$
☎ 312-266-1616; 1655 N Sedgwick St; mains $13-25; Ⓨ dinner; Ⓜ Brown, Purple Line to Sedgwick

Twin Anchors is synonymous with ribs, and Chicagoans can get violent if you leave town without sampling some of the smoky, tangy-sauced baby backs. The meat drops from the ribs as soon as you lift them. The restaurant doesn't take reservations, so you'll have to wait outside or around the neon-lit 1950s bar, which sets the tone for the place. An almost all-Sinatra jukebox completes the supper-club ambience.

ADOBO GRILL Map pp78-9 — Mexican $$
☎ 312-266-7999; 1610 N Wells St; mains $14-20; Ⓨ lunch Sat & Sun, dinner daily; Ⓜ Brown, Purple Line to Sedgwick

Adobo chef Paul LoDuca takes Mexican food and flavors to another dimension at his lively eatery near Second City. The yummy guacamole appetizer is made tableside, and the dishes that follow are no less extraordinary. Try the trout steamed in corn husk or the tender chicken breast in an Oaxacan black *mole* sauce. Thirsty? The margaritas are predictably good, but Adobo also has over 80 sipping tequilas on hand.

OLD JERUSALEM
Map pp78-9   Middle Eastern $

☎ 312-944-0459; 1411 N Wells St; mains $7-13;
🕓 11am-10:30pm Sun-Thu, to 11pm Fri & Sat;
Ⓜ Brown, Purple Line to Sedgwick

This friendly Middle Eastern joint has been pumping out falafel and pita sandwiches for over 30 years. For something leafy try the Greek salad, served with Lebanese flatbread. If the weather's good, get your food to go and feast in nearby Lincoln Park.

LAKE VIEW & WRIGLEYVILLE

It's best to eat your way through Lake View and Wrigleyville with broad expectations and a big appetite. Hungry wanderers will navigate chic bistros, late-night gay-friendly pizzerias and seemingly endless stretches of inexpensive ethnic eateries. On foot, there are three distinct areas to explore: Halsted St north of Belmont Ave in Boystown, Clark St as it unfurls on either side of Wrigley Field, and the restaurant row on Southport Ave between Belmont and Irving Park Rd. A batch of groovy bites also clusters in Roscoe Village, on Roscoe St just west of Damen Ave.

Note that dining in Wrigleyville before or after a Cubs game is challenging for those in search of a quiet meal.

TERRAGUSTO
Map pp86-7   Italian $$$

☎ 773-248-2777; 1851 W Addison St; 3-/4-course menu $30/40; 🕓 6-10pm Tue-Fri, 5-10:30pm Sat, 5-9pm Sun; Ⓜ Brown Line to Addison

Steps from the Brown Line, Terragusto makes its organic gnocchi, ravioli and other pastas daily (watch 'em in the front window; if you're inspired, you can learn how to do it yourself via their classes). Sturdy wooden tables prop up the heaping rustic dishes that arrive fragrant from the kitchen. If there are fewer than six in your party, you choose from the small, changing list of menu options; if more, the chef chooses. It's BYOB, and you'll need reservations.

CHILAM BALAM
Map pp86-7   Mexican $$$

☎ 773-296-6901; 3023 N Broadway St; mains $21-28; 🕓 dinner, closed Tue; Ⓜ Brown Line to Wellington

Chef-owner Chuy Valencia is only in his 20s, but he has already apprenticed under Rick Bayless and brought his 'farm to table' phi-

losophy to this vibrant brick-and-Spanish-tile eatery, which sits below street level. The close-set tables pulse with young foodies ripping into fiery halibut *ceviche*, mushroom empanadas, chocolate-chili mousse and other imaginative fare. It's BYOB.

YOSHI'S CAFÉ
Map pp86-7   Japanese $$

☎ 773-248-6160; 3257 N Halsted St; mains $16-27; 🕓 dinner Tue-Sun, brunch Sun; Ⓜ Brown, Purple, Red Line to Belmont

Yoshi and Nobuko Katsumura preside over one of the most innovative casual places in town – as they've done for two decades – with a changing Japanese- and French-flared menu. They treat all ingredients with the utmost respect, from the salmon to the tofu to the Kobe beef. Service in the low-lit, well-spaced room is every bit as snappy as the food.

HB
Map pp86-7   New American $$

☎ 773-661-0299; 3404 N Halsted St; mains $15-23; 🕓 dinner Wed-Sun; Ⓜ Red Line to Addison

The monogram stands for 'Home Bistro,' where chef-owner Joncarl Lachman serves careful comfort food in a warm wood-and-tile-lined space. Shout-outs go to the exquisite pork chops and the pan-roasted trout. Try to snag a seat by the front window, which entertains with Boystown people-watching. HB is BYOB.

MIA FRANCESCA
Map pp86-7   Italian $$

☎ 773-281-3310; 3311 N Clark St; mains $13-22; 🕓 dinner; Ⓜ Brown, Purple, Red Line to Belmont

Diners quickly fill up the room at this popular, family-run Italian bistro (part of a local chain), and energy swirls among the closely spaced tables, topped with white tablecloths and fresh flowers. The hand-written menu features earthy standards – seafood linguine, spinach ravioli, veal medallions – with aggressive seasoning from southern Italy. Other treats include wafer-thin pizzas and the often-overlooked staple of Italian kitchens: polenta.

TANGO SUR
Map pp86-7   Steak House $$

☎ 773-477-5466; 3763 N Southport Ave; mains $12-27; 🕓 dinner; Ⓜ Brown Line to Southport

This candlelit BYOB Argentine steak house makes an idyllic date location, serving classic skirt steaks and other tender grass-fed options. In addition to the traditional cuts, the chef's special is *bife Vesuvio*, a

EATING LAKE VIEW & WRIGLEYVILLE

prime strip stuffed with garlic, spinach and cheese – it's a triumph. In summer, tables outside expand the seating from the small and spare interior.

ARCOS DE CUCHILLEROS
Map pp86-7   Spanish $$

☎ 773-296-6046; 3445 N Halsted St; tapas $6-9, mains $12-17; ☽ dinner Tue-Sun; Ⓜ Red Line to Addison

The owners come from Madrid, and they have faithfully replicated a traditional Madrid family cafe, with a long bar, a narrow room, dark wood furniture and small plates of classics like sautéed lima beans, chickpea croquettes and *tortilla española* (a cold egg and potato omelet). Don't bother keeping track of how many pitchers of tangy sangria you drink; just keep ordering.

SHIROI HANA Map pp86-7   Japanese $$

☎ 773-477-1652; 3242 N Clark St; sushi per piece $2-3.50, mains $10-16; ☽ lunch Tue-Sat, dinner daily; Ⓜ Brown, Purple, Red Line to Belmont

Every large city, if it's lucky, has its Shiroi Hana – the dirt-cheap sushi place where the food is consistently good, if not overwhelming. There's a $20 all-you-can-eat special from 5pm to 8pm weekdays.

CHICAGO DINER Map pp86-7   Vegetarian $$

☎ 773-935-6696; 3411 N Halsted St; mains $9-14; ☽ 11am-10pm Mon-Fri, from 10am Sat & Sun; Ⓜ Red Line to Addison; Ⓥ

The gold standard for Chicago vegetarians, this place has been serving barbecue seitan, wheat meat and tofu stroganoff for decades. The tattooed staff will guide you to the best stuff, including the peanut butter vegan 'supershakes' and the 'Radical Ruben.' Vegans take note: even the pesto for the pasta can be had without a lick of cheese.

VILLAGE TAP Map pp86-7   Burgers & Hot Dogs $$

☎ 773-883-0817; 2055 W Roscoe St; mains $8-11; ☽ dinner daily, from noon Sat & Sun; Ⓜ Brown Line to Paulina

Even though it can get overly packed on the weekends, this neighborhood tavern does everything well: food, drink and atmosphere. The friendly bartenders give out free samples of the ever-changing and carefully chosen lineup of Midwestern microbrews. The kitchen turns out some great burgers, veggie burgers and chicken sandwiches, served with a side of hummus and grilled pita. Out back the beer garden contains a fountain; inside, the tables enjoy good views of the TVs for ball games.

EPICUREAN EXCURSIONS

Feed your mind *and* your stomach on one of these tours of Windy City foodstuffs:

Second City Pizza Tours (☎ 773-242-0084; www.secondcitypizzatours.com; 2.5hr tours adult/child $36/28; ☽ 11:30am Fri-Sun Apr–mid-Nov) Munch five slices by five different pizza purveyors on the a mile-long walk, which includes Giordano's, Gino's East and Pizzeria Uno. Departure is from Giordano's (p152).

Chicago Chocolate Tours (☎ 312-929-2939; www.chicagochocolatetours.com; 2.5hr tours per person $40; ☽ Wed-Sun) Walk to various candy makers, bakeries and shops to indulge. Departure times, locations and routes vary.

Fork & the Road (www.forkandtheroad.com; tours per person $40-60; ☽ late-May–Sep) Local foodies lead themed bike rides (eg barbecue, vegetarian, Asian) to various restaurants to chat with chefs and, of course, eat their wares. Departure times and locations vary; rides range from 12 to 22 miles.

Eli's Cheesecake Factory Tour (Map pp50-1; ☎ 773-736-3417; www.elicheesecake.com; 6701 W Forest Preserve Dr; 40min tour per person $3; ☽ 1pm Mon-Fri) How's a cheesecake made, decorated and packaged? Find out at the source. The Food Network rated Eli's the nation's number-one factory tour. Dig into a free slice at the end.

Chicago Food Planet Tours (☎ 212-209-3370; www.zerve.com/chicagofoods; 3hr tour per person $42; ☽ Apr-Nov) Nibble at seven restaurants while walking around either the Near North (departs 11am daily) or Bucktown and Wicker Park (departs 11:30am Tuesday to Saturday) neighborhoods.

City Provisions (☎ 773-293-2489; www.cityprovisions.com; per person $175) Takes foodies to area farms for tours and dining amid the fields. The price includes transportation on a biodiesel bus from Chicago, a five-course meal and beer pairings.

top picks

VEGGIE DELIGHTS

Some suggestions for when Chicago's bacon fixation gets a little old:

- **Chicago Diner** (opposite) The local scene's long-standing all-veg linchpin.
- **Victory's Banner** (below) New Age, meat-free bliss (and a great brunch) awaits.
- **Green Zebra** (p167) Chicago's highfalutin veg-out spot.
- **Karyn's on Green** (p171) Making vegan dining sexy.
- **Devon Avenue Indian eateries** (p164) A flavorful row of meatless curry houses.

CRISP Map pp86-7   Korean $
☎ 877-693-8653; 2940 N Broadway St; mains $7-12; 🕙 11:30am-9pm Tue-Thu & Sun, to 10:30pm Fri & Sat; Ⓜ Brown Line to Wellington
Music pours from the stereo and cheap, delicious Korean fusions arrive from the kitchen at this cheerful cafe. The 'Bad Boy Buddha' bowl, a variation on *bibimbap* (mixed vegetables with rice), is one of the best $8 lunches in town. On second thought, maybe that award goes to Crisp's burrito, filled with perfectly fried chicken in a savory soy-ginger sauce.

VICTORY'S BANNER Map pp86-7 Vegetarian $
☎ 733-665-0227; 2100 W Roscoe St; mains $7-10; 🕙 8am-3pm, closed Tue; Ⓜ Brown Line to Paulina; Ⓥ
The tough decision at this revered breakfast house is between the fresh, free-range-egg omelets and the legendary French toast, cooked in rich cream batter and served with peach butter. New Age tunes and muted colors give it a soothing Zen vibe, even when the place is mobbed on weekend mornings.

PENNY'S NOODLE SHOP Map pp86-7 Thai $
☎ 773-281-8222; 3400 N Sheffield Ave; mains $5-9; 🕙 lunch & dinner Tue-Sun; Ⓜ Brown, Purple, Red Line to Belmont; Ⓥ
Despite the presence of several other excellent Asian choices within a few blocks, this place attracts crowds most hours of the day and night. You'll see people waiting outside in all kinds of weather. Maybe these

hapless hordes are drawn by the place's minimalist decor, the low prices or – no doubt – the cheap, tasty noodle soups and stir-fries. Penny's is BYOB.

FALAFILL Map pp86-7   Middle Eastern $
☎ 773-525-0052; 3202 N Broadway St; mains $5-8; lunch & dinner; Ⓜ Brown, Purple, Red Line to Belmont; Ⓥ
Buy a falafel sandwich or falafel salad at the counter, then customize it at the topping bar with cilantro chutney, Moroccan olives, *zhug* (hot jalapeno sauce), tabbouleh, pickled ginger and 15 other fresh items. Soup, hummus and sweet-potato fries sum up the side dishes. Freshly squeezed carrot, orange and apple juices add to the healthy fast-food vibe.

BLEEDING HEART BAKERY
Map pp86-7   Bakery $
☎ 773-327-6934; 1955 W Belmont Ave; mains $5-8; 🕙 7am-7pm Tue-Sun; 🚌 77; Ⓥ
With punk-rock posters, hot-pink wallpaper, the relentless Sex Pistols soundtrack and tattooed counter staff, owners Michelle and Vinny Garcia opened the country's first wholly organic bakery. The 'punk rock pastries' are the draw, but smaller treats (many of which are vegan) and lunch sandwiches are pulled off with flamboyant flair.

CLARK STREET DOG
Map pp86-7   Burgers & Hot Dogs $
☎ 773-281-6690; 3040 N Clark St; mains $3-7; 🕙 9am-3am Sun-Thu, to 4am Fri & Sat; Ⓜ Brown, Purple Line to Wellington
Clark Dog is the brighter, friendlier version of the brash Wiener's Circle, with only a smidgeon of the confrontational attitude. Apart from hot dogs, carnivorous delights include the hearty combo – which marries Italian beef *and* Italian sausage on a single soggy bun – and the chili cheese fries. If all the salty dogs make you thirsty, head to the adjoining divey Clark Street Bar for some cheap cold ones.

IAN'S PIZZA Map pp86-7   Pizza $
☎ 773-525-4580; 3463 N Clark St; slices $3-4; 🕙 5pm-2am Tue-Fri, noon-2am Sat & Sun; Ⓜ Red Line to Addison
Need to soak up all those brewskis post Cubs game? Ian's can help. Crazy slices topped by macaroni and cheese (the

most popular), guacamole taco, barbecue chicken and about 20 other items are in high demand late at night, so prepare to queue for the pleasure.

ANDERSONVILLE, LINCOLN SQUARE & UPTOWN

Though they're a hike to get to, these northern neighborhoods are good for a delicious browse. Andersonville rewards with global eats, from Sicilian pastries to Belgian frites to much-ballyhooed American pizzas. The neighborhood's Swedish history lives on at the stalwart Swedish Bakery: just follow your nose to the cakes and cream puffs. Clark St is the main vein. Exit the Red Line at Berwyn and walk west about three-quarters of a mile to reach the compact strip.

Around the corner to the south, Uptown is a whole different scene, with Asian eateries clattering pots and pans on Argyle St. Most of the Thai and Vietnamese noodle houses lie between Broadway St and Sheridan Rd, though several also spill out along Broadway. Take the Red Line to Argyle, and you're in the fishy-smelling heart of it.

West of Uptown, Lincoln Square is a busy 'hood with a trove of eats. Stroll up N Lincoln Ave and you'll find casually upscale bistros and taverns to suit a range of tastes. Get there by taking the Brown Line train to Western.

ANDERSONVILLE

GREAT LAKE Map p90   Pizza $$
☎ 773-334-9270; 1477 W Balmoral Ave; 14in pizza from $21; ◷ 4:30-9:30pm Wed-Sat; Ⓜ Red Line to Berwyn
Hard to believe all the excitement this wee storefront generates, as it sits unobtrusively next to a shoe repair shop and barbershop. But everyone from *GQ* to Rachel Ray to the *New York Times* has crowned it the nation's best pizza maker. The perfectionist couple that owns Great Lake typically offers three pizza types per day using house-made mozzarella, house-ground sausage and small-farm produce atop a charred, chewy, between-thick-and-thin crust. There are just 12 seats, and no reservations – which explains the long lines and testy attitudes. This is indeed slowww food.

BISTRO CAMPAGNE Map pp50-1   French $$
☎ 773-271-6100; 4815 N Lincoln Ave; mains $14-26; ◷ dinner daily, brunch Sun; Ⓜ Brown Line to Western
True, Chicago has a lot of French bistros sprinkled around, but not many perfect the balance of fine but unfussy dining in a sophisticated but welcoming ambience the way Campagne does. The stained-glass-filled Lincoln Square favorite plates such classics as beef *bourguignonne*, chocolate soufflé and mussels (all you can eat on Tuesdays) alongside fat wines. Reservations are useful, especially if there's a concert at the nearby Old Town School of Folk Music.

LEONARDO'S RESTAURANT
Map p90   Italian $$
☎ 773-561-5028; 5657 N Clark St; mains $14-25; ◷ dinner Tue-Sun; Ⓜ Red Line to Bryn Mawr
A sleek yet quaint atmosphere and delicious traditional Tuscan fare make this a fiercely guarded local neighborhood favorite. No yawn-inducing pasta and meatballs, here. The champion of the menu is the 18 Hour Ravioli, stuffed with a mouthwatering combination of braised osso bucco and goat cheese, covered in caramelized pearl onions, sage and a succulent demi-glace. A whole boneless chicken tops the meat mains.

JIN JU Map p90   Korean $$
☎ 773-334-6377; 5203 N Clark St; mains $11-18; ◷ dinner; Ⓜ Red Line to Berwyn
One of only a handful of *nouveau* Korean restaurants in town, Jin Ju throws a culinary curveball by tempering Korean food to Western tastes. The minimalist candlelit interior of Jin Ju echoes softly with downbeat techno, and the stylish 30-something clientele enjoys mains like *haemul pajon* (a fried pancake stuffed with seafood) and *kalbi* (beef short ribs). The drinks menu must is the *'soju*-tini', a cocktail made with *soju,* a Korean spirit distilled from sweet potatoes.

HOPLEAF Map p90   New American $$
☎ 773-334-9851; 5148 N Clark St; mains $10-17; ◷ dinner; Ⓜ Red Line to Berwyn
A cozy, European-style tavern, Hopleaf draws crowds for its Montreal-style smoked brisket, cashew-butter-and-fig-jam sandwiches, organic sausages and the house specialty of *frites* and ale-soaked

EATING CHICAGO STYLE – BY THE BOOK

Books by Chicago chefs are a good way to bring the city's culinary character home. Here are some recent favorites:

- *The Seasons on Henry's Farm: A Year of Food and Life on an Organic Farm* (Agate Surrey, 2009) – A fifth-generation Illinois farming family takes you from soil to the supper table in this memoir by Terra Brockman, complete with recipes.
- *Alinea* (Ten Speed Press, 2008) – Celebrity chef Grant Achatz imparts the secret to making 'yolk drops with asparagus' and other molecular gastronomy in his Beard-award-winning cookbook.
- *Sweetness* (Agate Surrey, 2009) – Local pastry-shop owner Sarah Levy teaches amateurs to bake quality confections (while you salivate over the chocolaty pictures).
- *Soup & Bread Cookbook* (www.soupnbread.wordpress.com, 2009) – Each Wednesday in winter, local foodies, musicians and artists gather at the Hideout music club and take turns making a free feast of – yes – soup and bread. This book collects their funky recipes.
- *Mexican Everyday* (WW Norton & Company, 2005) – Rick Bayless, celebrated mind behind Frontera, writes euphoric prose to accompany his brilliant recipes.

mussels. It also pours 200 types of brew (30 are on tap), emphasizing craft and Belgian suds. You'll need patience for the queue, but it'll be worth it.

ANDIE'S Map p90   Mediterranean $$
☎ 773-784-8616; 5253 N Clark St; mains $10-16; ☾ 11am-11pm Sun-Thu, to 12:30am Sat & Sun; Ⓜ Red Line to Berwyn

Reliable Andie's has anchored Andersonville's restaurant row from the get-go, and it still draws crowds for smooth hummus, dill rice and much more in the cool Mediterranean interior. Check online for coupons.

SUNSHINE CAFE Map p90   Japanese $$
☎ 773-334-6214; 5449 N Clark St; mains $9-12; ☾ 4-9pm Mon-Sat, noon-9pm Sun; Ⓜ Red Line to Berwyn

Japanese comfort food fries in the pans at this humble storefront. *Gyozas* (dumplings), potato croquettes, *sakiyuki* (a sweet savory noodle dish with thinly sliced beef and veggies) and *tonkatsu* (breaded pork) are among the most popular dishes. The laid-back staff can help you decide what to order if you're new to the non-sushi scene.

KOPI, A TRAVELER'S CAFE
Map p90   Coffee Shop $

☎ 773-989-5674; 5317 N Clark St; mains $7-10; ☾ 8am-11pm Sun-Thu, to midnight Sat & Sun; Ⓜ Red Line to Berwyn; Ⓥ

Kopi wafts an Asian trekker-lodge vibe, from the pile of pillows to sit on by the front window to the bean-sprouty sandwiches, lefty clientele and flyer-filled

community bulletin board. The little shop in back sells travel books and fair-trade global gifts. Wine goes down the hatch for half price on Wednesdays.

PASTICCERIA NATALINA Map p90   Bakery $
☎ 773-989-5674; 5317 N Clark St; pastries $5-8; ☾ 7am-6pm Tue-Fri, 8am-5pm Sat & Sun; Ⓜ Red Line to Berwyn

A bright green awning announces the little bakery of Natalie and Nick Zarzour, who achieve the most authentic Italian sweets in the city by importing the hard-to-find ingredients (including pistachios, rosewater and Sicilian sheep's milk ricotta) from the motherland. The creations change daily, though all are made with unfailing attentiveness. The luckiest visitors pick up *cassata,* a Sicilian liqueur-soaked cake filled with sweet ricotta cream, and a box of old-fashioned Sicilian lemon cookies – bites of buttery, crumbly goodness.

SWEDISH BAKERY Map p90   Bakery $
☎ 773-561-8919; 5348 N Clark St; pastries $1.30-4; ☾ 6:30am-6:30pm Mon-Fri, to 5pm Sat; Ⓜ Red Line to Berwyn

Locals have been getting in line for custard-plumped eclairs, French silk tortes, chocolate-chip streusels and chocolate-drop butter cookies for more than 75 years. Free samples and coffee help ease the wait.

UPTOWN

HAI YEN Map p90   Vietnamese $$
☎ 773-561-4077; 1055 W Argyle St; mains $9-15; ☾ 10:30am-10pm Mon-Fri, from 9:30am Sat & Sun, closed Wed; Ⓜ Red Line to Argyle

Many of the dishes at this warm Argyle St eatery require some assembly, pairing shrimp, beef or squid with rice crepes, mint, Thai basil and lettuce. For an appetizer, try the *goi cuon*, fresh rolls of vermicelli rice noodles along with shrimp, pork and carrots. The *bo bay mon* consists of seven (yes, seven) different kinds of beef. Order sparingly, or ask for some help from your server – like the *bo bay mon,* many of the dishes are large enough to feed an army.

TWEET Map p90   Breakfast $$
☎ 773-728-5576; 5020 N Sheridan Rd; mains $7-14; ☽ 9am-3pm, closed Tue; Ⓜ Red Line to Argyle
A dish of perfect biscuits and gravy is a surprise just steps from the city's northern Asian enclave, but so are many of the reimagined breakfast standards made by former Charlie Trotter's chefs at this cozy morning spot. The 'Country Benedict' adds two poached eggs and a thick slab of sausage for a decadent opening meal. For something lighter, try the organic buckwheat pancakes.

THAI PASTRY Map p90   Thai $$
☎ 773-784-5399; 4925 N Broadway St; mains $7-11; ☽ lunch & dinner; Ⓜ Red Line to Argyle
A lunchtime favorite with workers from both Uptown and Andersonville, this Thai restaurant has a window filled with accolades and awards, and the food to back it up. The pad thai is excellent, and the spot-on curries arrive still simmering

in a clay pot. For a quick, cheap snack, visit the counter for a baked pastry.

TANK NOODLE Map p90   Vietnamese $$
☎ 773-878-2253; 4953 N Broadway St; mains $6-11; ☽ 8:30am-10pm, to 9pm Sun, closed Wed; Ⓜ Red Line to Argyle
The official name of this spacious utilitarian eatery is Pho Xe Tang, but everyone just calls it Tank Noodle. The crowds come for *banh mi*, served on crunchy fresh baguette rolls, and the *pho*, which is widely regarded as the city's best. The 200-plus-item menu sprawls on from there and includes *banh xeo* (crispy pancakes), catfish and squid dishes, and a rainbow array of bubble teas.

WICKER PARK, BUCKTOWN & UKRAINIAN VILLAGE

These three neighborhoods buzz with exciting eats – arguably Chicago's densest concentration of them. *Nouveau* comfort food? Organic pizza? Chic vegetarian? The Vienna Beef factory? All here, and that's just an appetizer of what the area holds. Exit the Blue Line at Damen and you're at the epicenter, where Bucktown meets Wicker Park and cool restaurants radiate along North, Milwaukee and Damen Aves. A half-mile south, Division St is another rich vein. It's especially happening in summertime, when sidewalk cafes pop

GETTING CURRIED AWAY

The blinking lights, aromatic spice shops and scads of Indian restaurants make Devon Ave west of Western Ave seem like a little side trip to India. The best curry in the city is here at Chicago's northern edge, though it is a long haul from downtown – about 30 minutes by car or an hour by public transportation. Take the Brown Line to Western and then transfer to bus 49B, or take the Red Line to Loyola and transfer to bus 155. Worth the trek.

Udupi Palace (Map pp50-1; ☎ 773-338-2152; 2543 W Devon Ave; mains $7-14; Ⓥ) This bustling all-vegetarian South Indian restaurant serves toasty, kite-sized *dosas* (crepes made with rice and lentil flour) stuffed with all manner of vegetables and spices, along with an array of curries. The room gets loud once it packs out with 20-something Anglo hipsters and a young Indian crowd.

Mysore Woodlands (Map pp50-1; ☎ 773-338-8160; 2548 W Devon Ave; mains $7-14; Ⓥ) It's another South Indian all-veg favorite, where friendly servers deliver well-spiced curries, *dosas* and *iddlies* (steamed rice-lentil patties) in the spacious low-lit room.

Sabri Nehari (Map pp50-1; ☎ 773-465-3272; 2502 W Devon Ave; mains $10-15) Fresh, fresh meat and vegetable dishes, distinctly seasoned, set this Pakistani place apart from its competitors on Devon. Try the 'frontier' chicken, which comes with a plate of freshly cut onions, tomatoes, cucumber and lemon, and enough perfectly cooked chicken for two. For dessert, check out the *kheer*, a creamy rice pudding.

open their umbrellas. Ukrainian Village spills south from here, offering eateries that are a bit edgier, centered on Chicago Ave. A cab or car might be best after dark in Ukie Village, as everything is more widespread.

WICKER PARK & BUCKTOWN

SCHWA Map pp96-7   New American $$$
☎ 773-252-1466; 1466 N Ashland Ave; 9-course menu $110; ⏰ dinner Tue-Sat; Ⓜ Blue Line to Division
Exceedingly popular – reservations for chef Michael Carlson's masterful restaurant should be booked around the same time as your airline ticket. The fact that Carlson worked at Alinea is apparent in an avant-garde, three- or nine-course menu (go for the nine) that redefines American comfort food via such dishes as apple-pie soup. The setup is progressive, too, with chefs also acting as servers. The intimate room is bookended by black wood floors and has a mirrored ceiling.

HOT CHOCOLATE Map pp96-7   American $$
☎ 773-489-1747; 1747 N Damen Ave; mains $13-27; ⏰ lunch Wed-Fri, dinner Tue-Sun, brunch Sat & Sun; Ⓜ Blue Line to Damen
'Come for dessert, stay for dinner' might be the motto at this cocoa-walled Bucktown restaurant. Run by renowned pastry chef Mindy Segal, the cute place feels exactly like the irresistible, upscale chocolate desserts it peddles. With six rich kinds of hot chocolate available (they're like dipping your mug into Willy Wonka's chocolate river), along with mini brioche doughnuts, you may forget to order the other food on offer, such as Kobe beef flank steak and beer-soaked mussels.

CRUST Map pp96-7   Pizza $$
☎ 773-235-5511; 2056 W Division St; mains $12-16; ⏰ lunch & dinner, closed Tue; Ⓜ Blue Line to Division; Ⓥ
Mind your semantics when you step into the first certified organic restaurant in the Midwest: that's no pizza, it's flatbread! The seemingly minor distinction allows for more sophisticated, global flavors (including many vegetarian options), with tender wood-fired crust. If you choose your patio seat wisely, you can even pick your own fresh herbs for garnish. For those more thirsty than hungry, explore the excellent selection of house-infused vodka.

PIECE Map pp96-7   Pizza $$
☎ 773-772-4422; 1927 W North Ave; small pizzas from $11; ⏰ lunch & dinner; Ⓜ Blue Line to Damen
The thin flour-dusted crust of 'New Haven–style' pizza at this spacious Wicker Park microbrewery offers a welcome reprieve from the city's omnipresent deep-dish. The best is the white variety – a sauceless pie dressed simply in olive oil, garlic and mozzarella – which makes a clean pairing with brewer Jon Cutler's award-winning beer. The easygoing, sky-lit ambience changes after dark, when ball games beam down from ubiquitous flat screens, an occasional band plugs in, and the 30-something patrons get a bit more boisterous.

DEE'S PLACE Map pp96-7   Southern $$
☎ 312-348-6117; 2114 W Division St; mains $10-16; ⏰ 11am-11pm Mon-Thu, to 12:30am Fri & Sat, to 8pm Sun; Ⓜ Blue Line to Division
Not many places waft an ambience of 1950s Harlem jazz house meets Soul Train. Photos of musical greats hang on the walls, and a stage hosting live jazz, blues and poetry readings takes up half the small room. Oh, the food? It has soul too, as in fried chicken, fried green tomatoes, fried okra and jerk chicken, along with seafood gumbo on weekends. In summer there's seating by the barbecue pit in the back garden. Dee's is BYOB.

HANDLEBAR Map pp96-7   Eclectic $$
☎ 773-384-9546; 2311 W North Ave; mains $9-14; ⏰ 10am-midnight Mon-Thu, to 2am Fri & Sat, to 11pm Sun; Ⓜ Blue Line to Damen; Ⓥ
The cult of the bike messenger runs strong in Chicago, and this restaurant-bar is a way station for tattooed couriers and locals who come for the strong, microbrew-centric beer list, vegetarian-friendly food (including West African groundnut stew and tofu fajitas) and festive back beer garden.

MIRAI SUSHI Map pp96-7   Japanese $$
☎ 773-862-8500; 2020 W Division St; rolls $2-6, dishes $8-15; ⏰ dinner; Ⓜ Blue Line to Division
This high-energy restaurant has an even higher-energy lounge upstairs; both are packed with happy, shiny Wicker Park residents enjoying some of the freshest sushi in the area. From the trance-hop electronic music to the young, black-clad

top picks

SWEET TREATS

- Margie's (right) Hot fudge sundaes.
- Hot Chocolate (p165) Signature drink and brioche doughnuts.
- Hoosier Mama Pie Company (p168) Banana-cream or chocolate chess pies.
- Swedish Bakery (p163) Chocolate eclairs.

staff, Mirai is where true connoisseurs of sashimi and *maki* (rolled sushi) gather to throw back a few cocktails between savory morsels of yellowtail and shiitake tempura lightly fried to perfection.

IRAZU Map pp96-7   Latin American $$
☎ 773-252-5687; 1865 N Milwaukee Ave; mains $7-13; ⏰ 11:30am-9:30pm Mon-Sat; Ⓜ Blue Line to Western
Chicago's unassuming lone Costa Rican eatery turns out burritos bursting with chicken, black beans and fresh avocado, and sandwiches dressed in a heavenly 'mystery sauce.' Wash them down with an *avena* (a slurpable oatmeal milkshake). For breakfast, the *arroz con huevos* (peppery eggs scrambled into rice) relieves hangovers. The small interior gets crowded; outdoor tables provide some relief when the weather warms. Cash only.

MILK & HONEY Map pp96-7   American $
☎ 773-395-9434; 1920 W Division St; mains $7-9; ⏰ 7am-8pm Mon-Fri, 8am-5pm Sat, to 4pm Sun; Ⓜ Blue Line to Division
A bright, stylish cafe, Milk & Honey has become the hangout *du jour* for discerning neighborhood socialites. The orange brioche French toast rocks the breakfast menu, while the thick-cut bacon, lettuce and tomato sandwich and crab-cake baguette please the lunch crowd. The fireplace and small list of beer and wine soothe when the weather blows.

LETIZIA'S NATURAL BAKERY Map pp96-7   Bakery $
☎ 773-342-1011; 2144 W Division St; sandwiches $6-8, pizzas from $20; ⏰ 6am-11pm; Ⓜ Blue Line to Division
Early risers can get their fix of fantastic baked goods here starting at 6am, and

everyone else can swing by at a more reasonable hour for Letizia's crunchy, toasty panini, slices of gourmet pizza and cups of mind-expanding coffee. The patio with plush seats wins kudos in summer.

PODHALANKA Map pp96-7   Polish $
☎ 773-486-6655; 1549 W Division St; mains $5-10; ⏰ 9am-8pm Mon-Sat, 10am-7pm Sun; Ⓜ Blue Line to Division
Since you're in the middle of the old 'Polish Broadway' area, why not eat like they did in the old 'Polish Broadway' days? This hole-in-the-wall holdover from the era serves up massive portions of potato pancakes, *pierogi*, dill-flecked borscht and other Polish fare on red vinyl seats as the Pope stares from the wall.

SULTAN'S MARKET
Map pp96-7   Middle Eastern $
☎ 773-235-3072; 2057 W North Ave; mains $5-9; ⏰ 10am-10pm Mon-Sat, to 9pm Sun; Ⓜ Blue Line to Damen; Ⓥ
Steps from the Blue Line, this Middle Eastern spot has meat-free delights like falafel sandwiches, spinach pies and a sizable salad bar. Carnivores can come in, too; many swear by the chicken shawarma.

MARGIE'S Map pp96-7   Dessert $
☎ 773-384-1035; 1960 N Western Ave; mains $4-8; ⏰ 9am-midnight Sun-Thu, to 1am Fri & Sat; Ⓜ Blue Line to Western
Margie's has held court at Bucktown's edge for over 80 years, dipping ice-cream sundaes for everyone from Al Capone to the Beatles (check the wall photos). Sure, you can admire the old-fashioned Tiffany lamps, the marble soda fountain and the booths with minijukeboxes. But the star is the hot fudge, unbelievably thick, rich and bountiful, served in its own silver pot. Burgers and sandwiches are just clumsy foreplay to the 50 massive sundaes on offer.

VIENNA BEEF FACTORY STORE & CAFE Map pp96-7   Burgers & Hot Dogs $
☎ 773-435-2277; 2501 N Damen Ave; mains $3-6; ⏰ 6am-4pm Mon-Fri, 10am-3pm Sat; 🚌 50
After you've eaten these hot dogs all over town, it's worth a trip to the source. The Vienna Beef Factory makes the majority of hot dogs sold in Chicago, and the factory's workers' deli is one of the freshest places to try the famous creations. Hot-dog haters

can nosh on corned-beef sandwiches or burgers. And Vienna diehards can pick up a case of the dogs at the on-site store to bring back home.

BIG STAR TAQUERIA

Map pp96-7   Mexican $

☎ 773-235-4039; 1531 N Damen Ave; tacos $3-4; ☽ 11:30am-2am; Ⓜ Blue Line to Damen
Once a filling station, now a taco-serving honky-tonk bar helmed by a big-name Chicago chef (Paul Kahan). So goes gentrification in Wicker Park. The place gets packed, but damn, those tacos are worth the wait – pork belly in tomato–guajillo chili sauce and lamb shoulder with *queso fresco* (creamy white cheese) accompany the specialty whiskey list. If the table-studded patio is too crowded, order from the walk-up window. Cash only.

ALLIANCE BAKERY Map pp96-7   Bakery $

☎ 773-278-0366; 1736 W Division St; items $2-5; ☽ 6am-9pm, from 7am Sun; Ⓜ Blue Line to Division
Order your macaroons, red-velvet cupcakes and other creamy-frosted goodies in the bakery, then take them to the 'lounge' next door (or out to the sidewalk tables) and make like a local by hanging out, reading or tap-tap-tapping on your laptop using the free wi-fi.

UKRAINIAN VILLAGE

GREEN ZEBRA Map pp96-7   Vegetarian $$$

☎ 312-243-7100; 1460 W Chicago Ave; small plates $8-15, 5-course menu $55; ☽ dinner daily, brunch Sun; Ⓜ Blue Line to Chicago; Ⓥ
Beard-award-winning chef Shawn McClain's slick, upscale veggie haven is anything but conventional. With a few nods to the meatily inclined via seafood, the menu focuses on creative seasonal odes to meatless fare. Rich broths, curries and dumplings all make appearances. It's a small-plate setup, so you'll have to order several to make a meal. Or opt for the five-course 'tasting' (four savory dishes and dessert). Add wine pairings for $35.

WEST TOWN TAVERN

Map pp96-7   New American $$

☎ 312-666-6175; 1329 W Chicago Ave; mains $17-25; ☽ dinner Mon-Sat; 🚌 Blue Line to Chicago
The owners hoped to create a

neighborhood restaurant that evoked Chicago of the '40s, and the exposed brick walls and tin ceiling in the handsome dining area do just that. The atmosphere – casual, ebullient and unpretentious – mirrors the contemporary comfort foods, and forking into the pot roast, pasta with turkey meatballs and slabs of lemon chess pie makes for a happy day.

MR BROWN'S LOUNGE

Map pp96-7   Jamaican $$

☎ 773-278-4445; 2301 W Chicago Ave; mains $9-15; ☽ noon-2am Tue-Sun; 🚌 66
Named after a Jamaican folklore tale that Bob Marley adapted into a song, this bar-restaurant cooks up such Jamaican staples as jerk chicken and stewed oxtail along with American riffs like 'island-style' maca-roni and cheese. Wash it down with a spicy rum punch. DJs spin reggae and dancehall tunes on weekends. Ya, mon.

FLO Map pp96-7   Mexican $$

☎ 312-243-0477; 1434 W Chicago Ave; mains $9-14; ☽ 8:30am-10pm Tue-Thu, 8:30am-11pm Fri, 9am-11pm Sat,9am-3pm Sun; Ⓜ Blue Line to Chicago
Think you've had a good breakfast burrito before? Not until you've eaten here. The Southwestern-bent dishes and jovial staff at this brunch hots pot draw hordes of late-rising neighborhood hipsters on the week-end. Tart, potent mojitos and fish tacos take over after dark, but the breakfast foods are the main draw.

TWISTED SPOKE Map pp96-7   American $$

☎ 312-666-1500; 501 N Ogden Ave; mains $9-14; ☽ lunch & dinner daily, brunch Sat & Sun; Ⓜ Blue Line to Grand
Don't let the motorcycle theme, burly burgers and steel finishing intimidate you: behind the macho facade at this popular brunch spot are artful dishes better cali-brated for nesting yuppies than hardscrab-ble Hell's Angels. If the smoky-sweet BBQ Kobe Brisket isn't tough enough for you, order the famous, though unfortunately named, 'Road Rash' Bloody Mary extra spicy, and chomp your way through its accompanying array of harpooned veggies.

BITE CAFÉ Map pp96-7   Eclectic $

☎ 773-395-2483; 1039 N Western Ave; mains $7-9; ☽ 8am-10:30pm Sun-Tue, to 11:30pm Wed-Sat; 🚌 49; Ⓥ

Join the shaggy rockers reading graphic novels and eating globe-spanning dishes like the veggie burrito with tofu, falafel plate and Thai green curry. The small room is industrial chic, with gray booths and funky artwork peppering exposed brick walls. Up until 8:30pm, you can bring booze over from the Empty Bottle bar–music venue next door to accompany meals.

TECALITLAN Map pp96-7   Mexican $

☎ 312-384-4285; 1814 W Chicago Ave; mains $6-12; ⏱ 10am-midnight Sun-Thu, to 3am Fri & Sat; Ⓜ Blue Line to Chicago or 🚌 66

Weighing in at more than a pound and costing less than $6, the *carne asada* (roast meat) burrito with cheese is not just one of the city's best food values, it's one of the city's best foods. Add the optional avocado and you'll have a full day's worth of food groups wrapped in a huge flour tortilla. The *horchata* (a rice-based beverage made with water, sugar, cinnamon, vanilla and lime) is creamy and refreshing.

BARI FOODS Map pp96-7   Deli $

☎ 312-666-0730; 1120 W Grand Ave; sandwiches $4-7; ⏱ 8am-6pm Mon-Sat; Ⓜ Blue Line to Grand

This Italian grocery store and butcher cuts a mean salami. If you're planning a picnic, drop by and pick up a 9in sub sandwich or two (the Italian meatball is particularly scrumptious) and a nice bottle of earthy red.

HOOSIER MAMA PIE COMPANY

Map pp96-7   Dessert $

☎ 312-243-4846; 1618 ½ Chicago Ave; slices $4; ⏱ 8am-7pm Tue-Thu, 8am-9pm Fri, 9am-5pm Sat, 10am-4pm Sun; 🚌 Blue Line to Chicago

There's a statistic out there saying one out of five people have eaten an entire pie solo. Hoosier Mama is your place to do it. Pastry chef Paula Haney hand rolls and crimps her dough, then plumps it with fruit or creamy fillings. Favorites include the fat banana cream, chocolate chess (nicknamed the 'brownie pie') and classic apple (flavored with Chinese five-spice powder). Fridays she offers a pie 'flight' (three small slices for $8). Seating is limited in the itty-bitty storefront.

LOGAN SQUARE & HUMBOLDT PARK

These two neighborhoods have a split personality when it comes to eating out. Their Latino roots show in the scads of hole-in-the-wall taquerias along Milwaukee Ave and the Puerto Rican *jibarito* joints along Division St. But popping up like truffles on odd street corners are inventive foodie meccas and crazy-fun burger and hot-dog sellers. Low rents have made it possible to take an idea and run with it here, and many chefs have done just that. Everything is spread out, so you'll have to work to reach your destination. But boy, will it be worth it.

BONSOIREE

Map p100   New American $$$

773-486-7511; 2728 W Armitage Ave; 4-/7-course menus $58/85; ⏱ dinner Tue-Sun; Ⓜ Blue Line to California

It started as an underground supper club for foodies, and Saturdays are still an invitation-only event (go to the website to get on the mailing list). Otherwise, dinner at Bonsoiree is a leisurely multicourse affair

---

MIDNIGHT MUNCHIES

Chicago is a town that treats midnight snacking with diligence. You can get a burger at any hour from the wealth of old-school, 24-hour family restaurants like the Golden Apple or the Golden Nugget chain. Or you can try one of the following:

- Handlebar (p165) Eat healthy fare and swill beer till midnight on weekdays and 2am on weekends.
- Lazo's Tacos (Map pp96-7; ☎ 773-486-3303; 2009 N Western Ave; mains $4-11; Ⓜ Blue Line to Western) The quintessential taco stop after a long night of drinking; open 24/7.
- El Taco Veloz (Map pp96-7; ☎ 312-738-0363; 1745 W Chicago Ave; mains $4-10; Ⓜ Blue Line to Chicago or 🚌 66) The other quintessential taco stop after boozing, with the bonus of occasional karaoke.
- Eggsperience (p153) Serving eggs and such around the clock.
- Purple Pig (p153) A communal downtown venue where you can eat well and clink wine glasses till midnight and beyond.

where the chefs whip up a set of inspired comfort foods (often with a Japanese bent) using seasonal ingredients. It's unusually casual for such fine dining, right up to being BYOB (though if you ask in advance they'll pair wine for you from a nearby shop). No Menu Sundays cost less, and are made from whatever the chefs pick up at the Logan Square farmers' market that day.

LULA CAFÉ Map p100 New American $$

☎ 773-489-9554; 2537 N Kedzie Ave; mains $18-27; ☾ 9am-10pm Sun-Mon & Wed-Thu, to 11pm Fri & Sat, closed Tue; Ⓜ Blue Line to Logan Square

Funky, arty Lula led the way for Logan Square's dining scene, and appreciative neighborhoodies still crowd in for the seasonal, locally sourced menu. Even the muffins here are something to drool over, and that goes double for lunch items like pasta *yiayia* (bucatini pasta with Moroccan cinnamon, feta and garlic) and dinners such as striped bass with pine-nut-peppered orzo. Mondays offer a prix fixe three-course Farm Dinner.

SMOQUE Map pp50-1 BBQ $$

☎ 773-545-7427; 3800 N Pulaski Rd; mains $11-21; ☾ lunch & dinner Tue-Sun; Ⓜ Blue Line to Irving Park

This squeaky-clean, family-friendly barbecue joint is all about slow-cooked meats. The baby-back and St Louis–style ribs are what line 'em up: they're smoked over oak and applewood and soaked in a tangy, slightly sweet sauce. The brisket and pulled pork aren't far behind in making carnivores swoon (including Guy Fieri, who featured it on Food Network's *Diners, Drive-Ins and Dives*). Brisket-flecked baked beans, cornmeal-crusted mac 'n' cheese, freshly cut fries, citrusy coleslaw and peach cobbler round out the trim menu. BYOB.

KUMA'S CORNER

Map p100 Burgers & Hot Dogs $$

☎ 773-604-8769; 2900 W Belmont Ave; mains $10-13; ☾ 11:30am-1am Mon-Fri, to 2am Sat, noon-11pm Sun; 🚌 77

Ridiculously busy and head-bangingly loud, Kuma's attracts the tattooed set for its monster 10oz burgers, each named for a heavy-metal band and hefted onto a pretzel-roll bun. The results can be straightforward (Black Sabbath comes blackened with chili and pepper jack),

top picks

FOODIE FAVORITES

- **Bonsoiree** (opposite) An underground supper club takes its *nouveau* comfort foods public.
- **Schwa** (p165) The waiters who serve your progressive multicourse dinner are also the chefs who cooked it.
- **Xoco** (p153) Celebri-chef Rick Bayless doles out responsibly sourced Mexican street food and hot chocolate.
- **Hot Doug's** (p170) The beloved hot-dog joint serves 'haute dogs' along with the city's best traditional, Chicago-style wiener.
- **Hopleaf** (p162) Lines twist down the block for the mussels, *frites* and 200-strong beer list.

esoteric (Led Zeppelin is piled with pulled pork, bacon, cheddar and pickles) or whimsical (Judas Priest has bacon, blue cheese, fruit and nuts). There's a mac 'n' cheese menu for vegetarians, and beer and bourbon for all. Be warned: on winter days there's no outside seating, so the prime-time wait can be two hours.

BORINQUEN RESTAURANT

Map p100 Latin American $$

☎ 773-442-8001; 1720 N California Ave; mains $7-15; ☾ 10am-10pm Sun-Thu, to midnight Fri & Sat; Ⓜ Blue Line to Western

The story goes that Borinquen owner Juan 'Peter' Figueroa created his signature dish after reading an article in a Puerto Rican newspaper about a sandwich that subbed plantains for bread – a flash of inspiration that birthed the *jibarito*, a popular dish that piles steak, lettuce, tomato and garlic mayo between two thick, crisply fried plantain slices. The idea caught on, and the *jibarito* is all the rage at local Puerto Rican eateries. It's the marquee item at Borinquen, though more traditional Puerto Rican fare is also available at this homey family spot.

EL CID 2 Map p100 Mexican $

☎ 773-395-0505; 2645 N Kedzie Ave; mains $6-14; 9am-midnight, to 2am Fri & Sat; Ⓜ Blue Line to Logan Square

The tart, fresh margaritas and fish tacos (not batter fried, simply grilled) steal the show at this bright, friendly Mexican, which is a stone's throw from the Logan Square El stop. On busy nights an acoustic minstrel sets up indoors, and when its warm patrons head out back to the romantic patio to dine under strings of lights.

FEED Map p100   Southern $

☎ 773-489-4600; 2803 W Chicago Ave; mains $6-12; ⊗ 8am-10pm Mon & Wed-Fri, 9am-10pm Sat, 9am-9pm Sun; 🚌 66

With red-checked tablecloths, a free-play jukebox piled with classic rock and country, and a menu of southern home cookin', Feed has the chipper feel of a lost *Hee Haw* set. All the framed portraits of poultry allude to the house specialty – juicy, tender rotisserie chicken – but the sides, including hand-cut fries, corn pudding and mac 'n' cheese, are equally stellar. Bulging fruit pie and vanilla-wafer banana pudding follow for dessert. Cash only; BYOB.

HOT DOUG'S
Map p100   Burgers & Hot Dogs $

☎ 773-279-9550; 3324 N California Ave; mains $3-8; ⊗ 10:30am-4pm Mon-Sat; 🚌 77 or 52

Doug's the man to fulfill all your hot-dog fantasies. He serves multiple dog styles (Polish, bratwursts, Chicago) cooked multiple dog ways (char grilled, deep fried, steamed). Confused? He'll explain it all. The chatty Cubs lover also makes gourmet 'haute dogs' – say blue-cheese pork with cherry cream sauce or sesame-ginger duck – that have reviewers dragging out their superlatives. On Friday and Saturday, Doug offers fries cooked in duck fat; be sure to ask for them. The line is lengthy but good natured (it's even been known to burst into a group sing-along). Cash only.

NEAR WEST SIDE & PILSEN

The West Side is vast, though our focus is on three relatively close neighborhoods: the West Loop, Little Italy and Greektown. Of these, the West Loop offers creative cuisine and hip atmospheres that outshine the sturdy stalwarts of the other two districts. Most options are along the Randolph St corridor. A cab or car is the easiest way to reach the area (the El leaves you about a half-mile afield).

There are few surprises in Little Italy and Greektown, but those seeking a heaping plate of pasta or a dish of flaming cheese will have plenty of options.

South of Little Italy, Pilsen is Chicago's most densely populated Latino community, where vendors sling watermelon pops and butter-slathered cobs of corn. A couple of foodie surprises crop up, too. The 18th St stop on the Pink Line puts you at the strip's west end.

WEST LOOP
BLACKBIRD
Map pp104-5   New American $$$

☎ 312-715-0708; 619 W Randolph; mains $27-35; ⊗ lunch Mon-Fri, dinner Mon-Sat; Ⓜ Green, Pink Line to Clinton

One of the most talked-about restaurants in Chicago, this chic dining destination for Chicago's young and wealthy perches atop best-of lists for its exciting, notably seasonal menu. The warm-ups – like the confit of suckling pig with concord grape, roasted chioggia beets, and house-made prosciutto – are a perfect introduction to the visionary mains, which pair well with the short, careful wine list.

PUBLICAN Map pp104-5   New American $$

☎ 312-733-9555; 837 W Fulton Market; mains $20-30; ⊗ 3:30-10:30pm Mon-Thu, to 11:30pm Fri & Sat, 10am-2pm & 5-10pm Sun; Ⓜ Green, Pink Line to Clinton

Set up like a swanky beer hall with urbanites young and old sitting across from each other at long communal tables, Publican specializes in oysters, hams and fine suds – all from small family farms and microbrewers. So you'll know your pork shoulder is from Dyersville, Iowa; your orange-honey turnips from Congerville, Illinois; and your oysters from Bagaduce River, Maine. There's a four-course special ($45) Sunday nights, often hosted by a local brewer who provides beer pairings ($15 to $20 extra). Many locals think the Sunday brunch is the best around – Publican does indeed know its bacon.

AVEC Map pp104-5   New American $$

☎ 312-377-2002; 615 W Randolph; mains $14-21; ⊗ 3:30pm-midnight Sun-Thu, to 1am Fri & Sat; Ⓜ Green, Pink Line to Clinton

Feeling social? This casual cousin to neighboring Publican gives diners a chance to rub elbows at eight-person communal tables. Dishes are meant for sharing (though you only have to share with people you know), and the food from Chef Koren Grieveson is exceptional. Sweet and savory, the bacon-wrapped dates are the must on the menu.

WISHBONE Map pp104-5   Southern $$
☎ 312-850-2663; 1001 W Washington Blvd; mains $8-17; ☽ breakfast & lunch daily, dinner Tue-Sat; Ⓜ Green, Pink Line to Clinton
They call it 'Southern reconstruction cooking,' which means such items as corn muffins, cheese grits, fried chicken, buttermilk rolls and crawfish patties top the tables. Wishbone sits a block from Oprah's studio, and indeed it's her kind of folksy, down-home, gravy-laden place. Wacky chicken and egg artwork splashes across the wall in the cavernous room, which was once a Goodyear Tire garage.

GREEKTOWN

PARTHENON Map pp104-5   Greek $$
☎ 312-726-2407; 314 S Halsted St; mains $13-27; ☽ lunch & dinner; Ⓜ Blue Line to UIC-Halsted; Ⓥ
This veteran has anchored Greektown for three decades, hearing countless yells of 'Opa' to accompany the flaming *saganaki* (sharp, hard cheese cut into wedges or squares and fried). Greeks returning to the city from their suburban retreats have made the Parthenon a favorite. Vegetarians and gluten-free eaters will find lots of options, all marked on the extensive menu. A plus for drivers: there's free valet service.

SANTORINI Map pp104-5   Greek $$
☎ 312-829-8820; 800 W Adams St; mains $11-23; ☽ lunch & dinner; Ⓜ Blue Line to UIC-Halsted
Fish, both shelled and finned, honor the legacies of Greek fishermen at this popular spot, where fresh whole fish can be prepared and served tableside. The boisterous room manages to seem cozy, thanks in part to the large Aegean fireplace. Everything from the bread to the baklava is well made, arriving in portions huge enough to encourage convivial sharing.

KARYN'S ON GREEN Map pp104-5 Vegetarian $$
☎ 312-226-6155; 130 S Green St; mains $10-15; ☽ lunch & dinner; Ⓜ Blue Line to UIC-Halsted; Ⓥ
Karyn Calabrese, who owns a handful of restaurants around town, is Chicago's

queen of raw foods, but this stylish place is her first foray into cooked fare. Her mission: to make vegan dining sexy. And she does a heckuva job in the loungey, low-lit room. Menu items include chicken legs, meatloaf, crab and salmon – but of course, they're vegan reinterpretations of the classics. The full bar pours more than 30 organic and sustainable wines and cocktails.

MELI CAFE Map pp104-5   Breakfast $$
☎ 312-454-0748; 301 S Halsted St; mains $8-15; ☽ 6am-3pm; Ⓜ Blue Line to UIC-Halsted
Meli is the Greek word for 'honey,' and it's apt for this sweet breakfast spot. Skillet dishes made from cage-free eggs (served over a bed of potatoes), goat cheese and fig omelets, and the decadent French toast (made from challah bread dipped in vanilla-bean custard) start the day off right. Meli is also a juice bar, so you can gulp beverages from wheat-grass shots to banana-maple smoothies.

ARTOPOLIS BAKERY & CAFE
Map pp104-5   Greek $$
☎ 312-559-9000; 306 S Halsted St; mains $7-15; ☽ 9am-midnight Mon-Thu, to 1am Fri & Sat, 10am-11pm Sun; Ⓜ Blue Line to UIC-Halsted
Like a good Greek salad, this place has many ingredients. One of the city's top bakeries – many of the nearby Randolph St joints get their bread here – which sells oozing baklava; a cafe-bar that opens onto the street, with tables along the front; and a food bar with classics like spinach pie, which you can eat in or get to go.

top picks
CHEAP EATS

- Cafecito (p149) Fat Cuban sandwiches.
- Feed (p170) Down-home chicken and mac 'n' cheese.
- French Market (p148) Artisanal wares in a train station.
- Podhalanka (p166) *Pierogi* and other Polish comfort food.
- Big Star Taqueria (p167) Tacos for Wicker Park foodies.

MR GREEK GYROS Map pp104-5 Greek $
☎ 312-906-8731; 234 S Halsted St; mains $6-9;
🕑 24hr; Ⓜ Blue Line to UIC-Halsted
Although there's no sign of Mrs, Ms or Mr
Greek, 'the Mr' is a classic gyros joint with
good prices. While the fluorescent lighting
and plastic decor may lack a little charm,
the gyros have a beauty of their own.
Carnivores: this is definitely your place in
the 'hood for late-night eats, as the UIC
students, club goers and occasional bum
will attest.

LITTLE ITALY

CHEZ JOEL Map pp104-5 French $$
☎ 312-226-6479; 1119 W Taylor St; mains $19-25;
🕑 lunch & dinner; Ⓜ Blue Line to Racine
Whether you're dining outside under the
big oak tree or tucked in a cozy corner,
the atmosphere and exceptional French
fare make Chez Joel – the renowned
namesake of chef Joel Kazouini – a
romantic favorite, though an odd duck
among the predominantly Italian stretch of
Taylor St. The menu is anchored by bistro
favorites such as duck leg *confit* and *coq au
vin,* and is complemented by an extensive
wine list.

ROSEBUD Map pp104-5 Italian $$
☎ 312-942-1117; 1500 W Taylor St; mains $15-23;
🕑 lunch & dinner; Ⓜ Pink Line to Polk
This location in Little Italy is the first branch
of an empire of quality Italian restaurants
that has spread throughout the city. It is
popular with politicos and old-school Taylor
St Italians, who slurp down colossal piles of
pasta and spinach gnocchi soaked in red
sauces. Bring a big appetite.

TUFANO'S VERNON PARK TAP
Map pp104-5 Italian $$
☎ 312-733-3393; 1073 W Vernon Park Pl; mains
$9-17; 🕑 lunch Tue-Fri, dinner Tue-Sun; Ⓜ Blue
Line to UIC-Halsted
Still family run after three generations,
Tufano's serves old-fashioned, hearty Italian
fare for modest prices. The blackboards
carry a long list of daily specials, which can
include such wonderful items as pasta with
garlic-crusted broccoli. Amid the usual
celebrity photos on the wall you'll see
some really nice shots of Joey DiBuono,
his family and their patrons through the
decades.

SWEET MAPLE CAFE Map pp104-5 Southern $$
☎ 312-243-8908; 1339 W Taylor St; mains $7-12;
🕑 7am-2pm; Ⓜ Blue Line to Racine
The creaking floorboards, matronly staff
and soulful home cookin' lend the
Sweet Maple Cafe the bucolic appeal of
a Southern roadside diner. The signature
dishes – inch-thick banana (or, seasonally,
peaches and cream) pancakes, cheddar
grits and fluffy, freshly baked biscuits that
come smothered in spicy sausage gravy
or as a part of a fried 'Chick'n Egg and
Cheeser' – earn the superlatives of locals,
but the egg dishes, sturdy muffins and
lunch sandwiches are done with equal
aplomb. If you only have time for one
breakfast in the city, this is the place.

MANNY'S DELI Map pp104-5 Deli $
☎ 312-939-2855; 1141 S Jefferson St; mains $7-14;
🕑 5am-8pm Mon-Sat; Ⓜ Blue Line to Clinton
Chicago's politicos and seen-it-all senior citizens get in the cafeteria-style line at Manny's
for the towering pastrami and corned-beef
sandwiches, matzo ball soup, potato
pancakes and other deli staples. Know what
you want before you join the fast-moving
queue. The newspaper clippings on the wall
provide a dose of city history – or you could
just eavesdrop on the table next to you to
hear deals being brokered that'll be
tomorrow's front-page story.

AL'S #1 ITALIAN BEEF
Map pp104-5 Italian $
☎ 312-226-4017; 1079 W Taylor St; mains $4-6;
🕑 9am-midnight Mon-Fri, from 10am Sat; Ⓜ Blue
Line to Racine
The original location of this local chain
might not be the place to grab lunch if you
want to get off your feet – there are no
tables, only a stand-up counter – but the
legendary namesake sandwich is a favorite
of Hillary Clinton (who ordered some for
her 50th birthday party). Piled high with
savory beef that soaks through the thick
bun, this inexpensive treat is one of the
city's culinary hallmarks.

MARIO'S Map pp104-5 Italian $
1068 W Taylor St; drinks $1-4; 🕑 10am-midnight,
closed Oct-Apr; Ⓜ Blue Line to Racine
At this cheerful box of a shop, super Italian
ice comes loaded with big chunks of fresh
fruit, which keeps crowds coming in the
summer. The owners have been serving the

EATING NEAR WEST SIDE & PILSEN

slushy goodness for a half-century. Lemon tops the list.

PILSEN

NIGHTWOOD Map pp104-5   New American $$
☎ 312-526-3385; 2119 S Halsted St; mains $19-30; ☯ dinner Mon-Sat, brunch Sun; 🚌 8
Staff members handwrite the menu each day based on what local farmers have provided to the chefs: maybe chicken with grits and red kale, or thick-cut hand-made pasta with Hungarian wax peppers. It has the same owners as Lula Cafe in Logan Square – so there's a hint of a hipper-than-thou vibe – but they've intensified their commitment to sustainably produced foods here at Nightwood. The warm, wood-toned room sports an open kitchen, and there's a big patio for al fresco dining.

NUEVO LEON Map pp104-5   Mexican $$
☎ 312-421-1517; 1515 W 18th St; mains $10-15; ☯ 7am-midnight; Ⓜ Pink Line to 18th St
Tour buses line up, disgorging dozens of gringo tourists to sample the famed cuisine of Pilsen's most celebrated restaurant. Sounds horrible, right? Wrong. This huge place is a well-deserved tour stop, and tourists are well outnumbered by the Latino families who fill the tables. Outstanding tacos, tamales and enchiladas are available, though the dish most likely to blow any meat eater's taste buds is the *assado de puerco* – tender roast pork served with homemade flour tortillas. The breakfast is also excellent.

HONKY TONK BBQ Map pp104-5   BBQ $$
☎ 312-226-7427; 1213 W 18th St; mains $8-18; ☯ 4-10pm Tue-Thu, to 11pm Fri & Sat, noon-8pm Sun; Ⓜ Pink Line to 18th St
Art-colored walls and a swell beer and wine list separate Honky Tonk from its Chicago barbecue brethren. It's a fun atmosphere, with live country music some nights and imaginative, changing side dishes like candied bacon and empanadas with shiitake mushrooms. That's all gravy, though, for the signature wood-roasted pork, beef and chicken.

CAFE JUMPING BEAN
Map pp104-5   Coffee Shop $
☎ 312-455-0019; 1439 W 18th St; mains $5-9; ☯ 6am-10pm Mon-Fri, 7am-7pm Sat & Sun; Ⓜ Pink Line to 18th St; 🛜

This ramshackle cafe will make you feel like a regular as soon as you step through the door. It serves excellent hot focaccia sandwiches, baked goods and strong coffee to the 20- and 30-something crowd of MFA-wielding local bohemians. Chess and domino games are always breaking out here, and the comfy confines make it an excellent spot for whiling away a couple of hours with a mocha, soaking up Pilsen's colorful surroundings.

DON PEDRO CARNITAS
Map pp104-5   Mexican $
☎ 312-829-4757; 1113 W 18th St; tacos $1.50-2; ☯ 6am-6pm Mon-Fri, 5am-5pm Sat, to 3pm Sun; Ⓜ Pink Line to 18th St
At this no-frills meat den, a man with a machete salutes you at the front counter. He awaits your command to hack off pork pieces, then wraps the thick chunks with onion and cilantro in a fresh tortilla. You then devour the taco at the tables in back. Lines twist out the door on weekends. Goat stew and tripe add to the meaty menu. Cash only.

SOUTH LOOP & NEAR SOUTH SIDE

Options are a bit thin on the ground in the South Loop, given all the visitor and condo-dweller traffic. The places that are here tend to be solid, reasonably priced cafes and restaurants – just the sort of vittles one needs after a Museum Campus expedition.

Chicago's small but busy Chinatown is nearby and easily reached by train. The Red Line's Cermak-Chinatown stop puts you between the neighborhood's two distinct parts: Chinatown Sq (basically an enormous bilevel strip mall) to the north holds several restaurants, and Wentworth Ave holds slightly grittier, more authentic eateries.

top picks

BEST BRUNCH

- Meli Cafe (p171)
- Lula Café (p169)
- Twisted Spoke (p167)
- Publican (p170)
- Sweet Maple Cafe (p172)

CHICAGO FIREHOUSE

Map pp112-13   American $$$

☎ 312-786-1401; 1401 S Michigan Ave; mains $20-35; ☺ lunch & dinner; Ⓜ Red, Orange, Green Line to Roosevelt

Situated in a carefully restored turn-of-the-century firehouse, this place offers traditional American cuisine in the South Loop. Ribs and steaks headline the show here, although they're pushed out of the spotlight when local resident Mayor Richard M Daley drops in.

CHICAGO CURRY HOUSE

Map pp112-13   Indian $$

☎ 312-362-9999; 899 S Plymouth Ct; mains $10-19; ☺ lunch & dinner; Ⓜ Red, Orange, Green Line to Roosevelt; Ⓥ

Even if it's just standard Indian food in a standard Indian restaurant ambiance, the Curry House provides a nice option for the South Loop and offers a rare bonus: Nepalese dishes. Standouts include *aloo tama bodi* (potatoes and black-eyed peas) and *khasi ko maasu* (goat meat on the bone). Sample them at the lunch buffet. Several menu items are vegetarian. A full bar helps wash it all down.

YOLK Map pp112-13   Breakfast $

☎ 312-789-9655; 1120 S Michigan Ave; mains $8-11; ☺ 6am-3pm Mon-Fri, from 7am Sat & Sun; Ⓜ Red, Orange, Green Line to Roosevelt

Slinking into one of the custom booths at this cheerful diner is worth the long wait – you'll dig into the best traditional breakfast in the South Loop. The omelets include lots of healthy options (the Iron Man is made from egg whites and comes loaded with veggies and avocado), and sweets lovers have stacks of cinnamon-roll French toast and peach-cobbler crepes to drench in syrup. Scores of big salads and burgers are on hand for those inclined to order lunch.

LAWRENCE FISHERIES

Map pp112-13   Southern $

☎ 312-225-2113; 2120 S Canal St; mains $6-12; ☺ 24hrs; Ⓜ Red Line to Cermak-Chinatown

There's not much to look at inside this 24-hour fish-and-chip joint, but the window at the end of the long dining room frames a stunning scene of the Willis Tower over the Chicago River. Not that you have much option but to stand agape once your order arrives – delicious treats like popcorn

shrimp, oysters and fish and chips are stalwarts, but frog legs and scallops round out the menu of batter-crusted goodies from the sea. At night the parking lot outside of this typically family-oriented joint is a prime location for locals to sit on car hoods and shop for suspiciously current DVDs.

PANOZZO'S Map pp112-13   Italian $

☎ 312-356-9966; 1303 S Michigan Ave; mains $6-10; ☺ 10:30am-7pm Tue-Fri, 10am-5pm Sat, 10am-4pm Sun; Ⓜ Red, Orange, Green Line to Roosevelt

Stock your picnic basket for the Museum Campus at Panozzo's. The neatly shelved Italian import store has a deli counter in back that'll stack take-away hot (house-made meatball) or cold (prosciutto and mozzarella) sandwiches, plus lasagna, rice balls and roasted chicken. Grab a bottle of wine or beer, Italian cookies or cheeses to accompany your selection.

EPIC BURGER

Map pp112-13   Burgers & Hot Dogs $

☎ 312-913-1373; 517 S State St; mains $6-9; ☺ lunch & dinner; Ⓜ Brown, Orange, Purple, Pink Line to Library

This sprawling, sunny-orange restaurant brings ecoconscious fast-food eaters the goods they crave: burgers made with all-natural beef, no hormones or antibiotics, topped with cage-free organic eggs and nitrate-free bacon; preservative-free buns; vanilla-bean-speckled milkshakes; and no petroleum-based packaging. The loud music and flat-screen TVs draw a student crowd from the surrounding college campuses in the South Loop.

CHINATOWN

LAO SZE CHUAN Map pp112-13   Chinese $$

☎ 312-326-5040; 2172 S Archer Ave; mains $12-20; ☺ 10:30am-midnight; Ⓜ Red Line to Cermak-Chinatown

Lao Sze Chuan is the most authentic option in heavily touristy Chinatown Sq. The house special is the three-chili chicken, which is tender and very spicy, though the extensive menu has excellent hot pots alongside dishes from the far reaches of the Szechuan province. If the choices are overwhelming, look for advice from watchful chef and owner 'Tony' Xiao Jun Hu.

PHOENIX Map pp112-13   Chinese $$

☎ 312-328-0848; 2131 S Archer Ave; mains $12-19; ⊙ breakfast, lunch & dinner; Ⓜ Red Line to Cermak-Chinatown

Though better sit-down dinner experiences in Chinatown are abundant, the draw here is the excellent dim sum. Small plates of *char siu bao* (barbecued pork buns), shrimp-filled rice noodles, egg custards and other popular vitals roll around the dining room in a seemingly endless parade of carts. The language barrier can be an issue, so keep in mind that if it looks like chicken feet, it probably is.

JOY YEE'S NOODLE SHOP

Map pp112-13   Asian $

☎ 312-328-0001; 2139 S China Pl, Chinatown Sq; mains $8-12; ⊙ lunch & dinner; Ⓜ Red Line to Cermak-Chinatown

Folks line up for bubble teas packed with fresh fruit at this brightly colored, hip cafe. Do yourself a favor, though, and save one of the deliciously sweet drinks for dessert after a bowl of udon, *chow fun* (rice noodles) or chow mein.

WAN SHI DA BAKERY

Map pp112-13   Chinese $

☎ 312-225-1133; 2229 S Wentworth Ave; items $1-3; ⊙ 7am-8pm; Ⓜ Red Line to Cermak-Chinatown

Offering the best, and cheapest à la carte lunch in Chinatown, this bright little bakery has fluffy barbecue pork buns, hot-dog buns (a Chinese variation on the pig in a blanket), bite-sized egg custards, coconut and winter-melon pastries and some dim sum fare. It's available to go, or to scarf down by the handful at the no-frills tables in the back. The more weather-beaten sister bakery across the street, Chiu Quon Bakery, has a nearly identical menu and more tourist foot traffic. Cash only.

HYDE PARK & SOUTH SIDE

Chicago's South Side isn't a heavily traveled dining destination, but if you ask around you'll find excellent African American soul food favorites like collard greens and fried chicken, and some of the city's best barbecue – with or without meat – around the so-called 'Barbecue Triangle.' Hyde Park, which surrounds the University of Chicago, has the

BYTES FOR YOUR BITES

Need help deciding where to eat? Check out the following websites, blogs and discussion boards (in addition to Yelp, of course).

Gapers Block (www.gapersblock.com/drivethru) An entertaining blog dedicated to 'Chicago bite by bite.'

LTH Forum (www.lthforum.com) Wide-ranging, friendly talk about the restaurant scene from a dedicated community of local-minded food lovers. This is the place to get breaking news and the latest buzz.

Chicago Gluttons (www.chicagogluttons.com) Entertaining source of unvarnished restaurant reviews by a group of foul-mouthed 'regular Joes'.

Local Beet (www.thelocalbeet.com) Advice on local and sustainable eating in the Windy City.

Chicago Brunch Blog (www.chicagobrunchblog .com) Dedicated to the meal Chicagoans love most.

requisite college-town fare at similarly low prices. The distances are much too far to walk, so it's best to take a car.

ARMY & LOU'S Map pp50-1   Southern $$

☎ 773-483-3100; 422 E 75th St; mains $8-15; ⊙ 9am-10pm

If you've never had soul food before, you've got to start at this warm and welcoming Chicago classic. It rises above the crowd of similar local establishments with its fried chicken, catfish, collard greens, sweet-potato pie and other classics at prices that are good for your soul. Don't be surprised if you see a few famous black politicians, led by Jesse Jackson. And don't be surprised if some white politicians show up for a photo op. You'll need a car to get here.

SOUL VEGETARIAN EAST

Map pp50-1   Vegetarian $$

☎ 773-224-0104; 205 E 75th St; mains $8-15; ⊙ 11am-9pm Mon-Thu, 11am-10pm Fri, 9am-10pm Sat, 9am-9pm Sun; Ⓥ

Finding soul food that meets the tenets of the vegan diet is such a rarity that the creative barbecue sandwiches and dinner plates at this comfy South Side place have earned a national reputation. Carnivores should head up the street to Lem's Bar-B-Q House (Map pp50-1; ☎ 773-994-2428; 311 E 75th St; mains $10-13) for more traditional fare; it sits atop Chicago's 'Barbecue Triangle.' You'll need wheels to get either place.

MEDICI Map p120 — American $$

☎ 773-667-7394; 1327 E 57th St; mains $7-14; Ⓜ Metra to 55th-56th-57th

The menu of thin-crust pizzas, sandwiches and salads draws U of C students to this colorful cafe and bakery. For breakfast, try the 'eggs espresso,' made by steaming eggs in an espresso machine. After your meal, check the vast bulletin board out front. It's the perfect place to size up the character of the community and possibly find the complete works of John Maynard Keynes for sale, cheap.

VALOIS CAFETERIA Map p120 — Southern $

☎ 773-667-0647; 1518 E 53rd St; mains $5-11; ☺ 5:30am-10pm; Ⓜ Metra to 53rd

It's a mixed crowd at Valois. In fact, the clientele is so socioeconomically diverse that a U of C sociology professor wrote a well-known book about it, titled *Slim's Table*. It seems hot, fast, Southern-style dishes like French toast, bacon, biscuits, pot pies and patty melts attract all kinds – even Barack Obama, who used to chow here regularly (enjoying steak and eggs, according to the sign at the counter). It's a real-deal cafeteria, so know what you want before reaching the front of the fast-moving line. Cash only.

top picks

- Violet Hour (p186)
- Billy Goat Tavern (p179)
- Happy Village (p184)
- Matchbox (p185)
- Schaller's Pump (p187)
- Old Town Ale House (p181)
- Ginger Man (p182)
- Delilah's (p180)
- Signature Lounge (p180)
- Revolution Brewing (p186)

DRINKING

A signed portrait of Sinatra beams down over the bar at Gene & Georgetti, an old-world Italian joint where the drinks menu bears a simple dedication 'to those merry souls of other days…who, whatever they may drink, prove able to carry it, enjoy it, and remain gentlemen.' By the abundance of taverns in Chicago, it's clear the city's residents enjoy drinking every bit as much as those merry souls. And the part about remaining gentlemen? Well, aside from the over-served coeds in Lincoln Park and the boisterous game-day mobs in Wrigleyville, the city approaches drinking with gentlemanly diligence. From knocking back bottles at a linoleum-floored Ukrainian Village tavern to consulting *haute* food pairings at a sophisticated lounge, Chicago's drinking culture is nothing if not a serious, widely cherished civic pastime.

DRINKING DESTINATIONS

To really toast Chicago's drinking culture, get the heck out of the Loop and into one of the outlying neighborhoods. There, the proud corner taverns populated by the immigrants who built this city are still marked by a swinging Old Style sign out front. But if your thirst for adventure accompanies one for rainbow-colored inebriants, it's easy to hail a cab and find a neighborhood to suit your taste. Lincoln Ave and Halsted St in Lincoln Park draw raucous DePaul students, while indie-rock jukebox bars on Damen and Milwaukee Aves in Wicker Park bring in hordes of postcollegiate hipsters. The Boystown stretch of Halsted in Lake View is an energetic epicenter of gay nightlife, while the posse of single older gents on the make and upscale singles earned the Gold Coast the nickname 'Viagra Triangle.'

PRACTICALITIES

Though a ban on public smoking sailed through city council back in 2005, it wasn't enforced until January 2008, when Chicago joined New York, Boston and Los Angeles by sending smokers outside to light up. Even so, loopholes in the ordinance ensure that indomitable smokers will still be able to find a hazy refuge – just ask around.

Also keep in mind that even though the vast majority of bars will run a tab on your credit card, it's a good idea to have cash on you. This is especially true at small neighborhood bars, some of which accept cash only.

The following listings are establishments where people primarily go to thin their blood and socialize. The Nightlife chapter (p189) has options if you're looking for an active night of dancing or live music, but if the evening's primary activity is lifting a pint glass, these are the best places to belly up.

Opening Hours

Most Chicago bars open at 11am and close at 2am daily, except on Saturday when they're permitted to stay open until 3am. Some bars have a special license that allows them to stay open until 4am daily, and 5am on Saturday. We've noted these late-night bars in the listings below, as well as provided the specific hours for any bars that deviate from the 11am to 2am norm.

Seasonally, summer is the best time to drink in Chicago, due to ubiquitous open-air patios where patrons toast the balmy evenings.

How Much?

The good news for spendthrift travelers is that drinking in Chicago can be done on a pittance compared to other big American cities. A bottle of Chicago's rank-and-file favorites, Pabst and Old Style, will set you back about $3. That doesn't mean there's a lack of options on the other end of the spectrum – in swish neighborhoods around the Loop, a $11 cocktail is common. A pint of beer averages $6 throughout the city.

DRINK DEALS

My Open Bar (www.chi.myopenbar.com) is 'your guide to free booze,' as the tagline says. Indeed, the website tells you what bars are dispensing drink specials day by day, so you'll know where to go for $1-off Belgian beers on Monday and $5 Stoli drinks on Wednesday – and then some. It's got a free iTunes app, too.

LOCAL SUDS

Chicago and environs have a cache of craft brewers, and they're ready to pour you a cold one. Keep an eye on the local taps for these slurpable beer makers:

Bell's Kalamazoo, MI

Founder's Grand Rapids, MI

Goose Island Chicago, IL

Great Lakes Cleveland, OH

Half Acre Chicago, IL

Lakefront Milwaukee, WI

New Holland Holland, MI

Three Floyds Munster, IN

Two Brothers Warrenville, IL

Tipping

Like elsewhere, the love and devoted attention of a bartender can usually be bought with courteous behavior and cold hard cash, and big tips often result in a heavy pour. Tipping a dollar per drink is the norm, though if you order a round for buddies, a $5 tip should suffice.

THE LOOP

Big hotels and office buildings loom over the Loop, which has plenty of options for a three-martini lunch, but limited choices at night. Add the Gage restaurant (p148) to the list below; its bar pours good whiskeys and suds. Move a few blocks onward to the Near North and the boozer bounty increases.

CAL'S BAR Map pp54-5   Bar
☎ 312-922-6392; 400 S Wells St; ☼ 7am-8pm Sun-Thu, to 2am Fri & Sat; Ⓜ Brown, Orange, Purple, Pink Line to LaSalle

The bartenders serve plenty of 'tude with the drinks at this family-owned dive bar and liquor store, which serves as a lone oasis for scruffy hipsters who find themselves lost among suits in the Loop. On weekend nights, punk-rock bands with names like Broadzilla and Johnny Vomit take the stage.

INTELLIGENTSIA COFFEE
Map pp54-5   Coffee Shop
☎ 312-920-9332; 53 E Randolph St; ☼ 6am-8pm Mon-Thu, 6am-9pm Fri, 7am-9pm Sat, 7am-7pm

Sun; Ⓜ Brown, Green, Orange, Purple, Pink Line to Randolph; ☜

This local chain roasts its own beans and percolates good strong stuff. Its baristas frequently win the national latte-making championship, and one went on to win the international version. They know their joe. It makes a good pre- or post–Millennium Park fuel up.

NEAR NORTH & NAVY PIER

Drinkeries here span the gamut, pouring Schlitz on one block and champagne on the next. The crowds tend to be a mix of tourists and office workers, neither of which seem to mind much about paying for the relatively pricey drinks.

BILLY GOAT TAVERN Map pp66-7   Bar
☎ 312-222-1525; lower level, 430 N Michigan Ave; ☼ from 6am Mon-Fri, from 10am Sat & Sun; Ⓜ Red Line to Grand

Somehow, despite the steady line of tourists that queue up for SNL-famous 'cheezborgers,' and the soulless franchise locations all over town, this subterranean haunt for Tribune and Sun-Times writers is an enduring, endearing classic. See p153 for details on the solids that can accompany your Schlitz.

CLARK ST ALE HOUSE Map pp66-7   Bar
☎ 312-642-9253; 742 N Clark St; ☼ 4pm-4am Mon-Thu, to 5am Fri & Sat, to 2am Sun; Ⓜ Red Line to Chicago

With one of the best beer selections downtown, the Ale House has a rotating assortment featuring several Midwestern microbreweries. Work up a thirst on the free pretzels, order a three-beer sampler for $5, and cool off in the beer garden out back. This place is tops in the 'hood.

TERRACE AT TRUMP TOWER
Map pp66-7   Lounge
☎ 312-588-8600; 401 N Wabash Ave; ☼ from 2:30pm Mon-Sat, from 4pm Sun; Ⓜ Brown, Orange, Green, Purple, Pink to State

Trump's view-a-riffic, 16th-floor al fresco lounge is for when you want to live large, with a glass of champagne in hand, looking at the Wrigley Building and the river from

top picks

HOP-HEADS' FAVORITES

- Hopleaf (p184)
- Quencher's (p186)
- Delilah's (below)
- Map Room (p186)
- Clark St Ale House (p179)

a bird's eye vantage point. It only seats 75 (no reservations), making it cozier than you'd think.

BREHON PUB Map pp66-7   Pub
☎ 312-642-1071; 731 N Wells St; Ⓜ Brown, Purple Line to Chicago
This Irish stalwart is a fine example of the corner saloons that once dotted the city. The ample selection of draft beer in frosted glasses is served to neighborhood crowds perched on the high stools.
The following are also recommended:

Harry Caray's (Map pp66-7; ☎ 312-527-9700; 700 E Grand Ave; ⏱ from 11am; 🚌 124) The local chain's Navy Pier outpost, with decent brewskis and a small sports memorabilia 'museum.'

Pop's for Champagne (Map pp66-7; ☎ 312-266-7677; 601 N State St; ⏱ from 3pm Sun-Fri, from 1pm Sat; Ⓜ Red Line to Grand) A mature crowd sips from a list of 100 sparkling wines.

Purple Pig (☎ 312-464-1744; 500 N Michigan Ave; ⏱ 11:30am-midnight Sun-Thu, to 1am Fri & Sat; Ⓜ Red Line to Grand) A long and lovely list of affordable vinos to match the hammy food (p153).

GOLD COAST

When the sun goes down, the bars of the Gold Coast swell with vivacious 30- and 40-somethings who are dressed to the nines and on the prowl. The small, triangular green space formed between Chicago, State and Rush Streets – coyly dubbed the Viagra Triangle by locals – is at the heart of the action. The three-sided catwalk offers unparalleled people-watching.

GIBSON'S Map pp72-3   Bar
☎ 312-266-8999; 1028 N Rush St; Ⓜ Red Line to Clark/Division
Gibson martinis (served with a cocktail onion) are the namesake item at this lively

bar attached to Gibson's steakhouse (p154). A piano player starts up at 5pm.

LODGE Map pp72-3   Bar
☎ 312-642-4406; 21 W Division St; ⏱ 2pm-4am Sun-Fri, to 5am Sat; Ⓜ Red Line to Clark/Division
Dressed up like a misplaced hunting cabin, the Lodge has a bit more polish than most of its neighbors on Division St. A Wurlitzer jukebox spins oldies, and the bowls of salty peanuts complement the abundance of beers on tap. The crowd of mostly 40-somethings drink like they mean it, sometimes until dawn.

COQ D'OR Map pp72-3   Lounge
☎ 312-787-2200; 140 E Walton St; Ⓜ Red Line to Chicago
This classy joint in the Drake Hotel opened the day after Prohibition was repealed. It offers a taste of old Chicago – burgundy-colored leather booths, a tuxedoed bartender and bejeweled women in furs sipping Manhattans. A piano player starts tickling the ivories around 7pm.

SIGNATURE LOUNGE
Map pp72-3   Lounge
☎ 312-787-7230; John Hancock Center, 875 N Michigan Ave; Ⓜ Red Line to Chicago
Have the Hancock Observatory view without the Hancock Observatory admission price. Shoot straight up to the 96th floor and order a beverage while looking out over the city. It's particularly gape-worthy at night. Ladies: don't miss the bathroom view. For Observatory details, see p71. For the restaurant, see p154.

LINCOLN PARK & OLD TOWN

The blood-alcohol levels run pretty high in Lincoln Park, where bars pour microbrews and Cosmopolitans for hard-drinking yuppies. The saloons around DePaul University heighten the party-hearty feel of the place, serving as beer-soaked launching pads for plenty of awkward conversations the following morning. In Old Town, the pace is slower and quirkier.

DELILAH'S Map pp78-9   Bar
☎ 773-472-2771; 2771 N Lincoln Ave; ⏱ from 4pm; Ⓜ Brown Line to Diversey

A bartender rightfully referred to this bad-ass black sheep of the neighborhood as the 'pride of Lincoln Ave,' a title earned by its underground rockers for the heavy pours and the best whiskey selection in the city. They know their way around a beer list, too, tapping unusual domestic and international suds (though cheap Pabst longnecks are always behind the bar, too).

ROSE'S LOUNGE Map pp78-9   Bar
☎ 773-327-4000; 2656 N Lincoln Ave; ⏰ from 4pm; Ⓜ Brown, Purple Line to Diversey
Once your eyes adjust to the dark of Rose's, the eclectic bric-a-brac, drop ceiling and dollar brews make it an odd duck amongst Lincoln Park's yupple lounges. The ultra-cheap beers are the big draw, bringing in a motley set of spendthrift regulars.

WEEDS Map pp78-9   Bar
☎ 312-943-7815; 1555 N Dayton St; ⏰ from 4pm, closed Sun; Ⓜ Red Line to North/Clybourn
This place has the tenacity of its namesake flora, sticking to its beatnik-meets-bohemia roots for years while the neighborhood gentrified around it. If the walls – or the bras hanging from the ceiling – could talk, you'd hear some strange yarns from the motley crew who work and drink here. Weeds hosts open-mic poetry (Monday), comedy (Tuesday) and sometimes live music, and you can quaff in the laid-back beer garden.

GOOSE ISLAND BREWERY
Map pp78-9   Brewery
☎ 312-915-0071; 1800 N Clybourn Ave; Ⓜ Red Line to North/Clybourn

top picks
BOOZING BLOCKS

- Rowdy night owls: Clark St in Lake View (Map pp86-7).
- Thirty-something hipsters: Division St in Wicker Park (Map pp96-7).
- Collegiate beer-chuggers: Lincoln Ave in Lincoln Park (Map pp78-9).
- Patio-hopping boozehounds: Damen Ave in Bucktown (Map pp96-7).
- Pan-genre bar-hoppers: Milwaukee Ave in Wicker Park (Map pp96-7).

Goose Island's popular beers are served in bars and restaurants around Chicago, but it tastes best here at the source. The pub pours the flagship Honker's Ale and 14 or so other potent brews. If you're lucky, the 10% Extra Naughty Goose or Maple Bacon Stout, served with a meaty slice, will be on tap. A four-beer flight (5oz per glass) costs $8. Tours ($7) take place on Sundays at 1:30pm, 3pm and 4:30pm and must be reserved in advance. Fine grub complements the brews; special kudos to the Stilton burger and chips.

RED ROOSTER CAFE & WINE BAR
Map pp78-9   Cafe
☎ 773-071-2100; 2100 N Halsted St; ⏰ 5-10:30pm Mon-Thu, to 11:30pm Fri & Sat, to 10pm Sun; Ⓜ Brown, Purple Line to Armitage
Connected to Cafe Bernard, this funky little wine bar makes a great stop before or after meals or the theater. Choose from plenty of wines by the glass.

OLD TOWN ALE HOUSE Map pp78-9   Pub
☎ 312-944-7020; 219 W North Ave; ⏰ 8am-4am Mon-Fri, to 5am Sat, noon-4am Sun; Ⓜ Brown, Purple Line to Sedgwick
Located by Second City and the scene of late-night musings since the 1960s, this unpretentious neighborhood favorite lets you mingle with beautiful people and grizzled regulars, seated pint by pint under the nude-politician paintings. Classic jazz on the jukebox provides the soundtrack for the jovial goings-on.

LAKE VIEW & WRIGLEYVILLE
The bars of Lake View flaunt the distinctive characteristics of the neighborhoods that surround them; there are bars full of high-fiving Cubs fans in Wrigleyville, high-stakes pool games near the Southport corridor, and high-energy gay clubs in Boystown. If you're arriving on a Cubs game day, prepare for traffic snarls and big crowds.

CLOSET Map pp86-7   Bar
☎ 773-477-8533; 3325 N Broadway St; ⏰ 2pm-4am Mon-Fri, noon-5am Sat, noon-4am Sun; Ⓜ Red, Brown, Purple Line to Belmont
One of the very few lesbian-centric bars in Chicago, the Closet changes mood and

tempo at 2am, when the crowd becomes more mixed, the music gets louder and things get a little rowdier.

GINGER MAN Map pp86-7   Bar
☎ 773-549-2050; 3740 N Clark St; ⏱ from 3pm Mon-Fri, from noon Sat & Sun; Ⓜ Red Line to Addison
A splendid place to pass an evening, this spot features a huge and eclectic beer selection, which is enjoyed by theater types and other creative folks. It offers respite from the Cubs mania of the rest of the strip by playing classical music and jazz during home games. Pool is free on Sunday.

HARRY CARAY'S Map pp86-7   Bar
☎ 773-327-7800; 3551 N Sheffield Ave; ⏱ closed Mon & Tue Oct-Mar; Ⓜ Red Line to Addison
Across from Wrigley Field and named after its famed announcer, this outpost of the local Harry Caray's chain caters to pre- and post-Cubs-game guzzlers a bit more demurely than its neighbors. If something feels familiar, almost gamelike, while you're bellied up to the 60ft-6in bar, well, that's the distance from the pitcher's mound to home plate.

HUNGRY BRAIN Map pp86-7   Bar
☎ 773-935-2118; 2319 W Belmont Ave; ⏱ from 8pm, closed Mon; 🚌 77
The kind bartenders, roving tamale vendors and well-worn, thrift-store charm are inviting at this Roscoe Village staple, which hosts sets of free live jazz from some of the city's best young players on Sunday nights; see p191 for more info. Cash only.

L&L Map pp86-7   Bar
☎ 773-528-1303; 3207 N Clark St; ⏱ from 2pm Mon-Fri, from noon Sat & Sun; Ⓜ Red, Brown, Purple Line to Belmont
The dim, inviting L&L is one of the few places on Clark St where ordering Sex on the Beach might get you 86ed. Instead, relax with $2 Pabst or a sip from the impressive assortment of Irish whiskey. It's an excellent dive bar in which to duck the Wrigleyville madness.

MURPHY'S BLEACHERS Map pp86-7   Bar
☎ 773-281-5356; 3655 N Sheffield Ave; Ⓜ Red Line to Addison
Getting well lubricated before the big game is the prerogative of Cubs fans at

top picks
BARS TO GET YOUR GAME ON
Though most of the city's bars cater to inebriated inactivity, there are plenty of arenas for time-tested boozy athletics.
- **Happy Village** (p184) Get aced by cheerful locals in the cutthroat ping-pong room.
- **Captain Morgan's** (p218) Cornhole, anyone? It's the beanbag version of horseshoes.
- **Southport Lanes** (p182) Bowl a few frames and try to pick up the illusive 7-10 split.
- **Ten Cat Tavern** (p183) Pool sharks test their mettle on the vintage tables.
- **Sluggers** (p215) Practice your home-run swing in the batting cages across from Wrigley Field.

this well-loved, historic watering hole, only steps away from the entrance to Wrigley Field's bleacher seats. They jam this place like sardines on game day.

SOUTHPORT LANES Map pp86-7   Bar
☎ 773-472-6600; 3325 N Southport Ave; ⏱ from noon; Ⓜ Brown Line to Southport
An old-fashioned, four-lane bowling alley with hand-set pins hides inside this busy neighborhood bar and grill. Those who prefer to shoot stick can chalk up at the six regulation pool tables. The main bar features an inspirational mural of cavorting nymphs, and tables sprawl onto the sidewalk in summer.

DUKE OF PERTH Map pp86-7   Pub
☎ 773-477-1741; 2913 N Clark St; ⏱ from 5pm Mon, from noon Tue-Sun; Ⓜ Brown, Purple Line to Wellington
The UK beers and more than 80 bottles of single-malt scotch are nearly overwhelming at this cozy, laid-back pub. After enough of them, try the fish and chips, which is all-you-can-eat for lunch and dinner for $9.50 on Wednesday and Friday.

GLOBE PUB Map pp86-7   Pub
☎ 773-871-3757; 1934 W Irving Park Rd; Ⓜ Brown Line to Irving Park
This warm, dark-oak pub is ground zero for English soccer and rugby fanatics, since it shows all the international league games on satellite TV. It even opens at 6am for big

matches so patrons can watch the action live. The kitchen cooks up a traditional English breakfast daily, and the taps flow with ales from the homeland.

GUTHRIE'S Map pp86-7 — Pub
☎ 773-477-2900; 1300 W Addison St; ☻ from 4pm; Ⓜ Red Line to Addison
A local institution, and the perfect neighborhood hangout, Guthrie's remains true to its mellow roots even as the neighborhood goes manic around it. The glassed-in back porch is fittingly furnished with patio chairs and filled with 30- and 40-somethings, and most tables sport a box of Trivial Pursuit cards.

TEN CAT TAVERN Map pp86-7 — Pub
☎ 773-935-5377; 3931 N Ashland Ave; ☻ from 3pm; Ⓜ Brown Line to Irving Park
Pool is serious business on the two vintage tables that Ten Cat co-owner Richard Vonachen refelts regularly with material from Belgium. The ever-changing, eye-catching art comes courtesy of neighborhood artists, and the furniture is a garage saler's dream. Regulars (most in their 30s) down leisurely drinks at the bar or, in warm weather, head to the beer garden.

ANDERSONVILLE, LINCOLN SQUARE & UPTOWN

Although Andersonville and Uptown are geared toward quieter outings and unlikely to attract hard-partying bar hounds, there are a number of worthy destinations, including one of Chicago's best beer bars and a couple of GLBT favorites.

BIG CHICKS Map p90 — Bar
☎ 773-728-5511; 5024 N Sheridan Rd; ☻ from 4pm Mon-Sat, from 3pm Sun; Ⓜ Red Line to Argyle
Uptown's Big Chicks has an enjoyable split personality. During the week, the bar is a cozily sedate place for gay and straight to socialize beneath the sizable collection of woman-themed art. On weekends, though, gay men pack the stamp-sized dance floor and boogie until all hours. Every Sunday, Big Chicks hosts a legendary free barbecue brunch.

CHICAGO BRAUHAUS Map pp50-1 — Bar
☎ 773-784-4444; 4732 N Lincoln Ave; ☻ 11am-midnight, closed Tue; Ⓜ Brown Line to Western
Unlikely as it may seem for a bar, the oompah soundtrack, rosy-cheeked staff and early last call give this spacious Bavarian-themed joint the all-ages appeal of a Disney ride. Dinnertime is best, when the 'world-famous' lederhosen-clad Brauhaus Trio starts bumping, and steaming plates of schnitzel seem heaven-sent. Bring your dancing shoes, too – there's polka action nightly.

HAMBURGER MARY'S Map p90 — Bar
☎ 773-784-6969; 5400 N Clark St; ☻ from 11:30am Mon-Fri, from 10:30am Sat & Sun; Ⓜ Red Line to Berwyn
This is Chicago's outpost of the campy San Francisco–based chain that bills itself as an 'open-air bar and grill for open-minded people.' Yes, they serve well-regarded burgers and weekend brunch in the downstairs restaurant, but the action's on the rowdy, booze-soaked patio. Mary's Rec Room next door brews its own beer and turns on the HDTVs for sports fans. The Attic lounge upstairs hosts cabaret, karaoke and DJs.

SIMON'S Map p90 — Bar
☎ 773-878-0894; 5210 N Clark St; Ⓜ Red Line to Berwyn
An Andersonville mainstay that has been around since 1934, Simon's is a dimly lit musicians' watering hole. The jukebox rocks an eclectic menu ranging from Robert Gordon to Elastica to Television to The Clash. In winter, in homage to its Swedish roots, Simon's serves *glogg* (spiced wine punch). A giant neon fish holding a martini glass marks the spot.

IN FINE SPIRITS Map p90 — Lounge
☎ 773-334-9463; 5420 N Clark St; ☻ 4pm-midnight Mon-Thu, 3pm-2am Fri & Sat, 3-11pm Sun; Ⓜ Red Line to Berwyn
For a cocktail lounge that shakes and stirs chichi artisanal drinks like the Tiki Bebado (with 'fresh-cut Brazilian mountain cane'), In Fine Spirits is surprisingly low-key. And the drinks – all 30 of them, many made with locally sourced booze à la North Shore Gin from suburban Lake Bluff – kick ass. Wine and bourbon flights and a small menu of flatbreads and appetizers round out the offerings.

HOPLEAF Map p90 — Pub

☎ 773-334-9851; 5148 N Clark St; ⏰ from 3pm; Ⓜ Red Line to Berwyn

Using the name of the national beer from his ancestral Malta, owner Michael Roper operates one of the city's best, classiest beer bars. The overwhelming selection – 200 brews, 30 on tap – is artfully selected by Roper, with an emphasis on Belgian and American craft brews. The kitchen serves excellent Belgian *frites* and mussels. No wonder the place is always packed to the rafters.

WICKER PARK, BUCKTOWN & UKRAINIAN VILLAGE

Taking the Blue Line to Damen puts you on the doorstep of some of Chicago's most eclectic nightlife. On one hand, highfalutin cocktail lounges and wine bars wet the whistles of 20- and 30-somethings on Damen and Milwaukee Aves. But back on the side streets, mom-and-pop bars serve pretty much the same shot-and-beer combos as in Nelson Algren's day.

BLUEBIRD Map pp96-7 — Bar

☎ 773-486-2473; 1749 N Damen Ave; ⏰ from 5pm; Ⓜ Blue Line to Damen

Rustic Bluebird's candlelit bar, oak tables and exposed brick walls give it a casually romantic, good-for-a-first-date ambience. The lengthy, well-curated beer list focuses on small-batch and global pours, and there are several wines available by the glass. To quell the stomach, order a cheese or charcuterie plate or perhaps a Belgian chocolate waffle.

top picks
BARS WITH GOOD FOOD

Or maybe they're restaurants with good booze? At any rate, you can eat and drink well simultaneously at these places.

- Bluebird (above)
- Big Star Taqueria (p167)
- Hopleaf (above)
- Gage (p148)
- Longman & Eagle (p187)

DANNY'S Map pp96-7 — Bar

☎ 773-489-6457; 1951 W Dickens Ave; ⏰ from 7pm; Ⓜ Blue Line to Damen

Little Danny's is a hipster magnet, featuring a comfortably dim and dog-eared atmosphere and occasional DJ sets of Stax 45s. Blessedly TV free, Danny's is a great place to come for conversation early in the evening, or to shake a tail feather at an impromptu dance party on the weekend.

ED & JEAN'S Map pp96-7 — Bar

2032 W Armitage Ave; ⏰ hr vary; Blue Line to Damen

It's one of the city's classic dive bars, where the wood paneling, kitschy knick-knacks and 'shot-ana-beer' orders impart authentic Chicago character. There's no phone number, and the hours are at Ed and Jean's whim, so it's good to have a backup plan like nearby Danny's or the Map Room.

GOLD STAR BAR Map pp96-7 — Bar

☎ 773-227-8700; 1755 W Division St; ⏰ from 4pm; Ⓜ Blue Line to Division

A vestige from the days when Division St was 'Polish Broadway,' the Gold Star remains a divey winner, drawing a posse of bike messengers – and people who dress like them – for cheapie libations and a great metal-and-punk jukebox.

HAPPY VILLAGE Map pp96-7 — Bar

☎ 773-486-1512; 1059 N Wolcott Ave; ⏰ from 4pm Mon-Fri, from noon Sat & Sun; Ⓜ Blue Line to Division

The sign boasting the 'happiest place in the east village' seems like an understatement on a summer evening when a strolling tamale vendor appears on the vine-covered patio here – then it's happiest place on Earth. Don't get too sauced before entering the table-tennis room adjoining the bar; the competition is fierce.

INNERTOWN PUB Map pp96-7 — Bar

☎ 773-235-9795; 1935 W Thomas St; ⏰ from 3pm; Ⓜ Blue Line to Division

A cigar-smoking moose and a bronze bust of Elvis overlook the crowd of artsy regulars playing pool and drinking cheap at this lovably divey watering hole. Order a Christmas Morning, a delightful shot of hot espresso and chilled Rumplemintz.

MATCHBOX Map pp96-7   Bar

☎ 312-666-9292; 770 N Milwaukee Ave; ☺ from 4pm; Ⓜ Blue Line to Chicago

Lawyers, artists and bums all squeeze in for retro cocktails. It's as small as – you got it – a matchbox, with about 10 barstools; everyone else stands against the back wall. Barkeeps make the drinks from scratch. Favorites include the pisco sour and the ginger gimlet, ladled from an amber vat of homemade ginger-infused vodka.

OLA'S LIQUOR Map pp96-7   Bar

☎ 773-384-7259; 947 N Damen Ave; ☺ from 7am Mon-Sat, from 11am Sun; ☒ 50

This classic 'slashie' – the term for a bar–liquor store combo, where the bar is stashed in the back room – has hours catering to third-shift locals and the most indomitable night owls. Order the advertised *zimne piwo* (Polish for 'cold beer') and blast some tunes on the juke in the same language.

RAINBO CLUB Map pp96-7   Bar

☎ 773-489-5999; 1150 N Damen Ave; ☺ from 4pm; Ⓜ Blue Line to Division

The center for Chicago's indie elite during the week, the boxy, dark-wood Rainbo Club has an impressive semicircular bar and one of the city's best photo booths. The service is slow and the place goes a little suburban on weekends, but otherwise it's an excellent place to hang out with artsy locals.

RICHARD'S BAR Map pp96–7   Bar

☎ 312-421-4597; 725 W Grand Ave; ☺ from 8am Mon-Fri, from 9am Sat, from noon Sun; Ⓜ Blue Line to Grand

The younger of the two main bartenders in this timeless dive is in his 70s. The bar –

top picks
HEAD-SPINNING COCKTAILS

- Violet Hour (p186)
- In Fine Spirits (p183)
- Matchbox (left)

with its tall, humming refrigerated coolers for to-go orders and a strange mix of Rat Pack and *Saturday Night Fever* on the jukebox – feels like something out of a Jim Jarmusch movie. Hang around long enough and the owner may bring out a huge platter of food for everyone.

FILTER Map pp96-7   Coffee Shop

☎ 773-904-7819; 1373 N Milwaukee Ave; ☺ 7am-11pm Mon-Fri, 7:30am-11pm Sat, 8am-10pm Sun; Ⓜ Blue Line to Division or Damen; ☺

Linger over good coffee at thrift-store tables and couches along with all the laptop-toting writers tapping out their screenplays. The in-house roasting system uses oil from the coffee beans to run the machine.

RODAN Map pp96-7   Lounge

☎ 773-276-7036; 1530 N Milwaukee Ave; ☺ from 6pm; Ⓜ Blue Line to Damen

This sleek, cinematic spot for 30-some-things slides from restaurant mode to bar mode around 10pm. Arty videos courtesy of Chicago artists are projected on the back wall, and the space often hosts interesting live collaborations between electronic composers and video artists.

DRINKING WICKER PARK, BUCKTOWN & UKRAINIAN VILLAGE

DIY: HOW TO FIND A REAL CHICAGO BAR

In a city that holds drinking in such high regard, it's telling that the highest honor to bestow on a drinking establishment is mystifyingly simple: 'That place,' a local is wont to say with a far-off look, 'is a *real* Chicago bar.' You'll know one when you walk in the door: these 'real Chicago bars' are the kind of family-owned-and-operated, work-a-day joints that were once on every corner of the city. Usually soaked in some kind of proud ethnic proclivity, they're filled with fiercely loyal regulars who gripe about the mayor and cheer whatever baseball club is within closer geographical proximity. There are no hard and fast rules for what makes a bar 'real' and another less so, but here are some things to look out for:

- An 'Old Style' beer sign swinging out front.
- A well-worn dart board and/or pool table inside.
- Patrons wearing Cubs-, White Sox– or Bears-logoed ball caps.
- Bottles of brew served in buckets of ice.
- Sports on TV (with the latter being a 1974 Zenith, not some fancy flat-screen thing).

VIOLET HOUR Map pp96-7   Lounge
☎ 773-252-1500; 1520 N Damen Ave; ⏱ from 6pm; Ⓜ Blue Line to Damen
This *nouveau* speakeasy isn't marked, so look for the poster-covered, wood-panel building and the door topped by a yellow lightbulb (U2 found it for their recent record-release party). Inside, high-backed booths, chandeliers and long velvet drapes provide the backdrop to elaborately engineered cocktails in which homemade bitters are applied with an eyedropper over six varieties of ice. As highbrow as it sounds, it's quite welcoming and accessible.

MAP ROOM Map pp96-7   Pub
☎ 773-252-7636; 1949 N Hoyne Ave; ⏱ from 6:30am Mon-Fri, from 7:30am Sat, from 11am Sun; Ⓜ Blue Line to Damen; 📶
At this map- and globe-filled 'travelers' tavern,' artsy types sip coffee by day and suds from the 200-strong beer list by night. Board games and *National Geographics* are within reach. There's free ethnic food Tuesdays at 7pm.

QUENCHERS Map pp96-7   Pub
☎ 773-276-9730; 2401 N Western Ave; 🚌 74; 📶
At the north end of Bucktown, Quenchers peddles a global selection of over 200 beers from more than 40 nations. Locals, artisans, laborers and visiting brew masters enjoy Earle Miller's hospitality. Even when the live music gets loud, the bargain prices are worth the noise.

LOGAN SQUARE & HUMBOLDT PARK

Hipsters in this area have been clamoring for cool places to slake their thirst, and their wishes are finally coming true. Several new establishments have opened recently, with more on the way.

FIRESIDE BOWL Map p100   Bar
☎ 773-486-2700; 2848 W Fullerton Ave; ⏱ from 6pm Sun-Fri, from 3pm Sat; Ⓜ Blue Line to California
In the not-so-distant past, the Fireside Bowl was a premiere venue for up-and-coming rock, punk and hardcore shows. The punk spirit, and most shows, were ditched in 2004, but the remodeled bar remains a great place to enjoy the time-honored marriage of frosty pints and clattering pins.

SMALL BAR Map p100   Bar
☎ 773-509-9888; 2956 N Albany Ave; ⏱ from 4pm Mon-Fri, from noon Sat & Sun; Ⓜ Blue Line to Logan Square
Its ace jukebox, affordable food menu and kindly staff make this unpretentious gem an easygoing place to spend an evening in the neighborhood. The mirror behind the bar dates back to 1907. Two sister Small Bars pop up in Lincoln Park and Wicker Park.

WHIRLAWAY LOUNGE Map p100   Bar
☎ 773-276-6809; 3224 W Fullerton Ave; ⏱ from 4pm; Ⓜ Blue Line to Logan Square
With threadbare couches and broken-in board games, this neighborhood fave has the homey charm of your uncle's '70s rumpus room – if your uncle had loads of hip pals with an insatiable thirst for Pabst. Sweetheart owner Maria Jaimes is downright saintly.

REVOLUTION BREWING Map p100   Brewery
☎ 773-227-2739; 2323 N Milwaukee Ave; ⏱ from 11am Mon-Fri, from 10am Sat & Sun; Ⓜ Blue Line to California
Raise your fist to Revolution, a mondo, industrial-chic brewpub that fills glasses

CANS, CHICAGO STYLE

The red and blue Old Style crest is emblematic of Chicago drinking, whether it hangs on a sign in front of a favored neighborhood tavern or toasts a double play at Wrigley. The beer itself – an inexpensive, unpretentious pilsner with proud Midwestern immigrant roots – is perfectly suited for the 'city that works.' Every refreshing clack of a pop-top honors the tradition of Gottlieb Heileman, a German-born brewer who set up shop in La Crosse, Wisconsin. Heileman's 'high end' product, Heileman's Old Style Beer, was first brewed in 1902 and quickly found favor with so-called 'flatlanders,' Chicagoans vacationing in the north woods. The beery migration was aided by its partnership with the Cubs, which started in 1950. Heileman Brewing Company survived myriad mergers through the '80s and '90s, until it was taken over by rival Milwaukee brewer Pabst Brewing Company, a kind of Capulet–Montague marriage of inexpensive swills that jointly dominate working-class bars throughout the city.

with heady beers like the 7% Eugene porter (named for Eugene Debs, the leader of Chicago's Pullman strike in 1894). The owner honed his craft at Goose Island (p181), so the constantly changing beer lineup is high quality. The *haute* pub grub includes house-smoked meat sandwiches and bacon-fat popcorn with fried sage. Since its opening in 2010, lines have been lengthy.

LONGMAN & EAGLE Map p100   Pub
☎ 773-276-7110; 2657 N Kedzie Ave; ☽ from 3pm; Ⓜ Blue Line to Logan Square
It's easy to walk right by this shabby-chic tavern, as the sign in the window is so subtle it's almost invisible. Inside, 52 bourbons and 26 whiskeys prop up the bar, along with several craft beers and fancy comfort food like wild-boar sloppy joes and Kobe beef meatballs. At press time, the owners were planning to open a six-room inn on the upper floor.

NEAR WEST SIDE & PILSEN

W Fulton Market in the West Loop and W 18th St in Pilsen are pretty plentiful stretches, but otherwise drinking holes are scattered in the area.

BEER BISTRO Map pp104-5   Bar
☎ 312-433-0013; 1061 W Madison St; 🚌 19 or 20
This bar near United Center fills with Bulls and Blackhawks fans, and it even runs a shuttle to the arena on game days. Ninety global beers (most in bottles) comprise the swill, and TVs flashing the requisite games circle the big room.

SKYLARK Map pp104-5   Bar
☎ 312-948-5275; 2159 S Halsted St; 🚌 8
The Skylark is the place to end a long night after exploring the southern reaches of the city. It's a bastion for artsy drunkards, who slouch into big booths sipping on strong drinks and eyeing the long room. It's a good stop after the Pilsen gallery hop.

SOUTH LOOP & SOUTH SIDE

In the South Loop, Michigan Ave is your best bet for bars, though it's not exactly lined with them. Farther south, Halsted St in the Irish

enclave of Bridgeport (near US Cellular Field) has some winners before or after a White Sox game.

BERNICE'S TAVERN Map pp50-1   Bar
☎ 312-326-9460; 3238 S Halsted St; ☽ from 3pm Mon-Fri, from 11am Sat & Sun, closed Tue; Ⓜ Red Line to Sox-35th or 🚌 8
A motley assemblage of local artists and neighborhood regulars haunts this workaday Bridgeport tavern, where the eclectic calendar includes weekly metal DJs and a folkie open mic. Order a *Starka*, a honey-flavored liqueur every bit as Lithuanian as the owners.

JIMMY'S WOODLAWN TAP
Map p120   Bar
☎ 773-643-5516; 1172 E 55th St; Ⓜ Metra to 55th-56th-57th
Some of the geniuses of our age have killed plenty of brain cells right here in one of Hyde Park's few worthwhile bars. The place is dark and beery, and a little seedy. But for thousands of University of Chicago students deprived of a thriving bar scene, it's home. Hungry? The Swissburgers are legendary.

SCHALLER'S PUMP Map pp50-1   Bar
☎ 773-376-6332; 3714 S Halsted St; ☽ 11am-2am Mon-Fri, 4pm-2am Sat, 3-9pm Sun; Ⓜ Red Line to Sox-35th or 🚌 8
Schaller's is Chicago's oldest continually operating tavern and is conveniently located across the street from the 11th Ward Democratic offices. It's a fine place to toast the city's infamous politicos (both Mayor Daleys have imbibed here) or the White Sox, whose ballpark is a short toss away.

LITTLE BRANCH CAFE Map pp50-1   Cafe
☎ 312-360-0101; 1251 S Prairie Ave; ☽ 7am-4pm Mon & Tue, to 10pm Wed-Fri, 8am-10pm Sat, 8am-4pm Sun; Ⓜ Red, Orange, Green Line to Roosevelt; 🛜
A good fortifier after the Museum Campus, Little Branch is probably more known for its food than its drinks, but it does indeed have a bar. And that bar stirs hot toddies, Irish coffees, gin-filled Corpse Revivers and serves a small roster of wines and beers. The café hides in a residential complex.

NIGHTLIFE

top picks

NIGHTLIFE

Finding something to do in Chicago on any given night is effortless, and the spectrum of entertainment that's available in every price range is overwhelming. Just flip through the city's newsweekly, the *Reader*, with its pages of club listings, theater openings and concert announcements, and Chicagoans' insatiable appetite for nocturnal amusement becomes apparent. The free publication comes out every Thursday. Or you can buy a copy of weekly entertainment mag *Time Out Chicago*, which also covers the scene at length.

So name your poison. Wanna bust a gut over edgy, experimental improv comedy or bust your eardrums in front of edgy jazz? No problem. How about dancing in a converted warehouse with sock puppets, or in a rugged beer hall that safeguards traditional Chicago blues? Easy.

Undaunted by the weather, or the work week, Chicagoans turn out en masse for everything from blockbusting hip-hop acts to groundbreaking hucksters. Ticket prices for live music and comedy varies wildly by venue. A $5 cover at the door will get front-row admittance for a local punk band, while nosebleed seats for a big rock band at United Center might start at $70. Popular concert venues will (reluctantly) offer tickets through the charge-by-phone ticket retailing giant Ticketmaster (☎ 866-448-7849, 800-745-3000; www.ticketmaster.com), an automated service that tacks on its own mysteriously expensive fees.

OPENING HOURS

Most nightlife options start the evening's entertainment at around 9pm, and stay open until 2am. A few clubs keep things going a bit later on weekends, until 4am or 5am. Opening hours are noted for places that stray from these standards – like piano bars and small jazz or blues clubs. For particulars on start times for other events, it's best to call the venue or check newspaper listings.

LIVE MUSIC

If the family tree of American pop and rock music takes root in the blues, it follows that Chicago's proud heritage as a capital of electric blues has inspired generation after generation of world-class performers. The good news is that many of the surly, guitar-wielding oldsters who put Chicago on the map are still wailing about what happened after they 'woke up this mornin',' often just blocks away from younger crowds who uphold the city's reputation for musical innovation. If the sound of a distorted guitar doesn't fit your mood, a cab to the city's ethnic strongholds offers a global soundtrack.

Music lovers who want to gorge should visit Chicago during the summer: blankets are spread and corks or cans are popped before a continuous string of outdoor music festivals. These happen on city blocks and in parks in every neighborhood, often with sounds reflecting the surrounding community. The band shells at Millennium Park and Grant Park host loads of free concerts to suit every taste.

Festivals requiring admission are also plentiful. The grunge-rocking '90s carnival Lollapalooza (www.lollapalooza.com) quit touring and made Chicago its permanent home in 2005, bringing marquee rock acts for a three-day-long event every August. Another star is the Pitchfork Music Festival (www.pitchforkmusicfestival.com), which is run in July by the widely influential local indie-rock tastemakers at *Pitchfork* magazine.

For more details on Lolla, Pitchfork and Chicago's many other music fests, see p12 or visit www.chicago.metromix.com/festivals.

BLUES & JAZZ

The fret-bending of blues icons such as Muddy Waters and Howlin' Wolf echo in clubs from north to south. Yes, some of those closest to downtown are a bit touristy. But the music still burns up the amps. If you have wheels you can head further afield for a more authentic experience.

Jazz fans will find that the nightly scene here runs the gamut – from traditional hard bop to the most progressive, noisy fusion. For gospel, the majority of action happens, appropriately, on Sunday, when historic South Side churches (p122) raise the roof.

Cover prices hover around $15 at most blues and jazz clubs.

ANDY'S Map pp66-7

☎ 312-642-6805; www.andysjazzclub.com; 11 E Hubbard St, Near North; ⏰ from 4pm; Ⓜ Red Line to Grand

This comfy jazz club programs a far-ranging lineup of local traditional, swing, bop, Latin, fusion and Afro-pop acts, along with the occasional big-name performer. It has been on the scene for several years, and its downtown location makes it a popular spot for postwork boppers.

BACK ROOM Map pp72-3

☎ 312-751-2433; www.backroomchicago.com; 1007 N Rush St, Gold Coast; Ⓜ Red Line to Clark/Division

This venerated Gold Coast jazz room is so cozy that there isn't a bad view in the house, even when you take in the stage via a long mirror. If the small main floor gets too tight, head up the spiral staircase and take things in from above. Bop purists be warned: the tunes here can get more than a little smooth. There's a two-drink minimum.

BLUE CHICAGO Map pp66-7

☎ 312-661-0100; www.bluechicago.com; 536 N Clark St, Near North; Ⓜ Red Line to Grand

If you're staying in the neighborhood and don't feel like hitting the road, you won't go wrong at this mainstream blues club. Commanding local acts like Big Time Sarah wither the mics nightly.

B.L.U.E.S. Map pp78-9

☎ 773-528-1012; www.chicagobluesbar.com; 2519 N Halsted St, Lincoln Park; Ⓜ Red, Brown, Purple Line to Fullerton

Long, narrow and high volume, this veteran blues club draws a slightly older crowd that soaks up every crackling, electrified moment. As one local musician put it, 'The audience here comes out to *understand* the blues.' Big local names like L'il Ed and the Blues Imperials grace the small stage.

BUDDY GUY'S LEGENDS Map pp112-13

☎ 312-427-1190; www.buddyguys.com; 700 S Wabash Ave, South Loop; ⏰ restaurant 11am-midnight, club from 9:30pm Sun-Thu, from 5:30pm Fri, from 6pm Sat; Ⓜ Red Line to Harrison

Top local and national blues acts wail on the stage of local icon Buddy Guy. The man himself usually plugs in his ax in January.

The location is a bit rough around the edges, but the acts are consistently excellent. The restaurant serves Cajun food, and diners are treated to a free acoustic set at lunchtime (between noon and 2pm) on weekdays.

GREEN MILL Map p90

☎ 773-878-5552; www.greenmilljazz.com; 4802 N Broadway St, Uptown; ⏰ from noon; Ⓜ Red Line to Lawrence

You can sit in Al Capone's favorite spot at the timeless Green Mill, a true cocktail lounge that comes complete with curved leather booths and colorful tales about mob henchmen who owned shares in the place (a trap door behind the bar leads to tunnels where they hid their bootlegged booze). Little has changed in over 70 years – the club still books top local and national jazz acts. On Sunday night it hosts a nationally known poetry slam, where would-be poets try out their best work on the openly skeptical crowd.

HUNGRY BRAIN Map pp86-7

☎ 773-935-2118; www.emergingimprovisers.org; 2319 W Belmont Ave, Lake View; ⏰ closed Mon; 🚍 77

The Sunday Transmission jazz series, hosted by the Emerging Improvisers collective, is the best time to get a feel for this unassuming, comfortable dive. On that and other nights, young jazzers drink cheap (see p182) and build their chops, often resulting in inspired sessions.

JAZZ SHOWCASE Map pp112-13

☎ 312-360-0234; www.jazzshowcase.com; 806 S Plymouth Ct, South Loop; Ⓜ Red, Orange, Green Line to Roosevelt

The Jazz Showcase disappeared from the scene for a while, but Chicago's top club for national names is back in biz in a gorgeous room in the historic Dearborn Station building. In general, local musicians take the stage Monday through Wednesday, with visiting jazz cats blowing their horns Thursday through Sunday.

KATERINA'S Map pp86-7

☎ 773-348-7592; www.katerinas.com; 1920 W Irving Park, North Center; Ⓜ Brown Line to Irving Park

The swish Southern European finish and soulful pan ethnic gypsy jazz and blues make Katerina's a stylish, soulful destination in the less-traveled North Center neighborhood, just west of Lake View. A sophisticated set of 30- and 40-somethings down martinis, dig the good tunes and hang here all night.

KINGSTON MINES Map pp78-9

☎ 773-477-4646; www.kingstonmines.com; 2548 N Halsted St, Lincoln Park; Ⓜ Red, Brown, Purple Line to Fullerton

Popular enough to draw big names on the blues circuit, Kingston Mines is so hot and sweaty that blues neophytes will feel as though they're having a genuine experience – sort of like a gritty theme park. Two stages, seven nights a week, ensure somebody's always on.

LEE'S UNLEADED BLUES Map pp50-1

☎ 773-493-3477; www.leesunleadedblues.com; 7401 S South Chicago Ave, South Side; ◷ closed Mon-Thu

Far off the tourist path and buried deep on the South Side, Lee's is a genuine juke joint with sweet blues. The local crowd dresses in their finest threads, and everyone jams until dawn. The cover is $5. You'll need wheels to get here.

NEW APARTMENT LOUNGE Map pp50-1

☎ 773-483-7728; 504 E 75th St, South Side; 🚍 3

The only night to come to this storefront venue on the far South Side is Tuesday, when octogenarian saxophonist Von Freeman leads his long-running, roof-raising jam to rousing calls from the ultracasual, deep-listening audience. The session starts at 10:30pm, but if you want to get into the tiny room, come early. Brave audience members can sit in with the legend.

NEW CHECKERBOARD LOUNGE
Map p120

☎ 773-684-1472; www.checkerboardhydepark .com; 5201 S Harper Ave, Hyde Park; 🚍 Metra to 53rd

When the original location of this Bronzeville blues room closed in 2003, enthusiasts mourned – until it reopened in this bigger, better-sounding space in Hyde Park. Although it's in a strip mall, the new location is more inviting for university kids, who often join locals for electric blues (Friday and Saturday) and jazz (Sunday and

Monday). There's a two-drink minimum in addition to the cover charge (usually $5 to $10).

ROSA'S LOUNGE Map p100

☎ 773-342-0452; www.rosaslounge.com; 3420 W Armitage Ave, Logan Square; ◷ closed Sun, Mon & Wed; 🚍 73

Rosa's is an unadorned, real-deal blues club that brings in top local talent and dedicated fans to a somewhat dodgy Logan Square block. The location is isolated from easy public transportation, so be sure to take a cab.

UNDERGROUND WONDER BAR
Map pp72-3

☎ 312-266-7761; www.undergroundwonderbar .com; 10 E Walton St, Gold Coast; ◷ from 3pm; Ⓜ Red Line to Chicago

This live-music venue run by musician Lonie Walker features little-known jazz- and bluesmen, along with the occasional rock or reggae player. The club is tiny, and Lonie herself takes the stage for her sultry show several nights a week.

VELVET LOUNGE Map pp112-13

☎ 312-791-9050; www.velvetlounge.net; 67 E Cermak Rd, Near South Side; ◷ closed Mon & Tue; Ⓜ Red Line to Cermak-Chinatown

Tenor saxophonist Fred Anderson (one of the founding members of the Association for the Advancement of Creative Musicians) owned the Velvet and played here regularly until he passed away in 2010 at age 81. Visiting jazz musicians often hang out here late at night. The place rocks especially hard during the Sunday night jam sessions.

ROCK, POP & INDIE

Just as the bossy electrified sound of Chicago shaped fledgling American rock 'n' roll, Chicago's rock scene has a national reputation for brazenly defying conventions and muddling sonic borders. Today, the city's rock scene is inventive, proud and broadly influential, from rootsy folk rock to jarring, jazz-influenced postrock. Chicago's most popular rock exports of the past couple decades, Wilco and the Smashing Pumpkins, both sprung from the city's bustling indie underground, which has been abuzz with creative, challenging, independent music makers for years. Rock fans visiting the city have no shortage of options for a big show, but the distinct flavor of the city is better savored at smaller venues like the Hideout or Empty Bottle, where you're certain to catch some great local rock and likely to rub shoulders with Chicago's self-made guitar heroes. Tickets range from $5 for lesser known names on a weeknight, up to $20 for a buzz band on a Saturday night.

ABBEY PUB Map pp50-1
☎ 773-478-4408; www.abbeypub.com; 3420 W Grace St, Irving Park; Ⓜ Blue Line to Addison
The Abbey is two places in one: a club where on-the-verge local and well-known national rock bands play; and a Guinness-pouring Irish pub where guitar and fiddle jam sessions have been known to erupt. The venue is a haul far from the city center, on the northwest side.

BEAT KITCHEN Map pp86-7
☎ 773-281-4444; www.beatkitchen.com; 2100 W Belmont Ave, Lake View; 🚌 77
Everything you need to know is in the name – entertaining beats traverse a spectrum of sounds, and the kitchen turns out better-than-average dinners. Dine early in the front of the house, since service is unhurried. Music in the homely back room can be funky or jammy, but a crop of Chicago's smart, broadly appealing songwriters dominates the calendar.

DOUBLE DOOR Map pp96-7
☎ 773-489-3160; www.doubledoor.com; 1572 N Milwaukee Ave, Wicker Park; Ⓜ Blue Line to Damen
Alternative rock that's *just* under the radar finds a home at this former liquor store, which still has the original sign out front and remains a landmark around the Wicker Park bustle. The cachet is such that groups like the Rolling Stones have plugged in too.

EMPTY BOTTLE Map pp96-7
☎ 773-276-3600; www.emptybottle.com; 1035 N Western Ave, Ukrainian Village; 🚌 49
Chicago's music insiders fawn over the Empty Bottle, the city's scruffy, go-to club for edgy indie rock, jazz and other beats. Monday's show is always free, and is usually by a couple of up-and-coming bands. You won't even have to spend much on booze – cans of Pabst are $1.50. Plus there's a cool photo booth in back.

top picks

LOW-KEY PLACES TO HEAR LOCAL TALENT

- **Empty Bottle** (below) In-the-know music fans come for the nightly buzz band lineup.
- **Hungry Brain** (p191) The proving ground for tomorrow's jazz improvisers has inexpensive drinks and no pretension.
- **Hideout** (below) It's in the middle of nowhere, but it feels leagues ahead of other small rock venues.
- **Whistler** (p194) Homegrown bands and DJs take the stage in this new, arty house.
- **Schubas** (p194) The intimate room cocoons alt-country singers and ascending indie bands in equal measure.

HIDEOUT Map pp96-7
☎ 773-227-4433; www.hideoutchicago.com; 1354 W Wabansia Ave, Wicker Park; 🚌 72
Maybe it's all the Pabst, the strangely industrial surroundings, or the room of sweaty thrift-store bedecked hipsters grinding to soul records at the postshow dance party, but an evening in this two-room lodge of indie rock and alt-country can be downright transcendent.
The owners have nursed an outsider, underground vibe, and the place feels like the downstairs of your grandma's rumpus room. Music and other events (bingo, literary readings etc) take place nightly.

LINCOLN HALL Map pp78-9
☎ 773-525-2501; www.lincolnhallchicago.com; 2424 N Lincoln Ave, Lincoln Park; Ⓜ Brown Red Purple Line to Fullerton; 🛜
Owned by the same folks as Schubas (see p194), clean-cut Lincoln Hall is larger but with the same acoustically perfect sound. Hyped national indie bands are the main players, but when they're not on, DJs and free movie nights take over. The front room has a kitchen that offers small plates, sandwiches and coffee from noon onward.

METRO Map pp86-7
☎ 773-549-0203; www.metrochicago.com; 3730 N Clark St, Wrigleyville; Ⓜ Red Line to Addison
The Metro is legendary for loud rock. Sonic Youth and the Ramones in the '80s. Nirvana and Jane's Addiction in the '90s. White

Stripes and Fall Out Boy in the new millennium. Each night prepare to hear noise by three or four bands who may be well be teetering on the verge of superstardom.

PHYLLIS' MUSICAL INN Map pp96-7
☎ 773-486-9862; 1800 W Division St, Wicker Park; Ⓜ Blue Line to Division
One of the all-time great dives, this former Polish polka bar features scrappy up-and-coming bands nightly. It's hit or miss for quality, but you've got to applaud them for taking a chance. If you don't like the sound you can always slip outside to the bar's basketball court for relief. Cheap brewskis, to boot.

REGGIES ROCK CLUB Map pp112-13
☎ 312-949-0121; www.reggieslive.com; 2109 S State St, South Loop; Ⓜ Red Line to Cermak-Chinatown
Bring on the punk and the all-ages shows. Graffitied Reggies books mostly touring hardcore bands at the Rock Club. Next door, Reggies Music Joint is for folks 21 and older, and hosts more mainstream (we use that term loosely) live music nightly, as well as trips to see the White Sox, the Bears and other sports teams.

WHISTLER Map p100
☎ 773-227-3530; www.whistlerchicago.com; 2421 N Milwaukee Ave, Logan Square; Ⓜ Blue Line to California
Hometown indie bands and DJs rock this arty bar most nights. There's never a cover charge, but you'd be a weenie if you didn't order at least one of the swanky cocktails to keep the scene going. Whistler hosts the very fun 'movieoke' the first Monday of the month (like karaoke, only you act along with the movie scenes playing on the screen behind you).

FOLK & COUNTRY

While Chicago lies a bit too far north of the Mason-Dixon to have much of a traditional country scene, the city is silly with roots alt-country acts, some of the best of which find a home on the local Bloodshot Records label and take the stage of Schubas. The traditional folk scene has a very centralized home in the acclaimed Old Town School of Folk Music.

CAROL'S PUB Map p90
☎ 773-334-2402; 4659 N Clark St; 🚌 22
The closest thing Chicago has to a honky-tonk, Carol's Pub offers (at times ironic)

boot-stompin', Bud-drinkin' good times to patrons, who come out on weekends to dance like crazy to the house country band.

OLD TOWN SCHOOL OF FOLK MUSIC Map pp50-1
☎ 773-728-6000; www.oldtownschool.org; 4544 N Lincoln Ave, Lincoln Square; Ⓜ Brown Line to Western
You can hear the call of the banjos from the street outside this venerable institution, where major national and international acts like Doc Watson, Richard Thompson and Joan Baez play when they come to town. Old Town also hosts lots of world music shows, including every Wednesday at 8:30pm when they're free (or a $5 donation if you've got it). Do-it-yourselfers can take guitar and other musical classes here.

SCHUBAS Map pp86-7
☎ 773-525-2508; www.schubas.com; 3159 N Southport Ave; Ⓜ Brown Line to Southport
Something of an alt-country legend, Schubas presents a host of twangy acoustic artists, plus indie rock acts on their way up (like My Morning Jacket and the Shins in their early days). Bands play nightly in the cozy back-room club, which is noted for its great sound, thanks to the all-wood construction. A friendly, boisterous bar pours microbrews in the front room.

PIANO BAR & CABARET

DAVENPORT'S PIANO BAR & CABARET Map pp96-7
☎ 773-278-1830; www.davenportspianobar.com; 1383 N Milwaukee Ave; ⏰ from 7pm, closed Tue; Ⓜ Blue Line to Damen
Old standards get new interpretations and new songs are heard for the first time at this swanky place on a rather lonely stretch of Milwaukee Ave. The front room is a fun, inclusive (read: sing-along) place, with the back reserved for more fancy-pants cabaret events (where singing along will get you thrown out).

HOWL AT THE MOON Map pp66-7
☎ 312-863-7427; www.howlatthemoon.com; 26 W Hubbard St, Near North; ⏰ from 5pm Mon-Sat, from 7pm Sun; Ⓜ Red Line to Grand
The Guns 'n' Roses covers, dirt-cheap happy hour specials and flirty singles scene here could make nearly anyone into a piano bar convert. Billy Joel? Sorry, how about AC/DC?

ZEBRA LOUNGE Map pp72-3

☎ 312-642-5140; www.zebraloungechicago.com; 1220 N State St; ⏱ from 5pm Mon-Fri, from 6pm Sat & Sun; Ⓜ Red Line to Clark/Division
The piano in the tiny, dark and mirrored room can get as scratchy as the voices of the crowd, which consists mainly of older folks who like to sing along. The ivory strokers here are veterans who know their stuff.

CLUBBING

Let's get the semantics out of the way: the clubs listed below differ from mere bars by putting an emphasis on entertainment, mostly by way of DJ sets, themed nights, and big dance floors. They also regularly charge a cover that can range from $10 to $30. (If you want an evening of simple drinking and socializing, turn back to the Drinking chapter (p177), which lists plenty of low-key options.)

Within that rudimentary taxonomy, the distinctions are vast. Chicago's club scene offers a huge breadth of experiences, from cavernous megaclubs where pretty people skirt beyond the velvet rope, to tiny spots where people come to get seriously sweaty and hold DJs to a high standard. Most clubs cluster in three main areas: the River North/West Loop stretch, where the clubs tend to be huge and luxurious (with dress codes); the Wicker Park/Ukie Village area, where they're typically more casual; and the Wrigleyville/Boystown area, where they fall in between the two extremes. Most clubs open their doors around 9pm, and most use social media to provide discounts on admission, so check the websites and links before heading out.

Time Out (www.timeoutchicago.com) magazine serves as the most succinct guide to Chicago's club scene, and its website lists several examples of what's on tap each day. For the more underground events, look for flyers at hip record stores like Gramaphone Records (p136) or the post-raver boutiques along Milwaukee Ave in Wicker Park.

For those who drive to a club and drink more than planned, call U Drink I Drive (☎ 888-808-8343; www.udrinkidrive.com). They'll drive you and your car home for the price of a taxi.

BEAUTY BAR Map pp96-7

☎ 312-226-8828; www.beautybar.com; 1444 W Chicago Ave, Ukrainian Village; ⏱ to 2am daily, to 3am Sat; Ⓜ Blue Line to Chicago

The owners of the Empty Bottle (see p193) had a hand in this new venue, which opened in 2010. The interior is an imported and restored late-1960s beauty salon from New Jersey. 'Martinis and manicures' are the shtick, and you can get the latter anytime for $10. Genre-spanning DJs spin nightly. If the Beauty Bar sounds familiar, it's because it's part of a chain with outposts in several US cities.

BERLIN Map pp86-7

☎ 773-348-4975; www.berlinchicago.com; 954 W Belmont Ave, Lake View; ⏱ to 4am daily, to 5am Sat; Ⓜ Red, Brown, Purple Line to Belmont
Stepping off the El at Belmont has long been one of the city's best bets for finding a packed, sweaty dance floor. Berlin caters to a mostly gay crowd midweek, though partiers of all stripes jam the place on weekends. Monitors flicker through the latest video dispatches from cult pop and electronic acts, while DJs take the dance floor on trancey detours.

DARKROOM Map pp96-7

☎ 773-276-1411; www.darkroombar.com; 2210 W Chicago Ave, Ukrainian Village; ⏱ to 2am daily, to 3am Sat; 🚌 66
Everyone from goths to reggae heads goes to this welcoming, brick-walled bar, which changes personality depending on what comes from its turntables. Resident

top picks
GAY & LESBIAN NIGHTLIFE

- Berlin (above) Right off the El, this is a great place to get sweaty on the dance floor, no matter your orientation.
- Closet (p181) This lesbian-centric hole-in-the-wall is fun and unpretentious.
- Big Chicks (p183) The dance floor is perfectly tiny at this mainstay.
- Spin (p197) 'Shower Night' makes a raunchy departure from the excellent action on the dance floor.
- Hamburger Mary's (p183) Cabaret, karaoke, burgers and a booze-soaked outdoor patio make for good times at this Andersonville hot spot.
- Chance's Dances (www.chancesdances.org) Organizes queer dance parties at clubs around town.

DJs lead nights of '80s, Britpop and house, among others. There's even the occasional sock puppet party.

DEBONAIR SOCIAL CLUB Map pp96-7
☎ 773-227-7990; www.debonairsocialclub.com; 1575 N Milwaukee Ave, Wicker Park; ⏲ to 2am Sun-Fri, to 3am Sat; Ⓜ Blue Line to Damen
It's mostly a younger, hipster crowd dancing their asses off at Debonair. The main action takes place on the upstairs floor. That's where Monday's youth-friendly Rehab party draws big crowds for the can't-sit-still oldies mash-ups, hard rock and new electro. The downstairs floor is less hot and packed, though still grooving with rock or whatnot. Reggae and burlesque shows entertain on other nights.

ENCLAVE Map pp66-7
☎ 312-654-0234; www.enclavechicago.com; 220 W Chicago Ave, River North; ⏲ to 2am Fri, to 3am Sat, closed Sun-Thu; Ⓜ Brown, Purple Line to Chicago
This club is *big* – 15,000 sq ft of former warehouse redone with glossy hardwood floors and lively art installations. Even with the platform dancers and coy martini menu, it's fairly classy, bringing in Chicago celebs and a downtown crowd who dance to mainstream pan-genre hits.

FUNKY BUDDHA LOUNGE Map pp96-7
☎ 312-666-1695; www.funkybuddha.com; 738 W Grand Ave, West Loop; ⏲ to 2am Thu, Fri & Sun, to 5am Sat, closed Mon-Wed; Blue Line to Grand
The Buddha shakes with hip-hop and house music (plus chunks of funk, neosoul and old-school rap). It's usually a mixed crowd dancing in the room, which is unobnoxiously decorated with antique lighting, mural-covered walls and big ol' Buddhas. Next door the sister venue, Butterfly Social Club, serves organic cocktails while DJs spin.

HYDRATE Map pp86-7
☎ 773-975-9244; www.hydratechicago.com; 3458 N Halsted St, Wrigleyville; ⏲ to 4am daily, to 5am Sat; Ⓜ Red Line to Addison
A wild night on the Boystown club circuit requires a visit to this frenzied spot, which boasts an open-air feel (thanks to retract-able windows) and a chatty pickup scene

top picks

DANCE CLUBS

- Late Bar (below) The dance crowd goes wild for the new-wave grooves and the vintage bar and cocktails.
- Darkroom (p195) It welcomes a wide range of music lovers with its eclectic spins.
- Leg Room (opposite) The friendliest place to gawk at the Rush St meat market.
- Smart Bar (opposite) This high-minded subterranean space has been programming great DJs for years.
- Debonair Social Club (left) Where the young and hip come to sweat the night away.

(thanks to $1 well drinks). It's not all roses; the service gets rude and the crowds unruly (also thanks to the $1 well drinks). Special events at the club include a male burlesque troupe and female impersonators.

LATE BAR Map p100
☎ 773-267-5283; www.latebarchicago.com; 3534 W Belmont Ave, Logan Square; ⏲ to 4am Tue-Fri, to 5am Sat, closed Sun & Mon; Ⓜ Blue Line to Belmont
Late Bar is off the beaten path on a forlorn stretch of Belmont Ave surrounded by auto repair shops and Polish bars, though it's easily reachable via the Blue Line train. A couple of DJs opened the club in 2010, and its weird, new-wave vibe draws fans of all stripes: mods, hooligans, rockers, punks, goths, scooterists and more. Saturday's Planet Earth alt/postpunk dance nights are popular.

LE PASSAGE Map pp72-3
☎ 312-255-0022; www.lepassage.com; 937 N Rush St, Gold Coast; ⏲ to 4am Thu & Fri, to 5am Sat, closed Sun-Wed; Ⓜ Red Line to Chicago
Take a hint from the faux-French name: this restaurant-nightclub is not without its affected pretensions. Once you're past the doorperson's clipboard, though, it's a beautiful club with French-colonial decor. It makes the appropriate backdrop for would-be models and their pursuers, all of whom try to maintain their poise while sucking down fruity Polynesian concoctions like the 'Scorpion Bowl.'

LEG ROOM Map pp72-3

☎ 312-337-2583; www.legroomchicago.com; 7 W Division St, Gold Coast; ☽ to 4am daily, to 5am Sat; Ⓜ Red Line to Clark/Division
The Leg Room wins few points for originality, with safari-print stools and schmoozing, scantily dressed singles, but the laid-back vibe and friendly staff make it the most inviting place to gawk at the Rush St pick-up scene.

ONTOURAGE Map pp66-7

☎ 312-573-1470; www.ontouragechicago.com; 157 W Ontario St, River North; ☽ to 2am Thu & Fri, to 3am Sat, closed Sun-Wed; Ⓜ Red Line to Grand
VIPs get all access to the exclusive recesses of this neon-lit hip-hop and house club, though it's arguably more fun to hang downstairs with the dressed-up common-ers. Ontourage has been here since 2005 and seems to have the staying power lacked by its predecessors, as the space has housed a revolving door of clubs.

SIDETRACK CIRCUIT Map pp86-7

☎ 773-477-9189; www.sidetrackchicago.com; 3349 N Halsted St, Wrigleyville; to 2am daily, to 3am Sat; Ⓜ Brown, Purple, Red Line to Belmont
Massive Sidetrack thumps dance music for a gay and straight crowd alike. Get ready to belt out your Broadway best at the good-time 'show tune nights' on Sunday and Monday. The clubs hosts stand-up comedy on Thursday. If the indoor action gets to be too much, the massive outdoor courtyard beckons.

SMART BAR Map pp86-7

☎ 773-549-4140; www.smartbarchicago.com; 3730 N Clark St, Wrigleyville; ☽ to 4am Wed-Fri & Sun, to 5am Sat, closed Mon & Tue; Ⓜ Red Line to Addison
This downstairs adjunct to the Metro (p193) is a dance and music lover's dream, and the DJs here are often more renowned than you'd expect the intimate space to accom-modate. A who's who of forward-looking break artists, house and trance DJs have held down the turntables.

SOUND-BAR Map pp66-7

☎ 312-787-4480; www.sound-bar.com; 226 W Ontario St, River North; ☽ to 4am Thu & Fri, to 5am Sat, closed Sun-Wed; Ⓜ Red Line to Grand
This 4000-sq-ft nightspot rises above the city's other sprawling megaclubs by way of superstar trance and house DJs (John Digweed, Dimitri from Paris etc). There's an amazing sound system and a dramatic setting of futuristic neon and steely, minimalist decor.

SPIN Map pp86-7

☎ 773-327-7711; www.spin-nightclub.com; 800 W Belmont Ave, Wrigleyville; ☽ to 2am Sun-Fri, to 3am Sat; Ⓜ Red Line to Belmont
Though its clientele consists mostly of gay men in their 20s, Spin has become

NIGHTLIFE CLUBBING

YOUR GIG IN CHICAGO

Open-mic nights in Chicago aren't much like the navel-gazing mopefests of other cities. Here, you get the sense that songwriters and musicians are in the room to hone their craft, not bare their souls. If you're a visiting musician, there's no better way to get an intimate feel for Chicago's music scene than to get into it firsthand. Guitar-picking songwriters or aspiring blues players have it easy – just head to a gig, sign up to play (if it's required) and politely ask around for a loaner ax. Open Mic Chicago (www.openmicchicago.com) lists events around town. The info can be a bit dated, so check with the venue before heading out.

For less traditional open mics, try the following:

Live Band Karaoke at Piece (Map pp96-7; ☎ 773-772-4422; 1927 W North Ave; Ⓜ Blue Line to Damen). Front the band at Piece (p165) every Saturday night at 11pm. The 'back-up' players know a million chestnuts from the rock and pop canon. For other spots around town to live the dream, see www.livebandkaraoke.com.

Uptown Poetry Slam at the Green Mill (p191). This is where slam poetry got started, and you can carve your name into the movement's history during the open session that precedes the slam competition (p211). The open-mic portion of the evening runs from 7pm to 8pm.

Open Mic Comedy at Rockit (Map pp86-7; ☎ 773-645-4400; www.rockitbarandgrill.com; 3700 N Clark St, Wrigleyville; Ⓜ Red Line to Addison) Heard the one about the hapless tourist who got heckled off the stage? C'mon, that won't happen here. Hopefully. (Though watch out if there has been a Cubs game in the neighborhood earlier that day…) The open mic is on Friday at 6.30pm.

a popular destination for hetero men and women on the weekends. Serious dancers hit the floor, while chatty cruisers orbit the large bar by the entrance. Don't miss Spin's shower contest every Friday night, when hopefuls of both genders bare (almost) all. There's also an outdoor beer garden, darts tournaments and drag queen bingo.

SUBTERRANEAN Map pp96-7
☎ 773-278-6600; www.subt.net; 2011 W North Ave, Wicker Park; ⏰ to 2am Sun-Fri, to 3am Sat; Ⓜ Blue Line to Damen

DJs spin hip-hop and other styles to a trendy crowd at this place, which looks slick inside and out. The cabaret room upstairs draws good indie rock bands and hosts popular open-mic events.

IMPROV & COMEDY

Dating back to the Compass Players – the 1950s cabaret that birthed Second City – Chicago has earned its reputation for bleeding-edge comedy one snicker at a time. Stand-up takes a backseat to group improv, and a sampling of the city's nightlife isn't complete without checking it out. It doesn't have to break the bank either: while Second City is the launching pad for tomorrow's kings and queens of comedy, lower-profile training stages and jokesters outside of the Second City empire are less expensive.

Chicago's famous comedic names and ensembles will descend on the city in the spring for the Chicago Improv Festival (☎ 773-935-9810; www.chicagoimprovfestival.org). If you're lucky enough to catch it, it's worth your while and easy to find – it takes over stages around the city.

ANNOYANCE THEATRE Map p90
☎ 773-561-4665; www.annoyanceproductions.com; 4830 N Broadway St, Uptown; Ⓜ Red Line to Lawrence

The Annoyance masterminds nutty and absurd shows, such as Co-Ed Prison Sluts, a naughty, late-night gem that has been running for nearly 15 years, and Scientology: The Musical. Both the shows and the theater itself (complete with chic front bar area) are of surprisingly high quality. Susan Messing's $5 Thursday night session always provides good yucks.

COMEDYSPORTZ Map pp86-7
☎ 773-549-8080; www.comedysportzchicago.com; 929 W Belmont Ave, Lake View; Ⓜ Red, Brown, Purple Line to Belmont

The gimmick? Two improv teams compete with deadly seriousness to make you laugh hysterically. The audience benefits from this comic capitalism, and all the fun is G-rated. You can bring in alcohol from the lobby bar. Wednesday's shows are free.

CORN PRODUCTIONS Map pp86-7
☎ 312-409-6435; www.cornservatory.org; 4210 N Lincoln Ave, North Center; Ⓜ Brown Line to Irving Park

Though Corn occasionally stages something serious, most of its productions are kitschy and inexpensive. With the seven-year engagement of Floss! it lampooned hoity dance programs. The theater is just west of Lake View in the North Center neighborhood.

HELL IN A HANDBAG PRODUCTIONS
☎ 312-409-4357; www.handbagproductions.org

This award-winning group of young actors, producers, designers and composers produces hilarious parodies of sundry pop-culture staples (a recent Halloween production was a send-up of Hitchcock's The Birds), often in musical form. The Christmastime reviews are an annual hit with Chicago audiences. The group takes up residence in spaces that vary depending on the production, so check the website for details.

iO (IMPROVOLYMPIC) Map pp86-7
☎ 773-880-0199; www.ioimprov.com; 3541 N Clark St, Wrigleyville; Ⓜ Red Line to Addison

The Olympic Committee forced this comic veteran to change the name to its initials in 2005, a suitably laughable development in a long career of chuckles. iO launched the careers of Tina Fey and Stephen Colbert, along with a host of other well-known comics (many cross over from iO to Second City). Shows hinge entirely on audience suggestions, and each turn can run 40 minutes or longer. If you're thoroughly motivated by what you see, iO offers a range of courses to suit every budget. Shows tend to be a little bawdier than at ComedySportz. Shows on Wednesday and Sunday are usually just $5.

PLAYGROUND IMPROV THEATER
Map pp86-7

☎ 773-871-3793; www.the-playground.com; 3209 N Halsted St, Lake View; Ⓜ Brown, Red Line to Belmont

This nonprofit temple of improv hosts irreverent pieces by some of Chicago's emerging improv ensembles. The lineup changes every night. Sunday's shows are usually free.

SECOND CITY Map pp78-9

☎ 312-337-3992; www.secondcity.com; 1616 N Wells St, Old Town; Ⓜ Brown, Purple Line to Sedgwick

A Chicago must-see, this club is best symbolized by John Belushi, who emerged from the suburbs in 1970 and earned a place in the Second City improv troupe with his creative, manic, no-holds-barred style. Belushi soon moved to the main stage, and then to *Saturday Night Live,* and then on to fame and fortune. A who's who of funny people have followed a similar path: Billy Murray, Steve Carell, Amy Poehler and many more. Second City's shows are sharp and biting commentaries on life, politics, love and anything else that falls in the crosshairs of the comedians' rapid-fire, hard-hitting wit. See Second City Etc for info on lower-cost shows and free improv sets.

SECOND CITY ETC Map pp78-9

☎ 312-337-3992; www.secondcity.com; 1608 N Wells St, Old Town; Ⓜ Brown, Purple Line to Sedgwick

Second City's second company often presents more risky work, as actors try to get noticed and make the main stage. Shows here cost less.

Both theaters, the Mainstage and Etc, offer the city's best comedy value after the last show of the evening (Friday excluded): free improv, when the performers let loose and riff for a half hour or so. The freebies begin at 10pm Monday to Thursday, 1am Saturday and 9pm Sunday. There are no tickets – just show up 15 minutes prior.

ZANIES Map pp78-9

☎ 312-337-4027; www.chicago.zanies.com; 1548 N Wells St, Old Town; Ⓜ Brown, Purple Line to Sedgwick

The city's main stand-up comedy venue regularly books big-name acts familiar to anyone with a TV, and also frequently invites comics you're *going to* hear about on TV. The shows last less than two hours and usually include the efforts of a couple of up-and-comers before the main act. The ceiling is low and the seating is cramped, which only adds to the good cheer.

THE ARTS

top picks

- Printers' Ball (p210)
- Grant Park Music Festival (p204)
- Uptown Poetry Slam (p211)
- Elastic Arts Foundation (p208)
- Redmoon Theater (p206)
- Chicago Moving Co (p207)
- Music Box Theatre (p210)
- Steppenwolf Theater (p206)
- Neo-Futurists (p206)
- Chicago Sinfonietta (p203)

THE ARTS

The following chapter casts the spotlight on the city's wealth of high culture – everything from classical music, theater and literature to film and dance. Chicago is a distinguished, world-class destination in all areas. If you're in the mood for a rowdy evening of thundering house music, howling electric blues or uproarious sketch comedy, turn back to the Nightlife chapter (p189) for Chicago's more boisterous hallmarks.

Not that art in Chicago is a buttoned-up, blue-haired affair. Audiences embody the city's open-minded, unpretentious spirit, rewarding daring artistic underdogs who take big risks and answering adventuresome programming at civic institutions like the Chicago Symphony with unwavering patronage.

Finally, some of the greatest rewards in Chicago's art scene are reserved for those who know how to find them. If an organization listed below doesn't have a specific street address it's likely because it will perform in sundry spaces around the city. Check the *Reader* or *Time Out* for their exact performance location. For more on the topic, see the boxed text They're Playing Where? (p202).

TICKETS

For discounted theater tickets try Hot Tix (www.hottix.org), which sells same-day seats for half-price. You can buy them online, or in person at booths in the Chicago Tourism Center (Map pp54-5; 72 E Randolph St, Loop) and Water Works Visitor Center (Map pp72-3; 163 E Pearson St, Gold Coast). Recently it has started to sell discounted tickets for later in the week (ie if you check on Monday, it may have seats available for performances through Sunday at certain venues). Hot Tix outlets also sell full-price tickets for upcoming shows. The booths are run by the League of Chicago Theatres (www.chicagoplays.com), so most big local venues fall under its purview.

For dance tickets and productions that aren't handled by Hot Tix, call the box office directly. Many theaters also sell 'rush' tickets – discounted seats available at the box office one hour before performance.

National ticket broker Goldstar (www.goldstar.com) sell lots of half-price tickets to Chicago performances. You'll fare best if you sign up at least three weeks ahead of time, as Goldstar typically releases its seats well in advance of shows.

CLASSICAL MUSIC & OPERA

The Chicago Symphony Orchestra (CSO) has been one of America's best orchestras for a generation, and wrestling seats out of the hands of season ticket holders is difficult. That doesn't mean that seeing an expert orchestral performance is impossible; per-formances by brilliant younger players of the Civic Orchestra of Chicago and the Grant Park Orchestra are stunning – and free.

Though competition for tickets to Chicago's Lyric Opera is as intense as for the CSO, there are worthy alternatives at various churches and smaller concert series throughout town.

Many classical performances will be listed in the *Reader* and *Time Out*, but the best resource for obtaining tickets and informa-tion about all classical events is the Chicago Classical Music website (www.chicagoclassicalmusic.org), which has the latest news, an accurate calendar and a ticket swap. If you're truly desperate to see the CSO or the Lyric Opera, it's worth hanging around the box office before the baton drops. Some generous swell might give you theirs for free.

THEY'RE PLAYING WHERE?

The more you know Chicago's entertainment venues, the more confused you'll be by who plays where and when. The booking style here involves a lot of club sharing by wildly different entertainment factions, meaning that the best reggae club in Chicago on Friday is a scooter-filled mod hangout on Saturday... and a gay musical theater group on Sunday. It's a game of musical chairs that keeps different scenes rotating to and from the same barstools each night. It's part of the fun mixing of cultures that helps make Chicago so exciting, but it also means that you'd do well to check the club listings carefully before you head back to your favorite reggae bar two nights running.

APOLLO CHORUS OF CHICAGO
☎ 312-427-5620; www.apollochorus.org
A 150-member vocal group founded in 1872, the Apollo often performs at Symphony Center (see Chicago Symphony Orchestra, p203), as well as various churches around town. Unless you plan *way* in advance, catching the chorus' Christmas performance of Handel's *Messiah* is impossible.

CHICAGO CHAMBER MUSICIANS
☎ 312-819-5800; www.chicagochambermusic.org
This 15-member ensemble is comprised of world-class soloists and CSO section leaders, known and revered for educational outreach programs and its two affiliated groups – the Chicago String Quartet and CCM Brass. It plays at halls and theaters all around town.

CHICAGO OPERA THEATER Map pp54-5
☎ 312-704-8414; www.chicagooperatheater.org; Harris Theater for Music & Dance, 205 E Randolph St, Loop; Ⓜ Brown, Green, Orange, Purple, Pink Line to Randolph
Tod Machover's *Death and the Powers* and Marc-Antoine Charpentier's *Medea* were offered on the spring 2011 schedule – mere indications of this innovative group's broad range. Under general director Brian Dickie, Chicago Opera Theater has soared to critical acclaim.

CHICAGO SINFONIETTA
☎ 312-236-3681; www.chicagosinfonietta.org
Led by Paul Freeman (at least through 2011, when he'll hand over the baton), this beloved organization is all about knocking down the cultural walls that surround traditional classical ensembles. Expect broad-minded premieres and wide-ranging guest artists, including jazz luminaries and ethnic folk musicians. Many of its concerts are at Symphony Center.

CHICAGO SYMPHONY ORCHESTRA
Map pp54-5
☎ 312-294-3000; www.cso.org; Symphony Center, 220 S Michigan Ave, Loop; Ⓜ Brown, Green, Orange, Purple, Pink Line to Adams
Riccardo Muti leads the CSO, one of America's best symphonies, known for fervent subscribers and an untouchable brass section. The season is from

THE PALACES OF THE LOOP

Chicago boasts some dreamboat old theaters, all of which have been renovated and reopened in recent years as part of the Loop theater district. Signs are posted in front of each palatial property, detailing the zaniness that went on during its heyday. Whether they're showing a Cuban ballet company or a Disney musical, these beauties are worth the price of admission alone. Broadway in Chicago (www.broadwayinchicago.com) handles tickets for most of them.

Auditorium Theatre (Map pp54-5; ☎ 312-922-2110; 50 E Congress Pkwy; Ⓜ Brown, Orange, Purple, Pink Line to Library)

Bank of America Theatre (Map pp54-5; ☎ 312-977-1700; 18 W Monroe St; Ⓜ Blue, Red Line to Monroe)

Cadillac Palace Theater (Map pp54-5; ☎ 312-977-1700; 151 W Randolph St; Ⓜ Brown, Orange, Purple, Pink Line to Washington)

Chicago Theatre (Map pp54-5; ☎ 312-462-6300; 175 N State St; Ⓜ Brown, Green, Orange, Purple, Pink Line to State)

Ford Center/Oriental Theater (Map pp54-5; ☎ 312-977-1700; 24 W Randolph St; Ⓜ Blue Line to Washington)

September to May at Symphony Center's Daniel Burnham–designed Orchestra Hall, though the orchestra also plays summer engagements at Ravinia (see Classical Music Festivals, p204).

CIVIC ORCHESTRA OF CHICAGO
Map pp54-5
☎ 312-294-3420; www.cso.org; Symphony Center, 220 S Michigan Ave, Loop; Ⓜ Brown, Green, Orange, Purple, Pink Line to Adams
Founded in 1919, this orchestra is something of the kid sibling to the CSO, made up of younger players who often graduate to the big-time professional symphonic institutions around the world. It's the only training orchestra of its kind in the world, and, amazingly, tickets to performances at Symphony Center are free.

LYRIC OPERA OF CHICAGO Map pp54-5
☎ 312-332-2244; www.lyricopera.org; Civic Opera House, 20 N Wacker Dr, Loop; Ⓜ Brown, Orange, Purple, Pink Line to Washington
By taking on a premiere of William Bolcom's *A Wedding* (an adaptation of a Robert

THE ARTS CLASSICAL MUSIC & OPERA

CLASSICAL MUSIC FESTIVALS

Though it was always popular, the Grant Park Music Festival (☎ 312-742-7638; www.grantparkmusicfestival.com) has recently become an indispensable part of summer in Millennium Park – the festival's name is a bit of a misnomer since it's no longer held in Grant Park. The orchestra and chorus are excellent, and though the programming targets populist choices like Bernstein and Beethoven, the directorial board wisely sneaks more challenging slices of orchestral rep on the picnicking lay audience.

These free concerts happen around twilight on Wednesday, Friday and Saturday evenings throughout the summer, although other big events like the Jazz Festival can alter the schedule. If you can't make the gig, catching a sparsely attended daytime rehearsal at the park (usually around noon) provides an intimate glimpse into the mechanics of the great ensemble.

In the summer the CSO heads to Ravinia (☎ 847-266-5100; www.ravinia.org; Green Bay & Lake Cook Rds), a vast open-air summer series in Highland Park on the North Shore. It's certainly a hike from downtown, but if you go, avoid the traffic and take the 45-minute Metra/Union Pacific North Line train from the Ogilvie Transportation Center to Ravinia Station ($9 round-trip). Trains stop both before and after the concerts right in front of the park gates.

Altman movie) for its 50th anniversary, the Lyric Opera showed its stripes. The seasons of this truly great modern opera company are popular with subscribers, who fill the ornate Civic Opera House for a shrewd mix of common classics and daring premieres from September to March. If your Italian isn't up to snuff, don't be put off; much to the horror of purists, the company projects English 'supertitles' above the proscenium.

MUSIC OF THE BAROQUE
☎ 312-551-1415; www.baroque.org
One of the largest choral and orchestral groups of its kind in the USA, Music of the Baroque (MoB) brings the music of the Middle Ages and the Renaissance to vibrant life. Its Christmas brass and choral concerts are huge successes. It performs at Harris Theater (Map pp54-5; 205 E Randolph St, Loop; Ⓜ Brown, Green, Orange, Purple, Pink Line to Randolph), as well as various churches around town.

THEATER

Steppenwolf is Chicago's world-renowned main stage, but the number of smaller curtains that rise in the city casts Chicago in a vigorous supporting role to great American acting cities like New York and Los Angeles. Though the international awareness might be less intense here, Chicago's actors and players are a passionate, busy lot and most productions are first-rate.

The listings below include both resident theater companies (those with their own performance spaces) and itinerant companies (those that perform in a variety of venues). For the latter, which tend to be the more low-key, adventurous and fringe groups, check the At the Fringes boxed text (p207), which lists theater locations where such companies tend to appear.

In general, expect to pay around $80 for tickets to a big Broadway production downtown, $50 to see a Steppenwolf-caliber show, and $20 to see a fringe or small theater performance.

And note that these listings represent a small, high-quality fraction of what's going on. Check the local press to find out what's hot, or maybe just ask your waiter.

ABOUT FACE THEATRE
☎ 773-784-8565; www.aboutfacetheatre.com
This itinerant ensemble primarily stages serious plays dealing with gay and lesbian themes at small but quality Chicago houses. Its three series include the Mainstage Season and a New Works Program.

AMERICAN THEATER COMPANY Map pp86-7
☎ 773-409-4125; www.atcweb.org; 1909 W Byron St, Lake View; Ⓜ Brown Line to Irving Park
ATC has been around for more than a quarter century, putting on both new and established works by American playwrights. To give a sampling: the 2010 season included Speed the Plow by David Mamet, a new R-rated version of the musical Grease and a world premiere by Dan LeFranc titled The Big Meal.

BLACK ENSEMBLE THEATER Map p90
☎ 773-769-4451; www.blackensembletheater .org; Uptown Center Hull House, 4520 N Beacon St, Uptown; Ⓜ Red Line to Wilson
This well-established group saw its fledgling production of The Jackie Wilson Story attract wide attention and national tours.

The focus here has long been on original productions about the African American experience through mostly historical, biographical scripts.

CHICAGO DRAMATISTS Map pp96-7
☎ 312-633-0630; www.chicagodramatists.org; 1105 W Chicago Ave, Ukrainian Village; Ⓜ Blue Line to Chicago

For a visit to the heart of Chicago's dramatic scene, step into this small, functional theater space, a testing ground for Chicago's new playwrights and plays. It's no surprise that this embracing environment has earned stunning results; current resident playwrights are Emmy nominee Susan Lieberman and Nambi E Kelly.

CHICAGO SHAKESPEARE THEATER
Map pp66-7
☎ 312-595-5600; www.chicagoshakes.com; 800 E Grand Ave, Navy Pier; 🚍 66

Snuggled into a beautiful, highly visible home on Navy Pier, this company is at the top of its game, presenting works from the Bard that are fresh, inventive and timeless.

COURT THEATRE Map p120
☎ 773-753-4472; www.courttheatre.org; 5535 S Ellis Ave, Hyde Park; Ⓜ Metra to 55th-56th-57th

---

A classical company hosted by the University of Chicago, the Court focuses on great works from the Greeks to Shakespeare, and various international plays not often performed in the USA. The 2010 season saw Edward Albee's Three Tall Women and Gershwin's Porgy and Bess among the lineup.

FACTORY THEATER Map p100
☎ 312-409-3247; www.thefactorytheater.com; 3504 N Elston Ave, Logan Square; 🚍 152

This company has been staging ridiculous (Poppin' and Lockdown 2: Dance the Right Thing) and marginally serious plays for over 15 years. It still maintains a nervy, irreverent edge that makes its schedule a must for Chicago theater and comedy fans.

GOODMAN THEATRE Map pp54-5
☎ 312-443-3800; www.goodman-theatre.org; 170 N Dearborn St, Loop; Ⓜ Blue, Brown, Green, Orange, Purple, Pink Line to Clark

The Goodman reigns with Steppenwolf as Chicago's top drama house, and its Theater District facility is gorgeous. It specializes in new and classic American productions, and has been cited several times as one of the best regional theaters in the USA. Its annual production of A Christmas Carol has become a local family tradition. Goodman's distinguished Artistic Collective is another great source of new work.

HOUSE THEATRE
☎ 773-251-2195; www.thehousetheatre.com

By throwing out the rule book, 'Chicago's most exciting young theater company' (Tribune) presents a mix of quirky, funny, touching shows written by untrained playwrights. Magic, music and good old-fashioned storytelling usually tie in somehow. House often performs at the Chopin Theatre (see At the Fringes, p207) in Wicker Park.

LOOKINGGLASS THEATRE COMPANY
Map pp72-3
☎ 312-337-0665; www.lookingglasstheatre.org; 821 N Michigan Ave, Gold Coast; Ⓜ Red Line to Chicago

This company took a step into the big time with the opening of its new, spacious digs on Michigan Ave. The ensemble cast – which includes cofounder David Schwimmer of TV's Friends – loves to use physical stunts and acrobatics to enhance its thought-provoking plays.

THEATER FESTIVALS

The most talked-about fest and granddaddy of the scene is the Rhinoceros Theater Festival (www.rhinofest.com), which has been treating Chicago to new dramatic works for over 20 years. It runs through the fall at various theaters. Check the website for more information.

The Goodman Theatre (p205) hosts the Latino Theatre Festival every other year. It brings in playwrights and produces works from Latino countries around the globe, usually throughout July.

Things get pretty raucous at the Abbie Hoffman Died For Our Sins Theatre Festival – aka Abbie Fest – for three days in mid-August at the Mary Arrchie Theatre Company (Map pp86-7; ☎ 773-871-0442; www.maryarrchie.com; 735 W Sheridan Rd, Lake View; Ⓜ Red Line to Sheridan). The event puts on over 50 straight hours of back-to-back-to-back, off-the-cuff performances to celebrate the anniversary of Woodstock.

At press time, some folks were trying to get a Chicago Fringe Festival (www.chicagofringe.org) up and running in summer. Check the website for progress.

NEO-FUTURISTS Map p90
☎ 773-275-5255; www.neofuturists.org; 5153 N Ashland Ave, Andersonville; Ⓜ Red Line to Berwyn
The theater is best known for its long-running *Too Much Light Makes the Baby Go Blind,* in which the hyper troupe makes a manic attempt to perform 30 plays in 60 minutes. It runs Friday and Saturday at 11:30pm and Sunday at 7pm. Admission cost is based on a dice roll. The group puts on plenty of other original works that'll make you ponder and laugh simultaneously. Well worth the northward trek.

NEXT THEATRE COMPANY Map pp50-1
☎ 847-475-6763; www.nexttheatre.org; 927 Noyes Street, Evanston; Ⓜ Purple Line to Noyes
Like many of Chicago's most exciting companies, Next was founded in the '80s and has grown into one of the region's most dynamic, celebrated performance spaces, encouraging local premieres.

PROP THTR Map p100
☎ 773-539-7838; www.propthtr.org; 3504 N Elston Ave, Logan Square; 🚌 152
This long-running troupe presents fresh stage adaptations of literary works by serious writers, from Nabokov to William Burroughs. The well-executed productions are typically dark in theme. Prop Thtr is a big part of the buzzed-about annual Rhinoceros Theater Festival.

REDMOON THEATER Map pp96-7
☎ 312-850-8440; www.redmoon.org; 1463 W Hubbard St, Ukrainian Village; Ⓜ Green, Pink Line to Ashland
The interaction of humans and puppets is key to the magical, haunting adaptations of classic works like *Moby Dick* and new commissions like *The Princess Club,* a fairly twisted look at children's fairy tales. The innovative nonprofit troupe, headed up by performance artists Blair Thomas and Jim Lasko, never fails to mesmerize. Be ready – the puppets can get downright creepy.

ROYAL GEORGE THEATRE Map pp78-9
☎ 312-988-9000; www.theroyalgeorgetheatre .com; 1641 N Halsted St, Lincoln Park; Ⓜ Red Line to North/Clybourn
The Royal George is actually three theaters in one building. The cabaret venue stages long-running mainstream productions such as *Late Nite Catechism*, a nun-centered comedy. The main stage presents works with big-name stars, and the gallery hosts various improv and small-troupe works.

STEPPENWOLF THEATER Map pp78-9
☎ 312-335-1650; www.steppenwolf.org; 1650 N Halsted St, Lincoln Park; Ⓜ Red Line to North/ Clybourn
This legendary name in Chicago theater was founded by Terry Kinney, Gary Sinise and Jeff Perry in a church basement. It quickly outgrew one space after another, won a Tony award for regional theater excellence, and is now a leading international destination for dramatic arts. Among the many famous alums who have gone on to illustrious careers are John Malkovich, Gary Cole and John Mahoney. Productions are of the highest quality. A tip to save dough: the box office releases 20 tickets for $20 for each day's shows. They go on sale at 11am Monday to Saturday and at 1pm Sunday, and are available by phone. They go fast.

THEATER OOBLECK

773-247-1041; www.theaterobleck.com
For over two decades Theater Oobleck has been creating works for the off-off-Loop intelligentsia. Some make you laugh, all make you think, but few have a title like *An Apology for the Course and Outcome of Certain Events Delivered by Doctor John Faustus on This His Final Evening*. Free if you're broke. The company often appears at Chopin Theatre (see At the Fringes, p207).

TRAP DOOR THEATRE Map pp96-7

☎ 773-384-0494; www.trapdoortheatre.com; 1655 W Cortland Ave, Bucktown; 🚌 9
This ragtag operation once had to hold a fundraiser to purchase a bathroom for its tiny theater, but it is starting to draw bigger audiences for its consistently great productions of European avant-garde plays and originals. A recent production of *The Bitter Tears of Petra Van Kant* won three illustrious local After Dark awards.

VICTORY GARDENS THEATER

Map pp78-9
☎ 773-071-3000; www.victorygardens.org; 2433 N Lincoln Ave, Lincoln Park; Ⓜ Brown, Red Line to Fullerton
Long established and playwright-friendly, Victory Gardens specializes in world premieres of plays by Chicago authors. The *Wall St Journal* called it 'one of the most important playwright theaters in the US.' It's located in the historic Biograph Theater, where bank robber John Dillinger – aka Public Enemy Number One – was shot in 1934.

DANCE

With a renowned ballet company and a classical ballet training center in town, it's not hard to see a pirouette while you're here, but Chicago's world of dance has far more innovative and eclectic depths for those who seek it.

Millennium Park's **Harris Theater for Music & Dance** (Map pp54-5; ☎ 312-334-7777; www.harristheaterchicago.org; 205 E Randolph Dr, Loop; Ⓜ Brown, Green, Orange, Purple, Pink Line to Randolph) has given Chicago's small but vibrant modern dance community a high-profile home. Long before the center was complete, though, jazz dance thrived in Chicago because of local pioneers like Gus Giordano. The Joffrey Ballet has also settled in to the city nicely since its relocation from New York City in 1995.

See Chicago Dance (www.seechicagodance.com) is the well-maintained online hub for information about companies that go far beyond the marquee names. You'll also find more information in the *Reader* or *Time Out* listings.

BALLET CHICAGO

☎ 312-251-8838; www.balletchicago.org
The repertoire of technician and choreographer George Balanchine, admired as a founding father of American ballet, makes the foundation of this preprofessional training center. The performance troupe wins wide acclaim, and leaps at various venues around town.

CHICAGO MOVING CO Map pp86-7

☎ 773-880-5402; www.chicagomovingcompany.org; 3035 N Hoyne Ave, Lake View; 🚌 77
Known for gutsy, energetic performances, this exciting group was founded over 30

THE ARTS DANCE

AT THE FRINGES

Looking for a tasty slice of Chicago fringe theater? Maybe something oddball, thought provoking or just plain silly? The following theaters often host Chicago's itinerant companies:

Apollo Theater (Map pp78-9; ☎ 773-935-6100; www.apollochicago.com; 2540 N Lincoln Ave, Lincoln Park; Ⓜ Red, Brown, Purple Line to Fullerton)

Chopin Theatre (Map pp96-7; ☎ 773-278-1500; www.chopintheatre.com; 1543 W Division St, Wicker Park; Ⓜ Blue Line to Division)

DCA Theater (Map pp54-5; ☎ 312-742-8497; www.dcatheater.org; 66 E Randolph St, Loop; Ⓜ Brown, Green, Orange, Purple Pink Line to Randolph)

Theatre Building (Map pp86-7; ☎ 773-327-5252; www.theatrebuildingchicago.org; 1225 W Belmont Ave, Lake View; Ⓜ Red, Brown, Purple Line to Belmont)

Viaduct Theatre (☎ 773-296-6024; www.viaducttheatre.com; 3111 N Western Ave, Lake View; 🚌 77)

years ago by Nana Shineflug, a pioneer of modern dance in Chicago. The works and performers are all local. Shows are at the Hamlin Park Fieldhouse.

DANCE CENTER AT COLUMBIA COLLEGE Map pp112-13

☎ 312-344-8300; www.colum.edu/dancecenter; 1306 S Michigan Ave, South Loop; Ⓜ Green, Orange Line to Roosevelt

More than an academic institution, the Dance Center is one of the most focused collegiate modern dance programs in the country and has carved out a fine reputation. Columbia College helps it to continue attracting quality dance from beyond the city's border.

ELASTIC ARTS FOUNDATION Map p100

☎ 773-772-3616; www.elasticrevolution.com; 2nd fl, 2830 N Milwaukee Ave, Logan Square; Ⓜ Blue Line to Logan Square

The calendar at Elastic Arts is far-reaching and impossible to pin down – one week the city's most exciting experimental choreographers will fill the space, and the next will see a performance of original art music by a cutting-edge international ensemble. Regardless, this is at the edge of Chicago's art community.

DANCE FESTIVALS

Plenty of dance festivals move the city, starting with SummerDance (☎ 312-742-4007; www .chicagosummerdance.org; ☺ 6pm Thu-Sat, 4pm Sun), where ordinary Chicagoans get free lessons and hone their ballroom and Latin dance moves to a live orchestra in the Spirit of Music Garden (Map pp112-13; 601 S Michigan Ave, South Loop; Ⓜ Red Line to Harrison).

For spectators, the Jazz Dance World Congress (☎ 847-866-9442; www.jazzdanceworldcongress .org) visits the city for a week in August at the Harris Theater for Music & Dance (Map pp54-5; ☎ 312-334-7777; www.harristheaterchicago.org; 205 E Randolph Dr, Loop; Ⓜ Brown, Green, Orange, Purple, Pink Line to Randolph), bringing a set of exciting performances by top jazz dance companies. November holds the city's biggest dance event, though. Dance Chicago (☎ 773-989-0698; www.dancechicago.com) brings dancers from across disciplines to the Theatre Building (Map pp86-7; 1225 W Belmont Ave, Lake View; Ⓜ Red, Brown, Purple Line to Belmont) for a month-long series in November.

GIORDANO JAZZ DANCE CHICAGO

☎ 874-866-6779; www.giordanojazzdance.com

This Chicago company was founded by one of the most important people in the history of American dance form, Gus Giordano. Now headed by his daughter Nan, the company is out on the road for much of the year, but still comes back for occasional performances in its hometown, often at the Harris Theater (Map pp54-5; 205 E Randolph St, Loop; Ⓜ Brown, Green, Orange, Purple, Pink Line to Randolph).

HUBBARD ST DANCE CHICAGO Map pp54-5

☎ 312-850-9744; www.hubbardstreetdance.com; Harris Theater for Music & Dance, 205 E Randolph Dr, Loop; Ⓜ Brown, Green, Orange, Purple, Pink Line to Randolph

Hubbard St is the preeminent dance group in the city, with a well-deserved international reputation to match. The group is known for energetic and technically virtuoso performances under the direction of the best choreographers in the world, including founder Lou Conte.

JOFFREY BALLET OF CHICAGO
Map pp54-5

☎ 312-386-8905; www.joffrey.com; 10 E Randolph St, Loop; Ⓜ Brown, Green, Orange, Purple, Pink Line to Randolph

This famous group has flourished since it relocated from New York in 1995. Noted for its energetic work, the company frequently travels the world and boasts an impressive storehouse of regularly performed repertoire. Joffrey practices and instructs in the swanky new Joffrey Tower on Randolph St in the Theater District, though it typically performs at the Auditorium Theatre (Map pp54-5; ☎ 312-922-2110; 50 E Congress Pkwy; Ⓜ Brown, Orange, Purple, Pink Line to Library).

MUNTU DANCE THEATER OF CHICAGO

☎ 773-602-1135; www.muntu.com

The word *muntu* means 'the essence of humanity' in Bantu. This company was founded in 1972 to perform African and American dances that draw on ancient and contemporary movement. The fiery performances of traditional dances from West Africa are an essential part of Muntu's signature. It performs at venues around town.

CHICAGO ARTS: PEOPLE YOU SHOULD KNOW

Martha Lavey A vet director and actor of the Goodman and Victory Gardens theaters, Lavey's post as artistic director of Steppenwolf has helped Chicago's reputation for 'serious' theater surpass even that of New York.

Ira Glass The creator and host of National Public Radio's *This American Life* is still equated with the city, though these days his show sports a New York address. *TAL* documents all facets of our perplexing, disturbing and ultimately lovable nation. It has broadened into a cable TV series, as well.

Studs Terkel The oral historian and master conversationalist put a small library's worth of amazing stories into print. He passed away in 2008 at age 96.

Chris Ware The first comic artist ever to have work in the Whitney Museum's biennial exhibit, Ware has forever raised the bar for the funny pages. Miserable weather? Grab a copy of Ware's *Jimmy Corrigan* at Quimby's bookstore (p139) and spend a wonderful afternoon under its spell.

Mary Zimmerman A director and ensemble member of Chicago's Lookingglass Theatre, Zimmerman is one of those bright suns around which entire scenes revolve.

RIVER NORTH DANCE COMPANY

☎ 312-944-2888; www.rivernorthchicago.com
This vibrant young company has quickly become one of Chicago's most admired modern companies, bringing a mixed bag of pop culture (including mime) and theatrical modern dance. It performs around the country, but when in town you're likely to find it at the Harris Theater (Map pp54-5; 205 E Randolph St, Loop; Ⓜ Brown, Green, Orange, Purple, Pink Line to Randolph).

FILM

Chicagoans will spend whole weekends in the cool, darkened confines of a movie theater during unbearably humid summer days, but movie houses are scarcely less packed in the winter, as folks will trudge through the snow to catch the latest art-house blockbuster.

Chicago is packed with movie theaters, but the following have been selected with the interests of travelers in mind. Show times are printed in the *Reader* or in either daily paper, or available via multiple online movie sites.

600 N MICHIGAN THEATERS Map pp66-7

☎ 312-255-9347; 600 N Michigan Ave, Near North; Ⓜ Red Line to Grand
Despite the name, the entrance to these centrally located theaters is off Rush St. This comfortable complex is quiet during the week and features six screens of various sizes, plus a café and a concession stand on each of its three floors.

AMC RIVER EAST Map pp66-7

☎ 312-596-0333; 322 E Illinois St, Near North; 🚌 65
The screens are huge and the sound will rumble your dental work loose at this high-tech theater – the perfect place to get out of the humidity, suck down buckets of Coke and take in an explosion-filled, scantily clad, special-effects-laden blockbuster. Parking is pricey, so take public transportation.

BREW & VIEW Map pp86-7

☎ 773-929-6713; www.brewview.com; Vic Theater, 3145 N Sheffield Ave, Lake View; Ⓜ Red, Brown, Purple Line to Belmont
Even the worst film gets better when you've got a pizza in front of you and a pitcher of beer at your side. As you watch second-run Hollywood releases, you can behave as badly as you would at home – in fact, the $2.75 mid-week drink specials encourage it. You must be 18 or over.

FACETS MULTIMEDIA Map pp78-9

☎ 773-281-4114; www.facets.org; 1517 W Fullerton Ave, Lincoln Park; Ⓜ Brown, Purple, Red Line to Fullerton
Facets' main business is as the country's largest distributor of foreign and cult films, so it follows that its 'cinematheque' movie house shows interesting, obscure movies that would never get booked elsewhere.

GENE SISKEL FILM CENTER Map pp54-5

☎ 312-846-2600; www.siskelfilmcenter.org; 164 N State St, Loop; Ⓜ Brown, Green, Orange, Purple, Pink Line to State

THE ARTS FILM

The former Film Center of the School of the Art Institute was renamed for the late *Chicago Tribune* film critic Gene Siskel. It shows everything from amateurish stuff by students to wonderful but unsung gems by Estonian directors. The monthly schedule includes theme nights of forgotten American classics.

LANDMARK'S CENTURY CENTRE
Map pp86-7
☎ 773-509-4949; www.landmarktheatres.com; 2828 N Clark St, Lake View; Ⓜ Brown, Purple Line to Diversey

This seven-screen high-tech cinema is a big bucket of popcorn better than typically roughshod art houses. It has stadium seating just like the multiplexes and a gourmet snack bar for the fanciest filmgoer.

MOVIES IN THE PARK
☎ 312-742-1134; www.chicagoparkdistrict.com

The Chicago Park District screens around 160 films throughout the summer at parks, beaches and museums all over the city. Bring a blanket, bug spray and popcorn, and settle in as darkness falls for movies ranging from family-friendly to classics to foreign-language flicks. Movies begin at dusk from June to September. Check the website for locations each day.

MUSIC BOX THEATRE Map pp86-7
☎ 773-871-6604; www.musicboxtheatre.com; 3733 N Southport Ave, Lake View; Ⓜ Brown Line to Southport

The current feature hardly matters; the Music Box itself is worth the visit. This perfectly restored theater dates from 1929 and looks like a Moorish palace, with clouds floating across the ceiling under twinkling stars. The programs are always first-rate, including a midnight roster of cult hits like *The Big Lebowski*. A second, small and serviceable theater shows held-over films.

SUMMER SCREENINGS PROGRAM
Map pp54-5
☎ 312-744-6630; www.cinemachicago.org; 78 E Washington St, Loop; Ⓜ Brown, Green, Orange, Purple, Pink Line to Randolph

The same group that puts on the Chicago International Film Festival hosts a free program in the summer showing foreign films in the Chicago Cultural Center's

CHICAGO FILM FESTIVALS

The Midwest Independent Film Festival (www .midwestfilm.com) – a monthly event dedicated to showcasing the best indie films from the Midwest – is a great way to catch a flick from Chicago's up-and-coming filmmakers. It happens the first Tuesday of the month at Landmark's Century Centre (p210).

The Chicago International Movies and Music Festival (www.cimmfest.org), or CIMM Fest, reels through the Windy City for a long weekend in early March. It spotlights global films in which music plays a central role. Screenings and concerts bring together the two disciplines at the Chicago Cultural Center and other venues around town.

In October, the Chicago International Film Festival (☎ 312-683-0121; www.chicagofilm-festival.com) is the main event. If your visit coincides, check the festival website for the complete schedule. For more unique offerings in a festival environment, check out the Chicago Underground Film Festival (www.cuff.org), which runs in late June.

Claudia Cassidy Theater (2nd floor). Each movie premieres on Wednesday at 6:30pm, and typically is repeated on Saturday at 2pm (though check to make sure). Seating is first come, first served. The program runs from early May through early September.

READINGS & SPOKEN WORD

Chicago's literary scene might be small but it is feisty, featuring local and out-of-towner readings in comfortable (often boozy) DIY settings. Quimby's (p139), Danny's (p184) and the California Clipper (see Guild Complex, p211) all host reliable events.

The more established (and sober) men and women of letters are likely to read at bookstores such as Barbara's (p142), Women and Children First (p137) or the Book Cellar (Map pp50-1; www.bookcellarinc.com; 4736 N Lincoln Ave, Lincoln Square; Brown Line to Western), where events are frequent. The only occasion that might bring all these scenes together is the annual Printers' Ball (www .printersball.org), which brings all sorts of performance and lit-based events to Chicago venues for a month-long literary hootenanny in July. It's been known to get downright out of hand; one year the cops even busted the closing party.

DANNY'S READING SERIES
☎ 773-489-6457; www.dannys.noslander.com;
1951 W Dickens Ave; 🚇 Blue Line to Damen
Held the second Wednesday of every month
at Danny's (p184), this is one of the city's best
places to see young poets from Chicago
and abroad. The atmosphere is casual
and the roster heady, making it Chicago's
quintessential younger poets' event.

GUILD COMPLEX LITERARY COMPLEX
☎ 877-394-5061; www.guildcomplex.org
The prose series and BYOP (P is for
'people,' of course) of this smart nonprofit
organization brings together the young,
old, hip and square of Chicago's literary
scene for free events at the brilliantly divey
California Clipper (Map p100; ☎ 773-384-2547; www
.californiaclipper.com; 1002 N California Ave, Humboldt
Park; 🚌 52). For Spanish speakers it also
organizes the bilingual Palabra Pura series.

HAROLD WASHINGTON LIBRARY CENTER READINGS
☎ 312-747-4050; www.chipublib.org; 400 S State
St, Loop; Ⓜ Brown, Orange, Purple, Pink Line to
Library
Several writers each month come to the
country's largest library, the Harold Washington
Library Center (p60), and give talks about their
current projects. Recent guests have included Salman Rushdie and *No Reservations*
author Anthony Bourdain. The library's
author calendar can be seen on its website,
or drop by the library for a flyer.

PAPER MACHETE Map pp50-1
☎ 773-227-4433; www.thepapermacheteshow
.com; 4644 N Lincoln Ave, Lincoln Sq; Ⓜ Brown
Line to Western
Poets, musicians, playwrights, comedians
and moms get together for this weekly 'live
magazine' discussing culture, politics and
wit. It's held at Ricochet's, a bar in Lincoln
Sq, at 3pm Saturday.

top picks
LITERARY BLOGS
- Literago (www.literago.org) This ace blog by
  Gretchen Kalwinski and Eugenia Williamson was
  founded to 'show the world Chicago isn't an illiter-
  ate sinkhole.'
- Book Slut (www.bookslut.com) A sharp monthly
  online lit magazine of reviews, headed by Jessa
  Crispin.
- Shoot the Messinger (www.shootthemessinger
  .com) A blog about literature and life by Jonathan
  Messinger, the cofounder of local indie publisher
  Featherproof Books.
- The Outfit (www.theoutfitcollective.blogspot
  .com) Chicago crime writers band together and talk
  about the writing lifestyle.

UPTOWN POETRY SLAM
☎ 773-878-5552; www.slampapi.com; 4802 N
Broadway St, Uptown; Ⓜ Red Line to Lawrence
This long-running event birthed the
national slam fad, and it's still going every
Sunday night at the Green Mill (p191). Watch
shaky first-timers take to the mic from 7pm
to 8pm, then for an hour after that a
featured guest has a go and the slam
competition begins in earnest. There's a
$6 cover.

WEEDS POETRY NIGHT Map pp78-9
☎ 312-943-7815; 1555 N Dayton St, Old Town;
Ⓜ Red Line to North/Clybourn
Verse comes in all shapes and sizes at
Weeds' weekly Monday night event
(10:30pm), when a cast of delightfully
eccentric poets get on the tavern's mic to
vent about love, sex, war, booze, urban
living and pretty much everything in
between. Some of it rhymes, some of it
rambles, but the proportions make for a
pretty cool scene.

SPORTS & ACTIVITIES

top picks

- Chicago Cubs (p220)
- Working Bikes Cooperative (p216)
- Lakefront Bike Trail (p216)
- Millennium Park Workouts (p214)
- Wateriders Kayaking (p220)
- Baseball Batting Cages at Sluggers (p215)
- North Avenue Beach (p219)
- Ice-Skating in Millennium Park (p217)
- Moksha Yoga (p215)
- Diversey-River Bowl (p216)

SPORTS & ACTIVITIES

Chicago is the USA's greatest sports town. There – we said it. Listen in at the office water-cooler on Monday morning and the talk is all about the Bears. Eavesdrop on a conversation between neighbors as they tidy their yards, and the chatter revolves around the Cubs or the White Sox.

Sports are deeply woven into the local fabric. This is a city that sees no conflict of interest in taking one of its most revered cultural icons – the Art Institute's lion sculptures – and plopping giant fiberglass Blackhawks helmets on them when the local team wins the Stanley Cup. The creatures also donned Bears helmets and White Sox caps when those teams played in recent championships. Even the city's staid skyscrapers get into the spirit, arranging their window lights to spell 'Go Hawks' or 'Go Cubs' when the teams make a run for the championship.

It's not all about passively watching sports, though. When the sun peeps out in April after the long, cold winter, everyone busts out of work and makes a dash for the lakefront to jog, skate or ride their bikes. Chicago provides plenty of places to get active via its city-spanning shoreline, 33 beaches and 552 parks.

OK, OK, it's true: the bars during a Bears game are still more crowded than a free 8am yoga class in Millennium Park. And statistics show that Chicagoans are not particularly fit as a whole (the city placed in the top five for chubbiness, according to a recent national study).

The point is, Chicago has a sweet array of sports and activity options, so whether you want to open your chakras, play a little bike polo or practice your home-run swing, the Windy City has you covered.

HEALTH & FITNESS

For a fun and free exercise session, try Millennium Park Workouts (www.millenniumpark.org). Every Saturday morning between 7am and 11am, from early June to mid September, the park hosts a workout on the Great Lawn (Map pp54-5). It starts with an hour of tai chi, followed by yoga (8am), Pilates (9am) and dance aerobics (10am).

Hotels almost always have either their own fitness facilities or agreements with nearby clubs. We've listed some additional options below. Gym day passes cost $20 to $25; yoga drop-in classes cost around $15.

HEALTH & DAY SPAS

AVEDA INSTITUTE Map pp86-7
☎ 773-883-1560; www.avedainstitutechicago.com; 2828 N Clark St, Lake View; ☼ 9am-4:30pm Tue-Fri, 8:30am-5pm Sat; Ⓜ Brown, Purple Line to Diversey

Aveda makes nice-smelling, plant-based beauty products. The Institute teaches future cosmetologists to use those products on people. So what you get here are discounted services by students who use Aveda goodies to beautify you. Haircuts ($14 to $16) are the most popular offering, but you can also get treatments such as the Caribbean seaweed body wrap and minimassage ($50); a Dead Sea salt exfoliation and massage ($45); and a variety of facials ($30 to $50), each of which includes a bonus foot soak with hot stones. Attention men: Aveda can remove your back hair (from $30).

FOUR SEASONS SPA Map pp72-3
☎ 312-280-8800; www.fourseasons.com/chicagofs; Four Seasons Hotel, 120 E Delaware Pl, Gold Coast; ☼ 8am-8pm; Ⓜ Red Line to Chicago

If you really want to do it in style, head to the Four Seasons Spa, where pleasures like the Sedona red-clay wrap ($145) and the lemongrass and ginger body polish ($65) will 'revitalize your energy meridians.' They also feel pretty great. You can do quick 30-minute sessions or have a luxurious all-day affair. Prices start sky high and go up from there.

RUBY ROOM Map pp96-7
☎ 773-235-2323; www.rubyroom.com; 1743-5 W Division St, Wicker Park; ☼ 10am-7pm Mon-Fri, 9am-7pm Sat, 10am-6pm Sun; Ⓜ Blue Line to Division

Ruby Room is a spa and 'healing sanctuary' serving up a wild array of services. The 'intuitive numerotherapy' option ($100 for 60 minutes) will help you figure out why you keep dating jerks and working at dead-end jobs. Or maybe you just need an energy healing ($100 for 60 minutes) to get your aura back to its proper color. More down-to-earth services – massages, facials, haircuts etc – are also on the menu. For details on lodgings here, see p241. For yoga classes, see Yogaview (p215).

YOGA & PILATES

Chicago has several options for exercising the body and mind. Call or check the websites for class times. In addition, yoga tog maker Lululemon (p135) offers free classes on Sunday in its shops.

BIKRAM YOGA Map pp96-7

☎ 773-395-9150; www.bycic.com; 1344 N Milwaukee Ave, Wicker Park; Ⓜ Blue Line to Division
For a great yoga-only experience, try this place in Wicker Park, where classes run daily and cost $15 per 90-minute session. This is 'hot' yoga, in a heated room, so arrive hydrated.

HARMONY MIND BODY FITNESS
Map pp78-9

☎ 773-296-0263; www.harmonybody.com; 1962 N Bissell, Lincoln Park; Ⓜ Brown, Purple Line to Armitage
A staff of fully certified Pilates purists offers classes in Pilates, Gyrotonic and other core-strengthening techniques. Group classes cost $20; private sessions run up to $80.

MOKSHA YOGA Map pp86-7

☎ 773-975-9642; www.mokshayoga.com; 3334 N Clark St, Lake View; Ⓜ Brown, Purple, Red Line to Belmont
Hatha, vinyasa, ashtanga and tantric-hatha classes happen throughout the day, seven days a week. Drop-in classes cost $12 to $17, depending on their length; students with ID receive a 20% discount. Moksha also offers a free 'community' class from 4pm to 5:30pm on Saturdays; its yoga style varies.

YOGAVIEW Map pp96-7

☎ 773-342-9642; www.yogaview.com; 1745 W Division St, Wicker Park; Ⓡ Blue Line to Division
Most Yogaview instructors teach some type of vinyasa, but individual teachers can lean toward an iyengar or ashtanga approach, too. All of the class here are 'pay what you

can,' with a suggested donation of $14. The studio is at the Ruby Room spa.

GYMS

FITNESS FORMULA CLUB Map pp86-7

☎ 773-755-3232; www.ffc.com; 3228 N Halsted St, Lake View; Ⓨ 24hr Mon-Thu, to 9:30pm Fri, 7am-9pm Sat, 8am-9pm Sun; Ⓜ Brown, Purple, Red Line to Belmont
This club is particularly well regarded for its strength training. Along with the usual workout machines, swimming pools and basketball courts, the half-dozen locations around town also offer spinning, yoga and Pilates classes.

LAKESHORE ATHLETIC CLUB Map pp54-5

☎ 312-616-9000; www.lsac.com; 211 N Stetson Ave, Loop; Ⓨ 5:15am-10pm Mon-Fri, 8am-6pm Sat, 8am-4pm Sun; Ⓜ Brown, Green, Orange, Purple, Pink Line to State
Located at the Illinois Center, Lakeshore offers a full range of exercise classes, a pool and squash courts, plus an impressive seven-story indoor climbing wall, for which day use and orientation fees cost $40. General-use gym rates are $25 per day.

WEST LOOP ATHLETIC CLUB Map pp104-5

☎ 312-850-4667; www.chicagoathleticclubs .com; 1380 W Randolph St, West Loop; Ⓨ 5am-11pm Mon-Thu, to 10pm Fri, 7am-9pm Sat & Sun; Ⓜ Green, Pink Line to Ashland
Part of a local chain, this outlet has a five-lane lap pool, a basketball court, a slew of cardio and strengthening machines, a long list of group classes and a steam room with a whirlpool. A day pass costs $25.

ACTIVITIES

When the weather warms, Chicagoans dash like sun-starved maniacs for the parks and beaches. On the first nice day (there's usually one in April), bikers, joggers and skaters jam the lakefront path – it's worse than anything on the local highways. Winter is quieter, though the hardy bundle up to ice-skate and ride sleds.

BASEBALL BATTING CAGES

Tired of watching your favorite Cubs or Sox player strike out, and think you could do better? Give it a try at Sluggers (Map pp86-7;

☎ 773-472-9696; www.sluggersbar.com; 3540 N Clark St), a popular bar and grill across from Wrigley Field. Sidestep the drunk fans and giant screen TVs and head to the 2nd floor, where there are four batting cages. Ten pitches cost $1; you'll begin feeling the pain pretty soon after your efforts.

CYCLING & IN-LINE SKATING

Curbs are the highest mountains you'll find in Chicago, making it ideal for biking and in-line skating. The popular 18.5-mile Lakefront Trail from Hollywood Ave in the north to 71st St in the south is an excellent way to see the city, and in hot weather the lake offers cool breezes. Lincoln Park is another good spot for biking and rolling, with paths snaking around the small lakes and the zoo. Another surprisingly good option for biking is the Loop on Sundays. The traffic clears out of the business district, giving wheeled tourists an exhilarating, stress-free opportunity to roll through the historic architecture of downtown.

Bicycling Magazine ranked Chicago as one of the nation's top-10 cities for bike friendliness, and bike culture is indeed taking root. The city's Department of Transportation (www .chicagobikes.org) offers a free map of bike-friendly streets, plus info on bike shops, publications, local regulations and a slew of other resources. The advocacy group Active Transportation Alliance (www.activetrans.org) is another gold mine for cyclists; it includes details on grassroots events such as 'veggie bike rides,' where enthusiasts get together for a ride and a meat-free meal.

The McDonald's Cycle Center (www.chicagobike station.com) at Millennium Park offers 300 bike storage spaces, repairs and showers to make bike commuting an appealing option for workers. It's also a convenient place to pick up rental bikes (per hour/day from $10/35), including road, hybrid, tandem and children's bikes. Bike Chicago (www.bikechicago.com) is the rental company doing the honors here, as well as from outlets on Navy Pier and at North Ave Beach. It also offers guided bike tours ($39 to $59, including equipment) several times daily, covering themes such as the lakefront, nighttime fireworks or Obama sights. In-line skates can also be rented at each of Bike Chicago's outlets for the same price as bikes. For details on rental locations, see p263. For tours, see p272.

If you're going to need a bike for more than a few days, consider buying a recycled two-wheeler from Working Bikes Cooperative (Map pp50-1; ☎ 773-847-5440; www.workingbikes.org; 2434 S Western Ave, Pilsen; ⌚ noon-7pm Wed, 10am-5pm Sat). The nonprofit group trawls local landfills and scrap yards for junked bikes, then brings them back to its warehouse and refurbishes them. Half get sold in the storefront shop; proceeds enable the group to ship the rest to developing countries. WBC now recycles 10,000 bikes annually this way. It's a great deal – you'll get a sturdy, well-oiled machine for the bargain price of about $50 or so. When you're finished, you can donate the bike back. Note you will have to factor in the cost of a lock and a helmet (rental companies provide these for free).

If you're looking for a very big, very slow group ride while you're in town, Chicago Critical Mass (www.chicagocriticalmass.org) organizes rides through the streets on the last Friday of the month. The rides, which are intended to celebrate bike use and disrupt the

---

CHICAGO'S LUCKY STRIKES

Bowling is a beloved Midwestern activity. People of all shapes, sizes and ages gather in boisterous groups to send balls crashing into pins. Talent is not a prerequisite, but a willingness to consume copious pitchers of cheap beer is. Bowling alleys draw the most crowds during the cold months.

Try your luck on the lanes at one of the following:

Diversey-River Bowl (Map pp86-7; ☎ 773-227-5800; www.drbowl.com; 2211 W Diversey Pkwy, Lake View; lanes per hr $19-32; 🚌 76) Nicknamed the 'rock 'n' bowl' for its late-night light show, fog machines and loud music.

Southport Lanes (Map pp86-7; ☎ 773-472-6600; www.sparetimechicago.com; 3325 N Southport Ave, Lake View; lanes per hr $15-20; Ⓜ Brown Line to Southport) Has old-fashioned, hand-set pins; slip a dollar into the ball when you roll it back, and the pin-setter might knock down a few extra ones on your behalf.

Waveland Bowl (Map pp86-7; ☎ 773-472-5900; www.wavelandbowl.com; 3700 N Western Ave, Lake View; per person per game $1-5; Ⓜ Brown Line to Addison, transfer to 🚌 152) Open 24/7, baby, so you can roll the ball and wear the spiffy shoes whenever the mood strikes (pun!).

car-dependent status quo, begin at Daley Plaza (cnr of Dearborn & Washington Sts) at 5:45pm. The mood is lighthearted and routes unfold spontaneously. Other Critical Mass rides take place in various neighborhoods on first and second Fridays; check the website for details. The Chicago Cycling Club (☎ 773-509-8093; www .chicagocyclingclub.org) sponsors three to four free rides per week April through October, as well as sporadic rides in winter. Just show up at the designated time and departure point (listed on the website); no reservations required. If you're in town over Memorial Day weekend, Bike the Drive (www.bikethedrive.org) lets riders have Lake Shore Dr all to themselves for one glorious morning; for event details, see p14.

FISHING

Between the fishing derbies organized by the mayor's office, the state-sponsored Urban Fishing Program and, of course, smelt season, anglers cast a lot more lines in the city than you might expect. The waters of Lake Michigan just off Northerly Island (p114) boast good fishing, as does the lagoon in Humboldt Park (p99). If the fish are biting, expect to catch smallmouth bass, largemouth bass, catfish and bluegill.

In April, it's all about smelt, the wee fish that swarm into Chicago's harbors to spawn. Anglers meet them with nets and deep-fat fryers from piers up and down the lakefront (beers and portable TVs are also part of the deal). No matter that smelt have been scarce in recent years – it remains a great excuse to gather and have a few pops by the water.

Anglers over 16 years of age will need a license (available online at http://dnr.state .il.us and at any bait shop for $5.50 per day). The Illinois Division of Fisheries (www.ifishillinois.org) is a good resource for maps and tips.

GOLF

Chicago golfers stretch the season as far as possible in both directions; basically you can play until it snows.

The Chicago Park District has six public golf courses and three driving ranges, all overseen by Kemper Golf Management (☎ 312-245-0909; www.cpdgolf.com). Call or go online to find out more about the courses, as well as to make your tee times.

DIVERSEY DRIVING RANGE Map pp78-9
☎ 312-742-7929; Diversey Pkwy, Lincoln Park;
☺ 7am-10pm; ➌ 151

top picks

BEST BIKE RIDES

- Lakefront Trail (p216)
- Lincoln Park (p77)
- South Side/Obama Tour with Bike Chicago or Bobby's Bike Hike (p272)
- Bike the Drive (p14)

If you just want to knock a bucket of balls around, this driving range in Lincoln Park will let you whack away to your heart's content. Rental clubs are available, and a bucket of 50 balls costs $9.

JACKSON PARK GOLF COURSE
Map pp50-1
☎ 773-667-0524; E 63rd St & Lake Shore Dr, South Side; ➌ 6, Ⓜ Metra to 63rd
The district's only 18-hole course is moderately challenging. Public fees range from $24 to $27. Reservations are recommended.

SYDNEY R MAROVITZ GOLF COURSE
Map pp86-7
☎ 312-742-7930; 3600 N Recreation Dr (Lake Shore Dr), Lake View; ➌ 151
The nine-hole course in the park enjoys sweeping views of the lake and skyline. The course is very popular, and in order to secure a tee time golfers cheerfully arrive at 5:30am. You can avoid that sort of lunacy by spending a few dollars extra to get a reservation. Public fees cost $22 to $25 in summer. You can also rent clubs here.

ICE-SKATING & SLEDDING

The Chicago Park District operates a first-class winter rink at Daley Bicentennial Plaza (Map pp54-5; ☎ 312-742-7650; 337 E Randolph St, Loop) and at the McCormick-Tribune Ice Rink (Map pp54-5; ☎ 312-742-5222; 55 N Michigan Ave, Loop) in Millennium Park. Admission is free to both; skate rental costs $6 to $10. They're open from late November to late February.

The Rink at Wrigley (Map pp86-7; www.rinkatwrigley .com) takes over the baseball stadium's parking lot in winter. There's an admission fee (adult/child $10/6) plus skate rental cost.

The Park District operates a free, 33ft sledding hill by Soldier Field (Map pp112-13; 425 F

McFetridge Dr, South Loop) in winter; bring your own gear. They fire up a snowmaking machine for times when the weather doesn't cooperate.

PICK-UP GAMES

Those looking to put in a little time on the basketball court will be especially excited by Chicago's offerings: casual hoops happen at almost every park in the city. You can get a game at Wicker Park (the park, not the neighborhood). Ultimate Frisbee (www .ultimatechicago.org) is also big in Chicago. There's typically a pick-up game Tuesday evening by Montrose Beach in warm weather; check the website's community forum for details.

RUNNING & WALKING

The Lakefront Trail (p216) also has a runner's side for those looking to get a little bipedal workout. Runners hit the trail around 5am. If you're looking for a good starting point, try Oak St Beach on the Gold Coast and head north. The path from the beach northward is largely cinder rather than asphalt, which your feet will appreciate.

If you find yourself getting distracted by the great city and park views, you can regain focus on the free cinder oval track at Lake Shore Park (Map pp72-3; 808 N Lake Shore Dr), at the intersection of Chicago Ave and Lake Shore Dr.

Any questions about running should be directed to the Chicago Area Runners Association (☎ 312-666-9836; www.cararuns.org), which sponsors training programs. The website provides a list of free, daily fun runs throughout the city.

For those looking to move at a more leisurely pace, walking through the city's parks is a great way to get exercise. The Chicago Park District (www.chicagoparkdistrict.com) offers extensive lists, maps and ratings of its hundreds of city-maintained walking trails on its website. The site even provides a flower and plant finder to help you identify any flora you see en route.

TENNIS

Some of Chicago's public tennis courts require reservations and charge fees (usually around $10 per hour), while others are free and players just queue for their turns on the court. Place your racket by the net and you're next in line. The season runs from mid-April to mid-October.

The following are good options:

Daley Bicentennial Plaza (Map pp54-5; ☎ 312-742-7648; 337 E Randolph St, Loop; Ⓜ Brown, Green, Orange, Pink, Purple Line to Randolph) Charges a fee for its 12 lit courts.

Grant Park (Map pp112-13; 900 S Columbus Dr near E Balbo Dr, South Loop; 🚌 6) No reservations are taken for the 12 lit courts, but fees are charged at peak times.

OFFBEAT ACTIVITIES

Bet you never expected to go surfing or become a cornhole master in Chicago, did you?

Snow Biking Whenever 2in or more of new snow falls, bundled-up cyclists meet at the Handlebar (p165) at 7pm for liquid courage before heading out to a random location to ride through the wintry wonderland. For more snow bike events, check www.bikewinter.org.

Bike Polo It's three mallet-wielding, spoked players against three in Garfield Park every Wednesday at 6:30pm and Sunday at 2:30pm. Newcomers are welcome, with beer and tricked-out bikes provided by the good folks at Chicago Hardcourt Bike Polo (www.chicagohardcourt.com).

Cornhole Get your mind out of the gutter; we're not talking porn here. We're talking corn, as in small corn-filled bags (aka beanbags) that participants toss into a sloped box with a hole in it. Bars are the place to see the game in action. The one attached to Wrigley Field, Captain Morgan Club (Map pp86-7; ☎ 773-404-4759; www.captainmorgan club.com; 1060 W Addison St, Wrigleyville), has leagues and tournaments on Wednesday nights where you can win free Cubs tickets.

Kitesurfing Pump up your adrenaline with Chicago Kitesurfing (www.chicagokitesurfing.com). Beginners can sign up for three- to four-hour lessons ($150 to $250, gear included). These take place at beaches outside the city, wherever wind conditions are best (but they're usually no more than an hour away). If you don't want to participate, you can always watch experienced kitesurfers go at it from Montrose Beach.

Surfing If you've got your own board, surfing is permitted at Montrose Beach and 57th St Beach. For rentals and lessons, you'll have to travel an hour and a half outside of town to New Buffalo, Michigan (p251), where you'll see dudes licking some tasty, if small, waves.

CHICAGO BEACHES

Visitors often don't realize Chicago is a beach town. In fact, it has 33 sandy stretches along Lake Michigan, all operated by the Park District (☎ 312-742-7529; www.chicagoparkdistrict.com). Call it the Miami of the Midwest – at least for a few months each year. Lifeguards patrol *Baywatch*-style from late May through early September. Most beaches have parking lots (average fee per hour $1). These are our favorites (from north to south):

Loyola Beach (Map pp50-1) Runs for more than eight blocks from North Shore Ave to Touhy Ave; features an upscale wooden playground for kids. It's fairly close to the Loyola El stop.

Montrose Beach (Map pp50-1) A wide, dog-friendly beach with a curving breakwater. You can rent kayaks here. Sometimes you'll see surfers and kitesurfers, and anglers frequently cast here. The Montrose Harbor bait shop sells ice for coolers. There's ample parking, but the walks to the beach can be long. Take bus 146 or 151.

Fullerton Beach (Map pp78-9) Fills with zoo day-trippers and Lincoln Parkers. The narrow beach can get jammed on weekends, but a five-minute walk south from Fullerton yields uncrowded vistas.

North Avenue Beach (Map pp78-9) Chicago's Southern California–style pocket, with loads of beautiful people, volleyball nets, a bar and million-dollar views; for more information, see p80.

Oak Street Beach (Map pp72-3) Lies at the north end of Michigan Ave, less than five minutes from the Water Tower. The hulking Lake Shore Dr condos cast shadows in the afternoon, but the beach remains packed. See p74 for more information.

Ohio Street Beach (Map pp66-7) Just a few minutes' walk from Navy Pier, this small beach is convenient for those who want a quick dip. The water's calmness makes it the preferred practice spot for triathletes.

12th Street Beach (Map pp112-13) Hidden behind the Adler Planetarium, it makes a great break from the myriad sights of the Museum Campus. Its out-of-the-way location gives the narrow enclave an exclusive feel. See p114 for more details.

57th Street Beach (Map p120) Just across Lake Shore Dr from the Museum of Science & Industry, 57th St Beach features an expanse of clean, golden sand. Surfers say it's the best beach to hang ten.

Jackson Park Beach (Map p120) A bit further south from 57th St Beach, this expanse contains a stately restored beach house with dramatic breezeways. It's next to a yacht harbor, and exudes a charm lacking at the beaches with more modern – and mundane – facilities.

Lake Shore Park (Map pp72-3; ☎ 312-742-7891; 808 N Lake Shore Dr, Gold Coast; Ⓜ Red Line to Chicago) Two very popular (and free) lit courts near the lake.

Waveland Tennis Courts (Map pp86-7; ☎ 312-742-8515; east side of N Lake Shore Dr where Waveland Ave meets Lincoln Park, Lake View; 🚌 151) Charges a fee for its 20 courts.

WATERSPORTS

Between Lake Michigan, the Chicago River and Chicago's public pools, there are limitless ways to make a splash in the city.

Lakefront beaches (see the boxed text, p219) have lifeguards in summer. However, you can swim at your own risk whenever you want, depending on what you think of the temperature. The water in August is usually in the 70°s F (21° to 26°C). If you're looking for chlorinated water, try the large pool at Holstein Park (Map pp96-7; ☎ 312-742-7554; 2200 N Oakley Ave; admission free; ⏰ 7am-8pm Mon-Fri, from 9am Sat & Sun) in the heart of Bucktown. Check for the 'open swim' hours.

Kayaking has taken off in the city. Outfitters rent vessels along the lakefront and the Chicago River. The latter is not the world's cleanest body of water, but that doesn't seem to be deterring anyone. Note that boat traffic can get heavy as you approach downtown. If you're a beginner, you might want to chat with the outfitter about local conditions to make sure you're up for the task. Rentals cost $15 to $20 per hour. Or opt for a guided paddle, which all of the companies below offer as well, from May through September.

CHICAGO RIVER CANOE & KAYAK
Map pp50-1

☎ 773-704-2663; www.chicagoriverpaddle.com; 3400 N Rockwell Ave; Ⓜ Brown Line to Addison, transfer to 🚌 152

The launch point is about 2 miles north of downtown, so it's better for beginners (ie away from traffic). Guided trips, like the Skyscraper Canyon tour ($50) on Sunday evenings, head downtown.

KAYAK CHICAGO Map pp50-1

☎ 630-336-7245; www.kayakchicago.com; Montrose Beach; 🚌 146 or 151

This group is best known for its lakefront paddles. Take a four-hour beginner's lesson ($85) or a two-hour tour ($50). They teach paddleboarding here too. Located in the beach's southeast corner.

WATERIDERS Map pp72-3

☎ 312-953-9287; www.wateriders.com; 950 N Kingsbury St; Ⓜ Brown, Purple Line to Chicago

Wateriders is closest to downtown. If you decide to go with a guided tour, it offers excellent daily 'Ghost and Gangster' trips ($60) that glide by notorious downtown sites.

SPECTATOR SPORTS

Almost every Chicagoan declares a firm allegiance to at least one of the city's teams, and the place goes absolutely nuts when one of them hits the big time. Take the Blackhawks' Stanley Cup win in 2010: an estimated two million people poured into the Loop for a raucous ticker-tape parade. When the White Sox won the World Series in 2005? Similar scene, only it also included F-16 fighter planes, Journey's Steve Perry and Oprah, all strangely woven together. And when the Bears went to the Super Bowl in 2007, the city couldn't talk about anything else. Businesses with coat-and-tie dress codes were suddenly requiring staff to wear their blue and orange jerseys to the office.

There are various ways to procure tickets, which we've described below. All sports teams save the Cubs use Ticketmaster (☎ 800-745-3000; www.ticketmaster.com) as their ticketing outlet. You can also check national ticket broker Goldstar (www.goldstar.com) for half-price tickets to venues.

BASEBALL

Chicago is one of only a few US cities to boast two Major League baseball teams. The Cubs are the lovable losers on the North Side, with record-breaking yuppie attendance year after year despite generally woeful play. The White Sox are the working man's team on the South Side, and thumb their nose at all the hoopla across town.

The two ballparks are also a study in contrasts: traditional Wrigley Field (p84) is

top picks

CHICAGO SPORTS BLOGS

- Bleed Cubbie Blue (www.bleedcubbieblue.com)
- South Side Sox (www.southsidesox.com)
- Windy City Gridiron (www.windycitygridiron.com)
- Blog-A-Bull (www.blogabull.com)

baseball's second-oldest park and about as charming as it gets in this sport. US Cellular Field is the new breed of stadium with such amenities as a chock-full food court (veggie burgers and burritos are among the eats at present) and fireworks if the Sox hit a home run at night.

The two stadiums are equidistant from the Loop: Wrigley is 4.5 miles north, while the Cell is 4.5 miles south. The Red Line train connects them both. The two teams play catch from early April through September.

CHICAGO CUBS Map pp86-7

☎ 773-404-2827; www.cubs.com; Wrigley Field, 1060 W Addison St, Wrigleyville; average ticket $53; Ⓜ Red Line to Addison

By far the local favorite, the Cubs play at Wrigley Field. Tickets are available at the box office, through the team's website, or by calling ☎ 800-843-2827 (within Illinois) or ☎ 866-652-2827 (from out of state). The cheapest tickets (about $18) are the 'upper deck, restricted view' ones, and they're not bad.

But know this: unless you plan waaaay ahead (like in March), the game you want likely will be sold out. No big deal – you still have options. First, try the box office for standing-room tickets ($15). They release these about two hours before the game if it's a sellout. Or check online the morning of the game, as the teams' unused tickets sometimes become available. Next, try the frightfully named 'scalpers.' These guys stand across from the ballpark entrance (on Clark St's west side and Addison St's south side). They typically charge above face value for tickets – until the third inning or so. Then tickets can be yours for a pittance. Private fans also try to unload tickets they can't use, usually at face value. Look for the sad-faced people walking around and asking, 'Anyone need tickets?' Finally, you can enquire about rooftop seats (ie those not in the park, but rather on the rooftops of the surrounding houses on Sheffield and Waveland Aves). They're usually booked out by groups, but not always, and they include food and drinks as part of the deal; check www.ballparkrooftops.com or www .goldstar.com (for half-price rooftop offers).

CHICAGO WHITE SOX Map pp50–1

☎ 312-674-1000; www.whitesox.com; US Cellular Field, 333 W 35th St, South Side; average ticket $39; M Red Line to Sox-35th

The White Sox play at US Cellular Field (aka the Cell, though often referred to by its pre-corporate-sponsorship name, Comiskey Park). Less loved than the Cubs despite their 2005 World Series win, the Sox resort to more promotions and cheaper tickets to lure fans to their southerly location. Thus, you might be treated to a pregame '80s hair band or a free hot dog with admission. Tickets are available through the team's website, at the ballpark box office or at any Ticketmaster outlet. Sellouts aren't usually an issue. The Cell sports a couple of cool features, such as the Bullpen Bar, where you sip your beer practically right freakin' on the field; and the pet check, which allows dog owners to bring Fido to the game and drop him off with a babysitter for a fee. The team offers half-price tickets most Mondays.

BASKETBALL

The Bulls, once the stuff of legend, haven't posed much of a threat since the 1997–98 season, when Michael Jordan led the team. The controversial

top picks

CHICAGO SPORTS SOUVENIRS

- Ditka T-shirt from Strange Cargo (p136)
- Cubs flask, ball cap or mini–Wrigley Field street sign from Sports World (p137)
- Ozzie Guillen bobblehead doll from US Cellular Field gift shop (p221)
- Cubs or Sox jersey for your pooch from Barker & Meowsky (p134)

owner Jerry Reinsdorf allowed Jordan, Zen coach Phil Jackson, Scottie Pippen and other key parts of the Bulls juggernaut to leave after that championship year, and since then the team has ranged from awful to so-so. The Bulls shoot their hoops on the West Side in the cavernous United Center. The season runs from November to April.

CHICAGO BULLS Map pp104–5

☎ 800-462-2849; www.nba.com/bulls; United Center, 1901 W Madison St, West Loop; average ticket $64; 🚌 19

They may not be the mythical champions of yore, but the Bulls are still well loved and draw good crowds. Tickets are available through the United Center box office – located at Gate 4 on the building's east side – and at Ticketmaster outlets. On game days, the Chicago Transit Authority runs a special express bus (number 19) on Madison St that heads west to the stadium.

A DAY AT THE FRIENDLY CONFINES

Let's assume you've already procured tickets (see p220), and let's assume you've already walked our Cubbyville tour (p85) around the environs. Now it's time to enter the pearly gates – after taking a keepsake photo under the main-entrance neon sign, of course.

Ahh. You scan around and see the green grass field, the hand-operated scoreboard and the ivy-covered outfield walls. It looks pretty much the same as when Babe Ruth batted here all those years ago. You order a hot dog and an Old Style beer, Wrigley's traditional fare, and head to your seat.

The Cubs are getting clobbered, and the guy next to you says it's the Curse. You nod, because you know all about Billy Sianis, owner of the Billy Goat Tavern (p153). When he tried to enter Wrigley Field with his pet goat in 1945, ballpark staff refused, saying the goat stank. Sianis threw up his arms, and called down a mighty hex: 'The Cubs will never win a World Series!' And they haven't.

And then – holy smoke – here comes a home-run ball straight at you! Unfortunately, the opposing team slugged it, so you're honor bound to throw it back onto the field. That's a Wrigley ritual, as is the seventh inning stretch sing-along of 'Take Me Out to the Ballgame.'

All too quickly the game ends. Another loss. 'Wait till next year,' everyone says. Another tradition – Cubbie hope, despite all odds.

FOOTBALL

Once upon a time the Chicago Bears were one of the most revered franchises in the National Football League. Owner and coach George Halas epitomized the team's no-nonsense, take-no-prisoners approach. The tradition continued with players such as Walter Payton, Dick Butkus and Mike Singletary and coach Mike Ditka. In 1986 the Bears won the Super Bowl with a splendid collection of misfits and characters, such as Jim McMahon and William 'the Refrigerator' Perry, who enthralled and charmed the entire city. Then came 17 years of mediocrity. Then came the 2007 Super Bowl! The Bears kicked serious ass to get there, then sadly, got their ass handed right back. The team has been up and down since.

But expectations are ever high, with fans flocking to Soldier Field. The season runs from August to December, when you can get snowed on.

CHICAGO BEARS Map pp112-13

☎ 847-615-2327; www.chicagobears.com; Soldier Field, 1410 S Museum Campus Dr, South Loop; average ticket $90; 🚌 146

Da Bears can be found, sleet, snow or dark of night, at Soldier Field. Since the inauguration of the new stadium in 2003, tickets have been hard to come by, and are available only through Ticketmaster. Arrive early on game days and wander through the parking lots – you won't believe the elaborate tailgate feasts people cook up from the back of their cars. And for crissake, dress warmly.

HOCKEY

What a difference a management change can make. After languishing at the bottom of Chicago's pro-sport pantheon for the past few decades, the Blackhawks have skated into prominence thanks to a young winning team and TV and radio deals that put them back in the mainstream. Oh, and they won the 2010 Stanley Cup, their first since 1961. The fervor picks up when rivals like the Detroit Red Wings and St Louis Blues skate into the United Center (which the Blackhawks share with the Bulls). The season runs October to April.

CHICAGO SPORTS HEROES PRIMER

Should you find yourself in a sports bar anywhere in the Windy City, a misty-eyed mention of any of the names below will help bond you to your fellow drinkers. Heck, someone might even buy you an Old Style.

Mike Ditka The Chicago Bears star (and current Chicago restaurateur), Ditka is the only person to have won a Super Bowl as a player, assistant coach and head coach. His mustache is legendary.

Michael Jordan The Chicago Bulls great ended his career of 15 seasons with the highest per-game scoring average in National Basketball Association (NBA) history.

Ryne Sandberg The Cubs second baseman played a record 123 consecutive games without an error, and in 2005 became the fourth Cubs player ever to have his number retired. Recently, he's been coaching the Cubs' minor league team in Iowa.

Dick Butkus Elected to the Pro Football Hall of Fame in 1979, the Bears player recovered 25 fumbles in his career, a record at the time of his retirement.

Walter Payton The Chicago Bears great is ranked second on the National Football League (NFL) all-time rushing list, and seventh in all-time scoring.

Ernie Banks Voted the National League's most valuable player (MVP) twice (1958 and 1959), he was the first baseball player to have his number retired by the Cubs.

Stan Mikita The Czech-born hockey star played his entire career with the Chicago Blackhawks, from 1959 to 1980, retiring with the second-most points of any player.

Bobby Hull Nicknamed 'The Golden Jet,' the Blackhawks left winger is considered one of hockey's all-time greats.

Ozzie Guillen Current White Sox coach and former player, known for his outspoken and politically incorrect comments. Still, many love him since he brought the World Series trophy to Chicago in 2005 – the first big win in almost 100 years.

Scottie Pippen Leading the Bulls through champion seasons throughout the 1990s, Pippen is known for pioneering the point forward position on the basketball court.

CHICAGO BLACKHAWKS Map pp104-5

☎ 312-455-7000; www.chicagoblackhawks.com; United Center, 1901 W Madison St, West Loop; average ticket $50; 🚌 19

Tickets have become difficult to get, with lots of sellouts since the team picked up steam. The box office and Ticketmaster do the honors. Be sure to arrive in time for the national anthem at the game's start. The raucous, ear-splitting rendition is a tradition. On game days, the Chicago Transit Authority runs a special express bus (number 19) on Madison St that heads west to the stadium.

SOCCER

Thanks to support from Chicago's large Latino and European communities, the city's soccer team, the Fire, attracts a decent-sized fan base (despite being largely ignored by the mainstream media). The team has made the Major League Soccer play-offs several times in recent years, and last won the championship in 1998.

The Fire play in their own stadium – Toyota Park – way the hell southwest of downtown. The regular season runs from April to September, and the finals take place in October.

WINDY CITY ROLLERS

The bang-'em-up sport of roller derby was born in Chicago in 1935, and it's made a comeback in recent years thanks to the battlin' beauties of the Windy City Rollers (www.windycityrollers.com) league. Players boast names like Sassy Squatch and Juanna Rumbel, and there is a fair amount of campy theater surrounding the bouts. But the action and the hits are real, and the players are dedicated to the derby cause. Matches take place once a month at the UIC Pavilion (525 S Racine Ave, Near West Side; Ⓜ Blue Line to Racine) from late January to mid June; tickets cost $20.

CHICAGO FIRE Map pp50-1

☎ 708-594-7200, 888-657-3473; www.chicago-fire.com; Toyota Park, 71st & Harlem, Bridgeview; tickets $20-50; 🚌 386

Fire tickets are available through Ticketmaster, and are fairly easy to come by. Less easy is getting to the stadium in suburban Bridgeview. If you get to Midway Airport via the Orange Line, you can catch the suburban Pace Bus number 386 Toyota Park Express, which runs on game days only. The full trip from the Loop will likely take an hour or so.

lonely planet Hotels & Hostels

Want more sleeping recommendations than we could ever pack into this little ol' book? Craving more detail — including extended reviews and photographs? Want to read reviews by other travelers and be able to post your own? Just make your way over to **lonelyplanet.com/hotels** and check out our thorough list of independent reviews, then reserve your room simply and securely.

SLEEPING

top picks

SLEEPING

From dramatic views and rose-petal bubble baths to hostel bunks and homestays, you'll find amenities at every level in Chicago. Finding something at a reasonable rate? That's more difficult. Chicago is the Midwest's biggest city and convention central, so demand is high year-round, and it gets near impossible to find value on summer weekends (June through August), when the festival season and tourism peak. If you're willing to be flexible with your dates, you'll have a better chance of finding a place to stay that won't break the bank. Consolidators and online room bookers are another way to go if cost cutting is your primary objective (for more, see Saving Strategies opposite).

More than 30,000 hotel rooms blanket the city, most in high-rise buildings. With so many choices, picking a place can be daunting. It helps to decide on a neighborhood first. If you're going to tromp up and down the Mag Mile and binge on shopping, the Gold Coast or slightly more moderately priced Near North are the places to lay your head. If you're interested in snoozing amid the architecture and museums of the Loop and South Loop, there are plenty of options in those central neighborhoods, almost all of which are located near El stations for easy transportation to anywhere in the city. These core areas have the greatest concentration of hotels, and generally speaking, the farther south you go, the lower the prices.

Less central, but more personal, are area bed-and-breakfasts. A few old townhomes – in Wicker Park, Lake View and Andersonville – have been turned into great places to stay. There are even a couple in the Gold Coast. Pluses such as free internet, quieter surrounds and some free parking give B&Bs more bang for the midrange buck. In addition to the properties listed here, check out Bed & Breakfast Chicago (www.chicago-bed-breakfast.com), which represents 18 local guesthouses. Most do have minimum stay requirements.

Vacation rentals in local apartments are also a good deal in Chicago, especially for traveling families.

Using search engines, you're likely to find the most affordable chain options close to Chicago's airports. Even though these are connected by reliable public transportation, it's worth it to put down a little extra to spare the long commute.

APARTMENT RENTALS: LONG- & SHORT-TERM

If you'll be in town a while, or you just like feeling 'at home,' it may make sense to rent an apartment or condo. Typically the price is comparable to a hotel, but the upside is more room to spread out and amenities such as a kitchen and a deck. Plus these properties often feel less sterile and put you in the midst of cool neighborhoods.

For long-term rentals of a week or more, you can occasionally find a bargain at Sublet.com (www.sublet.com), where apartment owners sublease their place by the week or the month. Only premium listings are free to contact, otherwise

you have to pay $25 to join. Rates run from $450 to $1500 a week for a one-bedroom rental. You can find a bedroom in a shared apartment (from $600 per month) or a whole studio or one-bedroom apartment to sublet (from $750 per month) at Craigslist (www.chicago.craigslist.org).

Several services offer short-term vacation rentals in addition to longer-term ones. Vacation Rental By Owner (www.vrbo.com) is an excellent online source for everything from high-rise condominiums to leafy graystone apartments in neighborhoods citywide. You work out all the details with the owner themselves; the website just acts as a clearinghouse. VacationsFRBO (www.vacationsfrbo.com) is another bountiful source for apartments (and even houseboats!) around the city. At Home in Chicago (☎ 312-640-1050, 800-375-7084; www.athomeinnchicago.com) rents out apartments and B&B rooms in Wrigleyville, Lincoln Park, Wicker Park and around; it's easy to search by neighborhood. With all of these services, be sure to check if there's a cleaning fee added,

PRICE GUIDE

$$$	over $250 a night
$$	$125-250 a night
$	under $125 a night

SAVING STRATEGIES

Don't think a $115 motel room qualifies as a budget buy? Neither do we. But that's Chicago. Unless you're willing to stay in a hostel, your low-end options are limited. A few saving strategies to try:

- Look for the **P** - Parking can add $45 a day in Chicago. Aim for places – motels, chains like Best Western and some B&Bs – that offer this service free. We mark them in the listings with a **P**.
- Added extras – Look for properties that give away breakfast and internet access. We mark free wi-fi with a 📶 and denote where there's free morning munchies.
- Shop around – Some chains have low price guarantees on their websites; at others, you'll get a better rate at a booking website such as www.hotrooms.com, www.travelocity.com or www.expedia.com.
- Be flexible – Hotel rates in Chicago change by the day. Call ahead and ask when it'd be best to come. The website www.hotels.com also has an excellent rate calendar. Once you click 'Select rooms and rates' for a particular date at a specific property, you're given an 'Flexible dates?' option which pulls up a calendar that shows the prices on different days.
- Take a gamble – When maximizing quality for the price is your main concern, consolidator websites such as www .priceline.com and www.hotwire.com are an excellent risk to take. They don't let you see the name of the property before you buy, but you can save up to 50%. The hotel gets to unload its unsold rooms (without sacrificing their rep by advertising it) and you benefit. Pick your neighborhood ('Gold Coast' yields lots of acceptable results), the hotel's star rating and how much you're willing to pay. Once you've bought and paid, you're told where you're staying. Note that making changes once you've reserved is harder than crossing Lake Shore Dr at rush hour. For more, see Bidding on a Bed (p232).
- Couchsurf or swap houses – Stay for free with a local who has offered his or her sofa through Couchsurfing (www.couchsurfing.com). You must become a member of the group first, but there's no fee to do so. Or trade houses with a local via Craigslist's 'housing swap' section (www.chicago.craigslist.org).

because it can be substantial (from $100). Also ask about parking and wi-fi costs.

For lodging that caters to the business traveler, try Habitat Corporate Suites Network (☎ 317-902-2092, 800-833-0331; www.habitatcsn.com), which runs several high-rise properties in Near North. Expect weekly maid service, and business and fitness centers on-site.

At press time, Chicago's city council had voted to license and regulate vacation rentals (the first US city to do so), which could change the local landscape. Property owners say the fees and bureaucracy will put them out of business. The city says its regulations will ensure safeguards for consumers. Stay tuned.

ROOM RATES

The rates listed in this chapter are for standard double-occupancy rooms with bathroom (unless otherwise indicated). Deluxe rooms are 10% to 20% more; suites are an additional 30% to 40% or more. The range noted takes into account seasonal fluctuations and the vagaries of weekend versus weekday lodging. The prices are for comparison purposes only, since a large convention in town can make them laughably off base.

Chicago's 15.4% hotel tax is not included in the rates listed, so factor in that extra cost. Other expenses can add up too. You'll pay

dearly for parking in Chicago, an average of $45 per night extra downtown (ouch!) and $22 per night in outlying neighborhoods. If you can leave your car at home, do. Most hotels have parking lots in the same building or very nearby. B&B parking is usually on street. We've used a **P** to indicate the rare and treasured establishment that offers a free, dedicated spot for your car.

Internet access is ubiquitous – unless otherwise noted, lodgings listed have wired and/or wireless in-room access. At many high-end hotels it'll cost you ($10 to $15 per day is common), though more and more properties are offering it for free. Lobbies sometimes serve as free wi-fi zones. If a place has complimentary in-room access we've marked it with 📶 . Otherwise, expect to pay up.

Some lodgings provide a free continental breakfast (rolls, pastries, fruit, juice, coffee). Listings will say so if it's part of the room rate.

Every lodging we list has air-conditioning (unless stated otherwise). Check-in time is usually around 3pm, check out at 11am.

THE LOOP

Fast-walking office workers whisk by you as the clack-clack-clack of an El train reverberates overhead. The business center of town pulses in the daytime, but the further you get from the lake or the river, the more it empties out at night. Every El and train line in the city converges on the Loop, making the boutique hotels and historic properties here superconvenient to everywhere. Millennium and Grant Park are just a Frisbee throw away, and you're no more than a 15-minute walk to River North dining and South Loop museums.

FAIRMONT Map pp54-5   Hotel $$$
☎ 312-565-8000, 866-540-4408; www.fairmont .com; 200 N Columbus Dr; r $279-499; Ⓜ Brown, Orange, Green, Purple, Pink Line to Randolph
Millennium Park here you come. All 687 luxury rooms and suites here are as close to the statues and fountains as you can stay. Upgrade above a standard room to get a park or lake view (those near the top of the hotel's 45 stories are the best). Accents like Asian ceramics combine with French empire chairs to create soft – if a bit stodgy – surrounds.

W CHICAGO CITY CENTER
Map pp54-5   Hotel $$$
☎ 312-332-1200, 877-946-8357; www.whotels .com/chicago; 172 W Adams St; r $229-499; Ⓜ Brown, Orange, Purple, Pink Line to Quincy; ✗
Employees all wear black at this hip hotel where the soaring 'living room' (lobby/bar) feels a little like a dance club, especially when the DJ gets going. Sleek urban rooms, in black and beiges, seem stark to some. Special gay pride packages include W Pride T-shirts and complimentary rainbow-themed cocktails, usually in summertime.

HOTEL MONACO Map pp54-5   Boutique Hotel $$$
☎ 312-960-8500, 866-610-0081; www.monaco -chicago.com; 225 N Wabash Ave; r $259-379; Ⓜ Brown, Orange, Green, Purple, Pink Line to State; ✗ 🛜 ♿
Had to leave your beloved poodle Fifi at home this trip? Pick up a complimentary pet goldfish to keep you company during your stay instead. Hotel Monaco's fun-loving nature comes out in the room decor too. Curvaceous couches offset bold moss green and white striped wallpaper and raspberry window-seat cushions. In the Rock and Roll Suite, a permanently suspended TV appears to have already been 'thrown' through the window. All this posh quirkiness and it also has free wi-fi

and a free wine happy hour (standard, as part of the Kimpton chain).

HARD ROCK HOTEL CHICAGO
Map pp54-5   Boutique Hotel $$$
☎ 312-345-1000; 866-966-5166; www.hardrock hotelchicago.com; 230 N Michigan Ave; r $259-359; Ⓜ Red Line to Lake; ♿
The Hard Rock tries hard to let you know it's hip – DJs work the lobby lounge, staff will loan you an electric guitar to wail in your room, rock star photos pop up everywhere (including the bathroom where you might find, say, David Bowie staring out over your toilet). Despite the price level, standard rooms are just that – standard, mod clean lines and all.

RENAISSANCE CHICAGO
DOWNTOWN HOTEL Map pp54-5   Hotel $$$
☎ 312-372-7200, 800-468-3571; www.renaissance hotels.com; 1 W Wacker Dr; r $250-359; Ⓜ Brown, Orange, Green, Purple, Pink Line to State; ✗
Don't be fooled by the bland exterior. Step into the lobby, where modern art, sink-right-in couches and lively earth tones exude warmth and style. Rooms are pretty typical contemporary stuff, but those with a water view (about $50 extra) have bay windows overlooking the skyline and the adjacent river.

WIT Map pp54-5   Hotel $$$
☎ 312-467-0200; www.thewithotel.com; 201 N State St; r from $229; Ⓜ Brown, Orange, Green, Purple, Pink Line to State; ✗
Holidaying hipsters and business travel-ers flock to the Wit in equal measure. The green-hued glass box glints between the Theater District and the river, and brings a few eco-amenities like dual-flush toilets and energy-efficient heating and lighting to the table. But it's the cozy, design-savvy vibe that's the big selling point. Rooms have vast windows and awesome views that you can take in from your turquoise couch with pink cushions. Guests can see what's showing in the 40-seat movie theater on-site or what's brewing at the swanky rooftop bar. It's part of the Doubletree chain.

HOTEL BURNHAM
Map pp54-5   Boutique Hotel $$$
☎ 312-782-1111, 877-294-9712; www.burnham hotel.com; 1 W Washington St; r $199-300; Ⓜ Blue Line to Washington; ✗ 🛜 ♿

The proprietors brag the Burnham has the highest guest return rates in Chicago; it's easy to see why. Housed in the landmark 1890s Reliance Building (precedent for the modern skyscraper), the superslick Burnham woos architecture buffs. Blue velvet headboards and gold and blue striped silk draperies make you feel like you're sleeping in a tufted jewel box. Mahogany writing desks and chaise longues add to the lavish setup. Like other Kimpton Hotels, this one has complimentary wi-fi, wine happy hours and yoga gear to borrow. For an only-in-Chicago experience, try to nab room 809, where Al Capone's dentist and partner in crime drilled teeth.

HOTEL ALLEGRO Map pp54-5   Hotel $$$

☎ 312-236-0123, 800-643-1500; www .allegrochicago.com; 171 W Randolph St; r $189-310; Ⓜ Brown, Orange, Purple, Pink Line to Washington; ⊠ 🛜 ♿

Boutique bliss. Hotel Allegro is another historic property, part of the fun and flirty Kimpton Hotel chain. After a $40 million makeover in 2008, the 483 rooms have emerged sporting a retro luxury cruise ship look, with funky patterned wallpaper and carpet in royal blue and snowy white tones. It's dramatic – which makes sense for a hotel right next to the Cadillac Palace Theater and its Broadway crowd. Flat-screen TVs, free wi-fi, free evening wine receptions and free yoga gear round out the stylish package.

A GREEN NIGHT'S SLEEP

Most of the city's properties do the usual by asking visitors to reuse towels and sheets, but a few have gone beyond that standard. Top of the heap are Hotel Felix (p234), Chicago's first downtown hotel to earn LEED certification for environmentally responsible construction, and Hotel Palomar (p232), Chicago's first hotel to have a green roof. The Felix even offers free parking to visitors driving hybrid cars.

Approximately 15 downtown hotels have received Green Seal (www.greenseal.org) certification. This means they've paid to go through an evaluation that checks for energy and water efficiency, recycling procedures and ecofriendly cleaning practices, among others. 'Silver' certified properties (the highest so far in Chicago) include the Fairmont (opposite), Hotel Allegro (above), Hotel Burnham (opposite), Hotel Monaco (opposite), Hotel Intercontinental, the Sheraton (p233), the Talbott and the Westin (p232 and p237).

SWISSÔTEL CHICAGO Map pp54-5   Hotel $$

☎ 312-565-0565, 888-737-9477; www.chicago .swissotel.com; 323 E Wacker Dr; r $209-259; Ⓜ Brown, Orange, Green, Purple, Pink Line to Randolph; ⊠ 🛜

Water vistas are just part of the attraction at this triangular-shaped, mirrored-glass high-rise at the confluence of river and lake. Families love the oversized layouts, separate shower and tub, and special kids' rooms with colorful furnishings and toys. Summer weekends book up fast. No wonder, since you can munch on homemade pastries in the on-site café or tackle a heck of a hunk of beef at the Palm steakhouse. Note that the pool costs extra.

BUCKINGHAM ATHLETIC CLUB
HOTEL Map pp54-5   Boutique Hotel $$

☎ 312-663-8910; www.bac-chicago.com; 440 S LaSalle St; r incl breakfast $199-210; Ⓜ Brown, Green, Orange Line to LaSalle; 🛜 🛀

Tucked onto the 40th floor of an office building, the 21-room Buckingham Athletic Club Hotel is far from easy to find. The benefit if you do? Quiet (on weekends and evenings especially) and expansive views south of town. Elegant rooms here are so spacious they'd be considered suites elsewhere. Take the elevator down to the namesake gym and dive into the lap pool, or work it out on the racquetball court, before your massage appointment.

HYATT REGENCY CHICAGO
Map pp54-5   Hotel $$

☎ 312-565-1234, 800-233-1234; www.chicago .hyatt.com; 151 E Wacker Dr; r $179-299; Ⓜ Brown, Orange, Green, Purple, Pink Line to State

With more than 2019 rooms and five restaurants and bars, the contemporary Hyatt Regency is best known for being big. And filled with conventioneers. And kind of blah. Drinkers will rejoice at the fact it makes claim to having the longest freestanding bar in North America. Lots of specials keep all those rooms filled in off-peak times.

HOTEL BLAKE Map pp54-5   Boutique Hotel $$

☎ 312-986-1234; www.hotelblake.com; 500 S Dearborn St; r incl breakfast $149-259; Ⓜ Blue Line to LaSalle; 🛜

The old customs house building has found new life as a boutique hotel at the Loop's southern edge. It's a unique location midway between downtown's core and the Museum Campus, though not much goes on in the evenings. The mod, black and red furnishings are spread out in the well-sized rooms; the bathrooms are flat-out huge. However, if rates swing up to the high end of the spectrum, you'll probably get better bang for your buck elsewhere.

SILVERSMITH

Map pp54-5   Historic Hotel $$

☎ 312-372-7696; www.silversmithchicagohotel .com; 10 S Wabash Ave; r $159-229; Ⓜ Brown, Orange, Green, Purple, Pink Line to Madison; ☒

Another Loop architectural gem, this one was built in 1894. Although the exterior was designed by Daniel Burnham's firm, the hotel's interior recalls Frank Lloyd Wright: the chunky wood furniture has a distinct Prairie School charm. Too bad that windows overlook the El tracks, or face right onto another building. Ah well, it's a small price to pay for the core Loop location by the Art Institute and Millennium Park.

PALMER HOUSE HILTON

Map pp54-5   Historic Hotel $$

☎ 312-726-7500, 800-445-8667; www.hilton.com; 17 E Monroe St; r $129-279; Ⓜ Brown, Orange, Green, Purple, Pink Line to Adams; 🖥 🏊

Chicago legend Potter Palmer set many worldwide hotelier records with his 1875 hotel (first to use electric lighting, first to have in-room telephones, invention of the brownie…). Today the Palmer House lobby still has an 'Oh my God' opulence – Tiffany chandeliers, ceiling frescos – that makes a look-see imperative. The 1600-plus guest rooms give off a more updated vibe: graphic swirl prints on draperies and countertop bowl sinks seem like an up-dated play on antique design. The location is steps from the Art Institute and Millennium Park.

CENTRAL LOOP HOTEL

Map pp54-5   Hotel $$

☎ 312-601-3525, 866-744-2333; www .centralloophotel.com; 111 W Adams St; r $119-171; Ⓜ Blue Line to Monroe; 🖥

The Central Loop has a good location (the name doesn't lie) and good prices if you're stuck paying rack rates. It's acces-sorized for business folk, though not so useful for families given the rooms'

top picks

OVER-THE-TOP AMENITIES

- A $60,000 proposal package – with ring – at the James (p232).
- A goldfish (and bowl) you can borrow during your stay at the Hotel Monaco (p228).
- A sound pillow with harmonic sleep CD at Affinia Chicago (p234).
- A butler to walk your dog at the Peninsula (opposite).
- An electric guitar and lessons, if you need them, at the Hard Rock Hotel (p228).

smallish size. A fine pub pours drinks down-stairs. The owners have another, similar property called Club Quarters at 75 E Wacker Dr.

HOSTELLING INTERNATIONAL-CHICAGO Map pp54-5   Hostel $

☎ 312-360-0300; www.hichicago.org; 24 E Congress Pkwy; dm incl breakfast $26-38; Ⓜ Brown, Orange, Purple, Pink Line to Library

By far the best hostelling option in town. Kick back in the giant common room with free wi-fi (the computer room has 10 terminals for rent, too), ping-pong, tons of sofas and chairs – and a concierge. Sign up for daily field trips to interesting neighborhoods, bar hopping or sightseeing. In the morning, toast, cereal and pastries await in the enormous dining room and kitchen. Throughout, a clean, dormlike feel pervades. That's probably because half of the 500 beds go to Columbia College students during the school year. Some of the single-sex, six-bed rooms have bathrooms en suite. Linens included.

NEAR NORTH & NAVY PIER

A little bit nicer than the Loop and slightly less pricy overall than the Gold Coast (but walking distance to both), Near North is a good compromise – which is helpful, since it holds the lion's share of hotels in town. This is often where you'll end up if you bid on a room. Art galleries are to the west, Navy Pier to the east. Bars and restaurants are everywhere.

PENINSULA Map pp66-7   Hotel $$$

☎ 312-337-2888, 866-288-8889; www.peninsula
.com; 108 E Superior St; r $450-650; Ⓜ Red Line to
Chicago; ⊠ ⚅

The over-the-top Peninsula is the premier
lodging in town. Nestled in the neoclassical rooms, among the equestrian statues
and the marquetry furnishings, are five
phones. Lighting and electronics tie into
impressively complicated high-tech
systems. Two-story walls of glass enclose
the pool, where you can swim after your
essence-of-rubies spa facial. How's the
service? Buttoned down. Staff members
are even required to take personal
grooming classes. This is where
Hollywood stars check in when they
come to town.

PARK HYATT Map pp72-3   Hotel $$$

☎ 312-335-1234, 800-633-7313; www.park
chicago.hyatt.com; 800 N Michigan Ave; r $415-505;
Ⓜ Red Line to Chicago; ⊠

Want every inch of your suite covered
in rose petals, with candles lit and your
bath water run? They've done it before
at this ask-and-it-shall-be-granted luxury
flagship of the locally based Hyatt chain.
From the miniature TVs in the bathroom
to the butler and the courtesy car service,
no expense has been spared. Bow-shaped
tubs hide behind rolling window shades
in some rooms so you can soak and still
admire the view. Terrace kings have small
balconies looking out across the street
to the Water Tower and the lake beyond.
C'mon – if it's good enough for U2 when
they rock through town, you know it's got
street cred.

TRUMP HOTEL & TOWER

Map pp66-7   Hotel $$$

☎ 312-588-8000, 877-458-7867; www.trump
chicagohotel.com; 401 N Wabash Ave; r from $400;
Ⓜ Brown, Orange, Green, Purple, Pink to State;
⊠ ⊡ ⊠

The Donald opened his glassy Chicago
handiwork, which rose to be the city's
second-tallest building, in 2008. The
manly, earth-toned rooms are high in
the sky with floor-to-ceiling windows,
kitchens full of stainless-steel appliances
(except for the 'spa' rooms) and bottled
water you can buy for $5 to $25. The views
are sweet, and service is as polished as
you'd expect.

SAX CHICAGO Map pp66-7   Hotel $$$

☎ 312-245-0333, 877-569-3742; www.thompson
hotels.com; 333 N Dearborn St; r $259-409; Ⓜ Red
Line to Grand; ⊠

Fluff up your best feather boa and head for
the bar – the crystal-drenched chandeliers
and deep-tufted red velvet sofas would
make any high-class madam feel right
at home. An odd lighting-related theme
continues throughout. The reception desk
looks like a crystal shop, faux chandelier
shadows are painted on guest room walls
and flickering lights illuminate (sort of) the
dark corridors. This former House of Blues
hotel (redesigned in 2007) is still highly
theatrical. Rooms are comparatively staid,
small and gray toned; renovations are
reportedly upcoming.

W CHICAGO-LAKESHORE

Map pp66-7   Hotel $$$

☎ 312-943-9200, 877-946-8357; www.whotels.com
/chicago; 644 N Lake Shore Dr; r $239-379; ⊡ 66;
⊠ ⚅

Lobby chairs appear to be carved out of
tree trunks and river rocks fill a public
bathroom troughlike sink… The earthy
aesthetic feels entirely appropriate here on
the lakefront. You can see the water from
telescopes by the windows in the eleva-
tor bays, from 'spectacular' rooms and
'fantastic' suites. Navy Pier and oceanlike
expanses stretch before you while you run
on the treadmill or lie on the pool deck.
The small Whisky Sky bar glows from the
33rd floor.

CONRAD CHICAGO Map pp66-7   Hotel $$$

☎ 312-645-1500; 800-445-8667;
http://conradhotels1.hilton.com; 520 N Michigan
Ave (main entrance on N Rush St); r $230-365;
Ⓜ Red Line to Grand; ⊠ ⊡ ⚅

Euro sleek, urban chic. Slide into 500-
thread-count Italian linens and put your
favorite CD on the Bose surround-sound
stereo. That is, if you're not too busy
watching the 42in plasma TV or docking
your iPod – these rooms are wired. Adding
to the discreet sense of luxury, the lobby is
hiding on the 6th floor of Michigan Ave's
North Bridge Shops. Lounging alfresco
on the padded rattan sofas at the terrace
bar is surpassed only by splurging on the
grand suite, with 1000 sq ft of terrace all
to yourself.

BIDDING ON A BED

In the following nonscientific study, we asked friends and colleagues to share their recent experiences with the two main hotel booking sites. The result: it's possible to get a three-star hotel by the Magnificent Mile for less than $110 in high summer season.

- Case 1 – Agreed to a $90 rate for a three-star, 'Water Tower – Gold Coast area' hotel at www.hotwire.com. Turned out to be the Tremont (p238). No frills, but good location next to the Hancock Center and free wi-fi. Regular cost: $129.
- Case 2 – Agreed to a $109 rate for a three-star, 'Magnificent Mile – Streeterville area' hotel at www.hotwire. com. It showed having breakfast, internet access, pool, laundry, business center. Turned out to be the Embassy Suites Chicago-Lakefront (p233). A huge two-room suite overlooking the lake, superclose to Navy Pier. The hot breakfast was colossal. A night at the hotel rate? $331.
- Case 3 – Bid $96 for a three-star River North hotel at www.priceline.com. Rejected. Instead booked a $106 room at a 3½-star Mag Mile hotel on www.hotwire.com. The Wyndham Chicago (p234) room was plush and palatial. No view, limited TV channels, but only two blocks from Mag Mile. Regular rate? $279.

JAMES Map pp66–7   Boutique Hotel $$$
☎ 312-337-1000, 877-526-3755; www.jameshotels .com; 616 N Rush St; r $259-499; Ⓜ Red Line to Grand; 🛜 🛝

Low and loungey chairs sidle up to over-sized tripod lamps. Strings of silver beads act as a dividing curtain between the platform bed and the living room. Porthole windows allow you to peep through sliding bathroom doors. Fans of mid-century modern design must stay here. But everyone can appreciate the little luxuries: Kiehl's bath products, Turkish cotton towels, a bar that has half bottles instead of minis… You can tell from the gym and spa that the co-owner created Equinox fitness centers. An overwhelmingly gracious staff helps work out any service kinks, like rooms not being ready on time.

OMNI CHICAGO HOTEL
Map pp66–7   Hotel $$$
☎ 312-944-6664, 800-444-6664; www.omnihotels .com; 676 N Michigan Ave (entrance on E Huron St); r $179-479; Ⓜ Red Line to Chicago; 🛝

Each room is really two. French doors connect the bedroom with the sitting area; both are decked out in rich colors and cherrywood. Girls' night packages come with chick-flick DVDs, wine and chocolate; guys' nights include sports DVDs, beer and chips. Ask ahead and kids receive suitcases full of games to keep them entertained – if they aren't swimming in the pool or watching the plasma TV.

HOTEL PALOMAR Map pp66–7   Hotel $$
☎ 312-755-9703, 877-731-0505; www.hotel palomar-chicago.com; 505 N State St; r $175-305; Ⓜ Red Line to Grand; ✗ 🛜 🛝 🛝

Here we go again: another excellent, green-tinged property in the Kimpton chain (like the Burnham, the Monaco and the Allegro, all in the Loop). Note of distinction: the 17-story, 261-room Palomar has a green roof, Chicago's first for a hotel. Arty decor – little sculptures, original paintings on the wall – add to the fashionable but businesslike decor. There's an indoor rooftop pool, and a free wine hour each evening.

WESTIN RIVER NORTH Map pp66–7   Hotel $$
☎ 312-744-1900, 877-866-9216; www.westin rivernorth.com; 320 N Dearborn St; r $189-369; Ⓜ Brown, Green, Orange, Purple, Pink Line to State; ✗ 🛝

Yet another riverfront chain hotel. At least this one has a decent sushi bar and vaguely Asian decor – a rock garden, lots of orchids – to set it apart. Frequent travelers choose the Westin chain for the 'heavenly beds,' with superthick mattresses and high-thread-count sheets. Sorry, no pool here, but the showers have dual spa heads – hopefully that helps.

HOTEL CASS Map pp66–7   Boutique Hotel $$
☎ 312-787-4030, 800-799-4030; www.casshotel .com; 640 N Wabash Ave; r incl breakfast $199-350; Ⓜ Red Line to Grand; 🛜

It's hard to imagine that this property was a bare-bones budget option not too long ago. In late 2007 expensive hardwoods, Kohler fixtures and other upscale treatments transformed what was an aging 1920s hotel into a Holiday Inn Express–affiliated boutique. Small room spaces are maximized with modern flair: hanging flat-screen TVs, mod C-shaped tables and armless couches. The breakfast bar includes bacon, eggs and a few other hot items.

EMBASSY SUITES CHICAGO-
LAKEFRONT Map pp66-7   Extended Stay $$
☎ 312-836-5900, 866-866-8095; www.chicago embassy.com; 511 N Columbus Dr; ste incl breakfast $209-245; 🛏 66; 🐾

Peer out through the shutters of your living-room window onto the forest of beech trees growing in the atrium, an outside-in arrangement that's quite interesting. The rooms are pretty darn big. The bedroom of each suite (with microwave and refrigerator) fronts the street, away from the noisy hubbub of the monumental hot breakfast buffet that takes over the courtyard each morning. Lines form early. Located just a few blocks from Navy Pier.

AMALFI HOTEL CHICAGO
Map pp66-7   Boutique Hotel $$
☎ 312-395-9000; 877-262-5341; www.amalfihotel chicago.com; 20 W Kinzie St; r $149-299; Ⓜ Red Line to Grand; ⊠ 🛜 🐾

The Amalfi lobby blooms like a bird of paradise: vivid oranges contrast with deep turquoise hues on thoroughly mod furnishings. Upstairs, the rooms are a bit more subdued, in jewel tones, but the whole hotel is clearly high end and modern-design driven. Each floor has a sumptuous spread of pastries and bagels laid out every morning, and you can borrow CDs and DVDs for free.

HILTON GARDEN INN Map pp66-7   Hotel $$
☎ 312-595-0000, 800-774-1500; www.hilton gardeninn.com; 10 E Grand Ave; r $117-329; Ⓜ Red Line to Grand; 🛜 🐾

Lather up with Neutrogena products in the shower before you head down to the Weber Grill restaurant for an evening cookout... hang on, make that a cook in. If your honey thinks you smell too good to leave the room, that's OK; area restaurants deliver to this up-to-date 23 story hotel. And you can keep the leftovers in the fridge and nuke them in your room the next day. Rates vary wildly, so you may get a steal.

EMBASSY SUITES CHICAGO-
DOWNTOWN Map pp66-7   Extended Stay $$
☎ 312-943-3800, 800 362 2779; www .embassysuiteschicago.com; 600 N State St; ste incl breakfast $162-279; Ⓜ Red Line to Grand; 🐾

Cooked-to-order eggs, and pancakes, and waffles, and, and… An enormous breakfast buffet comes standard with the two-room suites. Families know it, too; boy, do they mob the place. The pool's hardly big enough to hold all the little ones. Good thing that they usually head out to nearby River North shopping for the day. Eighteen suites have special equipment such as knock detectors and vibrating bed alarms for the disabled. Note there's another Embassy Suites a half-mile east that's closer to the lake.

HOTEL INTER-CONTINENTAL
CHICAGO Map pp66-7   Hotel $$
☎ 312-944-4100, 800-327-0200; www.icchicago hotel.com; 505 N Michigan Ave; r $179-279; Ⓜ Red Line to Grand; ⊠ 🐾 🦽

Once the Medina Athletic Club, the ornate original tower (c 1929) retains many of the eclectic details meant for rich men's eyes only. Thank goodness now everyone can float by the Neptune fountain in the mosaic-tiled indoor swimming pool area. Historic rooms have a similarly elegant, heavily draped look, with thick brocades and sumptuous silks. A more conservative, masculine feel – angular lines, neutral earth tones – characterizes the main building rooms. Moorish-inspired lamps add a touch of whimsy.

CHICAGO MARRIOTT HOTEL
Map pp66-7   Hotel $$
☎ 312-836-0100, 800-228-9290; www.marriott .com; 540 N Michigan Ave; r $179-269; Ⓜ Red Line to Grand; ⊠ 🐾

A Magnificent Mile address is the primary draw card of this 46-story behemoth. You have to upgrade to a 'studio' room to get the size (320 sq ft) most people expect at these rates. The downy duvets and flat-screen TVs will do, though. Packages include everything from museum tickets to American Girl shopping discounts.

SHERATON CHICAGO HOTEL &
TOWERS Map pp66-7   Hotel $$
☎ 312-464-1000, 877-242-2558; www.sheraton chicago.com; 301 E North Water St; r $199-219; 🛏 56; ⊠ 🐾

From this riverfront location you can stroll along the esplanade to catch a water taxi or an architectural tour. River-view upgrades are worth the $50 or so, but dark accent walls and contemporary corporate decor make all the rooms acceptable. Be warned, you may be the only person staying at this 1204-room hotel who's not part of a group.

CROWNE PLAZA AVENUE HOTEL
Map pp66-7   Hotel $$
☎ 877-283-5110, 877-227-6963; www.avenue hotelchicago.com; 160 E Huron St; r $190-270; Ⓜ Red Line to Chicago; ✕ 🛜 📺 🛝
Guests cite the Avenue's classy yet unfussed vibe, its large rooms and the try-hard staff as the reasons to key in here. The small heated rooftop pool and sundeck offer cool views. The hotel's rainbow-hued 'family' rooms are impressive, with beanbag chairs, drawing easels and other toys for kids.

ALLERTON HOTEL Map pp66-7 Historic Hotel $$
☎ 312-440-1500; www.theallertonhotel.com; 701 N Michigan Ave; r $171-279; Ⓜ Red Line to Chicago; ✕
High atop the Italianate red-brick facade shines the red neon Allerton Tip Top sign, a reminder of the hotel's past. From the 1920s to the '50s, the penthouse Tip Top Club was a happening place. All the big bands and early radio stars played here. Thankfully, a recent renovation launched the Allerton's rooms out of that era and into modern times with marble bathrooms, flat-screen TVs and comfy bedding. Standard rooms are by no means large (and the 'classic' rooms are downright tiny), but they can be a bargain off-peak.

AFFINIA CHICAGO Map pp66-7 Boutique Hotel $$
☎ 312-787-6000; 866-246-2203; www.affinia.com; 166 E Superior St; r $159-269; Ⓜ Red Line to Chicago; ✕ 🛝
The rooms are clean lined and white bedded, and the lobby new and shiny after a recent renovation. The staff have the enthusiastic 'What can I do for you?' down. A pillow menu (buckwheat, memory foam…), a personal shopper and free 'experience kits' (ie walking-tour kits with music-loaded iPods, walking-tour books and pedometers) are a few things they've thought of to make your stay top-notch. The swank rooftop bar is a local hot spot.

WYNDHAM CHICAGO Map pp66-7 Hotel $$
☎ 312-573-0300, 877-999-3223; www.wyndham .com; 633 N St Clair St; r $159-269; Ⓜ Red Line to Grand; ✕ 📺

You and 15 of your closest friends could sack out on the floor for a slumber party, the space in a base level room is so great. Cushy beds and soft neutrals, like beige and cream, are far too refined for that. Several energetic concierges field travel requests deftly, all day and evening long, for the 17-story hotel.

COMFORT INN & SUITES
DOWNTOWN Map pp66-7   Hotel $$
☎ 312-894-0900, 888-775-4111; www.chicago comfortinn.com; 15 E Ohio St; r $159-249; Ⓜ Red Line to Grand
Can a hotel have multiple personality disorder? It would explain the convergence of an art-deco-style 1920s building, a Tudoresque dark wood lobby and the contemporary dusty blue and beige guest rooms. Though it's classier than the typical Comfort Inn, prices are overinflated. There's free wired internet access in the rooms, but no wi-fi (though it is available in the lobby).

HOTEL FELIX Map pp66-7 Boutique Hotel $$
☎ 312-447-3440, 877-848-404; www.hotelfelix chicago.com; 111 W Huron St; r $149-189; Red Line to Chicago; ✕ 🛜
Opened in 2009 in the Near North, the 225-room, 12-story Felix is downtown's first hotel to earn ecofriendly LEED certification (Silver status, to be exact). The earth-toned, mod-furnished rooms are small but efficiently and comfortably designed. It's more of a place for urban hipsters than families, but who doesn't appreciate a rainfall showerhead, a flat-screen TV and soft cotton sheets? Parking is free if you drive a hybrid.

FOUR POINTS CHICAGO
DOWNTOWN Map pp66-7   Extended Stay $$
☎ 312-981-6600, 800-368-7764; www.fourpoints chicago.com; 630 N Rush St; ste $149-239; Ⓜ Red Line to Grand; ✕ 📺 🛜
Constructed in 2005, this Sheraton-affiliated hotel has more soundproofing and less wear than many of the other big name chains in town. Setting it apart style-wise are six of renowned artist Dale Chihuly's abstract paintings and the small glass *Amethyst* sculpture in the lobby. Every room has microwaves, minifridges, coffee makers and free wi-fi that come standard. (Balconies and whirlpool tubs extra.)

DOUBLETREE MAGNIFICENT MILE

Map pp66-7   Hotel $$

☎ 312-787-6100; www.doubletreemagmile.com; 300 E Ohio St; r $144-209;  66;

Relax on your window seat and look out at the sliver of a lake view many rooms have here in Streeterville, near Navy Pier. If you're not looking for anything fancy (ie average space, generic faux-wood decor), you've found it. But there is a 50,000-sq-ft athletic club, two pools (outdoor free, indoor charge is $15), a café and a restaurant, and free wi-fi in the lobby. This three-star property pops up at lower rates on discount booking websites quite often.

HAMPTON INN & SUITES-CHICAGO

DOWNTOWN Map pp66-7   Hotel $$

☎ 312-832-0330, 800-426-7866; www.hampton suiteschicago.com; 33 W Illinois St; r incl breakfast $119-239; Ⓜ Red Line to Grand;

Thick oak desks and angular leaded-glass lamps give the two-story lobby a Prairie School feel, and historic Chicago photos line the hallways. But the Frank Lloyd Wright influence is less apparent once you get to the contemporary rooms. Nearly half are studio and one-bedroom suites, some with full kitchens. The roominess, and a big hot breakfast, attract families and business travelers.

BEST WESTERN RIVER NORTH

Map pp66-7   Hotel $$

☎ 312-467-0800, 800-780-7234; www .bestwestern.com/rivernorthhotel; 125 W Ohio St; r $109-199; Ⓜ Red Line to Grand;

Think seven-story motel. Surprisingly cheery, well-maintained rooms with maple veneer beds and desks make this a River North value. Free parking and wi-fi seal the deal. Oh, and did we mention the giant indoor pool and the attached Italian restaurant?

INN OF CHICAGO Map pp66-7 Boutique Hotel $

☎ 312-787-3100, 800-557-2378; www .innofchicago.com; 162 E Ohio St; r $109-199; Ⓜ Red Line to Grand;

The Inn has shed its Best Western skin and emerged more boutique-like than ever. Zebra-striped ottomans prowl the lobby; lime green and chocolate color schemes look delicious. And prices are right – it's just too bad the rooms are so darn 1920s-era

top picks

PET FRIENDLY

- Palmer House Hilton (p230)
- Hotel Allegro (p229)
- W Chicago-Lakeshore (p231)
- Peninsula (p231)
- Hotel Monaco (p228)

small. Don't try to take two steps in the stylish bathroom: one is all there's room for.

HOWARD JOHNSON INN Map pp66-7 Motel $

☎ 312-664-8100, 800-446-4656; www.hojo.com; 720 N LaSalle St; r $99-169; Ⓜ Brown Line to Chicago;

Ah, the outdated charm of a cheap motel. At least this one's in the city, is on the edge of respectable, in far west River North. Sure the rooms could use a serious re-do. If you care about furniture more than free parking, look elsewhere.

RED ROOF INN Map pp66-7   Hotel $

☎ 312-787-3580, 800-466-8356; www.redroof chicago-downtown.com; 162 E Ontario St; r $90-140; Ⓜ Red Line to Grand;

If you snag one of the lower rates, it might be worth your while to stay here, steps from the Michigan Ave shopping bonanza. But just how much money are you willing to pay for stained couches, faded wallpaper and barely enough space to walk around two beds?

OHIO HOUSE MOTEL Map pp66-7   Motel $

☎ 312-943-6000, 866-601-6446; www.ohio housemotel.com; 600 N LaSalle Dr; r $85-120; Ⓜ Red Line to Grand;

The retro stylings of Ohio House (ie a diamond-shaped marquee, a diner in the parking lot and more) are by no means put on. This place really is from the 1960s. Given the dingy cement-block detailing on the outside, it's a pleasant surprise to find the rooms within are modern (if a bit basic) and quite clean. The neighborhood to the west near the highway feels a bit ragged, but you're still in River North so you're close to transport and loads of restaurants to the east. And believe it, people: there's free parking.

GOLD COAST

Many of the truly top-end digs in town are in the chi-chi Gold Coast. Michigan Ave and Magnificent Mile shopping and dining are outside your door, and the lake is rarely more than five blocks away. Don't expect to be alone here, though – even the sidewalks have traffic jams.

ELYSIAN Map pp72-3   Hotel $$$

☎ 312-646-1300; www.elysianhotels.com; 11 E Walton St; from $400 per night; Ⓜ Red Line to Chicago; ✕ 🛜 🏊 🐾

The Elysian is one of Chicago's newest uberluxury hotels and models itself on 1920s Parisian glamour. We gotta say: it delivers. Rooms are large – they have to be, to hold the fireplaces, the bars, the marble soaking tubs, the beds with 460-thread-count sheets and the fully wired work spaces and other techno gadgets. There's a fancy gym with a lap pool, a high-rollin' bar and a couple spiffy restaurants.

FOUR SEASONS HOTEL
Map pp72-3   Hotel $$$

☎ 312-280-8800, 800-332-3442; www.four seasons.com/chicagofs; 120 E Delaware Pl; r $385-560; Ⓜ Red Line to Chicago; 🛜 🏊

Service is taken seriously here. Call for food day or night and they'll attempt to fulfill any request, on the menu or not. Even the little ones are pampered – with munchkin-sized bathrobes, a 'bedtime story butler' and a special teen-interest concierge in summer. Slip into the spa for a Sedona red-clay wrap.

Then relax further, dipping into the pool beneath the Romanesque domes. Crisp, cool bedding and a marble soaking tub are standard in the elegantly tailored, blue and taupe rooms. And an oddity in high-end lodging: the Four Seasons has free wi-fi.

RITZ-CARLTON Map pp72-3   Hotel $$$

☎ 312-266-1000, 800-621-6906; www.four seasons.com/chicagorc; 160 E Pearson St; r $385-560; Ⓜ Red Line to Chicago; 🛜 🏊

Just think of all the shopping you can do without leaving the building if you stay in one of the 32 stories above Water Tower Place. High-backed tapestry chairs, Renaissance paintings and porcelain vases containing stunning floral displays characterize the Franco-Asian elegance of the lobby. Guest rooms follow suit with antique armoires and expensive fabrics in fine prints. (Nonfeather duvets and anti-irritant cleaners are used in 'allergy sensitive' rooms.) The 12th floor's Art Deco brasserie plates decadence like a 10-layer chocolate cake, which you may need after an exhausting day burning up the credit cards.

DRAKE HOTEL Map pp72-3   Historic Hotel $$$

☎ 312-787-2200, 800-553-7253; www.thedrake hotel.com; 140 E Walton St; r $229-329; Ⓜ Red Line to Chicago

Queen Elizabeth, Winston Churchill, Charles Lindbergh, Dean Martin, Princess Di...the Reagans, the Bushes, the Clintons... Who hasn't stayed at the elegant Drake Hotel since it opened in 1920? The grande dame commands a striking location at the north

LOCAL VOICES: MARK TUNNEY

For more than 20 years Mark Tunney has worked at the marketing end of the hospitality industry. Since 2007 he has been the Managing Director of Convention Sales for the Chicago Convention and Tourism Bureau.

Hotel rates in Chicago seem hugely tied to conventions. Everyone says watch out when the radiologists are in town. Why? Quite frankly, there are shows that sell out every hotel room in the city, every year. The Radiological Society of North America convention, usually the Friday and Saturday after Thanksgiving, is one of them.

So, what months should leisure travelers avoid, convention-wise? Spring and fall are the busiest, but it changes by the week. The restaurant show is usually around the third weekend in May, but Mother's Day, the week before, is pretty quiet. The best thing to do is call the hotel and ask what dates are the least expensive.

When are there the fewest groups in town? Holidays are always a good time to come. December and January are slow. People think they should avoid Chicago in the winter, but it's not actually a bad time. We get snow, but not the arctic temperatures. And there's the ice rink at Millennium Park and lots of Broadway-quality shows to see.

by Lisa Dunford

end of Michigan Ave, near Oak St Beach. Embroidered gold silk coverlets and Grecian urn lamps are almost as impressive as the water views from the junior suites. Whether enjoying lobster in the Cape Cod Room (as Marilyn Monroe did) or having a drink accompanied by a local jazz artist in the Palm Court, you'll feel like somebody special too.

SOFITEL CHICAGO WATER TOWER
Map pp72-3   Hotel $$
☎ 312-324-4000, 800-763-4835; www.sofitel .com; 20 E Chestnut St; r $199-310; Ⓜ Red Line to Chicago

The Sofitel looks a little like some state-of-the-art Mac computing device from the outside, its triangular glass tower leaning gracefully forward into space. Inside, stylish staff members tend to stylish 30- and 40-something guests, who come here for the minimalist vibe (think blond wood and rectangular lines). The on-site restaurant, Café des Architectes, with its sculptural food served in a striking red and black dining room, fits right in.

WESTIN MICHIGAN AVENUE
Map pp72-3   Hotel $$
☎ 312-943-7200, 888-625-5144; www.westin .com/michiganave; 909 N Michigan Ave (entrance on E Delaware Pl); r $197-319; Ⓜ Red Line to Chicago; ✗

Bloomingdale's, the 900 Shops, Oak St boutiques: they're all within easy pouncing distance, about a block from this Michigan Ave address. After a hectic day of walking and spending, stepping into the soft contemporary lobby is a calming relief – low-profile brown leather sofas and retro armchairs wait to embrace you. Crisp bed linens offset moss green loungers in the smoke-free rooms. Lake views available.

RAFFAELLO HOTEL
Map pp72-3   Boutique Hotel $$
☎ 312-943-5000; 800-898-7198; www.chicago raffaello.com; 201 E Delaware Pl; r $189-279; Ⓜ Red Line to Chicago; ✗

If only you could live in the silk-draped modernity of these guest rooms. Oh, wait, you can – they're condominiums, too. Smart suites have microwaves and minifridges in marble cooking centers in addition to roomy seating areas or separate living rooms. Double rooms are smaller, but

top picks
SWEET VIEWS

- W Chicago-Lakeshore (p231)
- Park Hyatt (p231)
- Wit (p228)
- Trump Hotel & Tower (p231)
- Swissôtel Chicago (p229)

they have similar upscale amenities, such as rainforest shower heads and high-thread-count linens. A swanky Italian seafood restaurant tempts on-site.

SUTTON PLACE HOTEL
Map pp72-3   Boutique Hotel $$
☎ 312-266-2100, 866-378-8866; www.chicago .suttonplace.com; 21 E Bellevue Pl; r $187-275; Ⓜ Red Line to Clark/Division

Walking into one of the all-business guest rooms might just remind you of a man's suit: oversized gray stripes on the wall, a tailored grayish bedspread, and marine blue on singular accent pillows, which could easily be the color of a tie or an ascot. The contemporary decor is accented by Robert Mapplethorpe's floral photos (the controversial stuff is over at the Museum of Contemporary Art). Plush robes and Gilchrist & Soames bath products do at least seem to have been chosen with a woman in mind. The on-site Whiskey Bar has a local following.

RESIDENCE INN BY MARRIOTT
Map pp72-3   Extended Stay $$
☎ 312-943-9800; 866-596-7890; www.marriott .com; 201 E Walton St; r incl breakfast $179-279; Ⓜ Red Line to Chicago; ✗ 🛜

What to say about a totally generic extended-stay hotel… Well, it's got all the extras families crave: weekday happy hour, kitchens, laundry facilities, free wi-fi, pantry shop. They'll even run out and buy groceries for you. Studios, one and two bedrooms available. No pool though – sorry, kids.

HOTEL INDIGO
Map pp72-3   Boutique Hotel $$
☎ 312-787-4980, 800-972-2494; www.hotelindigo .com; 1244 N Dearborn St; r $179-259; Ⓜ Red Line to Clark/Division; 🛜 🐾

A pile of blueberries, a hyacinth bush, sea glass or a cable knit sweater: any of these may be the subject of your room's macro photo wall mural – as long as they're indigo in color. Hardwood floors and neon green, orange and sunny yellow accent fabrics perk up the rooms further. It feels more like your hip friend's apartment than a hotel. The location is quieter than other Gold Coast places, yet still within easy walking distance to shopping, nightlife and the lakefront – though you'll be hard-pressed to leave the just-right bed.

SENECA HOTEL & SUITES
Map pp72-3   Boutique Hotel, Extended Stay $$
☎ 312-787-8900, 800-800-6261; www.seneca hotel.com; 200 E Chestnut St; r incl breakfast $179-239; Ⓜ Red Line to Chicago; ✗ ⊚

It's the rare street in downtown Chicago that's quiet and tree lined, but you'll find the Seneca on one. A middle-aged and older clientele seems to favor this serene spot. Ornate brass drawer pulls on the dressers and carved finial headboards are decidedly colonial. Two-room suites have full kitchens and discounted rates for extended stay. Long-term guests love the laundry facilities and free wi-fi.

FLEMISH HOUSE Map pp72-3   B&B $$
☎ 312-664-9981; www.innchicago.com; 68 E Cedar St; r incl breakfast $175-250; Ⓜ Red Line to Clark/Division; ✗ ⊚

A wall full of framed line drawings, coffered panels and rosette woodwork, an exquisite porcelain collection atop the armoire: indeed, you can tell that one of the co-owners of this 1892 row house is an architect. Travelers check into these self-service apartments (with full kitchens) for the quiet remove. Don't expect the typical B&B socializing; breakfast supplies are stocked in the fridge before you arrive. The closest parking is a lot a couple blocks away. No children under six.

MILLENNIUM KNICKERBOCKER
HOTEL Map pp72-3   Historic Hotel $$
☎ 312-751-8100; www.millenniumhotels.com; 163 E Walton Pl; r $160-260; Ⓜ Red Line to Chicago; ✗

Built in 1927, the Knickerbocker Hotel has a notorious history. The 14th floor once contained a casino (now it's banquet space). Al

Capone slipped out more than once through the secret passageway from there down to the street. Then in the 1970s, this became the Playboy hotel. You'd never suspect anything from the elegance of the public spaces (peek into the lobby-level ballroom) and the neotraditional guest rooms.

WHITEHALL HOTEL
Map pp72-3   Historic Hotel $$
☎ 312-944-6300, 866-753-4081; www.thewhite hallhotel.com; 105 E Delaware Pl; r $160-240; Ⓜ Red Line to Chicago; ⊚

Tallyho, my good chap, we're off to the fox hunt. Cozy rooms, hunting-dog paintings and clubby furniture: this old Chicago hotel speaks with a decidedly British accent. It's extremely popular with wedding parties; you'll often see gown-clad beauties flowing by. Families who belong to the Disney Vacation Club, of which the hotel is a part, stay here too. Michigan Ave is supremely close.

GOLD COAST GUEST HOUSE
Map pp72-3   B&B $$
☎ 312-337-0361; www.bbchicago.com; 113 W Elm St; r incl breakfast $129-229; Ⓜ Red Line to Clark/Division; ✗ ⊚

Innkeeper Sally Baker has been making stays memorable for more than 20 years. She'll lead you to a happy-hour bargain on lobster, make a discounted tour reservation or supply you with the most recent *Time Out* magazine. Her 1873 classic three-story townhouse has a delightful secret garden, and rooms made light and airy by muted taupes, blues and creams. Self-serve coffee, juices, breads and cheeses are among the breakfast choices. Help yourself to sodas and snacks around the clock. Wi-fi and computer use are free, parking (on street with permit) is $25. She also rents apartments nearby. No children under 10.

TREMONT HOTEL Map pp72-3   Hotel $$
☎ 312-751-1900, 866-716-8139; www.tremont chicago.com; 100 E Chestnut St; r $129-219; Ⓜ Red Line to Chicago; ✗ ⊚

Here are the Tremont's pros: you're steps from the Magnificent Mile in a ritzy 'hood, and the property often turns up dirt cheap on Hotwire. Do the rooms tend toward faded upholstery and peeling wallpaper? Yes, but you can help the situation by asking for a room with good natural light at check-in. Old-school touches, like the parlor that's studded with leather chairs and has a fireplace, evoke nostalgia, as does the on-site meaty restaurant of former Bears coach Mike Ditka. Look elsewhere if room prices slide toward the high end of the range. Starwood Hotels–affiliated.

LINCOLN PARK & OLD TOWN

Staying here, you're close to some great neighborhood nightlife. Townhouses are more common than high-rises and dog walkers outnumber business suits on the street two to one. You may be able to walk to the zoo and the beach from area lodgings, and museums in the Loop are a 15-minute El or bus ride south.

BELDEN-STRATFORD HOTEL
Map pp78-9   Extended Stay $$
☎ 773-281-2900, 800-800-8301; www.belden stratfordhotel.com; 2300 N Lincoln Park W; r incl breakfast $129-209; ▣ 22, 151; ☒ ⊚
You can get a darn good deal in this 1924 building, though don't be fooled by all the 'luxury' lingo the B-S throws around (yes, we're aware of initials). The common areas are elegant, but the rooms themselves are fairly dated. No problem, because there's a big upside: the rooms resemble apartments, which means they're larger than typical hotel quarters and are equipped with kitchens. Some even have lake views. The location is particularly good for families since it's steps from the zoo and the beach. Free wi-fi and continental breakfast are included.

DAYS INN LINCOLN PARK NORTH
Map pp78-9   Hotel $$
☎ 773-525-7010, 888-576-3297; www.lpndaysinn .com; 644 W Diversey Pkwy; r incl breakfast $120-180; Ⓜ Brown, Purple Line to Diversey; ⊚
This is a busy hotel on a busy intersection. The Days Inn caters to the budget-minded with value-added punches like free wi-fi, health club access and hot waffle breakfasts. Avoid the standard doubles if you're claustrophobic; kings are much roomier. And if you see a big shiny bus outside, that's because touring indie bands stay here, since it's one of the few hotels near the north side's music venues.

CHICAGO GETAWAY HOSTEL
Map pp78-9   Hostel $
☎ 773-929-5380; www.getawayhostel.com; 616 W Arlington Pl; incl breakfast dm $31-33, r $62-112; ▣ 22 or Ⓜ Brown, Purple, Red Line to Fullerton; ☒ ⊚
The Getaway Hostel gets points for trying, thanks to new management that's doing its best to spruce up the once-dingy budget stalwart. Most rooms have a fresh coat of paint, and the owners have started to install air-conditioning (at press time it still wasn't in all rooms). Dorms are single sex, sleeping six to 12 people. The private rooms are small and either have a full bathroom, a half bathroom or share one down the hall. The hostel attracts a mostly a college-aged crowd who strum the house guitars, use the free wi-fi and head out to nightlife-rich Clark and Halsted Sts (the hostel is equidistant between the two). There's no curfew or lockout times.

LAKE VIEW & WRIGLEYVILLE

The beer-pounding, bar-hopping parade that is Wrigleyville makes up just part of this prime neighborhood. Bunches of shops and eateries provide services for all the locals that live in area condos. Boystown gay nightlife is nearby. And frequent buses and trains provide easy access to the Loop, 20 minutes south. Streets still bustle, but here you've escaped the high-rise jungle.

WILLOWS HOTEL Map pp86-7   Hotel $$
☎ 773-528-8400, 800-787-3108; www.willows hotelchicago.com; 555 W Surf St; r incl breakfast $159-229; ▣ 22; ☒ ⊚
Small and stylish, the Italianate Willows wins an architectural gold star. The chic little lobby provides a swell refuge of overstuffed chairs by the fireplace (a fine spot to curl up and munch free cookies in the afternoon). The 55 rooms, done up in shades of peach, cream and soft green, impart a 19th-century French countryside vibe. There's free wi-fi throughout; parking costs $22. The hotel's owners also run the City Suites and Majestic hotels. The Willows is the farthest south, at Lake View's edge, so you're near the zoo and lakefront parklands.

top picks

GAY STAYS

- Villa Toscana (right)
- House 5683 (opposite)
- Flemish House (p238)
- Best Western Hawthorne Terrace (below)
- W Chicago City Center (p228)

MAJESTIC HOTEL Map pp86-7   Hotel $$

☎ 773-404-3499, 800-727-5108; www.majestic
-chicago.com; 528 W Brompton Ave; r incl breakfast
$159-229; 🚌 151; ✕ 🛜

Nestled into a row of residential housing,
the Majestic is walking distance to Wrigley
Field, Boystown and the lakefront.
From the lobby fireplace and dark-wood
furnishings to the Laura Ashley–style floral
decor, the interior has the cozy feel of an
English manor. Rooms are slightly larger
than those at sibling hotels the City Suites
and Willows, and the location is more
remote and therefore quieter. Wi-fi is free;
parking costs $22.

CITY SUITES HOTEL Map pp86-7   Hotel $$

☎ 773-404-3400, 800-248-9108; www.chicago
citysuites.com; 933 W Belmont Ave; r incl breakfast
$159-229; Ⓜ Brown, Purple, Red Line to Belmont;
✕ 🛜

The City Suites may remind European
visitors pleasantly of home. The mod, art-
deco-tinged rooms and lobby buzzing just
off Belmont Ave are vaguely reminiscent
of Amsterdam. The El races right by the
hotel, so light sleepers should ask for a
room away from the tracks. Compared to
the Majestic and Willows, the owners'
other two properties, the City Suites skews
a bit younger and livelier. As with the
others, there's free wi-fi throughout and a
pass to nearby Bally's fitness club. Parking
costs $22.

BEST WESTERN HAWTHORNE
TERRACE Map pp86-7   Hotel $$

☎ 773-244-3434, 888-860-3400; www.hawthorne
terrace.com; 3434 N Broadway St; r incl breakfast
$159-209; 🚌 36; 🛜

The earthy Hawthorne Terrace attracts the
most mixed crowd of the neighborhood's
hotels. Sporty Cubs fans check in next to

gay groups, with everyone primed to go
out and have some fun. Standard-issue
furnishings fill the rooms, but the free wi-fi,
microwaves and minifridges are nice perks,
along with the continental breakfast and a
small fitness room. The 1920s Federal-style
apartment building may not be the newest
place around, but it retains a classic appeal
inside and out. Parking (in a garage next
door) costs $22.

VILLA TOSCANA Map pp86-7   B&B $$

☎ 773-404-2643, 800-404-2643; www.thevilla
toscana.com; 3447 N Halsted St; r incl breakfast
$109-159; 🚌 8; ✕ 🛜

A 1890s Victorian home seems out of
place, set next to Gay Mart on the busiest
of Boystown streets. Wander through the
leafy front garden and you're transported.
Purple silks evoke Morocco in one room,
toile recalls France in another. All eight
diminutive lodgings (five with private
bathrooms) are often booked, so plan
ahead. Enjoy breakfast pastries on the rear
sundeck in nice weather. Free wi-fi and
broadband.

OLD CHICAGO INN Map pp86-7   B&B $$

☎ 773-472-2278; www.oldchicagoinn.com; 3222 N
Sheffield Ave; r incl breakfast $100-215; Ⓜ Brown,
Purple, Red Line to Belmont; ✕ 🛜

Sure the street din may seep into this
century-old, 10-room graystone three-flat,
but that's the price you pay for being smack
in a high-energy shopping and nightlife
hub. For quiet, ask for the cozy room in
the rear (hardly big enough to stretch your
arms out). Much bigger is the Wrigleyville
basement suite, where you could organize
a decent game of catch. Ballpark pics and
a neon sign get you in the mood. In addition to continental breakfast, you get a $10
gift certificate for food at the owner's pub,
Trader Todd's, two doors down. There's free
wi-fi and on-street parking (though you may
have to search a bit).

ANDERSONVILLE
& UPTOWN

Homey Andersonville makes a unique
getaway. What you trade in access (the
Loop is 30 minutes south by El or bus),
you gain in tranquility in this residential,
gay-friendly 'hood.

HOUSE 5683 Map p90 B&B $$

☎ 773-944-5555; www.house5863.com; 5683 N Glenwood Ave; r incl breakfast $99-179; Ⓜ Red Line to Thorndale; ✗ 🛜

Hip and urban, sleek and sophisticated: House 5683 is a thoroughly modern B&B. You'll find no frilly ruffles here, just clean-lined furnishings and abstract art in an old apartment house. Lounge on the black leather sofa in the common living room and watch the plasma TV, or use the free wi-fi throughout. Adirondack chairs invite lolling about in the backyard. Neither N Broadway nor N Clark St are far, but a party place this neighborhood ain't. Garage parking available ($20).

WICKER PARK, BUCKTOWN & UKRAINIAN VILLAGE

If you prefer a crash pad away from the tourist masses, surrounded by eclectic shopping and trendy lounges, then Wicker Park, Bucktown and Ukrainian Village are your answer. B&Bs are the only option in these mostly residential neighborhoods, though at press time the gastro-pub Longman & Eagle (www .longmananandeagle.com) in nearby Logan Square was scheduled to open an English-style inn on its top floor.

RUBY ROOM Map pp96-7 B&B $$

☎ 773-235-2323; www.rubyroom.com; 1743-5 W Division St; r $155-185; Ⓜ Blue Line to Division; ✗ 🛜

Take an Anusara yoga class, go on a guided intuitive journey or get your chakra massaged. Ruby Room is primarily a spa and 'healing sanctuary.' Eight simplified rooms are boiled down to the essence of comfort. No TVs, no telephones, no elevator, no breakfast. Instead, expect 500-thread-count sheets, pristine white interiors, pillow-top mattresses, free wi-fi and Aveda products. No children under 12.

WICKER PARK INN BED & BREAKFAST
Map pp96-7 B&B $$

☎ 773-645-9827; www.wickerparkinn.com; 1329 N Wicker Park Ave; r incl breakfast $149-199; Ⓜ Blue Line to Damen; ✗ 🛜

This classic brick row house is steps away from Chicago's most rockin' restaurant and nightlife scene. The sunny rooms aren't huge, but all have hardwood floors, soothing pastel colors schemes, terry-cloth robes and small desk spaces where you can use the free wi-fi. Across the street, two apartments with kitchens provide a self-contained experience (sans the baked-good-rich breakfast). Rooms have varying minimum-stay requirements. Children are welcome.

HOUSE OF TWO URNS BED & BREAKFAST Map pp96-7 B&B $$

☎ 773-235-1408, 877-896-8767; www.twourns .com; 1239 N Greenview Ave; r incl breakfast $129-199; Ⓜ Blue Line to Division; ✗ 🛜

Artists own these two houses at Wicker Park's edge, so it's no surprise both are fancifully furnished with old cameras, cobalt glass and other odd antiques, as well as original art. Rooms are more homey than luxurious. Those at the lower end of the spectrum share a bathroom, while those at the upper end have a Jacuzzi tub and include free off-street parking. Guests all gather in the main dining room for a cooked breakfast (banana French toast, for example), though you can request a self-serve continental breakfast if you prefer. Your helpful hosts also lend out umbrellas, provide free snacks and share their 200-plus DVDs. Children are welcome in certain rooms.

NEAR WEST SIDE & PILSEN

Greektown isn't bad for a stay, since it's restaurant laden and convenient to public transportation (you can also walk to the Loop in about 15 minutes). Beyond that there's no compelling reason to stay on the West Side, unless you're visiting the University of Illinois at Chicago or the medical district.

CHICAGO MARRIOTT AT MEDICAL DISTRICT/UIC Map pp104-5 Hotel $$

☎ 312-491-1234, 800-356-3641; www.marriott .com; 625 S Ashland Ave; r $179-269; Ⓜ Blue Line to Medical District; ✗

The Marriott is gussied up after a 2009 renovation that upgraded the beds, brightened the decor and added HDTVs, work-friendly desks and a minifridge in each room. Most guests are visiting friends and family at the huge medical center complex nearby. A complimentary bus shuttles you to the hospital door, to the University or to Little Italy – anywhere within a mile radius. Parking costs $28.

CHICAGO PARTHENON HOSTEL

Map pp104-5   Hostel $

☎ 312-258-1399, 304-268-8981; www.parthenon hostel.com; 310 S Halsted St; dm/r incl breakfast from $30/61; Ⓜ Blue Line to UIC-Halsted; ☒ ⓦ
Guests young and old, international and American, check in to this well-run hostel that sits next to the Parthenon Restaurant. It feels more like a hotel with bunk beds rather than a traditional hostel. Tidy dorms and private rooms come in myriad configurations; the typical single-sex dorm has eight beds. There's a small common area with a TV, games and books. The free continental breakfast in the restaurant's banquet area is a nice start to the day. Dorm dwellers must pay $3 extra for linens.

SOUTH LOOP & NEAR SOUTH SIDE

Proximity to the Museum Campus, and potential lake views along S Michigan Ave, attract sightseers to the South Loop hotels. That and also a desire for a bargain. In general, prices here are less than in the Near North, but that's because you're a 15-minute train or bus ride from its action. Restaurants are fewer and farther between, too.

BLACKSTONE HOTEL

Map pp112-13   Historic Hotel $$

☎ 312-447-0955, 800-468-3571; www.blackstone renaissance.com; 636 S Michigan Ave; r $199-309; Ⓜ Red Line to Harrison; ☒ ⓦ
This 1910, neoclassical, beaux-arts landmark was shuttered for several years, until Marriott paid $128 million and restored it to its former glamour in 2008. Known as the 'hotel of presidents' (more than a dozen have slumbered here), the 23-story beauty now caters to a high-falutin' business crowd. Rooms are urban stylish (downy bedding, white-marbled bathrooms, abstract artworks); several have lake views (for which you'll pay about $50 extra). Check out the painting-filled Art Hall.

HILTON CHICAGO

Map pp112-13   Historic Hotel $$

☎ 312-922-4400, 800-445-8667; www.hilton.com; 720 S Michigan Ave; r $164-309; Ⓜ Red Line to Harrison; ☒ ⓦ
When built in 1927 (for $30 mil), this was the world's largest hotel, having close to 3000 rooms (and a hospital, and a theater…). Renovations brought that total down to a mere 1544, but the gilt grandeur and crystal-dripping class have remained. Anecdotes abound at the Hilton: in the 1940s it served as an army barracks. At the height of the 1968 Democratic National Convention riots, police tossed protesters through the front plate-glass windows. The rooms? They're reasonable, standard-issue Hilton types, with heavy drapes, cherrywood decor and comfy beds. A lake view upgrade (about $30) makes a nice enhancement.

HYATT REGENCY MCCORMICK PLACE

Map pp112-13   Hotel $$

☎ 312-567-1234, 800-633-7313; www .mccormickplace.hyatt.com; 2233 S Martin Luther King Jr Dr; r $149-359; Ⓜ Metra to McCormick Place; ⓦ
If you're manning a show booth at McCormick Place, you can't beat the short walk to your bed in this attached hotel. Lobby monitors help you keep track of meeting schedules, and the business center computers are free to use. However, if you're not a conventioneer, even the

top picks

HOTELS FOR ARCHITECTURE BUFFS

Several of Chicago's lodgings are in historically significant, landmarked buildings.

- Hotel Burnham (p228) In the terra-cotta-clad Reliance Building, whose design helped pave the way for the skyscraper.
- Blackstone (left) A neoclassical, beaux-arts beauty.
- Palmer House Hilton (p230) An old-time Chicago property with a lobby like no other.
- Hard Rock Hotel (p228) In the art-deco, champagne-bottle-esque Carbide & Carbon building.

skyline views may not be reason enough to stay in one of these 800 modern rooms, 2 miles south of the Loop.

BEST WESTERN GRANT PARK
Map pp112-13   Hotel $$

☎ 312-922-2900, 800-780-7234; www.best western.com; 1100 S Michigan Ave; r incl breakfast $110-199; Ⓜ Green, Orange Line to Roosevelt; 📶 🅿

This very basic Best Western attracts for its location near the Museum Campus, free wi-fi and lower-than-usual downtown parking rate ($24 per day). Though the lobby's gone modern, rooms are standard faux-oak and floral-bedspread decor. Outside convention time, it can be a bargain. But if the rates ratchet up, remember you're getting a no-frills room for that dough.

ESSEX INN Map pp112-13   Hotel $

☎ 312-939-2800, 800-621-6909; www.essexinn .com; 800 S Michigan Ave; r $109-189; Ⓜ Red Line to Harrison; 🅿
Walk out to the 4th-floor rooftop garden and soak in the sun, or swim protected in the giant glass-enclosed pool, which looks like a bit like an Olympic pavilion. Both are a pleasant surprise at this low-end price. Plus, a free shuttle takes you north to the Mag Mile. Brightly colored pendant lights

and low-slung lobby leather say mod, as do the rooms, which were revamped in 2008 and now include flat-screen TVs, minirefrigerators and work-friendly desks. Wi-fi costs $6 per day.

TRAVELODGE CHICAGO
DOWNTOWN Map pp112-13   Hotel $

☎ 312-427-8000, 800-211-6706; www.travelodge hoteldowntown.com; 65 E Harrison St; r $109-139; Ⓜ Red Line to Harrison; ☒ 📶
The nearby Essex and Best Western typically offer better quality with more amenities, but the Travelodge's prices are more consistently low. What do you say about lackluster motel-like rooms? Um, they're there. Parking costs $28.

HYDE PARK & SOUTH SIDE

BENEDICTINE B&B Map pp50-1   B&B $$

☎ 773-927-7424, 888-539-4261 ext 202; www .chicagomonk.org; 3111 S Aberdeen St; r incl breakfast $165-255; 🚌 8; ☒
This is unusual for the city: a B&B run by monks. The B&B is two simple apartments, to be exact, which means you get loads of space and kitchen facilities. One is a two-bedroom garden apartment with a deck and self-serve breakfast; the other is a three-

AIRPORT ACCOMMODATIONS

Got an early flight to catch? Given the crazy Chicago traffic, or long El commute (45 minutes from the Loop), resting your head at one of the dozens of airport hotels may be your best bet. Most (including those listed here) run free 24-hour airport shuttles.

O'Hare

Aloft Chicago O'Hare (Map pp50-1; ☎ 847-671-4444; www.aloftchicagoohare.com; 9700 Balmoral Ave, Rosemont; r $89-169; Ⓜ Blue Line to Rosemont; 📶) It offers the chain's typical compact, efficiently designed, industrial-toned rooms and clubby, game-filled lobby. About 3.5 miles from the airport.

O'Hare Hilton (Map pp50-1; ☎ 773-686-8000, 800-445-8667; www.hilton.com; O'Hare International Airport; r $139-279; Ⓜ Blue Line to O'Hare; 🅿) Attached to the airport via an underground tunnel. Relax in the sauna, take a refreshing dip in the indoor pool and then retire to your soundproofed contemporary room.

Midway

Hilton Garden Inn (Map pp50-1; ☎ 708-496-2700, 800-445-8667; www.hiltongardeninn.com; 6530 S Cicero Ave, Bedford Park; r $149-219; Ⓜ Orange Line to Midway; 🅿 📶) One of the newest in the Midway Hotel Center complex of nine hotels.

Sleep Inn (Map pp50-1; ☎ 708-594-0001, 877-424-6423; www.choicehotels.com; 6650 S Cicero Ave, Bedford Park; r incl breakfast $79-149; Ⓜ Orange Line to Midway; ☒ 📶) Slightly cheaper, but in the same complex. The modern modular rooms are perfectly acceptable. Free hot breakfast is a nice touch.

SLEEPING HYDE PARK & SOUTH SIDE

bedroom loft with breakfast prepared by the monks. It's in the Bridgeport neighborhood, about a mile and a half from US Cellular Field. You'll fare best if you have a car.

RAMADA LAKE SHORE Map p120   Motel $
☎ 773-288-5800; www.ramada-chicago.com; 4900 S Lake Shore Dr; r $79-129; 🚌 6; Ⓟ 🛜 🛋

Rooms at this two-story motel may not be the freshest, and the door jambs may be scuffed. But who cares when you're across from the lake, parking is free and you're paying under $100? A free shuttle takes you up to Michigan Ave, or you can hop on the bus for the 15-minute ride. The outdoor pool is open summers only.

DAY TRIPS & EXCURSIONS

Certainly Chicago has enough sky-high buildings, rockin' live-music clubs, beaches, boozers and ballparks to keep you occupied for weeks. But let's say you want to scale sand dunes, see a giant spaceman or nibble a hunk of freshly made cheese – you're out of luck in the city limits. Which means you'll have to hit the road to broaden your experience. The destinations in this chapter range from 20-minute jaunts to 3½-hour journeys, many reachable by bus or train for those without a car, and they fan out beyond Illinois into Wisconsin, Indiana and Michigan.

Oak Park is a short El ride from downtown, though it seems a world away with its huge old houses, wrap-around porches and sprawling green yards. Frank Lloyd Wright designed many of the town's buildings and had his studio here. Ernest Hemingway was born a few blocks away, and his home is now a museum.

Beach bums will want to proceed east to Indiana Dunes, where those heaps of sand provide opportunities for shoreside lounging and dune hiking. Just beyond in New Buffalo and Harbor Country, visitors can surf Lake Michigan's waves or sip reds and whites at local vineyards. Farther up Michigan's 'gold coast' lies Saugatuck, a favorite getaway for boaters, artists, antique hounds and gay couples. And the scene stretches onward: more rugged beaches, waterfront camping and mango-colored sunsets unfurl along the road to Holland and beyond.

Turning the wheel north to Wisconsin rewards the road-tripper with two worthy cities: down-to-earth Milwaukee, which admirably balances Harleys and beer with world-class art and cultural festivals; and liberal, leafy Madison, the small state capital loaded with coffee shops, bookstores, farmers' markets and cheap, international places to grab a bite. Of course, there's no escaping the Dairy State without cheese, so we provide a trek to the nation's densest cheesemaking area.

Back in Illinois, Route 66, the nostalgic 'Mother Road', starts in downtown Chicago in front of the Art Institute, and carries travelers south through a trail of kitschy roadside attractions, pie shops and scattered shrines to local hero Abe Lincoln. Genteel Galena, a B&B-stuffed, Civil War-era town near the Mississippi River, transports visitors back to a slower, horse-drawn age.

The prices listed here are for peak season, which runs from late May to early September. During the off-season, many places reduce their hours and some even close entirely.

ACTIVE ENDEAVORS

C'mon, haul your buns off the couch and get out there. The region offers activities for all seasons and experience levels, and the scenery will knock your socks off. Visitors can paddle Old Man River in Galena (p256); hike, swim and cross-country ski in Indiana Dunes (p249); cycle past orchards and vineyards near Three Oaks (p251); and surf, paddleboard and sandboard in New Buffalo (p251).

FOODIE FORAGES

Make sure to wear expandable trousers when you embark. Crane's Pie Pantry (p252) near Saugatuck is famed for its fruit pies; the blueberries, raspberries and other fillings come straight from the surrounding orchard. Madison's Dane County Farmers' Market (p255) is the premier place to chomp into Wisconsin specialties like beer-cooked brats and artisanal cheeses. Or travel south to Monroe (p256), where more cheesemakers reside than anywhere else in the country. Learn Great Foods (p257) in Galena offers culinary tours to local farms and markets. There's good sippin' in the wineries (p251) that blanket the land around New Buffalo and Harbor Country. Foodies who want to stay overnight at a farm can tuck into Inn Serendipity (p256) in Wisconsin or Tryon Farm (p251) in Indiana.

ART & HISTORY

Impress your friends by returning from your Midwest excursion more knowledgeable about art, architecture and history. Architecture buffs can be unleashed in Oak Park to view Frank Lloyd Wright's studio (p248) and a couple of streets' worth of homes he designed; Taliesin (p256), outside Madison, is his ubersite. The Milwaukee Art Museum (p253) sports unusually cool folk and outsider art galleries in a Santiago Calatrava–designed

246

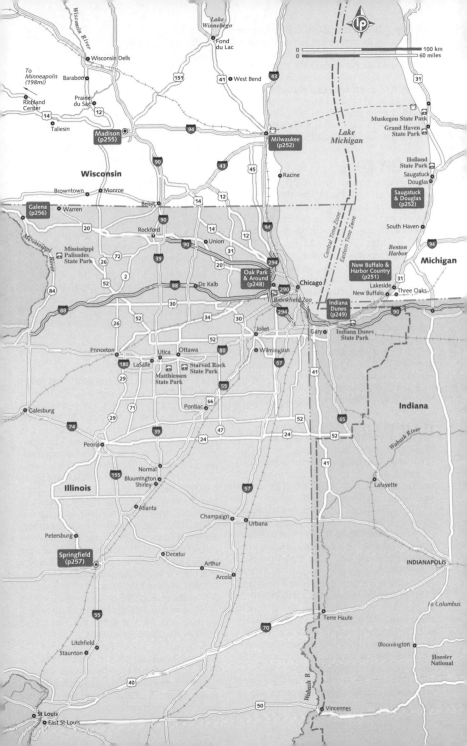

building. Three Oaks (p251) and Saugatuck (p252) are both gallery-rich towns and home to multiple artists. Novelist Ernest Hemingway hailed from Oak Park, where the Hemingway Museum (opposite) tells his story (using words sparingly, of course). Springfield houses a trio of historical Abraham Lincoln sights (p259), including his tomb. Galena offers historical insight on another Civil War–era president at the Ulysses S Grant home (p256).

KITSCHY KOOL

Once you've wowed your pals with your high-brow art and history knowledge, show them you're no snob, because you're a connoisseur of not-so-high culture, too. The giant fiberglass spaceman outside the Launching Pad Drive-in (p257) and the hot-dog-clutching Paul Bunyan statue by the Palms Grill Cafe (p258) are just two of Route 66's many kitschy wonders. It doesn't get much wackier than the Racing Sausages (aka guys dressed in mondo meat costumes) at Miller Park (p253). Another Milwaukee treasure: the polka band with bubble machine at Lakefront Brewery's fish fry (p253). Pig-bedecked Oink's Dutch Treat (p251) is the start of a kitschy array of roadside shops as you head north through Michigan's coastal towns. And finally, Annie Wiggins Ghost Tour (p257) provides a healthy dose of hoke in Galena.

OAK PARK & AROUND

The suburb of Oak Park spawned two famous sons: Ernest Hemingway was born here, and architect Frank Lloyd Wright lived and worked here from 1889 to 1909. The town's main sights revolve around these men.

During Wright's 20 years in Oak Park, he designed a whole heap of houses. Stop at the visitors center (☎ 888-625-7275; www.visitoakpark .com; 158 N Forest Ave; ☉ 10am-5pm) and ask for the architectural site map (a free photocopied page), which gives their locations. Ten of them cluster within a mile along Forest and Chicago Aves; the homes are privately owned, so all gawking must occur from the sidewalk. Moore House (333 N Forest Ave) is particularly noteworthy. First built in 1895, it's Wright's bizarre interpretation of an English manor house. In his later years, Wright called the house 'repugnant' and said he had only taken the commission because he needed the money. He claimed that he walked out of his way to avoid passing it.

TRANSPORTATION: OAK PARK & AROUND

Direction To Oak Park 10 miles west; to Brookfield Zoo 14 miles west

Travel time To Oak Park 20 minutes; to Brookfield Zoo 25 minutes

Car To Oak Park, take I-290 west, exiting north on Harlem Ave; take Harlem Ave north to Lake St and turn right. For the zoo, go west on the Eisenhower Expressway (I-290) to the 1st Ave exit, then south to 31st St and follow the signs.

El Take the Green Line to its terminus at the Harlem stop, which lands you about four blocks from the visitors center. The trip (one way $2.25) takes 20 minutes; be aware that the train traverses some bleak neighborhoods before emerging into Oak Park's wide-lawn splendor.

Metra The Union Pacific West Line has an Oak Park stop; trains depart from Ogilvie Transportation Center (one way $2.50). Brookfield Zoo is reachable via the Burlington Northern Santa Fe (BNSF) Line from Union Station; exit at the Hollywood stop (one way $3.50).

To get inside a Wright-designed dwelling, you'll need to visit the Frank Lloyd Wright Home & Studio (☎ 708-848-1976; www.gowright.org; 951 Chicago Ave; adult/child 4-17yr $15/12) at the corner of Forest and Chicago Aves. Tours generally take place between 11am and 3pm daily (a bit later in summer), every 20 minutes or so. The hour-long walk-through reveals a fascinating place, filled with the details that made Wright's style distinctive. Note how he molded plaster to look like bronze and how he stained cheap pine to look like rare hardwood. Always in financial trouble, spendthrift Wright was adept at making the ordinary seem extraordinary. He remained here until 1909, when he ran off to Europe with a female client, leaving behind his wife, six kids and his architecture practice. He later explained his infidelity, saying that as a 'thinking man,' he didn't have to follow the rules of the ordinary man. He set up shop next at Taliesin in Wisconsin, where he lived with his new lady until a deranged servant murdered her in 1914.

Self-guided audio tours ($15) of the neighborhood are also available. Or you can combine the guided home tour with the neighborhood audio tour for $25. Get tickets at the Home & Studio or online. Advance reservations recommended.

The Unity Temple (☎ 708-383-8873; www.unitytemple -utrf.org; 875 Lake St; adult/child $8/6; ⊗ 10:30am-4:30pm Mon-Fri, 10am-2pm Sat, 1-4pm Sun) is the only other Wright building that devotees can go inside; it requires a separate admission fee for a self-guided look around. If you're short on time or money, skip this one and head to the Home & Studio instead.

Despite Hemingway calling Oak Park a 'village of wide lawns and narrow minds,' the town still pays homage to him at the Ernest Hemingway Museum (☎ 708-848-2222; www.ehfop .org; 200 N Oak Park Ave; adult/child $10/8; ⊗ 1-5pm Sun-Fri, 10am-5pm Sat). The exhibits begin with his middle-class Oak Park background and the innocent years before he went off to find adventure. The ensuing displays focus on his writings in Spain and during WWII. Admission includes entry to Hemingway's birthplace (339 N Oak Park Ave), where you can see his first room. 'Papa' was born here in 1899 in the large, turreted home of his maternal grandparents. The telephone number and opening hours are the same as for the museum.

To see the array of animals Hemingway likely shot and killed on his famed hunting expeditions, head southwest from Oak Park to the Brookfield Zoo (☎ 708-485-0263; www .brookfieldzoo.org; 8400 W 31st St, Brookfield; adult/child 3-11yr $13.50/9.50, parking per vehicle $9; ⊗ 9:30am-6pm, reduced hr Sep-May). With 2700 animals over 215 acres, the zoo can easily sustain a day's wanderings. More extensive than the free Lincoln Park Zoo in Chicago, Brookfield features a wildly impressive bear habitat, African- and Australian-themed exhibits, several primate areas, a kids' zoo and a ton more.

Because most visitors use the north gate and tend to stop at the nearby attractions first, you can avoid some of the crowds by starting in the southern part of the zoo and working back north.

INDIANA DUNES

Lake Michigan's prevailing winds created the 21 miles of beaches and sandbanks that comprise Indiana Dunes National Lakeshore (☎ 219-926-7561, 800-959-9174; www.nps.gov/indu; admission free excluding West Beach). Behind the sands, large areas of woods and wetlands have become major wildlife habitats and the breeding grounds for an incredible variety of plant life. Everything from cacti to pine trees sprouts here.

Preserving this rare ecosystem, which stretches from Gary east to Michigan City, has

always been a struggle. The smoke-belching steel mills that pop up amid the bucolic beauty show which way the fight has often gone, and give visitors a whiff (literally – just breathe in that Gary air) of the horrors that might have spread had activists such as Dorothy Buell and Illinois Senator Paul Douglas not stepped in to protect the region.

Today the dunes attract huge crowds in summer months, when people from Chicago to South Bend flock to the shores for good swimming and general frivolity. Swimming is allowed anywhere along the national lakeshore. On busy days, a short hike away from the clogged developed beaches will yield an almost deserted strand. In winter the lake winds and pervasive desolation make the dunes a moody and memorable experience. You may well hear the low hum of the 'singing sands,' an unusual sound caused by the zillions of grains hitting each other in the wind.

The best place to start is the Dorothy Buell Memorial Visitor Center (☎ 219-926-7561; Hwy 49; ⊗ 8:30am-6:30pm Jun-Aug, to 4:30 Sep-May). It can provide beach details; a schedule of ranger-guided walks and activities; and hiking, biking and birding maps.

Most beaches are open from 7am to sunset daily. Central Beach is a good place to escape the masses, and it leads to a set of steep dune cliffs. Mt Baldy Beach boasts the highest dunes, with namesake Mt Baldy offering the best views all the way to Chicago from its 120ft peak. This beach is by far the busiest of the lot. West Beach (per car $6), nearest to Gary, draws fewer crowds than the others and features a number of nature hikes and trails. It's also the only beach with an on-duty lifeguard.

For those who'd rather be hiking than sunbathing, the park service has done a fine job of developing trails through a range of terrain and environments. The 2½-mile Bailly/ Chellberg Trail begins at the Bailly/Chellberg Visitor Center (☎ 219-926-7561; Mineral Springs Rd; ⊗ 11am-4:30pm Sat & Sun), east of the Buell Center. It winds through the forest past a fur-trading outpost from the 1820s and a farm built by Swedes in the 1870s. The latter hosts family-friendly activities, like feeding the animals, on weekends. Nearby, the 5-mile walk at Cowles Bog Trail combines marshes and dunes.

At the park's western edge, the 1½-mile Miller Woods Trail passes dunes, woods and ponds. At West Beach the 1.6-mile Long Lake Trail is a classic wetlands walk around an inland lake. The easy 2-mile Heron Rookery Trail winds around

INDIANA DUNES

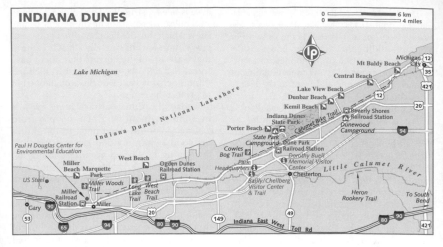

a breeding ground for the great blue heron; it's located inland, southeast of Buell Center. Dawn and dusk are the best times to view the tall, regal birds wading in the water. Since they are elusive, it's wise to stop into the Buell Center first and have staff give you sighting tips.

Much of the national park area is good for cycling, although the traffic and the narrow shoulders on US 12 can make that road dangerous. The Calumet Bike Trail runs west from near Michigan City almost to the Chellberg Farm in the lakeshore's midst. In winter, cross-country skiers glide

TRANSPORTATION: INDIANA DUNES

Direction 50 miles southeast

Travel time 60 to 75 minutes

Car Take I-90 east out of Chicago to Indiana (be prepared to pay about $5 worth of tolls). After Gary take exit 21 to merge onto I-94 east (toward Detroit). Soon after, take exit 22B to merge onto US 20 toward Porter. This will get you to the middle of the park near the Buell Visitor Center. Parking is difficult on weekends unless you arrive before 10am. West Beach is the best bet, though it charges $6 per car.

Metra South Shore Line trains (☎ 800-356-2079; www.nictd.com) depart frequently from Randolph St/Millennium Station in the Loop and stop at Miller, Portage/Ogden Dunes, Dune Park and Beverly Shores (one way $5.50 to $7.50). Note that the various stations are a mile or two from the beach.

inland, especially along the trails described above.

Indiana Dunes State Park (☎ 219-926-1952; www .dnr.in.gov/parklake; per walk-in/car $2/10; ☺ beaches 9am-sunset, park 7am-11pm) is a 2100-acre shoreside pocket within the national lakeshore; it's located at the end of Hwy 49, near Chesterton. It has more amenities, but also more regulation and more crowds (plus the $10 vehicle entry fee). Away from its mobbed beaches, the park does offer secluded natural areas. In winter cross-country skiing is popular, while summertime brings out the hikers. Seven numbered trails zigzag over the sandscape: Trail 4 climbs up Mt Tom, the highest dune at 192ft; Trail 2 is good for spring flowers and ferns and is well-used by skiers; and Trail 8 surmounts three of the highest dunes, paying off with killer views of the region.

Unfortunately, the parks do not rent bicycles or skis, so you'll have to bring your own with you.

The dunes are an easy day trip from Chicago and give a sense of being far from the city. Those who want to make a night of it can camp or pull up the covers at a B&B.

INFORMATION

Porter County Convention & Visitors Bureau (☎ 800-283-8687; www.indianadunes.com)

EATING

Other than a couple of beachfront snack bars you won't find much to eat in the parks.

Lucrezia (☎ 219-926-5829; 428 S Calumet Rd; mains $17-27; ☻ 11am-10pm Sun-Thu, to 11pm Fri & Sat) It's a homey, Italian favorite in Chesterton.

Miller Bakery Cafe (☎ 219-938-2229; 555 Lake St; lunch $11-16, dinner mains $18-29; ☻ 11:30am-2pm Tue-Fri, 5-9pm Tue-Thu, 5-10pm Fri & Sat, 4-8pm Sun) This foodie favorite pops up in Miller Beach.

SLEEPING

Tryon Farm Guesthouse (☎ 219-879-3618; www.tryon farmguesthouse.com; r incl breakfast $100-190; ☒ ▣ ☞) This five-room B&B nestles in a turn-of-the-century farmhouse near Michigan City. It's part of a larger conservation community, in which 50 families share farm duties and an organic garden.

Indiana Dunes State Park Campground (☎ 866-622-6746; www.camp.in.gov; campsites $17-28; ☻ year-round) These campsites are modern and closer to the beach than Dunewood. Reserve in advance in summertime.

Dunewood Campground (☎ 219-395-8914; www.nps .gov/indu; campsites $15; ☻ Apr-Oct) The national lakeshore's seasonal campsites are rustic (no electricity) and first come, first served (no reservations).

NEW BUFFALO & HARBOR COUNTRY

About 25 miles up the road from Indiana Dunes, just over the Michigan border, the little town of New Buffalo beckons with its well-loved beach, dreamy ice cream and – believe it, people – surfing.

The VW-bus-driving dudes at Third Coast Surf Shop (☎ 269-932-4575; www.thirdcoastsurfshop .com; 22 S Smith St; ☻ 10am-6pm Jun-Aug, reduced hr spring & fall, closed Jan-Mar) will help you catch that Lake Michigan wave. They provide wetsuits and boards for surfing, skimboarding and paddleboarding (rentals per day $20 to $35). For novices, they offer 1½-hour lessons (including equipment $50 to $70) right from the public beach from June through September. It's a great place to learn since the waves are nice and gentle in summer. The shop also offers sandboarding lessons ($50) at nearby Warren Dunes.

New Buffalo is the largest town in Harbor Country, which refers to the eight beachy communities closest to the Michigan border. Three Oaks is the only Harbor community that's inland (6 miles in, via US 12). Here Green Acres meets Greenwich Village in a funky blends of farms and arts. By day, rent bikes at Dewey Cannon Trading Company (☎ 269-756-3361; 3 Dewey Cannon Ave; bikes per day $15; ☻ 10am-4pm Sun-Fri, to 9pm Sat, reduced hr in winter) and cycle lightly used rural roads past orchards and wineries. By evening, catch a provocative play or art-house flick at Three Oaks' theaters.

Antique shops and wineries are Harbor Country's other big draws. The Lake Michigan Shore Wine Trail (www.miwinetrail.com) provides a downloadable map of vineyards and tasting rooms. Most are signposted off the highway. Connoisseurs often regard Tabor Hill Winery (☎ 800-283-3363; www.taborhill.com; 185 Mt Tabor Rd, Buchanan; tours & tastings free; ☻ tours noon-4:30pm May-Oct, weekends only Nov-Apr, tastings from 10am Mon-Sat, from noon Sun), with its dry reds and crisp sparkling whites, as the region's best.

INFORMATION

Harbor Country Chamber of Commerce (☎ 269-469-5409; www.harborcountry.org)

EATING

Redamak's (☎ 269-469-4522; 616 E Buffalo St; mains $4.50-10; ☻ noon-10:30pm, closed Nov-Feb) After you've been surfing, refuel at this burgers-and-beer roadhouse dating from the 1940s. The spicy curly fries reign supreme.

Oink's Dutch Treat (☎ 269-469-3535; 227 W Buffalo St; ☻ 11:30am-10pm Sun-Thu, to 11pm Fri & Sat) Conveniently located by both the beach and surf shop, piggy-decorated Oink's scoops 55 creamy flavors, including Mackinac Island Fudge.

TRANSPORTATION: NEW BUFFALO

Direction 75 miles east

Travel time 1½ hours

Car Take I-90 east out of Chicago to Indiana. After Gary take exit 21 to merge onto I-94 east (toward Detroit). Drive for 30 miles to the Michigan border, then take exit 1 for New Buffalo, and go left on LaPorte Rd into town. Note that I-90 is a toll road, so be prepared to pay around $5 en route.

Train There are Amtrak (☎ 800-872-7245; www .amtrak.com) trains to/from New Buffalo ($13 to $22, 75 minutes) twice per day, typically in the late afternoon and evening.

SLEEPING

Lakeside Inn (☎ 269-469-0600; www.lakesideinns.com; 15251 Lakeshore Rd, Lakeside; r in summer $115-200, in winter $90-175) Thirty-one simple rooms spread over three floors in this atmospheric century-old lodge with a private beach. It's in Lakeside, 6 miles north of New Buffalo.

SAUGATUCK & DOUGLAS

Saugatuck is one of Michigan's most popular resort areas, known for its strong arts community, numerous B&Bs and gay-friendly vibe. Douglas is its twin city a mile or so south, and they've pretty much sprawled into one. It's a touristy but funky place, with ice-cream-licking families, yuppie boaters and martini-drinking gay couples sharing the waterfront. The area shows its independent streak by steering clear of chain businesses – there's nary a Starbucks or a McDonald's in sight.

The best thing to do in Saugatuck is also the most affordable. Jump aboard the clackety Saugatuck Chain Ferry (foot of Mary St; one way $1; ⊙ 9am-9pm late May-early Sep), and the operator will pull you across the Kalamazoo River. On the other side, walk to the dock's left and soon you'll come to Mt Baldhead, a 200ft-high sand dune. Huff up the stairs to see the grand view, then race down the north side to beautiful Oval Beach. Can't get enough sand? The Saugatuck Dune Rides (☎ 269-857-2253; www.saugatuckduneride.com; 6495 Blue Star Hwy; adult/child 3-11yr $17/10; ⊙ 10am-7:30pm Mon-Sat, 11:30am-7:30pm late Jul & Aug, to 5:30pm late Apr-Jun & Sep, weekends only Oct) provide a half-hour of good, cheesy fun zipping over nearby mounds.

Galleries and shops proliferate downtown on Water and Butler Sts. Antiquing prevails on the Blue Star Hwy running south for 20 miles. The odd shops often look like just a bunch of junk in someone's front yard, but pull up at the right time and that old traffic light or Victorian sled can be yours for a song. Blueberry U-pick farms share this stretch of road and make a juicy stop, too.

Come evening, folks eat and drink at the casually upscale restaurants that ring the harbor. Or they chill at their Victorian B&Bs. And that pretty much sums up the main attractions: partying and puttering.

INFORMATION

Saugatuck/Douglas Visitors Bureau (☎ 269-857-1701; www.saugatuck.com)

TRANSPORTATION: SAUGATUCK & DOUGLAS

Direction 140 miles northeast

Travel time 2½ hours

Car Take I-90 east toward Indiana for about 30 miles (be prepared to pay about $5 worth of tolls). After Gary, merge onto I-94 east, and stay on it for about 65 miles. After Benton Harbor merge onto I-196/US 31 north, and take it for about 40 miles, until the Saugatuck/Douglas exit.

EATING & DRINKING

Crane's Pie Pantry (☎ 269-561-2297; 6054 124th Ave, Fennville; pie slices $3.75; ⊙ 9am-8pm Mon-Sat, 11am-8pm Sun May-Oct, reduced hr Nov-Apr) Buy a bulging slice at the restaurant, or pick your own fruit in the surrounding apple and peach orchards. Located in Fennville, 3 miles south on the Blue Star Hwy, then 4 miles inland on Hwy 89.

Saugatuck Brewing Company (☎ 269-857-7222; 2948 Blue Star Hwy, Douglas; ⊙ 11am-11pm Sun-Thu, to midnight Fri & Sat) Locals like to hang at this Douglas pub and sip the house-made suds. There's live music various nights, and occasional beer-brewing classes.

Marro's Italian Restaurant (☎ 269-857-4248; 147 Water St, Saugatuck; pizzas $19-23; ⊙ 5-11pm Tue-Sun, closed mid-Oct–mid-Apr) It gets props for its pizzas.

SLEEPING

Frilly B&Bs abound. Most are tucked into century-old homes and range from $125 to $300 a night per couple in the summer high season.

Bayside Inn (☎ 269-857-4321; www.baysideinn.net; 618 Water St, Saugatuck; r incl breakfast $150-280; ⊛) This former boathouse has 10 rooms and an outdoor tub on Saugatuck's waterfront.

Pines Motorlodge (☎ 269-857-5211; www .thepinesmotorlodge.com; 56 Blue Star Hwy, Douglas; r incl breakfast $129-189; ⊛) Retro-cool tiki lamps, pinewood furniture and communal lawn chairs add up to a fun, social ambience amid the firs in Douglas.

MILWAUKEE

No one gives much consideration to Milwaukee, Wisconsin, standing as it does in Chicago's shadow. That's a shame, because with its line-up of beer, motorcycles, world-class art and a ballpark of racing sausages, it makes a rollicking getaway.

Germans first settled the city in the 1840s. Many started small breweries, but a few decades later the introduction of bulk brewing technology turned beer into a major industry. Milwaukee earned its 'Brew City' and 'Nation's Watering Hole' nicknames in the 1880s, when Pabst, Schlitz, Blatz, Miller and 80 other breweries made suds here. Alas, only Miller and a few microbreweries remain today.

So why not make the Miller Brewing Company (☎ 414-931-2337; www.millercoors.com; 4251 W State St; admission free; ⏱ 10:30am-3:30pm Mon-Sat Sep-May, 10:30am-4:30pm Mon-Sat, to 2pm Sun Jun-Aug) your first stop, and join the legions of drinkers lined up for the free tours? Though the mass-produced beer may not be your favorite, the factory impresses by its sheer scale: you'll visit the packaging plant, where 2000 cans are filled each minute, and the warehouse, where half a million cases await shipment. And then there's the generous tasting session at the tour's end, where you can down three full-sized samples. Don't forget your ID.

For more swills, head to Lakefront Brewery (☎ 414-372-8800; www.lakefrontbrewery.com; 1872 N Commerce St; 1hr tours $6, fish fry $10; ⏱ Mon-Sat), across the river from the Brady St entertainment district. It has afternoon tours, but the swellest time to visit is on Friday nights, when there's a fish fry, 16 house-crafted beers to try, and a polka band letting loose. Tour times vary throughout the week, but there's usually at least a 3pm walk-through.

In 1903 local schoolmates William Harley and Arthur Davidson built and sold their first Harley-Davidson motorcycle. A century later the big bikes are a symbol of American manufacturing pride. The Harley-Davidson Museum (☎ 877-436-8738; www.h-dmuseum .com; 400 W Canal St; adult/child 5-17yr $16/10; ⏱ 9am-6pm Fri-Mon & Wed, to 8pm Tue & Thu May-Oct, 10am-6pm Fri-Wed, to 8pm Thu Nov-Apr) pays homage in a sprawling industrial building just south of downtown. Hundreds of bikes show styles through the ages, including the sweet rides of Elvis and Evel Knievel.

Hog heads can get another fix at the Harley-Davidson plant (☎ 414-343-7850, 877-883-1450; www .harley-davidson.com; 11700 W Capitol Dr; admission free; ⏱ 9:30am-2pm Mon-Fri, plus 10am-1pm Sat in summer), in the suburb of Wauwatosa, a 20-minute drive west of downtown. This is where engines are built (body assembly goes on in York, Pennsylvania, and Kansas City, Missouri.) The one-hour tours are kind of technical, but the ultimate payoff comes when you get to sit in the saddle of a vintage bike. No open shoes are permitted.

Even those who aren't usual museum goers will be struck by the lakeside Milwaukee Art Museum (☎ 414-224-3200; www.mam.org; 700 N Art Museum Dr; adult/child 13-18yr $12/10; ⏱ 10am-5pm Tue-Sun, to 8pm Thu), which features a stunning winglike addition by Santiago Calatrava. It soars open and closed every day at noon, which is wild to see. There's a permanent display on architect Frank Lloyd Wright, and fabulous folk and outsider art galleries.

And about those racing sausages: they're at Miller Park (☎ 414-902-4000; www .milwaukeebrewers.com; 1 Brewers Way, near S 46th St; tickets $15-50), the spiffy, retractable-roofed stadium where the Milwaukee Brewers play baseball. Only here will you see such a sight – a group of five people in giant sausage

DETOUR: HOLLAND & BEYOND

Holland lies 11 miles north of Saugatuck via US 31. Yes, there's plenty of kitschy tulips, windmills and clogs. But there's also an excellent brewery and an ecohotel hiding in town. They sit a block apart, making it way too easy to raise another Dragon's Milk ale at the New Holland Brewing Company Pub (☎ 616-355-6422; www.newhollandbrew.com; 66 E 8th St, Holland; pints $4-5; ⏱ 11am-midnight Mon-Thu, to 1am Fri & Sat, noon-10pm Sun) before stumbling into your bamboo sheets at the Gold-LEED-certified City Flats Hotel (☎ 616-796-2100; www.cityflatshotel.com; 61 E 7th St, Holland; r $119-219; 🛜).

Outdoor enthusiasts can pitch a tent on the beach at popular Holland State Park (☎ 616-399-9390; 2215 Ottawa Beach Rd; ⏱ closed Nov-Mar). Or kick it up a notch at Grand Haven State Park (☎ 616-847-1309; 1001 Harbor Ave; ⏱ closed Nov-Mar), 22 miles north. It sprawls along the beach and connects via a scenic walkway to the resorty town of Grand Haven. A lighthouse, an active surf scene and a giant musical fountain also make appearances here. Farther north, Muskegon State Park (☎ 231-744-3480; 3560 Memorial Dr; ⏱ year-round) offers 12 miles of trails through rugged, wooded dunes. The town of Muskegon itself is no great shakes, but it is the jumping-off point for the Lake Express ferry (☎ 866-914-1010; www.lake-express.com; one way adult/child $85/45; ⏱ May-Oct, 2.5hr crossing) to Milwaukee. All state park entries require a vehicle permit (per day/year $8/29). Campsites cost $16 to $33.

TRANSPORTATION: MILWAUKEE

Direction 92 miles north

Travel time 1½ to 2 hours

Boat The Lake Express ferry (☎ 866-914-1010; www.lake-express.com; one way adult/child $85/45; ☼ May-Oct) sails from Milwaukee to Muskegon, Michigan, and provides easy access to Michigan's beach-lined coast. The crossing takes 2½ hours. The terminal is a few miles south of downtown.

Bus The drop-off for Megabus (☎ 877-462-6342; www.megabus.com) is at the downtown Amtrak station. The service runs frequently between Chicago and Milwaukee (from $12, two hours). Badger Bus (☎ 414-276-7490; www.badgerbus.com; 635 N James Lovell St) goes to Madison ($19, 1½ hours); its terminal is across the street from Amtrak.

Car Take I-90/94 west from downtown, and follow I-94 when it splits off. The interstate goes all the way into Milwaukee. It's a busy road, and travel times can be horrendous in peak hours. It's also a toll road, costing about $3.

Public transportation The Milwaukee County Transit System (☎ 414-344-6711; www.ridemcts.com) provides efficient local bus service ($2.25). Bus 31 goes to Miller Brewery; bus 90 goes to Miller Park. Catch them along Wisconsin Ave.

Train Perhaps the quickest way to Milwaukee given the snail-crawl pace of highway traffic is via Amtrak (☎ 800-872-7245; www.amtrak.com), which runs the Hiawatha train seven times per day to/from Chicago ($22, 1½ hours). The main station (433 W St Paul Ave) is downtown; there's also one at Milwaukee's airport (MKE; www.mitchellairport.com).

costumes who sprint down the field in the middle of the 6th inning, vying for meat supremacy.

In summertime, festivals unleash revelry by the lake most weekends. Summerfest (www.summerfest.com; day passes $15) is the granddaddy – dubbed 'the world's largest music festival' – and indeed, hundreds of rock, blues, jazz, country and alternative bands swarm its 10 stages over 11 days in late June/early July. There's also PrideFest (www.pridefest.com; mid-Jun), Polish Fest (www.polishfest.org; late Jun), Irish Fest (www.irishfest.com; mid-Aug) and a slew of others.

Good areas to wander for shops, food and drink include N Old World 3rd St downtown; the fashionable East Side by the University of Wisconsin-Milwaukee; hip, Italian-based Brady Street by its intersection with N Farwell Ave; and the gentrified Third Ward, anchored along N Milwaukee St, south of I-94.

INFORMATION

Milwaukee Convention and Visitors Bureau (☎ 800-554-1448; www.visitmilwaukee.org)

EATING & DRINKING

Check the free weekly Shepherd Express (www.expressmilwaukee.com) for additional restaurant and entertainment listings. Many bars and restaurants host a traditional fish fry on Friday.

Milwaukee Public Market (☎ 414-336-1111; 400 N Water St; ☼ 10am-8pm Mon-Fri, 8am-6pm Sat, 10am-6pm Sun) Wine and ethnic food vendors fill this sprawling Third Ward warehouse. Big-name chefs do cooking demos.

Trocadero (☎ 414-272-0205; 1758 N Water St; mains $7-17; ☼ 11am-11pm Mon-Fri, from 9am Sat & Sun) A glorious wine list, cheese plates, crepes, baguettes with jam, mussels and *frites* – we're in Paris, *oui*? Nope, we're near Brady St at Trocadero, a romantic coffee house–restaurant-bar with a year-round patio (it's heated in winter).

Palm Tavern (☎ 414-744-0393; 2989 S Kinnickinnic Ave) Located in the southside neighborhood of Bay View, this warm, jazzy little bar has a mammoth selection of unusual beers and single-malt scotches.

Kopp's (☎ 414-961-2006; 5373 N Port Washington Rd; ☼ 10:30am-11:30pm) It's a popular purveyor of frozen custard (a local specialty like ice cream, only richer and smoother). Located in suburban Glendale, about 15 minutes north.

SLEEPING

Book ahead in summer due to festival crowds.

Comfort Inn & Suites Downtown Lakeshore (☎ 414-276-8800, 800-328-7275; www.choicehotels.com; 916 E State St; r incl breakfast $110-170; ⊠ ⊛) Check in here and you'll be laying low in the same contemporary rooms as the touring indie bands who come to town. Parking costs $10.

County Clare Irish Inn (☎ 414-272-5273, 888-942-5273; www.countyclare-inn.com; 1234 N Astor St; r incl breakfast $139-179; ⚒ ⚟) Rooms have a snug Irish-cottage feel, with four-poster beds, white wainscot walls and whirlpool baths. There's free parking and an on-site Guinness-pouring pub, of course.

Iron Horse Hotel (☎ 888-543-4766; www.theironhorse hotel.com; 500 W Florida St; r $159-239; ⚒ ⚟) Classy, loft-style rooms fill this old factory building. Motorcycle riders get special perks. Parking costs $25.

MADISON

Madison reaps a lot of kudos – most walkable city, best road-biking city, most vegetarian-friendly, ecofriendly, and just plain all-round friendliest city in the USA. Ensconced on a narrow isthmus between Mendota and Monona lakes, it's a pretty combination of small, grassy state capital and liberal, bookish college town. An impressive foodie/locavore scene has been cooking here for years.

The X-shaped Capitol Building (☎ 608-266-0382; admission free; ⚟ 8am-6pm Mon-Fri, to 4pm Sat & Sun), the largest outside Washington, DC, marks the heart of downtown. Tours are available on the hour most days. On Saturday, the Dane County Farmers' Market (www.dcfm .org; ⚟ 6am-2pm late Apr–early Nov) takes over Capitol Sq. It's one of the nation's largest markets, famed for its artisanal cheeses. Arriving on a nonmarket day? Walk around the corner to Fromagination (☎ 608-255-2430; www.fromagination .com; 12 S Carroll St; ⚟ 9:30am-6pm Mon-Fri, 8am-4pm Sat), which specializes in small-batch and hard-to-find local hunks. Be sure to pick up some cheese curds to experience their squeaky bite.

State St runs from the capitol west to the University of Wisconsin. The lengthy avenue is lined with free-trade coffee shops, parked bicycles and incense-wafting stores selling hackeysacks and flowy Indian skirts. State St also holds the impressive Museum of Contemporary Art (☎ 608-257-0158; www.mmoca.org; 227 State St; admission free; ⚟ noon-5pm Tue-Thu, noon-8pm Fri, 10am-8pm Sat, noon-5pm Sun), which hosts works by Frida Kahlo, Claes Oldenburg and others, plus a rooftop sculpture garden, a cinema and a martini lounge.

The campus has its own attractions, including the 1260-acre Arboretum (☎ 608-263-7888; 1207 Seminole Hwy; admission free; ⚟ 7am-10pm), dense with lilac, and the Memorial Union

(☎ 608-265-3000; 800 Langdon St), with its festive outdoor bar and free live music, films and internet access.

It'd be a shame to leave town without taking advantage of the city's lakes and 120 miles of trails. For wheels, head to Budget Bicycle Center (☎ 608-251-8413; 1230 Regent St; bike rental per day $20; ⚟ 9am-9pm Mon-Fri, to 7pm Sat, 10am-7pm Sun), about 1½ miles from Capitol Square, near the university and good trails. For water-faring craft, try Rutabaga Paddlesports (☎ 608-223-9300, 800-472-3353; www.rutabaga.com; 220 W Broadway; canoe/kayak rental per half/full day $25/40; ⚟ 10am-8pm Mon-Fri, to 6pm Sat, 11am-5pm Sun), about 5 miles southeast of Capitol Sq and right on the water.

INFORMATION

Madison Convention and Visitors Bureau (☎ 608-255-2537, 800-373-6376; www.visitmadison.com)

EATING

Graze Gastropub & L'Etoile Restaurant (☎ 608-251-0500; 1 S Pinckney St; pub mains $9-15, restaurant mains $29-42; ⚟ pub lunch Mon-Fri, dinner Mon-Sat, brunch Sat & Sun, restaurant dinner Mon-Sat) Slow-food pioneer Odessa Piper offered farm-to-table dinners at L'Etoile for 30 years. These days, chef Tory Miller does the cooking, with seasonal ingredients sourced at the farmers' market. Graze slings organic sandwiches, burgers and mussels during the day, and the attached bakery wafts pastries.

Himal Chuli (☎ 608-251-9225; 318 State St; mains $8-15; ⚟ 11am-9pm Mon-Sat, noon-8pm Sun) Cheerful, cozy

TRANSPORTATION: MADISON

Direction 150 miles northwest

Travel time Three hours

Bus The Van Galder Bus (☎ 800-747-0994; www .vangalderbus.com) service runs between Chicago (both O'Hare airport and downtown) and Madison's Memorial Union (one way $27, 3¼ hours) several times daily. Badger Bus (☎ 414-276-7490; www .badgerbus.com) goes to Milwaukee (one way $19, 1½ hours) from the Union.

Car Take I 90/94 west out of Chicago; stay on I-90 west when it splits off. Remain on the interstate going west to Rockford, then north. On the outskirts of Madison get onto US 18/12 west for about 6 miles, and then take the Park St exit into downtown. Parts of I-90 require tolls.

Himal Chuli serves homemade Nepalese fare, including vegetarian dishes.

Weary Traveler Free House (☎ 608-442-6207; 1201 Williamson St; mains $7-11; ☷ 4pm-2am Mon, 11:30-2am Tue-Sun) It's global comfort food at this dark-wood pub, including Hungarian goulash and vegan chili. Local brewers Capital and New Glarus provide the accompanying suds.

SLEEPING

Arbor House (☎ 608-238-2981; www.arbor-house.com; 3402 Monroe St; r incl breakfast weekday $110-175, weekend $150-230; ☷) This 1853 tavern is now an eight-room, wind-powered, vegetarian-breakfast-serving B&B. It's located about 3 miles southwest of the capitol, near the Aboretum and accessible to public transportation. The owners hook you up with free mountain bikes, too.

HI Madison Hostel (☎ 608-441-0144; www .madisonhostel.org; 141 S Butler St; dm $22-25, r $49-52; ☐) It's by the capitol. Parking costs $5.

University Inn (☎ 608-285-8040, 800-279-4881; www .universityinn.org; 441 N Frances St; r $89-129; ☷) The rooms are nothing special but the handy location by the State St action is.

GALENA

Wee Galena, Illinois, draws hordes of Chicagoans to its perfectly preserved Civil War–era streets. While it sometimes gets chided as a place for the 'newly wed and the nearly dead' – thanks to all the tourist-oriented B&Bs, fudge and antique shops – there's no denying the little town's beauty. It spreads across wooded hillsides near the Mississippi River, amid rolling, barn-dotted farmland. Redbrick mansions in Greek Revival, Gothic Revival and Queen Anne styles fill the streets, left over from Galena's heyday in the mid-1800s, when local lead mines made it rich. Throw in cool kayak trips, foodie farm tours and back-road drives on an old stagecoach route, and you've got a lovely, slow getaway.

The visitors center (101 Bouthillier St), in the 1857 train depot visible as you enter town from the east, is a good place to start. Get a map, leave your car in the lot ($3 per day) and explore on foot.

Elegant old Main St curves around the hillside and the historic heart of town. Among numerous sights is the Ulysses S Grant Home (☎ 815-777-3310; www.granthome.com; 500 Bouthillier St; adult/child $4/2; ☷ 9am-4:45pm Wed-Sun Apr-Oct, reduced hr Nov-Mar), which was a gift from local Republicans to the victorious general at the Civil War's end. Grant lived here until he became the country's 18th president. The elaborate Italianate Belvedere Mansion (☎ 815-777-0747; 1008 Park Ave; adult/child $12/6; ☷ 11am-4pm Sun-Fri, to 5pm Sat late May-Oct) hangs the green drapes from *Gone With the Wind*.

Outdoors enthusiasts should head to Fever River Outfitters (☎ 815-776-9425; www.feverriver

---

DETOUR: CHEESE & TALIESIN

Wisconsin is cheesy and proud of it – which you may have figured out already. The state pumps out 2.4 billion pounds of cheddar, Gouda and other smelly goodness annually from its cow-speckled farmland. Local license plates read 'The Dairy State' with udder dignity. So embrace the cheese thing. And how better than via a road trip to the USA's largest concentration of cheesemakers, who happen to reside around Monroe, 50 miles south of Madison?

Follow your nose to Roth Käse (☎ 608-328-2122; www.rothkase.com; 657 2nd St; ☷ 9am-6pm Mon-Fri, to 5pm Sat, 10am-5pm Sun), a store and factory where you can watch cheesemakers in action from the observation deck (weekday mornings only). Bite into a fresh limburger-and-raw-onion sandwich at Baumgartner's (☎ 608-325-6157; 1023 16th Ave; sandwiches $4-7; ☷ 8am-11pm), an old Swiss tavern on the town square. At night, catch a flick at the local drive-in movie theater (south of town on Hwy 69), then climb into bed at Inn Serendipity (☎ 608-329-7056; www.innserendipity.com; 7843 County Rd P; r incl breakfast $105-120), a two-room, wind- and solar-powered B&B on a 5-acre organic farm, about 8 miles southwest of Monroe (toward Browntown). For more on local dairy producers and plant tours, pick up the Traveler's Guide to America's Dairyland map (☎ 608-836-8820; www.eatwisconsincheese .com). It's free from area shops and visitors centers (or call ahead to have one sent to you).

Also in the vicinity, 40 miles west of Madison and 3 miles south of Spring Green, Taliesin was the home of native son Frank Lloyd Wright for most of his life, and is the site of his architectural school. It's now a major pilgrimage destination for fans and followers. Wright's house was built in 1903, the Hillside Home School in 1932, and the visitors center (☎ 608-588-7900; www.taliesinpreservation.org; Hwy 23; ☷ 9am-5:30pm May-Oct) in 1953. A wide range of guided tours ($16 to $80) cover various parts of the complex; reservations are a good idea for the lengthier ones. The one-hour Hillside Tour ($16) provides a nice introduction to Wright's work. For additional Wright sights, see Oak Park (p248).

outfitters.com; 525 S Main St; ☺ 10am-5pm, closed Tue-Thu early Sep-late May), which rents canoes, kayaks, bicycles and snowshoes. It also offers guided tours, such as two-hour kayak trips ($45 per person, equipment included) on the Mississippi River.

On weekend evenings, set out on the hokey but fun Annie Wiggins Ghost Tour (☎ 815-777-0336; www.anniewiggins.com; 1004 Park Ave; 1hr tour $10.75; ☺ Fri & Sat evenings May-Oct). Or visit local bison ranches, artisanal cheesemakers and herb farms on a culinary tour with Learn Great Foods (☎ 866-240-1650; www.learngreatfoods.com; tours $50-105). Excursions vary; check online for the schedule and locations.

For a pretty drive, pick up the Stagecoach Trail downtown. It morphs from Field St (aka County Rd 3) and rolls for 26 narrow, twisty miles northeast to Warren. And yes, it really was part of the old stagecoach route between Galena and Chicago.

INFORMATION

Galena Visitors Center (☎ 815-777-4390, 877-464-2536; www.galena.org; 101 Bouthillier St; ☺ 9am-5pm)

EATING

111 Main (☎ 815-777-8030; 111 N Main St; mains $13-24; ☺ 11am-9pm Sun-Thu, to 10pm Fri & Sat) Meatloaf, pork and beans and other Midwestern favorites arrive at the table, using ingredients sourced from local farms.

Victory Cafe (☎ 815-777-4407; 200 N Main St; mains $4-8; ☺ 6am-2pm) It serves biscuit-and-gravy breakfasts and lunchtime sandwiches.

SLEEPING

Galena brims with B&Bs – you can't throw a quilt without it landing on a four-poster bed at one of the zillion properties in town. Most B&Bs cost $100 to $200 nightly, and they fill up on weekends. The visitors center website provides contact information.

Ryan Mansion B&B (☎ 815-777-2750; www.ryanmansiongalena.com; 11373 US 20; r incl breakfast $95-205; ☒ ☺) Parlors, marble fireplaces and a library of historic tomes stuff this Victorian country estate 2 miles northwest of town.

DeSoto House Hotel (☎ 815-777-0090; www.desotohouse.com; 230 S Main St; r $128-200; ☒ ☺) Grant and Lincoln stayed in the well-furnished rooms here, and you can too. The hotel dates from 1855.

Grant Hills Motel (☎ 877-421-0924; www.granthills.com; 9372 US 20; r $69-79; ☒ ☒) It's a no-frills option 1.5 miles east of town, with countryside views, an outdoor pool and a horseshoe pitch.

ROUTE 66 TO SPRINGFIELD

The classic highway from Chicago to Los Angeles once cut diagonally across Illinois to St Louis and beyond. Though now superseded by I-55, the old route – affectionately called Main St, USA – still exists in scattered sections, carrying road-trippers through time-warped small towns. Prepare for an onslaught of drive-in movies and burger joints, oddball attractions, corn dogs and pie.

The road kicks off in downtown Chicago on Adams St just west of Michigan Ave. Keep an eye out for brown 'Historic Route 66' signs, which pop up at crucial junctions to mark the way. Our first stop rises from the cornfields 60 miles south in Wilmington. Here the Gemini Giant – a 28ft fiberglass spaceman – stands guard outside the Launching Pad Drive In (☎ 815-476-6535; 810 E Baltimore St; burgers $2-6; ☺ 10am-9:30pm). To reach it, exit I-55 at Joliet Rd, and follow it south as it becomes Hwy 53 into town.

Motor 45 miles onward to Pontiac and the tchotchke- and photo-filled Route 66 Hall of Fame (☎ 815-844-4566; 110 W Howard St, Pontiac; admission free; ☽ 11am-3pm Mon-Fri, 10am-4pm Sat). Cruise another 50 miles to Shirley and Funk's Grove (☎ 309-874-3360; www.funksmaplesirup.com; 5257 Old Route 66), a pretty 19th-century maple-syrup farm and nature preserve. Call for seasonal hours.

Ten miles later you'll reach the throwback hamlet of Atlanta. Pull up a chair at the Palms Grill Cafe (☎ 217-648-2233; 110 SW Arch St, Atlanta; mains $4-9; ☽ 8am-5pm Sun-Thu, to 8pm Fri & Sat), where thick slabs of gooseberry, sour cream raisin

and other retro pies tempt from the glass case. Then walk across the street to snap a photo with Tall Paul, a sky-high statue of Paul Bunyan clutching a hot dog. Old-time murals color the walls of local buildings, and there's a museum in the little grain elevator that explains how corn was stored years ago.

The small state capital of Springfield, 50 miles further on, harbors a trio of Route 66 sights. All must stop to hail the corn dog's birthplace at the Cozy Dog Drive In (☎ 217-525-1992; 2935 S 6th St, Springfield; items $2-4; ☽ 8am-8pm Mon-Sat). It's a Route 66 legend, with memorabilia and

DETOUR: MIDWESTERN METRO GETAWAYS

Minneapolis, Detroit and Cleveland aren't far from Chicago. They range from five to nine hours away by car, and little more than an hour by air if you cop a cheap flight (check Southwest or Delta Airlines; the latter has hubs in Minneapolis and Detroit). Amtrak and Megabus also run to all three cities. Pick up a copy of Lonely Planet's USA for more in-depth explorations.

Detroit

Ah, the Motor City. Once the pride of the nation for its car savvy (GM, Ford and Chrysler all launched here), the city fell to pieces when the auto industry tanked. Today, once-grand buildings lie boarded up with trash blowing about their bases, and wide swaths of downtown are downright vacant. While this contributes to a sort of bombed-out, apocalyptic vibe, it's these same qualities that fuel a raw urban energy you won't find anywhere else.

The city sports a trio of top-tier attractions. Spend a day wandering through the Henry Ford Museum/Greenfield Village Complex (☎ 313-982-6001; www.thehenryford.org; 20900 Oakwood Blvd; adult/child 5-12yr $32/24; ☽ 9:30am-5pm, Ford open year-round, Greenfield Village closed in winter) in suburban Dearborn. The two museums contain a fascinating wealth of American culture such as the chair Lincoln was sitting in when he was assassinated, Edgar Allan Poe's writing desk, the bus on which Rosa Parks refused to give up her seat and, of course, vintage cars. Parking is $5. The Motown Historical Museum (☎ 313-875-2264; www.motownmuseum.com; 2648 W Grand Blvd; adult/child $10/8; ☽ 10am-6pm Tue-Sat, plus Mon Jul & Aug) is a string of unassuming houses that became known as 'Hitsville USA' after Berry Gordy began Motown Records – and the careers of Stevie Wonder, Marvin Gaye et al – with an $800 loan in 1959. Diego Rivera's mural Detroit Industry fills a room at the renowned Detroit Institute of Arts (☎ 313-833-7900; www.dia.org; 5200 Woodward Ave; adult/child 6-17yr $8/4; ☽ 10am-4pm Wed & Thu, to 10pm Fri, to 5pm Sat & Sun).

Detroit may be Motown, but in recent years it's been rap, techno and hard-edged rock that have pushed the city to the forefront of the music scene; homegrown stars include the White Stripes and the Von Bondies. St Andrew's Hall (☎ 313-961-6358; 431 E Congress St) and Magic Stick (☎ 313-833-9700; www.majesticdetroit.com; 4120 Woodward Ave) are where the coolest bands plug in their amps.

If you fancy something mellower than a live show but still want that grungy rocker ambience, head to The Bronx (☎ 313-832-8464; 4476 2nd Ave; mains $4-8; ☽ 11:30am-2am), where the Stripes used to hang. There's not much inside the dimly lit dive bar besides a pool table and couple of juke boxes filled with ballsy rock and soul. But that's the way the neighborhood regulars and local musicians like it. They're also fond of the beefy burgers fried up late at night.

The Inn on Ferry Street (☎ 313-871-6000; www.innonferrystreet.com; 84 E Ferry St; r incl breakfast from $149) harbors 40 guest rooms in a row of Victorian mansions right by the art museum. Free wi-fi, a hot breakfast and a shuttle to downtown are included.

Cleveland

Does it or does it not rock? You'll have to visit to decide.

Certainly Cleveland's top attraction is the Rock & Roll Hall of Fame & Museum (☎ 216-781-7625, 888-764-7625; www.rockhall.com; 1 Key Plaza; adult/child 9-12yr $22/13; ☽ 10am-5:30pm, to 9pm Wed year-round, to 9pm Sat Jun-Aug). It's more than a collection of rock-star memorabilia, though it does have Jimi Hendrix's Stratocaster and Ray Charles' sunglasses. Interactive multimedia exhibits trace the history and social context of rock music and the

souvenirs in addition to the deeply fried main course. Shea's Gas Station Museum (☎ 217-522-0475; 2075 Peoria Rd, Springfield; admission $2; ☽ 8am-4pm Tue-Fri, to noon Sat) lets visitors fill up with Route 66 pumps and signs. And there's nothing better on a warm summer evening than catching a flick under the stars at the Route 66 Drive In (☎ 217-698-0066; www.route66-drivein.com; Recreation Dr, Springfield; adult/child 4-12yr $6/4; ☽ nightly Jun-Aug, weekends mid-Apr–May & Sep).

Springfield also has a certifiable obsession with local hero Abraham Lincoln, who practiced law here from 1837 to 1861. Many of the attractions are walkable downtown and cost little to nothing.

To visit the top-draw Lincoln Home, you must first pick up a ticket at the Lincoln Home Visitors Center (☎ 217-492-4150; www.nps.gov/liho; 426 S 7th St, Springfield; admission free; ☽ 8:30am-5pm). A tour guide will then take you through the house where Abraham and Mary Lincoln lived from 1844 until they moved to the White House in 1861. You'll see considerably more than just the home, as the whole block has been preserved.

The Lincoln Presidential Library & Museum (☎ 217-558-8844; www.alplm.org; 212 N 6th St, Springfield; adult/

performers who created it. Why is the museum in Cleveland? Because this is the hometown of Alan Freed, the disc jockey who popularized the term 'rock 'n' roll' in the early 1950s, and because the city lobbied hard and paid big. Be prepared for crowds.

Cultural attractions cluster at University Circle (the area around Case Western Reserve University, Cleveland Clinic and other institutions), 5 miles east of downtown, including the excellent Cleveland Museum of Art (☎ 216-421-7340; www.clevelandart.org; 11150 East Blvd; admission free; ☽ 10am-5pm Tue-Sun, to 9pm Wed & Fri). Busy Little Italy is along Mayfield Rd, near University Circle (look for the Rte 322 sign).

For stylish eating and drinking, head to the Ohio City and Tremont neighborhoods, which straddle I-90 south of downtown. Food Channel celebrity chef (and local boy) Michael Symon serves Iowa prosciutto, mussels and Neapolitan-style pizzas with cold craft beer at his bistro Lolita (☎ 216-771-5652; 900 Literary Rd; mains $9-17; ☽ 5-11pm Tue-Thu, to 1am Fri & Sat, 4-9pm Sun). The nearby West Side Market (www.westsidemarket.org; cnr W 25th St & Lorain Ave; ☽ 7am-4pm Mon & Wed, to 6pm Fri & Sat) overflows with fresh produce and prepared foods that are handy for picnicking or road-tripping. Great Lakes Brewing Company (☎ 216-771-4404; 2516 Market Ave; ☽ closed Sun) wins prizes for its brewed-on-the-premises beers. Added historical bonus: Eliot Ness got into a shootout with criminals here; ask the bartender to show you the bullet holes.

For accommodation try the Hilton Garden Inn (☎ 216-658-6400, 877-782-9444; www.hiltongardeninn.com; 1100 Carnegie Ave; r $110-169) downtown by the baseball park. Rooms have comfy beds and wi-fi-rigged work stations, and there's a pool.

Minneapolis

Minneapolis is the artiest town on the prairie, with all the trimmings of progressive prosperity – swank art museums, rowdy rock clubs, organic and ethnic eateries, and enough theaters to be nicknamed Mini-Apple (second only to the Big Apple, New York City). It's always happenin', even in winter.

Top attractions include the Walker Art Center (☎ 612-375-7622; www.walkerart.org; 725 Vineland Pl; adult/child 13-18yr $10/6, admission free Thu evening; ☽ 11am-5pm Tue-Sun, to 9pm Thu), with big-name US painters and great US pop art, and the whimsical Sculpture Garden (admission free; ☽ 6am-midnight) next door. Walk the 2-mile trail by St Anthony Falls (on the north edge of downtown at the foot of Portland Ave), the power source of the timber and flour mills that gave rise to this Mississippi River city. Within a mile or two of downtown, a ring of lakes circles the inner-city area. Cedar Lake, Lake of the Isles, Lake Calhoun and Lake Harriet are all surrounded by parks and paths.

Browse for eats in the punk-yuppie Uptown neighborhood. A workingman's bowling alley meets epicurean food at the Bryant-Lake Bowl (☎ 612-825-3737; 810 W Lake St; sandwiches $7-9, mains $11-16; ☽ 8-12:30am). Artisanal cheese plates, mock-duck rolls, cornmeal-crusted walleye strips and organic oatmeal melt in the mouth, complemented by a wide-ranging beer selection (including several local brews). The on-site theater always has something intriguing and odd going on.

Acts such as Prince and post-punk bands like Hüsker Dü and the Replacements cut their chops in Minneapolis. First Avenue & 7th St Entry (☎ 612-338-8388; www.first-avenue.com; 701 1st Ave N) is the bedrock of the city's music scene, and it still pulls in top bands and big crowds. Triple Rock Social Club (☎ 612-333-7499; www .triplerocksocialclub.com; 629 Cedar Ave) is a popular punk-alternative club.

Cheery, 10-bedroom Wales House (☎ 612-331-3931; www.waleshouse.com; 1115 5th St SE; r with/without bathroom from $75/65) caters to scholars at the nearby University of Minnesota, and is a fine place to lay your head. Two-night minimum stay required.

child 5-15yr $10/4; ☺ 9am-5pm) contains the most complete Lincoln collection in the world. Real-deal artifacts like Abe's shaving mirror and briefcase join whiz-bang exhibits and Disney-esque holograms that keep the kids agog.

After Lincoln's assassination, his body was returned to Springfield, where it lies today. The impressive Lincoln's Tomb sits in Oak Ridge Cemetery (☎ 217-782-2717; 1441 Monument Ave; admission free; ☺ 9am-5pm Mar-Oct, to 4pm Nov-Feb), north of downtown. The gleam on the nose of Lincoln's bust, created by visitors' light touches, indicates the numbers of those who pay their respects here.

INFORMATION

Illinois Route 66 Scenic Byway (☎ 866-378-7866; www .illinoisroute66.org) Provides hard-copy and downloadable maps and resources.

Route 66 Association of Illinois (www.il66assoc.org) Information on route sights and events.

Springfield Visitors Center (☎ 800-545-7300; www .visitspringfieldillinois.com; 109 N 7th St, Springfield; ☺ 8:30am-5pm Mon-Fri) Produces a good visitors guide booklet.

SLEEPING

The following options are in Springfield.

Statehouse Inn (☎ 217-528-5100; www.the statehouseinn.com; 101 E Adams St, Springfield; r incl breakfast $95-145; ⊠ �) It looks concrete-drab outside, but inside the Statehouse shows its style. Comfy beds and large baths fill the rooms; a mod bar fills the lobby.

Inn at 835 (☎ 217-523-4466; www.innat835.com; 835 S 2nd St, Springfield; r incl breakfast $125-175; ⊠) This 10-room B&B in a historic home offers the classiest digs in town.

TRANSPORTATION

Flights, tours and rail tickets can be booked online at www.lonelyplanet.com/travel _services.

AIR

O'Hare International Airport is the nation's second-busiest airport, transporting about 65 million passengers a year. It's a hub for United Airlines (headquartered here) and American Airlines, but scads more domestic and international carriers use the airport too. Direct flights depart for London, Sydney, Tokyo… Smaller Midway Airport is used mostly by Southwest and other domestic carriers. Between the two airports you'll likely find a way here from there – wherever that is.

Foul weather can cause delays getting in to and out of Chicago, especially from November through February. O'Hare is more prone than Midway to make you wait. Call ahead and check your flight, but still head out to the airport. If the weather clears and the plane can leave earlier, it will. If you miss it, that's your responsibility. Non-weather-related delays have plagued O'Hare in recent years. Runway expansion is in the works.

If you have an early flight, you might consider avoiding traffic and spending a night near the airport. See Airport Accommodations (p243) for more info.

Airlines

Airlines flying in to and out of Chicago include:

Air Canada (☎ 888-247-2262; www.aircanada.com)

Air France (☎ 800-237-2747; www.airfrance.us)

American Airlines (☎ 800-433-7300; www.aa.com)

British Airways (☎ 800-247-9297; www.britishairways .com)

Continental Airlines (☎ 800-523-3273; www .continental.com)

Delta Airlines (☎ 800-221-1212; www.delta.com)

Frontier Airlines (☎ 800-432-1359; www.frontier airlines.com)

Japan Airlines (☎ 800-525-3663; www.jal.com)

JetBlue (☎ 800-538-2583; www.jetblue.com)

KLM Royal Dutch Airlines (☎ 800-447-4747; www .klm.com)

Lufthansa (☎ 800-645-3880; www.lufthansa.com)

Porter Airlines (☎ 888-619-8622; www.flyporter.com)

Southwest Airlines (☎ 800-435-9792; www.southwest .com)

Spirit Airlines (☎ 800-772-7117; www.spiritair.com)

CLIMATE CHANGE & TRAVEL

Climate change is a serious threat to the ecosystems that humans rely upon, and air travel is the fastest-growing contributor to the problem. Lonely Planet regards travel, overall, as a global benefit, but believes we all have a responsibility to limit our personal impact on global warming.

Flying & Climate Change

Pretty much every form of motor transport generates carbon dioxide (the main cause of human-induced climate change) but planes are far and away the worst offenders, not just because of the sheer distances they allow us to travel, but because they release greenhouse gases high into the atmosphere. The statistics are frightening: two people taking a return flight between Europe and the US will contribute as much to climate change as an average household's gas and electricity consumption over a whole year.

Carbon Offset Schemes

Climatecare.org and other websites use 'carbon calculators' that allow travellers to offset the greenhouse gases they are responsible for with contributions to energy-saving projects and other climate-friendly initiatives in the developing world – including projects in India, Honduras, Kazakhstan and Uganda.

Lonely Planet, together with Rough Guides and other concerned partners in the travel industry, supports the carbon offset scheme run by climatecare.org. Lonely Planet offsets all of its staff and author travel.

For more information check out our website: www.lonelyplanet.com.

THINGS CHANGE...

The information in this chapter is particularly vulnerable to change. Check directly with the airline or a travel agent to make sure you understand how a fare (and ticket you may buy) works and be aware of the security requirements for international travel. Shop carefully. The details given in this chapter should be regarded as pointers and are not a substitute for your own careful, up-to-date research.

United Airlines (☎ 800-241-6522; www.united.com)

US Airways (☎ 800-428-4322; www.usairways.com)

Virgin Atlantic (☎ 800-821-5438; www.virgin-atlantic .com)

In addition to the airline companies' own websites, some of which may have internet-only deals, a number of third-party sites can be helpful in finding flight discounts:

www.airfarewatchdog.com

www.expedia.com

www.hotwire.com

www.orbitz.com

www.priceline.com

www.smartertravel.com

www.travelocity.com

www.travelzoo.com

http://us.lastminute.com/

Airports

In conjunction with Mayor Daley's focus on making Chicago greener and cleaner, both airports have increased the number of recycling bins around the terminals. Posters and info-center pamphlets educate visitors about ways to save energy while traveling.

O'HARE

The larger of the two airports, O'Hare International (ORD; Map pp50-1; ☎ 800-832-6352; www.ohare.com) is 17 miles northwest of the city. The four operational terminals (1, 2, 3 and 5) bustle day and night. Travel through the glass-and-steel Terminal 1 building, designed by architect Helmut Jahn, to Terminal 2 and you'll experience a psychedelic neon and colored glass moving sidewalk.

ATMs and phones (including TTY phones) are available in every terminal. The airport has wireless internet access throughout ($6.95 per day). The bus-shuttle center is in the ground level of the central parking garage. Follow signs to get there from Terminals 1, 2 and 3. Terminal 5, the international terminal, has its own pickup area.

Airport services:

Airport information desks Terminals 1, 3 and 5.

Back Rub Hub (☒ 9am-9pm) Upper level, Terminal 3.

Children's Museum Exhibit Upper level, Terminal 2.

Currency exchange (☎ 773-462-9973) All terminals.

Police kiosk/lost and found Upper levels of all terminals.

Post office (☒ 9am-5pm Mon-Fri) Upper level, Terminal 2.

Travelers & Immigrants Aid Office (☎ 773-894-2427; ☒ 8:30am-9pm Mon-Fri, from 10am Sat & Sun) Upper level of Terminal 2. Provides information, directions and special assistance.

UIC Medical Center (☎ 773-894-5100) Upper level, Terminal 2.

Visitor Information (☒ 9am-5pm) Lower level, all terminals. Brochures available 24/7.

MIDWAY

Fast-growing, but still a manageable size, Midway Airport (MDW; Map pp50-1; ☎ 773-838-0600; www .flychicago.com) was redeveloped in the early 2000s and still has that shiny-new-airport smell. No matter which of the three concourses (A, B, C) you depart from, you enter and exit through the New Terminal, home to almost all of the airport's services and amenities. ATMs and pay phones (some TTY capable) are found throughout. Wireless internet access is available for $6.95 per day.

Airport police and Travelers Aid are located in the New Terminal building. Additionally, there are two visitor information brochure kiosks; the first is in the lower-level baggage-claim area, and the other is on the top floor, in the center of the restaurant and shopping boulevard.

BICYCLE

Riding along the 18.5-mile long Lakefront Bike Path is a great way to see the city. Though there are 120 miles of bike lanes around town, traffic can be less than respectful, making street peddling a bit more of a challenge. Request a free bike map from the city's Department of Transportation (www.chicagobikes.org).

Bikes are allowed on all CTA trains, save for during high-use commuter hours (7am to 9am and 4pm to 6pm Monday to Friday).

GETTING INTO TOWN

Chicago Transit Authority (CTA) train service is available from both airports, but it's a bit of a hike. So if you're lugging a load, shared shuttle van service is the way to go. Airport Express (☎ 888-284-3826; www.airportexpress.com) has a monopoly on services between the airports and downtown lodgings. Once in the center, you may have to ride around while others are dropped off before you. You may also have to wait until the van is full before you leave the airport. From O'Hare the fare is $29 per person ($20 a piece for two). Midway to the Loop costs $24 per person. For shuttle rides between Midway and O'Hare airports, use the Omega Shuttle (☎ 773-734-6688; www.omegashuttle .com; per person $25).

Van Galder/Coach USA (☎ 800-747-0994; www.coachusa.com/vangalder) buses serve southern Wisconsin, suburban Illinois and northwest Indiana from O'Hare and Midway airports.

O'Hare

The CTA offers 24-hour train service on the Blue Line to and from the Loop (about 45 minutes, $2.25). Unfortunately, the O'Hare station is buried under the world's largest parking garage. Finding it can be akin to navigating a maze — directional signs are variously marked as 'CTA,' 'Rapid Transit' and 'Trains to City.' Unless you are staying right in the Loop, you will likely have to transfer to complete your journey. A good alternative is to ride the El as close as you can get to your hotel and then take a taxi for the final few blocks.

Each terminal has one taxi stand outside the baggage-claim area; you may have to line up. The fare to Near North and the Loop runs about $45, including a 10% to 15% tip. Note that traffic affects the fare: meters keep running even when the car is at a standstill. During rush hours, the train can be quicker than a taxi.

If you've rented a car, take I-190 east from the airport to I-90 east into the Loop.

Midway

You can take the CTA Orange Line from Midway to the Loop (about 30 minutes, $2.25). To reach the CTA station, follow the signs from the lower-level baggage claim. You have to walk a ways through a not-very-climate-controlled parking garage to get there.

Follow the signs to 'ground transportation' to catch a taxi. Costs are based on the meter (there are no flat-rate rides), and will likely run about $30 to $40 including tip into the Loop.

If you've rented a car at the airport, take S Cicero Ave north to I-55N east into town.

Many CTA buses are equipped with a bike rack on the front, which accommodates two bikes at a time.

Rental

Bike Chicago (www.bikechicago.com) and Bobby's Bike Hike (www.bobbysbikehike.com) rent wheels for $10 an hour or $35 per day (helmets and locks included). Reserve online and you'll save money. Child seats and tandem bikes are available, as are guided tours (see p272).

Rental locations abound. Here are some of the most convenient:

Bike Chicago Millennium Park (Map pp54-5; 239 E Randolph St; ☉ 6:30am-8pm Mon-Fri & 8am-8pm Sat & Sun Jun-Aug, 6:30am-7pm Mon-Fri & 9am-7pm Sat & Sun Apr-May & Sep-Oct; 6:30am-6:30pm Mon-Fri, closed Sat & Sun Nov-Mar; Ⓜ Brown, Green, Orange, Purple, Pink Line to Randolph) The associated McDonald's Cycle Center has bike parking, lockers and showers for members ($20 per month).

Bike Chicago Navy Pier (Map pp66-7; 600 E Grand Ave; ☉ 8am-10pm Jun-Aug, 9am-7pm Apr-May & Sep-Oct, closed Nov-Mar; 🚌 66)

Bike Chicago North Ave Beach (Map pp78-9; 1603 N Lakeshore Dr; ☉ 8am-8pm Jun-Aug, 9am-7pm May & Sep, closed Oct-Apr; 🚌 151)

Bobby's Bike Hike (Map pp66-7; Ogden Slip at River East Docks, 465 N McClurg Court; ☉ 8:30am-7pm Jun-Aug, reduced hr Mar-May & Sep-No, closed Dec-Feb; Ⓜ Red Line to Grand)

Another option is the bike-sharing program B-cycle (☎ 773-672-2000; www.bcycle.com; ☉ May-Oct). Self-serve kiosks at the Museum Campus, the Hancock Center, the Buckingham Foundation and various other downtown locations rent cruiser-style bikes for $10 for the first hour and $2.50 each hour thereafter. You can drop off at any kiosk. Locks are included, helmets are not.

BOAT

Taking a Shoreline Sightseeing Water Taxi (Map pp66-7; ☎ 312-222-9328; www.shorelinesightseeing.com; ☉ 10am-6pm) is an interesting alternative to walking or busing between major sights. The Lake Taxi transports you from Navy Pier (at the southwestern corner) to the South Loop's Shedd Aquarium (one way adult/child $7/4). The River Taxi connects Ogden Slip/ Gateway Park (just west of Navy Pier) to Willis Tower/Union Station (via the Adams St bridge's southeast side) for the same price. The Commuter Taxi glides from the Michigan Ave bridge (northeast side, near the Tribune Tower) to Willis Tower/Union Station (one way adult/child $4/2).

The Chicago Water Taxi (Map pp66-7; ☎ 312-337-1446; www.chicagowatertaxi.com; ⏱ 6:30am-7pm) is another service, aimed primarily at commuters. It plies the river from the Michigan Ave bridge (northwest side, by the Wrigley Building) to Madison St (near the Metra Ogilvie Transportation Center), stopping at LaSalle/ Clark en route. On summer weekends it continues on to Chinatown. A one-way ride is $2; an all-day pass is $4 ($6, including Chinatown, on weekends).

BUS

Long-distance bus carrier Greyhound (Map pp104-5; ☎ 312-408-5800, 800-231-2222; www.greyhound.com; 630 W Harrison St; Ⓜ Blue Line to Clinton) sends dozens of buses in every direction every day, stopping along the way to pick up people traveling from small towns. Prices are least if you purchase with 21 days' advance notice. Sample one-way fares and times include: Detroit ($27 to $41, seven hours), Minneapolis ($36 to $63, nine hours) and New York City ($84 to $118, 20 hours). The station's ticketing windows are open 24 hours.

Upstart Megabus (Map pp54-5; ☎ 877-462-6342; www.megabus.com/us) provides an alternative for major Midwestern cities. Booked ahead, a one-way seat to Detroit (5½ hours) or Cleveland (seven hours) costs only $8, and service runs much more efficiently than the big dog (though less often). Megabus has no terminals – drop-off and pickup are streetside, and all purchases must be made online in advance (you cannot buy a ticket from the driver). In Chicago, Megabus departs near Union Station, on Canal St (east side) between Jackson Blvd and Van Buren St. Most vehicles are equipped with free wi-fi.

Pace (www.pacebus.com) buses connect to outlying suburbs.

CAR & MOTORCYCLE

Driving in Chicago is no fun. Traffic snarls not only at rush hours, but also just about every hour in between. Especially for short trips in town, use public transportation to spare yourself the headache.

Parking

Parking is another good reason to leave the car behind. Garages cost about $29 per day, but will save you time and traffic tickets. Meter spots and on-street parking are plentiful in outlying areas, but the Loop, Near North, Lincoln Park and Lake View neighborhoods can require up to an hour of circling before you find a spot. Valet parking, even at $12, can be worth it in these congested neighborhoods. Some meter-free neighborhoods require resident parking passes, some don't. Read signs carefully. Most importantly: never park in a spot or a red-curbed area marked 'Tow-Away.' Your car will be towed. Period. Tow-truck drivers in Chicago circle like vultures; fees start at $150, plus the cost of the cab ride to retrieve your car.

Note that 'meter' is a bit of a misnomer – you actually feed coins or a credit card into a pay box that serves the entire block. Decide how much time you want, then the box spits out a receipt to display on the car's dashboard. Per-hour costs range from $1.25 in outlying areas to $4.25 in the Loop, and they'll likely be higher by the time you're reading this. In many areas, you do not have to pay between 9pm and 8am. Check the pay box's instructions.

Rental

Just about every big-name rental chain you can think of has outlets at both O'Hare and Midway airports, in addition to offices in town. If your taste runs to the more exotic and expensive, you might rent a Porsche Boxter or a Harley-Davidson motorcycle from specialist firms.

You'll need a credit card to rent, and many agencies only do business with those 25 and older. Expect to pay $40 to $60 per day (including tax) for a compact car, with rates going down somewhat if you rent for an entire week. Prices are also lower on weekends, sometimes dramatically so. Booking online has become commonplace (and firms may offer internet-only, no-cancellation rates), but if it's last minute, calling might get you a better deal. At Hotwire (www.hotwire .com) and Priceline (www.priceline.com) you can bid for lower rates. They guarantee the type of car, but they don't tell you the name of the rental agency (all well-known brands) until you've paid. You can't make any changes after you've committed, but we've seen rates from $15 to $25 per day accepted.

Most agencies' cars come with unlimited mileage; if they don't, ask about it – the per-mile costs can add up quickly. Also, be aware of redundant liability and medical insurance coverage. Many credit cards have built-in liability coverage on car rentals, so check with yours before you agree to add supplemental insurance to your rental bill.

If you need a car only infrequently during a longer stay in Chicago, you might consider using Zipcar (☎ 866-494-7227; www.zipcar.com). You have to join ($50 annual fee, plus $25 one-time application fee) and pick up your ID card, but after that, all you have to do is call to reserve one of the cars parked in various locations around the city (business parking lots, residential areas). You'll be given the key access code and you return the car to the same parking spot at the agreed-upon time (from $8 an hour). Cars are usually fuel-efficient models. Gas and insurance included.

Rental agencies:

Ace Rent a Car (☎ 800-323-3221; www.acerentacar .com) Off-airport independent by O'Hare, with lower than average rates. Call for airport shuttle (10 minutes to site).

Alamo (☎ 800-462-5266; www.alamo.com)

Avis (☎ 800-331-1212; www.avis.com)

Budget (☎ 800-527-0700; www.budget.com)

Chicago Exotic Car Rental (☎ 312-204-7227; www .chicagoexoticrentals.com) Ferraris, Porsches and Lamborghinis go for anywhere from $250 to $2000 per day.

Dollar (☎ 800-800-4000; www.dollar.com)

Eaglerider Harley-Davidson (☎ 773-767-7280, 888-736-8660; www.eaglerider.com) Motorcycle rentals start at $140 per day; the shop is near Midway Airport.

Enterprise (☎ 800-867-4595; www.enterprise.com)

Hertz (☎ 800-654-3131; www.hertz.com)

National (☎ 800-227-7368; www.nationalcar.com)

Thrifty (☎ 800-527-7075; www.thrifty.com)

PUBLIC TRANSPORTATION

The **Chicago Transit Authority** (CTA; ☎ 312-836-7000; www.transitchicago.com) operates the city's buses and the elevated/subway train system (aka the El). The train network consists of eight color-coded lines. Two of them – the Blue Line from O'Hare airport to the Loop, and the Red Line from Howard to 95th/Dan Ryan

– operate 24 hours a day. The other lines run from about 5am to midnight daily, every five to 15 minutes. Buses follow major arterial roads, and most operate from early morning until late evening. CTA Bustracker (www.ctabustracker .com) is a handy, GPS-facilitated service that lets you check real-time progress of your bus and when it will arrive to pick you up (thus reducing lengthy waits outdoors in freezing weather). Between the buses and the trains, you can explore the furthest reaches of the city. Pick up useful, free system maps at any CTA station, or plan your trip on its website.

CTA is striving to reduce its carbon footprint. So far, it has put 170 diesel-electric buses into service, with more to come (900 hybrids were supposed to be in service already, but funding issues have slowed down the switchover).

Fares

CTA buses cost $2 and the El costs $2.25 per ride; transfers cost 25¢. The plastic card tickets, aka Transit Cards, have magnetized strips that allow you to add as much credit as you'd like. Fares (and transfers) are deducted automatically when you enter the El system or board the bus. Transit Cards are sold from vending machines at all train stations. On buses, you're also allowed to pay with cash (though it requires exact change only, and the price goes up to $2.25).

The best bet for travelers is to buy a Visitor Pass for one day ($5.75), three days ($14) or seven days ($23), which allows unlimited rides. These are available from vending machines at both O'Hare and Midway airport El stations, the Red Line's Chicago station, Union Station, both visitor centers (p275), and at some hotels, hostels and currency exchanges. The CTA website has a full list. You can also buy the passes online (with no shipping fees), and they'll arrive at your residence within 10 days.

Fares are slated to increase in 2012.

TAXI

Taxis are plentiful in the Loop, north to Andersonville and west in Wicker Park. Simply stand on the curb and raise your arm to hail one. In other parts of the city, you can either call a cab or face what may be a long wait for one to happen along. Fares start at $2.25 when you get into the cab, $1.80 for each additional mile and about 40¢ per minute;

the first additional passenger is $1, any extra passengers after that are 50¢ apiece. Drivers expect a 10% to 15% tip. All major companies accept credit cards. To report a taxi incident, take down the driver's name and cab number, and call the Department of Customer Services Complaint Hotline (☎ 311).

Reliable companies:

American-United Taxi (☎ 773-248-7600)

Flash Cab (☎ 773-561-1444; www.flashcab.com)

Yellow Cab (☎ 312-829-4222; www.yellowcabchicago .com)

TRAIN
Amtrak

Chicago's Union Station (Map pp54-5; 225 S Canal St) is the hub for Amtrak (☎ 800-872-7245; www.amtrak .com), and it has more connections than any other US city. Trains chug toward faraway cities like San Francisco ($182 to $227, 53 hours) and New York ($84 to $137, 20½ hours). They also connect to closer Midwestern cities such as Milwaukee ($22, 1½ hours) and Detroit ($29 to $41, 5½ hours). Booking several weeks in advance will usually save you money. Amtrak typically is faster than traveling by Greyhound, and runs pretty much neck-in-neck with Megabus, though it's much more comfortable than both.

Metra

A web of 11 commuter trains running under the Metra (☎ 312-322-6777; www.metrarail .com) banner serves 245 stations in the suburbs surrounding Chicago. Some of the Metra lines run frequent schedules seven days a week; others operate only during weekday rush hours. The four end-of-the-line Metra stations in Chicago are Ogilvie Transportation Center, Union Station, La-Salle St Station and Millennium Station. Each station has schedules available for all the lines, as well as other information. Short trips start at $2.25; buy tickets from agents and machines at major stations.

BUSINESS HOURS

Normal business hours:

Banks & most businesses 9am to 5pm Monday to Friday

Bars & pubs 11am to 2am, some bars until 4am or 5am

Nightclubs 9pm to 2am, some clubs until 4am or 5am

Restaurants 11am to 10pm

Shops 11am to 7pm Monday to Saturday, noon to 6pm Sunday

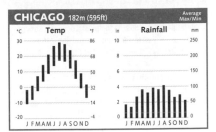

CHILDREN

From the dinosaurs at the Field Museum to the carousel on Navy Pier, to a bike ride along the lakefront and a beach swim, Chicago will endlessly entertain children. Most museums have special areas to amuse and educate wee ones. See the boxed text on p68 for a list of Chicago's top kid-friendly attractions.

Lonely Planet's *Travel With Children* (by Brigitte Barta et al) is a goldmine for planning ahead. Chicago-specific resources include the following:

Chicago Kids (www.chicagokids.com) Website packed with kid-friendly ideas for locals and visitors alike.

Chicago Parent (www.chicagoparent.com) Free monthly publication available at libraries, the Children's Museum and elsewhere.

Time Out Chicago Kids (www.timeoutchicagokids.com) Quarterly magazine ($3); the website provides excellent daily online listings.

Babysitting

Check with your hotel's concierge for a list of recommended sitters. American Childcare Services (☎ 312-644-7300; www.americanchildcare.com; per hr $18.50, plus $20 agency fee) provides professional babysitters who will come to your hotel (four-hour minimum service). It's recommended you book a couple days ahead of time.

CLIMATE

The nickname 'Windy City' actually has nonmeteorological origins. It was coined by newspaper reporters in the late 1800s in reaction to the oft-blustery boastfulness of Chicago's politicians. Nevertheless, Chicago is windy, with everything from cool, God-sent lake breezes at the height of summer to skirt-raising gusts in the spring, to spine-chilling, nose-chiseling blasts of icy air in the winter. The city experiences all four seasons, with late spring and early fall being generally warm, clear and dry times. Winter and summer behave as expected, but early spring and late fall can freely mix pleasant days with rather wretched ones. Chicago has no true rainy season; its 34in of average annual precipitation are spread throughout the course of the year.

COURSES

You can learn a lot during your time in Chicago, from blues harmonica to improv to scarf crocheting.

If you'll be in town less than a week, try these options:

Chopping Block (Map pp50-1; ☎ 773-472-6700; www.thechoppingblock.net; 4747 N Lincoln Ave, Lincoln Square; Ⓜ Brown Line to Western) Offers both demonstration and hands-on cooking classes daily; wide-ranging topics include how to prepare locally sourced meals and how to put together tailgate-party chow for Bears games (two- to three-hour classes, $40-135). Classes are also held at the Merchandise Mart (Map pp66-7) outlet.

Second City (Map pp78-9; ☎ 312-664-3959; www.secondcity.com; 1616 N Wells St, Old Town; Ⓜ Brown Line to Sedgwick) Laugh while learning to write and perform improv comedy at Second City's famed Training Center. Intensive Friday-to-Sunday workshops ($285) are offered frequently, along with traditional eight-week sessions. For the schedule, go to the website's 'Training Centers' link, then 'Chicago.'

Specimen/Chicago School of Guitar Making (Map p100; ☎ 773-489-4830; www.specimenproducts.com; 1240 N Homan Ave, Humboldt Park; 🚌 70) Sure you can learn to play the guitar, but why not go a step further and actually build your own stringed beauty? Luthier courses, as well as classes to build your own tube amp or learn roadie repair techniques, take place over a series of weekend-long workshops; costs from $220 per workshop.

World Kitchen (Map pp54-5; ☎ 312-742-8497; www .explorechicago.org; 66 E Randolph St, Loop; Ⓜ Brown, Orange, Green, Purple, Pink Line to Randolph) Ethnic cooking classes ($30 for 2.5 hours) at city-run Gallery 37.

Several local shops offer one-off classes: see Loopy Yarns (p143) for knitting, Beadniks (p138) for jewelry making and Wolfbait & B-girls (p141) for bookbinding and other crafts.

For those who will be in town for a longer duration (at least four weeks), try the following:

Lillstreet Art Center (Map pp86-7; ☎ 773-769-4226; www.lillstreet.com; 4401 N Ravenswood St. Lake View; Ⓜ Brown Line to Montrose) Fire up the saws, kilns, easels and other arty implements at Lillstreet's glass-blowing, block-printing, painting, pottery and jewelry-making classes; four weeks for $130.

Old Town School of Folk Music (Map pp50-1; ☎ 773-728-6000; www.oldtownschool.org/classes; 4544 N Lincoln Ave, Lincoln Square; Ⓜ Brown Line to Western) Ever wanted to impress your friends by wailing on the banjo, fiddle, blues harmonica or guitar? The Old Town School will teach you well; seven weeks for $140.

CUSTOMS REGULATIONS

For a complete list of US customs regulations, check the **US Customs and Border Patrol** (www.cbp.gov) portal. The 'Know Before You Go' section covers the basics. In general, you're allowed to bring in 1L of liquor and 200 cigarettes (or 100 non-Cuban cigars) duty free, as well as gifts totaling up to $100. You can bring in, or take out, as much as $10,000 cash without formality. While there's no maximum limit, larger amounts must be declared. Declare any food you've brought, though most prepackaged items will be allowable. Drug paraphernalia is forbidden, and penalties for drug smuggling are especially severe.

DISCOUNT CARDS

If you don't mind hitting the pavement hard, the **Go Chicago Card** (www.gochicagocard.com) is a discount pass to visit an unlimited number of museums for a flat fee. It's good for one, two, three, five or seven consecutive days. For instance, the one-day pass costs $67/45 per adult/child and provides admission to approximately 30 top-draw sights and tours.

If you prefer a more leisurely pace, the lump-sum **CityPass** (www.citypass.com; adult/child 3-11 yr $69/59) might be best. It gives access to five of Chicago's most popular attractions – the Shedd Aquarium, the Field Museum, the Adler Planetarium, the Museum of Science & Industry and either the Hancock Observatory or the Willis Tower Skydeck – over a nine-day period once activated.

Both the Go Card and the CityPass let you skip the regular ticket lines, though be aware you'll still have to wait in some sort of queue (our recent experience at the Willis Tower showed the regular and pass lines to be equal). Buy the passes online; some attractions also sell them.

The Chicago Office of Tourism offers coupons (www.chicagoofficeoftourism.org/chicagocoupons) online that can save you a few bucks on various museums, tours, restaurants and shops; you'll have to print them beforehand for use.

Students who present ID will often receive reduced museum admission. Discounts are also commonly offered for seniors, children and the disabled. In these cases, however, no special cards are issued (you get the savings on-site when you pay). American Auto Association (AAA) members frequently receive hotel and motel discounts, as well as other travel-related savings.

ELECTRICITY

Electric current in the US is 110-120V, 60Hz AC. Outlets accept North American standard plugs, which have two flat prongs and an occasional third round one. If your appliance is made for another system, you will need a converter or adapter. These are best bought in your home country. Otherwise, try a travel bookstore. Check www.kropla.com for further useful details on electricity and adaptors.

EMBASSIES & CONSULATES

Most countries have their embassies in Washington, DC. For a full list see www .embassy.org. Many countries also have a consulate in Chicago.

Australia (Map pp54-5; ☎ 312-419-1480; www.usa .embassy.gov.au; 123 N Wacker Dr, The Loop; ☯ 8:30am-4:30am Mon-Fri)

Canada (Map pp54-5; ☎ 312-616-1860; www.chicago.gc .ca; 180 N Stetson Ave, The Loop; ☯ 9am-5pm Mon-Fri)

France (Map pp54-5; ☎ 312-327-5200; www.consul france-chicago.org; Suite 2400, 205 N Michigan Ave, The Loop; ☺ 9am-12:30pm & 2-4:30pm Mon-Fri)

Germany (Map pp66-7; ☎ 312-202 0480; www.germany .info; Suite 3200, 676 N Michigan Ave, Near North; ☺ 9am-noon Mon-Fri)

India (Map pp66-7; ☎ 312-595-0405; www.chicago .indianconsulate.com; Suite 850, 455 N City Front Plaza Dr, Near North; ☺ 9am-5pm Mon-Fri)

Italy (Map pp66-7; ☎ 312-467-1550; www.conschicago .esteri.it; Suite 1850, 500 N Michigan Ave, Near North; ☺ 9am-noon Mon-Fri & 2-4pm Wed)

Spain (Map pp54-5; ☎ 312-782-4588; www.consulate -spain-chicago.com; 180 N Michigan Ave, The Loop; ☺ 9am-2pm Mon-Fri)

UK (Map pp66 7; ☎ 312 970 3800; www.ukinusa.fco.gov .uk/en/about-us; 400 N Michigan Ave, Near North; ☺ 9am-12:30pm Mon-Fri)

EMERGENCY

For all emergencies (police, ambulance, fire), call ☎ 911. For nonemergency police matters call ☎ 311.

GAY & LESBIAN TRAVELERS

Chicago has a flourishing gay and lesbian scene; for details, check the free weekly publications of Chicago Free Press (www .chicagofreepress.com) or Windy City Times (www .windycitymediagroup.com). The massive new Chicago Area Gay & Lesbian Chamber of Commerce (Map pp86-7; ☎ 773-303-0167; www.glchamber .org; 3656 N Halsted St, Lake View; ☺ 9:30am-6pm Mon-Fri; Ⓜ Red Line to Addison) also provides useful visitor information. Chicago Greeter (see Organized Tours, p273) offers personalized sightseeing trips.

The biggest concentration of bars and clubs is on N Halsted St between Belmont Ave and Grace St, an area known as Boystown. Andersonville, aka Girls' Town, is another area with plenty of choices. For the gay and lesbian nightlife lowdown see p195.

HEALTH

No special vaccines are required or recommended for travel to the United States. All travelers should be up-to-date on routine immunizations. Because of the high level of hygiene, infectious diseases will not be a significant concern for most travelers (though note HIV infection does occur throughout the USA).

Insurance

The United States offers possibly the finest health care in the world. The problem is that unless you have good insurance, it can be prohibitively expensive. It's essential that you purchase travel health insurance if your regular policy doesn't cover you when you're abroad.

Bring any medications you may need in their original containers, clearly labeled. A signed, dated letter from your physician that describes all medical conditions and medications, including generic names, is also a good idea.

If your health insurance does not cover you for medical expenses abroad, consider supplemental insurance. Check the Lonely Planet website (www.lonelyplanet.com/bookings/insurance.do) for more information. Find out in advance if your insurance plan will make payments directly to providers or reimburse you later for overseas health expenditures.

HOLIDAYS

Chicago's governmental offices and services shut down on public holidays, as do some city shops. Public transportation runs on a reduced schedule. Locals celebrate many of the holidays with parades and other fanfare. To find out how you can join in the fun, see Festivals (p12). Major public holidays include the following:

New Year's Day January 1

Martin Luther King Jr Day Third Monday in January

President's Day Third Monday in February

Pulaski Day First Monday in March

Memorial Day Last Monday in May

Independence Day July 4

Labor Day First Monday in September

Columbus Day Second Monday in October

Veteran's Day November 11

Thanksgiving Day Fourth Thursday in November

Christmas Day December 25

INTERNET ACCESS

Public libraries remain the best bet for free internet access, offering computer terminals for visitor use and wi-fi for those with their own devices. The Harold Washington Library (p60) is cream of the crop; get a 'day pass' at the counter.

Many restaurants and coffee shops in the Loop, Near North, Lincoln Park and Bucktown have free wi-fi. Try Map Room (p186) or Goose Island Brewery (p181). The Chicago Cultural Center (p58) also has free wi-fi.

Practically all lodgings in Chicago have in-room wi-fi. At many high-end hotels it'll cost you ($10 to $15 per day is common). B&Bs and midrange places usually offer it for free. Lobbies sometimes serve as free wi-fi zones. If a Sleeping, Eating or Drinking establishment listed in this book has free wi-fi, we've marked it with 🛜.

LEGAL MATTERS

The basics of Chicago's legal system are identical to that of other US cities. If stopped and questioned by the police, you should cooperate, though you are not required to give them permission to search either your person or your car (though they can do both if they determine they have 'probable cause'). If arrested, you have the right to remain silent – which you should do – and the right to make one phone call from jail. If you don't have a lawyer, friend or family member to help you, call your consulate. The police will give you the number upon request.

It's generally against the law to have an open container of any alcoholic beverage in public, whether in a car, on the street, in a park or at the beach. But during festivals and other mass events, this rule is usually waived. The drinking age of 21 is strictly enforced. If you're younger than 35 (or just look like it), carry an ID. The legal driving age is 16, the age of consent is 17 and the voting age is 18. There is zero tolerance at all times for any kind of drug use.

MAPS

The maps in this book will probably suffice for casual touring. You'll find general maps for free at the tourist information offices (see p275) and detailed maps for sale at bookstores. You can pick up free maps of the Chicago transit system at any CTA station, or download one from www.transitchicago.com.

MEDICAL SERVICES

If you are ill or injured and suspect that the situation is in any way life threatening, call ☎911 immediately. This is a free call from any phone.

Clinics & Emergency Rooms

The following hospitals offer medical services through their emergency rooms. If your condition is not acute, call first, because many also operate clinics that can see you in a more timely and convenient manner. None of their services come cheap, so make sure you have insurance. If you are broke and don't have insurance, head to Stroger Cook County Hospital. If your problem is not life threatening, you will be seated in a waiting room where you will do just that, sit, for perhaps 12 hours while you're surrounded by people sicker than yourself. Another option for minor ailments is the Walgreens clinic listed below.

Advocate Illinois Masonic Medical Center (Map pp86-7; ☎ 773-975-1600; 836 W Wellington Ave, Lake View; Ⓜ Brown, Purple Line to Wellington)

Children's Memorial Hospital (Map pp78-9; ☎ 773-880-4000; 2300 N Lincoln Ave, Lincoln Park; Ⓜ Brown, Purple, Red Line to Fullerton) Note the hospital will move to a new downtown facility in 2012.

Northwestern Memorial Hospital (Map pp66-7; ☎ 312-926-5188; 251 E Erie St, Near North; Ⓜ Red Line to Chicago)

Stroger Cook County Hospital (Map pp104-5; ☎ 312-864-6000; 1900 W Polk St, Near West Side; Ⓜ Blue Line to Medical District)

University of Chicago Hospital (Map p120; ☎ 773-702-1000; 5841 S Maryland Ave, Hyde Park; Ⓜ Metra to 55th-56th-57th)

Pharmacies

Walgreens pharmacies are convenient places to get your prescriptions filled.

Walgreens (Map pp66-7; ☎ 312-664-8686; 757 N Michigan Ave, Near North; ◷ 24hr; Ⓜ Red Line to Chicago)

Walgreens (Map pp54-5; ☎ 312-346-5727; 79 W Monroe St, Loop; ◷ 7am-7pm Mon-Fri; Ⓜ Red, Blue Line to Monroe) This Walgreens also has a health clinic inside, staffed by a nurse practitioner to treat minor infections, allergies and injuries; no appointment needed.

MONEY

The US currency is the dollar ($), divided into 100 cents (¢). Coins come in denominations of 1¢ (penny), 5¢ (nickel), 10¢ (dime), 25¢ (quarter), 50¢ (half dollar – rare) and $1 (silver dollar – rare). Notes (bills) come in denominations of $1, $2 (rare), $5, $10, $20, $50 and $100.

See p18 for how your money will be spent in Chicago. For exchange rates, see Quick Reference on the inside front cover of this book.

ATMs

You can find ATMs everywhere in Chicago, with many convenience stores getting in on the action as well. All machines are connected to Cirrus and Plus, the world's two largest banking networks.

Unless you find an ATM belonging to your bank, you will be charged a fee upward of $2 to withdraw money from one of the machines. The exchange rate you get by taking money out of the ATM is usually the very best available (though the fees may nullify that advantage).

Changing Money

You'll find that exchanging foreign cash and non–US dollar traveler's checks in Chicago is a hassle, although it can be done. One cautionary note: shortly after arriving in Chicago, you will begin noticing 'currency exchanges' on many street corners. These primarily serve people without bank accounts who want to cash checks, and will not exchange foreign currencies. Head instead to the following banks and exchange places.

Traveler's checks are usually just as good as cash in the USA, provided they are in US dollars. Most places will accept them as long as you sign them in front of the cashier, waiter etc.

To exchange international monies or traveler's checks for dollars, you can visit the arrivals areas of O'Hare's Terminals 3 or 5, which have foreign-exchange services. Otherwise, you try one of the following places in the Loop or Near North:

American Express (Map pp66-7; ☎ 312-943-7840; 605 N Michigan Ave, Near North; ☻ 9am-6pm Mon-Fri, to 5pm Fri; Ⓜ Red Line to Grand)

Chase Building (Map pp54-5; ☎ 312-732-6009; 21 S Clark St, Loop; ☻ 7:30am-6pm Mon-Fri; Ⓜ Blue Line to Washington)

Northern Trust Bank (Map pp54-5; ☎ 312-630-6000; 50 S LaSalle St, Loop; ☻ 8am-5pm Mon-Fri; Ⓜ Brown, Orange, Purple, Pink Line to Washington)

Travelex (Map pp54-5; ☎ 312-807-4941; 19 S LaSalle St, Loop; ☻ 9am-5pm Mon-Fri; Ⓜ Brown, Orange, Purple, Pink Line to Washington)

World's Money Exchange (Map pp54-5; ☎ 312-641-2151; Suite M-11, upper fl, 203 N LaSalle St, Loop; ☻ 9am-5pm Mon-Fri; Ⓜ Blue, Brown, Orange, Green, Purple, Pink Line to Clark)

Credit Cards

Major credit cards are widely accepted by car-rental firms, hotels, restaurants, gas stations, shops, large grocery stores, movie theaters, ticket vendors, taxicabs and other places. In fact, you'll find certain transactions impossible to perform without a credit card: you can't reserve theater or other event tickets by phone without one, nor can you guarantee room reservations by phone, or rent a car. The most commonly accepted cards are Visa and MasterCard. American Express is widely accepted but not universally. Discover and Diners Club cards are usually good for travel tickets, hotels and rental cars, but they're less commonly accepted in other situations.

If your credit card is lost or stolen, call the card issuer.

American Express (☎ 800-528-4800)

Diners Club (☎ 800-234-6377)

Discover (☎ 800-347-2683)

MasterCard (☎ 800-307-7309)

Visa (☎ 800-336-8472)

NEWSPAPERS & MAGAZINES

For further details on these publications, see p42.

Chicago Magazine (www.chicagomag.com) Monthly magazine with articles and culture coverage slanted toward upscale readers.

Chicago Reader (www.chicagoreader.com) Free weekly alternative newspaper with comprehensive arts and entertainment listings; widely available at bookstores, bars and coffee shops.

Chicago Sun-Times (www.suntimes.com) The *Tribune's* daily, tabloid-style competitor.

Chicago Tribune (www.chicagotribune.com) The city's stalwart daily newspaper. Its younger, trimmed-down, free version is *RedEye*.

Crain's Chicago Business (www.chicagobusiness.com) Weekly publication covering business news.

Time Out Chicago (www.timeoutchicago.com) Hip, service-oriented weekly magazine with all-encompassing listings.

ORGANIZED TOURS

Tours can get you out on the water and into less-visited neighborhoods (the Obama bike tours are particularly good at that). Many companies offer discounts if you book online. Don't forget to look into kayak tours (p219) and foodie tours (p160), too.

Bike Tours

Two companies offer two- to four-hour tours ($30 to $45, including bikes) that cover themes like the lakefront, nighttime fireworks or Obama sights. They go daily in summer; times vary.

Bike Chicago (Map pp54-5; ☎ 888-245-3929; www .bikechicago.com; 239 E Randolph St, Loop; Ⓜ Brown, Orange, Green, Purple, Pink Line to Randolph) It's in Millennium Park; the company also has departure points at Navy Pier, North Ave Beach and elsewhere.

Bobby's Bike Hike (Map pp66-7; ☎ 312-915-0995; www.bobbysbikehike.com; Ogden Slip at River East Docks, 465 N McClurg Court, Near North; Ⓜ Red Line to Grand) Bobby's earns raves from riders.

Boat Tours

Most run May to November, several times daily.

Chicago Architecture Foundation (CAF; Map pp54-5; ☎ 312-922-3432; www.architecture.org; 90min tours $32; Ⓜ Brown, Green, Orange, Purple, Pink Line to State) CAF offers the gold standard in boat tours, cruising along the Chicago River. Departs from the Michigan Ave Bridge's southeast corner. Buy tickets at the dock, online or at CAF (224 S Michigan Ave, Loop).

Mercury Chicago Skyline Cruises (Map pp54-5; ☎ 312-332-1353; www.mercuryskylinecruiseline.com; 90min tours $24; Ⓜ Brown, Green, Orange, Purple, Pink Line to State) Glides on both the river and the lake. Be aware that passing through the locks to and from the lake can take up a fair part of the excursion. Architecture lovers: the info here is perfunctory; you're better off with CAF. Departs from the Michigan Ave Bridge's southeast corner.

Mystic Blue Cruises (Map pp66-7; ☎ 877-299-7783; www.mysticbluecruises.com; tours from $35; 🚌 124) Plies the lakefront, departing from Navy Pier. It caters to a younger crowd and offers lunch, dinner, cocktail and moonlight tours accompanied by bands or DJs.

Wendella Sightseeing Boats (Map pp66-7; ☎ 312-337-1446; www.wendellaboats.com; 90min tours $25; Ⓜ Red Line to Grand) Offers a similar river-and-lake tour as Mercury. Departs from the Michigan Ave Bridge's northwest corner.

Windy (Map pp66-7; ☎ 312-595-5555; www.tallship windy.com; 60-75min tours $24; 🚌 124) The four-masted schooner sets sail from Navy Pier. Trips have different themes (pirates, architecture, sailing skills etc). With only the sound of the wind in your ears, these tours are the most relaxing way to see the skyline from offshore.

Bus Tours

The Chicago Architecture Foundation (p272) also operates bus tours (from $45) of the lakefront, Prairie Ave, Hyde Park, Oak Park and other areas.

Chicago Neighborhood Tours (Map pp54-5; ☎ 312-742-1190; www.chicagoneighborhoodtours.com; Chicago Cultural Center Visitors Center, 77 E Randolph St, Loop; 3/4hr tours $20/30; Ⓜ Brown, Orange, Green, Purple, Pink Line to Randolph) The Department of Cultural Affairs offers tours on Friday and Saturday mornings. They're OK, but you pretty much just sit on a bus and stare out the window – though they do go into offbeat neighborhoods ignored by more mainstream companies. Departs from the Chicago Cultural Center Visitors Center.

Chicago Trolley Co (☎ 773-648-5000; www.chicago trolley.com; 2hr tours $35) Offers a guided, 13-mile tour that stops at all the major sights throughout downtown and the Near North. It's handy that you can hop on and off wherever you want, all day long. Departure points vary.

Untouchable Gangster Tours (Map pp66-7; ☎ 773-881-1195; www.gangstertour.com; cnr N Clark St & W Ohio Ave, Near North; 2hr tours $28; Ⓜ Red Line to Grand) Comic, costumed actors take you by van to some of Chicago's famous gangster sights. Departs outside McDonald's several times per week.

Weird Chicago Tours (Map pp66-7; ☎ 888-446-7859; www.weirdchicago.com; cnr N Clark & W Ontario Sts, Near North; 3hr tours $30; ⏰ 7pm Thu-Sat; Ⓜ Red Line to Grand) Takes visitors to ghost, gangster and red-light sites. Departs outside the Hard Rock Cafe.

Downloadable Tours

These tours are all available for free, so load 'em up on your iPod and hit the road.

Chicago Blues Tour (www.downloadchicagotours.com /bluesmedia) Buddy Guy leads you to the city's blues shrines. You'll need a car to cover all the ground, though it's equally rewarding to just listen to the narrative.

Chicago Loop Alliance (www.chicagoloopalliance.com) It offers three downloads covering different themes downtown: Art Loop, Landmark Loop and Theater Loop.

Chicago Movie Tour (www.onscreenillinois.com) Tour sites made famous in flicks such as *The Blues Brothers, Ferris Bueller's Day Off* and *The Untouchables*.

Chicago Poetry Tour (www.downloadchicagotours.com) Famous poets give the lowdown on literary hot spots around the city; the first six stops cover the Loop.

Walking Tours

Chicago Architecture Foundation (see p272) CAF offers heaps of great walking tours, such as the 'Historic Downtown: Rise of the Skyscraper' (two hours, $16). It departs daily at 10am (plus 3pm in summer) from CAF's headquarters. The $5 lunchtime tours Monday through Friday are a bargain, in which visitors explore one landmark building for 45 minutes and get backstage access to its intricacies. There are even 7:30am tours for 'Early Risers.'

Chicago Greeter (☎ 312-744-8000; www.chicagogreeter .com; tours free) Pairs you with a local city dweller who takes you on a personal two- to four-hour tour customized by theme (architecture, history, gay and lesbian, and more) or neighborhood. Travel is by foot and/or public transportation. Reserve seven business days in advance.

Chicago History Museum (Map pp78-9; ☎ 312-642-4600; www.chicagohs.org; 1601 N Clark St, Lincoln Park; tours $10-45) The museum counts pub crawls, kayak jaunts and cemetery walks among its tour arsenal. Departure points and times vary.

InstaGreeter (Map pp54-5; ☎ 312-744-8000; www .chicagogreeter.com; Chicago Cultural Center Visitors Center, 77 E Randolph St, Loop; tours free; 🕐 10am-4pm Fri & Sat, 11am-4pm Sun) The quicker version of Chicago Greeter, offering one-hour tours on the spot from the Cultural Center Visitors Center. Instagreeter also has outlets open on summer Saturdays at both Second City (1616 N Wells St, Old Town) & Hyde Park Art Center (5020 S Cornell Ave, Hyde Park) for local walk-abouts.

PHOTOGRAPHY

Central Camera (p129) has it all: camera sales, supply sales, equipment repairs, traditional film processing and CD/DVD image transfers to free up digital camera memory card space. You can also buy digital camera memory cards at most Walgreens and Target stores, as well as transfer digital images to CDs at Walgreens.

POST

For 24-hour information, including post office locations, hours and rates, contact the reliable US Postal Service (USPS; ☎ 800-275-8777; www .usps.com).

It costs 44¢ to mail a 1oz 1st-class letter within the USA, and 28¢ to mail a postcard domestically. International airmail rates (except to Canada and Mexico) are 98¢ for a 1oz letter or a postcard; to Canada it's 75¢, and to Mexico it's 79¢.

Parcels mailed to foreign destinations from the USA are subject to a variety of rates. First class can be very expensive. The cheapest option is 'priority mail,' which takes six to 10 business days. (The US postal service discontinued its '4th class' service, which used to be the least expensive way to go.)

If you'd like to get mail while traveling but don't have an address, have it sent to you in Chicago via 'general delivery.' This is the same

as poste restante. Letters should be addressed as follows:

Your Name

c/o General Delivery (Station Name)

Chicago IL (Zip Code)

USA

General-delivery mail is held for at least 10 days (sometimes as long as 30) before being returned to the sender. Bring photo ID when you come to pick up your mail. Full-service post offices that also accept general delivery include the following:

Fort Dearborn Station (Map pp66-7; ☎ 312-644-0485; 540 N Dearborn St, Chicago, IL 60610; 🕐 8am-6:30pm Mon-Fri, 7:30am-3pm Sat, 9am-2pm Sun)

Loop Station (Map pp54-5; ☎ 312-427-4225; 211 S Clark St, Chicago, IL 60604; 🕐 7am-6pm Mon-Fri)

Main Post Office (Map pp54-5; ☎ 312-983-8182; 433 W Harrison St, Chicago, IL 60699; 🕐 7:30am-midnight)

RADIO

CHIRP Radio (www.chirpradio.org) Awesome online community radio station run by hipsters who know their tunes.

The Loop (97.9FM) Classic rock, where you'll find your Journey, Van Halen and U2.

WBEZ (91.5FM) National Public Radio affiliate airing news, political and cultural programs 24/7.

WGN (720AM) Local talk shows, plus broadcasts all of the Cubs and Blackhawks games.

WHPK (88.5FM) University of Chicago's eclectic station of public affairs, rockabilly, calypso and beyond.

WSCR (670AM) Local sports 24/7; broadcasts all White Sox games.

WXRT (93.1FM) Modern, classic and local rock music.

Vocalo (www.vocalo.org) Online station affiliated with WBEZ, where listeners can interact with hosts and upload their own playlists and stories to the shows. Also broadcast (weakly) at 89.5FM.

RELOCATING

If you're looking for a long-term apartment rental while awaiting more permanent digs, see the ideas we've provided in the Sleeping chapter, (p226). A good web resource for finding fellow expats in Chicago is Meet Ups (http://expatriates.meetup.com/cities/us/il/chicago/). For information on working in the Windy City, see p276.

SAFETY

For the most part, serious crime in Chicago has been dropping in recent years, and the areas written about in this book are all reasonably safe during the day. At night, the lakefront, major parks and certain neighborhoods (especially south and west of the Loop) can become lonely and forbidding places. The Loop, Near North, Gold Coast, Old Town, Lincoln Park, Lake View and Bucktown, on the other hand, are tolerably safe night and day. That doesn't mean you shouldn't be vigilant and be careful solo at night.

You've probably heard about Chicago's high murder rate (458 homicides in 2009 compared to 471 in New York City, which has three times the population), but know this is mostly concentrated in certain far west and far south neighborhoods. If you like to know before you go, visit Everyblock Chicago (http://chicago.everyblock.com/crime). The site breaks down crime by type and neighborhood, and probably shouldn't be viewed by those who are on the fence about coming to the Windy City. (It's safe! We swear!)

TAXES

The basic sales tax is 9.75% – the nation's highest (in a tie with Los Angeles). Some grocery items are taxed at only 2.25%, and newspapers and magazines, but not books, are tax free. The hotel tax is 15.4%; the car-rental tax is 19%. And for meals in most parts of town, there's an 11% tax added to the bill.

TELEPHONE

Area & Country Codes

The city has three area codes. The area code ☎ 312 serves the Loop and an area bounded roughly by North Ave to the north, Ashland Ave to the west and 18th St to the south. The rest of the city falls in area code ☎ 773. Recently ☎ 872 was added for new numbers (wherever they're located in the city), since the other two area codes are at capacity. The northern suburbs use area code ☎ 847, suburbs to the west and south use ☎ 708, and the far west suburbs use ☎ 630.

The country code for the US is ☎ 1. The international access code is ☎ 011 for calls you dial directly.

Cell Phones

In the USA cell phones use GSM 1900 or CDMA 800, operating on different frequencies from other systems around the world. The only foreign phones that will work here are GSM tri- or quad-band models.

You can buy a cheap cell phone with a set amount of prepaid call time for as little as $30. T-Mobile (www.t-mobile.com) and Virgin Mobile (www.virginmobileusa.com) are US companies that provides this service. Many vendors in downtown Chicago sell their wares; type in a zip code at the website to find one near you. Online retailers such as Telestial (www.telestial.com) and Planetfone (www.planetfone.com) sell phones internationally. Most cost around $90 and up, including voicemail, some prepaid minutes and a rechargeable SIM card. A good place in Chicago to poke around and possibly find a better deal is on Devon Ave (p138), where several shops sell cell phone equipment to a mostly Indian and European clientele. Electronics retailer Best Buy (www.bestbuy.com) also sells international SIM cards at various local branches.

Note that talking on your hand-held cell phone while driving in Chicago is illegal.

Dialing

All phone numbers within the USA and Canada consist of a three-digit area code followed by a seven-digit local number. If you are calling from within the US to another area code, dial ☎ 1 + the three-digit area code + the seven-digit local number. In the city, you must dial the same way – ☎ 1 + the area code + seven-digit local number (even if you're calling within the same area code).

To make an international call from Chicago (or anywhere in the USA), dial ☎ 011, then the country code, followed by the area code and the phone number. To find out the country code of the place you're trying to call, look in the front of the local phone directory.

Toll-free phone numbers start with the area codes ☎ 800, ☎ 877 or ☎ 888. Numbers that begin with ☎ 900 will cost you a small fortune (up to several dollars per minute). Local directory assistance can be reached by calling ☎ 411. If you are looking for a number outside of your local area code but know what area code it falls under, dial ☎ 1 + the area code + 555-1212. These calls are no longer free, even from pay phones. Online phone directories include www.411.com and www.yellowpages.com.

Pay Phones & Hotel Phones

Unfortunately, pay phones do not use the same high-tech card systems in the USA that they do in Europe. This is fine for local calls, which cost 35¢ to 50¢ for about 10 minutes of talk time. But trying to make a long-distance call at a pay phone if you don't have a credit-card calling card or a prepaid calling card requires an outrageous amount of change. When using hotel phones, know that some places will charge up to $2 per local call. Ask in advance to avoid a shock later.

Phonecards

Prepaid phonecards usually offer some of the best per-minute rates for long-distance and international calling. They come in denominations of $5, $10, $20 and $50 and are widely sold in drugstores, supermarkets and convenience stores. Beware of cards with hidden charges such as 'activation fees' or per-call connection fees, and see if your card has a toll-free access number. A surcharge for calls made from public pay phones is common. AT&T sells a reliable phonecard that's available at many retailers.

TIME

Chicago falls in the US Central Standard Time (CST) zone. 'Standard time' runs from the first Sunday in November to the second Sunday in March. 'Daylight saving time,' when clocks move ahead one hour, takes over for the rest of the year, from mid March to early November.

Chicago is one hour behind Eastern Standard Time (EST), which encompasses nearby Michigan and Indiana, apart from the northwestern corner of Indiana, which follows Chicago time. The border between the two zones is just east of the city.

The city is one hour ahead of Mountain Standard Time (MST), a zone that includes much of the Rocky Mountains, and two hours ahead of Pacific Standard Time (PST), the zone that includes California. Chicago is six hours behind London, UK.

TOILETS

There's not much in the way of public toilets. You can try the facilities at the visitors centers (see p275). Another decent option is the Borders bookshop (p132) in the Gold Coast; you'll need to get the key from a staff member to enter.

TOURIST INFORMATION

The Chicago Office of Tourism (☎ 312-744-2400, 877-244-2246; www.explorechicago.org) provides a 24-hour

hotline to answer questions about sights, events and lodging. The website is chock-full of neighborhood and event info. Sign up for the Twitter feed to get the daily lowdown on free things going on. The two well-stocked visitors centers have free wi-fi and places to sit and chill. It's tough to beat the one in the Chicago Cultural Center for sheer tonnage of multilanguage maps and leaflets; it has a restaurant concierge, too. The second location, in the Water Works Pumping Station, is close to the Near North and Gold Coast sights and shops. It has a pie cafe inside, and a machine to buy CTA train passes.

Chicago Cultural Center Visitors Center (Map pp54-5; 77 E Randolph St, Loop; ☺ 8am-7pm Mon-Thu, 8am-6pm Fri, 9am-6pm Sat, 10am-6pm Sun; Ⓜ Brown, Green, Orange, Purple, Pink Line to Randolph) Many tours also depart from here.

Water Works Visitors Center (Map pp72-3; 163 E Pearson St, Gold Coast; ☺ 8am-7pm Mon-Thu, 8am-6pm Fri, 10am-6pm Sat, 10am-4pm Sun; Ⓜ Red Line to Chicago)

TRAVELERS WITH DISABILITIES

Chicago can be a challenge for people with reduced mobility. The preponderance of older buildings means that doorways are narrow and stairs prevalent. All city buses are accessible, but many El stations are not. If you do find a station with an elevator, make sure that there's also one at your destination. To see a list of wheelchair-accessible El stations, check www.transitchicago.com (click 'Riding the CTA', then 'Accessibility') or call ☎ 888-968-7282 (press 5 for the Elevator Status Hotline).

For hotels, you're best off with the newer properties. But call the hotel itself – not the 800 number – and confirm that the room you want to reserve has the features you need. The phrase 'roll-in showers' is interpreted very loosely by some properties.

The Mayor's Office for People with Disabilities (☎ 312-744-7050, TTY 312-744-4964; www.cityofchicago.org/disabilities) is a good place to call to ask questions about the availability of services. Easy Access Chicago (www.easyaccesschicago.org) is another useful resource.

VISAS

A reciprocal visa-waiver program applies to citizens of certain countries, who may enter the USA for stays of 90 days or fewer without having to obtain a visa. Currently these countries include Andorra, Australia, Austria, Belgium, Brunei, Czech Republic, Denmark, Estonia, Finland, France, Germany, Hungary, Iceland, Ireland, Italy, Japan, Latvia, Liechtenstein, Lithuania, Luxembourg, Malta, Monaco, the Netherlands, New Zealand, Norway, Portugal, San Marino, Singapore, Slovakia, Slovenia, South Korea, Spain, Sweden, Switzerland and the UK.

If you are a citizen of a visa-waiver country, you do not need a visa *only if* you have a passport that meets current US standards (ie is 'machine-readable') *and* you have gotten approval from the Electronic System for Travel Authorization (ESTA) in advance. Register online with the Department of Homeland Security (https://esta.cbp.dhs.gov) at least 72 hours before arrival. Once travel authorization is approved, your registration is valid for two years (note there's a $14 fee for processing and authorization).

The US State Department (www.travel.state.gov/visa) maintains the most comprehensive visa information, providing downloadable forms, lists of US consulates abroad and even visa wait times calculated by country.

Requests for visa extensions in Chicago are entertained at the office of US Citizenship & Immigration Services (Map pp54-5; ☎ 800-375-5283; www.uscis.gov; 101 W Congress Pkwy, Loop; Ⓜ Blue Line to LaSalle). Meetings are all by appointment only. To make one, visit http://infopass.uscis.gov. Be sure to get the paperwork moving well before your visa expires.

You can also visit www.lonelyplanet.com/chicago for up-to-date visa information, or check with the US embassy or consulate in your home country.

WOMEN TRAVELERS

Women will be safe alone in most parts of Chicago, though they should exercise a degree of caution and awareness of their surroundings.

The El is safe, even at night, though you might want to seek out more populated cars or the first car, to be closest to the driver.

In the commonly visited areas of Chicago, you should not encounter troubling attitudes from men. In bars some men will see a woman alone as a bid for companionship. A polite 'no thank you' should suffice to send them away. Chicagoans are very friendly, so don't be afraid to protest loudly if someone is hassling you. It will probably send the offending party away and bring helpful Samaritans to your side.

WORK

It is very difficult for foreigners to get legal work in the United States. Securing your own work visa without a sponsor – meaning an employer – is next to impossible. If you do have a sponsor, the sponsor should normally be able to assist you, or do all the work themselves to secure your visa. Contact your embassy or consulate for more information.

Doing Business

Many large international companies have their headquarters and distribution centers in Chicago. O'Hare is the main airport used for shipping and transportation. For services such as copying, overnight shipping, emailing and videoconferencing, FedEx (☎ 800-463-3339; www.fedex.com) has multiple locations around town that can get the job done.

Volunteering

If you're interested in doing some volunteer work while you're in town, check out the listings on the Chicago Community Resource Network (www.chicagovolunteer.net) or look through the opportunities listed in the community section of the Craigslist message board (www.chicago.craigslist.org).

BEHIND THE SCENES

THIS BOOK

This 6th edition of Chicago was written by Karla Zimmerman. Karla also coordinated and wrote the 5th edition, with contributions from Nate Cavalieri and Lisa Dunford. Previous editions were written by Chris Baty, and Ryan Ver Berkmoes. This guidebook was commissioned in Lonely Planet's Oakland office, laid out by Cambridge Publishing Management, UK, and produced by the following:

Commissioning Editors Jennye Garibaldi, Emily Wolman

Coordinating Editors Karen Beaulah, Penelope Goodes

Coordinating Cartographer Jolyon Philcox

Coordinating Layout Designer Donna Pedley

Senior Editor Katie Lynch

Managing Editor Melanie Dankel

Managing Cartographers Alison Lyall, Amanda Sierp

Managing Layout Designer Celia Wood

Assisting Editors Hazel Meek, Ceinwen Sinclair

Assisting Cartographers Valeska Canas, Anthony Phelan

Assisting Layout Designer Paul Queripel

Cover Research Pepi Bluck

Internal Image Research Sabrina Dalbesio

Color Designer Julie Crane

Indexer Amanda Jones

Thanks to Sasha Baskett, Jessica Boland, Bruce Evans, Michelle Glynn, Yvonne Kirk, Lisa Knights, Katie Lynch, Naomi Parker, Rebecca Skinner,

Cover photographs Low angle view of buildings, Marina City Towers, Panoramic Images (top); Experimental mirror room at the Museum of Science & Industry, Patrick Frilet (bottom)

Internal photographs All images are copyright of the photographer unless otherwise indicated. Many of the images in this guide are available for licensing from Lonely Planet Images: www.lonelyplanetimages.com.

THANKS
KARLA ZIMMERMAN

Thanks to all my local amigos (you know who you are) for good-heartedly answering my relentless questions and sharing your favorite hot spots. A tip of the hat to the kindly people at Chicago's Office of Tourism. Gratitude to Jennye, Emily, Bruce and Sasha at LP for guidance and advice, and to all the LP *Chicago* writers who tread before me. Thanks most of all to Eric Markowitz, the world's best partner-for-life, who fed me, drove me and kept the house from falling apart while I wrote this book.

THE LONELY PLANET STORY

Fresh from an epic journey across Europe, Asia and Australia in 1972, Tony and Maureen Wheeler sat at their kitchen table stapling together notes. The first Lonely Planet guidebook, *Across Asia on the Cheap*, was born.

Travelers snapped up the guides. Inspired by their success, the Wheelers began publishing books to Southeast Asia, India and beyond. Demand was prodigious, and the Wheelers expanded the business rapidly to keep up. Over the years, Lonely Planet extended its coverage to every country and into the virtual world via lonelyplanet.com and the Thorn Tree message board.

As Lonely Planet became a globally loved brand, Tony and Maureen received several offers for the company. But it wasn't until 2007 that they found a partner whom they trusted to remain true to the company's principles of traveling widely, treading lightly and giving sustainably. In October of that year, BBC Worldwide acquired a 75% share in the company, pledging to uphold Lonely Planet's commitment to independent travel, trustworthy advice and editorial independence.

Today, Lonely Planet has offices in Melbourne, London and Oakland, with over 500 staff members and 300 authors. Tony and Maureen are still actively involved with Lonely Planet. They're traveling more often than ever, and they're devoting their spare time to charitable projects. And the company is still driven by the philosophy of *Across Asia on the Cheap*: 'All you've got to do is decide to go and the hardest part is over. So go!'

OUR READERS

Many thanks to the travelers who used the last edition and wrote to us with helpful hints, useful advice and interesting anecdotes:

Sonja Bauer, Judith Berkshire, Jeff and Pavla Bowyer, Ron Broadfoot, Dean Buckfield, Sahrah Dermish, Gustavo Dessal, Brian Friedopfer, George Gardiner, Ellen Goodman, Laura Hayes, Brandi Hughes Anderson, Jabari Jordan-Walker, Gregor Kos, Tim Lewis, Steve McInnes, Oliver Metzerott, Harald Olsen, Priscilla Poor, George Pudlo, Emily Quinn, Thomas Seymour, Meg Viezbicke, Howard Weiner

SEND US YOUR FEEDBACK

We love to hear from travelers — your comments keep us on our toes and help make our books better. Our well-traveled team reads every word on what you loved or loathed about this book. Although we cannot reply individually to postal submissions, we always guarantee that your feedback goes straight to the appropriate authors, in time for the next edition. Each person who sends us information is thanked in the next edition and the most useful submissions are rewarded with a free book.

To send us your updates — and find out about Lonely Planet events, newsletters and travel news — visit our award-winning website: lonelyplanet.com/contact.

Note: We may edit, reproduce and incorporate your comments in Lonely Planet products such as guidebooks, websites and digital products, so let us know if you don't want your comments reproduced or your name acknowledged. For a copy of our privacy policy visit lonelyplanet.com/privacy.

BEHIND THE SCENES

INDEX

A

accessories, *see* Shopping *subindex*
accommodations 225-44, *see also* Sleeping *subindex*
at airports 243
apartment rentals 226-7
costs 18, 226, 227, 232
Achatz, Grant 149, 156, 163
activities 215-20, *see also individual activities*, Sports & Activities *subindex*
air travel 261-2
airports 262
accommodations 243
to/from airports 263
Algren, Nelson 94
ambulance 269
Amtrak 266
Andersonville 89, 92-3, **90**
accommodations 240-1
drinking 183-4
food 162-3
shopping 137-8
transportation 89
walking tour 92-3, **92**
Andersonville Midsommarfest 14
apartments, *see* Sleeping *subindex*
aquariums 111, 118
architecture 36-9, 56, 119
area codes, *see inside front cover*
Art Institute of Chicago 29, 52-3, 57, 62, **5**
Artropolis 13
arts 28-36, 201-11, *see also individual arts*, Arts & Shopping *subindexes*
tickets 202
venues 202
ATMs 271

B

B&Bs, *see* Sleeping *subindex*
babysitters 267
bars 185, *see also* Drinking *subindex*
baseball 215-16, 220-1
basketball 218, 221
bathrooms 275
Bayless, Rick 149, 150, 153, 163
beaches 219, **8**, *see also* Sights *subindex*
Bean, the, *see Cloud Gate*
beer 179, 186
bicycling 14, 216-17, 262-3
bike polo 218
blues music 30, 123, 190-2, **4**, *see also* Nightlife *subindex*
boat travel 70, 118, 263-4, *see also* kayaking, paddleboats
books 21, 33-4, 35, 163, *see also* Shopping *subindex*
bowling 216
Boystown 85
breweries, *see* Drinking *subindex*
Bridgeport 124
Bronzeville 122-3
Bucktown 94-5, **96-7**
accommodations 241
drinking 184-6
food 165-7
shopping 138-41
transportation 94
buildings, *see* Sights *subindex*
Burnham, Daniel 22, 23, 39, 56
bus travel 264
business hours 267, *see also inside front cover*

bars 178
nightlife 190
restaurants 147
shops 128

C

cabaret 194-5
cafes, *see* Drinking *subindex*
Capone, Al 23, 24, 81
car travel 264-5
cathedrals, *see* Sights *subindex*
cell phones 274
cemeteries, *see* Sights *subindex*
chemists 270
Chess Brothers 23
Chicago Auto Show 12
Chicago Cubs 84, 220-1, **8**
Chicago fire of 1871 22
Chicago River 21, 22, 72
Chicago Spire 65
Chicago Theatre 60, 61, 203, **5**
Chicago Transit Authority 265
Chiditarod 13
children, travel with 267
attractions 68
theaters 205
Chinatown 116, 174-5
churches, *see* Sights *subindex*
Cinco De Mayo Festival & Parade 13
cinema 36, 209-10, *see also* Arts *subindex*
classical music 202-4
Cleveland 258-9
climate 12, 261, 267
clothing, *see also* Shopping *subindex*
sizing chart 131
Cloud Gate 53, 56, 62, **7**
clubs 195-8
comedy 13, 14, 33, 198-9
consulates 268-9
costs 17-18, *see also inside front cover*
accommodations 18, 226, 227, 232
discount cards 268
drinking 178

food 18, 147-8
free attractions 74, 111
transportation 265
country music 194
courses 267-8
credit cards 271
crime 274
CTA 265
customs regulations 268
cycling, *see* bicycling

D

Daley, Richard J 23, 25
Daley, Richard M 27, 39
dance 34-5, 207-9
day spas 214-15
day trips 246-60, **247**
Detroit 258
disabilities, travelers with 275
discount cards 268
Douglas 252
drinks 177-87, *see also* Drinking & Shopping *subindexes*
drive-ins 257, 258, 259
driving, *see* car travel
drugstores 270

E

El, the 59, 80, 265
electricity 268
Elliot, Graham 149, 150
embassies 268-9
emergencies 269
environmental issues 39-40
exchange rates, *see inside front cover*

F

farmers' markets 60, 148, 157, **6**
fashion 44, *see also* Shopping *subindex*
festivals 12-17, 254
art 30
cinema 210
classical music 204
dance 208
literature 34
theater 206
film, *see* cinema

000 map pages
000 photographs

GREENDEX

GOING GREEN

Almost everyone seems to be going 'green'. But how can you know which businesses really are ecofriendly? The following listings have been handpicked by our author because they are committed to lowering their impact on the environment. Some are locally owned and operated; others are actively involved in resource conservation.

If you think we've omitted somewhere that should be listed here, email us at www.lonelyplanet.com/contact. For more information about sustainable tourism and Lonely Planet, see www.lonelyplanet.com/about/responsible-travel.

MAP LEGEND

ROUTES

........Tollway
........Freeway
........Primary
........Secondary
........Tertiary
........Lane
........Under Construction
........Unsealed Road
........One-Way Street

........Mall/Steps
........Tunnel
........Pedestrian Overpass
........Walking Tour
........Walking Tour Detour
........*Walking Trail*
........*Walking Path*
........*Track*

TRANSPORT

........Ferry
........Metro

........Rail
........Rail (Underground)

HYDROGRAPHY

........River, Creek
........Swamp

........Canal
........Water

BOUNDARIES

........International

........State, Provincial

AREA FEATURES

........Airport
........Area of Interest
........Beach
........Building
........Campus
........Cemetery, Christian

........Land
........Mall
........Market
........Park
........Sports

POPULATION

◎ **CAPITAL (NATIONAL)**
● **Large City**
● Small City

◉ ....CAPITAL (STATE)
● ....Medium City
○ ....Town, Village

SYMBOLS

Information
🏧 ....Bank, ATM
➕ ....Hospital, Medical
❶ ....Information
@ ....Internet Facilities
⊗ ....Police Station
⊗ ....Post Office
☎ ....Telephone
🚻 ....Toilets

Sights
🏖 ....Beach
✝ ....Christian
✡ ....Jewish
🏛 ....Monument
🏛 ....Museum, Gallery
● ....Point of Interest
🦓 ....Zoo, Bird Sanctuary

Shopping
🛍 ....Shopping

Eating
🍴 ....Eating

Drinking
☕ ....Drinking
☕ ....Cafe

Nightlife
♣ ....Nightlife

The Arts
🎭 ....Arts

Sports & Activities
🏊 ....Pool
🏃 ....Trail Head

Sleeping
🛏 ....Sleeping

Transport
✈ ....Airport, Airfield
🚌 ....Bus Station
🅿 ....Parking Area
🚕 ....Taxi Rank

Geographic
🔭 ....Lookout
▲ ....Mountain, Volcano
🏞 ....National Park
)(........Pass, Canyon
🕳 ....Waterfall

Published by Lonely Planet Publications Pty Ltd
ABN 36 005 607 983

Australia (Head Office)
Locked Bag 1, Footscray, Victoria 3011,
☎03 8379 8000, fax 03 8379 8111,
talk2us@lonelyplanet.com.au

USA 150 Linden St, Oakland, CA 94607,
☎510 250 6400, toll free 800 275 8555,
fax 510 893 8572, info@lonelyplanet.com

UK 2nd fl, 186 City Rd, London, EC1V 2NT,
☎020 7106 2100, fax 020 7106 2101,
go@lonelyplanet.co.uk